DIMENSIONS OF THINKING
AND COGNITIVE INSTRUCTION

DIMENSIONS OF THINKING
AND COGNITIVE INSTRUCTION

EDITED BY

BEAU FLY JONES
North Central Regional Educational Laboratory

LORNA IDOL
Institute for Learning and Development

**NORTH CENTRAL REGIONAL
EDUCATIONAL LABORATORY**
Elmhurst, Illinois 60126

 LAWRENCE ERLBAUM ASSOCIATES, PUBLISHERS
1990   Hillsdale, New Jersey   Hove and London

This publication is based in part on work conducted under Contract No. 400-86-0004 with the Office of Educational Research and Improvement (OERI), U.S. Department of Education. The opinions expressed do not necessarily reflect the position or policy of OERI and no official endorsement should be inferred.

Lawrence Erlbaum Associates, Inc., Publishers
365 Broadway
Hillsdale, New Jersey 07642

Library of Congress Cataloging-in-Publication Data

Dimensions of thinking and cognitive instruction / edited by Beau Fly
    Jones, Lorna Idol.
        p.   cm.
    Includes bibliographical references and indexes.
    ISBN 0-8058-0346-7
    1. Thought and thinking—Study and teaching.   2. Cognitive
learning.   I. Jones, Beau Fly.   II. Idol, Lorna.
LB1590.3.D58   1990
370.15'2—dc20   90-35752
                                                             CIP

Printed in the United States of America
10 9 8 7 6 5 4 3 2 1

Contents

CONCLUSIONS   *511*
Beau Fly Jones and Lorna Idol

Acknowledgments

We are deeply indebted to many people for helping us develop this series. First, there were several inhouse reviewers from the North Central Regional Educational Laboratory: Larry Friedman, Beverly Walker, Margaret Tinzmann, Trish Stephens, and Jane Arends.

Second, there were numerous external reviewers, some of whom are authors, to whom owe our extended thanks: Zulfi Ahmad, Cincinnati Public Schools; Jonathon Barron, University of Pennsylvania; Carole Wegley Brown, Texas Education Agency; Robert Clasen, University of Wisconsin, Madison; Mary Gick, Carleton University; John Hayes, Carnegie Mellon University; Carolyn Hughes, Oklahoma City Public Schools; Susan Johnson, University of Texas, Austin; Susan Markle, University of Illinois, Chicago; William Nagy, University of Illinois, Champaign-Urbana; Annemarie Sullivan Palincsar, Michigan State University; Scott Paris, University of Michigan; Kathleen Roth, Michigan State University; Sigmund Tobias, City Colleges of New York; and Claire Weinstein, University of Texas at Austin. Each of these persons gave valuable time and insight to the chapters they read, but we of course are ultimately responsible for the contents of both Volumes.

Third, we are truly grateful to our husbands, James V. Davis (married to Beau Fly Jones), and James Frederick West, married to Lorna Idol. Both of them gave endless encouragement for all the activities related to developing this series and help in editing our various chapters.

Finally, we would like to thank two deans who generously gave both financial and research assistance to our authors in order to help them do the work for their chapters: John Palmer, Dean, University of Wisconsin, Madison, and Nancy Cole, then Dean, University of Illinois, Champaign-Urbana. Both deans gave this assistance out of their commitment to the work of the Laboratory.

Introduction

American education is experiencing a period of unprecedented change. One significant change is the focus on restructuring schools. Throughout the nation, there are initiatives for "school-based management," "empowerment," "alternative schools," "essential schools," "accelerated schools," "involvement of parents," and "community/business partnerships" as different approaches to restructuring schools.

A second change is the growth of the movement to improve students' ability to think using cognitive instruction, which helps students to develop so-called "higher order" thinking skills and to become self-regulated learners. This thrust comes largely from two different sources: (a) the number of commercially developed thinking skills programs and study skill courses offered as adjunct courses, and (b) the recent movement to infuse the teaching of thinking across the subject areas so that every teacher teaches thinking.

This movement to teach thinking is refreshing and long overdue. However, there is much confusion among educators, policymakers, and researchers alike about what thinking is and how best to teach it. Also, we have great concerns that the movement to teach thinking is not linked directly to the initiatives to restructure schools. Equally important, this ground swell to teach thinking characteristically does not address issues of equity of access to quality curricula and appropriate cognitive instruction.

The two volumes of this book address these issues. Volume 1 provides research-based descriptions of skilled thinking and self-regulated learning within each of the various dimensions of thinking, factors that influence thinking, and the instructional implications of these descriptions. *Educational Values and Cognitive Instruction: Implications for Reform* explores cognitive instruction in the specific subject areas, key contextual variables in classrooms that inhibit or promote cognitive instruction, issues of equity in access to knowledge and quality instruction, and the implications of research on thinking and cognitive instruction for restructuring schools.

Both volumes are written for two inter-related audiences who must necessarily form closer partnerships if educational reform is to be effective: researchers interested in educational reform and practitioners interested in research on thinking. This includes researchers and practitioners interested in various areas of cognitive psychology, expert teaching and teacher education, socio-linguistics, instructional technology, and the change process. It also includes philosophers, program developers, curriculum specialists and staff developers, policymakers, and teachers on the cutting edge of research and practice.

The remainder of this introduction sets the stage for the two volumes. The first section identifies changes in society that most impact on the need to teach all students to learn how to think. The second section considers the context of educational reform and discusses the need to link the movement to teach thinking to the current emphasis on restructuring schools, paying special attention to issues of equity and excellence. The third section describes how this book grew out of a unique research-into-practice collaboration. Finally, the fourth section provides a brief description of each of the chapters.

THE NEED FOR TEACHING THINKING

Although many economic trends are important for understanding reform in schools, the primary concern is the shift away from traditional manufacturing to a focus on information and services. A universal implication of this shift is that society is decreasing its dependence on the human hand and increasing its dependence on the human brain (Catterall, 1988). Thus, excellence in the future will increasingly depend on the capabilities of the intellect.

Ironically, the human resources available for the growth of these technology-driven, mind-expanding tasks are shrinking dramatically. According to Hodgkinson (1985), there will be steep declines in the number of students who graduate from high school and college in the next few decades. Complicating these problems is the surge of unskilled laborers with non-English speaking backgrounds (Hodgkinson, 1985). We must also consider the spread of an increasingly violent element in our society that continues to sap the constructive energies of those within it and of its victims (*U.S. News,* 1988). Thus, there is some serious question as to whether there will be enough educated persons to satisfy the nation's needs for technology, the military, and health services, as well as other occupations including teaching.

Moreover, various indicators suggest that far too many students are either unskilled or very limited in their capability to read and write with fluency and to solve problems effectively (Berlin & Sum, 1988; Venezky, Kaestle, & Sum, 1987; cf. Catterall, 1988). The traditional concept of schooling was developed at the turn of the century to help students acquire basic skills so that they could fill the nation's need for manufacturing and other industries (Tucker, 1988). Schools themselves were designed like factories (Keating & Oakes, 1988). However, as more jobs require processing information and providing services, the "product" yielded by the nation's schools does not seem to fit the needs of a changing society. According to Tucker (1988), we must create organizations capable of vastly increasing students' capacity for higher-order thinking. We must improve students' capability to acquire, analyze, and apply complex information; to locate, communicate, and produce information effectively; to solve problems quickly and efficiently; and to be committed to lifelong learning.

These economic and social changes have important implications for education. First, the deficit in skilled workers, including teachers, will place unprecedented cognitive and psychological demands on those who are able to process complex information and provide services—both to do the work with fewer resources and to train others. Therefore, there is an increased need to understand the nature of thinking and cognitive instruction. Second, these changes will place unprecedented demands on schools to reduce the deficit of skilled workers.

THE CONTEXT FOR EDUCATIONAL REFORM

Although there is a great national need to improve the ability to think for all students, schools are in a crisis that is both widespread and historically significant in two respects:

1. The exceptionally high dropout rates, low achievement levels, and other deficits in learning suggest that traditional concepts of schooling are essentially bankrupt (e.g., Carnegie Foundation Special Report, 1988; Levin, 1986; Ornstein & Levine, in press). American schools do not provide effective curricula, instruction, and assessment for America's future economic needs or for a critical democracy. And there is mounting evidence that students do not attend school, or are failing school, in part because of their needs for social bonding to the mainstream of social

and economic opportunities; and in part because of barriers to learning created by poverty (Fennimore, 1988; Fernandez, Geary, Lesko, Rutter, Smith, & Wehlage, 1987; National Coalition of Advocates for Students, 1985). Thus, future schools may need to redefine the boundaries of school services needed to support academic achievement for those who are poor and/or disconnected from society (e.g.; Council of Chief State School Officers, 1987a; Farrar & Hampel, 1987; Parnell, 1986).

2. There are crucial issues of equity at the heart of these problems. Students at risk of academic failure are disproportionately poor and minorities. Moreover, they continue to be placed in basic skills programs and lower tracks that are inferior in quality, compared to instruction in the regular classroom (Resnick & Resnick, 1985). Thus, even when students *successfully* exit from basic skills programs, they may be able to decode and compute with efficiency but be unable to read, write, and solve problems with fluency (Berlin & Sum, 1988; Jones, in press; Shanker, 1988). Increasingly, there are arguments that this differential access to quality education is as serious in its consequences as the inequalities that led to *Brown vs. Board of Education* in 1954 and later the Kerner Report (see Jones, 1988; Keating & Oakes, 1988; National Coalition of Advocates for Students, 1985; National Education Association, 1988).

The movement to restructure schools and the movement to teach thinking are responses to these problems. Although both movements are needed, they are currently disconnected. That is, many of the people and resources that are involved in restructuring schools to provide for school-based management, parental involvement, community-business partnerships, and improvements in teacher education are essentially separate from the people and resources identified for improving students' academic achievement and ability to think. Moreover, in most networks for restructuring schools, concepts such as school-based management and parent/community involvement are ends in themselves; they are not driven by the need to improve student achievement, some exceptions notwithstanding (e.g., Chion-Kenney, 1987).

Additionally, the popular movement to teach thinking skills in adjunct programs fails to address key issues of equity and excellence. Perhaps the most serious equity problem is that thinking skills programs are frequently designed for and distributed to high-achieving students (Feuerstein, Volume 2), leaving low-achieving students, who need them the most, to suffer the limitations of poorly coordinated and poor quality basic skills approaches. Regarding excellence, the most serious problem is transfer. Students who master the skills in adjunct programs undoubtedly enhance their repertoire of thinking strategies. Yet, with some exceptions, there is little evidence that they can readily apply these strategies to improve achievement in studying literature and other disciplines (Resnick, 1987).

Aware of the limitations of the movement to teach isolated thinking skills, researchers, practitioners, and policy makers increasingly argue that the best instruction for thinking is the infusion approach. According to this approach, thinking occurs within the context of specific tasks; therefore, instruction for thinking should be situated in specific problems and functional contexts that are embedded in the disciplines, rather than in adjunct programs taught as ends in themselves. This approach has also yielded powerful instructional strategies calling for a change in the role of the teacher away from giving information to teacher as model, decision maker, mediator, strategist, and collaborator. Moreover, in most cases, these strategies are as appropriate and effective for low-achieving students as they are for high-achieving students, for example, reciprocal teaching (see Paris & Winograd, Vol. 2).

Unlike the thinking skills adjunct approach, the concepts in the infusion approach cannot merely be imported as a commercial thinking skills program and added to the curriculum. Infusing instruction for thinking requires restructuring curriculum, instruction, and assessment in each content area as well as teacher education and models of instructional leadership generally.

To support this approach, we must have both fundamental restructuring and a focus on teaching thinking in every classroom. If we do not link the movement to restructure schools to the movement to teach thinking and to improve student performance, initiatives for educational change will become ends in themselves, that is, merely reorganizations for adults without transformations in learning for students. In the final analysis, that is what the these two volumes are about: to engender in educators, researchers, and policymakers a vision of schooling that is based on a thorough understanding of the various dimension of thinking, cognitive instruction, and the full implications of these concepts for schooling.

Without exception, the recommendations for teaching thinking in both volumes require fundamental changes in defining curriculum objectives, instructional strategies, assessment, and policies for grouping. Further, if these changes are to occur, we must consider models of change that involve a paradigm shift in our thinking about the purpose of schools and the characteristics of the people who will run them.

However, before we describe the individual chapters, it is important to understand how the organization of the first volume grew out of a collaboration between the North Central regional Educational Laboratory (NCREL) and the Association for Supervision and Curriculum Development (ASCD).

THE DIMENSIONS OF THINKING PROJECTS:
A UNIQUE COLLABORATION

In 1985, Ronald Brandt assembled seven educators to prepare a framework for school districts and other agencies committed to teaching thinking. Their efforts culminated in the book, *Dimensions of Thinking* (Marzano et al, 1988). The project identified six dimensions of thinking that were distinguished in the research literature:

1. metacognition
2. cognitive processes (conceptualizing, principle formation, comprehending, composing, oral discourse, scientific enquiry, problem solving, and decision making)
3. core thinking skills such as representation, summarizing, and elaboration
4. critical thinking
5. creative thinking
6. the role of content knowledge

These dimensions were not conceptualized as a hierarchical taxonomy of mutually exclusive categories of thinking. From the outset, the dimensions were seen as providing a framework for conceptualizing research on thinking as well as curriculum and instruction. The thinking operations themselves were seen as frequently overlapping and nonlinear in their relations, often used in clusters that function recursively, and often engaged simultaneously. Thus, the learner could be thinking both critically and creatively at the same time or use a core thinking skill such as summarizing as a means to some comprehension monitoring (a metacognitive behavior) or problem solving (a cognitive process). Moreover, although the ASCD authors (Marzano et al., 1988) clearly focused on defining the various dimensions, they stressed throughout the book that instruction for thinking should be infused into the curriculum, rather than taught separately in adjunct programs with the possible exception of thinking skills programs for students at risk.

Because the authors wanted the fruits of their labors to be consistent with recent research, they arranged for extensive and frequent reviews of the various drafts. Toward this end, ASCD scheduled a conference at Wingspread in which over 60 participants (half researchers and half practitioners) offered suggestions for revisions. On their advice, the book was completely rewritten. After additional rounds of feedback, revisions, editing, and more revisions, the final draft was prepared. In other words, *Dimensions of Thinking* was truly a collaborative effort (Brandt, 1988).

Early in the ASCD project, it was evident that its authors needed to be more systematically informed about the various dimensions of thinking. As they began to seek out research on the various dimensions, it was also clear that cognitive psychologists and philosophers who were expert in one area of thinking often were uninformed about research in other areas. This is a point of considerable importance if we are to understand the nature and process of thinking better and if we are to develop a common language for learning and instruction. Additionally, it was critical for both practitioners and researchers to consider systematically and in depth the implications of the dimensions of thinking concept for instruction and student assessment as well as for the process of systemic change. To address these concerns, the North Central Regional Educational Laboratory (NCREL) supported the development of this parallel work, comprised of this two-volume series.

Thus, our intent from the outset was that the two projects would be interactive. We would use the ASCD framework as a "road map" for the organization of Volume 1 focusing on the dimensions of thinking concept, and the ASCD authors would use materials from the development of this series as they became available. No claim is made that the specific terms used in these volumes are necessarily defined in the same way as those in the ASCD book, nor are any of the authors in these volumes necessarily commited to the ASCD framework.

THE ORGANIZATION OF THESE VOLUMES

Volume 1. The two volumes that comprise this series are organized as follows. Volume 1 has at least one chapter on each of the dimensions of thinking in the ASCD framework as well as separate chapters for all but one of the cognitive processes (principle formation). Each author was asked to describe how thinking operates in a given domain or process, to identify key issues that affect that operation, and to pursue the instructional implications of their research.

Volume 1 begins with two chapters on *metacognition*. In Chapter 1 Paris and Winograd propose to limit the construct of metacognition to knowledge about cognitive states and abilities that can be shared among individuals, as well as to expand that knowledge to include the affective and motivational characteristics of thinking. Much of their chapter is devoted to defining the judgments, beliefs, and choices that will determine successful and unsuccessful self-appraisal and self-regulation. They also consider four instructional strategies that foster these characteristics in the classroom. In Chapter 2, Borkowski, Carr, Rellinger, and Pressley discuss how self-concept and attributional aspects of personal control influence the course of new strategy acquisition, the likelihood of strategy transfer, and the quality of self-understanding.

In Chapter 3, Klausmeier explains the mental operations involved in learning concepts that have specifiable intrinsic, functional, and/or relational attributes, concepts such as *triangle, noun, comprehension,* and *metacognition.* According to him, students, when properly instructed, attain concepts at four successively higher levels, starting with discriminating an example of any given concept as something different from its surroundings through understanding the concept at the level of the expert. Klausmeier identifies the instructional conditions that facilitate concept attainment at the four successively higher levels and indicates that, in general, students require focused instruction to attain the highest level.

In the ASCD framework, principle formation is discussed after concept formation. However, the editors chose not to have a separate chapter on principle formation because there is relatively little research on that topic and because we believe that it operates in similar ways as concept formation and conceptual development as discussed by Klausmeier and Roth.

In Chapter 5, Kline and Delia refer to various approaches to *oral communication,* but they focus on the constructionist perspective they developed on how learners think about oral communication. They define three design logics that are successively more sophisticated: (a) expressive communications designed to tell the listener about the self without necessarily attending to the interests and prior knowledge of the listener, (b) conventional communication designed to secure a desired response, and (c) rhetorical design logics. The latter views the speaking context as created and negotiated by the persons involved to define and construct our social selves and situations.

In Chapter 6 on *comprehension,* Pearson and Raphael differentiate skilled versus unskilled learning in terms of specific thinking skills in a series of examples. However, the chapter focuses on a framework of factors that decades of research have shown to influence reading comprehension and instruction: historical/cultural context, social factors, instructional variables, task, text, and the characteristics of the reader. Finally, they discuss how the thinking skills movement might avoid some of the mistakes of research and practice in reading comprehension. In a parallel chapter on *composition,* Chapter 7, Hayes provides both a vision of the skilled writer and factors in the environment that influence writing and writing instruction: task definition, perception, spatial aspects of text, the physical environment, cultural context, and social context.

The next two chapters focus on processes in specific content areas. In Chapter 8 on *problem solving*, Silver and Marshall discuss factors that relate to successful problem solving in mathematics and science, issues that influence learning problem-solving skills and problem-solving instruction, and the inadequacy of current conceptions of problem-solving expertise. In Chapter 9 on *scientific thinking*, Tweney and Walker discuss three concerns: (a) the discrepancy between the nonlinear and value-laden reasoning processes used to think scientifically and the orthodox categories of formal reasoning used to express the end result of scientific reasoning that is value free; (b) the process of utilizing "expert" knowledge in science; and (c) recent research on the process of problem solving.

In the ASCD framework, problem solving and decision making are closely parallel operations. Although the two processes do indeed have fundamental similarities, the corresponding chapters in these volumes are not parallel. This is because there was very little empirical research on decision making that was not in a specific context such as teaching or the business world. For obvious reasons, *teaching* was selected. It is labelled as teaching because teacher thinking is described largely in terms of teacher decision making and because decision making in other contexts may have important differences. In Chapter 10, Borko and Shavelson review recent research on teacher planning and interactive decision making, provide a framework for analyzing teacher decision making, examine research on teacher decision making using their framework, and suggest implications for future research.

In Chapter 11, Derry's focus is on *learning strategies,* rather than the term skills, as defined in the ASCD framework, in part because of the concern voiced earlier about learning skills as being ends in themselves. Strategies and skills are defined in this series and her chapter as a means to learning. However, Derry's definition of learning strategies is highly consistent with the ASCD framework in substance and she discusses many of the same skills within the context of a discussion of how declarative and procedural knowledge is acquired.

Chapter 12, by Bransford, Vye, Kinzer, and Risko, defines what is needed to teach *content.* The authors focus on two key issues: the importance of specific knowledge and problems in accessing information. Basically, the authors argue for an integrated approach that is designed to teach specific content knowledge in the context of problem solving. Toward this end, they provide principles of anchored instruction that situates instruction in the context of specific problems and real-life contexts.

In Chapter 13 on *creative thinking,* Perkins provides a fine-tuned specification of the nature of creative thinking such as the effects of values. Then Perkins considers how creative thinking is related to each of the other dimensions of thinking, how to assess creative thinking, and how to teach creative thinking. In Chapter 14 on *critical thinking*, the last chapter, Paul provides an equally fine-tuned description of the philosophical mind, focusing heavily on how values are related to thinking. Paul also wishes to place the contributions of philosophy in perspective. Toward this end, he contrasts the differences between philosophy and psychology within a number of categories related to learning and instruction; later, he uses the same categories to show areas of agreement between psychology and philosophy, in contrast to traditional assumptions. Thus, it is fitting that his chapter is the last in the framework because it summarizes some of the themes in other chapters.

Given that both ASCD's framework and these volumes call for fundamental educational reform, their implementation will not be easy or without controversy. Specifically, we would like to call attention to two sets of criticisms. First, NCREL commissioned Raymond Nickerson (1987) to write a critique of the ASCD framework for the Wingspread conference to help ASCD authors to revise their framework. Specifically, he argues that our choice of the word dimensions of thinking is problematic in important ways, that the breakdown of dimensions into core skills and processes implies a componential approach which may not be warranted, that there is the risk of reification in developing an organizational framework, and that there are some neglected issues. Although focused explicitly on the ASCD book, many of the comments apply to the this Volume. Therefore, we have included it in this Volume with our conclusions in the spirit of critical thinking.

Second, Richard Paul wrote a formal protest at Wingspread concerning ASCD's framework for its bias favoring research from psychology over the contributions of philosophy (Paul, 1986). Because we believed there was much merit in Paul's comments, we invited Paul to publish his criticisms in this book, and we tried to give more attention to philosophy. We did this for two reasons: (1) because its contributions deserve far more attention from psychologists, teacher educators, teachers, policy makers; and (2) because we believe that philosophers may also benefit from exchanges with psychologists. We are particularly gratified that Paul's chapter reflects both the differences between philosophy and psychology as well as the similarities. However, the bias he describes is still present in these volumes and in ASCD's framework, largely because philosophers tend not to conduct empirical quantitative research in the classroom or write in popular journals to the same degree as other researchers. We hope that such exchanges will increase communication and exchange of ideas among the two groups in both academic and popular forums.

In *Educational Values and Cognitive Instruction: Implications for Reform*, Idol and Jones have introduced each of the chapters in the Preface of that volume, so we will not describe them here. Instead, we would like to comment about the overall organization. Volume 2 is in three parts. Part 1 focuses directly on the issue of integrating the teaching of thinking in subject matter disciplines. Specifically, there are chapters on critical thinking, reading, and writing with a special focus on infusing these dimensions of thinking in the content areas. Other chapters discuss intervention programs for students at risk, cognitive instruction and technology, and the assessment of thinking.

Part 2 discusses contextual factors that affect thinking and teaching thinking in the classroom: grouping, student motivation, policy for students at risk and their access to quality information, and the role of language and culture in the life of the classroom. Part 3 considers the implications of research on thinking and cognitive instruction for changes in schooling and teacher education. The book ends appropriately with a chapter by Marzano, the first author of ASCD's *Dimensions of Thinking*, describing the paradigm shift in education that will be needed if we are to fully address the implications of the position that thinking should be infused in all classrooms.

Finally, we conclude with a tribute to the authors. Throughout the description of their chapters, it has been very difficult to be dispassionate about the very fine writing and insights of each set of authors. Their chapters are thought-provoking and thorough in scope. And certainly their contributions are most timely. We are indebted to them for their expertise and perseverance.

Beau Fly Jones
Lorna Idol

REFERENCES

Berlin, G., & Sum, A. (1988). *Toward a more perfect union: Basic skills, poor families, and our economic future.* New York: The Ford Foundation.

Brandt, R. S. (1988). The development of *Dimensions of Thinking.* In B. F. Jones (Ed.), *Perspectives on Dimensions of Thinking* (pp. 1–6). Elmhurst, IL: North Central Regional Educational Laboratory.

Brown v. Board of Education of Topeka, 347 U.S. 483,484 (1954).

Carnegie Foundation Special Report. (1988). *An imperiled generation: Saving urban schools.* Princeton, NJ: The Carnegie Foundation for the Advancement of Teaching.

Catterall, J. (1988, March). *Tomorrow's workforce: Over-credentialled and under-prepared?* Paper presented at the conference Can California be Competitive and Caring?, sponsored by the Institute of Industrial Relations, University of California at Los Angeles.

Chion-Kenney, L. (1987). A report from the field: The Coalition of Essential Schools. *American Educator, 12*(4), 18–24.

Council of Chief State School Officers. (1987, November). *Assuring school success for students at risk* (A Council Policy Statement). Washington, DC: Council of Chief State School Officers.

Farrar, E., & Hampel, R. L. (1987). Social services in American high schools. *Phi Delta Kappan, 69*(3), 297–303.

Fennimore, T. (1988). *A guide for dropout prevention: Creating an integrated environment in secondary schools.* Columbus, OH: National Center for Research on Vocational Education.

Fernandez, R., Geary, P. A., Lesko, N., Rutter, R. A., Smith, G., & Wehlage, G. (1987, December). *Dropout prevention and recovery: Fourteen case studies.* Madison, WI: University of Wisconsin-Madison.

Hodgkinson, H. (1985). *All one system: Demography of schools, kindergarten through graduate school.* Washington, DC: Institute for Instructional Leadership.

Jones, B. F. (1988). Toward redefining curriculum and instruction for students at risk. In B. Z. Presseisen (Ed.), *Students at risk and thinking: Issues and research perspectives* (pp. 76–103). Washington, DC: National Education Association.

Jones, B. F. (1989). *Students at risk versus the Board of Education.* Proposal submitted to the Public Broadcasting Service.

Keating, P., & Oakes, J. (1988). *Access to knowledge: Breaking down school barriers to learning.* Denver, CO: The Education Commission of the States.

Levin, H. M. (1986). *Educational reform for disadvantaged students: An emerging crisis.* Washington DC: National Education Association.

Marzano, R., Brandt, R. S., Hughes, C., Jones, B. F., Presseisen, B. Z., Rankin, S., & Suhor, C. (1988). *Dimensions of thinking.* Alexandria, VA: Association for Supervision and Curriculum Development.

National Coalition of Advocates for Students. (1985). *Barriers to excellence: Our children at risk.* Boston, MA: National Coalition of Advocates for Students.

National Education Association. (1988). *. . . And justice for all: The NEA Executive Committee Study Group Reports on ethnic minority concerns.* Washington, DC: National Education Association.

Nickerson, R. (1987). *Dimensions of thinking: A critique* (Tech. Rep. HST-10). Elmhurst, IL: North Central Regional Educational Laboratory.

Ornstein, A. C., & Levine, D. U. (in press). Providing equal educational opportunity. In A. C. Ornstein & D. U. Levine (Eds.), *Introduction to foundations of education* (4th ed.). Boston, MA: Houghton Mifflin.

Parnell, D. (1986). *The neglected majority.* Washington, DC: Community College Press.

Paul, R. (1986). *The cognitive psychological bias of Dimensions of Thinking.* Unpublished paper.

Resnick, D. P., & Resnick, L. B. (1985). Standards, curriculum, and performance: A historical and comparative perspective. *Educational Researcher, 14,* 5–21.

Resnick, L.B. (1987). *Education and learning to think.* Washington, DC: National Academy Press.

Shanker, A. (1988, May 29). New Rx needed: Education better but not good enough. *New York Times* (Sect. 4), p. 7.

Tucker, M. S. (1988). Peter Drucker: Knowledge, work, and the structure of schools. *Educational Leadership, 45,* 44–46.

U.S. News. (1988, May 9). Kids who sell crack. pp. 20–33.

U.S. National Advisory Committee on Civil Disorders. (1968). *The Kerner Report* Washington, DC: U.S. Printing Office and Bantam.

Venezky, R., Kaestle, C. F., & Sum, A. M. (1987). *The subtle danger: Reflections on the literary ability of America's young adults.* Princeton, NJ: Center for the Assessment of Educational Progress, Educational Testing Service.

How Metacognition Can Promote Academic Learning and Instruction

Scott G. Paris
University of Michigan

Peter Winograd
University of Kentucky

This chapter is about metacognition and academic learning. The central message is that students can enhance their learning by becoming aware of their own thinking as they read, write, and solve problems in school. Teachers can promote this awareness directly by informing students about effective problem-solving strategies and discussing cognitive and motivational characteristics of thinking. The twin benefits of this "consciousness-raising" are: (a) it transfers responsibility for monitoring learning from teachers to students themselves, and (b) it promotes positive self-perceptions, affect, and motivation among students. In this manner, metacognition provides personal insights into one's own thinking and fosters independent learning.

A great deal of research supports the importance of metacognition in cognitive development and academic learning (Brown, Bransford, Ferrara, & Campione, 1983; Paris & Lindauer, 1982; Paris, Wasik, & van der Westhuizen, 1988; Pressley, Borkowski, & O'Sullivan, 1985). In the first section of this chapter we review this research noting both the virtues and the problems associated with metacognition, and we argue that it is time to develop a new perspective on the construct. In the second section of the chapter we define metacognition as knowledge about cognitive states and abilities that can be shared among individuals while at the same time expanding the construct to include affective and motivational characteristics of thinking.

The remainder of the chapter illustrates how students and teachers share and apply metacognition in classrooms. In the third section we discuss how students' understanding of academic tasks and perceptions of themselves as learners influence their judgments and beliefs about their personal learning. These judgments and beliefs affect the strategies they choose and the effort they expend in school. In the final section of the chapter we discuss instructional methods that enhance metacognition and learning. We describe methods that facilitate metacognitive dialogues in the classroom because such discussions allow teachers and students to exchange their views about strategies and motivation required to master academic tasks. Knowledge about learning is shared explicitly among teachers and students in these dialogues. We describe how instructional interactions that promote metacognition facilitate self-regulated learning. Our point is *not* to establish metacognition as a curriculum objective, but rather to show how students' understanding of their own thinking can be enhanced by teachers.

ELUSIVE DEFINITIONS AND FUZZY CONCEPTS

A reasonable starting point is to define metacognition but most researchers eschew rigid or operational definitions. Instead, they use examples of students' thinking about thinking in order to illustrate metacognition. Consider the following reflections of expert readers as they think aloud about text they are reading (from Afflerbach & Johnston, 1986):

> . . . I don't understand very well this word . . . but . . . my guess right now . . . is that it's—it's many things put together somehow . . . so—what I'll try to do . . . probably is try to understand this word . . . I'll expect to understand it after reading . . . the rest of the text . . . because . . . it's obvious that the word is very important . . . (p. 59)

> . . . I would be skeptical immediately . . . uh—to be quite honest . . . uhm . . . but—but . . . that's because of my knowledge of the subject . . . and perhaps I ought to concentrate more on . . . exactly how they're saying this . . . (p. 67)

> . . . I kind of feel insecure reading these things so I would . . . I'm gonna try to read it again . . . (p. 69)

These vignettes show how readers try to evaluate the importance of ideas in text and check their understanding as they construct meaning. They assess their own knowledge, confidence, and strategies. These are clearly cognitive judgments about their own cognitive states and abilities, and they conform to conventional descriptions of metacognition.

Flavall (1978), in his pioneering work, chose to emphasize the learner's knowledge about variables related to the person, task, and strategy in order to compartmentalize metacognitive knowledge that might be germane to remembering. Brown (1978) reviewed the same early research on metacognition but emphasized aspects of executive cognition such as planning, monitoring, and revising one's thinking. Most researchers have now blended those twin approaches into a definition that emphasizes (a) knowledge about cognitive states and processes and (b) control or executive aspects of metacognition (Borkowski, 1985; Brown et al., 1983; Wellman, 1985). This familiar dichotomy of the mind is consistent with information processing accounts of declarative and procedural knowledge and captures two essential features of metacognition—self-appraisal and self-management of cognition.

Cognitive Self-Appraisal

Self-appraisal includes personal reflections about one's knowledge states and abilities. Metacognitions of this sort answer questions such as, "Do I know the capital of Idaho? Can I memorize a list of 20 words in 10 minutes? Can I derive a formula to calculate the area of a trapezoid?" These questions interrogate particular bits of knowledge or one's ability to meet a cognitive goal. In Flavell's terms, they are judgments about one's personal cognitive abilities, task factors that influence cognitive difficulty, or cognitive strategies that may facilitate or impede performance. The appraisals often reflect static judgments because people are asked to assess knowledge or gauge ability in a hypothetical situation. Paris, Lipson, and Wixson (1983) described metacognitive knowledge in terms of declarative, procedural, and conditional knowledge because self-appraisal answers questions about *what* you know, *how* you think, and *when* and *why* to apply knowledge or strategies.

Many students have shown that students are not adept at cognitive self-appraisal. For example, young students often mistakenly believe that they understand what they hear or read (Markman & Gorin, 1981). They have an illusion of comprehension following reading because they rarely monitor their knowledge (Wagoner, 1983). Paris and Myers (1981) observed that 10-year-olds failed to identify many scrambled phrases and nonsense words while reading. Similarly, young students often believe they are ready for a test before the information has been retained well (Flavell, 1978; Pressley, Snyder, Levin, Murray, & Ghatala, 1987). Children's abilities to appraise various reading purposes, strategies, and their own understanding improves with age and reading ability (Canney & Winograd, 1979; Forrest-Pressley & Waller, 1984; Myers & Paris, 1978).

Cognitive Self-Management

In contrast, self-management refers to "metacognitions in action"—in other words, how metacognition helps to orchestrate cognitive aspects of problem solving. For example, the ability of students to form good plans, to use a variety of strategies, and to monitor and revise ongoing performance are executive cognitions that help guide and coordinate thinking (Baker & Brown, 1984). Self-management is reflected in the plans that learners make before tackling a task, in the adjustments they make as they work, and in the revisions they make afterwards. Paris and Lindauer (1982) described these executive actions as evaluating, planning, and regulating. Students who engage these tactics are good trouble-shooters, indeed, even trouble-avoiders, because they are resourceful at repairing their own problem solving (Wittrock, 1986).

Cognitive self-management is a popular aspect of metacognition because it has direct implications for students' performance and subsequent instruction. Researchers and teachers alike are less interested in what children report about what they know and are much more interested in the efficiency and effectiveness of their actual thinking skills (Winne & Marx, 1987). Self-management of thinking applies to virtually any domain of problem solving in or out of school, and thus provides a rich source of information about learning and development because metacognition helps students interpret and adapt to learning experiences.

Virtues of Metacognition

These two aspects of metacognition, self-appraisal and self-management of thinking, have helped cognitive and educational psychologists to focus on important areas of children's learning that have often been neglected. Thus, metacognition as a psychological construct and a dimension of thinking has several virtues (Marzano et al., 1987). First, it focuses our attention on the role of awareness and executive management of our own thinking. Metacognition helps learners become active participants in their own performance rather than the passive recipients of instruction and imposed experiences. It is consistent with constructivist accounts of learning and development (Paris & Byrnes, 1989). Second, because metacognition emphasizes *personal* appraisal and management, it is oriented to analyses of individual differences in cognitive development and learning. Such a perspective has been sorely lacking in developmental and educational psychology despite the plea for theories that are sensitive to individual differences in styles and abilities. Third, metacognition is obviously embedded in cognitive development and represents the kind of knowledge and executive abilities that develop with experience and schooling. It is both a product and producer of cognitive development.

A fourth general virtue of metacognition is that the constructive, personal, strategic thinking that is involved in metacognition is amenable to classroom instruction. Teachers can encourage metacognitive dialogues and promote self-appraisal and self-management skills (Paris, Wasik, & Turner, in press). A fifth virtue, which we discuss later, is that self-appraisal and self-management invite both cognitive and motivational explanations because skill and will are interwoven in reflections and anticipations about learning (Corno & Mandinach, 1983; Covington, 1983; Nicholls, 1983; Paris & Cross, 1983). Thus, traditional educational problems such as the transfer of learning, production and generalization of strategies, and learned helplessness can be analyzed from new perspectives provided by metacognition. In our view, many of these traditional problems have been intransigent to theoretical solutions or instructional interventions because the analyses did not focus on the combined cognitive, metacognitive, and motivational aspects of academic learning (Johnston & Winograd, 1985; Winograd & Paris, 1989).

Persistent Problems

Despite the many virtues of metacognition for developmental and educational psychology, the definition of metacognition remains a thorny issue. *Any* cognition that one might have relevant to knowledge and thinking might be classified as a metacognition, and thus inclusive definitions are impossible. That is precisely why Wellman (1985) defined metacognition as a "fuzzy concept" and is perhaps the reason why Brown, Flavell, and others have used prototypical examples of metacognition to illustrate metacognition rather than operational definitions that may constrain the construct. Thus, metacognition remains open-ended and definitions of metacognition almost become projective tests. Researchers bemoan the imprecision of the term and attribute to it those things that they feel are important about thinking and learning. As Flavell (1985) has noted, the really important things about cognitive development are usually difficult to pin down, define, and demarcate.

The disadvantages of fuzzy definitions of metacognition are numerous. First, there is a fundamental disagreement about whether metacognition means conscious awareness of thinking. Some researchers argue that metacognition can be unconscious, tacit, and inaccessible (e.g., Pressley, Borkowski, & Schneider, 1987). These views tend to emanate from people oriented to the executive functions of metacognition and self-management. Other researchers focus on reports of cognitive self-appraisal derived from interviews, think-aloud protocols, and subjective reports. Thus, various orientations to metacognition have invited different methodologies and definitions.

A second disadvantage of fuzzy definitions involves measurement. If metacognition is equated with verbal reports and awareness, there are serious issues of validity and reliability. Critics point out that subjects' verbal reports are often inaccurate (Garner, 1987), although verbal reports about performance seem to be more accurate when they are collected immediately following performance and the questions are designed to interrogate specific aspects of thinking (Afflerbach & Johnston, 1984; Garner, 1988). The problem of measurement is severe when considering the performance of experts who may be unaware of the complexity of their thinking or novices who may be unable to explain their thinking. Perhaps in both cases subjects have knowledge about their mental states and abilities but cannot access or report the information.

The consequences of open-ended definitions and difficult measurement of metacognition reveal a third disadvantage with the construct, namely, it cannot have explanatory power. It is gratuitous to attribute performance variation to levels of metacognition when it can only be inferred from performance itself. Attributions to good or poor metacognition when it is not measured independently are simply attributes to the "ghost in the machine" and add no psychological explanation.

A fourth disadvantage of the construct metacognition is that prescriptions for instruction or intervention are unclear without a better understanding of how metacognition facilitates or impedes learning and performance. We believe that these problems are serious and may hinder research and conceptual development on the issue of metacognition. The important aspects of self-appraisal and self-management can be infused in other kinds of theories and research that avoid these problems in definition and measurement, and thus it may not be surprising to see the term gather growing criticism among academic researchers (Cavanaugh & Perlmutter, 1982) while simultaneously achieving popularity among educators who are seeking new ways of fostering cognitive instruction and self-regulated learning. What are we to do?

NEW PERSPECTIVES ON METACOGNITION

We believe that the construct of metacognition is too important to be set adrift. There is widespread enthusiasm for the emphasis on metacognition, both in teachers' instruction and in students' independent learning.

Revived interest in Vygotsky's theory of socially mediated learning has initiated searches for cognitive variables that are amenable to social exchange. Metacognition is an excellent candidate because insight about self-appraisal and self-management can be promoted by other people as well as by self-discovery. In a sense, metacognition is a mirror on one's knowledge and thinking, and the reflection can come from within the individual or from other people (Paris, Jacobs, & Cross, 1987). It is our belief that metacognition fits well within the new social/cultural/cognitive emphases on learning and development and forms an appropriate model for education that has not been provided by behavioral, Piagetian, or information processing theories.

Our proposal is straightforward. First, we propose to limit the construct of metacognition to knowledge about cognitive states and abilities that can be shared among people. Second, we propose to expand the scope of metacognition to include affective and motivational characteristics of thinking. We outline each of these proposals in the following sections.

Metacognition as Shared Knowledge

Awareness and verbal reporting are the most likely ways to exhibit or share knowledge about thinking, but other ways are possible (e.g., indirect verbal prompts, teaching strategies, written accounts, and so forth). Shared knowledge is observable, verifiable, and measurable. Yet, we explicitly want to counter two traditional criticisms. First, accuracy of verbal reports is not the critical issue. Instead it is the relation between what people say and how they act that determines the *functional role* of the person's thoughts and feelings about thinking. For example, if a woman believes that listening to foreign language records while sleeping will increase language learning and she acts accordingly, then her metacognition is important for guiding her attempts to learn. Likewise, a boy who believes himself incapable of learning to multiply fractions and subsequently gives up trying is acting in accordance with his cognitive self-appraisal.

When cognitive regulation is the context in which metacognition is viewed, then the important issue becomes the correspondence between metacognition and action. How do thoughts and feelings of learners guide their thinking, effort, and behavior? The significance of what subjects report about their own self-appraisal and self-management can be deeply significant or epiphenomenal depending on the impact it has on their own behavior. Thus, the emphasis on regulation, whether by self or other people, reorients metacognition as a functional means to learning rather than a goal in itself. This reinforces our second point—metacognition should not be regarded as a final objective for learning or instruction. It is embedded in ongoing thinking and problem solving and is an intermediate step to proficiency. Although we have praised the virtues of metacognition, we seek to bury it in student learning. The goal of education is not to create reflective thinkers who are cautious and self-conscious about their own thinking. That would immobilize learning instead of enhancing it. Instead, metacognition can provide students with knowledge and confidence that *enables* them to manage their own learning and *empowers* them to be inquisitive and zealous in their pursuits.

We believe that metacognition is often relatively brief and infrequent in the classroom, yet it can play a powerful role. Three situations in particular are influenced by the knowledge about thinking that is shared among teachers and students. First, as children acquire new knowledge and skills, they achieve mastery. Metacognition may be critical for this phase because it allows students to understand their own thinking and learning. The awareness stimulated in the mastery phase of learning is particularly vulnerable to outside intervention by teachers and peers. A second occasion for metacognition is in the realm of trouble-shooting or debugging. When problems are encountered, students may need recourse to other strategies such as monitoring their performance or revising their plans. They may also seek help from others. Awareness of the cognitive demands of the task and the benefits of various strategies may provide explicit information about appropriate solutions. A third occasion in which metacognition may be particularly useful is initial teaching. Describing a new skill to be learned and the steps required to master it requires a tutor to dissect the task and present it in a meaningful way to a novice. Whether the instruction is provided by an expert, teacher, or peer, metacognitive understanding of the task at hand can facilitate instruction. These occasions are important for classroom learning, yet they may involve relatively brief "bursts of metacognitive exchanges" among teachers and students.

Metacognition provides cognitive tools for accomplishing the craft of schooling. These tools are the means whereby students achieve self-appraisal and self-management of their own thinking. For example, a common metacognitive tool in elementary reading instruction is the reminder to think about a topic before reading about it. Children are encouraged to read a title and think about what they know in order to activate relevant background knowledge (Langer, 1984; Ogle, 1983). When writing a composition, they are reminded to plan a series of ideas and a conclusion before they begin. Among older students the cognitive tools include a list of strategies such as skimming, summarizing, paraphrasing, predicting, and self-questioning as one reads, writes, or solves problems (Paris et al., 1983). These strategies can be domain specific such as the use of algorithms to check mathematical computations, or they can be general heuristics for solving problems such as planning and monitoring. The breadth of application of the cognitive tool is an empirical issue, not a definitional issue.

The metaphor of cognitive tools is consistent with conceptualizations offered by Vygotsky (1978) and others. Collectively, they focus on the use of problem-solving techniques and the coordination of particular tools to solve particular problems. A good craftsman is not a person who simply collects a wide assortment of tools; good craftsmen use tools selectively to accomplish particular purposes. Good craftsmen use tools wisely and independently. The analogy works well with the acquisition of cognitive strategies and metacognition for enhancing the craft of school learning (Collins, Brown, & Newman, in press; Paris & Oka, 1982). Students should be taught to use particular strategies in particular settings to accomplish specific purposes and not simply taught an inventory of strategies. Exhortations to "be strategic" or "be metacognitive" are not sufficient to teach students how to use cognitive tools. We will have more to say shortly about instructional models that facilitate the development of the craft of learning, but the metaphor of "apprentice" provides an appropriate foreshadowing.

Motivational Characteristics of Metacognition

Cognitive evaluations are rarely dispassionate assessments. If children are asked, "Are you a good reader? Do you like math? Why did you get such a high/low grade? Do you think you can solve this problem? Which course will you choose?," they will respond with strong emotions. Flavell (1985) referred to the emotional accompaniments of cognitive self-appraisal as "metacognitive experiences." They color what students think about themselves as learners with strong emotions such as doubt, shame, and helplessness, or confidence, pride, and self-assuredness. Consider the anecdote reported by Brown et al. (1983) of a 10-year-old boy named Daniel who was labeled "learning disabled."

> Upon encountering his first laboratory task, Daniel volunteered this telling comment: "Is this a memory thing? (It wasn't.) Didn't they tell you I can't do this stuff—Didn't they tell you I don't have a memory." (p. 147)

Is self-appraisal devoid of affect? Not usually. Consider this example of an adult's recollection of learning to read.

Oh, I can remember those agonies but I don't know when that was, of passing the story around the room deal. "OK, Johnny, you read the first four sentences," (Groans and pretends to read.) "Your turn Lee." And you go (strangled sound) (laughs), you just choke right there. God, I read badly. To this day I have difficulty spelling anything except my name. That was probably the worst experience of my life . . . I think probably that is the most humiliating, embarrassing, and most horrible thing that teachers do to kids. Maybe it was just because I was the one who couldn't do it. "It's your turn to read," and you didn't even know what page they were on. (Laughs) I was off someplace but even if I knew what page they were on and you read over a word and you botch the word and you didn't know what it was or they make you "sound it out." You didn't even know what it sounded like. Yuk. No (laughs), I don't remember enjoying that ever. (D. Taylor, 1983, *Family Literacy,* p. 10)

Self-appraisal and self-management are personal assessments filled with affect. A view of metacognition in the service of academic learning and the development of schoolcraft necessarily entails motivated, social interactions. Our focus on academic learning is decidedly different than the view noted by Brown et al. (1983) who said, "Bleak though it may sound, academic cognition is relatively effortful, isolated, and cold" (p. 78). We concur that classroom learning is effortful, but the long-term goal is to lessen the effort required for different cognitive activities so that they flow automatically and smoothly. However, neither the long-term goals of schooling nor the initial stages of learning appear to us to be isolated, unmotivated, or unemotional. Consider the following episode of Charlie, age 11, who is engaged in a routine writing task in sixth grade.

Charlie knows he will write today because every Friday after lunch is writing time in English. He wonders what the topic will be this week. This is his most hated moment in the week because he has problems with everything related to writing. These problems have been pointed out to him since third grade. Charlie takes his seat. The dreaded words come his way: "Clear your desks, paper out, pencils at the ready. This week's assignment is to write about a day you might have with Abraham Lincoln. You have all heard about Abraham Lincoln. I want you to write now about what it would be like if you could spend a day with him. Class, what are you going to look out for? Anyone? Yes, Sandy."

"No spelling or punctuation errors, Mr. Chase?"

"You've got it, Sandy. This time I take off five points for any misspelled word, two for any word that is illegible, and two for any misplaced punctuation marks. Begin."

Charlie stares at his empty paper, his mind blank as usual in these first moments. It takes him five minutes to get over the shock of the assignment.

He feels his heart beating in his ear lobes. "Fucking bastard," he mutters to himself. He doesn't know if he hates Mr. Chase more than Abraham Lincoln.

"Better get crackin', Charles. A clean sheet of paper will never win a Nobel Prize for literature," breathes Mr. Chase over his shoulder.

"Up yours," mutters Charlie when Mr. Chase is out of earshot. The white piece of paper is still there. Would that it might be a flag of truce declaring, "No Writing Today." Charlie leans over to a friend and whispers, "Hey Andy, look, I haven't made any mistakes yet." (Graves, 1983. p. 166)

Charlie approaches the task of writing with low expectations for success and few strategies for composing. His apprehension turns to anger and sarcasm because he does not know how to begin the task. His coping tactics circumvent thinking and writing instead of attacking the problem with brainstorming, projection, imagery, outlining, or similar tactics. It is impossible to separate Charlie's lack of strategies and his anxiety. That is precisely why metacognition involves motivational dynamics as well as cognitive knowledge.

Self-appraisal and self-management can be interpreted according to several motivational frameworks. For example, in an expectancy–value orientation (e.g., Feather, 1982), Charlie has low expectations for success and attributes minimal value to writing a composition about Abraham Lincoln. The exercise is onerous and risky because his chances of failure are high. In an attributional frame of reference (e.g., Weiner, 1986), Charlie attributes failure to his own poor ability to write and to the lack of help provided by the teacher. Charlie feels angry toward Mr. Chase and ashamed that he cannot complete the task. It is easier for him to feel guilty about not trying and sarcastic in his remarks to his friends than to try hard at the task and fail. Charlie's expectations, perceptions of the task, and attributions for success and failure can all be regarded as emotionally charged metacognitions. In fact, when one analyzes the scenario of Charlie struggling to write, it is impossible to identify his metacognitions about person, task, and strategy without reference to the affect that accompanies the thoughts.

We believe that metacognition helps students to exhibit intellectual curiosity and persistence, to be inventive in their pursuits of knowledge, and to be strategic in their problem-solving behavior. If metacognition is knowledge about thinking that can be shared among people, then individuals can report it to others, use it to direct another's performance, or use it to analyze and manage their own thinking. Metacognition then becomes a way of facilitating problem solving with "cognitive tools." The tools are used with guidance from others and provide the medium through which teachers can help students construct deeper, richer, better forms of learning. Teachers who understand the ways in which their students think and learn are better prepared to motivate their students and encourage their development in appropriate directions. In the following two sections we illustrate the functions of metacognition in instructional contexts and how teachers can promote the appropriate use of metacognition for academic learning.

JUDGMENTS, BELIEFS, AND CHOICES

In this section of the chapter we discuss three ways in which metacognitions are embedded in classroom learning. We emphasize how students use personally constructed knowledge about themselves and academic tasks to marshall appropriate effort and cognitive strategies. Metacognitions inform and guide these decisions. These episodes of metacognition usually occur at critical junctures in learning, such as initial acquisition, trouble-shooting, and instruction delivered to others. Metacognition influences students' orientations to tasks and their beliefs in their personal abilities. Students' motivational investment flows from these personal beliefs about learning. That is precisely why metacognition is essential for the development of self-regulated learning.

Metacognitive Judgments

Children frequently encounter situations in classrooms where they must make judgments about themselves or the task at hand. For example, students may ask themselves, "What do I know about this topic? Is this task hard or easy? How much should I try? Do I care if I get a good grade? Do I need to check my work? What are the consequences of doing well or poorly?" Of course, there are endless questions that students may ask themselves, but in these instances they are making judgments about the task of learning in particular situations. Questions about effort, expectations, difficulty, and outcomes necessarily include social interactions, motivational dispositions, and consequences of learning. All of these judgments involve self-appraisal of cognition in some form or another. Certainly the evaluation of task demands and difficulty reflects an appreciation of the task complexity and effort required to solve it.

Students' judgments about aspects of the learning situation are the forerunners of their actions. If they judge themselves as having little knowledge and little expectation for success, they will probably expend little effort in learning (Butkowsky & Willows, 1980; Johnston & Winograd, 1985). Therefore, a critical aspect of instruction includes the on-going assessment of children's judgments of the cognitive characteristics of the learning situation. Any attempt to intervene and provide instruction must be predicated on both the child's abilities and cognitive judgments within the setting.

Judgments of the learning situation are metacognitive self-appraisals because they involve a cognitive dimension of evaluation. For example, students can judge their level of comprehension while reading, or preparedness for a test while studying. Judgments like these usually include a standard generated by the self or another person, are specific to a situation, and are open to both cognitive and affective biases. Some students may mistake the goal of the task or exaggerate their perceptions of effort or skill required to master it. Such judgments have been documented by researchers (Canney & Winograd, 1979; Garner, 1987; Paris & Myers, 1981) and may underlie students' avoidance of academic tasks, reluctance to try hard, and self-defeating views of their own abilities. Metacognitive judgments are important because they determine which tasks students find worthwhile and how they choose to engage them.

Metacognitive Beliefs

Metacognitive beliefs are expectations that students hold with regard to thinking and learning. The most well-known example of metacognitive beliefs involve attributions for success and failure (e.g., Abramson, Seligman, & Teasdale, 1978; Dweck, 1986). Weiner (1979, 1986), for example, outlined an attributional model of success and failure in academic situations that included postulated causes that could be classified along the dimensions of stability, locus, and control. For example, personal ability is classified as an internal, stable characteristic over which an individual has little control compared to effort that is internal but unstable and controllable (see Hiebert, Winograd, & Danner, 1984).

How do personal interpretations of success and failure foster metacognitive beliefs? When students are stimulated to think about the reasons for their success or failure in academic situations, they typically mention effort, ability, luck, or other people as the primary reasons. For example, Butkowsky and Willows (1980) studied fourth-grade boys who were labeled learning disabled and found that they had lower expectations for success than other students and attributed their failures to poor ability. More skilled peers had higher expectations and attributed their failures to effort and their successes to ability. This well-known pattern has led some theorists, such as Dweck (1986), to characterize children as either mastery-oriented or helpless. Mastery-oriented children attribute success to ability and believe that effort can overcome failure. In contrast, children who have learned to be helpless believe that they are unable to master a task and that further effort is futile.

In general, children's beliefs about the role of ability, effort, luck, and other factors in academic achievement show marked differences among children who succeed or do not succeed in classrooms. Johnston and Winograd (1985) described how children often adopt passive attitudes toward reading and resign themselves to failure. These beliefs are debilitating because they discourage effort and self-esteem. Some metacognitive beliefs in the classroom can be viewed as rationalizations or coping responses. As Covington (1983) pointed out, students who try hard and fail are left with no other reasonable attribution except that they have low ability. The choice between being viewed as lazy or stupid is not an appealing alternative for students who oftentimes cope with academic tasks by expending minimal effort and inventing a range of excuses so that they can always maintain that performance would have been better if they had tried harder, cared about the task, or had not been interfered with by other circumstances.

Metacognitive beliefs also include students' perceptions of self-efficacy and self-control. For example, students select challenging tasks and persevere on them when they believe that they can accomplish the tasks with reasonable effort (Bandura, 1982; Schunk, 1984). Thus, self-efficacy involves attributions to both effort and ability and results in a positive perception of competence. Skinner, Chapman, and Baltes (1988) have proposed a theory of motivated actions in which individuals' beliefs can be classified into three categories: "*control beliefs,* defined as expectations about the extent to which agents (e.g., the self) can obtain desired outcomes; *means-ends beliefs,* defined as expectations about the extent to which potential means or causes produce outcomes; and *agency beliefs,* defined as expectations about the extent to which agents possess or can obtain potential means" (Skinner et al., 1988, p. 117).

How can we conceptualize the role of metacognitive beliefs? We propose (following Skinner et al., 1988, and Paris, Newman, & Jacobs, 1985) that students' beliefs reveal four cognitive dimensions that influence their orientation to school learning: agency, instrumentality, control, and purpose. First, students develop beliefs about themselves as learners and their own cognitive capabilities. They perceive themselves as skillful in particular areas or as generally competent or incompetent. They can develop beliefs about their ability to use particular strategies successfully. Students' metacognitive beliefs must include this view of themselves as intentional, self-directed, and self-critical learners.

A second dimension of their beliefs is the instrumental relations that are perceived between educational strategies and outcomes. Students need to realize the cognitive utility of strategies such as summarizing, note-taking, and planning for learning. Negative or erroneous views about the usefulness of strategies constitute maladaptive beliefs that can thwart effort and achievement. A third dimension is the control they exert over their own thinking. In order to avoid learned helplessness, students must believe in their own power to control and direct their thinking. Otherwise, they develop passive or antagonistic attitudes toward learning and a view of themselves as ineffectual (Johnston & Winograd, 1985). They need to believe that their actions are responsible for successful performance (when it is appropriate) and that failure is neither inevitable nor uncontrollable. Indeed, failure must be regarded as a normal part of learning that can be used constructively to shape future efforts (Clifford, 1984).

Fourth, students need to believe in the purpose of their own learning. They need to have positive expectations for their performance and value success. School learning is goal oriented, but there are a number of short-term or erroneous goals that may impede learning. Students who view the completion of worksheets or the dodging of tasks as legitimate goals in classrooms are forming dangerous metacognitive beliefs about the purposes of learning (Doyle, 1983; Winograd & Smith, 1987).

Maehr (1983) described four kinds of goals relevant to academic situations: ego, task, extrinsic, and social goals. Many tasks are approached for the goal of ego enhancement whereby one person's self-worth is elevated at the expense of another through competition. Success can also be achieved for the purpose of obtaining external rewards or for gaining social approval or social solidarity. But Maehr (1983), Nicholls (1983), and others argue that the best purpose for learning is task involvement in which engagement and mastery of the task provide their own reward. Students who have this metacognitive belief about learning to read, to write, to calculate, and so forth develop a different orientation to the craft of schooling than students who choose to learn for other reasons. Thus, students' metacognitive beliefs about agency, instrumentality, control, and purpose shape their orientations to school learning. Although these dimensions of children's learning are often emphasized by teachers and educators, they are rarely targets of research on metacognition. We strongly suggest that metacognition be enlarged as a construct to facilitate the combined emphasis on children's thoughts and feelings so that we can examine how metacognitive beliefs influence students' orientations to school learning.

Choices and Actions

Metacognitive judgments reflect the knowledge that students develop about cognitive states and abilities. Metacognitive beliefs involve expectations that reflect affective biases, self-concepts, and motivational dispositions. Together these bits of knowledge, expectations, and values influence what students do at particular choice points in school learning. One of the unresolved issues in the study of metacognition, however, is how students' metacognitions actually function to direct behavior. We believe that metacognitive judgments and beliefs guide decision making at critical junctures in classroom learning. There are three prototypical situations in which this arises. First, students can choose to do task A or task B. The choice depends on their perceptions of many different factors, including the expected payoff, their expectations for success, and the amount of effort required to accomplish the task. However, all of these judgments are metacognitive and the resulting choice reflects an interactive tradeoff among these various factors.

A second situation involves the choice of expending effort or not. When a student is given an assignment in class, the option is there to try or not try, or at least to put forth minimal effort on the task. What determines the student's choice? Certainly the range of distractions and available alternatives are important. However, there is also the student's perceptions of the task and the eventual attributions for success or failure. Is it worth the risk to try hard on a task in which the expectations for success are low? Most students would rather avoid a task than to work hard for little gain. Conversely, many students are not motivated to expend effort on a task that is easy to master and offers little sense of enjoyment or mastery. Pride and self-competence are not cultivated by either circumstance.

Third, there are specific situations in which metacognitive choices are made. For example, when students choose to do task A and choose to expend effort, they may direct their thinking in a variety of ways. The particular strategy that is chosen is dictated by judgments of the appropriateness of different tactics for that task. Considerable research on children's choices of memory strategies has shown that children's awareness of the strategies and their understanding of the utility of the strategies guides their choices (O'Sullivan & Pressley, 1984; Paris, Newman, & McVey, 1982). Thus, choices within academic contexts, whether they refer to particular strategies, investments of effort, or selection of one task over another, involve choices based on metacognitive judgments and beliefs. We cannot adequately understand how students choose learning tactics or act with different degrees of motivation without assessing their thoughts and feelings about the various metacognitive aspects of the learning situation. It is precisely for this reason that ongoing assessments of students' metacognition must be linked directly to instruction provided in the classroom (Jacobs & Paris, 1987; Winograd & Niquette, 1988). In the following section we discuss several orientations to the social exchange of metacognition in the classroom.

METACOGNITIVE DIALOGUES:
SHARING KNOWLEDGE TO GUIDE LEARNING

An analysis of children's beliefs, judgments, and choices has important implications for instruction because it calls attention to the affective, motivational, and social interactions involved in learning and instruction. One important consequence of research on metacognition is the renewed appreciation that effective instruction and learning requires both "skill and will" (Paris & Cross, 1983). Brown et al. (1983) touched on this issue with the following comments:

> In our previous discussion of training studies we portrayed parents, teachers, and researchers as dispensers of "pearls of cognitive wisdom." Effective mediators do much more than focus on particular concepts and strategies that may improve task performance; they respond to *individuals* who may feel confident, enthused, threatened, defiant, and so forth . . .
>
> Many of the activities employed by effective mediators are specifically focused on "cold cognitive" aspects of instruction, on particular concepts, factual knowledge, or strategies, for example. But effective mediators do much more than impart cognitive lore. They encourage children, try to help them stay on task, express joy at the children's accomplishments, and so forth. Learning proceeds smoothly when child and mediator are in "synchrony." But, it is often very difficult to establish and maintain this synchrony; many of the moves made by effective mediators are designed to do just this. (p. 148)

Effective teachers display both empathy and expertise; they guide students' learning with sensitivity. Classroom practices should allow teachers and students to discuss their thoughts and feelings about learning in order to promote metacognition and motivation. In the following section, we discuss four approaches that incorporate metacognition in literacy instruction and are designed to facilitate social exchanges of shared knowledge. They illustrate innovative features that are adaptable to many curricula. These four, often overlapping, approaches are direct explanation, scaffolded instruction, cognitive coaching, and cooperative learning. We attempt to identify particular strengths of each approach as well as limitations and unresolved questions.

Direct Explanation

A number of researchers have designed instructional programs that provide children with clear explanations about the instruction they are receiving. These instructional programs can trace their roots to research on direct instruction (e.g., Carnine & Silbert, 1979; Gersten & Carnine, 1986; Rosenshine, 1979), although their current popularity can be linked to several other factors. First, the need for better explanations was revealed by research studies that showed that much of what teachers tell students about reading comprehension is vague and confusing. Durkin (1978–1979), for example, reported that teachers rarely provided children with adequate explanations that would help them work out the meaning of connected text. Durkin characterized what the teachers did say about comprehension as "mentioning—say just enough about a skill, requirement, or topic to allow for an assignment related to it" (Durkin, 1985, p. 4). Although Durkin's research has been criticized on the grounds that her definition of comprehension instruction was too narrow (Hodges, 1980) or that her observational scheme was too simplistic (Heap, 1982), her contention that teachers need to provide students with more detailed explanations about what they are learning has been supported by other researchers (e.g., Duffy et al., 1986; Hare & Milligan, 1984; Pearson, 1984).

A second factor contributing to the popularity of direct explanation has been the recent advances in our understanding of the kinds of knowledge that underlie expert behavior (e.g., Brown, Campione, & Day, 1981; Bruner, 1972; Resnick, 1983). In order to read strategically, students need to know: (a) about the existence of relevant strategies, the impact of task characteristics, and their own personal abilities (declarative knowledge), (b) about the execution of various actions and how to monitor and regulate comprehension (procedural knowledge), and (c) about when and why to apply various strategies and knowledge (conditional knowledge). One efficient way of helping children acquire these different kinds of knowledge is by direct explanation (Duffy & Roehler, 1987; Paris, Cross, & Lipson, 1984).

Winograd and Hare (1988) summarized how direct explanation has been approached across several instructional studies designed to help children become more adept in their use of reading comprehension strategies. Their review revealed that many researchers focused their explanations on five key features:

1. *What the strategy is.* Researchers described critical features of the strategy or provided a definition or description of the strategy.
2. *Why the strategy should be learned.* Researchers explained to the students the purpose and potential benefits of the strategy.
3. *How to use the strategy.* Researchers explained each step in the strategy as clearly as possible. When the individual steps in a strategy were hard to explicate, as in getting the main idea,

researchers used analogies, think-alouds, and other instructional aids.

4. *When and where the strategy is to be used.* Researchers explained to students the appropriate circumstances under which strategies should be employed.

5. *How to evaluate the use of the strategy.* Finally, researchers often explained to students how to tell whether using the strategy had proven helpful and what to do if it had not.

A study by Duffy and his colleagues (Duffy et al., 1986) provides a specific illustration of direct explanation. These researchers trained fifth-grade teachers to be more explicit when teaching their low reading groups to use reading skills strategically. The teachers were trained in "(a) how to recast prescribed basal text skills as strategies useful when removing blockages to meanings, (b) how to make explicit statements about the reading skills being taught, when it would be used, and how to apply it, and (c) how to organize these statements for presentation to students" (Duffy et al., 1986, p. 244). The central tenet of this research is that teachers can assume metacognitive control of their instruction to enhance student awareness and achievement.

The results of this 6-month study were mixed. On the positive side, teachers did increase the explicit nature of their instruction. They provided more detailed explanations about strategies to students. In general, students' metacognition increased, although no data are provided that link individual students' awareness and the kinds of explanations they received. On the negative side, there were no differences between the control and treatment groups on the standardized reading test. Duffy et al. (1987) suggested that one reason for the variable effects was that several of the trained teachers found it difficult to use explicit explanations consistently. Indeed, finding the appropriate level of detail and explanation about various mental strategies is a central problem for teachers and researchers alike.

Duffy et al. (1987) repeated the same kind of study with 20 third-grade teachers and their low readers. The training helped teachers to provide more detailed explanations to their students about the purposes of basal reading lessons and the strategies they were using. Students in the treatment groups also increased their metacognition as measured by open-ended questions such as, "What were you learning in the lesson you just saw?" and "What do good readers do?" The researchers also found better word study and oral reading by third-graders in the treatment groups but there were no differences on basal skills or comprehension tests. The results of both studies show that teachers can be trained to provide better explanations about the cognitive strategies that students are learning and using. In turn, these explanations increase students' metacognition and strategic reading.

Despite some limitations, direct explanation is one useful way to structure learning so that teachers and students can engage in the social exchange of shared knowledge. There are three particular advantages worth noting. First, direct explanation about academic tasks and relevant strategies helps students decompose difficult tasks and equips them with useful tactics for problem solving. It helps identify learning goals and effective ways to reach them. Second, direct explanation requires teachers to understand the cognitive demands of the task and thus forces them to do more than mention objectives and distribute assignments. Third, direct explanation can be done with large groups or whole classes and is therefore an economical means of teaching. Individualized and small group instruction is costly for teachers' time and management of all students' learning; direct explanation is an effective alternative to these practices.

Scaffolded Instruction

A second line of instructional research that will influence future curricula has been labeled scaffolded instruction. The distinguishing feature of scaffolded instruction is the prominent role of dialogue between teacher and student. The purpose of this dialogue is to provide the learner with just enough support and guidance to achieve goals that are beyond unassisted efforts (Wood, Bruner, & Ross, 1976). Scaffolded instruction includes at least six components:

1. recruitment—The tutor must enlist the child's interest.
2. reduction in degrees of freedom—The tutor must reduce the size of the task to the level where the learner can recognize a fit with task requirements.
3. direction maintenance—The tutor must keep the child in pursuit of the task.
4. marking critical features—The tutor must accentuate certain features of the task that the learner can use to compare what was actually produced with the desired "correct" production.
5. frustration control—The tutor must help reduce stress—to make the tutorial situation less stressful than if the adult had not been present.
6. demonstration—The tutor must demonstrate an "idealization" of the task by means of completing the task or explicating a solution with the expectation that the learner will "imitate" it back in a more appropriate form (Langer & Applebee, 1986, p. 177).

Scaffolded instruction derives its theoretical support from theorists such as Vygotsky (1978), Wertsch (1984), and Feuerstein (1980) who assert that children learn higher order intellectual functions first by being exposed to them in interpersonal situations. Vygotsky (1978), for example, stated that:

> Any higher mental function which has emerged in the process of human historical development appears on the scene twice. It first appears as a form of interaction and co-operation among people, as an interpsychological category. Then it appears as a form of individual adaptation, as a part of an individual's psychology, as an intrapsychological category. (p. 128)

An important feature of Vygotsky's view of socially mediated learning is the notion of the zone of proximal development. Vygotsky (1978) defined this as "the distance between the actual developmental level as determined by independent problem-solving and the level of potential development as determined through problem-solving under adult guidance or in collaboration with more capable peers" (p. 76). Reciprocal teaching is a way that teachers can use dialogues to support and guide students by focusing instruction in the zone of proximal development.

Reciprocal teaching designed by Palincsar and Brown (1984) emphasizes interactive communication and a mutual flow of information in contrast to direct instruction in which information generally flows from teachers to students. Palincsar and Brown concentrated on four strategies—predicting, questioning, clarifying, and summarizing—because they are commonly used to foster and to monitor reading comprehension. Palincsar and Brown embedded these four activities in training sessions in which the investigator and seventh-grade students took turns leading a dialogue focusing on the text. When the texts were new, the dialogue leaders asked for predictions based on the title. As the texts were read, the dialogue leaders would ask questions, and offer summaries, clarifications, and further predictions when appropriate.

During the initial reciprocal teaching sessions, students had difficulties acting as dialogue leaders. The teacher provided support and guidance by modeling effective strategies and producing responses that the students could emulate. As the training sessions progressed, students became more competent in the role of dialogue leaders. The teacher responded to the students' increasing independence by reducing the amount of support and guidance. This gradual fading of support is what is captured in the metaphor of the scaffold because a scaffold offers support that is adjustable and temporary (Gavelek, 1986). Palincsar and Brown (1984) observed significant improvements following reciprocal teaching. The 34 poor readers in seventh-grade who received 20 days of training with the four target strategies showed significant improvements in summarizing relevant information and detecting errors in text. They also transferred these strategies to lessons in science and social studies.

It is important to note, however, that although an impressive amount of evidence has been gathered in favor of scaffolded instruction, some important limitations and unresolved issues remain. For example, such an approach is extremely labor-intensive (Pressley, Snyder, & Cariglia-Bull, 1987). In addition, scaffolded instruction requires an empathetic teacher who is skilled in guiding students to engage in dialogues. The teacher (or tutor) must be sensitive to the learners' needs in order to provide the optimum level of support. Teachers who consistently misjudge their students' level of competence could frustrate and confuse students.

Teachers engaged in scaffolded instruction need to be knowledgeable as well as empathetic. Many fluent readers are not as aware of various reading strategies as might be expected. Palincsar, Brown, and Martin (1987) spent several days teaching prospective tutors the components of various reading strategies and credit some of the success of their reciprocal teaching study to this preparation. Palincsar et al. also noted that it is difficult to teach students to evaluate and correct each other's comprehension. For example, in one session a tutee requested clarification of the words "antitoxin" and "antivenins." The tutor clarified in the following manner:

> Well, what antivenins and antitoxins is, is, I kind of know because my brother, when we lived in our other house, my brother got bit by a water mocassin and what it is is a thing that they put in a snake bite and it pumps out the blood—takes out all the poison. Like, they took the cut, and had a big hole around it, and then they pumped the blood and put this thing in it and sterilized it. (p. 250)

The occasional transfer of misinformation between tutor and tutee is certainly not limited to scaffolded instruction, but it is an issue that researchers in all varieties of collaborative learning need to address more fully in the future.

Reciprocal teaching may contribute to students' learning in a number of ways. It seems reasonable to assume that the dialogues and roles exchanged between tutors and tutees foster more explicit descriptions of reading strategies, how to use them, when they are helpful, and why students should use them. Strategy training, metacognition, social incentives, and other factors may all contribute to the benefits of scaffolded instruction. We believe that students' understanding about strategies plays a significant role. Metacognition is probably enhanced because nearly all the effectiveness of reciprocal teaching is due to students' improved use of two strategies, paraphrasing and summarizing. The gains reported by Palincsar and Brown (1984) followed 20 days of practice on these strategies and it seems plausible that this concentrated strategy practice and socially negotiated reading comprehension significantly increased students' metacognition about two useful strategies.

In conclusion, scaffolded instruction as a way of sharing and developing students' metacognitive knowledge has several attractive features. First, data from several studies indicate that scaffolded instruction is an effective approach compared to a variety of more traditional forms of instruction. Second, interactive dialogues between teachers and students offer a natural context for exploring beliefs about learning. These opportunities allow students to share rationales for why they made certain judgments and choices in the classroom. Third, scaffolded instruction enhances the social relationships among teachers and students and provides additional motivation for learning (Winograd & Smith, 1987).

Cognitive Coaching

Many training studies include multiple components of direct explanation and scaffolded instruction. For example, Brown et al. (1981) taught junior college students summarizing strategies with instruction that emphasized both knowledge about good tactics and the self-controlled application of strategies. Griffin and Cole (1984) developed an intervention for children that helped them reconceptualize the nature of reading. Children were encouraged to ask questions about the meaning of words and sentences, to elaborate ideas, and to make predictions. These activities took place in groups with student discussion about the processes of reading. Helping and sharing knowledge were key components that allowed children to focus on meaning in text and to pursue knowledge construction more actively while reading.

Cognitive coaching includes mutual dialogues, direct explanation, modeling, and encouragement. These features are evident in the classroom intervention program developed by Scott Paris and colleagues at the University of Michigan (e.g., Paris et al. 1984; Paris & Jacobs, 1984; Paris & Oka, 1986) that includes a series of instructional modules, posters, and activities. Each module is focused on a particular strategy, such as finding main ideas in text, and has three, separate 45-minute lessons designed for whole group instruction. The important instructional features were the use of metaphors, materials, and discussions to promote children's understanding about reading strategies. Paris and his colleagues tried to make the mysterious, invisible, mental processes of reading tangible for 8- to 10-year-olds through metaphors such as "Be a Reading Detective," "Tracking Down the Main Idea," "Rounding Up Ideas," and "Planning Your Reading Trip." The analogies provided concrete representations of mental actions that are illustrated on posters and worksheets. The analogies help to initiate group discussions about *what* strategies are, *how* they operate, *when* they should be applied, and *why* they are useful. Reading and writing activities were interwoven with these discussions. Thus, direct explanation of strategies was incorporated into metacognitive dialogues and instructional activities that were enjoyable and sensible for children.

The data revealed significant advantages of the instruction. Measures of metacognition, strategy utility, error detection, and cloze reading performance all revealed significant improvement from pre- to posttests for children in the experimental classes compared to their peers in other classes. Paris (1986) suggested that three aspects of cognitive coaching may contribute to the effectiveness of metacognitive instruction. First, teachers and students have common goals in coaching situations that provide for cooperation and mutual striving. Sharing knowledge about reading strategies improves students' reading achievement and satisfaction. Second, coaching involves ongoing assessment of students' levels of performance so that task difficulty and expectations can be adjusted to challenging levels. Third, coaching involves mutual regulation. An important component of the dialogues was teachers' understanding of students' complaints and misconceptions. Reciprocity allowed students to share their thoughts and feelings about the thinking processes they were learning instead of focusing only on the content of reading selections.

Cognitive coaching combines assessments of learning with sensitive instruction; it integrates cognitive explanations and motivational encouragement. Many new approaches to cognitive instruction include these characteristics (Marzanno et al. 1987). For example, "procedural facilitation" described by Bereiter and Scardamalia (1985) as a means of enhancing composition processes helps students make more thoughtful decisions while writing. Students can be encouraged to choose appropriate words and topics, to reorganize the order of sentences, and to revise ideas to achieve text coherence. Bereiter and Scardamalia (1985) concluded that procedural facilitation is particularly helpful when task demands exceed the current levels of students' ability—exactly the kind of tasks that are encountered in schools.

Eclectic approaches to instruction that involve cognitive coaching explain processes of thinking, provide clear goals for academic tasks, and stimulate reciprocal interactions (Weinstein & Underwood, 1985). Moreover, they facilitate five essential components of effective instruction

(Langer & Applebee, 1986): ownership, appropriateness, structure, collaboration, and transfer of control. Ownership refers to students' sense of personal goals and products. Learning is mindless, compliant, or purposeless if students' cannot develop a sense of ownership about what they do in classrooms. Second, effective instruction builds on "ripening skills" so it is developmentally progressive and appropriate. Third, academic learning must be embedded in tasks that recontextualize the significance of the activities and provide a meaningful structure to the experiences (Paris & Cross, 1983). Fourth, instruction is most effective when it is collaborative and mutually informative. Authoritarian and critical attitudes stifle enthusiasm and interactions. Fifth, an overarching goal of instruction is to transfer control to the students so that they take responsibility for their own self-regulated learning (Corno & Mandinach, 1983; Gavelek, 1986; Paris & Oka, 1986).

Cooperative Learning

The fourth instructional approach that seems particularly suited to facilitating the social exchange of shared knowledge is cooperative learning. In cooperative learning, students "usually work together to complete tasks, whereas students in other settings work at their seats or receive instruction in large groups in which most interaction occurs between teacher and student" (Webb, 1982, p. 421). Researchers have been studying cooperative learning for most of this century and the long list of studies available in the literature attests to the number and complexity of the issues associated with it (e.g., Johnson & Johnson, 1975; Maller, 1929; Slavin, 1980; Webb, 1982).

Some of the issues pertaining to cooperative learning are particularly relevant to our discussion of metacognition as shared knowledge. First, one of the social interaction variables used to explain the positive effects of cooperative learning is helping behavior. After reviewing a number of studies, Webb (1982) concluded that both providing and receiving help resulted in higher achievement. Webb also noted that helping behavior itself is quite complex and that, logically, help seems more beneficial when it is given to students who need it rather than when it was provided to those who do not. Moreover, "help consisting of explanations has a greater chance of eliminating confusion than does help consisting only of a correct answer" (Webb, 1982, p. 426).

A second variable that contributes to the positive outcomes of cooperative learning is the nature of the cognitive processes that help group members learn. A number of researchers (e.g., Slavin, 1977; Wittrock, 1974; Yager, Johnson, & Johnson, 1985) have suggested that oral discussion among group members is an effective means of helping individuals restructure their ideas. Other researchers (e.g., Johnson & Johnson, 1975; Lindow, Wilkinson, & Peterson, 1985; Piaget, 1932) have emphasized the role that conflicts among group members play in learning. Disagreements among group members force individuals to seek new information or seek to understand old information from a new perspective.

A third variable that we find particularly interesting concerns the socioemotional variables that may mediate achievement in cooperative learning situations (Webb, 1982). Studies indicate that students in cooperative learning situations may be more motivated (e.g., Slavin, 1978) and less anxious (e.g., Haines & McKeachie, 1967) than students working in other instructional settings. Donald Dansereau and his colleagues have investigated these variables in a variety of cooperative learning situations. They reason that cognitive, affective, metacognitive, and social processes (CAMS) can be affected differently in a variety of cooperative situations. In one study, Lambiotte et al. (1987) asked college students to read and study passages in pairs. There were three different scripts for cooperative interactions in which partners read some or all of the information that they needed to learn. Researchers found that students who engaged in a teaching role remembered significantly more information than students who simply read passages together.

In a subsequent study, O'Donnell, Dansereau, Hall, and Rocklin (1987) compared the performance of college students who learned material with scripted or unscripted dyadic interaction. The researchers found that scripts provided important information about learning strategies that helped them learn the information and evaluate their own performance. The scripts also relieved anxiety and facilitated the social perceptions of their partners. Thus, students working in groups who follow a standardized set of procedures can improve their cognitive performance, social relationships, and metacognition. In a follow-up study of the CAMS model, Hall et al. (1988) investigated individual difference variables that contribute to the effectiveness of cooperative learning. College students learned a four-step study strategy, used the strategy in dyads or alone, and took subsequent memory tests for the materials. These data were compared to a variety of individual difference measures. The researchers found that cooperative learning was more effective than studying the materials alone, but proved most beneficial to students who scored high in cognitive ability and had an extroverted social orientation. They also found that high anxiety interfered with learning but good study skills contributed to successful learning. The researchers claim that the cognitive and social factors are independent, but that anxiety and metacognition are strongly and negatively related.

This pattern certainly confirms the importance of the interaction of metacognition, motivation, and affect described earlier.

Cooperative learning often involves a mixture of many instructional practices including modeling, direct explanation, scaffolded instruction, and group activities. This kind of eclectic program is illustrated by the Cooperative Integrated Reading and Composition model (CIRC) described by Stevens, Madden, Slavin, and Farnish (1987). Instruction in the CIRC model begins with the direct teacher explanation and cognitive modeling. Practice activities occur in cooperative groups where oral reading among pairs of students is common. Partners focus on the content of the stories as well as on strategies for predicting, summarizing, and analyzing story structure. In writing and language arts, students use peer conferences for planning, revising, and editing each other's compositions. The model is characterized by a combination of direct instruction and team practice that is integrated across reading and writing activities. Data collected from 43 classes of third- and fourth-grade students revealed significant improvements on standardized measures of reading comprehension, reading vocabulary, language mechanics, language expression, and spelling. The students who participated in CIRC activities also were significantly better on measures of writing and oral reading.

In summary, cooperative learning provides an arena for teachers and students to discuss the nature of learning and academic tasks. In cooperative settings, students' judgments, beliefs, and choices are often negotiated publicly and are at least open to self-examination when there is a strong emphasis on metacognition in the curriculum. There are three fundamental aspects of instruction that are apparent in these brief excerpts that are worth reiterating. First, learning is student-centered rather than teacher-directed. Each of these methods gives credibility to students' interpretations and perceptions of their learning tasks and situation (Shulman, 1986). Second, when teachers provide information or structure opportunities for learning, they must fit the curriculum to the developmental levels of their students. Third, teachers need to make learning sensible and personally relevant for students. They need to model explicitly the fact that learning is enjoyable and enriching (Brophy, 1986). This emphasis on sense-making and personal satisfaction can be achieved with many different methods that focus on metacognitive dialogues in the classroom.

Toward a Balanced Curriculum

We have identified some current instructional approaches that can promote effective teaching and self-regulated learning, but we have included some discussion of limitations and unresolved issues in the hope that such approaches are incorporated thoughtfully and not as panaceas. Winograd and Johnston (1987), for example, argued that if current advances in comprehension instruction are to continue, then we must address several issues. First, we must pay careful attention to the conditional applicability of the various instructional approaches in our repertoire. It is unreasonable to assume that one instructional technique (e.g., direct explanation, scaffolded instruction) can be used with equal effectiveness for all kinds of tasks, for all kinds of texts, and for all kinds of students. Yet, the history of instruction is littered with examples of reasonable approaches that were generalized beyond reasonable limits (Paris, Wixson, & Palincsar, 1986).

Second, researchers and educators need to expand the definition of reading that currently dominates literacy instruction in our schools (Winograd & Johnston, 1987; Wixson & Peters, 1984). Currently, children spend a majority of allocated reading time focusing on discrete aspects of reading instruction and relatively little time practicing the entire process while reading meaningful texts (e.g., Fisher et al., 1978). Recent research and common sense both emphasize the role that motivation plays in developing reading ability and we would argue that time spent helping children discover the aesthetic (Nell, 1988; Rosenblatt, 1978; Winograd & Smith, 1987) side of reading is an essential aspect of any effective curriculum.

Third, if curricular changes are to be effective, then they need to help teachers cope with the complex and often conflicting demands of teaching. For example, our recommendation that students be exposed to the aesthetic side of reading is likely to go unheeded if teachers are overly concerned about preparing children to do well on accountability measures that focus on discrete skills (Winograd & Greenlee, 1986). Likewise, more metacognitive dialogues in classrooms are unlikely if teachers are overly concerned with matters of discipline or management.

In summary, we hope that curricula of the future can provide students and teachers with time and methods to share and discuss their beliefs, judgments, and choices about academic tasks. Direct explanation, scaffolded instruction, cognitive coaching, and cooperative learning offer some ways that teachers can organize their instruction in order to promote students' metacognition about learning.

CONCLUSIONS

Recent research in educational and developmental psychology has revealed the importance of student learning that is self-regulated, independent, and flexible (Brown et al., 1983). Young children and less-skilled learners in particular need to manage their own learning by planning, evaluating, and regulating their performance on academic tasks (Paris & Cross, 1983). They need to set reasonable goals for themselves, persist in the face of failure, and adopt intrinsic standards for success. the cognitive consequence of self-regulated learning is that students become *enabled* to select and attack problems strategically. The motivational consequence is that students feel *empowered* to be successful and thereby invest effort in relevant and challenging tasks. These twin concepts summarize many of the virtues of instruction designed to increase students' metacognition about learning.

One of the broad goals of education is to encourage the application and transfer of skills, rather than simple demonstrations of knowledge or competence in the classroom. Using knowledge to solve problems in everyday tasks is at the heart of strategic learning. But independent learning requires the effective management of one's time, effort, and external resources. Self-regulated learning involves choices of tasks in which to engage and the degree of help to solicit. Self-management uses all available resources, both internal and external, and is thus a balance of personal motivation and cognitive abilities. Self-management allows students to make decisions about the academic tasks they confront and the potential workload and satisfaction associated with them. Metacognitive beliefs, judgments, and choices enable students to become independent learners. Thus, enhancing students' understanding of academic tasks and learning processes are appropriate goals for instruction as long as they are means to the larger goal of self-regulated learning.

The cognitive dimension of self-regulated learning should not be emphasized exclusively in accounts of teaching and learning. Equally important are the motivational consequences for students because self-regulated learning depends on a positive view of one's self-competence and expectations for future achievements. Effort, persistence, and pride emanate from intrinsic motivation and self-standards (Rohrkemper & Corno, 1988). Empowerment, the will to achieve a goal, is as essential as enablement, the ability to achieve a goal. The will or motivation to use one's skills has been examined from a variety of cognitive approaches using constructs that include causal attributions (Weiner, 1986), self-efficacy (Bandura, 1982), perceived competence (Harter, 1983), self-worth (Covington, 1983), and beliefs about control (Skinner, 1985). What these approaches have in common is the central role assigned to personal beliefs about learning and self-perceptions about one's competence. The selection of goals, the selection of tasks, and the persistence and vigor of students' efforts all reflect a pattern of beliefs about one's one learning potential. Novices in the classroom, whether by virtue of age or experience, are particularly vulnerable to erroneous beliefs about learning and their own achievement. We believe that optimistic beliefs of self-competence *empower* students to expend effort, persist, and choose challenging tasks. Positive self-evaluations of competence, control, purpose, and instrumental functions of academic strategies contribute to students' sense of power in the classroom. These feelings promote ownership of ideas and authority of knowledge-seeking so that students are willing to risk failure to achieve greater understanding.

In summary, we believe that research on metacognition has illustrated the positive values of students gaining greater awareness about their own mental processes and the purposes of academic learning. Instruction that promotes this awareness can encourage students to make better cognitive judgments, beliefs, and choices in academic situations. Instruction in a variety of formats can promote metacognition in students and teachers. We reviewed the principles of direct explanation, scaffolded instruction, cognitive coaching, and cooperative learning to illustrate new approaches to instruction that combine an emphasis on cognitive skills and motivational encouragement. We remain optimistic that students' thinking skills and positive attitudes toward learning can be promoted through these new types of instruction.

REFERENCES

Abramson, L. Y., Seligman, M. P., & Teasdale, J. D. (1978). Learned helplessness in humans: Critique and reformulation. *Journal of Abnormal Psychology, 87,* 49–74.

Afflerbach, P., & Johnston, P. (1984). On the use of verbal reports in reading research. *Journal of Reading Behavior, 16,* 307–322.

Afflerbach, P., & Johnston, P. (1986). What do expert readers do when the main idea is not explicit? In J. F. Baumann, (Ed.), *Teaching main idea comprehension* (pp. 49–72). Newark, DE: International Reading Association.

Baker, L., & Brown, A. L. (1984). Metacognitive skills and reading. In P. D. Pearson, M. Kamil, R. Barr, & P. Mosenthal (Eds.), *Handbook of reading research* (pp. 353–394). New York: Longman.

Bandura, A. (1982). Self-efficacy mechanism in human agency. *American Psychologist, 37* 122–147.

Bereiter, C., & Scardamalia, M. (1985). Cognitive coping strategies and the problem of "inert knowledge." In S. F. Chipman, J. W. Segal, & R. Glaser (Eds.), *Thinking and learning skills: Research and open questions* (Vol. 2, pp. 65–80). Hillsdale, NJ: Lawrence Erlbaum Associates.

Borkowski, J. G. (1985). Signs of intelligence: Strategy generalization and metacognition. In S. Yussen (Ed.), *The development of reflection in children* (pp. 105–144). San Diego, CA: Academic Press.

Brophy, J. (1986). Teacher behavior and student achievement. In M. Wittrock (Ed.), *The handbook of research on teaching*, (3rd ed.). Riverside, NJ: Macmillan.

Brown, A. L. (1978). Knowing when, where, and how to remember: A problem of metacognition. In R. Glaser (Ed.), *Advances in instructional psychology* (Vol. 1, pp. 77–165). Hillsdale, NJ: Lawrence Erlbaum Associates.

Brown, A. L., Bransford, J. D., Ferrara, R. A., & Campione, J. C. (1983). Learning, remembering, and understanding. In J. H. Flavell & E. M. Markman (Eds.), *Carmichael's manual of child psychology* (Vol 1, pp. 77–166). New York: Wiley.

Brown, A. L., Campione, J. C., & Day, J. D. (1981). Learning to learn: On training students to learn from texts. *Educational Researcher, 10,* 14–21.

Bruner, J. (1972). Nature and uses of immaturity. *American Psychologist, 27,* 687–708.

Butkowsky, I. S., & Willows, D. M. (1980). Cognitive-motivational characteristics of children varying in reading ability: Evidence of learned helplessness in poor readers. *Journal of Educational Psychology, 72,* 408–422.

Canney, G., & Winograd, P. (1979). *Schemata for reading and reading comprehension performance* (Tech. Rep. No. 129). Urbana, IL: Center for the Study of Reading.

Carnine, D., & Silbert, J. (1979). *Direct instruction in reading.* Columbus, OH: Charles E. Merrill.

Cavanaugh, J., & Perlmutter, M. (1982). Metamemory: A critical examination. *Child Development, 53,* 11–28.

Clifford, M. (1984). Thoughts on a theory of constructive failure. *Educational Psychologist, 19,* 108–120.

Collins, A., Brown, J. S., & Newman, S. E. (in press). Cognitive apprenticeship: Teaching the craft of reading, writing and methematics. In L. B. Resnick (Ed.), *Knowing, learning, and instruction: Essays in honor of Robert Glaser.* Hillsdale, NJ: Lawrence Erlbaum Associates.

Corno, L., & Mandinach, E. (1983). The role of cognitive engagement in classroom learning and motivation. *Educational Psychologist, 18,* 88–108.

Covington, M. V. (1983). Motivated cognitions. In S. Paris, G. Olson, & H. Stevenson (Eds.), *Learning and motivation in the classroom* (pp. 139–164). Hillsdale, NJ: Lawrence Erlbaum Associates.

Doyle, W. (1983). Academic work. *Review of Educational Research, 53,* 159–200.

Duffy, G., & Roehler, L. (1987). Improving classroom reading instruction through the use of responsive elaboration. *Reading Teacher, 40,* 514–521.

Duffy, G. D., Roehler, L. R., Meloth, M. S., Vavrus, L. G., Book, C., Putnam, J., & Wesselman, R. (1986). The relationship between explicit verbal explanations during reading skill instruction and student awareness and achievement: A Study of reading teacher effects. *Reading Research Quarterly, 21,* 237–252.

Duffy, G., Roehler, L., Sivan, E., Rackliffe, G., Book, C., Meloth, M., Vavrus, L., Wesselman, R., Putnam, J., & Bassiri, D. (1987). Effects of explaining the reasoning associated with using strategies. *Reading Research Quarterly, 22,* 347–368.

Durkin, D. (1978–1979). What classroom observations reveal about reading comprehension instruction. *Reading Research Quarterly, 14,* 481–533.

Durkin, D. (1985). Teachers' manuals in basal reading programs. In J. Osborn, P. Wilson, & R. Anderson (Eds.), *Reading education: Foundations for a literate America* (pp. 1–10). Lexington, MA: Lexington Books.

Dweck, C. S. (1986). Motivational processes affecting learning. *American Psychologist, 41,* 1040–1048.

Feather, N. T. (1982). *Expectations and actions: Expectancy-value models in psychology.* Hillsdale, NJ: Lawrence Erlbaum Associates.

Feuerstein, R. (1980). *Instrumental enrichment: An intervention program for cognitive modifiability.* Baltimore, MD: University Park Press.

Fisher, C., Berliner, D., Filby, N., Narliave, R., Cohen, L., Dishaw, M., & Moore, J. (1978). *Teaching and learning in elementary school: A summary of the beginning teacher evaluation study.* San Francisco, CA: Far West Laboratory of Educational Research and Development.

Flavell, J. H. (1978). Metacognitive development. In J. M. Scandura & C. J. Brainerd (Eds.), *Structural/process theories of complex human behavior.* The Netherlands: Sijthoff & Noordoff.

Flavell, J. H. (1985). *Cognitive development.* Englewood Cliffs, NJ: Prentice-Hall.

Forrest-Pressley, D., & Waller, T. G. (1984). *Cognition, metacognition, and reading.* New York: Springer-Verlag.

Garner, R. (1987). *Metacognition and reading comprehension.* Norwood, NJ: Ablex.

Garner, R. (1988). Verbal-report data on cognitive and metacognitive strategies. In C. Weinstein, E. Goetz, & P. Alexander (Eds.), *Learning and study strategies: Issues in assessment, instruction, and evaluation* (pp. 63–76). San Diego, CA: Academic Press.

Gavelek, J. R. (1986) The social contexts of literacy and schooling: A developmental perspective. In T. Raphael (Ed.), *Contexts of school-based literacy* (pp. 3–26). New York: Random House.

Gersten, R., & Carnine, D. (1986). Direct instruction in reading comprehension. *Educational Leadership, 43,* 70–78.

Graves, D. H. (1983). *Writing: Teachers and children at work.* Portsmouth, NH: Heinemann Educational Books.

Griffin, P., & Cole, M. (1984). Current activity for the future: The zo-ped. In B. Rogoff & J. Wertsch (Eds.), *Children's learning in the "Zone of Proximal Development"* (pp. 45–65). San Francisco, CA: Jossey-Bass.

Haines, D. B., & McKeachie, W. J. (1967). Cooperation versus competitive discussion methods in teaching introductory psychology. *Journal of Educational Psychology, 58,* 386–390.

Hall, T. H., Rocklin, T. R., Dansereau, D. F., Skaggs, L. P., O'Donnell, A. M., Lambiotte, J. G., & Young, M. D. (1988). The role of individual differences in the cooperative learning of technical material. *Journal of Educational Psychology, 80,* 172–178.

Hare, V. C., & Milligan, B. (1984). Main idea identification instructional explanations in four basal reader series. *Journal of Reading Behavior, 16,* 189–204.

Harter, S. (1983). Developmental perspectives on the self-system. In E. M. Hetherington (Ed.), *Handbook of child psychology: Vol. 4, Socialization, personality and social development* (4th ed., pp. 275–386). New York: Wiley,

Heap, J. L. (1982). Understanding classroom events: A critique of Durkin, with an alternative. *Journal of Reading Behavior, 14*, 391–411.

Hiebert, E. H., Winograd, P., & Danner, F. (1984). Children's attributions for failure and success in different aspects of reading. *Journal of Educational Psychology, 76*, 1139–1148.

Hodges, C. (1980). Commentary: Toward a broader definition of comprehension instruction. *Reading Research Quarterly, 15*, 290–306.

Jacobs, J., & Paris, S. (1987). Children's metacognition about reading: Issues in definition, measurement, and instruction. *Educational Psychologist, 22*, 255–278.

Johnson, D. W., & Johnson, R. T. (1975). *Learning together and alone.* Englewood Cliffs, NJ: Prentice-Hall.

Johnston, P., & Winograd, P. (1985). Passive failure in reading. *Journal of Reading Behavior, 17*, 279–301.

Lambiotte, J. G., Dansereau, D. F., O'Donnell, A. M., Young, M. D., Skaggs, L. P., Hall, R. H., & Rocklin, T. R. (1987). Manipulating cooperative scripts for teaching and learning. *Journal of Educational Psychology, 79*, 424–430.

Langer, J. (1984). Examining background knowledge and text comprehension. *Reading Research Quarterly, 19*, 468–481.

Langer, J. A., & Applebee, A. N. (1986). Reading and writing instruction: Toward a theory of teaching and learning. In E. Rothkopf (Ed.), *Review of research in education* (Vol 13, pp. 171–194). Washington, DC: AERA.

Lindow, J. A., Wilkinson, L. C., & Peterson, P. L. (1985). Antecedents and consequences of verbal disagreements during small group learning. *Journal of Educational Psychology, 77*, 658–667.

Maehr, M. (1983). On doing well in science: Why Johnny no longer excells. Why Sarah never did. In S. Paris, G. Olson, & H. Stevenson (Eds.), *Learning and motivation in the classroom* (pp. 179–210). Hillsdale, NJ: Lawrence Erlbaum Associates.

Maller, J. B. (1929). *Cooperation and competition.* New York: Teachers College, Columbia University.

Markman, E., & Gorin, L. (1981). Children's ability to adjust their standards for evaluation comprehension. *Journal of Educational Psychology, 73*, 320–325.

Marzano, R. J., Brandt, R., Hughes, C., Jones, B. F., Presseisen, B., Rankin, S., & Suhor, C. (1987). *Dimensions of thinking.* Alexandria, VA: Association for Supervision and Curriculum Development.

Myers, M., & Paris, S. (1978). Children's metacognitive knowledge about reading. *Journal of Educational Psychology, 70*, 680–690.

Nell, V. (1988). The psychology of reading for pleasure: Needs and gratifications. *Reading Research Quarterly, 23*, 6–50.

Nicholls, J. (1983). Conceptions of ability and achievement: A theory and its implications for education. In S. Paris, G. Olson, & H. Stevenson (Eds.), *Learning and motivation in the classroom* (pp. 211–237). Hillsdale, NJ: Lawrence Erlbaum Associates.

O'Donnell, A. M., Dansereau, D. F., Hall, R. H., & Rocklin, T. R. (1987). Cognitive, social/affective, and metacognitive outcomes of scripted cooperative learning. *Journal of Educational Psychology, 79*, 431–437.

Ogle, D. S. (1983). K-W-L: A teaching model that develops active reading of expository text. *The Reading Teacher, 37*, 564–570.

O'Sullivan, J. T., & Pressley, M. (1984). Completeness of instruction and strategy transfer. *Journal of Experimental Child Psychology, 38*, 275–288.

Palincsar, A. S., & Brown, A. (1984). Reciprocal teaching of comprehension-fostering and comprehension-monitoring activities. *Cognition and Instruction, 1*, 117–175.

Palincsar, A. S., Brown, A. S., & Martin, S. M. (1987). Peer interaction in reading comprehension instruction. *Educational Psychologist, 22*, 231–253.

Paris, S. G. (1986). Teaching children to guide their reading and learning. In T. Raphael (Ed.), *Contexts of school-based literacy* (pp. 115–130). New York: Random House.

Paris, S. G., & Byrnes, J. P. (1988). The constructivist approach to self-regulation and learning in the classroom. In B. Zimmerman & D. Schunk (Eds.), *Self-regulated learning and academic achievement: Theory, research, and practice.* New York: Springer-Verlag.

Paris, S. G., & Cross, D. R. (1983). Ordinary learning: Pragmatic connections among children's beliefs, motives and actions. In J. Bisanz, G. Bisanz, & R. Kail (Eds.), *Learning in children* (pp 137–168). New York: Springer-Verlag.

Paris, S. G., Cross, D. R., & Lipson, M. Y. (1984). Informed strategies for learning: A program to improve children's reading awareness and comprehension. *Journal of Educational Psychology, 76*, 1239–1252.

Paris, S. G., & Jacobs, J. E. (1984). The benefits of informed instruction for children's reading awareness and comprehension skills. *Child Development, 55*, 2083–2093.

Paris, S. G., Jacobs, J. E., & Cross, D. R. (1987). Toward an individualistic psychology of exceptional children. In J. Borkowski & J. Day (Eds.), *Intelligence and cognition in special children: Comparative approaches to retardation, learning disabilities, and giftedness* (pp. 215–248). New York: Ablex.

Paris, S. G., & Lindauer, B. K. (1982). The development of cognitive skills during childhood, In B. Wolman (Ed.), *Handbook of developmental psychology* (pp. 333–349). Englewood Cliffs, NJ: Prentice-Hall.

Paris, S. G., Lipson, M. Y., & Wixson, K. K. (1983). Becoming a strategic reader. *Contemporary Educational Psychology, 8*, 293–316.

Paris, S. G., & Myers, M. (1981). Comprehension monitoring, memory, and study strategies of good and poor readers. *Journal of Reading Behavior, 13*, 5–22.

Paris, S. G., Newman, R. S., & Jacobs, J. E. (1985). Social contexts and functions of children's remembering. In C. J. Brainerd & M. Pressley (Eds.), *The cognitive side of memory development* (pp. 81–115). New York: Springer-Verlag.

Paris, S. G., Newman, R. S., & McVey, K. A. (1982). Learning the functional significance of mnemonic actions: A microgenetic study of strategy acquisition. *Journal of Experimental Child Psychology, 34*, 490–509.

Paris, S. G., & Oka, E. R. (1986). Schoolcraft. *Academic Psychology Bulletin, 4*, 291–299.

Paris, S. G., & Oka, E. R. (1986). Children's reading strategies, metacognition, and motivation. *Developmental Review, 6*, 25–56.

Paris, S. G., Wasik, B., & Turner, J. (in press). The development of strategic readers. In P. D. Pearson (Ed.), *Handbook of reading research* (2nd ed). New York: Longman.

Paris, S. G., Wasik, B. A., & van der Westhuizen, G. (1988). Meta-metacognition: A review of research on metacognition and reading. In J. Readance & S. Baldwin (Eds.), *Dialogues in literacy research*. (pp. 143–166). Chicago, IL: National Reading Conference, Inc.

Paris, S. G., Wixson, K. K., & Palincsar, A. S. (1986). Instructional approaches to reading comprehension. In E. Rothkopf (Ed.), *Review of research in education* (Vol 14, pp. 91–128). Washington, DC: American Educational Research Association.

Pearson, P. D. (1984). Direct explicit teaching of reading comprehension. In G. Duffy, L. Roehler, & J. Mason (Eds.), *Comprehension instruction: Perspectives and suggestions* (pp. 222–233). New York: Longman.

Piaget, J. (1932). *The language and thought of the child* (2nd ed.). London: Routledge & Kegan Paul.

Pressley, M., Borkowski, J. G., & O'Sullivan, J. T. (1985). Children's metamemory and the teaching of memory strategies. In D. L. Forrest-Pressley, G. E. MacKennon, & T. G. Waller (Eds.), *Metacognitive, cognition, and human performance* (pp. 111–153). San Diego, CA: Academic Press.

Pressley, M., Borkowski, J. G., & Schneider, W. (1987). Cognitive strategies: Good strategy users coordinate metacognition and knowledge. In R. Vasta (Ed.), *Annals of child development* (Vol. 4, pp. 89–129). Greenwich, CT: JAI Press.

Pressley, M., Snyder, B., & Cariglia-Bull, T. (1987). How can good strategy use be taught to children?: Evaluation of six alternative approaches. In S. Cormier & J. Hagman (Eds.), *Transfer of learning: Contemporary research and applications*. Orlando, FL: Academic Press.

Pressley, M., Snyder, B., Levin, J., Murray, H., & Ghatala, E. (1987). Perceived readiness for examination performance (PREP) produced by initial reading of text and text containing adjunct questions. *Reading Research Quarterly, 23,* 219–236.

Resnick, L. B. (1983). Toward a cognitive theory of instruction. In S. Paris, G. Olson, & H. Stevenson (Eds.), *Learning and motivation in the classroom* (pp. 5–38). Hillsdale, NJ: Lawrence Erlbaum Associates.

Rohrkemper, M., & Corno, L. (1988). Success and failure on classroom tasks: Adaptive learning and classroom teaching. *The Elementary School Journal, 88,* 297–312.

Rosenblatt, L. M. (1978). *The reader, the text, the poem.* Carbondale, IL: Southern Illinois University Press.

Rosenshine, B. V. (1979). Content, time, and direct instruction. In P. L. Peterson & H. J. Walberg (Eds.), *Research on teaching: Concepts, findings, and implications* (pp. 28–55). Berkeley, CA: McCutchan.

Schunk, D. (1984). Self-efficacy perspective on achievement behavior. *Educational Psychologist, 19,* 48–58.

Shulman, L. (1986). Paradigms and research programs in the study of teaching: A contemporary perspective. In M. Wittrock (Ed.), *Handbook of Research on Teaching.* (3rd ed., pp. 3–36). New York: Macmillan.

Skinner, E. (1985). Action, control judgments, and the structure of control experience. *Psychological Review, 92,* 39–58.

Skinner, E. A., Chapman, M., & Baltes, P. B. (1988). Control, means-ends, and agency beliefs: A new conceptualization and its measurement during childhood. *Journal of Personality and Social Psychology, 54,* 117–133.

Slavin, R. E. (1977). Classroom reward structure: An analytical and practical review. *Review of Educational Research, 47,* 633–650.

Slavin, R. E. (1978). Student teams and achievement divisions. *Journal of Research and Development in Education, 12,* 39–49.

Slavin, R. (1980). Cooperative learning. *Review of Educational Research, 50,* 315–342.

Stevens, R. J., Madden, N. A., Slavin, R. E., & Farnisch, A. M. (1987). Cooperative integrated reading and composition: Two field experiments. *Reading Research Quarterly, 22,* 433–454.

Taylor, D. (1983). *Family literacy.* London: Heinemann Educational Books.

Vygotsky, L. (1978). *Mind in society.* (M. Cole, V. John-Steiner, S. Scribner, & E. Souberman, Trans.). Cambridge, MA: Harvard University Press.

Wagoner, S. (1983). Comprehension monitoring: What it is and what we know about it. *Reading Research Quarterly, 28,* 328–346.

Webb, N. M. (1982). Student interaction and learning in small groups. *Review of Educational Research, 52,* 421–445.

Weiner, B. (1979). A theory of motivation for some classroom experiences. *Journal of Educational Psychology, 71,* 3–25.

Weiner, B. (1986). *An attributional theory of motivation and emotion.* New York: Springer-Verlag.

Weinstein, C. E., & Underwood, V. L. (1985). Learning strategies: The how of learning. In J. Segal, S. Chipman, & R. Glaser (Eds.), *Thinking and learning skills: Relating instruction to basic research* (pp. 241–258). Hillsdale, NJ: Lawrence Erlbaum Associates.

Wellman, H. (1985). The origins of metacognition. In D. L. Forrest-Pressley, G. E. MacKinnon, & T. G. Waller (Eds.), *Metacognition, cognition, and human performance* (Vol. 1, pp. 1–31). Orlando, FL: Academic Press.

Wertsch, J. V. (1984). The zone of proximal development: Some conceptual issues. In B. Rogoff & J. Wertsch (Eds.), *Children's learning in the zone of proximal development* (pp. 7–18). San Francisco, CA: Jossey-Bass.

Winne, P. H., & Marx, R. W. (1987). The best tool teachers have—their students' thinking. In D. C. Berliner & B. Rosenshine (Eds.), *Talks to teachers: A festschrift for N. L. Gage* (pp. 267–304). New York: Random House.

Winograd, P., & Greenlee, M. (1986). Providing leadership in reading: The need for balance. *Educational Leadership, 43,* 16–21.

Winograd, P., & Hare, V. C. (1988). Direct instruction of reading comprehension strategies: The nature of teacher explanation. In E. T. Goetz, P. Alexander, & C. Weinstein (Eds.), *Learning and study strategies: Assessment, instruction, and evaluation* (pp. 121–140). New York: Academic Press.

Winograd, P., & Johnston, P. (1987). Some considerations for advancing the teaching of reading comprehension. *Educational Psychologist, 22,* 212–230.

Winograd, P., & Niquette, G. (1988). Assessing learned helplessness in poor readers. *Topics in Language Disorders, 8,* 38–55.

Winograd, P., & Paris, S. G. (in press). A cognitive and motivational agenda for reading instruction. *Educational Leadership.*

Winograd, P., & Smith, L. (1987). Improving the climate for reading comprehension instruction. *Reading Teacher, 41,* 304–310.

Wittrock, M. C. (1974). Learning as a generative process. *Educational Psychologist, 11,* 87–95.

Wittrock, M. C. (1986). Students' thought processes. In M. C. Wittrock (Ed.), *Handbook of research on teaching* (3rd ed., pp. 297–314). New York: Macmillan.

Wixson, K. K., & Peters, C. W. (1984). Reading redefined: A Michigan reading association position paper. *The Michigan Reading Journal, 17,* 4–7.

Wood, P., Bruner, J., & Ross, G. (1976). The role of tutoring in problem-solving. *Journal of Child Psychology and Psychiatry, 17,* 89–100.

Yager, S., Johnson, D. W., & Johnson, R. T. (1985). Oral discussion, group to individual transfer, and achievement in cooperative learning groups. *Journal of Educational Psychology, 77,* 60–66.

Self-Regulated Cognition: Interdependence of Metacognition, Attributions, and Self-Esteem

John G. Borkowski, Martha Carr, Elizabeth Rellinger
University of Notre Dame

Michael Pressley
University of Western Ontario

The history of psychology is replete with examples of theories that interrelate motivation with learning, cognition, and performance (Bower & Hilgard, 1975). On the one hand, the Yerkes-Dodson (1908) law—which states that moderate levels of arousal are optimal for performance—represents a commonly held view that respects differences and distinctions among motivation, learning, and performance. Similarly, drive (D) in the Hull-Spence theory represents a unique concept that combines with the learning construct (H) to determine performance (Spence, 1956). In these examples, motivation serves to activate or energize prior learning, with the result often being an alteration in the course of behavior.

In contrast, other performance models emphasize a closer, more intimate connection between the concepts of motivation, learning, and cognition. For instance, the concept of incentive motivation in the Hull-Spence system (cf. Spence, 1956) was introduced to show how need states per se can produce a classically conditioned anticipatory response that combines with habit strength and drive to influence instrumental performance. Similarly, in the area of cognition, Weiner and Walker (1966) and Zubrzycki and Borkowski (1973) have demonstrated that motivational variables influence the trace formation, or encodability, stage of short-term memory. These positions reflect a common theme that serves as the focus of this chapter: Although motivational states often direct and energize human behavior, they also play more subtle roles in determining the actual strength, shape, or functioning of cognitive processes.

We advance the position in this chapter that metacognitive theory is particularly suited for understanding more about the interface of motivation, attitudes, and cognition. The basic argument is that strategy-based actions directly influence self-concept, attitudes about learning, and attributional beliefs about personal control. In turn, these personal-motivational states determine the course of new strategy acquisition and, more importantly, the likelihood of strategy transfer and the quality of self-understanding about the nature and function of mental processes (cf. Borkowski, Johnston, & Reid, 1987; Oka & Paris, 1987).

METACOGNITION THEORY; THE INTERRELATION OF COGNITION, MOTIVATION, AND PERSONALITY

First Generation Research on Metacognition

The history of research on metacognition can be divided into two periods. In the initial wave of metacognitive research, direct relationships among knowledge about memory events or processes—referred to as metamemory by John Flavell (1971)—and relevant memory performance were assessed. This approach was based on the assumption that children's memory was influenced by, and possibly determined by, their knowledge of what actions were appropriate and beneficial in solving memory problems. Children were assumed to use a strategy if they knew when and in what situations strategy use was appropriate. The research technique was typically a variant of the correlational method: Children were asked several questions about their memory knowledge and then presented with a memory task; the quality of their performance was then related to verbalized metamemorial awareness about the task. Schneider (1985), in a thorough review of the metamemory literature, detailed the conceptually and statistically significant relationships between meta-memory and memory behavior. His meta-analysis yielded an overall correlation of .42, suggesting a substantial connection between what one knows about memory processes and subsequent memory performance.

Metacognition: Second Generation Research and Theory

The second wave of research on metamemory can be characterized by increased theoretical complexity, manipulative rather than correlational methods, use of multiple tasks and strategies, and mini-longitudinal designs (Paris, Newman, & McVey, 1982; Pressley, Levin, & Ghatala,

1984). In this section, we describe these shifts in research orientation from the perspective of a model of cognition first developed by Pressley, Borkowski, and O'Sullivan (1985) and later extended by Borkowski et al. (1987) and Pressley, Borkowski, and Schneider (1987). In describing the model, we emphasize the importance of attributional and attitudinal components, because they serve as the focus for the remainder of this chapter.

We have conceptualized metacognition in terms of a number of interactive, mutually related components. At this stage of model building, several major components deserve independent theoretical specification because they appear to have unique developmental histories, are differentially influenced by experience and instruction, and fill distinctive roles in explaining differences in learning and memory performance among normal, gifted, mentally retarded, and learning disabled children. The major components of metamemory are the following: Specific Strategy Knowledge, General Strategy Knowledge, and Metamemory Acquisition Procedures (Pressley et al., 1985). In the following sections, we outline the function of each metamemory component and expand the function of General Strategy Knowledge to include motivational properties that seem useful in explaining academic achievements. The main focus is on connections between metacognitive knowledge and motivational-attitudinal factors—including the ascription of success and failure experiences to effort and the emergence of self-esteem—and how these interactive components play pivotal roles in the maintenance and generalization of potentially useful learning strategies.

Specific Strategy Knowledge. At the core of the model is specific strategy knowledge. Each strategy has a base of knowledge associated with it. The child with well-developed specific strategy knowledge knows the task demands that dictate the use of particular strategies but not others, when to use these strategies, and how to apply them efficiently with the least possible effort. From this perspective, the appearance of a strategy on a transfer test suggests that the learner possessed sufficient information about its attributes so that the new task was recognized as solvable through the application of one of several available strategies (Borkowski, 1985).

Metamemory Acquisition Procedures. Metamemory acquisition procedures (MAPs) are strategies that operate on other strategies. Thus, learners can compare strategies with one another or conduct personal experiments, extending strategies that they know to new situations. MAPs allow the on-line regulation and monitoring of strategies, so that effective and efficient strategies are maintained but strategies detected as ineffective and inefficient are discarded.

For example, when applying a study strategy, good learners often employ self-testing. The self-test is a MAP, yielding information about whether the activated strategy works well in the current situation. In the long term, this information is stored as more detailed specific strategy knowledge about the activated strategy (i.e., that the strategy works well in a narrow or wide range of situations). In the short term, information gained from self-testing is used to guide the continued use of the activated strategy (if learning is going well) or results in a strategy shift (if the original strategy is inefficient).

Consider the following illustrative case. Not so many years ago, one of the authors was confronted with the task of learning 25 new Latin words a week. One of the most challenging yet essential aspects of the task was to learn the gender-determined ending for each vocabulary item. For some time, a rote rehearsal method was used. For *arca,* which means box, he said *"arca, arca, arca."* One day this student thought of another approach: Make an image between the word's referent and a male or female. Thus, for *arca,* an image of Raquel Welch carrying a box should increase the likelihood of remembering that the word for box is feminine and takes the -a ending. He tried this method for half the items on study lists for each of 3 weeks and informally compared acquisition of gender information for these words with the items that were rehearsed. It soon became clear that gender information was acquired more efficiently using imagery than using rehearsal, a fact now confirmed by research (Desroches & Begg, 1987). The important point is that the student used a simple MAP, comparing two strategies. By doing so, he realized that the imagery strategy worked well, which motivated continued use of the strategy during high school Latin. Metacognitive information that was produced by the MAP also permitted the application of the same imagery strategy while learning French several years later. This example points to the importance of MAPs for adult learners.

In a similar manner, even young children can be taught to compare the relative potencies of available strategies to enhance specific strategy knowledge (Ghatala, Levin, Pressley, & Goodwin, 1986; Ghatala, Levin, Pressley, & Lodico 1985; Lodico, Ghatala, Levin, Pressley, & Bell, 1983). Self-instructional routines, like those proposed by Meichenbaum (1977), also include MAPs, particularly instructions to check ongoing performance. Consistent with the theoretical perspective that MAPs produce specific strategy knowledge that increases the probability of durable strategy use, Elliott-Faust and Pressley (1986) found greater long-term maintenance of reading comprehension strategies by children when the strategies were taught with MAP-embellished self-instruction than when they were taught conventionally.

Metacognitive acquisition procedures boil down to self-experimentation. As such, they represent extremely sophisticated approaches to deliberate reflection about strategies. For evidence on this point see Neuringer's (1981) discussion of how self-experimentations has played a prominent role in the evaluation of strategies by prominent scientists. One of the most famous is Herman Ebbinghaus, who studied long-term memory by comparing his own performances under different conditions. Neuringer also discussed evidence supporting the position that university students can be taught to self-evaluate alternative strategies in order to learn about their relative efficacy—in our terms, to acquire Specific Strategy Knowledge. He also argued that it is desirable to teach directly these evaluation procedures. We agree and suggest that a great deal of metacognitive information could be derived by students who are shown how to try out various strategic approaches and to detect their relative costs, benefits, and ranges of applicability.

General Strategy Knowledge and Attributional Beliefs. One form of general strategy knowledge is the child's understanding that effort is required to apply strategies, with an eventual payoff in improved performance. Another is the general understanding that well-chosen strategies produce efficient performance. A third form is understanding that rudimentary strategic plans should be made before trying to carry out a task, with the additional recognition that the plan may need to be modified as the task proceeds. These aspects of general strategy knowledge increase the likelihood that an individual will search for, modify, and apply appropriate strategies (Clifford, 1984).

How does general knowledge develop? Feedback about the effects of strategy use on performance is one way to increase the general knowledge that strategies can facilitate performance. For instance, Kennedy and Miller (1976) showed that verbal feedback about effectiveness following training of a rehearsal strategy significantly improved strategy maintenance. Similarly, a brief film depicting the gains produced by an active mediational strategy preceding training enhanced strategy maintenance for first grade children (Borkowski, Levers, & Gruenenfelder, 1976).

Another way to enhance general knowledge is to provide general information to children explicitly. Thus, prompting children to be more strategic and to value strategies seems to enhance the production and use of strategies (Borkowski & Cavanaugh, 1979). Simply alerting children to the general effectiveness of strategies is, in itself, an effective method for enhancing the likelihood of spontaneous strategy use (Borkowski & Krause, 1985). When these prompts are internalized, the child becomes more aware of the value of specific strategies and of strategies in general, leading eventually to more durable and general strategy use (Lawson & Fuelop, 1980).

General knowledge about the efficacy of strategies has been hypothesized to have motivational properties (Borkowski & Krause, 1985). The motivational correlates of metacognition include positive self-esteem, an internal locus of control, and constructive attributional beliefs about the causes of success and failure. We believe that general strategy knowledge, and its associated motivational factors, are bidirectionally related, each contributing to the development of the other component. High self-esteem, an internal locus of control, and the tendency to attribute success to effort are the consequences of a history of consistent, successful, strategy-based habits of responding to learning and memory tasks. Good performance following strategy use strengthens general strategic knowledge, which promotes positive self-esteem and attributions of success to effort rather than to uncontrollable factors such as ability or luck. In turn, positive self-esteem and effort-related attributional beliefs enhance the likelihood of strategy generalization. Motivational factors play a key role in subsequent "spontaneous" strategy use by providing incentives necessary for deploying strategies, especially on challenging transfer tasks.

The model we have advanced provides a heuristic framework that sketches the interacting factors that promote strategic behavior. Knowledge about the attributes of specific strategies, self-regulating mechanisms (MAPs), and general beliefs about the efficacy of goal-oriented behaviors are three components that jointly determine the likelihood of strategy use (Borkowski, Carr, & Pressley, 1987). Next, we turn to the major focus of this chapter: an expansion of the conception of general strategy knowledge to include new perspectives about the nature of self-esteem and how, in combination, they potentiate behavior. The first objective is to show how cognitive, motivational, and personality constructs interact in a coherent system that shapes academic performance. Then we describe research in which this system is applied to select groups of special children. Finally, we present new research directions that have educational and theoretical relevance as well as raise new issues regarding the interface of cognitive, metacognitive, and motivational variables in classroom settings.

Metacognition and the Self-System

A review of existing research suggests that the self-system—which includes constructs such as self-efficacy, self-esteem, locus of control, achievement motivation, and attributional beliefs—is a complex, interdependent system that supports both metacognitive functions and academic performance (McCombs, 1986). For example, the development of attributional beliefs is closely tied to attitudes about self-efficacy (Eccles, 1983; Harter, 1982a), self-esteem (Carr & Borkowski, 1987), and intrin-

sic motivation (Watkins, 1984). Self-esteem and other self-system constructs, in turn, predict achievement (Calsey & Kenney, 1977; Marsh,
1986; Oka & Paris, 1987; Purkey, 1970).

The self-system is important because it appears to underlie the development of the metacognitive system and helps to determine the quality
of academic achievement. We know that children enter school with a
well-developed belief system (McCombs, 1986). Parents influence their
preschool child's self-esteem, self-confidence, and motivation for success
explicitly, through placement in preschools, and implicitly, through
home-based learning experiences. An example of familial influence in
the development of one aspect of the self-system, attributional beliefs,
can be found in a recent cross-cultural study by Kurtz, Schneider, Carr,
Borkowski, & Turner (1988).

One hundred and eighty-four West German and 161 American elementary school children were assessed on measures of attributional beliefs, metacognitive knowledge, and a memory task. Parents were then
asked to complete a questionnaire about the attributional beliefs they
ascribe to their children and the type of strategy training they provide in
the home. Americans were more likely to emphasize the need for effort
whereas Germans were equally likely to subscribe to the importance of
effort and ability in determining success. Furthermore, parental attributional beliefs paralleled children's attributional beliefs. More important,
the attributional beliefs of parents in both countries correlated with their
children's metacognitive knowledge, suggesting that attributional beliefs
of parents are tied to the development of metacognitive knowledge in
children, despite cultural differences. Furthermore, children's self-perceptions, combined with parental instruction of learning strategies and
metacognitive knowledge, accounted for some of the differences in
learning performance between and within the two countries.

Despite considerable contributions from family, school, and society to
cognitive development, children are, nonetheless, largely responsible for
their own cognitive development. From this perspective, McCombs
(1987) has recently outlined several general principles that relate to the
emergence of automaticity or self-regulated learning. First, children
have an inherent motivation for self-determination and self-development. This motivation is intrinsic (Deci & Ryan, 1985). Children will
work autonomously in order to reach the goals of self-determination and
self-development (cf. White, 1959). It is their inherent need to learn and
achieve self-determination that promotes learning through the development of cognitive, motivational, and affective processes. Achievement-
oriented behaviors are, in part, the product of children's repeated attempts to structure their self and metacognitive systems, with the goal of
maintaining a sense of control.

Children's achievement of self-determination and self-control is determined by the interacting components of the self and the metacognitive systems. According to McCombs (1987), the goal of self-directed achievement, produced via self-control and automaticity, is accomplished by fostering attribution belief patterns, in the form of effort-related beliefs about success, that maximize self-worth and foster the evaluation of outcome variables in terms of self-efficacy. This perspective is supported by evidence suggesting that the self-system is nonhierarchical and self-enhancing (Connell & Ryan, 1984). Children continuously self-evaluate their performance and, more importantly, their personal control and abilities (Harter, 1982). Hence, effort-related attributions are likely to motivate children to acquire and use new strategies and metacognitive knowledge in general. Metacognitive and cognitive processes thrive on these functional attributional patterns. In contrast, children who fail to develop positive attributions are in jeopardy of developing maladaptive and dysfunctional self and metacognitive systems. From this perspective, cognitive psychologists have advanced explanations about the development of functional (and dysfunctional) attributional beliefs, and how these beliefs affect the acquisition of self-control and metacognitive knowledge and skills (Borkowski, Johnston, & Reid, 1987; Oka & Paris, 1987). A number of recent investigators have approached the issue of self-regulated cognitive behavior through the analysis of motivational and personality determinants, including self-worth (Covington, 1985), self-concept (Harter, 1982b; McCombs, 1987), and affect (Covington & Omelich, 1979a, 1979b; Oka & Paris, 1987).

Self-Determination Through Self-Worth.   A sense of control over experience is one way that individuals achieve self determination. According to Covington (1985), self-worth is maintained by the manipulation of attributional beliefs about success and failure. In self-worth theory, Covington sees achievement behavior as the individual's attempt to maintain a positive self-image of ability and competency, especially when risking failure. Self-worth theory assumes that society equates human value with ability (Gardner, 1961) and that self-aggrandizement is a primary force in human behavior (Epstein, 1973). If these assumptions hold, failure becomes something to avoid because it implies low ability. When failure becomes unavoidable, the individual attempts to attribute failure to factors other than ability. For example, attributing failure to unstable factors (such as insufficient effort) or external factors (such as task difficulty) are preferred to internal, stable attributions about ability (Heider, 1958; Kelley, 1973). From this perspective, effort expenditure in the face of possible failure becomes a potential threat to the individual because high effort expenditure resulting in failure increases the probability of a low ability attribution (Kun & Weiner, 1973). This can be seen in Dweck and Repucci's (1973) work with learned helpless children who differ primarily from average children in that they have little sense of control over events; hence, helpless children believe that effort is useless in the face of inevitable failure. Children who believe that failure is due to the lack of effort, however, are more likely to escalate their efforts and are persistent in their attempts to obtain their goals (Dweck, 1975; Dweck & Repucci, 1973; Oka & Paris, 1987; Rotter, 1966; Weiner & Kukla, 1970). In respect to Covington's self-worth theory, children who maintain effort-related attributions are likely to use strategies aggressively in order to gain success; for these children, failure is caused by lack of effort. Helpless children, however, have poor effort-related attributions, leading to the conclusion that failure (and success) is the product of external forces (luck) or poor ability. These attributions about the reasons for performance are not likely to promote the further growth of the self-system.

From a more global perspective, Dweck (1987) has found that some children believe that their intellectual competence consists of a repertoire of skills that can be expanded through their own efforts. These children are called incremental theorists because they persist in achievement attempts, in part, to enhance cognitive development. They believe that the outcome of effortful-strategic behavior is increased intelligence. As would be predicted by the metacognitive-motivational model, persistent incremental-minded children search out tasks that allow for learning opportunities. On the other hand, other children who attribute performance outcomes to ability are called entity theorists (Dweck, 1987). Entity theorists view intelligence as a global and stable trait that cannot be increased through effort. Because these children view the exertion of effort as being a sign of lower intelligence (Dweck, 1975), they do not pursue alternate strategies when faced with the possibility of failure nor do they welcome challenging tasks as opportunities to expand cognitive skills or to enrich metacognitive knowledge. Hence, children classified as entity theorists tend to seek out tasks that provide an opportunity to avoid mistakes and yet receive competence judgments from others.

Covington's and Dweck's models focus on attributional development and help to explain how and why various attributional patterns about the role of effort in learning emerge in children and adolescents. The models suggest that appropriate attributions, in the form of Covington's effort-related attributions about success and Dweck's entity "theorists," facilitate achievement by fostering feelings of positive self-worth. Similarly, inappropriate attributional beliefs may interfere with cognitive development by blocking the development of positive self-worth. Hence, children are likely to achieve self-determination when they feel personally responsible for a successful outcome and understand that their success is due, in part, to the acquisition and application of appropriate metacognitive knowledge.

Self-Determination and Self-Concept. McCombs (1987) has suggested that the self-system promotes children's progress toward self-determination by influencing the processing, transformation, and encoding of information. That is, children with positive self-concepts, along with effort-related attributions (among other self-system constructs), are likely to store and use newly learned information in such a way as to maximize the later usefulness of that information. Children with dysfunctional self-systems, however, are unlikely to take full advantage of new information. They do not make the best of learning opportunities and tend to avoid learning challenges (Dweck, 1987). In addition, Harter (1986) found that individuals develop good or poor self-concepts depending on the amount of discrepency between their actual performance and their perceptions of the importance of the task at hand. In this sense, the self-system and the cognitive system are closely intertwined.

One way the self-system alters information processing is by determining how children perceive and integrate new information with existing knowledge in the same (and related) domains. Although perceptions of information may reflect certain global traits of the child, it also appears that children process new information in terms of task-specific relationships in concert with other self and metacognitive system constructs. For example, Marsh (1986), in a study of individuals ranging from 7 to 31 years-of-age found that math and reading self-concepts were unrelated despite correlations between math and reading achievement scores. Such task-specific perceptions may be due to a maturing self-system. Task-specific perceptions may also make it easier for the child to develop positive self-esteem, and accompanying metacognitive knowledge about specific tasks and strategies. This line of reasoning is similar to an argument that we will advance later: Attributional beliefs influence the quality of encoding processes, especially in recognizing the key attributes of new learning skills and strategies.

Self-Determination and Affect. Affective responses to task demands and task outcomes are a product of, and reinforce the development of, the self and metacognitive systems by modifying affective states, such as pride, sadness, or joy (Harter, 1982). For example, Weisz (1978) found that pride in success was enhanced by perceptions of personal causality. Furthermore, pride is maximized when success is perceived to be the result of a combination of high ability and effort (Covington & Omelich,

1979a), whereas shame and guilt are intensified when one believes the outcome is indicative of low effort and low ability (Covington & Omelich, 1979b, Weiner & Kukla, 1970). In a similar manner, it is believed that anxiety reactions to failure are the product of cognitive mediators that change with achievement circumstances (Covington, 1985). Hence, affective responses to success and failure are another metacognitively linked component. In short, children respond emotionally to outcomes, and these emotional responses, in turn, support or undermine metacognitive and cognitive development depending on self-perceptions.

Because attributional beliefs about success and failure play a significant role in metacognitive development and functioning, it is not surprising that differing attributional patterns evoke different emotional responses. Attributing success or failure to internal factors promotes pride or happiness in success (Stipek & Weisz, 1981). This is particularly apparent in Covington's work on attributions and self-worth. Covington (1987) suggested that achievement distress—such as self-blame, humiliation, and self-derogation—follow from the belief that one is personally unable to manage events that others seem able to control.

For instance, Covington and Omelich (1979a) have shown that failure following high effort maximizes negative emotional reactions. Introductory psychology students were given a number of hypothetical achievement situations involving failure on a college exam. These hypothetical exams were similar to the tests administered in the course. Each subject was told to imagine that he or she had failed the test under a given condition. The four conditions were the following: little effort without excuse, little effort with excuse, high effort without excuse, and high effort with excuse. The highest amount of public shame and personal dissatisfaction occurred under the condition of high effort without excuse. Public shame and dissatisfaction were reduced when the students had excuses to explain their failure despite effort, or an excuse that externalized the cause of failure. Excuses that allow the student to attribute failure to something other than their ability reduced the threatening linkage of high effort with low ability.

In addition, Covington and Omelich (1979b) found that failure, despite great effort, leads to decreasing expectancies. Covington and Omelich suggested that this is another way that the implication of low ability hinders children's affective and metacognitive development. From a more applied perspective, test-taking situations often are anxiety provoking because individuals may act to maximize success and to avoid failure (Epstein, 1973). In the end, humiliation, and other negative emotional responses based on ability-linked reactions to failure, further increase the distress experience (Covington & Omelich, 1984) and may inhibit metacognitive development.

Integrating Metacognitive
and Motivational Constructs

Given that self-system is instrumental for academic achievements, and that metacognition seems to be one conduit for explaining its influence via skilled learning, the model of Pressley et al. (1985) and Borkowski, Johnston & Reid (1987) may be useful in delineating how cognitive, affective, motivational, and attributional constructs influence achievement. From the perspective of the metacognitive model, children who feel good about themselves and their ability—those who are intrinsically motivated to learn and who have effort-related attributions—are more likely to believe in strategic behavior and to develop complex, mature strategy knowledge. Attributional beliefs that place control outside of the individual undermine intrinsic motivation—a necessary ingredient for self-determination and an emerging sense of self-efficacy (Deci & Ryan, 1985).

In this sense, self-system constructs power metacognition by giving children reasons to learn. Attributional beliefs are of particular importance for metacognitive development because children must first believe in the utility of their strategy-related effort (Clifford, 1984) before they will apply those efforts in situations that demand strategic behavior. Effort is actualized in the form of well-chosen strategies that are carefully and thoughtfully applied to difficult tasks. It follows that children with positive self-systems are more likely to acquire specific strategy knowledge, and to apply this knowledge on new tasks because they have a general belief in the utility of strategies and effort. That is, they have a well-developed general strategy knowledge component in their metacognitive system.

Emotional responses to success and failure may also foster metacognitive development. That is, children who have a sense of pride in their work and who seek success as a function of their effort, are likely to acquire and use metacognitive knowledge. These children will seek challenging experiences, in part, to increase feelings of pride and self-fulfillment. It follows that children must first be capable of experiencing positive affective feelings as a result of early successful strategic actions that lead to positive attributional patterns. Later on these attributional patterns about controllability determine whether children persist in strategic behaviors when they prove initially unsuccessful. Hence, children who feel good about themselves as learners are likely to continue to be strategic and to increase their metacognitive knowledge because these processes have paid off in the past, elevating performance and enhancing self-esteem.

Although the self-system provides the necessary motivation and affective states to foster children's progress toward self-determination, it is the metacognitive system that provides the means to reach that goal. In order for the metacognitive system to work, children must have adequate information about both general and specific strategy knowledge—about why, when, where, and how to use strategies. Effort-related attributions are of little use to a child who does not have the necessary accompanying specific strategic knowledge. Such children will end up "spinning their wheels," for instance, having high motivation and energy to use appropriate strategies but not knowing how to select the one to employ for a particular task. Hence, intervention programs must focus on the development of both the self and the metacognitive systems in order to maximize children's academic performance.

In summary, the development of the metacognitive system may be dependent on children's initial acquisition of appropriate attributions, motivation, and affective states. In general, children acquire these self-beliefs from their families and early school experiences. Successful students believe that their effort is instrumental in producing their successes. On the other hand, patterns of motivational and metacognitive development may also be disadvantageous. Children who have immature, inaccurate beliefs about success and failure (e.g., attributing success to luck and failure to a lack of talent) may produce the tendency to avoid strategic behavior in the face of challenging academic tasks (Dweck, 1987; Kurtz & Borkowski, 1984). These so-called "helpless" children often fail to develop functional self-systems that would facilitate their progress through school. The failure to develop a functional self-system, and corresponding metacognitive skills and knowledge, is likely to result in poor performance as well as the reinforcement of negative self-perceptions and beliefs.

Implications for Special Populations: Attributions and Skilled Learning

If self-system development occurs prior to metacognitive development, different developmental patterns among self-system constructs may differentially influence metacognitive development. That is, self-perceptions and beliefs may determine the development of the metacognitive system (Heckhausen, 1983). For example, positive self-esteem in average-ability children enhances their metacognition, whereas underachieving children have low self-esteem, which makes the development of basic metacognitive skills and achievements in school less likely (Carr &

Borkowski, 1987). This is not to say that the characteristics of the self-system determine whether a child will be learning disabled or gifted. Rather, these characteristics help determine the extent to which children develop, expand (e.g., remembering information that adults provide about specific strategies) and utilize their learning potentials. Within various subgroups of special children, different patterns of self-perceptions and beliefs seem to determine how children perceive task goals, solve problems, and assess the meaning of performance outcomes. Hence, differences within children's self and metacognitive systems account, in part, for between-group differences among gifted, learning disabled, and average-ability children who are classified as "helpless."

Perspectives on Giftedness.   In the case of gifted and talented children, an integrated pattern of motivational and metacognitive development generally leads to academic achievements. High intrinsic motivation and task-commitment in gifted children (Feldman, 1979), as well as healthy self-concepts (Ketcham & Snyder, 1977), are products of early success experiences. For the gifted child, consistent success, together with the encouragement of their families and teachers, set the stage for the emergence of a positive self-system and superior metacognitive development. Given this, it is not surprising that among gifted children, self-concept is correlated with academic achievement, such as reading skill (Anastaziow, 1964).

In terms of metacognitive theory, heightened perceptual speed and superior sensory-based skills characteristic of gifted preschoolers establishes the groundwork for the development of mature self and metacognitive systems (Borkowski & Peck, 1986). Gifted children acquire specific strategy knowledge more efficiently than average children (i.e., they both are more likely to figure out when it is appropriate to use skills that they learn and to remember that information when it is provided to them). Their consistent and early successes in initial strategic behaviors build positive self-systems, promoting the development of a more mature, complex, and integrated metacognitive system. Partial support for these claims were obtained by Borkowski and Peck (1986), who studied average and gifted 7- and 8-year-old children. The groups were compared on measures of metamemory, strategy use, and strategy generalization. Although no initial differences were found on strategy use, gifted children were more likely to generalize elaboration strategies and had more advanced metamemorial knowledge than average children. They also gave evidence of superior MAPs in that they tended to "fill-in-gaps" when given incomplete strategy instructions and demonstrated advanced monitoring skills.

We believe that gifted performance is characterized by high self-esteem, intrinsic motivation, and effort-related attributional beliefs. These characteristics of general strategy knowledge, combined with perceptual efficiency and more detailed specific strategy knowledge, promote the development of higher-order metacognitive knowledge (MAPs). It is the establishment of these advanced metacognitive components that eventually sets gifted children apart from average children (Borkowski & Kurtz, 1987), enabling the emergence of creative and inventive behaviors.

Perspectives on Learning Disabilities. Learning disabled (LD) children are assumed to have physiologically-based perceptual and/or cognitive deficits (Ceci, 1986). These perceptual deficits often result in an inability to adequately decode and process information presented visually or orally. Furthermore, because LD children are most often diagnosed after a period of failure, they often develop both metacognitive and motivational problems. For example, Jacobsen, Lowery, and DuCette (1986) interviewed learning disabled and non-learning disabled children and found that the learning disabled have self-systems that are unlikely to promote achievement behaviors. Instead of attributing success to effort and failure to external causes, learning disabled children tended to attribute success to external factors and failure to effort, an attributional pattern that, according to Covington's theory, would result in poor self-worth and dysfunctional metacognitive and self-systems. The dysfunctional metacognitive and motivational components of LD children, in turn, increases the likelihood of failure and reinforces negative self-evaluations, thus perpetuating the failure cycle.

Although many of the specific perceptual and intellectual deficits of LD children are not easily modifiable, the same is less true for the attributional beliefs and self-perceptions that accompany these physiologically based deficits. Children who have developmental learning deficits must always deal with their specific deficits, and it is the orientation of their self and metacognitive systems that may determine whether they succeed or fail in dealing with their disabilities. In this light, Douglas (1980) has proposed treatment programs for hyperactive and learning disabled children that address the dysfunctional cognitive, metacognitive, and motivational components. Specifically, children should be (a) taught to understand that their deficiencies are treatable, (b) given general problem-solving skills and accompanying attributional and motivational components, and (c) presented specific strategies for a wide variety of tasks (Douglas, 1982). Using Douglas' framework as a heuristic guide, Reid and Borkowski (1987) have developed a training program based on these principles which has shown considerable success in improving the learning skills of hyperactive children. The work of Douglas and Reid and Borkowski suggests that academic performance in children with physiologically based learning deficits may be altered by the addition of attributional or motivational components to strategy training. In addition, the importance of the self-system may also be seen in the inability of many intervention programs that focus solely on strategic training, such as the training program by Gelzheiser (1984), to remediate impaired performance effectively.

Perspectives on Learned Helplessness. A widely cited outcome of poorly functioning metacognitive and self-systems in average ability children is learned helplessness (Dweck, 1987). Helpless children react to failure by abandoning problem-solving strategies when intensification or modification of strategic behavior would be more appropriate (Diener & Dweck, 1978; Dweck, 1975; Dweck & Repucci, 1973). These children appear to have dysfunctional attributional beliefs. That is, learned helpless children believe that ability, and not effort, is the cause of success. As a result, they fail to apply effort because they perceive it to be useless. In contrast, children with more positive self-orientations and advanced metacognitive systems are "mastery-oriented." These children increase their efforts, and presumably utilize and/or acquire metacognitive understanding, in the face of learning challenges. The intensification of effort by mastery-oriented children may result in the development of more mature problem-solving strategies. Hence, learned helpless children do not benefit from their experiences, whereas mastery-oriented children often gain new insight into the applicability of specific strategies to novel situations. As a result, mastery-oriented children place themselves in a position of acquiring new MAPs, such as knowing how to select the best strategy or how to change strategies when they are dysfunctional.

For example, when Dweck and Repucci (1973) gave children a set of insolvable tasks followed by solvable tasks they found that, although some children actively pursued alternate solutions upon encountering failure, other children abandoned their strategies. As a result, the latter group of children were incapable of solving the problems that they had previously easily solved. This occurred despite no differences between groups on the initially solvable tasks. What distinguished the two groups was their attributional belief patterns. Dweck and Repucci (1973) found that children who did not persist in the face of failure placed significantly less emphasis on motivational factors as determinants of outcomes. That is, children most likely to abandon the tasks were those who either took less responsibility for their successes and failures or who attributed their performance outcome to ability rather than effort. Furthermore, Licht and Dweck (1984) found learned helplessness was related to an inability to cope when faced with difficulties in achievement-oriented situations.

Covington and Omelich's (1981) work supports Dweck's conceptualizations of learned helplessness by showing that attributions of low ability intensify both the affective and cognitive reactions that accompany performance deterioration. According to Covington's (1985) self-theory, learned helplessness is the product of negative affective and cognitive reactions to failure, such as anxiety. These affective and cognitive reactions are due to feeling personally incapable of altering the course of events (Covington, 1985). Covington believes that self-handicapping tactics, such as procrastination and blaming others, may be used by individuals in an attempt to circumvent personal responsibility for their failures. In the end, learned helpless children become "failure accepting" in order to avoid the implication of low ability (Covington & Omelich, 1981, 1984).

Learned helplessness can be explained in terms of the metacognitive model as dysfunctional attributional beliefs, a component of General Strategy Knowledge. As can be seen in Dweck's work, learned helpless children have adequate but not advanced specific strategy knowledge. Learned helpless children differ from average children in that learned helpless children lack strong commitments to strategic behaviors, the wherewithal to deploy strategies, or the ability to fill in the gaps when strategy knowledge is incomplete (one of the functions of MAPs). Strategic behavior may be elicited from both learned helpless and average children. Learned helpless children, however, do not seem to possess the underlying motivational states, attributional beliefs, and metacognitive processes (such as MAPs) that support specific strategy knowledge, particularly in the face of failure. Learned helpless children do not believe that they will succeed through effort. As a result, these children are unlikely to develop or use higher-order executive processes.

In the case of learned helpless children, General Strategy Knowledge may be the pivotal metacognitive component. Children with good general strategy knowledge understand the value of effort in producing good performance, and believe that thoughtful, strategic actions are effective ways to expend effort. Children who are deficient in general strategy knowledge exhibit helpless behavior because they do not believe that effort, in the form of strategic development, will prove fruitful in the face of challenging situations. On the other hand, children who believe that success is a result of effort persist in appropriate problem-solving behavior. In sum, learned helpless children, as opposed to learning disabled children, appear to be deficient in general strategy knowledge (and perhaps MAPs) as well as the motivational and affective states necessary for consistent patterns of academic achievement.

METACOGNITION AND ATTRIBUTIONS: METHODOLOGICAL PERSPECTIVES

The metacognitive model previously discussed lends itself to new research methodologies that are useful for analyzing and assessing multi-componential models. Two methodological approaches that have been particularly useful in early stages of model building are the structural equations modeling and instructional approaches. Each methodology provides different types of information about the complex phenomenon being studied. As an illustration of their importance for model testing, we focus next on the topic of underachievement, discussing two recent studies that interrelate the motivational, affective, and metacognitive factors believed to influence achievement and underachievement in elementary school children.

According to Kerwin, Howard, Maxwell, and Borkowski (1987), structural equation modeling is a sophisticated multivariate technique that has the capacity to test two models simultaneously: a measurement model and a structural model. The measurement model focuses on the relationship between the measured, observed variables and the hypothetical, unobserved constructs the variables are supposed to measure. The structural model describes the interrelationship between the constructs. In doing so, structural equation modeling allows alternative theoretical models to be compared. Although structural equations modeling does not confirm the significance of a particular theory, it does provide an indication of a theory's plausability. Hence, the goal of the first study to be described is to show the utility of structual equation modeling in the development of a complex theory of underachievement. The purpose was to compare achievers and underachievers in order to determine possible differences in causal relationships among affective, motivational, and cognitive constructs.

A second study will be used to illustrate the roll of the manipulative, intervention research approach, which can be useful in assessing the role of individual components in multi-factor instructional programs. Intervention programs, based on the instructional approach (cf. Belmont & Butterfield, 1977), are particularly useful when theoretically-based components are assumed to determine complex performance. In the study to be described, children who received strategy-plus-attribution training were expected to perform better on reading tasks than children who received strategy-only training or no training at all. Hence, the main thrust of the two studies to be described is to illustrate how motivational and metacognitive variables combine to influence achievement, using different research methodologies—correlational and maniputative.

Study 1: Models of
Underachievement and Achievement

One hundred and five underachievers and 110 achievers from the third, fourth, and fifth grades of several midwestern school systems participated (Carr & Borkowski, 1987). The selection of underachievers was based on a four-step process: (a) third-, fourth-, and fifth-grade teachers were asked to nominate children who were currently receiving C or D grades and yet who appeared capable of working at a higher level of performance. It should be added that none of the nominated children were participating in special classes; (b) next, children were given two tests of ability—the Slossen IQ and the Peabody Picture Vocabulary tests. Averaged ability scores were transformed to z-scores using national norms; (c) reading grades were then averaged over two semesters, and individual grades were transformed to z-scores using reading distributions from the local school system; (d) finally, each child's z-score for reading was subtracted from his or her z-score for intelligence. Children with difference scores of .5 or above were considered underachievers. Approximately half of the children originally nominated by the teachers were eventually classified as underachievers. Teachers also nominated achievers through the same process. Achievers were children who were currently receiving C or B grades and appeared to be working at their grade level. These children were given the same ability tests as the underachievers. Children with transformed difference scores between .49 and −.49 were considered achievers. Both groups were then given a battery of tests assessing the five constructs that are depicted in Figure 2.1. An analysis of mean differences revealed that achievers, in contrast to underachievers, had high self-esteem, a belief in the utility of effort, enhanced reading awareness, better academic performance, and were more intrinsically motivated. Structural equation modeling was then used to determine if a single model, with both constrained and free paths, best fit the two data sets.

The hypothesized model (see Figure 2.1) suggests that underachievers differ from achievers primarily in their failure to connect extant ability with their attributions about the causes of success and failure. To test this hypothesis, all paths in the models were constrained to be equal except for the free path between ability and attributions. Thus,

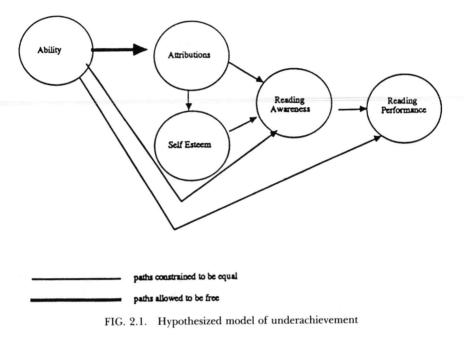

—————————— paths constrained to be equal

—————————— paths allowed to be free

FIG. 2.1.   Hypothesized model of underachievement

metacognitive systems for both achievers and underachievers were highly similar, with the exception of the relationship between the ability and
attribution components (see Figure 2.2). For both achievers and underachievers, ability facilitated reading performance as well as the development of reading awareness. Performance was also mediated by attributions, self-esteem, and reading awareness. It was the connection between
ability and attributional beliefs that distinguished the two groups. Apparently, underachievers failed to associate ability with the expenditure
of effort; that is, they did not take credit for their prior performance.
The failure to make this connection may have retarded the development
of the underachiever's metacognitive system. On the other hand, attributional beliefs of achievers developed in tandem with their ability; that is,
achievers credited themselves, at least to some extent, for their prior
performance. In short, the acquisition of appropriate attributional patterns most likely augmented the development and coordination of other
components in the metacognitive system of achievers.

    Despite the significant contribution of ability and reading awareness
to reading performance, a belief in the utility of effort and a sense of self-
esteem may be additional components in the development of a functional metacognitive system that promotes academic achievements. The
path from ability to attributions (and through attributions to self-esteem,
reading awareness, and performance) was the only path that discrimi-

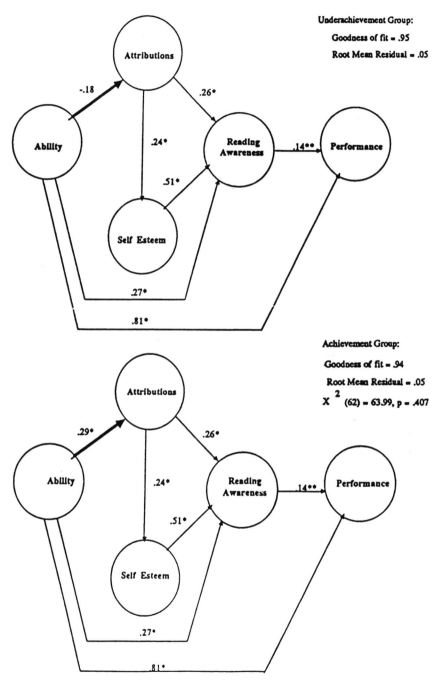

Achievement Group:
Goodness of fit = .94
Root Mean Residual = .05
$X^2 (62) = 63.99$, p = .407

FIG. 2.2.   A comparison of models of underachievement and achievement

nated underachievers from achievers. This supports earlier research suggesting that the acquisition of appropriate attributional beliefs is critical for the development of the metacognitive system; for instance, attributional beliefs have been shown to lead to enhanced self-esteem (Durr & Collier, 1960). In turn, attributional beliefs and positive self-esteem predict the use of appropriate metacognitive and cognitive strategies. In the case of underachievers, dysfunctional attributional beliefs may produce less intrinsic motivation and lower self-esteem. Hence, attributional beliefs would determine, in part, whether or not children succeed in academic settings.

These findings hint at the importance of motivational and affective states for metacognition development. Children enter school with an already well-developed self-system including self-esteem, attributional beliefs, and intrinsic motivation (McCombs, 1986). Motivational and affective states may determine the pattern of later metacognitive development, particularly during the elementary school years. These metacognitive and cognitive skills become increasingly important as the child matures and advances academically.

Study 2: The Instructional Approach to Attributions and Performance

If the metacognitive model is correct in implicating attributions and achievement, then an intervention program aimed at the dysfunctional components of underachievement (especially specific strategy knowledge and attributional beliefs) should improve learning performance. That is, intervention aimed at two key components, specific strategy knowledge and attributional beliefs, should enhance comprehension performance and heighten attributional beliefs about the importance of effort.

The "direct instructional" method was used in Study 2 to train both strategies and attributions (cf. Belmont & Butterfield, 1977). The direct instructional method was chosen because it can be used to instruct reading strategies. The goals of direct instruction are to shift from overt to covert performance, from simple to complex exemplars, from prompted performance to unprompted performance, from immediate feedback to delayed feedback, from emphasis on the teacher as source of information to the teacher as elicitor of new skills, and from much practice to little practice (Becker, Engleman, Carnine, & Rhine, 1981).

Direct instruction in Study 2 was used to inform children explicitly about the existence and effectiveness of metacognitive knowledge about reading. Such knowledge is necessary for the maintenance of cognitive strategies (Paris & Cross, 1983; Paris, Lipson, & Wixson, 1983; Pressley, Borkowski, & O'Sullivan, 1985). During training, students practiced the strategies by first observing the instructor going through the steps of the strategy. The instructor provided explicit steps and then gave information about how these steps should, and should not, be applied. For instance, the instructor told the children not to use a particular sentence because it did not fulfill the definition of the strategy being taught. Children were then allowed to practice the strategies by first going through every step of the strategy verbally and gradually shifting to internal processing. The focus was on mastery learning. Hence, the children mastered each step of the strategy, and understood its necessity, before they advanced to the next stage of strategy training.

We hypothesized that an intervention program that contained strategy-plus-attribution training would be maximally effective in producing changes in performance. This assumption was based on the belief that underachievers do not so much lack knowledge of strategies, but a full understanding that strategic behavior in tandem with effort results in reading achievements. This "misunderstanding" was hypothesized to be a major underlying cause of underachievement.

Fifty-two underachieving students were randomly assigned to one of three conditions. In a strategy-plus-attribution condition, underachieving students were given direct instructional training in reading comprehension strategies and attributional training. Children were taught the steps to each strategy (e.g., first read the entire paragraph and make sure you understand what you read). For the strategy-plus-attribution group, at each step of the strategy, the instructor reinforced the need for effort in the form of attentiveness to the strategy. The instructor then suggested that reading and searching for meaning require considerable effort but that this extra effort is necessary for successful recall.

Attributional beliefs were the focus of the training program for two reasons. First, the data from the structural equations modeling approach suggested that attributional beliefs power the development of the self-esteem and other motivational components in achievers. Hence, changes in attributional beliefs were thought to affect self-esteem in the long run and reading awareness in the short run. Second, earlier studies have indicated that dysfunctional attributional beliefs can be modified. For example, Dweck (1975) taught helpless children to attribute failure to controllable causes such as insufficient effort. The training resulted in increased motivation and improved performance. In addition, metacognitive knowledge and general strategy knowledge have also been modified by training specific strategies together with attributions in hyperactive (Reid & Borkowski, 1987) and learning disabled children (Borkowski, Weyhing, & Turner, 1986).

Each of three strategies (topic sentence, summarization, and questioning) was trained over two half-hour sessions, for a total of six training sessions. Children in the strategy-only condition received strategy training through direct instruction without attributional training. The control group received the same tasks as the treatment groups without training.

Three weeks following the final training session, students were posttested on measures of reading awareness, self-esteem, and attributions about the causes of performance. Comprehension strategies and prose recall were also tested. Underachievers who were given strategy-plus-attribution training were expected to alter their attributional beliefs about effort as well as their understanding about the components of reading awareness more so than the other groups. Furthermore, children in the strategy-plus-attribution training group should use the trained strategies to improve reading comprehension more so than any other group. The strategy-only group was expected to use the trained strategies, but not perform as well as the strategy-plus-attribution training group. No changes in attributions were expected in the strategy-only or control groups.

The addition of the attributional component to the training program produced significant gains in strategy use, recall performance, reading grades, and attributional beliefs. Not only did the strategy-plus-attribution condition promote the maintenance of the trained strategies, it facilitated generalization of the strategies to the classroom. That is, reading awareness increased in both strategy-plus-attribution and strategy-only training groups, suggesting that strategic training alone might be effective in improving this aspect of metacognitive development. It should be noted that these positive generalization effects are not commonly found in instruction research with poor readers. Increased metacognitive knowledge, however, did not translate into increased performance in the strategy-only condition. It was the addition of the attributional component that bridged the gap between knowledge about reading and actual reading performance. Finally, it should be pointed out that no type of training increased self-esteem. Longer, or more intense, instruction which would produce extensive generalized use of the strategy in classroom contexts may be necessary to alter self-esteem.

Retraining of attributional beliefs may be necessary to alter dysfunctional attributions, because intensive strategic training alone did not modify attributional beliefs about the utility of effort. This is probably because attributional beliefs are deeply embedded within cultural and familial contexts (Kurtz et al., 1988) and are often reinforced by parent's and teacher's attributions about the causes of success and failure. Hence, the results of the present study suggest that strategy-based interventions should explicitly provide important motivational components aimed at modifying attributional beliefs.

Implications for Underachievement and Reading Instruction

Several major conclusions about processes that distinguish achievement and underachievement can be drawn from the results of these studies. In contrast to much of the earlier work on underachievement, this research brings together many of the major variables—including affective, motivational, and cognitive processes—that have hitherto been studied in isolation. The structural equations modeling approach was used to shed new light on the relationships among affective, motivational, and metacognitive processes in both achiever and underachiever groups. The results of the modeling techniques suggested that a primary difference between underachievers and achievers is the connection between extant ability and attributional beliefs. Attributional beliefs appear to power the other components (such as reading awareness and self-esteem). As a result, the entire system suffers when children fail to develop appropriate attributional beliefs in concert with their achievements. Furthermore, the structural equations modeling study and the training study suggested that underachieving children need to be instructed, not only in specific strategies, but also in accompanying effort-related beliefs and metacognitive knowledge, in order for that knowledge to be translated into successful reading performance.

The training program also produced several interesting results. First, the combination of strategy and attributional training produced sizable gains in recall performance, strategy use, and more importantly, reading grades. The gains in performance are notable because some earlier training programs have found the modification of reading achievement difficult to accomplish (Paris, Cross, & Lipson, 1984; Paris & Oka, 1987; Ryan, Ledger, Short, & Weed, 1982). More positively, Palincsar and Brown (1984) trained learning disabled students to use four comprehension strategies: clarifying, summarization, questioning, and predicting through reciprocal training. Learning disabled students were initially taught the strategies, along with information about the text and the value of strategies. During part of the training the students were allowed to teach these strategies. Children trained using the reciprocal teaching method did better on comprehension tests and were able to generalize this knowledge to classroom settings.

One reason why the reciprocal training and direct instruction methods are effective may be their emphasis on teacher explanation. Consider a recent study by Duffy and colleagues (1987). Classroom teachers taught reading skills, such as the analysis of compound words, to low-ability readers in their usual reading groups. Teachers in the control group taught these skills as they normally would. Teachers in the experimental condition were taught to explain the skills explicitly and to provide information about when the strategy should be used. The teachers were taught to explain the strategies, model their use, and to interact with students as they tried to use the skills, providing feedback and additional explanations as required. Detailed analyses of experimental and control teachers' explanations confirmed that the trained teachers did in fact produce more complete explanations. The more explicit explanations paid off: Students of experimental teachers were more aware of when and how to use the new reading skills. More importantly, students in the experimental classrooms outperformed students in the control classrooms on standardized reading measures—even measures taken the subsequent academic year. The evidence was compelling that highly explicit teaching of strategies is much more effective than teaching that consists of nothing more than the explanation of strategies and skills (Duffy et al., 1987).

Implications for the General
Metacognitive Model

Structural equations modeling supported the metacognitive–motivational model proposed by Borkowski and Krause (1985). The structural equations modeling approach used in Study 1, expanded on the general motivational–metacognitive model in that the attributional beliefs and self-esteem were included as separate factors and as precursors to metacognitive awareness about reading. Borkowski and Krause (1985) included the motivational–affective component, but did not specify how this component interacted with its metacognitive counterparts. The present results suggested that attributions and self-esteem are integral parts of the metacognitive system; that is, metacognitive models need to include corresponding affective and motivational components in order to fully account for differences in achievement performance. Furthermore, the structural equation modeling suggested that behaviors of special populations may be due to differences in the ways attributional beliefs and the other motivational and affective factors are related to metacognitive development.

The acquisition of effort-related attributional beliefs seems to provide an appropriate context for the acquisition and use of strategies. Motivation that is necessary to notice and acquire specific strategy knowledge may depend on the development of constructive attributional beliefs, such that good performance is seen as due to use of appropriate strategies. This is evident in the training program where the addition of attributional training to strategy training increased the effectiveness of that training. Children who received the additional attributional training maintained and generalized comprehension strategies, but this was not the case for children who received no training or were taught only specific strategies and when to use them. In other words, once children understand that good performance depends on the use of appropriate strategies, they may be more motivated to learn when it is and is not appropriate to use a particular strategy.

In addition to attributional beliefs, self-esteem also seems instrumental in the development and maintenance of specific strategy knowledge and general strategy knowledge. In the structural equation model of Study 1, self-esteem may be interpreted as developing as a function of the childrens' attributional beliefs. Furthermore, self-esteem significantly predicted reading awareness that was, in turn, associated with strategic performance. In short, positive feelings associated with self-esteem may be an important impetus for the development and use of strategic knowledge. If children believe that they are capable of controlling their performance, then their self-esteem may promote effortful performance. The cycle continues on: Successful performance strengthens positive attributional beliefs and self-esteem. It is the interdependencies among metacognition, motivational, and personality constructs that influence the emergence of self-regulated cognitive acts. It is to the question of their development in classroom contexts that we now turn.

TEACHING AND MOTIVATING
STRATEGY USE IN THE CLASSROOM

The theoretical and experimental work reviewed thus far suggests that important benefits follow from motivationally embellished strategy instruction. The purpose of this section is to address issues of educational relevance. In doing so, we need to emphasize that the type of strategy instruction that we favor is far from common and difficult to implement. We argue, however, that strategy instruction that is metacognitively–motivationally based is not only possible but a preferred alternative to the status quo. The coverage is limited to three instructional issues: (a) Motivating teachers to instruct strategies, (b) motivating students to use strategies, and (c) inducing students to believe in their own self-efficacy (i.e., teach students that they have control over their learning experiences).

Motivating Teachers to Teach
Strategies in the Classrooms

The learning strategies identified by cognitive psychologists are rarely explicitly taught. There is little evidence of classroom teaching of empirically validated strategies for reading comprehension (Durkin, 1979), memory (Moely et al., 1986), writing (Applebee, 1984, 1986), or mathematical problem solving (Thompson, 1985). Even when strategy instruction occurs, it rarely involves the type of complete explanations, explicit modeling, and monitored progress that constitute effective strategy teaching (e.g., Duffy et al., 1987).

On a more positive note, the scientific community is at work developing and evaluating strategies that facilitate performance on school tasks, as well as developing effective methods for implementing those strategies in classrooms. There are also explicit efforts to disseminate new strategies and methods of strategy instruction to the educational community. Entire issues of journals—explicitly targeted to teachers—have been devoted to strategy instruction (e.g., *Exceptional Children* (October 1986); *Educational Leadership* (April 1986)). In addition, there are a number of journals, intended for teachers, that regularly publish articles detailing helpful strategies and how to teach them (e.g., *The Reading Teacher, The Elementary School Journal*). Textbooks on strategy instruction that are well-informed by recent research are now available (e.g., T. G. Devine's *Teaching and study skills: A guide for teachers* (1986); E. Gagne's *The cognitive psychology of school learning* (1985)). In short, recent efforts have been made to heighten the awareness of educators about strategy instruction, based on the assumption that knowledge about these procedures and their effects on student achievement will motivate teachers to incorporate strategy training into classroom practices.

Even more promising, however, is the incorporation of the strategy instructional perspective into teacher-education programs, with well-regarded leaders in the teacher-educator community spearheading the effort. For instance, Laura Roehler and Gerald Duffy at Michigan State have developed two such innovative courses, both of which have at their core the development of teachers who know how to provide detailed strategy instruction. In both programs, the preservice teachers have extensive opportunities to observe good strategy instruction, and also receive extensive instruction in cognitive strategies that can be taught to children. The necessity of providing specific strategy knowledge is emphasized, as is the necessity of explicitly modeling the use of cognitive strategies for students. Novice teachers learn to provide extensive practice in strategy execution, to monitor student progress carefully, and to provide individualized instruction as required. Over the course of 2 years, young teachers are given thorough instruction in how to teach strategies, how to provide specific strategy knowledge, and how to motivate student use of strategies. These procedures are outlined in Duffy and Roehler's (1986) text, *Improving classroom reading instruction: A decision-making approach*.

There is a potential problem of maintaining strategy instruction in classroom settings where reinforcing events and retraining opportunities may be minimal. After learning to teach study methods, teachers might have little motivation to continue to teach strategies, especially if strategy instruction has a poor learning payoff to effort ratio, as might be the case in the initial stages of training. Imagine the blow to a teacher's self-esteem if student performance is unchanged following the expenditure of considerable effort on a strategy that was represented as a panacea for many learning or comprehension problems. Negative attributional consequences could follow for those students who experienced failures and then concluded that even powerful procedures that *always help others, cannot save them!*

Because of the possibility that strategy instruction can backfire, and actually discourage teachers and students, we believe that great caution should be exercised in recommending strategies to teachers for classroom implementation. Every effort should be made to provide teachers with strategies that provide a "big bang for the buck." In addition, support and guidance should be provided in order to develop rich metacognitive knowledge about the to-be-learned strategies. Because most strategies designed for ecologically valid tasks like reading, writing, and elementary arithmetic are fairly new and not extensively evaluated, there is great challenge for the research community, which needs to identify those strategies that pay off, to determine when and how benefits can be maximized, and systematically to disseminate to the educational community the alternative training programs that seem most promising. For more extensive commentary on the challenges associated with translating strategy research from the journals to the classrooms, see Pressley, Goodchild, Fleet, Zajchowski, and Evans (in press).

Motivating Students' Use of Strategies

It is important to motivate students to use the potent strategies that they already know and to induce them to deploy ones that they are currently being taught. Students need to understand that they can achieve success in school by mastering strategies that are well-matched to task demands. Unfortunately, however, even when strategy instruction occurs, educators often fail to explain to their students why they are learning specific skills and procedures (Anderson, Brubaker, Alleman-Brooks, & Duffy, 1984; Brophy, Rohrkemper, Rashid, & Goldberger, 1983; Doyle, 1983; Rohrkemper & Bershon, 1984). In short, teachers generally do little to motivate the use of strategies and to promote appropriate attributions relevant to prolonged strategy use. Can strategies be taught in classrooms so that students are interested in acquiring and employing them and yet understand the intricate relationships between the use of strategies and competent performance, especially when the early stage of training might show little performance change?

The motivational literature offers several suggestions about how classroom instruction of skills and strategies could be conducted so to enhance continued strategy use, with Brophy (1986) providing a comprehensive review of the available procedures. Brief mention of some of Brophy's recommendations will make clear that there are existing motivational procedures that can be applied in the school that are not used extensively at present.

Students should be taught strategies that provide appropriate challenges (i.e., the strategy and task are not so difficult that they cannot be mastered with reasonable effort, nor so easy that almost no effort is required to learn the procedures). The strategies should be ones that are clearly worth learning in that they assist the acquisition of materials or mastery of tasks that students perceive as important. Students need to experience success using the strategies being taught. This can be done by having them practice strategies with appropriately difficult tasks, but also through explicit, detailed teaching, including careful monitoring of students as they practice procedures and assisting those students who experience difficulties. Steady progress, even if slow, must be reinforced. As long as students exert appropriate effort consistent with their abilities, there needs to be acknowledgment of whatever minimal achievements follow. The goals of strategy teaching should be made clear to students, with attainable standards as visible indicators of successful performance. Specific, detailed, and constructive feedback should be provided when students fall short of performance goals. Students can be taught to self-reinforce for achieving success, perhaps by reminding themselves that they had the ability and made the effort to achieve the designated learning goal (Brophy, 1986; Brophy & Kher, 1986).

Consistent with themes discussed earlier in this chapter, Brophy (1986) has argued that students need to be convinced that effort is an investment in cognitive development more than a risk to self-esteem. It should be made clear that the road to consistent strategy use is often filled with errors and that failure does not imply low ability. Students need to be assured that the development of intellectual skills is incremental, to use Dweck's term, and that the tedious path of mastering diverse strategies and skills is how cognitive advancement *normally* occurs.

Students can also be given explicit rewards and incentives for acquiring and using strategies appropriately. This can take the form of praise, which provides the teacher an opportunity to point out that success follows effort that is directed to strategy deployment. In addition, teachers can prompt students to notice how the strategies that they learn in school can enrich their lives in general, such as permitting them access to opportunities that depend on educational success (Brophy, 1986). In summary, teachers have many motivational tools at their disposal that can be used to induce students to learn strategic skills and to recognize that these skills will influence important aspects of their present and future lives.

One obstacle is that teachers are generally not equipped with information about available methods for motivating students (Brophy et al., 1983). An antidote is to provide teachers with instruction about how to motivate students and to evaluate what happens. Brophy and Merick (1987) did just that, in a study in which 11 teachers participated 6 to 8 hours in workshops that specified how motivational methods could be used in their classrooms. Each teacher was instructed to employ the motivational principles in one section of their seventh- or eighth-grade social studies course and their normal teaching method in another section that covered the same content with similar students. Although there was more improvement in social studies achievement in the experimental condition, differences in achievement gains favoring the children in the experimental condition were small—about one-third of a standard deviation. One possible reason for the small effect-size was that, although the teachers did in fact behave somewhat differently in the experimental and control classrooms, their differences in behavior were not very great. But given significant achievement gain following only brief teacher training and less than complete implementation of the motivational recommendations made by Brophy, there is reason to anticipate that more detailed teacher training and more adequate teacher implementation practices might produce more striking effects on both teacher and student performances.

Inducing Students to Believe
They Can Become Good Strategy Users

All of the suggestions about strategy instruction and the enhancement of motivation have focused on the acquisition and use of skills that improve current academic performance. We believe, however, that the overarching objective of strategy-based education should be to develop good strategy users (Pressley et al. 1987). The good strategy user possesses a vast repertoire of strategic skills. Many of these skills are practiced to the point of automaticity and efficient use in appropriate situations. The good strategy user also possesses well-organized metacognitive knowledge about specific strategies, which can be called upon to facilitate deployment of appropriate strategies when performance is not completely automatic. The good strategy user has appropriate motivational beliefs, the most central of which is an understanding that competent performance is often mediated by use of strategies that are well-matched to a task. Academic self-esteem is high because the good strategy user performs competently in many situations.

What should be apparent is that an enormous amount of strategic learning must occur in order to reach the endstate of being a good strategy user. Because we subscribe to Dweck's incremental point of view regarding children's beliefs about their mind's development, we have little difficulty imagining that a fifth grader who is currently struggling to master a few basic comprehension skills could develop into a good strategy user. Indeed, many children grow to fill competent roles in society, roles that require advanced skills and executive strategies. Understanding that such transformations are not only possible but occur frequently should motivate us to continue working on refinements in methods and models that might increase the likelihood that more children will acquire the knowledge and skills necessary to fit the model of a good strategy user.

A major instructional problem is how to teach students to believe in themselves—to believe that they can become more efficient and effective learners. Hazel Markus and her associates (e.g., Cantor, Markus, Niedenthal, & Nurius, 1986; Markus & Nurius, 1986) have developed a theory of "possible selves" that may be of use in achieving this objective:

> Possible future selves, for example, are not just *any* set of imagined roles or states of being. Instead, they represent specific, individually significant hopes, fears, and fantasies. I am *now* a psychologist, but I *could* be a restaurant owner, a marathon runner, a journalist, or the parent of a handicapped child . . . What others are now, I could become. (Markus & Nurius, 1986, p. 954)

One of the most important hypothesized functions of possible selves is their motivational consequences. A possible self can provide "direction and impetus for action, change, and development" (Markus & Nurius, p. 960). They can provide energy for behaviors that reduce the distance between the current true self and the possible self that one aspires to become. Thus, Markus' theory suggests that there might be value in trying to induce young children to believe that they can become good strategy users, that the good strategy user is a "possible self." Part of the process would be to help children understand that the many competent adult roles, from teacher to airplane pilot to diplomat, are largely accomplished by people carrying out strategic skills in interaction with other forms of domain-specific knowledge they have acquired. Children need to realize that the skills and knowledge of the competent expert were achieved slowly, a little bit at a time, and include at their core the skills and knowledge taught in school. Children also need to realize that the people running the world today were once very similar to themselves, grade-school children struggling to acquire basic literacy and mathematical skills. Understanding the stages and pace of cognitive development might in itself be a motivational factor for strategy acquisition.

Increased awareness about "possible selves" should enhance the motivation to acquire strategic skills, although it seems likely that consistent reminders may be necessary to link today's lessons with future possible selves. There is merit in constantly reminding children in very concrete terms how the incremental learning of strategies and other skills is tied to competency in future roles they will face. Brophy (1986) summarized the argument:

> Basic language arts and mathematics skills are used daily when shopping, banking, driving, reading instructions for using some product, paying bills and carrying on business correspondence, and planning home maintenance projects or family vacations . . . In general, a good working knowledge of the information, principles, and skills taught in school prepares people to make well-informed decisions that result in saving time, trouble, expense, or even lives, and it empowers people by preparing them to recognize and take advantage of the opportunities that society offers . . . Do what you can to rekindle this appreciation in your students by helping them to see academic activities as enabling opportunities to be valued. (p. 30)

In short, children need to be "convinced" that it is possible for them someday to perform life's many functions competently, and that a key ingredient for success is here-and-now learning of the strategies and knowledge presented in school. If children can be led to believe that they are acquiring powerful and important tools, self-esteem and self-confidence should also increase. Given the many real-world reinforcements for literacy and numerical competence, motivation to learn new skills should be heightened. And so it goes, competent strategy use affects motivation and self-esteem, which jointly fuel additional learning and facilitate the transfer and modification of strategies.

ACKNOWLEDGMENTS

The writing of this chapter was supported, in part, by NIH grant HD-21218 and, in part, by a grant from the Natural Sciences and Engineering Research Council of Canada.

REFERENCES

Anastaziow, N. J. (1964). "Success" in first grade as seen by teachers: Gough's Adjective Check List and teachers' ratings. *Psychological Reports, 13,* 403–407.

Anderson, L., Brubaker, N., Alleman-Brooks, J., & Duffy, G. (1984). *Making seatwork work.* (Research Series No. 142). East Lansing, MI: Michigan State University, Institute for Research on Teaching.

Applebee, A. N. (1984). *Contexts for learning to write.* Norwood, NJ: Ablex.

Applebee, A. N. (1986). Problems in process approaches: Toward a reconceptualization of process instruction. In A. R. Petrosky, D. Bartholomae, & K. J. Rehage (Eds.), *The teaching of writing: Eighty-fifth yearbook of the National Society for the Study of Education* (pp. 95–113). Chicago, IL: University of Chicago Press.

Becker, W. C., Engleman, S., Carnine, D. W., & Rhine, W. R. (1981). Direct instructional model. In W. R. Rhine (Ed.), *Making schools move effective* (pp. 95–151). New York: Academic Press.

Belmont, J. M., & Butterfield, E. C. (1971). Learning strategies as determinants of memory deficiencies. *Cognitive Psychology, 4,* 236–248.

Belmont, J. M., & Butterfield, E. C. (1977). The instructional approach to developmental cognitive research. In R. Kail & J. Hagen (Eds.), *Perspectives on the development of memory and cognition* (pp. 29). Hillsdale, NJ: Lawrence Erlbaum Associates.

Borkowski, J. G. (1985). Signs of intelligence: Strategy generalization and metacognition. In S. Yussen (Ed.), *Development of reflection in children* (pp. 105–144). San Diego, CA: Academic Press.

Borkowski, J. G., Carr, M., & Pressley, M. (1987). Spontaneous strategy use: Perspectives from metacognitive theory. *Intelligence, 11,* 61–75.

Borkowski, J. G., & Cavanaugh, J. C. (1979). The metamemory-memory connection: Effects of strategy training and maintenance. *Journal of General Psychology, 101,* 161–174.

Borkowski, J. G., Johnston, M. B., & Reid, M. K. (1987). Metacognition, motivation and controlled performance. In S. Ceci (Ed.), *Handbook of cognitive, social, and neurological aspects of learning disabilities* (Vol. 2, pp. 147–174). Hillsdale, NJ: Lawrence Erlbaum Associates.

Borkowski, J. G., & Krause, A. J. (1985). Metacognition and attributional beliefs. In G. d'Ydewalle (Ed.), *Proceedings of the XXIII International Congress of Psychology* (pp. 557–568). Amsterdam: Elsevier.

Borkowski, J. G., & Kurtz, B. E. (1987). Motivation and executive control. In J. G. Borkowski & J. D. Day (Eds.), *Cognition in special children* (pp. 123–150). Norwood, NJ: Ablex.

Borkowski, J. G., Levers, S., & Gruenenfelder, T. M. (1976). Transfer of mediational strategies in children: The role of activity and awareness during strategy acquisition. *Child Development, 47,* 779–786.

Borkowski, J. G., & Peck, V. (1986). Causes and consequences of metamemory in gifted children. In R. Sternberg & J. Davidson (Eds.), *Conceptions of giftedness* (pp. 182–200). Cambridge, England: Cambridge University Press.

Borkowski, J. G., Weyhing, R., & Turner, L. (1986). Attributional retraining and the teaching of strategies. *Exceptional Children* on "Competence and instruction: Contributions from cognitive psychology," *53*, 130–137.

Bower, G. H., & Hilgard, E. R. (1975). *Theories of learning* (4th ed.). Englewood Cliffs, NJ: Prentice-Hall.

Brophy, J. (1986). *On motivating students*. Occasional Paper 101. East Lansing, MI: Michigan State University, Institute for Research on Teaching.

Brophy, J., & Kher, N. (1986). Teacher socialization as a mechanism for developing student motivation to learn. In R. Deldman (Ed.), *Social psychology applied to education* (pp. 257–288). Cambridge, England: Cambridge University Press.

Brophy, J., & Merick, M. (1987, April). *Motivating students to learn: An experiment in junior high social studies classes*. Paper presented at the annual meeting of the American Educational Research Association, Washington, DC.

Brophy, J., Rohrkemper, M., Rashid, H., & Goldberger, M. (1983). Relationships between teachers' presentations of classroom tasks and students' engagement in those tasks. *Journal of Educational Psychology, 75*, 544–552.

Calsey, R. J., & Kenney, D. A. (1977). Self-concept of ability and perceived evaluation of others: Cause or effect of academic achievement. *Journal of Educational Psychology, 69*, 136–145.

Cantor, N., Markus, H., Niedenthal, P., & Nurius, P. (1986). On motivation and self-concept. In R. M. Sorrentino & E. T. Higgins (Eds.), *Motivation and cognition: Foundations of social behavior* (pp. 99–127). New York: Guilford.

Carr, M., & Borkowski, J. G. (1987, April). *The importance of attributional retraining for the generalization of comprehension strategies*. Paper presented at the annual meeting of the American Educational research Association, Washington, DC.

Ceci, S. J. (1986). *Handbook of cognitive, social, and neuropsychological aspects of learning disabilities* (Vol. 1). Hillsdale, NJ: Lawrence Erlbaum Associates.

Ceci, S. J., & Baker, J. G. (1986). How shall we conceptualize the language problems of learning-disabled children? In S. J. Ceci (Ed.), *Handbook of cognitive, social, and neuropsychological aspects of learning disabilities* (Vol. 2, pp. 103–114). Hillsdale, NJ: Lawrence Erlbaum Associates.

Clifford, M. M. (1984). Thoughts on a theory of constructive failure. *Educational Psychologist, 19*, 108–120.

Connell, J. P., & Ryan, R. M. (1984). A developmental theory of motivation in the classroom. *Teacher Education Quality, 11*, 64–77.

Covington, M. V. (1985). Anatomy of failure-induced anxiety. The role of cognitive mediators. In R. Schwarzer (Ed.), *Self-related cognitions in anxiety and motivation* (pp. 247–263). Hillsdale, NJ: Lawrence Erlbaum Associates.

Covington, M. V. (1987). Achievement motivation, self-attributions, and the exceptional learner. In J. D. Day & J. G. Borkowski (Eds.), *Intelligence and exceptionality* (pp. 355–389). Norwood, NJ: Ablex.

Covington, M. V., & Omelich, C. L. (1979a). It's best to be able and virtuous too: Student and teacher evaluative responses to successful effort. *Journal of Educational Psychology, 71*, 688–700.

Covington, M. V., & Omelich, C. L. (1979b). Are causal attributions causal? A path analysis of the cognitive model of achievement motivation. *Journal of Personality and Social Psychology, 37,* 1487–1504.

Covington, M. V., & Omelich, C. L. (1981). As failures mount: Affective cognitive consequences of ability demotion in the classroom. *Journal of Educational Psychology, 73,* 796–808.

Covington, M. V., & Omelich, C. L. (1984). Controversies over consistencies: A reply to Brown and Weiner. *Journal of Educational Psychology, 76,* 159–168.

Deci, E. L., & Ryan, R. M. (1985). *Intrinsic motivation and self-determination in human behavior.* New York: Plenum.

Desroches, A., & Begg, I. (1987). A theoretical account of encoding and retrieval processes in the use of imagery-based mnemonic techniques: The special case of the keyword method. In M. A. McDaniel & M. Pressley (Eds.), *Imagery and related mnemonic processes: Theories, individual differences, and applications* (pp. 56–77). New York: Springer-Verlag.

Devine, T. G. (1986). *Teaching study skills: A guide for teachers.* New York: Allyn & Bacon.

Diener, C. I., & Dweck, C. S. (1978). An analysis of learned helplessness: Continuous changes in performance, strategy, and achievement cognitions following failure . *Journal of Personality and Social Psychology, 97,* 161–168.

Douglas, V. I. (1980). Treatment and training approaches to hyperactivity: Establishing internal and external control. In C. K. Whalen & B. Henks (Eds.), *Hyperactive children: The social psychology of identification and treatment* (pp. 283–317). New York: Academic Press.

Douglas, V. I. (1982). Higher mental processes in hyperactive children: Implications for training. In R. M. Knights & D. J. Bakker (Eds.), *Treatment of hyperactive and learning disordered children* (pp. 65–91). Baltimore: University Park Press.

Doyle, W. (1983). Academic work. *Review of Educational Research, 53,* 159–199.

Duffy, G. G., & Roehler, L. R. (1986). *Improving classroom reading instruction: A decision-making approach.* New York: Random House.

Duffy, G. G., Roehler, L. R., Sivan, E., Rackliffe, G., Book, C., Meloth, M., Vavrus, L., Wesselman, R., Putnam, J., & Basiri, D. (1987). The effects of explaining the reasoning associated with using reading strategies. *Reading Research Quarterly, 16,* 403–411.

Durkin, D. (1979). What classroom observations reveal about reading comprehension instruction. *Reading Research Quarterly, 14,* 481–438.

Durr, W. K., & Collier, C. C. (1960). Recent research on the gifted. *Education, 81,* 163–169.

Dweck, C. S. (1975). The role of expectations and attributions in the alleviation of Learned Helplessness. *Journal of Personality and Social Psychology, 31,* 674–685.

Dweck, C. (1987, April). *Children's theories of intelligence: Implications for motivation and learning.* Paper presented at the annual meetings of American Educational Research Association, Washington, DC.

Dweck, C. S., & Repucci, N. D. (1973). Learned helplessness and reinforcement responsibility in children. *Journal of Personality and Social Psychology, 25,* 109–116.

Eccles, J. (1983). Expectancies, values, and academic behaviors. In J. T. Spence (Ed.), *Research on motivation in education: The classroom milieu* (pp. 77–113). San Francisco: W. H. Freeman.

Elliott-Faust, D. J., & Pressley, M. (1986). Self-controlled training of comparison strategies increases children's comprehension monitoring. *Journal of Educational Psychology, 78,* 27–33.

Epstein, S. (1973). The self-concept revisited: Or a theory of a theory. *American Psychologist, 28,* 404–416.

Feldman, D. H. (1979). The mysterious case of extreme giftedness. In A. H. Passow (Ed.), *The gifted and the talented: Their education and development* (pp. 335–351). The Seventy-Eight Yearbook of the National Society for the Study of Education, Chicago, IL: University of Chicago Press.

Flavell, J. H. (1971). First discussant's comments: What is memory development the development of? *Human Development, 14,* 272–278.

Gagne, E. D. (1985). *The cognitive psychology of school learning.* Boston, MA: Little, Brown.

Gardner, J. (1961). *Excellence: Can we be equal and excellent too?* New York: Harper & Row.

Gelzheiser, L. (1984). Generalization from categorical memory tasks to prose by learning disabled adolescents. *Journal of Educational Psychology, 76,* 1128–1138.

Ghatala, E. S., Levin, J. R., Pressley, M., & Goodwin, D. (1986). A componential analysis of the effects of derived and supplied strategy utility information on children's strategy selections. *Journal of Experimental Child Psychology, 22,* 199–216.

Ghatala, E. S., Levin, J. R., Pressley, M., & Lodico, M. G. (1985). Training cognitive strategy monitoring in children. *American Educational Research Journal, 22,* 199–216.

Harter, S. (1982a). A developmental perspective on some parameters of self-regulation in children. In P. Karoly & F. Kanfer (Eds.), *Self-management and behavior change: From theory to practice* (pp. 165–204). Elmsford, NY: Pergamon.

Harter, S. (1982b). Processes underlying self-concept formation in children, In J. Sals & A. Greenwald (Eds.), *Psychological perspectives on the self* (pp. 136–182). Hillsdale; NJ: Lawrence Erlbaum Associates.

Harter, S. (1986). Processes underlying the construction, maintenance, and enhancement of the self-concept in children. In S. Suls & A. Greenwald (Eds.), *Psychological perspectives on the self* (Vol. 3, pp. 136–182). Hillsdale, N.J.: Erlbaum.

Heckhausen, H. (1983). The development of achievement motivation. In W. W. Hartup (Ed.), *Review of child development research* (pp. 600–668). Chicago: University of Chicago Press.

Heider, F. (1958). *The psychology of interpersonal relations.* New York: Wiley.

Jacobsen, B., Lowery, B., & DuCette, J. (1986). Attributions of learning disabled children. *Journal of Educational Psychology, 78,* 59–64.

Kelley, H. H. (1973). The process of causal attribution. *American Psychologist, 28,* 107–128.

Kennedy, B. A., & Miller, D. J. (1976). Persistent use of verbal rehearsal as a function of information about its value. *Child Development, 47,* 566–569.

Kerwin, M. L., Howard, G. S., Maxwell, S. E., & Borkowski, J. G. (1987). Implications of covariance structure analysis (LISREL) versus regression models for counseling research. *Counseling Psychologist, 15,* 287–310.

Ketcham, B., & Snyder, R., (1977). Self-attitudes of gifted students as measured by the Piers-Harris Children's self-concept scale. *Psychological Reports, 40,* 111–116.

Kun, A., & Weiner, B. (1973). Necessary versus sufficient causal schemata for success and failure. *Journal of Research in Personality, 7,* 197–207.

Kurtz, B. E., & Borkowski, J. G. (1984). Children's metacognition: Exploring relationships among knowledge, process, and motivational variables. *Journal of Experimental Child Psychology, 3,* 335–354.

Kurtz, B. E., Schneider, W., Carr, M., Borkowski, J. G., & Turner, L. A. (1988). Sources of memory and metamemory development: Societal, parental, and educational influences. In M. Gruneberg, P. Morris, & R. Sykes (Eds.), *Practical aspects of memory* (Vol. 2, pp. 537–542). New York: Wiley.

Lawson, M. J., & Fuelop, S. (1980). Understanding the purpose of strategy training. *British Journal of Educational Psychology, 50,* 175–180.

Licht, B. G., & Dweck, C. S. (1984). Determinants of academic achievement: The interaction of children's achievement orientations with skill area. *Developmental Psychology, 20,* 628–636.

Lodico, M. G., Ghatala, E. S., Levin, J. R., Pressley, M., & Bell, J. A. (1983). Effects of metamemory training on children's use of effective learning strategies. *Journal of Experimental Child Psychology, 35,* 263–277.

Markus, H., & Nurius, P. (1986). Possible selves. *American Psychologist, 41,* 954–969.

Marsh, H. W. (1986). Verbal and math self-concepts: An internal-external frame of reference model. *American Educational Research Journal, 23,* 129–150.

McCombs, B. L. (1986, April). *The role of the self-system in self-regulated learning.* Paper presented at the annual meeting of the American Educational Research Association, San Francisco.

McCombs, B. L. (1987, April). *The role of affective variables in autonomous learning.* Paper presented at the annual meeting of American Educational Research Association, Washington, DC.

Meichenbaum, D. (1977). *Cognitive behavior modification: An integrative approach.* New York: Plenum.

Moely, B. E., Hart, S. S., Santulli, K., Leal, L., Johnson, T., Rao, N., & Burney, L. (1986). How do teachers teach memory skills? *Educational Psychologist, 21,* 55–72.

Neuringer, A. (1981). Self-experimentation: A call for change. *Behaviorism, 9,* 79–94.

Oka, E. R., & Paris, S. C. (1987). Patterns of motivation and reading skills in underachieving children. In S. Ceci (Ed.), *Handbook of cognitive, social, and neurological aspects of learning disabilities* (Vol. 2, pp. 115–145). Hillsdale, NJ: Lawrence Erlbaum Associates.

Palincsar, A., & Brown, A. L. (1984). Reciprocal teaching of comprehension fostering and monitoring activities. *Cognition and Instruction, 1,* 117–175.

Paris, S. C., & Cross, D. R. (1983). Ordinary learning: Pragmatic connections among children's beliefs, motives, and actions. In J. Bisanz, G. L. Bisanz, & R. Kail (Eds.), *Learning in children* (pp. 137–170). New York: Springer-Verlag.

Paris, S. C., Cross, D. R., & Lipson, M. Y. (1984). Infant strategies for learning: A program to improve children's reading awareness and comprehension. *Journal of Educational Psychology, 76,* 1239–1252.

Paris, S. C., Lipson, M., & Wixson, K. K. (1983). Becoming a strategic reader. *Contemporary Educational Psychology, 8,* 293–316.

Paris, S. C., Newman, R. S., & McVey, K. A. (1982). Learning the functional significance of mnemonic actions: A microgenic study of strategy acquisition. *Journal of Experimental Child Psychiatry, 34,* 490–509.

Pressley, M., Borkowski, J. G., & O'Sullivan, J. T. (1985). Children's metamemory and the teaching of memory strategies. In D. L. Forrest-Pressley, G. E. MacKennon, & T. G. Waller (Eds.), *Metacognition, cognition, and human performance* (p. 111–153). San Diego, CA: Academic Press.

Pressley, M., Borkowski, J. G., & Schneider, W. (1987). Cognitive strategies: Good strategy users coordinate metacognition and knowledge. In R. Vasta (Ed.), *Annals of child development* (Vol. 4, pp. 80–129). Greenwich, CT: JAI Press.

Pressley, M., Goodchild, F., Fleet, J., Zajchowski, R., & Evans, E. D. (in press). The challenges of classroom strategy instruction. *The Elementary School Journal.*

Pressley, M., Levin, J. R., & Ghatala, E. S. (1984). Memory strategy monitoring in adults and children. *Journal of Verbal Learning and Verbal Behavior, 23,* 270–288.

Purkey, W. W. (1970). *Self-concept and school achievement.* Englewood Cliffs, NJ: Prentice-Hall.

Reid, M. K., & Borkowski, J. G. (1987). Causal attributions of hyperactive children: Implications for training strategies and self-control. *Journal of Educational Psychology, 79,* 296–307.

Rohrkemper, M., & Bershon, B. (1984). Elementary school students' reports of the causes and effects of problem difficulty in mathematics. *Elementary school Journal, 85,* 127–147.

Rotter, J. B. (1966). Generalized expectancies for internal versus external control of reinforcement. *Psychological Monographs, 80* (1, Whole No. 609).

Ryan, E. B., Ledger, G. W., Short, E. J., & Weed, K. (1982). Promoting the use of active comprehension strategies by poor readers. *Topics in learning and learning disabilities, 21,* 53–60.

Schneider, W. (1985). Developmental trends in the metamemory-memory behavior relationship: An integrative review. In D. L. Forrest-Pressley, G. E., MacKinnon, & T. G. Waller (Eds.), *Metacognition, cognition, and human performance* (pp. 57–105). San Diego, CA: Academic Press.

Spence, K. W. (1956). *Behavior theory and conditioning.* New Haven, CT: Yale University Press.

Stipek, D. J., & Weisz, J. R. (1981). Perceived personal control and academic achievement. *Review of Educational Research, 51,* 101–137.

Thompson, A. G. (1985). Teachers' conceptions of mathematics and the teaching of problem solving. In E. A. Silver (Ed.), *Teaching and learning mathematical problem solving* (pp. 281–294). Hillsdale, NJ: Lawrence Erlbaum Associates.

Watkins, D. (1984). Student learning processes: An exploratory study in the Philippines. *Human Learning, 3,* 33–42.

Weiner, B., & Kukla, A. (1970). An attributional analysis of achievement motivation. *Journal of Personality and Social Psychology, 15,* 1–20.

Weiner, B., & Walker, E. L. (1966). Motivational factors in short-term retention. *Journal of Experimental Psychology, 71,* 190–193.

Weisz, J. R. (1978) . Choosing problem-solving rewards and Halloween prizes: Delay of gratification and preference for symbolic reward as a function of development, motivation, and person of investment. *Developmental Psychology, 14,* 66–78.

White, R. W. (1959). Motivation reconsidered: The concept of competence. *Psychological Review, 66,* 297–333.

Yerkes, R. M., & Dodson, J. D. (1908). The relation of strength of stimulus to rapidity of habit formation. *Journal of Comparative Neurological Psychology, 18,* 459–482.

Zubrzycki, C. R., & Borkowski, J. G. (1973). Effects of anxiety on storage and retrieval processes in short-term memory. *Psychological Reports, 33,* 315–320.

3

Conceptualizing

Herbert J. Klausmeier
University of Wisconsin - Madison

Our concern in this chapter is with conceptualizing—the learning of concepts. We may think of concepts as the tools of thought, the fundamental agents of all thinking processes. Indeed, concepts are to thinking as words are to speaking, as notes are to music scores.

Developmentally conceptualizing begins in early infancy, peaks during the school years, and continues through the life span. Relative to learning, concepts, along with many misconceptions, are acquired at an elementary level of understanding and use, through unguided experiences in and out of school. On the other hand, carefully designed instruction enables students to avoid misconceptions and to learn concepts to the same high level of understanding and use as that of the scholars in the various subject fields.

In this chapter I discuss the nature of concepts and present an overview of theories that attempt to explain concept learning. This background information is essential to understanding the design for teaching concepts that is given in the last part of the chapter.

THE NATURE OF CONCEPTS

An individual's concept of something, for example, of *metacognition* or *problem solving*, is his or her mental construct of the thing. The term *concept* also refers to the scholars' meaning of the word or words that name the concept, the scholars' meaning being the societally standardized concept of people who speak the same language. Societally standardized concepts provide much of the curriculum of English, mathematics, the natural sciences, and the social sciences, and a lesser amount of all other subject fields. Accordingly, students' attainment of concepts is properly a major educational goal at all school levels.

Concepts differ in many ways, including on a concrete–abstract dimension. Concepts that have attributes that are readily observable in concept examples or pictures or drawings of examples are at the concrete pole of the continuum. Included here are concepts of inanimate objects and places (*cutting tool, triangle, Hudson River*); animate objects (*tree, bird, onion*); events and processes (*presidential inauguration, swimming*); qualities and states (*red, thick, healthy*); and spatial relationships (*edge, between*). At the abstract end of the continuum are concepts that either have examples and attributes that are verbal (*participial phrase, square root*) or do not have examples (*infinity, soul*).

Mental Constructs

A concept as a mental construct consists of a person's organized information about an item or a class of items that enables the person to discriminate the item or the class of items from other items and also to relate it to other items and classes of items (Klausmeier, 1985, p. 276). The information may be in iconic, symbolic, or semantic form. A person's concepts are unique to the person; they are what persons (a) construct from their informal and formal learning experiences, (b) represent internally, and (c) store in memory. A person's concept of any given item or class of items is attained at increasingly higher levels of understanding and use with informal and formal learning experiences. Thus, concepts as mental constructs are the critical components of a maturing individual's continuously changing, enlarging cognitive structure.

Words and Word Meanings

Words are entities that speakers of the same language use in communicating with one another; words are symbols that *name* concepts, not concepts, per se. All the words of the six form classes of words—nominals, verbals, adjectivals, adverbials, conjunctivals, and prepositionals name concepts, except possibly signs or markers such as *the* and *an* (Carroll, 1964).

There is general agreement that words have meanings and that a word and its meaning are different (Engelkamp, 1983). Persons must hold the same meaning of words to communicate precisely and without misunderstanding (Carroll, 1964). In this chapter, the view is that the meanings of words that students should eventually attain are the meanings held by scholars in the various disciplines.

We may now relate word meanings and concepts. Our representation of any given concept varies with the level at which the concept is learned and the nature of the concept. To illustrate, an infant who forms an object concept for the first time, for example, *ball,* represents one or more of the observable attributes as part of the visual image of the particular ball that has been experienced (Gibson & Spelke, 1983). All of the observable attributes are eventually represented and patterned as components of the image when the concept, *ball,* is attained at the level of the expert (Biederman, 1987). The expert has also acquired the name of the concept and its meaning. The meaning of the name (word) is encoded semantically. Accordingly, the word meaning is not the same as the iconic representation of the observable attributes. Thus, scholars may have stored greatly different images with any given word meaning, for example, of "mother"; however, their meaning of "mother" is the same.

Many concepts do not have any observable attributes; *infinitive,* for example. Instead, the attributes are in verbal form as are also the examples of the concept. Inasmuch as both the defining attributes and examples of *infinitive* are not observable, the expert's meaning of *infinitive* and his/her concept of *infinitive* are approximately the same. Recognizing this close relationship, Carey (1982) and Macnamara (1982) treat the meaning of a word as being the same as the concept named by the word.

A few other points may be made regarding concepts, words, and word meanings: (a) some same-sounding words (*hear* and *here*) name two different concepts; (b) concepts can be named by groups of words as well as by individual words (*suits with pin stripes*) and these are referred to as complex concepts by Medin and Smith (1984); (c) some words do not have a universally accepted meaning (equally expert theologians give different meanings of *God* and *soul* and also have different concepts regarding them); and (d) the expert states word meanings in terms of the defining attributes of the concept, whereas the novice does not (Clark, 1983).

The relationship between concepts and word meanings is complex. Clark (1983) discussed the difference between concepts and word meanings, presented her theory regarding the acquisition of word meanings, and pointed out gaps in our current knowledge regarding the relationship of word meanings and concepts.

Markle (1975) also described gaps and indicated that most of the definitions of words provided in *Webster's Unabridged Dictionary,* textbooks, and other instructional materials are incomplete both as word meanings and as definitions of the concepts named by the words. The reader is referred to Clark (1983) and Markle (1975) for a fuller discussion of these problems.

Attribute Structure
and Fuzzy Concepts

An *intrinsic attribute* refers to an invariant property of an observable thing or class of things that typically can be pointed to (see Klausmeier & Allen, 1978, p. 11, 12 for a more complete discussion of attributes). All of the attributes of *equilateral triangle* are intrinsic: "plane figure," "closed figure," "simple figure," "three sides of equal length," and "three equal angles" (Feldman & Klausmeier, 1974). A *functional attribute* refers both to how something functions and what it is used for. Some of the attributes of *hand cutting tool* are intrinsic; others are functional: "used to carry out work of a mechanical kind," "used to cut" (DiLuzio, Katzenmeyer, & Klausmeier, 1975a).

A *relational attribute* refers to an invariant relationship between two or more items; for example, "the cardinal point directly opposite to north" is an attribute of *south;* "observing is prerequisite to inferring" is an attribute of *inferring* (Klausmeier, Swanson, & Sipple, 1976). When a concept is learned, its attributes are incorporated as the core of the individual's representation of the concept and are used in relating the concept to other concepts as well as in identifying newly encountered items as examples or nonexamples of the concept (Miller & Johnson-Laird, 1976).

The *defining attributes* of a concept are those invariant intrinsic, functional, and/or relational attributes that together differentiate the examples of any given concept from examples of all other concepts. The nondefining, or variable, attributes of a concept are those properties, dimensions, or values of the concept examples that are also present in examples of other concepts of the related group. The variable attributes of *equilateral triangle* are area, orientation, and possibly color of the interior surface. *Critical attributes* are those attributes of one coordinate class of a taxonomy that differentiate the members of the class from the members of all other coordinate classes. The critical attributes of *tree* are: "has a single main stem" that "is woody" (DiLuzio, Katzenmeyer, & Klausmeier, 1975b). These attributes differentiate trees from shrubs and herbs.

Most concepts have clearly demarcated boundaries specified by defining attributes such that, with exceedingly rare or no exceptions, any item encountered in the physical or social world can be generalized as an example or discriminated as a nonexample. Concepts that do not have clear boundaries are called "fuzzy" (Neisser, 1967; Oden, 1987).

Concepts may be fuzzy for a number of reasons (Rey, 1983). One is that some items cannot be classified because they have the attributes of two or more classes; for example, the organism Euglena as *plant* or *animal* and platypus as *mammal, reptile,* or *bird* (Howard, 1987). A second contributor to fuzziness is that a person does not know the defining attributes of the concept sufficiently well to classify the least typical instances; to illustrate, leeches were classified as insects (McCloskey & Glucksberg, 1978). We should expect lack of knowledge of the defining attributes of concepts to be widespread except among persons who have attained the concepts at a level approximating that of the experts in the various disciplines.

A third cause of fuzzy concepts is that the category system has not been constructed well. Poorly constructed category systems are widespread, especially in the social sciences. However, categories for which the defining attributes are specified by experts are continually being constructed to eliminate fuzziness, particularly in the legal field, for example, *juvenile, small business,* and *unemployed* (Howard, 1987, p. 64; Wicklegren, 1979; Zadeh, 1965). Experts tend to specify attributes precisely and only they have sufficient knowledge to construct nonfuzzy categories.

Misconceptions and Incomplete Concepts

Misconceptions result from ascribing incorrect defining attributes to a concept and are widespread at all levels of schooling. For example, children of various ages conceptualized the world as a flat disc (Nussbaum, 1979). Fifth graders are reported to hold misconceptions of *light* and *vision* (Anderson & Smith, 1984); 13- and 14-year-olds hold a misconception of *matter* (Nussbaum & Novick, 1981). Eleventh-grade students' understanding of science concepts correlated positively with their concept understanding/misconception scores (Shepherd, 1985). Some students of age 13 to 20 years had misconceptions of *mass, volume,* and *density* (Hewson & Hewson, 1984). Other misconceptions include those of *life* by college students (Brumby, 1984). Misconception always occurs when defining attributes are treated as nondefining and nondefining attributes are treated as defining (Tiemann & Markle, 1985). This results in some examples not being classified as examples and some nonexamples being classified as examples.

Misconceptions are difficult to eliminate even through focused instruction (Anderson & Smith, 1984; Nussbaum & Novick, 1981). Instruction to teach a concept is incomprehensible to students having a misconception if the instruction assumes that they have already attained the concept at an incomplete but correct lower level (Osborne & Wittrock, 1985). Novak and Gowin (1986) presented detailed information on eliminating misconceptions through focused instruction.

A misconception is not the same as an incomplete concept attained at a low level of understanding and use. To illustrate, a child has attained a concept of *noun* as a word that names something and is used as the subject of a sentence, does not know any of the other attributes of *noun*, and is able to recognize as nouns only a few words in simple sentences only. This child has an incomplete, or an inadequate concept (Gagnè, 1985), not a misconception.

CLASSICAL THEORY

Classical theory traces its origin philosophically to Artistotle. Bruner, Goodnow, and Austin (1956) presented a psychological approach. Classical theory incorporates three major propositions (Smith & Medin, 1981). First, a learner forms a concept either by abstracting the intrinsic attributes from some of its examples or by being given the attributes (the intrinsic attributes of *triangle* are "plane figure," "closed figure," "simple figure," "three sides," and "three interior angles" [Klausmeier & Feldman, 1975]). Second, each attribute is necessary to define the concept. All of the attributes combined are sufficient to specify the concept (every example of *triangle* must have each attribute and any geometric form having all five attributes is a triangle). The third proposition is that the attributes of the higher order concept are nested in all of its subordinate concepts and their subclasses (the five attributes of *triangle* are present in the subordinate concepts—*isosceles triangle* and *scalene triangle*—and their subclasses; however, the relative length of the sides and the relative size of the three angles vary from one subclass to another.

Smith and Medin (1981) pointed out what they consider to be four limitations of classical theory. First, the defining attributes of a concept are intrinsic only. Second, the intrinsic attributes of many concepts cannot be specified, even by experts. Third, classical theory is relevant only to conjunctive concepts. Fourth, the theory cannot handle unclear examples (fuzzy concepts).

With regard to the first limitation, our programmatic research demonstrated that defining attributes are not only intrinsic, but also functional and relational. This vastly increases the number of concepts that can be defined in terms of attributes. Relevant to the second limitation, our research teams,[1] working with scholars in various disciplines, were

---

[1]The analyses of these ten sets of concepts are found in the following technical reports of the Wisconsin R & D Center for Cognitive Learning: Nos. 116, 224, 243, 226, 434, 435, 436, 437, 357, and 428, respectively.

able to specify a summary set of intrinsic, functional, and/or relational attributes of each and every concept that we selected for study: *quadrilateral; population, habitat,* and *community; bilateral symmetry, rotational symmetry,* and *translational symmetry; biodegradable material, biodegradable agent,* and *biodegradable process; cutting tool; equilateral triangle; noun;* and *tree; reinforcement, positive reinforcement, negative reinforcement,* and other behavior modification concepts; and *inferring, predicting,* and other process concepts of science. All of these are conjunctive concepts (third limitation), as are nearly all concepts included in the school curriculum. With respect to unclear cases (fourth limitation) we identified and/or constructed instances. All instances had an attribute structure of each concept that could be generalized either as examples or discriminated as nonexamples. Markle (1975, 1978) reported the same procedure and results.

In summary, orthodox classical theory as interpreted by Medin and Smith (1981) has limitations. The two most critical limitations pertain to concepts being defined only by intrinsic attributes and the theory being applicable only to conjunctive concepts. Other limitations will be noted later in the introduction to a theory of concept learning and development.

PROTOTYPE THEORY

According to prototype theory (Rosch, 1975, 1978), a concept is learned and represented as a prototype of a class of objects. A prototype of a class is an image constructed from experiences with example(s) of the class. The prototype includes the typical features of the class, not all of the defining attributes as in classical theory. After a prototype is formed, newly encountered instances are identified by comparison with the prototype.

Formation of a Prototype

A prototype may be formed in a number of ways. The first is by exposure to one typical example that reflects the characteristic features of the class (a robin rather than a chicken as example of *bird*). A second way is by abstracting the characteristic features of two or more examples of the class: "has feathers," "flies," "sings," "lays eggs," "lives in trees" (notice that not all of these features are true of all birds). This results in an idealized prototype, reflecting the averaged characteristics of two or more examples (Rosch, 1978). Idealized prototypes have been demonstrated by Posner and Keele (1968, 1970) and Greenberg and Kuczaj

(1982). A third way to form a prototype is to be presented the typical features (Medin, Altom, & Murphy, 1984). Regardless of how the prototype is formed, one member of the class may have all of the prototype features; another only part of them; still another may have some features not included in the prototype. (See Bruner, Goodnow, & Austin, 1956, pp. 64–65, for an earlier account of a typical and an idealized representation.)

A prototype may either shift or be extended as new examples of a class are encountered. For example, a child's initial experiences are with atypical examples of *dog* (beagles only). When later encountering typical examples (collies, terriers), the child's prototype shifts from the beagle characteristics to those of the collies and terriers (Greenberg & Kuczaj, 1982). A prototype may be extended; for instance, as young children are exposed to prunes and dates, their prototype of *fruit* is extended to include the typical characteristics of prunes and dates (Bell & Freyberg, 1985).

The Theory

Prototype theory focuses heavily on the so-called basic level concepts of taxonomies (Mervis & Rosch, 1981; Rosch, 1978). A basic level concept is a subordinate concept rather than either the superordinate concept or a subclass of the subordinate. For example, *bird* is a basic level concept, *animal* is the superordinate, and *robin* is a subclass of bird. Rosch, Mervis, Gray, Johnson, and Boyes-Braem (1976) found that (a) basic level concepts are attained before concepts of other levels, (b) response times for verifying instances as belonging to a basic level concept are shorter for most typical examples than for least typical examples, and (c) objects are recognized as examples of basic level concepts more rapidly than as examples of concepts of superordinate and lower level concepts. In addition, basic level concepts are learned more easily and more accurately if initial exposure is only to most typical examples (Mervis & Pani, 1980). With one exception to be noted shortly, these findings have been supported. We should recognize here that they are based on research *limited to object concepts of taxonomies*, only a portion of real-world concepts.

Eysenck (1984) summarized the overall limitations of prototype theory as follows: (a) nondefining attributes of the concept may be learned as characteristic features (e.g., "lives in trees" for *bird*), (b) prototypes cannot be formed for abstract categories (e.g., *justice, eternity*) and for superordinate categories (e.g., *a work of art, plant*), and (c) a distinction is not made between the prototypes of naive persons and those of the expert (e.g., the naive person categorizing a small tree as a shrub).

Another limitation of prototype theory was identified by Osherson and Smith (1981). They indicated that the core of a concept consists of its defining attributes thus enabling the concept to be related to other concepts, as well as to thought in general. In contrast, the identification aspect of a concept consists of the information used in making quick decisions as to whether or not instances are examples of the concept. Prototype theory provides insights into the latter, "the superficial aspect," but tells us little about the core, or to what Eysenck (1984) referred to as the essential elements. With respect to the exception given earlier to one of the findings of Rosch, et al. (1976), examples of some subclasses (e.g., *racing car*) were responded to as rapidly as examples of the basic level, *car,* and in addition, were identified as racing cars before being identified as cars (Murphy & Brownell, 1985).

A Comparative Taxonomy by Novices and Experts

It is instructive to compare a partial taxonomy of concepts involving *tool* developed independently by two research groups and the attributes assigned to the concepts (see Table 3.1). The left column is the partial

TABLE 3.1
Comparison of a Partial Taxonomy of Tool Developed Independently by
a Novice Group Versus an Expert Group

SUPERORDINATE CONCEPT*	SUPERORDINATE CONCEPT**
tool:	*tool*:
make things	implement or object
fix things	used for carrying on work
metal	
ONE BASIC LEVEL CONCEPT	TWO SUBORDINATE CONCEPTS
saw:	*hand cutting tool*:
(others not indicated)	(the other is *power cutting tool*)
handle	used to cut
teeth	sharp edge
sharp	hard edge
cuts	tough edge
edge	blade that is either smooth or toothed
wooden handle	
SUBCLASSES	SUBCLASSES
cross-cutting hand saw:	*smooth-edged cutting tools*:
used in construction	(e.g., seven kinds of knives)
	smooth edge
hack hand saw:	*tooth-edged cutting tool:*
(no additional attributes)	(e.g., several kinds of saws)
	toothed edge

NOTE. *Developed by Rosch et al., 1976   **Developed by DiLuzio et al., 1975a taxonomy developed by one research group, followed with the attributes as specified by university students (Rosch et al., 1976). The right column is the partial taxonomy and the attributes specified by a second research group with expertise in analyzing concepts, aided by a professor of engineering as the content expert (DiLuzio et al., 1975a). The attributes of each concept lower in the taxonomy include those of the higher concept but are not repeated.

A quick glance at the two columns shows that the experts' taxonomy and attributes of *tool* are very different from those of novices (university students). But the more important point is that prototype theory indicates outcomes that follow from instruction unaided by experts. Thus, even though novices may be able to identify cross-cut and hack saws with considerable accuracy, other possible unintended outcomes are a misconception of *tool;* an incomplete taxonomical structure that does not include the many subordinate classes of *tool* (*cutting tool* is only one); and an incomplete and partially incorrect set of defining attributes of *saw* and its subclasses that may lead to undergeneralization. The Concept Learning and Development (CLD) theory, to be discussed next, describes concept learning as it occurred in many experiments in which experts participated in developing taxonomies and other organizations of concepts and in specifying the defining attributes. In these experiments, focused instruction was provided to bring the learner's concept, regardless of age or grade in school, as close as possible to that of the expert.

Rosch (1978) has demonstrated that correct classification of many examples follows after a prototype is formed. A grave error would be made if practitioners were to assume from this that concepts could be taught effectively without using not only typical and nontypical examples, but also nonexamples (Klausmeier, 1976b; Klausmeier, Ghatala, & Frayer, 1974; Klausmeier & Sipple, 1980; Markle, 1975, 1978; Tennyson & Cocchiarella, 1986; Tiemann & Markle, 1985). The use of examples and nonexamples will be discussed later.

THEORY OF CONCEPT LEARNING
AND DEVELOPMENT

The theory of concept learning and development (CLD) is comprehensive and differs in important ways from the preceding theories.[2] It in-

---

[2]CLD theory is based on many years of programmatic research. The first 10 experiments were conducted from 1961 to 1964 and focused on identifying strategies of concept attainment (Klausmeier, Harris, & Wiersma, 1964). The next 19 were carried out from 1964 to 1967 and focused on identifying the processes involved in concept learning, the basic abilities underlying concept attainment, and cognitive styles associated with concept

cludes many more items as concepts than does either classical theory or prototype theory. It integrates principles of learning and development. Related to learning, it describes (a) how a given concept is attained at four successively higher levels of understanding, (b) specifies the mental processes involved in attaining each higher level of the concept, (c) indicates the uses made of the concept when attained at each higher level, and (d) specifies the instructional conditions that facilitate learning at the successively higher levels. These learning aspects of the theory are derived from controlled experimentation. Related to development, the use of CLD allows one to chart the course of normative conceptual development during the school years as it occurs without focused instruction, pinpoints the range of interindividual differences in concept attainment, and highlights the intraindividual variability in attaining the concepts of different subject fields. These aspects of the theory are based on cross-sectional and longitudinal research.

Four Levels of Concept Attainment and Related Mental Processes

We attain concepts at four successively higher levels: concrete, identity, classificatory, and formal. The four levels and the uses made of a concept when learned at each level are shown in Figure 3.1. Individuals progress from one level to the next as certain mental processes become functional. The processes become functional as a product of the interaction of neural maturation and learning. We should note that neural maturation by itself does not insure that a process will become functional.

Concrete Level and Processes. The concrete level of a concept is attained when an item is discriminated as an entity different from its

---

attainment (Klausmeier, Harris, Davis, Ghatala, & Frayer, 1968). Later research and theory formulations that precede the present one are reported in Klausmeier (1971); Klausmeier, Ghatala, and Frayer (1974, pp. 1–246); Klausmeier (1976a); Klausmeier and Allen (1978, pp. 1–250; 267–299);Klausmeier and Associates (1979, pp. 1–225); and Klausmeier (1985, pp. 275–300). In general, series of related experiments were first reported in publications of the Wisconsin Center for Education Research and then in a book or book chapter rather than in journal articles.

A design for teaching concepts was formulated that involved testing all aspects of the design through research in school settings. Successive formulations of the design are found in Klausmeier, Ghatala, and Frayer (1974, pp. 247–267); Klausmeier (1976b); Klausmeier and Allen (1978, pp. 207–265); Klausmeier and Sipple (1980, pp. 1–210); and Klausmeier (1985, pp. 300–312).

Although CLD theory, as well as the design for teaching concepts, draws heavily from our programmatic research, I wish also to recognize the contributions of many other researchers, including those cited in this chapter.

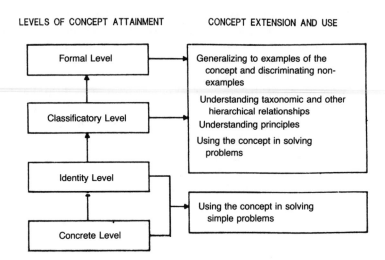

LEVELS OF CONCEPT ATTAINMENT   CONCEPT EXTENSION AND USE

FIG. 3.1.   Levels of attaining a concept and related uses of the concept.

surrounds and then later is recognized as the same entity when still in the same spatial orientation or other context. For example, an infant recognizes a pencil on the floor as the same object seen there earlier; a third-grader identifies the word *dog* as a noun (used as the subject of a sentence) that appears in the same sentence studied earlier; a ninth-grader recognizes an amoeba as the amoeba seen before on the same slide. For all three persons this marks the beginning level of the formation of a concept of which the discriminated item is an example. Of course, this occurs provided the discrimination is made on the basis of one or more defining attributes of the concept rather than on the basis of a property that is nondefining. The latter results in a misconception rather than an incomplete concept.

The mental processes employed in learning a concept at the concrete level are as follows:

— Attending to an item.
— Discriminating the item as an entity different from its surrounds on the basis of one or more of its defining attributes.
— Representing the item in long-term memory.
— Attending to and discriminating the item at a later time.
— Retrieving the representation and using it in recognizing the item as the same entity discriminated earlier.
— Storing the concrete level representation in long-term memory and being able to retrieve it.

The name of the concept and one or more of its defining attributes may or may not be learned concurrently. If no verbalization accompanies the learning, the concept is represented in the form of a visual image of the item.

Identity Level and Processes. Attainment of a concept at the identity level is inferred when the individual recognizes an item as the same one previously encountered when the item is observed in a different spatial orientation or other context. For example, the infant who recognizes a pencil on the table as being the same one seen earlier on the floor has attained the concept *pencil* at the identity level. Similarly, the child who recognizes the word *dog* as a noun (used as the subject) in a different sentence has attained the concept *noun* at the identity level. The mental processes follow:

— Attending to an item and one or more of its defining attributes.
— Discriminating the item as an entity different from other elements of the environment.
— Representing the item in long-term memory.
— Attending to and discriminating the item when observed in a different context.
— Retrieving the representation and generalizing that the item is the same entity discriminated earlier.
— Storing and being able to retrieve the identity level representation.

Generalizing an item to be the same entity when experienced in a different context is the new operation postulated to emerge as a product of learning and maturation and to make possible attainment at the identity level. Having attained the concept or being able to attain it at the concrete level is prerequisite to attainment of the identity level. The name of the concept and the names of the defining attributes may or may not be learned at this level. If names are learned, they may be represented in symbolic or semantic form with the visual image of the item.

Classificatory Level and Processes. The classificatory level of a concept is attained when two or more examples of the concept are generalized as equivalent. For example, the preschool child generalizes that a blue pencil and a red pencil are equivalent, and the elementary school child generalizes that the words dog and cat are nouns (words used as subjects of sentences). The processes employed are as follows:

— Attending to at least two examples of the concept.
— Generalizing the two examples as being equivalent on the basis of one or more defining attributes of the concept.
— Representing the classificatory level examples and attributes.
— Attending to and generalizing at least one new example as equivalent.
— Discriminating the example from nonexamples.
— Storing and being able to retrieve the classificatory level representation.

The new mental operation that becomes functional and is necessary for attaining a concept at the classificatory level is *generalizing that two or more examples are equivalent.* At the beginning classificatory level, generalization may be based on only part of the defining attributes of the concept; only some examples may be identified; and the concept name and the names of the defining attributes may not have been acquired. At the mature classificatory level most or all of the defining attributes have been learned; few if any errors are made in classifying; and the name of the concept and the names of some or all of the defining attributes have been attained. The concept at this level is presumed to be represented both in imagery and semantically. Attainment of two identity level concepts, each based on a different example of the concept, is prerequisite to attainment of the beginning classificatory level (an oak tree and a maple tree as identity level concepts of *tree*).

Formal Level and Processes.   The prerequisites and the mental operations involved in attaining a concept at the formal level are given in Figure 3.2 (Klausmeier & Allen, 1978, p. 20). Thus, people demonstrate a concept of *tree* at the formal level, if, when shown trees, shrubs, and herbs, (a) they identify any tree and call it a "tree," (b) identify and name all of the defining attributes of *tree,* (c) give a definition of the word, *tree* in terms of its defining attributes, and (d) evaluate how any example of *tree* differs from any example of *shrub* and *herb* in terms of the presence or absence of the defining attributes of *tree.*

Notice that there are four requirements for attainment of the formal level, all of which call for verbalization. As we shall see later, Klausmeier and Allen (1978) found that students identified members of a class and discriminated nonmembers (attained the classificatory level) before being able to perform the other three processes. Moreover, the students who had attained the formal level understood principles and solved

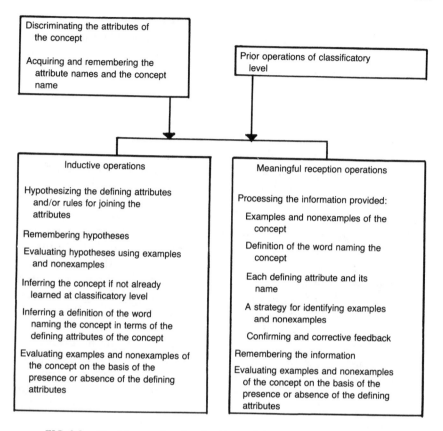

FIG. 3.2. Mental operations involved in attaining a concept at the formal level.

problems involving the concept much more effectively than students who had attained only the classificatory level. We interpreted these findings as supporting a level of concept attainment higher than the classificatory level, fully recognizing that some researchers (e.g., Tennyson & Cocchiarella, 1986; Tiemann & Markle, 1985) treat concept formation as being completed when the classificatory level is attained.

A question may arise as to whether all concepts are attained at the four successively higher levels of understanding and use. The four levels apply to concepts that (a) have more than one example; (b) have observable three-dimensional examples or examples that can be expressed in words, drawings, or other symbols; and (c) are defined or can be defined by experts in the various disciplines in terms of intrinsic, functional, and/or relational attributes. Most concepts are of this kind. Others that do not meet all three criteria can be attained at one or more of the four levels.

Validation of the Levels and Processes

The first validation of the levels and processes was through a cross-sectional study (Klausmeier et al., 1974, pp. 217–246). Subsequently, a longitudinal study was conducted to chart the course of conceptual development from kindergarten through grade 12 and to gain more definitive information regarding the levels, processes, and uses (see Klausmeier & Allen, 1978, pp. 44–47, for the design and pp. 135–206 for the findings).

The findings of this study are regarded as fully validating the four levels and the related processes. Other findings regarding the uses of concepts and individual differences follow later. Space does not permit a presentation of normative development across the school years. Brief summaries of the principles of development are given in Klausmeier (1976a, 1987) and Klausmeier and Sipple (1980, pp. 45–52).

Development in terms of four levels of concept attainment bears a superficial likeness to Piaget's four stages; however, the differences far outweigh the likeness. Orthodox Piagetian theory (Piaget, 1970) explains conceptual development in terms of changes in cognitive structures, whereas CLD explains it in terms of mental processes. The mental processes can be taught; the cognitive structures cannot. Second, Piagetian stage theory proposes a uniform timetable in which all concepts move enmasse through four stages—sensorimotor, preoperational, concrete operations, and formal operations (Brainerd, 1979; Piaget, 1970). Our research shows that the grade at which any of the four levels of concrete and abstract concepts are attained varies greatly; for example, the classificatory level of *equilateral triangle* was attained to the same mastery criterion (85%) in grade 1 as *noun* was in grade 10 (Klausmeier & Allen, 1978, p. 164). Piagetian stage theory cannot accommodate this normal but wide difference in concept acquisition. Third, Brainerd's (1979) comparison of the two theories indicates that according to Piagetian theory development of the cognitive structures must precede the learning of concepts; whereas CLD indicates that the learning of concepts provides the basis for the development of the cognitive structure. Brainerd's (1979) experiments support the latter view. For further discussion of factors contributing to the declining status of orthodox Piagetian stage theory, the reader is referred to Flavell and Markman (1983), Gelman and Baillargeon (1983), Klausmeier and Sipple (1982), and Siegel and Brainerd (1978).

Elaboration of the Processes

We now turn to a discussion of the mental processes involved in learning concepts. Understanding the processes aids educators in several ways. First, the processes can be taught concurrently while teaching the concepts. Second, during instruction the teacher can assess how well a student carries out a process such as discriminating or hypothesizing and can base subsequent teaching activities on the results of the assessment. Third, curriculum developers and evaluation specialists can construct tests to assess students' understanding of the processes as concepts and their ability to use the processes. The tests can be administered to ascertain students' status with respect to the processes prior to starting instruction (see Klausmeier & Allen, 1978, pp. 41–44; and Klausmeier & Sipple, 1980, pp. 126–132 for test construction procedures).

Selective Attention. Attending is involved in learning concepts at all four levels. To attend selectively is to respond to relevant stimulus information and not respond to the irrelevant. Presenting pairs of concept examples and nonexamples in a continuous pattern, in comparison with a noncontinuous pattern, resulted in fewer pairs needed to attain concepts (Sims, 1984). This finding was attributed to the continuous presentation that involved changing the defining attributes one at a time in the presence of the learner, thus focusing attention on each particular attribute. Attention directed toward the application of a rule also produced more effective learning (Carlson & Dulaney, 1985).

Discrimination and Generalization. Discrimination and generalization are widely accepted as two fundamental processes of concept learning (Homa, Rhoads, & Chambliss, 1979; Klausmeier et al., 1974; pp. 29–55, 86–94; Tennyson & Cocchiarella, 1986; Tiemann & Markle, 1985). To discriminate is to perceive two items as different and to respond differently to them. Thus, instances of a concept that share some but not all of the defining attributes of the target concept are discriminated as nonmembers of the target concept; a right triangle is discriminated as a nonmember, or nonexample, of *equilateral triangle*. At a more basic level, "three sides" is discriminated as a defining attribute of *triangle* and "length of sides" as a nondefining variable attribute.

Although discrimination is involved in attaining concepts at all levels, we cannot assume that students with typical instruction learn to discriminate the defining attributes of concepts as Figure 3.3 shows for *tree* (TR), *cutting tool* (CT), *equilateral triangle* (ET), and *noun* (NN) (Klausmeier & Allen, 1978, p. 70). We see that as late as grade 9 the mean scores were

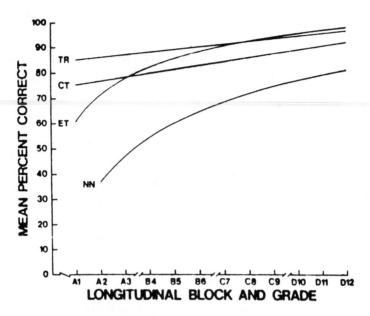

FIG. 3.3.   Discrimination of the defining attributes of concepts during the school years.

90% correct for *equilateral triangle* and *tree*, 80% for *cutting tool*, and 70% for *noun*.

To generalize at the identity level of concept learning is to respond to any given item as the same item when it is experienced in a different context, and at the classificatory level to respond to two or more items as equivalent or meaning the same. Fascinating studies of infant reaching clarify the discrimination of objects (corresponding to concept attainment at the concrete level), as well as to generalization across contexts (corresponding to the identity level) (Gibson & Spelke, 1983). Reaching starts at about 4½ months. At this age infants' reaching is adapted to some degree to an object's visually given distance, direction, and size. After repeated explorations the size of the object is perceived as an unchanging, or invariant, whole. Perception of the invariance enables the infant to recognize it as the same object thereafter (attainment of the concrete level). Attributes of objects, places, and events that infants are found to discriminate and perceive as being invariant include substance—being rigid or flexible, texture, shape, size, and animacy.

Gibson and Spelke (1983) provided a lucid account of how early identity-level generalization pertaining to animate and inanimate objects proceeds as either the object or the child moves.

The separateness of an object from the background is specified, as the object or the observer moves, by the accretion and deletion of background texture at the edges of the object. The unity of a moving object is further specified by the relationship between the movement of its parts. If the object moves rigidly, its projection at the eye undergoes a continuous series of perspective transformations, with all the invariant properties of projective geometry (Gibson & Gibson, 1957). Perception of objects depends on the detection of such invariants . . .

The ability to generalize increases across the first, third, and fifth grades (Anziano, 1984). With increasing age, children gain more information from nontypical examples and use less obvious attributes in generalizing.

Hypothesizing and Meaningful Reception Learning. To hypothesize involves making a best guess as to what the concept is, based on the information one has, and then testing the hypothesis against reality. Hypothesizing may occur at the identity and classificatory levels of concept learning. However, the formation and testing of hypotheses has been studied most extensively at the formal level, following the experimental method of Bruner et al. (1956). Here the subject is provided instances of many different but related concepts and is asked to identify a particular concept that the experimenter has in mind (Bruner et al., 1956; Klausmeier, Harris, Davis, Ghatala, & Frayer, 1968; Levine, 1975; Tumblin & Gholson, 1981). The subject examines successive instances of the concept population, offers a hypothesis as to what the concept is after examining a specified number of instances, is told whether the hypothesis is or is not the concept, and then continues the process until an hypothesis is confirmed as being the concept. There is a strong tendency for persons to seek additional information that confirms rather than disconfirms an hypothesis, even though disconfirming information may be equally useful in arriving at a correct hypothesis (Klayman & Young-Won, 1987).

Some college students are successful in attaining concepts without receiving instruction in hypothesizing, but many are not (Klausmeier, Harris, & Wiersma, 1964) The highly successful offer successive hypotheses, test each hypothesis, identify the defining attributes, and then quite suddenly progress from making many errors to performing perfectly (Mathews, Stanley, Buss, & Chinn, 1985). Moderately successful subjects fail to identify the attributes, but memorize the instances that they find to be examples and nonexamples and use this as the basis of classifying. The unsuccessful do neither, give up, and perform at a chance level.

Hypothesizing is used consistently by scientists at the frontiers of research, for example, by those who identified the defining attributes of *AIDS* (Howard, 1987, pp. 109–111). Children, too, use hypothesis testing both in learning the names of concepts that they already have attained at a beginning level and in extending their concepts to a higher level (Carey, 1982).

To attain a concept by meaningful reception learning is to process information that is provided about the concept. Starting at grade 4, instruction based on meaningful reception learning is clearly superior to that based on unguided discovery learning in terms of the amount of time required for students to attain the many concepts included in the school curriculum (Ausubel, 1966, 1977; Fredrick & Klausmeier, 1968a). We should recognize that meaningful reception learning is not the same as expository instruction that proceeds from general to specific, or rule to example; and it involves no rote memory of concept examples, word definitions, or lists of concept attributes. To the contrary, concept lessons based on meaningful reception learning engage the learner in guided discovery learning throughout the lesson (Klausmeier & Sipple, pp. 120–126).

Meaningful reception learning of concepts may occur through reading text. Sternberg (1984) described how the reader *inductively* attains verbal concepts, corresponding to word meanings, by processing the information given in the text. Williams (1984) showed how readers use the examples provided in a paragraph in attaining the macro-structure, or main idea, of the paragraph, that is, the global concept of the paragraph. This, too, is an inductive process of reception learning that involves using the meaningful information provided in the paragraph.

Both of the preceding theories represent a serious and long overdue attempt to relate some of the vast knowledge about concepts and concept learning to reading comprehension. However, material for teaching concepts at the classificatory and formal levels must include examples, nonexamples, and the defining attributes of the target concepts to be effective (Feldman, 1972; Klausmeier & Feldman, 1975; Markle, 1975; Tiemann & Markle, 1985). In general, authors do not include these, assuming that the learner either knows the concepts or that the teacher will teach the concepts before assigning the material. For this reason, Davis (1984) and McKeown, Beck, Omanson, and Pople (1985) recommended teaching the concepts embedded in the text rather than assuming that students will attain them inductively.

Uses of Concepts Attained
at the Various Levels

The extent to which any given concept can be used depends on the level at which it is attained. Students' attainment of the concrete or the identity level as their highest performance is rarely accompanied with understanding principles, understanding taxonomic relations, or with solution of problem-solving exercises (Klausmeier & Allen, 1978, pp. 171–181). Attainment of the identity level as the highest performance was accompanied with roughly 3% mastery of the three uses, the classificatory level 16%, and the formal level 67%.

These findings tell us that if we wish our students to become proficient in attaining a high level of cognitive functioning, we should teach them concepts at the formal level as soon as they are ready. Moreover, we should not cease teaching a concept when attained only at the classificatory level. Ceasing at the classificatory level will insure a lifetime of cognitive functioning at an elementary school level.

How does the understanding and use of concepts relate to educational achievement? We identified the correlations at grade 6, between 11 standardized educational achievement tests and the CLD tests at the classificatory level, the formal level, and each of the three uses of each of the four concepts (a total of 20 tests) (Klausmeier & Associates, 1979, pp. 116–118). The highest correlations between a CLD test and the 11 achievement tests were for the formal level of *noun*. Here the 11 correlations ranged from .52 to .68. Arithmetic concepts and listening comprehension had the highest correlations with the 20 CLD tests; 13 of the 20 correlations between arithmetic concepts and the CLD tests ranged from .31 to .68 and 14 correlations between listening comprehension and the CLD tests ranged from .30 to .60.

Interindividual Differences and Intraindividual Variability

The uniqueness of human beings is nowhere more apparent than in their rate of attaining and using concepts. Conditions associated with the individual, the home and neighborhood, and the school that contribute to the differences are given in Klausmeier and Allen (1978, pp. 185–205). Other studies have identified specific factors associated with below average concept attainment: low socioeconomic status (Nelson & Klausmeier, 1974); global cognitive style (Davis & Klausmeier, 1970); lack of language that provides labels for superordinate concepts (Bruner, 1973); and ineffective schooling (Bruner, 1973; Klausmeier, 1977).

Table 3.2 shows interindividual differences only for the formal level pertaining to *equilateral triangle*. We see that 3% of the grade 3 students had attained the formal level and 97% had not; whereas 79% of the grade 12 students had and 21% had not. The difference between individuals of the different grades is even more striking: 3% of the grade 3 students had attained the formal level whereas 21% of the grade 12 students had not.

Intraindividual variability in attaining and using concepts becomes increasingly differentiated from grade 4 to grade 6 (Klausmeier & Associates, 1979, pp. 112–116). The sharp differentiation that occurs by grade 6 continues through grade 12. Other factor analyses show intrain-

TABLE 3.2
Percentage of Four Longitudinal Groups (A-D)
of Students of Various Grades Who Did
and Did Not Attain the Formal Level
of Equilateral Triangle

Group and Grade	Attained Formal Level	
	Did	Did Not
A1	0	100
A3	3	97
B6	52	48
C9	75	25
D12	79	21

dividual variability in concept achievement to be closely related to the subject fields of English, mathematics, science, and social studies (Harris & Harris, 1973; Shaycoft, 1967). Clearly, curriculum specialists and teachers should not expect most students to learn concepts from these different subject fields at the same rate.

DESIGN FOR TEACHING CONCEPTS

A specific age or grade at which to teach all concepts at any of the four successive levels of understanding and use cannot be specified because of three conditions (Klausmeier & Allen, 1978, pp. 207, 208). First, concepts that have observable attributes are learned at all levels years earlier than abstract concepts. Second, a number of years elapse between the time the easiest and most difficult examples of a concept are learned at any level of attainment. Third, there are great differences among students in the age at which any given concept is attained at any level. Because of these conditions, I have combined (a) the concrete and identity levels and (b) the classificatory and formal levels in the discussion of the interaction phase of instruction. Although the levels are combined here, instruction should be started at the level appropriate for the individual child and proceed as far as possible within reasonable time limits. Teachers are aided immeasurably in doing this if three kinds of analyses are carried out prior to starting the interactive phase.

PREINSTRUCTION ANALYSES

Concept analysis, learning-developmental analysis, and instructional analysis provide the information that is essential for effective concept instruction (see Klausmeier & Sipple, 1980, pp. 59–79 for a discussion of the three analyses).

Concept Analysis

Conducting an analysis to ascertain what is required to perform an instructional task is now widespread (Gardner, 1985). Conducting a concept analysis is a demanding task that requires two areas of expertise. One area involves comprehensive knowledge regarding the nature of concepts, conceptual learning and development, and concept instruction. The second area includes expertise regarding the concepts of the particular subject field, the relationships among the concepts, and the uses of the concepts. Both kinds of expertise contribute to carrying on the activities that follow:

1. The first analysis activity is to organize the concepts of the subject field. The organization may be a taxonomy (Klausmeier, 1976b); a schematic arrangement showing prerequisite dependency and parallel relationships such as of the process concepts of science (Klausmeier & Sipple, 1980, pp. 62–64); a whole-part relationship (Miller & Johnson-Laird, 1976); or a network or some other schematic arrangement (Howard, 1987, pp. 30–52; Markle, 1978; Oden, 1987). The teacher uses the organizational arrangement in presenting an overview of the group of concepts to be learned and in determining the sequence in which to teach the concepts. The learner uses the organization to construct a schema of the related group of concepts. Having a schema markedly facilitates the learning of the concepts (Harty, Hamrick, & Samuel, 1985; Novak & Gowin, 1986; Novak, Gowin, & Johansen, 1983).

A partial taxonomy pertaining to the concept *equilateral triangle* and a schematic arrangement of the dependency and parallel relationships among the basic processes concepts of science follow. These and the other illustrations given in the next pages are drawn from Klausmeier (1976b) where conducting a concept analysis is discussed more fully.

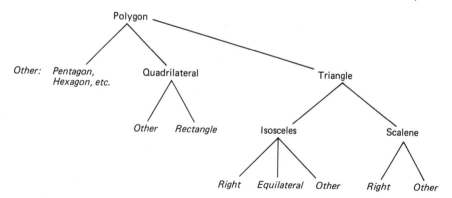

Schematic arrangement showing dependency relationships (solid lines) and parallel relationships (broken lines) among science concepts:

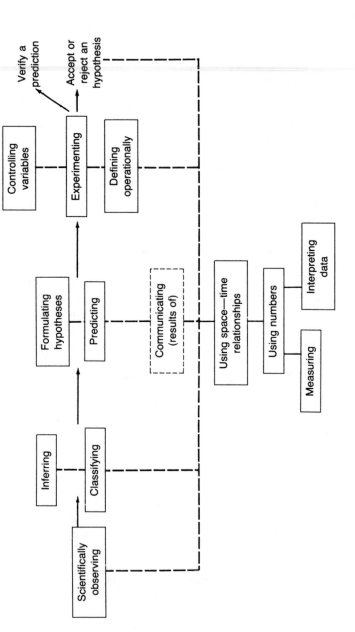

2. The attribute structure of the concept population is specified and the word that names each concept is defined in terms of its defining attributes. Specifying the attribute structure indicates the clarity of the concept boundaries. If an instance is identified that does not conform to the structure, it is noted and it is subsequently taught as an exception. If an attribute structure cannot be identified, this, too, is noted and this fact is taught to the students concurrently with the concept(s).

Definitions of "equilateral triangle" and "observing scientifically" follow. The five intrinsic attributes of *equilateral triangle* are boldface, as are the three functional (subprocess) attributes of *observing scientifically:*

Equilateral triangle: A **plane, simple, closed figure** with **three equal sides** and **three equal angles.**

Observing scientifically: **Using one or more of the senses** in critically **examining objects or events** and precisely **recording data about those objects or events.**

We should note that the defining attributes of the concept, **conceptualizing,** were given earlier in terms of the mental subprocesses involved at each of the four levels of attainment. The first two attributes of **conceptualizing at the classificatory level** are:

"Attending to at least two example of the concept," "Generalizing the two examples as being equivalent on the basis of one or more of the defining attributes."

3. Examples ranging from most typical to least typical, and nonexamples that vary in similarity from the typical examples are identified for use in teaching and in testing for attainment (Tiemann & Markle, 1985).

Descriptions of possible examples and nonexamples of *equilateral triangle* and *observing scientifically* follow:

Examples of *equilateral triangle:* drawings of equilateral triangles of various sizes in various spatial orientations.

Nonexamples of *equilateral triangle:* drawings of open, nonsimple, nonplane figures and of right triangles and quadrilaterals of various sizes in various orientations.

Example of *observing scientifically* (a verbal example in which all three defining attributes are included): Bill looked at a marshmallow carefully, felt it, tasted it, and smelled it. Then he put it over the flame of a Bunsen burner and watched as it turned from white to black. He smelled it as it burned. After it cooled, he felt it and noticed that it felt crisp. He tasted it and thought that it tasted like charcoal. He recorded these things in his report book. (This event could also be demonstrated by the teacher or a student.)

Nonexamples of *observing scientifically:* Examples of other process concepts of science and verbal descriptions in which one or more of the defining attributes are not included: Cecil saw the mailman deliver a box to the principal. Cecil thought to himself, "The principal said he was going to order a new microscope for the school." Cecil saw his friend, Jim, and told him that the new microscope had arrived.

4. Principles that range in difficulty of understanding are identified so that the learner may be taught to use the concept in understanding principles.

Illustrative Principles Involving *Equilateral Triangle:*

   (a) If the three sides of a triangle are of equal length, the angles of the triangle are equal in the number of degrees.

   (b) A line that bisects any angle of an equilateral triangle forms two equal angles (and lines) when it intersects the opposite side.

   (c) The perimeter of an equilateral triangle is three times the length of any side.

Illustrative Principles Involving *Observing Scientifically:*

   (a) Observing objects and events is a prerequisite for drawing inferences regarding them.

   (b) Using more than one of the senses in observing objects and events increases the probability of gaining more precise information.

   (c) Quantitative observation permits drawing more precise inferences than does qualitative observation.

5. Problem-solving exercises ranging from suitable for the novice to the expert are identified so that the learner may be taught to use the concept in solving problems.

Problem-solving exercises for *equilateral triangle* and for *observing scientifically* follow:

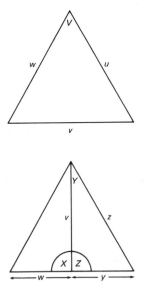

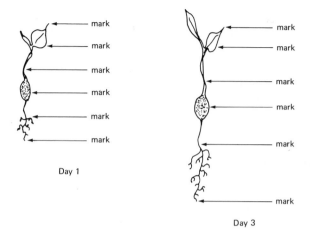

6. A vocabulary list is constructed that includes the name of each concept, the names of the defining attributes, and other key vocabulary. This list is used at the beginning of instruction so that students will be able to recognize the words and have their meanings before starting to read.

Vocabulary for *equilateral triangle:* angle, side, equal, equilateral, triangle, figure, closed, plane, simple.

Vocabulary for *observing scientifically:* observing, scientifically, senses, critically, examine, record, accurately, data, information, precisely.

Applications of the preceding guidelines may be found in an analysis of the process concepts of science (Klausmeier, Swanson, & Sipple, 1976) and in analysis of behavior management concepts (Bernard, 1975). Taxonomies of the concepts of most curricular fields of study may be found in Doherty and Peters (1978).

Concept analyses should be directed toward the formal level of attainment and should be expressed in vocabulary appropriate for senior high school students. Even though instruction may be at a lower school level, teachers should have attained the concepts at the formal level and should have technical vocabulary appropriate for high school instruction.

Learning Analysis

Carrying out a learning analysis identifies the mental operations involved in learning a concept at each of the four successively higher levels and the internal conditions of learning that are necessary and sufficient for attaining each level. Knowing the mental operations not only enables the teacher to guide the learning process effectively, but also to teach a process with which the learner may be experiencing difficulty. In addition, understanding the necessary and sufficient internal conditions given earlier in the discussion of the levels and processes enables the teacher to assess individual childrens' readiness and to arrange instruction accordingly.

Instructional Analysis

An instructional analysis is made to identify the external conditions that facilitate learning. The main conditions, treated as variables, are indicated in the ensuing discussion of the design for teaching concepts. Other variables to be considered are (a) instructional materials, supplies, and equipment and (b) modes of instruction, such as individual assignments, cooperative small-group activities, and whole-class activities.

Our observations, as we carried on experiments as part of the ongoing science instruction in two schools, indicated that teachers had not been prepared to conduct either a concept analysis or a learning-developmental analysis (Klausmeier & Sipple, 1980). Moreover, they needed to understand the results of these analyses before being able to carry out the instructional analysis. For these reasons we prepared illustrated printed lessons for the students and supplemented the lessons with inservice education.

Before turning to the interactive phase of the design, we should recognize that conducting the three analyses is not a trivial undertaking. Expertise is required regarding concept learning, the content of the given subject field, and curriculum development and instruction. Thus, a cooperative effort involving scholars and practitioners is required to conduct analyses that will guide the instructional program in a subject field, preschool through grade 12.

Looking ahead toward the interactive phase, we will see that teaching a concept as well as it should and can be taught at the successively higher levels takes time. Accordingly, a sensible strategy is to identify and organize only the major concepts of the given subject field, conduct the analyses for these concepts, and then introduce and teach them at the various school levels to an appropriate level of understanding and use. Implementing this strategy may enable students to move from the current memorizing of vast amounts of unorganized factual information to acquiring powerful conceptual structures of knowledge and the related enduring learning processes.

INTERACTIVE AND FOCUSED INSTRUCTION

Concrete Level and Identity Level

Both identity concepts (e.g., *George Washington*, the *Earth's moon*), and the identity level of equivalence concepts (e.g., *inanimate object, bacteria*) are learned at all school levels. Instruction is typically directed toward concurrent attainment of the concrete and identity levels of equivalence concepts inasmuch as the example of the concept used in instruction is not presented in an identical context. The ensuing discussion of instructional variables pertains more to attaining the identity level of equivalence concepts than identity concepts.

1. *Making available the concept example and focusing attention.* Concept teaching at the identity level starts with making available one example of the concept and calling student attention to it. Examples of many different concepts are found in the classroom. When an example is not available, the teacher or a student may supply it.

The first concept of a taxonomy to be taught might well be basic level rather than superordinate (Rosch, 1978). The first concept of a learning hierarchy (Gagnè, 1985) or a dependency group (Klausmeier & Sipple, 1980, pp. 62, 64) necessarily is the one that is prerequisite for attaining the next one. A most typical example should be used (Brooks, 1978, 1986; Rosch, 1978).

2. *Providing for naming.* The name of the item is presented concurrently with the example so that the example and the name are represented together. Thereafter, the name can be used to retrieve the concept.

Names can be associated with objects at a relatively young age and naming facilitates concept attainment (Nelson & Bonvillian, 1973). During a 6-month period mothers taught their children of 16 to 18 months of age to identify objects new to them. The 16 objects included *barrel, pulley, silo,* and *whetstone*. At the end of the 6 months, the objects that the mothers taught with names were identified much more reliably than those without names.

3. *Guiding examination of the item.* We are aware that unguided experience yields misconceptions as well as concepts. Accordingly, whether teaching an *identity concept,* such as *President Lincoln,* or the identity level of an equivalence concept, such as *word,* we guide the learner's study of the item to insure that its defining attributes are learned. Nelson (1973) found nearly unbelievable effects by guiding children's examination of concept examples and nonexamples. The experiment involved attain-

ment of the concept of *equilateral triangle* by 3-year-old and 5-year-old children, each of whom received only 16 minutes of active instruction. The experimental materials were 36 blocks varying in shape, color, size, and thickness. The edges of 12 blocks were examples of *equilateral triangle*, 12 *right triangle*, and 12 *square*.

Each child was assigned to one of five conditions: (a) visual inspection of the blocks, (b) visual inspection along with verbal orienting instruction that called attention to the defining attributes of *equilateral triangle*, (c) visual inspection and free-haptic activity that involved the child in being told to pick up the 36 blocks, one at a time, and play with them, and tactile-kinesthetic instruction that involved telling the child to pick up the blocks, one at a time in a given sequence, and to trace the edges of the block in certain ways and to press the block, (d) all of the preceding combined—visual inspection, verbal orienting instruction, free-haptic activity, and tactile-kinesthetic instruction, and (e) unrelated play activity without blocks (control). Two transfer tests were administered, one with blocks patterned after those used in the experimental session (near transfer) and another the line drawings of the figures (far transfer). Both tests assessed the children's attainment of *equilateral triangle* at the concrete level, the identity level, and the classificatory level.

Conditions 2, 3, and 4 yielded significantly better results than 1 and 5 at all three levels of attainment for both age groups under both near transfer and far transfer testing. Condition 4 (combined instruction) was most effective. Many more 3-year-olds receiving the combined instruction attained the concrete and identity levels than did the 3-year-olds not receiving instruction. Moreover, the mean attainment of the classificatory level by the 3-year-olds receiving the combined instruction exceeded that of the 5-year-olds without instruction. Thus, with 16 minutes of focused, individually guided instruction, 3-year-olds moved ahead of 5-year-olds who did not receive instruction.

4. *Aiding discrimination of the defining attributes.* Guiding the examination of the item is accompanied with aiding the learner discriminate one or more of the defining attributes of the concept. How many of the defining attributes to teach and whether or not to provide the names of the attributes depends both on the nature of the concept and the vocabulary level and other characteristics of the learner. As we saw earlier, infants without instruction attain concepts of objects at the identity level by discriminating one or more invariant properties of the objects (Gibson & Spelke, 1983); however, calling attention to the defining attributes using verbal, visual, and tactile techniques facilitates the discrimination (Nelson, 1973).

Unfortunately the invariant properties that are discriminated without instruction may be nondefining properties rather than defining attributes. For instance, related to *ball,* an infant discriminates the non-defining properties "red color" and "large size" as well as the defining attribute, "shape." Although the infant attains a concept of this object at the identity level, yellow balls of any size and small red balls may not subsequently be generalized as balls at the classificatory level.

5. *Providing feedback.* Feedback to the learner regarding correctness of actions and responses may be provided by the teacher verbally and by gesturing and other means. Learners may be able to secure feedback independently if correct responses are available to them by visual comparison or other means. Feedback may be either confirming or corrective.

Concepts may be attained without externally provided feedback (Nelson & Bonvillian, 1973); however, research reviews by Clark (1971) and Frayer and Klausmeier (1971) indicate that both externally arranged confirming feedback and externally provided corrective feedback have facilitative effects. Homa and Cultice (1984) found learning to be greatly facilitated by confirming feedback. Both confirming and corrective feedback provided by microcomputer resulted in higher initial concept attainment and better retention after 3 months than did no feedback (Armour-Thomas, 1985).

The view here is that externally arranged *confirming feedback* is facilitative in any instructional situation in which the learner cannot secure feedback independently. *Corrective feedback* is facilitative unless the learner responds to it with negative affect. Being told that a response is wrong as part of corrective feedback may be interpreted as a punishment and produce negative affect.

6. *Insuring attainment.* Insuring that the concept has been attained is accomplished by assessment. The assessment may involve recognition of the items in a context different from that in which it was taught. However, if instruction at the classificatory level follows immediately, being able to use the identity concept in attaining the classificatory level is a feasible test.

We may recall the mental processes involved in learning the identity level of a concept: selectively attending to an item, discriminating one or more defining attributes, and generalizing that the item, when observed in a different context, is the same one experienced earlier. These processes can probably be taught not only separately, but in combination as a strategy for attaining identity concepts and the identity level of equivalence concepts.

Classificatory and Formal Levels.   The rationale was given earlier for considering these two levels together. We recognize, however, that only the classificatory level may be taught when first introducing a concept whereas only the formal level is taught after the classificatory level is mastered. Moreover, some abstract concepts, for example, *DNA, infinity,* are taught meaningfully only at the formal level.

Concepts are taught much more effectively at the combined classificatory and formal levels as related sets rather than one at a time as unrelated items (Klausmeier, 1976b; Markle, 1978). The instructional variables that follow are the same for teaching the two levels concurrently or singly; however, their application varies. The applications also must take into account the age and other characteristics of the learner and the nature of the concepts. Thus, specific applications of the variables are not presented in any detail.

1. *Providing orienting instruction.* Orienting instruction is provided in many different ways for five purposes: (a) focus the student's attention, (b) alert the student to the idea that concepts are to be learned rather than other outcomes, (c) aid the student in constructing a schema of the concepts to be learned, (d) provide the student a global strategy for learning the concepts, and (e) generate student intention to learn the concepts. The orienting instruction is more comprehensive when a group of concepts is first introduced, rather than later after the initial concepts of the group have been attained.

Fredrick and Klausmeier (1968b) told students that they were to attain concepts, gave the names of the concepts and their attribute structure, provided a schematic arrangement of the concepts, and demonstrated a strategy for attaining the concepts. These orienting instructions were presumed to attain all five purposes; they yielded significantly better results than simply starting the experiment by having the student learn the first concept of the series. Bernard (1975) used similar instructions; however, the concepts were organized in a taxonomy. Klausmeier and Meinke (1968) found that an algorithmic strategy aided students in using the information about the attribute structure. Schwartz and Raphael (1985) proposed a schematic arrangement for introducing a concept definition in general, whereas Hewson and Posner (1984) outline a schematic arrangement for introducing the generic and highly abstract concept, *change.*

Creating student intention to learn merits a special note. Miller and Johnson-Laird (1976) treat "intend" as the process for consciously controlling the direction of one's thinking. An intention is the motivational component of a plan, or strategy, for attaining a goal. As long as the intention remains, activity continues toward goal attainment. Thus, creating an intention to learn the target concepts is a most critical aspect of orienting instruction.

2. *Providing or eliciting a definition.* Providing or eliciting a definition

stated in terms of the defining attributes of the concept assists the learner in delimiting what is to be learned. The defining attributes provide cues as to what to search for when examining items to be classified as examples or discriminated as nonexamples.

For maximum effectiveness a definition must be stated in appropriate terminology. A definition stated in common-usage vocabulary proved to be more effective for fourth-grade students than the same definition stated in technical vocabulary, whereas a technically stated definition was more effective with eighth-graders (Feldman & Klausmeier, 1974).

Definitions facilitate but are not sufficient for concept attainment (Anderson & Kulhavy, 1972; Feldman, 1972; Johnson & Stratton, 1966; Markle, 1978; Mayer, Dyck, & Cook, 1984; Merrill & Tennyson, 1978). A definition presented to fourth-graders has been found to have about the same amount of facilitation as one rational set (to be described later) of examples and nonexamples (Klausmeier & Feldman, 1975). A definition combined with one rational set was more effective than a definition or one set alone; and a definition combined with three sets showed greatest facilitation. Presenting college students a definition and examples and nonexamples accompanied either by explanation or with questioning and feedback led to significantly higher attainment than the same examples and nonexamples without the definition (Dunn, 1983).

3. *Providing for recall.* Many different techniques may be used in aiding students retrieve conceptual information from long-term memory. Retrieval reinstates in working memory the relevant information that has been learned.

During the retrieval process, the teacher ascertains whether misconceptions have occurred. Detailed methods for ascertaining students' misconceptions have been identified by Sutton (1980). Means of changing misconceptions have been demonstrated by Hewson and Hewson (1984), Novak and Gowin (1986), and Posner, Strike, Hewson, and Gertzog (1982).

In printed lessons the same guided recall is provided to all students at the beginning of each successive lesson, at the beginning of each main part of a lesson, and at the end of each lesson (Schilling & Klausmeier, 1975). Guided recall may be provided to aid the individual student in retrieving the specific information that he or she needs at any point in the learning sequence. It can be managed effectively by computer-aided learning (Tennyson & Cocchiarella, 1986). Teachers provide it orally.

4. *Using examples and nonexamples.* We might infer from prototype theory (Rosch, 1978) that instruction that uses only typical examples is highly effective. However, instruction that uses nonexamples as well as examples markedly reduces both overgeneralization and misconception (Klausmeier et al., 1974, pp. 195–200; Tiemann & Markle, 1985; Shum-

way, White, Wilson, & Brombacher, 1983; Swanson, 1972; Tennyson, Woolley, & Merrill, 1972).

Markle and Tiemann (1969) proposed a procedure for selecting a "rational set" of examples and nonexamples to be used in teaching concepts one at a time. The number of examples needed to promote generalization to all examples of the concept is a function of the range of values of the variable (nondefining) attributes. To illustrate, examples of *chair* may have all sorts of values of the attribute *foot:* wheels, rockers, ball feet, straight feet, a pedestal foot, or even none (if suspended from the ceiling). The prototypical chair is probably the one with *straight* feet on four straight legs, one value of the variable *feet* (and of the variable *number of legs*).

To foster adequate generalization, learners should work with enough (that is a judgment on the teacher's part) different kinds of *feet* on different kinds of chairs to accept variation in this attribute. Good students might generalize to chairs with rockers if they had seen straight feet, wheels, and a pedestal foot, whereas slower learners might not generalize so readily. Where the variable attribute is continuous, *size* being the most obvious continuum, learners should see enough of the range to accept very large and very small values as well as the prototypical mid-range (e.g., the Saint Bernard and the Chihuahua as well as the *average* dog).

In interactive instruction, the teacher decides when a sufficient number of examples and nonexamples have been used. However, when preparing instructional material to teach concepts, a rule is needed for developing a rational set. The rule is to include a number of nonexamples equal to the number of the concept's defining attributes and a number of examples equal to the number of the concept's variable attributes. Thus, for a concept having three defining attributes and four variable attributes, a rational set would consist of three nonexamples and four examples.

The use of rational sets is designed to reduce classifying some nonexamples as examples (overgeneralizing), rejecting some examples as nonexamples (undergeneralizing), and the combined error, misconception. As shown by Feldman (1972) and Feldman and Klausmeier (1974), one rational set included in a printed lesson may be insufficient for student attainment of the concept. The teacher who finds this to be the case provides additional examples and nonexamples or complete rational sets as may be necessary.

Several reasearchers (Houtz, Moore & Davis, 1973; Klausmeier & Feldman, 1975; Tennyson, Woolley, & Merrill, 1972) refined the idea of rational sets. They found classification to be most effective when the examples ranged from easy to difficult, subsequent examples differed from prior examples in their nondefining attributes, and each example was paired and presented with a nonexample.

Presenting a "best" example in the first paired set of examples and nonexamples yields good results (Park, 1984; Tennyson & Cocchiarella, 1986). It facilitates identifying the examples and discriminating the non-examples that follow in the subsequent pairs.

We now turn to teaching two or more related concepts either concurrently or in close time proximity. Here the nonexamples used in teaching one concept are examples of one or more of the related concepts. Thus, examples of one coordinate concept of a taxonomy (e.g., *equilateral triangle*) are nonexamples of a coordinate concept (e.g., *right triangle*) (DiLuzio et al., 1975a); examples of the prerequisite concept, *observing*, are nonexamples of the dependent concepts, *predicting* and *inferring* (Klausmeier & Sipple, 1980). Making examples available in an easy-to-difficult sequence produces excellent results (Houtz, Moore, & Davis, 1973; Klausmeier & Feldman, 1975; Tennyson & Park, 1980; Tennyson, Woolley, & Merrill, 1972).

In the instructional sequence, the learner is informed that certain instances are examples. Other instances are introduced that the learner is asked to identify as examples or nonexamples and confirming or corrective feedback follows (Klausmeier, 1976b; Schilling & Klausmeier, 1975). A strategy for aiding the learner in making the identification without error is discussed later.

Examples and nonexamples of most concepts are three-dimensional objects or processes, pictures, drawings, or verbal descriptions. Some abstract concepts have none of these kinds of examples; for instance, *light year* and *universe* (Herron, Cantu, Ward, & Srinivasan, 1977). Here, models, diagrams, analogies, and metaphors are used (Howard, 1987).

5. *Aiding students discriminate the defining attributes.* Merely providing the names of the defining attributes in a definition of the concept facilitates learning (Feldman, 1972; Johnson & Stratton, 1966; Merrill & Tennyson, 1978). Emphasizing the attributes by verbal and nonverbal means, referred to as attribute prompting, markedly improves immediate concept attainment and later transfer and retention (Klausmeier et al., 1974, pp. 200–208). Prompting yields better results than permitting the students to discover the attributes independently (Clark, 1971).

Aiding students in discriminating observable examples of defining attributes should start early in life. Previously we saw that 3- and 5-year olds profited from having defining attributes pointed out, along with examination of the examples (Nelson, 1973). First-graders, too, learned concepts better from instruction that involved pointing out the defining attributes than instruction that presented examples of the concepts (Musser, 1984). Not knowing the attributes seriously impedes attainment of a concept at both the classificatory and formal level.

6. *Providing strategies.* Klausmeier and Meinke (1968) gave experimental subjects one of three kinds of instruction: (a) told the student that he/she was to attain concepts, (b) gave the prior instruction and pointed out the defining attributes of the concept population, and (c) gave the prior instruction and taught an algorithmic strategy for determining whether an instance was or was not an example of the concept. In addition, each prior set of instructions either was or was not accompanied with a principle indicating how to use information that could be gotten from examples and nonexamples in attaining successive concepts. The results were unequivocal. Teaching the strategy yielded higher attainment than the instruction without the strategy; the strategy combined with the principle yielded far better results than any other kind of instruction.

The algorithmetic strategy involves using all of the defining attributes of the concept in ascertaining whether or not a given item is or is not an example of the concept as shown in Figure 3.4. The learner is instructed in using the strategy, including being told that if any question is answered "No" the item is not an example of the concept. (See Klausmeier, 1976b, or Klausmeier & Sipple, 1980, pp. 123, 124, for a more complete discussion of how the strategy is taught.)

Use of the strategy greatly reduces the demands on memory during initial attainment of the concept. Using the strategy to learn concepts promotes active learning of the strategy and promotes long-term retention, not only of the strategy but of the defining attributes of the concept. Tennyson and Cocchiarella (1986) recommended use of this algorithmic strategy in connection with "interrogatory examples" of an instructional sequence in contrast with "expository examples."

7. *Providing feedback.* The means of providing feedback and the ef-

---

Remember, your job is to tell if the figure is an equilateral triangle. Be sure to circle yes or no to each of the five questions. Then circle yes or no after the question: Is it an equilateral triangle?

	1.	Does it have three straight sides of equal length?	Yes No
	2.	Does it have three equal angles?	Yes No
	3.	Is it a plane figure?	Yes No
	4.	Is it a closed figure?	Yes No
	5.	Is it a simple figure?	Yes No
	6.	Is it an equilateral triangle?	Yes No

FIG. 3.4. Algorithmic strategy for identifying concept examples and nonexamples.

fects of confirming and corrective feedback are essentially the same here as given earlier for concept attainment at the concrete and identity levels. With respect specifically to the classificatory level, attaining ill-defined concepts inductively in the absence of feedback of any kind is typically less than 10% above the chance level (Homa & Cultice, 1984). However, corrective feedback after each hypothesis greatly facilitates attainment, not only of ill-defined concepts, but also concepts with a well-defined structure. After eight trials, 87% of the ill-defined concepts were attained with feedback and 30% without feedback; the corresponding percentages for well-defined concepts were 100% after the third trial with feedback and 82% without feedback. Moreover, with practice the percentage of correct hypotheses increased consistently across trials with feedback; without feedback it did not increase at all for ill-defined concepts and only moderately for well-defined.

   8. *Insuring attainment of the concept.* The primary test of attainment of a concept at the classificatory level is how well the learner can identify examples and discriminate nonexamples. Tests for attainment of the formal level are as follows: Can the learner (a) identify least typical examples of the concept and discriminate nonexamples of the related concepts, (b) discriminate and name the defining attributes of the concept, (c) give a definition in terms of the defining attributes, and (d) evaluate how any example of the concept differs from any example of any related concept in terms of the presence or absence of the defining attributes? Tests of uses of the concept can also be carried out: Can the learner (a) specify the relationships among the concepts, such as the inclusive and exclusive relations among superordinate, subordinate, and coordinate concepts of a taxonomy; (b) use the concept in understanding principles of which the concept is a part; and (c) use the concept in solving problems involving understanding of the concept?

   Paper-and-pen tests might be constructed to measure each aspect of attainment. However, arranging situations wherein the learner applies the knowledge is more effective in terms of insuring permanent learning.

POWERFUL ENDURING EFFECTS
OF FOCUSED INSTRUCTION

Earlier we saw that 16 minutes of one-on-one focused instruction enabled 3-year-olds to progress beyond the level of 5-year-olds who received no instruction (Nelson, 1973). Similar results were attained with older students in which the preceding variables were incorporated in the instruction.

   Two lessons of 35 minutes each were used to teach fourth-grade students *equilateral triangle* (McMurray, Bernard, Klausmeier, Schilling, Feldman, 1977). Of the two experimental groups that received the lessons, 60% and 64% attained the formal level, whereas only 7% and 11% of two control groups did. Two months later the results were 46% and 52% for the experimental groups and 7% and 8% for the control groups. The comparable attainment of the formal level of *tree* by a third-grade experimental group that received two lessons and a control group were 68% and 14%; no retention measure was obtained. In another experiment three lessons were used to teach high school seniors eight concepts dealing with behavior modification procedures (Bernard, 1975). The experimental group in this study receiving the most effective instruction scored 70%; the control students 30%.

Thirteen experiments were conducted over a period of 2 years as part of the ongoing science instruction of four elementary schools—two experimental, E1 and E2, and two control, C1 and C2 (Klausmeier & Sipple, 1980, pp. 137–190). The teachers of all four schools provided instruction in the classroom and science laboratory to aid their students carry on the processes of science, for example, *predicting* and *inferring,* not to understand the processes as concepts, per se. In addition, the experimental teachers used printed lessons prepared by the research team, supplemented with oral instruction, to aid the children in understanding the same processes as concepts.

The percentages attaining mastery and the mean scores of the experimental children were significantly higher than those of the controls in most of the 52 comparisons of their understanding the process concepts and their achievement of the curriculum content. The control children were not higher than the experimental children in any of the comparisons. Moreover, the fourth-graders of the first year who were fifth-graders in the second year in general attained higher than the fifth-graders of the first year, suggesting a positive cumulative effect of the instructional program. In sum, this series of experiments and the earlier ones indicate the power of the design when the prior variables are implemented properly.

SUMMARY

The first section of this chapter explored the nature of concepts. Concepts were described as being both mental constructs and word meanings, as having attribute structure, and as being "fuzzy" when they do not have clear boundaries. I discussed the differences between misconceptions and incomplete concepts, the former resulting from treating incorrect defining attributes as if correct and the latter simply being a more primitive form of initial concept formation.

From this I moved to the differences between classical theory of concept learning and prototype theory. In the former a concept consists of a summary representation of the intrinsic attributes of the concept. In prototype theory, a concept is thought of as the representation of a best example or the average of two or more typical examples of the concept. The limitations of both theories led to development of a more complex and comprehensive theory of concept learning and development. This theory explains attaining a concept at successively higher levels of understanding: concrete level, identity level, classificatory level, and formal level. This theory was followed with a related research-validated design for teaching concepts, organized into two major components: analysis prior to instruction and interactive instruction that is focused on learning concepts at each of the four levels.

A most important idea is that concepts, when attained at the formal level, are used both more widely and more effectively in understanding principles and taxonomic relations and in solving problems than when attained only at the classificatory level (Klausmeier & Allen, 1978, pp. 177–181). This fact adds highest importance to the use of carefully designed, focused concept instruction inasmuch as the acquisition of knowledge structures, the understanding and use of principles, and the development of convergent and divergent problem-solving processes are major desired outcomes of schooling.

ACKNOWLEDGMENTS

Recognition is given to the following former graduate advisees of the author who served as members of research teams and participated in developing concept analyses: Michael E. Bernard, J. Kent Davis, Kathryn V. Feldman, Dorothy A. Frayer, Elizabeth Ghatala, Richard M. Gargiulo, Selena E. Katz, Richard S. Marliave, Dean L. Meinke, Gerald W. Miller, Gregory Mize, Barbara A. Nelson, Gordon K. Nelson, Winston E. Rampaul, James G. Ramsey, Joan M. Schilling, Joseph A. Scott, James E. Swanson, Keith M. White, and Suzanne P. Wiviott.

Research assistants and research scientists to whom I am indebted are Patricia S. Allen, Geneva J. DiLuzio, Linda J. Ingison, Conrad G. Katzenmeyer, Nancy E. McMurray, Thomas S. Sipple, and William Wiersma.

REFERENCES

Anderson, C. W., & Smith, E. L. (1984). Children's preconceptions and content-area textbooks. In G. G. Duffy, C. R. Roehler, & J. Mason (Eds.), *Comprehen-*

sion instruction: Perspectives and suggestions (pp. 187–201). New York: Longman.

Anderson, R. C., & Kulhavy, R. W. (1972). Learning concepts from definitions. *American Educational Research Journal, 9,* 385–390.

Anziano, M. C. (1984). The concept of similarity: Age-related changes in the composition of children's categories. *Dissertation Abstracts International, 45*(9-B), 3091–3092.

Armour-Thomas, E. (1985). Microcomputer teaching concepts: Types of computer feedback in learning of relational concepts at kindergarten level. *Dissertation Abstracts International, 46*(3-A), 650.

Ausubel, D. P. (1966). Reception learning and the acquisition of concepts. In H. J. Klausmeier & C. W. Harris (Eds.), *Analyses of concept learning* (pp. 157–175). New York: Academic Press.

Ausubel, D. P. (1977). The facilitation of meaningful verbal learning in the classroom. *Educational Psychologist, 12,* 162–178.

Bell, B., & Freyberg, P. (1985). Language in the science classroom. In R. Osborne & P. Freyberg (Eds.), *Learning in science* (pp. 29–40). Auckland, New Zealand: Heinemann.

Bernard, M. E. (1975). *The effects of advance organizers and within-text questions on the learning of a taxonomy of concepts* (Tech. Rep. No. 357). Madison, WI: University of Wisconsin, Wisconsin Center for Education Research. (ERIC Document Reproduction Service No. ED 120 625)

Biederman, I. (1987). Recognition by components: A theory of human image understanding. *Psychological Review, 94*(2), 115–147.

Brainerd, C. J. (1979). Concept learning and developmental stage. In H. J. Klausmeier & Associates, *Cognitive learning and development: Information processing and Piagetian perspectives* (pp. 225–245). Cambridge, MA: Ballinger.

Brooks, L. (1978). Non-analytic concept formation and memory for instances. In E. Rosch & B. B. Lloyd (Eds.), *Cognition and Categorization* (pp. 169–215). Hillsdale, NJ: Lawrence Erlbaum Associates.

Brooks, L. (1987). Decentralized control of categorization: The role of prior processing episodes. In U. Neisser (Ed.), *Concepts and conceptual development: Ecological and intellectual factors in categorization* (pp. 141–174). Cambridge, MA: Cambridge University Press.

Brumby, M. N. (1984). Misconceptions about the concept of natural selection by medical biology students. *Science Education, 68,* 493–503.

Bruner, J. S. (1973). Culture and cognitive growth. In J. S. Bruner & J. M. Anglin (Eds.), *Beyond the information given* (pp. 368–393). New York: Norton.

Bruner, J. S., Goodnow, J. J., & Austin, G. A. (1956). *A study of thinking.* New York: Wiley.

Carey, S. (1982). Semantic development: The state of the art. In E. Wanner & L. R. Gleitman (Eds.), *Language acquisition: The state of the art* (pp. 347–389). New York: Cambridge University Press.

Carlson, R. A., & Dulaney, D. E. (1985). Conscious attention and abstraction in concept learning. *Journal of Experimental Psychology: Learning, Memory, and Cognition,11,* 45–58.

Carroll, J. B. (1964). *Language and thought.* Englewood Cliffs, NJ: Prentice-Hall.

Clark, D. C. (1971). Teaching concepts in the classroom: A set of prescriptions derived from experimental research. *Journal of Educational Psychology Monograph, 62,* 253–278.

Clark, E. V. (1983). Meaning and concepts. In J. H. Flavell & E. M. Markman (Eds.), *Handbook of child psychology: Vol. 3. Cognitive development* (pp. 787–840). New York: Wiley.

Davis, G. H. (1984). The relationship between the ability to categorize, level of concept used, and reading achievement. *Dissertation Abstracts International, 45* (6-A), 1700.

Davis, J. K., & Klausmeier, H. J. (1970). Cognitive style and concept identification as a function of complexity and training procedures. *Journal of Educational Psychology, 61,* 423–430.

DiLuzio, G. J., Katzenmeyer, C. G., & Klausmeier, H. J. (1975a). *Technical Manual for the conceptual learning and development series II: Cutting tool* (Tech. Rep. No. 435). Madison, WI: University of Wisconsin, Wisconsin Center for Education Research.

DiLuzio, G. J., Katzenmeyer, C. G., & Klausmeier, H. J. (1975b). *Technical Manual for the conceptual learning and development series IV: tree* (Tech. Rep. No. 437). Madison, WI: University of Wisconsin, Wisconsin Center for Education Research.

Doherty, V. W., & Peters, L. B. (1978). *K-12: Program goals and subject matter taxonomies for course goals in art, biological and physical sciences, business education, health education, home economics, industrial education, language arts, mathematics, music, physical education, second language, social science, and career education* (Tri-County Goal Development Project). Portland, OR: Commercial-Educational Distributing Services.

Dunn, C. S. (1983). The influence of instructional methods on concept learning. *Science Education, 67,* 647–656.

Engelkamp, J. (1983). Word meaning and recognition. In Th. B. Seiler & W. Wannenmacher (Eds.), *Concept development and the development of word meaning* (pp. 17–33). Berlin: Springer-Verlag.

Eysenck, M. W. (1984). *A handbook of cognitive psychology.* Hillsdale, NJ: Lawrence Erlbaum Associates.

Feldman, K. V. (1972). *The effects of number of positive and negative instances, concept definition, and emphasis of relevant attributes on the attainment of mathematical concepts* (Tech. Rep. No. 243). Madison, WI: University of Wisconsin, Wisconsin Center for Education Research.

Feldman, K. V., & Klausmeier, H. J. (1974). Effects of two kinds of definition on the concept attainment of fourth and eighth graders. *The Journal of Educational Research, 67*(5), 219–223.

Flavell, J. H., & Markman, E. M. (Eds.). (1983). *Handbook of child psychology.* New York: Wiley.

Frayer, D. A., & Klausmeier, H. J. (1971). *Variables in concept learning: Task variables* (Theo. Paper No. 28). Madison, WI: University of Wisconsin, Wisconsin Center for Education Research.

Fredrick, W. C., & Klausmeier, H. J. (1968a). Concept identification as a function of the number of relevant and irrelevant dimensions, presentation method, and salience. *Psychological Reports, 23,* 631–634.

Fredrick, W. C., & Klausmeier, H. J. (1968b). Instructions and labels in a concept-attainment task. *Psychological Reports, 23,* 1339–1342.

Gagnè, R. M. (1985). *The conditions of learning* (4th ed.). New York: Holt, Rinehart & Winston.

Gardner, M. K. (1985). Cognitive psychological approaches to instructional task analysis. In E. W. Gordon (Ed.), *Review of research in education* (Vol. 12, pp. 157–195). Washington, DC: American Educational Research Association.

Gelman, R., & Baillargeon, R. (1983). A review of some Piagetian concepts. In J. H. Flavell & E. M. Markman (Eds.), *Handbook of child psychology: Vol. 3. Cognitive development* (pp. 167–230). New York: Wiley.

Gibson, J. J., & Gibson, E. J. (1975). Continuous perspective transformations and the perception of rigid motion. *Journal of Experimental Psychology, 54,* 129–138.

Gibson, E. J., & Spelke, E. S. (1983). The development of perception. In J. H. Flavell & E. M. Markman (Eds.), *Handbook of child psychology: Vol. 3. Cognitive development* (pp. 1–76). New York: Wiley.

Greenberg, J., & Kuczaj, S. (1982). Toward a theory of substantive word-meaning acquisition. In S. Kuczaj (Ed.), *Language development, Vol. I: Syntax and semantics* (pp. 275–311). Hillsdale, NJ: Lawrence Erlbaum Associates.

Harris, M. L., & Harris, C. W. (1973). *A structure of concept attainment abilities: Wisconsin monograph series.* Madison, WI: University of Wisconsin, Wisconsin Center for Education Research.

Harty, H., Hamrick, L., & Samuel, K. V. (1985). Relationships between middle school students' science concept structure interrelatedness competence and selected cognitive and affective tendencies. *Journal of Research in Science Teaching, 22,* 179–191.

Herron, J. D., Cantu, L. L., Ward, R., & Srinivasan, V. (1977). Problems associated with concept analysis. *Science Education, 61,* 185–199.

Hewson, P. W., & Hewson, M. G. (1984). The role of conceptual conflict in conceptual change and the design of science instruction. *Instructional Science, 13,* 1–13.

Hewson, P. W., & Posner, G. J. (1984). The use of schema theory in the design of instructional materials: A physics example. *Instructional Science, 13,* 119–139.

Homa, D., & Cultice, J. (1984). Role of feedback, category size, and stimulus distortion on the acquisition and utilization of ill-defined categories. *Journal of Experimental Psychology: Learning, Memory, and Cognition, 10,* 83–94.

Homa, D., Rhoads, D., & Chambliss, D. (1979). The evolution of conceptual structure. *Journal of Experimental Psychology: Human Learning and Memory, 5,* 11–23.

Houtz, J. C., Moore, J. W., & Davis, J. K. (1973). Effects of different types of positive and negative instances in learning "nondimensional" concepts. *Journal of Educational Psychology, 64,* 206–211.

Howard, R. W. (1987). *Concepts and schemata: An introduction.* Philadelphia: Taylor and Frances.

Johnson, D. M., & Stratton, R. P. (1966). Evaluation of five methods of teaching concepts. *Journal of Educational Psychology, 57,* 48–53.

Klausmeier, H. J. (1971). Cognitive operations in concept learning. *Educational Psychologist, 9,* 1–8.

Klausmeier, H. J. (1976a). Conceptual development during the school years. In J. R. Levin & V. L. Allen (Eds.), *Cognitive learning in children: Theories and strategies* (pp. 5–29). New York: Academic Press.

Klausmeier, H. J. (1976b). Instructional design and the teaching of concepts. In J. R. Levin & V. L. Allen (Eds.), *Cognitive learning in children: Theories and strategies* (pp. 191–217). New York: Academic Press.

Klausmeier, H. J. (1977). Educational experience and cognitive development. *Educational Psychologist, 12,* 179–196.

Klausmeier, H. J. (1985). *Educational psychology* (5th ed.). New York: Harper & Row.

Klausmeier, H. J. (1987). Conceptual learning and development. In R. J. Corsini (Ed.), *Concise encyclopedia of psychology* (pp. 231–233). New York: Wiley.

Klausmeier, H. J., & Allen, P. (1978). *Cognitive development of children and youth: A longitudinal study.* New York: Academic Press.

Klausmeier, H. J., & Associates. (1979). *Cognitive learning and development: Information-processing and Piagetian perspectives.* Cambridge, MA: Ballinger.

Klausmeier, H. J., & Feldman, K. V. (1975). Effects of a definition and a varying number of examples and nonexamples on concept attainment. *Journal of Educational Psychology, 67,* 174–178.

Klausmeier, H. J., Ghatala, E. S., & Frayer, D. A. (1974). *Conceptual learning and development: A cognitive view.* New York: Academic Press.

Klausmeier, H. J., Harris, C. W., Davis, J. K., Ghatala, E., & Frayer, D. (1968). *Strategies and cognitive processes in concept learning* (U.S. Office of Education Project No. 2850). Washington, D.C.: U.S. Department of Health, Education, and Welfare, Office of Education, Bureau of Research.

Klausmeier, H. J., Harris, C. W., & Wiersma, W. (1964). *Strategies of learning and efficiency of concept attainment by individuals and groups* (U.S. Office of Education Project No. 1442). Washington, D.C.: U.S. Department of Health, Education, and Welfare, Office of Education, Bureau of Research.

Klausmeier, H. J., & Meinke, D. L. (1968). Concept attainment as a function of instructions concerning the stimulus material, a strategy, and a principle for securing information. *Journal of Educational Psychology, 59*(3), 215–222.

Klausmeier, H. J., & Sipple, T. S. (1980). *Learning and teaching process concepts: A strategy for testing applications of theory.* New York: Academic Press.

Klausmeier, H. J., & Sipple, T. S. (1982). Factor structure of the Piagetian stage of concrete operations. *Contemporary Educational Psychology, 7,* 161–180.

Klausmeier, H. J., Swanson, J. E., & Sipple, T. S. (1976). *The analysis of the process concepts in elementary science* (Tech. Rep. No. 428). Madison, WI: University of Wisconsin, Wisconsin Center for Education Research.

Klayman, J., Young-Won, H. (1987). Confirmation, disconfirmation, and information in hypothesis testing. *Psychological Review, 94,* 211–228.

Levine, M. (1975). *A cognitive theory of learning: Research on hypothesis-testing.* Hillsdale, NJ: Lawrence Erlbaum Associates.

Macnamara, J. (1982). *Names of things.* Cambridge, MA: MIT Press.

Markle, S. M. (1975). They teach concepts, don't they? *Educational Researcher, 4,* 3–9.

Markle, S. M. (1978). Teaching conceptual networks. *NSPI Journal, 17*(1), 4–7.

Markle, S. M., & Tiemann, P. W. (1969). *Really understanding concepts: Or in frumious pursuit of the jabberwock.* Champaign, IL: Stipes.

Mathews, R. C., Stanley, W. B., Buss, R. R., & Chinn, R. (1985). Concept learning: What happens when hypothesis testing fails? *Journal of Experimental Education, 53,* 91–96.

Mayer, R. E., Dyck, J. L., & Cook, L. K. (1984). Techniques that help readers build mental models from scientific text: Definitions pretraining and signaling. *Journal of Educational Psychology, 76*(6), 1089–1105.

McCloskey, M. E., & Glucksberg, S. (1978). Natural categories: Well defined or fuzzy sets? *Memory & Cognition, 6,* 642–672.

McKeown, M., Beck, I., Omanson, R., & Pople, M. (1985). Some effects of the nature and frequency of vocabulary instruction on the knowledge and use of words. *Reading Research Quarterly, 20,* 222–235.

McMurray, N.E., Bernard, M.E., Klausmeier, H. J., Schilling, J. M., & Feldman, K. (1977). Instructional design for accelerating children's concept learning. *Journal of Educational Psychology, 69,* 660–667.

Medin, D. L., Altom, M. W., & Murphy, T. D. (1984). Given versus induced category representations: Use of prototype and exemplar information in classification. *Journal of Experimental Psychology: Learning, Memory, and Cognition, 10,* 333–352.

Medin, D. L., & Smith, E. E. (1984). Concepts and concept formation. *Annual Review of Psychology, 35,* 113–138.

Merrill, M. D., & Tennyson, R. D. (1978). Concept classification and classification errors as a function of relationships between examples and non-examples. *Improving Human Performance, 7,* 351–364.

Mervis, C. B., & Pani, J. R. (1980). Acquisition of basic object categories. *Cognitive Psychology, 12,* 496–522.

Mervis, C. B., & Rosch, E. (1981). Categorization of natural objects. *Annual Review of Psychology, 32,* 89–115.

Miller, G. A., & Johnson-Laird, P. N. (1976). *Language and perception.* Cambridge, MA: Harvard University Press.

Murphy, G. L., & Brownell, H. H. (1985). Category differentiation in object recognition: Typicality constraints on the basic category advantage. *Journal of Experimental Psychology: Learning, Memory, and Cognition, 11,* 70–84.

Musser, M. P. (1984). The acquisition and representation of natural language-like concepts: A developmental study. *Dissertation Abstracts International, 45*(3-B), 1041.

Neisser, V. (1967). *Cognitive psychology.* New York: Appleton, Century, Crofts.

Nelson, G. K. (1973). *Sensory-motor and verbal foundations of concept acquisition: A study in early childhood* (Tech. Rep. No. 272). Madison, WI: University of Wisconsin, Wisconsin Center for Education Research.

Nelson, G. K., & Klausmeier, H. J. (1974). Classificatory behavior of low-socioeconomic-status children. *Journal of Educational Psychology, 66,* 432–438.

Nelson, K. E., & Bonvillian, J. D. (1973). Concepts and words in the 18-month-old: Acquiring concept names under controlled conditions. *Cognition, 2,* 435–450.

Novak, J. D., & Gowin, D. B. (1986). *Learning how to learn.* Cambridge, England: Cambridge University Press.

Novak, J. D., Gowin, D. B., & Johansen, G. T. (1983). The use of concept mapping and knowledge mapping with junior high school science students. *Science Education, 67,* 625–645.

Nussbaum, J. (1979). Childrens' conceptions of the Earth as a cosmic body: A cross age study. *Science Education, 63,* 83–93.

Nussbaum, J., & Novick, S. (1981). Brainstorming in the classroom to invent a model: A case study. *School Science Review, 62,* 771–778.

Oden, G. C. (1987). Concept, knowledge, and thought. *Annual Review of Psychology, 38,* 203–227.

Osborne, R., & Wittrock, M. C. (1985). The generative learning model and its implications. *Studies in Science Education, 12,* 59–87.

Osherson, D. N., & Smith, E. E. (1981). On the adequacy of prototype theory as a theory of concepts. *Cognition, 9,* 35–58.

Park, O. (1984). Example comparison strategy versus attribute identification strategy in concept learning. *American Educational Research Journal, 21,* 145–162.

Piaget, J. (1970). Piaget's theory. In P. H. Mussen (Ed.), *Carmichael's manual of child psychology* (Vol. 1, 3rd ed., pp. 703–772). New York: Wiley.

Posner, M. I., & Keele, S. W. (1968). On the genesis of abstract ideas. *Journal of Experimental Psychology, 77,* 353–363.

Posner, M. I., & Keele, S. W. (1970). Retention of abstract ideas. *Journal of Experimental Psychology, 83,* 304–308.

Posner, G. J., Strike, K. A., Hewson, P. W., & Gertzog, W. A. (1982). Accommodation of a scientific conception: Toward a theory of conceptual change. *Science Education, 66,* 221–227.

Rey, G. (1983). Concepts and stereotypes. *Cognition, 15,* 237–262.

Rosch, E. (1975). Cognitive representations of semantic categories. *Journal of Experimental Psychology: General, 104,* 192–233.

Rosch, E. (1978). Principles of categorization. In E. Rosch & B. Lloyd (Eds.), *Cognition and categorization* (pp. 9–31). Hillsdale, NJ: Lawrence Erlbaum Associates.

Rosch, E., Mervis, C. B., Gray, W. D., Johnson, D. M., & Boyes-Braem, P. (1976). Basic objects in natural categories. *Cognitive Psychology, 8,* 382–439.

Schilling, J. M., & Klausmeier, H. J. (1975). *Lesson on the basic process concept of "inferring" intended for use in elementary science with fifth grade students.* Madison, WI: University of Wisconsin, Wisconsin Center for Education Research.

Schwartz, R. M., & Raphael, T. E. (1985). Concept of definition: A key to improving students' vocabulary. *Reading Teacher,* 198–205.

Shaycoft, M. G. (1967). *The high school years: Growth in cognitive skills.* Pittsburgh, PA: American Institutes of Research.

Shepherd, D. L. (1985). A study of conceptual understandings of concrete and formal biological science concepts as related to state of intellectual development and background variables. *Dissertation Abstracts International, 45*(8-A), 2472–2473.

Shumway, R. J., White, A. L., Wilson, P., & Brombacher, B. (1983). Feature frequency and negative instances in concept learning. *American Educational Research Journal, 20,* 451–459.

Siegel, L. S., & Brainerd, C. J. (Eds.). (1978). *Alternatives to Piaget: Critical essays on theory.* New York: Academic Press.

Sims, E. V. (1984). Effects of continuous versus noncontinuous presentation and magnitude of difference between examples and nonexamples on acquisition and transfer of a comparative concept. *Dissertation Abstracts International, 46,*(4-B), 1366.

Smith, E. E., & Medin, D. L. (1981). *Categories and concepts.* Cambridge, MA: Harvard University Press.

Sternberg, R. J. (1984). A theory of knowledge acquisition in the development of verbal concepts. *Developmental Review, 4,* 113–138.

Sutton, C. R. (1980). The learner's prior knowledge: A critical review of techniques for probing its organization. *European Journal of Science Education, 2,* 107–120.

Swanson, J. E. (1972). *The effects of number of positive and negative instances, concept definition, and emphasis of relevant attributes on the attainment of three environmental concepts by sixth-grade children* (Tech. Rep. No. 244). Madison, WI: University of Wisconsin, Wisconsin Center for Education Research.

Tennyson, R. D., & Cocchiarella, M. J. (1986). An empirically based instructional design theory for teaching concepts. *Review of Educational Research, 56,* 40–71.

Tennyson, R. D., & Park, O. (1980). The teaching of concepts: A review of instructional design research literature. *Review of Educational Research, 50,* 55–70.

Tennyson, R. D., Woolley, F. R., & Merrill, M. D. (1972). Exemplar and nonexemplar variables which produce correct concept classification behavior and specified classification errors. *Journal of Educational Psychology, 63,* 114–152.

Tiemann, P. W., & Markle, S. M. (1985). *Analyzing instructional content* (2nd ed.). Champaign, IL: Stipes.

Tumblin, A., & Gholson, B. (1981). Hypothesis theory and the development of conceptual learning. *Psychological Review, 90,* 102–104.

Wicklegren, W. A. (1979). *Cognitive psychology.* Englewood Cliffs, NJ: Prentice-Hall.

Williams, J. P. (1984). Categorization, macrostructure, and finding the main idea. *Journal of Educational Psychology, 76,* 874–879.

Zadeh, L. S. (1965). Fuzzy sets. *Information and Control, 8,* 338–375.

Developing Meaningful Conceptual Understanding in Science

Kathleen J. Roth
Michigan State University

Elementary and secondary schools have not been successful in teaching students how to use and apply the facts and vocabulary they memorize in social studies and science classes or the computational and reading skills they master in mathematics and language arts classes. Many recent studies document that students can memorize facts and procedures but are unable to use those facts and skills to build arguments, to make predictions, to explain observed phenomena, to solve real-world problems, or to read critically (Anderson & Smith, 1983a; Applebee, Langer, & Mullis, 1986; Carey, 1986; Champagne & Klopfer, 1977, 1984; Champagne, Klopfer, & Gunstone, 1982; Johnson & Wellman, 1982; McKnight et al., 1987; National Assessment of Educational Progress, 1978, 1979a, 1979b, 1979c, 1979d, 1983; Roth, 1984; Roth, Smith, & Anderson, 1983; Travers & McKnight, 1985). As a result of these studies, many educators advocate a change from the current emphasis on facts and procedures in K-12 teaching to a new emphasis on teaching for meaningful conceptual understanding (Anderson & Smith, 1987; Armento, 1986; Committee on Research in Mathematics, Science, and Technology Education, 1985; Fey, 1979; Hiebert, 1984; Hiebert, 1986; Minstrell, 1982; National Academy of Sciences, 1982; National Council of Teachers of Mathematics, 1980; National Research Council, 1979, 1985; National Science Foundation, 1983; Romberg & Carpenter, 1986).

The argument is that students need better organized and deeper knowledge of a limited number of central concepts (rather than broad but superficial knowledge of many facts and formulae) in order to develop the higher level abilities that would enable them to use and apply their understandings in meaningful ways. What is meant by "meaningful conceptual understanding?" Is such conceptual understanding a reasonable and attainable goal for school learning?

This chapter explores these questions in the domain of science. A description of the nature and roles of conceptual understanding in the discipline of science and an analysis of schema theory views of the learning process are used to define what is meant by meaningful conceptual understanding in science. Next a review of recent research exploring students' difficulties in developing such conceptual understandings in science is presented. This review provides both additional insights into the nature of meaningful conceptual learning and explanations for why traditional instructional methods do not help most students develop such understandings. Finally, the possibilities of teaching for conceptual understanding in science classrooms are discussed in light of recent classroom research.

A central premise of the chapter is that meaningful conceptual learning should be a central goal in science teaching and that such learning is possible when instruction takes into consideration recent cognitive research about student learning. This research suggests that students' development of higher order thinking skills (such as problem solving or the application of ideas) depends on rich, domain-specific conceptual networks of knowledge. Developing such conceptual networks in science often requires students to go through a difficult process of conceptual change, a process that is not supported well by traditional methods of science instruction.

THE NATURE OF "MEANINGFUL CONCEPTUAL UNDERSTANDING" IN SCIENCE

Defining Meaningful Conceptual Understanding in Science: The Scientists' View

For practicing scientists, conceptualization is at the core of their work. Conceptualization is a process of representing observations and experiences in ways that make clear patterns and organization. Pines (1985) described concepts as "packages of meaning (that) capture regularities (similarities and differences), patterns, or relationships among objects, events, and other concepts" (p. 108). He emphasized that concepts represent different ways of organizing or "slicing up" the world. Concepts vary along a continuum from simple labels for concrete entities (such as "the sun," "plant," "soil," etc.) to higher level abstract representations that describe complex relationships among many subordinate concepts (Pines, 1985; Reif, 1985).

Reif (1985) argued that it is these higher level, or property, concepts that are at the heart of science. Scientists continually strive to create such conceptual networks and representations, because these kinds of under-standings provide satisfying descriptions and explanations of the world. But such higher level conceptualizations are not important only as *goals* in science. Rich understandings of particular concepts and of the variety of relationships among them are also important *cognitive tools,* which are needed in order to create new meaningful conceptualizations. Thus, scientists use the conceptual core of science to deduce important conse-quences, to make predictions, to solve problems, to generate hypotheses, and to develop research questions and research programs (Reif, 1985).

For scientists, then, meaningful conceptual understanding in science goes far beyond knowing facts and labels. Rather, conceptual knowledge becomes meaningful only when it can be used to explain or explore new situations.

Scientists' concern for the importance of conceptual organization and higher level conceptual abstractions in science was reflected in their in-put during the post-Sputnik science curriculum reform efforts. In these National Science Foundation (NSF)-sponsored curriculum development projects, scientists for the first time played a major role in deciding how science should be represented in school curricula. Their contributions to science education during that era are often summarized as awakening educators to the need for teaching the *processes* of science (predicting, observing, recording observations, inferring). However, the scientists' reorganization of the *content* of science curricula also represented a dra-matic change.

Scientists clearly viewed conceptualizations of the disciplines as crit-ical, and this was evidenced in the organization of materials they helped develop. These materials at both the elementary and secondary level were organized in ways that emphasized the major conceptual frame-works within scientific disciplines rather than the traditional topical ap-proach of school science curricula. In high school biology, for example, textbooks traditionally organized the discipline as a series of related but fairly discrete topics—the cell, unicellular organisms, multicellular plants (algae, mosses and ferns, seed plants), and multicellular animals (invertebrates, vertebrates, man). Connecting ideas/concepts among these units of instruction were few and primarily concerned classification and evolutionary issues. The materials developed in the 1960s and 1970s, however, emphasized different conceptual organizations of the discipline. Biology was organized in one Biological Sciences Curriculum

Study (BSCS) high school text (1968a), for example, around the bio-
chemical and cellular regularities among all living things. Transport systems of both plants and animals were considered simultaneously and
were linked to studies of photosynthesis, respiration, digestion, and so
forth, under an umbrella organizing concept of energy utilization in
living things. Another conceptual organization concerned unifying systems in multicellular organisms. Regulatory systems in both plants and
animals were compared and contrasted in exploring this set of concepts
in biology. Another text produced by the BSCS team (Biological Sciences
Curriculum Study, 1968b) and the elementary program developed by
the Science Curriculum Improvement Study (Knott, Lawson, Karplus,
Their, & Montgomery, 1978) organized biology around concepts describing the interdependency of all living things. In these curricula, central concepts about interactions among organisms were emphasized and
elaborated throughout a year-long sequence. Thus, in representing science in school curricula in ways that reflected the nature of the discipline, scientists emphasized the development of meaningful conceptual
understandings and networks of concepts.

Defining Meaningful Conceptual Understanding
in Science: A Teacher's Perspective

An example from my own teaching illustrates how I was able to recognize, at a gut level, when meaningful conceptual learning was occurring
in my classroom. This episode took place in a seventh-grade life science
class in which we were using curriculum materials that were developed as
part of the NSF post-Sputnik thrust and that were organized around
conceptual themes in biology. Using these materials, the class studied
units about photosynthesis, about cells' needs for food and oxygen,
about the circulatory systems of both plants and animals, about digestive
systems, about cell respiration, and about excretory systems. I wanted
students to connect these ideas together - to see how human body systems interacted to supply cells with needed materials and energy, and
how this whole process was ultimately dependent on plants' ability to
make food. Everyone listened quietly, apparently unimpressed by this
fascinating grand scheme. But then Mindy Hawkins, a hardworking
average student who normally would never speak out without raising her
hand and being called on, let out a loud *"Oh! I get it! That's neat!."* She
proceeded to ask clarifying questions that clearly indicated she did "have
it" and could apply the ideas to explain a variety of phenomena. She
asked questions, for example, that started, "So does that mean . . . ?"
"Then what if . . . ?" "Is that why . . . ?" As a teacher I was ecstatic that

one of my average students had developed such good understanding. In retrospect, however, I wonder about the rest of the class who sat staring at Mindy in disbelief that she was so excited about all this. Their lack of involvement suggested that they were not making the connections among concepts that Mindy was making. Undoubtedly, many of them did very well on my unit test, but did they achieve the kind of meaningful understanding that Mindy clearly had? I doubt that they did. The fact that Mindy's reaction to instruction is so prominent in my memory today attests to the rare occurrence of such learning.

Why did so few of my students experience that same kind of meaningful learning that Mindy had? These students were learning *something*, but they were not developing the meaningful network of concepts that Mindy had. Why? Cognitive psychologists' research on the role of prior knowledge in the learning process provides critical insights about why concept learning is not always meaningful learning for students.

Defining Meaningful Conceptual Understanding in Science: A Perspective From Schema Theory

Cognitive psychologists investigating internal mental processes during complex kinds of learning—including physics problem solving, chess playing, and reading of text—have emphasized the critical role a person's prior knowledge plays in the learning process. Learning is not simply a process of adding in knowledge into the head; rather, learning is an active process in which the learner takes information from the environment and *constructs* personal interpretations and meanings. The learner's interpretations are influenced not only by the external environment (words in a text or by what a teacher says), they are also shaped by the learner's prior knowledge and experience.

This prior knowledge is not just bits of information floating around randomly in a person's memory. Instead, a person makes sense of experience by organizing it into memory clusters that researchers have variously referred to as schemata (Anderson, Spiro, & Anderson, 1978; Rumelhart, 1980), frames (Davis, 1981; Minsky, 1975), cognitive structures (Champagne, Gunstone, & Klopfer, 1985; West, Fensham, & Garrard, 1985), or conceptual networks. A schema is a cluster of knowledge specifying a set of concepts and the relationships among them that describe a more complex superordinate concept. According to schema theorists (Anderson, Reynolds, Schallert, & Goetz, 1977; Bransford & Franks, 1976; Kintsch, 1974; Rumelhart & Ortony, 1977; Schank & Abelson, 1977; Smith, 1975; Thorndyke & Hayes-Roth, 1979), learning involves relating new experiences to what the person already knows; that is, to the person's relevant schema. Thus, learning can only occur if new information that is received by the learner is integrated into an already existing schema in the learner's head.

Schema theory specifies three conditions necessary for learning to take place (Mayer, 1983):

1. The learner must receive presented material.
2. The learner must have relevant prior knowledge, or schema.
3. The learner must activate that relevant prior knowledge.

What do schema theory and these prerequisites for learning have to say about the kinds of learning that can occur when students are presented with information about scientific concepts in their science classes? Examples of different ways that students might relate new information about one science concept (photosynthesis) to their existing knowledge will be used to contrast meaningful conceptual understanding with other types of conceptual learning. What might happen when students are taught about the concept of photosynthesis—that plants have a unique ability to use sunlight, carbon dioxide, and water to create their own energy-containing food?

Rote Memorization. It is possible that some students may not have any relevant schemata in which to fit this new information. They may not have a schema for "plants" or "energy." More likely, students will have relevant schemata, but they may not recognize that their real-world knowledge about plants and how to keep them healthy is relevant to a discussion of formal science and photosynthesis. Therefore, they may fail to activate the relevant schema. Lacking a place to link the new knowledge to prior knowledge, students simply will add the facts about photosynthesis to their memory as isolated bits of information unrelated to other ideas or schemata. This kind of rote memorization is familiar to teachers who recognize that many of their students "get by" experiencing primarily this kind of learning. Students can answer questions like "What is photosynthesis?" by recalling that isolated bit from memory, but that memorized definition is not linked to other concepts, including the students' prior knowledge. Therefore, the student is unable to use that definition to explain why plants die in the dark or to predict what would happen to a plant deprived of carbon dioxide. Thus, this is not the kind of conceptual "learning" that scientists would value—it is a kind of nonmeaningful conceptual learning. Students can label the concept but do not use it in trying to better understand the world.

Overreliance on Prior Knowledge. Another kind of nonmeaningful learning can occur when learners receive the presented concept(s) and activate relevant prior knowledge, but that prior knowledge is in conflict with the new information. To reconcile two inconsistent conceptualizations, students may distort or ignore the new information. In order to make sense of photosynthesis, for example, students need to activate a schema or conceptual network for "food" that is consistent with the scientific view. The scientists' concept of food includes a critical distinction between energy-containing substances (that can *only* be made by plants during photosynthesis) and other kinds of nutrients that support life but do not provide energy (minerals, vitamins, water, carbon dioxide). Students often lack this disciplinary schema but have an alternative schema for food that they have developed from their everyday experiences with food and eating. Thus, they "know" that people eat lots of different kinds of food and that people get that food from the external environment. Thus, food is defined as anything taken into the body that is needed to live. There is an important conflict between the scientists' conceptualization of food and the students' everyday schema for food.

Lacking knowledge of the scientific schema for food, students may come to understand the information about photosynthesis by activating and using their everyday schema about "food" for plants. In order to make the new information fit with the conflicting real-world schema, however, students may distort new concepts or selectively ignore some of the new concepts. Kevin, a seventh-grade student in one of my studies (Roth, 1986), had a rich prior knowledge about plants and food. He "knew" that plants, like people, have multiple sources of food that they take in from the external environment. He wrote on a pretest:

> Food (for plants) can be sun, rain, light, bugs, oxygen, soil, and even other dead plants. Also warmth or coldness. All plants need at least three or four of these foods. Plus minerals.

When Kevin read a text that explained that minerals are not food for plants but that plants make their own food during photosynthesis, he ignored the statement that minerals are not considered food (even after a second reading of the key paragraph). This allowed him to incorporate inappropriately the concept of photosynthesis into his own schema of multiple foods for plants:

> I: Could you summarize where does the plant get its food?
> K: Whew, from lots of places! From the soil for one, for the minerals and water, and from the air for oxygen. The sunlight for the sun, and it would change chemicals to sugars. It sort of makes its own food and gets food from the ground. And from air.

Because of an overreliance on his prior knowledge about plants, Kevin's learning about photosynthesis is distorted. His prior conception that anything plants need is their food and that plants have multiple sources of food was unchanged. As a result, he missed the critical understanding that the food made during photosynthesis is different from the raw materials taken into the plant. Although Kevin could accurately define photosynthesis, he could not use that concept to explain why all living things are dependent on green plants or to predict what would happen if only one leaf of a large plant received sunlight.

Posner, Strike, Hewson, and Gertzog (1982) called this kind of distorted learning "conceptual capture," a name that highlights how bits of disciplinary concepts are captured and integrated inappropriately into the student's conflicting, real-world schema. This is a kind of non-meaningful learning that occurs often in science classrooms (as shown in the next section of this review). In addition, this is a kind of learning that is frequently *not* noticed by teachers.

Meaningful Integration Learning. When students are able to call up an appropriate schema from their memory and fit new information into that schema, meaningful learning can occur. For example, a student who understands cells and the notion that certain cells are specialized for specific functions can easily assimilate into that schema the notion that only certain leaf cells that contain chlorophyll are capable of photo-synthesizing. Thus, they are able to easily integrate their prior knowledge with new knowledge, giving meaning to the new information. This integrative learning is a fairly straightforward process, as it is usually just a matter of fitting new instances of a concept into an already existing schema.

This kind of learning, called "assimilation" by Piaget (1929) and Posner et al. (1982) and "integration" by Hewson and Hewson (1984), is the kind of learning that teachers generally strive for. Because they assume that students will use scientists' way of organizing information in memory, they expect that students will understand if the scientific concepts are presented clearly to them. When students fail to learn, teachers attribute this failure to students' lack of effort or lack of intelligence. However, the studies reviewed in the next section demonstrate that students rarely bring schemata to the learning situation that are compatible with the scientific schema they are expected to learn. Thus, meaningful integration learning is often not possible for students, because they lack relevant, compatible schemata. As a result, learning is not the straight-forward process that teachers expect.

Meaningful Conceptual Change Learning. In thinking about students' prior knowledge about a topic, most teachers tend to think only about what the student already knows that is compatible with the scientific notion. In my own teaching, for example, I assumed that students would have a relevant schema for plants that was consistent with the scientific view but merely impoverished. For example, seventh grade students probably know that plants take in carbon dioxide and release oxygen. What they know is correct; the teacher's role is simply to elaborate, add to, and deepen that correct conceptual knowledge. Thus, I viewed the teaching task as enriching and adding to an impoverished but accurate schema.

However, recent research on science learning has established that students often come to instruction holding their own well-developed "theories" about many scientific phenomena. They have developed these naive theories, or misconceptions, about how the world works from their sense impressions and their experiences with everyday phenomena and everyday language. We have seen, for example, how Kevin thought about plants as having multiple, external sources of food. Students like Kevin must make significant changes in their own schema before the scientific explanations will make personal sense. Thus, learners must take apart or rearrange concepts in their everyday schemata in order to integrate new concepts appropriately. Posner et al. (1982) have called this type of learning conceptual change.

In order for this kind of learning to occur, students need to see (a) that the scientific concept is in conflict with their own conceptions, (b) that their own notions are inadequate, incomplete, or inconsistent with observable evidence, and (c) that a scientific conceptualization provides a more convincing and powerful alternative to their own notions. Using the photosynthesis example again, students must not only call up relevant prior knowledge about food for plants, they must also recognize that their schema is in conflict with the scientific schema. They must modify the idea that food is simply defined as "anything living things need" and use a new definition of "food" to reconstruct their understandings of food for plants. Their notion that plants' food is the stuff plants take in from the soil can no longer serve as the central, organizing concept in their schema of food for plants. Instead, new concepts about photosynthesis must be built into the core of their conceptual network. Materials taken in by the roots must take on a new, subsuming position in the "food for plants" schema. It is not enough for students to build up a totally new schema about how plants make food internally during photosynthesis. To have meaning, this new schema must be integrated with the previously held schema. Although the previously held schema about external, multiple sources of food for plants may still function adequately in students' everyday lives, the scientific schema will be seen as more useful to the student in explaining the hows and whys of life processes. This kind of learning is complex and requires a great deal of cognitive (and metacognitive) work by the learner.

Such conceptual change learning has been called accommodation by

Posner et al. (1982), following Piaget, and reconciliation or exchange by Hewson and Hewson (1984). Champagne et al. (1985) described it as the restructuring of conceptual systems. A key feature of this kind of learning is that existing schemata or conceptual networks are in conflict with what is being taught. Meaningful learning cannot occur until students' everyday, "real-world knowledge" is appropriately changed and integrated with disciplinary conceptual knowledge. Pines and West (1983) have used a vine metaphor that captures well the nature of this kind of learning:

> Our view of mature conceptual learning . . . is the integration of knowledge from these two sources. We find a vine metaphor useful in understanding this. We imagine two vines, representing these different sources of knowledge, the one originating from the child's intuitive knowledge of the world (which we call the upward growing vine to emphasize that it is part of the growth of the child), the other originating from formal instruction (which we call the downward growing vine to emphasize its imposition on the child from above). Mature concept learning involves the intertwining of these two vines. (p. 47)

Summary. Scientists and teachers can agree that students should experience conceptual change learning in science. This was clearly the kind of understanding that my student, Mindy Hawkins, achieved. Her understanding of the interconnections among a number of central concepts in biology is impressive not because she could rattle off detailed recapitulations of what her teacher or textbook said. Rather, the reason this kind of rich conceptual learning is so compelling as a central goal for science education is because of the questions it stimulated Mindy to ask. Having developed a rich conceptual system, Mindy was able to use that knowledge to generate questions that had never occurred to her before. Thus, she was using conceptual knowledge much like scientists do.

Schema theory suggests that the development of such rich, domain-specific conceptual knowledge depends on the successful integration of a learner's prior knowledge with the domain knowledge. If prior knowledge and disciplinary knowledge never connect and intertwine, learning of scientific concepts is reduced to rote memorization of facts that are not useful in developing better explanations of the world. When prior knowledge is rich and compatible with the scientific conceptualization, it can be intertwined with disciplinary knowledge in a fairly smooth way, with the learner simply finding the appropriate spot to twist together the two "vines." However, prior knowledge is problematic when it is well organized but in clear conflict with scientists' conceptualizations. In this case, learners must not only make connections between the two conflicting frameworks, or vines, they must also change their own conceptualizations to make them consonant with scientific views.

The rest of this chapter explores this kind of meaningful conceptual change learning. Why is such meaningful conceptual understanding so difficult for students to achieve? How is it supported or discouraged by instruction? What changes can be made in science teaching that will help more students achieve meaningful conceptual understandings?

STUDENTS' DIFFICULTIES IN ACHIEVING MEANINGFUL CONCEPTUAL UNDERSTANDING IN SCIENCE CLASSROOMS

A line of research focusing on science learning has investigated students' misconceptions, or prior knowledge that is in conflict with scientists' conceptions. Understandings developed from this research about the contrasts between children's ways of structuring the world and scientists' ways of organizing concepts help to explain *why* students are failing to achieve meaningful conceptual understandings in science classrooms. This section reviews how this line of research has developed critical understandings about the learner's "vine" of everyday knowledge.

Research Identifying Students' Misconceptions in Science

Although the bulk of the schema theory research in reading has focused on the *facilitative* effects of prior knowledge for learning, much of the research on science learning has been concerned with how students' incompatible prior knowledge often *constrains* comprehension of scientific theories and concepts. Labels for this incompatible prior knowledge have included: "misconceptions" (Helm, 1980), "preconceptions" (Anderson & Smith, 1984), "alternative frameworks" (Hewson & Hewson, 1984; Nussbaum & Novick, 1982a), "naive theories" (Resnick, 1983), "alternative conceptual systems" (Champagne et al., 1982), "alternative conceptions" (Driver & Easley, 1978), "children's science" (Gilbert, Osborne, & Fensham, 1982), "theories-in-action" (Rowell & Dawson, 1980), "intuitive theories" (McCloskey, 1983), and "qualitatively different conceptions" (Johansson, Marton, & Svensson, 1985). Each researcher has theoretical reasons for preferring one name over another. In fact, a great deal of discussion at the first International Seminar on Misconceptions in Science and Mathematics (Helm & Novak, 1983) concerned the nuances of meaning contained in different names. Thus, for example, many are concerned that the notion of *mis*conceptions puts too much emphasis on the "wrongness" of students' ideas rather than on the more complex picture of individually constructed conceptual schemes that contain some "correct" (i.e., in accord with accepted scientific theories) notions connected in various ways with "incorrect" or "partially correct" ideas. Others defend the use of the term in spite of this fault, because it is one that communicates easily to teachers and the general public. Gilbert and Watts (1983) discussed in detail this issue of terminology and the differences in meaning implied by different words.

However, the researchers in this group are all basically investigating the same thing. They all talk about children's conceptions of the world, the "substance of the actual beliefs and concepts" (Erickson, 1979) held by students. They all look at how the student constructs, organizes, and structures knowledge about the world and how that knowledge organization (schemata) differs from that of the scientific community, the teacher, and the textbook. They all recognize the need to understand students' ways of thinking and interpreting instruction if meaningful conceptual understanding is to be a realistic goal of science instruction.

A large number of the studies in this area have focused on documenting students' misconceptions on a variety of topics in the science curriculum and contrasting students' misconceptions with scientific conceptions. The purpose of these studies is to understand the workings of children's minds. Using Pines and West's aforementioned vine metaphor, these researchers are studying the structure of the lower vine—the vine that represents the children's construction of knowledge based on their everyday experiences in the world. The goal of this research is to understand in detail the nature of the children's "vines" in order to understand how they are different and similar to the disciplinary "vines" that students are expected to make sense of in school science classrooms.

The earliest studies in this area focused on college students' problems with physics concepts. More recently research has studied (a) misconceptions about topics in many other branches of science including biology, chemistry, and earth science, (b) children of all ages, and (c) cross-cultural similarities and differences in misconceptions. Because misconceptions about motion have been researched heavily, a review of studies in this area will be used to illustrate both how knowledge about students' misconceptions is growing and how students' misconceptions represent conceptual *systems* rather than simple errors in labeling of entities.

Students' Conceptions of Force and Motion. Several researchers have identified striking student misconceptions about the motion of objects that appear to be embedded in a systematic, "intuitive" theory of motion that is inconsistent with Newtonian mechanics (McCloskey, 1983). In fact, McCloskey found these "intuitive" theories to be surprisingly similar to Aristotelian ideas. For example, McCloskey asked college students to imagine a ball tied to a string and whirled over a person's head in a circular path. What would happen to the ball if the string suddenly broke? Whereas Newtonian mechanics predicts that an object moves in a straight line unless acted on by an external force, one-third of the students predicted a curved trajectory for the ball. On another task, students were asked to walk across the room and, while they walked, to drop a golf ball so it would hit a target on the floor. Only 45 percent of the students acted in a way that reflected an understanding that the ball would travel forward as it fell.

Subsequent discussions with the students about a variety of tasks revealed many of them held consistent notions that objects are kept in motion by an internal force that gradually dissipates. Similar to the impetus theory held by 16th-century scientists, this naive theory holds that an object acquires this impetus only when it is pushed or thrown, not when it is passively carried. Therefore, when a carried object is dropped, it falls straight down. Even at high speeds (like a plane dropping a bomb) students explained there was no force to move the bomb forward so it would fall straight down.

In another study, 90% of one teacher's high school students (Minstrell, 1982, 1984) explained that a frictionless wheeled cart rolling with a constant velocity across a horizontal, smooth table top must have a constant forward force or push to keep it going. In their motion schema, these students believed that a push produces motion, an idea consistent with Aristotelian physics and McCloskey's findings with college students.

Similar results have been obtained in a number of studies with university students. For example, Clement (1982) used written tests and videotaped problem-solving interviews to detail several characteristics of this "motion implies force" conceptual system in college freshmen. He noted how "deep-seated" and "pervasive" these notions are. In addition, he noted the diversity of situations in which this misconception surfaces. Viennot (1979) showed how highly self-consistent this misconception is and how functional it is in everyday experience: "It is not primitive . . . It represents a worked-out and effective system of thought, despite being in conflict with the yet more worked-out and effective Newtonian scheme. It deals without contradiction with most situations encountered in daily life" (p. 213). Champagne, Klopfer, Solomon, and Cahn (1980) and Leboutet-Barrell (1976) found the same misconceptions in both high school and college students, and Sjberg and Lie (1981) documented identical Aristotelian beliefs among 16- to 19-year-old Norwegian secondary school students. Gilbert and Watts (1983) described a number of other international studies that consistently report similar misconceptions among high school and college students.

DiSessa (1982) extended these findings to younger students. Eight sixth-graders interacted with a microcomputer program, Dynaturtle. Interviews with these students and analysis of their interactions with the Dynaturtle program showed the students held surprisingly robust and consistent Aristotelian notions that objects should go in the direction they are pushed. In addition, there was a surprising degree of commonality in the students' misconceptions. They were also nearly identical to the misconceptions held by older students reported in other studies. Langford and Zollman (1982) also found that elementary students held strong beliefs in the "constant motion requires constant force" misconception. Thus, students believed that unless an object receives constant force, motion is "used up" until some other force, like gravity, takes over.

In sum, although these studies investigating misconceptions about force and motion span students of different ages, aptitudes, and nationalities, they all identify a few commonly shared misconceptions. In exploring student conceptions relevant to other phenomena commonly addressed in the school science curriculum, researchers have found similar patterns of student thinking. Table 4.1 presents in abbreviated form a sampling of studies to indicate the range of these results.

Taken as a whole, this body of research demonstrates that students have "descriptive and explanatory systems" for many scientific concepts that they have developed from their real-world experiences (Champagne et al., 1982). Students do not just make random errors; instead, they rely on consistent, strongly held patterns of thinking based on their everyday experiences. Posner et al., (1982) borrowed Toulmin's (1972) notion of a conceptual ecology to describe a learner's organized set of current concepts. The notion of a conceptual *ecology* to describe students' conceptions is particularly appealing because it emphasizes that students' conceptions, like scientists' conceptions, are organized into interconnected sets of concepts or ideas. This interconnectedness of students' conceptions helps explain why instruction so often fails to help students change their ideas and to help them construct understandings more compatible with scientists' explanations. In the vine metaphor, these student conceptions are just as tightly intertwined as the vine representing disciplinary knowledge. Thus, they are difficult for students to unravel.

Research on the Effects of Traditional
Science Instruction on Students' Misconceptions

In the process of identifying student misconceptions and comparing them to scientific conceptions, researchers began to sense that instruction was failing to promote conceptual change learning. Therefore, researchers began to explore the effects of commonly used instructional strategies on students' misconceptions. How was instruction promoting or constraining

TABLE 4.1
Examples of Studies of Student Misconceptions

Researchers	Nature of Misconceptions	Students
Anderson and Smith, 1983a	light enables us to see by shining on objects and brightening them up	fifth graders
Stead and Osborne, 1980	light from a candle goes further at night	8–11 yr olds
Bell and Osborne, 1981	electric current is used up in a light bulb	8–11 yr olds
Champagne, Klopfer, Solomon, & Cahn, 1980	heavier objects fall faster than lighter objects	beginning college physics students, Australian
Johnson and Wellman, 1982	the brain is for thinking and dreaming and is irrelevant to walking, talking, sneezing, breathing, etc.	fifth graders
Novick and Nussbaum, 1978	matter is continuous (vs. particulate theory of matter)	14 yr old, Israeli
Nussbaum and Novak, 1976	"down" directions at different points on earth are always parallel to each other	fourth–eighth grades, Israeli
Nussbaum and Sharoni-Dagan, 1983		second grade, U.S.
Mali and Howe, 1979	"people can only live on the top of the earth"	cross-age, Nepali
Duncan and Johnstone, 1973	one mole of a compound will always react with one mole of another	14–15 yr olds
Rowell and Dawson, 1977	explain floating and sinking in terms of heavier/lighter (vs. relative density)	ninth grade, Australian

meaningful conceptual change learning? To answer this question, researchers studied instruction from the *students'* points of view, attempting to track students' conceptual change (or lack of change).

From this research comes the unequivocal conclusion that school science learning for most students is not meaningful conceptual change learning (Nussbaum & Novick, 1982b; Champagne et al., 1982). Students memorize facts and formulae, they plug in these facts and formulae to pass tests, and they use these to solve "textbook" problems. However, they do not use these facts and formulae to explain real-world phenomena that they observe and experience. To students, the facts and formulae are school knowledge, perhaps a third vine to add to the Pines and West (1983) metaphor. Students use this vine of knowledge to "get by" in school. However, this vine is unconnected with the disciplinary vine, and it is totally irrelevant to students' everyday ways of thinking— their intuitive knowledge vine. Thus, students end instruction still finding their intuitive theories, or misconceptions, as most useful in explaining their world. Connections between their own understandings and the disciplinary concepts are rarely made.

A number of studies of college level physics instruction support such conclusions. Several researchers documented the surprising robustness of students' misconceptions. Clement (1982) found, for example, that an alarmingly high number of college students passed a one-semester introductory course for engineers and science majors but continued to use intuitive theories and misconceptions to explain phenomena involving pendulums, coin tosses, and rocket paths. In explaining coin toss situations, for example, 88% of the students relied on misconceptions prior to instruction and 75% of the students continued this pattern after the course. Leboutet-Barrell (1976) found a similar persistence of misconceptions about force and motion in both high school and college students. Champagne, Klopfer, Solomon, and Cahn (1980) also studied college students' learning about classical mechanics. They concluded that students distorted observations and interpretations of experiments to make them fit with their prior conceptions.

These studies of the effects of college level instruction have focused on students' pre- and postinstructional conceptions. Other researchers have looked specifically at what goes on during instruction. How does instruction influence students' conceptions?

In one such classroom study Anderson and Smith (1983a, 1983b) conducted naturalistic observations of fifth-grade science teaching. Pre- and posttests and clinical interviews designed to reveal student misconceptions about light and seeing and about photosynthesis were used to trace student learning. After 4-6 weeks of "good" science instruction using a textbook, demonstrations, and discussion, 78% of the students studying about light remained committed to the idea that seeing is unconnected to the reflection of light. In the students' view, light shines on objects and brightens them up so that we can look out and see the object. Although the teachers' unit tests showed that students had successfully memorized definitions for terms like transparent, translucent, and opaque, the students failed to connect those terms with their ways of thinking about light and seeing. When asked to explain everyday situations about light and seeing, they did not talk about reflection of light. They relied instead on their everyday, prior conceptions. These intuitive ideas remained more personally sensible to them in explaining their observations than the scientific explanations they had studied.

Students learning about photosynthesis in a hands-on approach (part of the SCIIS curriculum; Knott et al., 1978) also failed to use instruction to change their prior conceptions in intended ways. They grew plants in the light and the dark and discussed their ideas about why the plants in the dark were dying and how plants get their food. Their teachers presented photosynthesis as a way of explaining the observations. On the posttests, however, students described plants' food and why plants die in the dark in ways that were nearly identical to what they had written on the pretest. At best, students added in plants' making of food to their list of plants' multiple, external sources of food. Only 7% of the students gave up these notions about external food for plants and described photosynthesis as plants' only source of energy-supplying food.

Thus, instruction in both textbook-based classrooms and in inquiry, hands-on classrooms failed to help students change their misconceptions so they could be appropriately intertwined with the disciplinary "vine." Analysis of actual instruction and students' interpretations of instruction revealed important insights into the reasons for this lack of change. In the textbook-centered classrooms, a critical problem was that the students' misconceptions and ideas were largely invisible to both the teachers and the students themselves. Instruction focused students' attention on *scientists'* explanations and terminology. Discussion and test questions focused on repeating scientists' ideas. When students were asked to apply concepts to explain everyday situations (which occurred rarely), the emphasis was on coming up with the "right" answer rather than exploring the nature of students' wrong answers.

In contrast to the textbook-centered classrooms, students' ideas and misconceptions were often the center of discussion in the activity-based classrooms. Students conducted experiments and talked about their observations and their own explanations for the observations. Thus, students had opportunities to explore their own ways of thinking about the phenomena. However, students in these classrooms did not spend much time exploring scientists' explanations. After listening to students' explanations, most of the teachers then presented the concepts about photosynthesis. Teachers assumed that the experimental results would provide powerful evidence to support and make obvious the power of the scientific explanation. They did not spend a lot of time discussing these explanations with students. Students listened attentively to these teacher explanations, but the presentation of concepts about photosynthesis did not cause students to reconstruct their own explanations about food for plants. These explanations did not appear to students to be more sensible than their own. At the end of the unit, students knew that they had studied photosynthesis, but they did not integrate this concept with their personal theories about real-world plants and how they get food.

Osborne and Wittrock (undated) reported similar findings from naturalistic observations done by Tasker (1981). Like Anderson and Smith, the teachers in this study were unaware that their students held misconceptions and that their students developed understandings of experiments and other instructional activities that were quite different from those intended. Students spent most of their time making "executive type decisions" (What do we do now?) and very little time actually thinking about science concepts. Typical assessment practices stressed neatly written laboratory reports and the production of appropriate statements on tests, instead of assessments that searched out how students really think. This kind of assessment encouraged nonmeaningful kinds of "learning."

In order to understand why it is so difficult for students to change their conceptions when presented with scientists' alternative conceptions in science classrooms, it is helpful to keep in mind Posner's notion of the *ecological* nature of students' conceptions. Their ideas are not random bits of wrong information that can be simply exchanged for correct bits. Rather, each student's conceptual ecology represents a complex network of interdependent concepts, attitudes, and goals. For example, Kevin's ideas (shown earlier) that plants take in their food from multiple, external sources depended on his understanding about the nature of living things, about food, about his own eating, and about plants' ability to take in materials from the soil. His conceptual ecology also was influenced by his own self-perceptions (I am a person who understands science; I know a lot about plants). It is not enough to simply *tell* Kevin that minerals are not food for plants. That minerals are food for plants is a *central* idea in Kevin's conceptual ecology. To remove it would threaten the integrity of his whole conceptual ecosystem. It is easier for Kevin to ignore such statements than to risk the confusion that would result from removing it.

It is also difficult for students to make sense of scientists' explanations when these explanations are presented as being remote from students' everyday experiences. Traditional science instruction too often ignores students' ways of explaining the natural world. Instead, explanations are organized in ways that make sense to scientists; they use a technical and abstract language that appears removed from students' experiences. Students study about reflection, transparent, and opaque but do not connect those concepts with their own experiences in seeing objects. They learn about photosynthesis, chlorophyll, and glucose but do not recognize that these concepts have to do with how plants and animals get food.

What conclusions can be drawn from these studies of the failures of instruction to change students' incompatible prior knowledge and to help them develop meaningful conceptual understandings? The most important conclusion is that formal instruction normally does not help students think about the relationships between their everyday notions about scientific phenomena and scientific explanations of the same phenomena. The two "vines" of everyday knowledge and disciplinary knowledge are not brought into contact. As Gunstone and White (1981) concluded from their study of physics instruction; "Students know a lot of physics but do not relate it to the everyday world" (p. 298). To reconcile the differences between their own notions and those presented by the teacher, students either (a) ignore or reject the scientific notion, and cling to their misconceptions, (b) distort the scientific conception to fit their own naive framework, or (c) rotely memorize the new conception without connecting it in any way to their own "real-world" conceptions. Current teaching practice often unintentionally encourages the last of these approaches to "learning" and fails to help students achieve meaningful learning. The next section explores how instruction might be changed in order to promote the development of meaningful conceptual understanding.

INSTRUCTION FOR MEANINGFUL CONCEPTUAL UNDERSTANDING IN SCIENCE: PROMISING DIRECTIONS

Goals of Conceptual Change Instruction: Linking Two Worlds of Knowledge

Science instruction that has meaningful conceptual understanding as its goal must somehow engage students in making connections between disciplinary conceptual knowledge and "real-world" knowledge (Pines & West, 1983). The challenge of instruction, then, is to enable students to intertwine those two vines of knowledge in appropriate ways. Lest the vine metaphor make this sound like an easy task, remember that students' experiential knowledge is organized and sensible to the student— a conceptual ecology. Changing, abandoning, or replacing even one small part of that ecology has effects on every other part of the conceptual ecology and has the potential to cause a total collapse of the "ecosystem," leaving the student in uncomfortable confusion. It is much easier to keep the two vines separate, using one for everyday living and the other for passing science courses, than to risk the double blow of being confused and not passing science tests.

Instruction that supports meaningful conceptual learning must help students recognize and reconcile the differences between two different worlds of thinking. Students need to be helped to rearrange their own ways of organizing concepts and to make new kinds of conceptual connections. Several researchers have proposed models of conceptual change instruction to achieve this goal. Their models share an emphasis on creating conceptual conflict and on engaging students in constructing meaning.

Key Features of Conceptual Change Instruction

Emphasis on Conceptual Conflict. Instruction that fosters conceptual change helps students see the conflicts between their own ways of thinking about a phenomenon and scientific ways of thinking about it. Hewson and Hewson (1984) asserted that without such conceptual conflict, students are inhibited from understanding the accepted view. Once conflict is recognized, the conflict can then be reconciled as the student makes sense of the new concept in light of his or her present knowledge or understanding (Hewson, 1983). Reconciliation, or meaningful conceptual learning, implies that there are now links between the two concepts, that there are no (or at least fewer) contradictions between them, that they are consistent with one another, and that they are parts of the same integrated set of ideas (Hewson, 1983).

Nussbaum and Novick (1982a, 1982b) described the following components in a conceptual change model of instruction:

1. Initial exposure of students' alternative conceptions through their responses to an "exposing event."
2. Sharpening student awareness of their own and other students' alternative conceptions through discussion and debate.
3. Creating conceptual conflict by having students attempt to explain a discrepant event.
4. Encouraging and building cognitive accommodation and the invention of a new conceptual model consistent with the accepted scientific conception.

Hewson (1983) criticized this model because it fails to give explicit help in identifying the conditions that determine whether students will recognize the conflict or not. He proposed that for a student to recognize conflict between two competing conceptions, the following three conditions must be met:

1. Both conceptions must be intelligible to the student.
2. The student must compare the two conceptions and find them to be in conflict.

3. The student must resolve the conflict by accepting the more plausible one and rejecting the other.

These notions have been built into a model of conceptual change proposed by Posner et al. (1982). They have proposed four conditions that must be fulfilled if students are likely to make changes in their central concepts by integrating new concepts with existing knowledge:

1. *There must be dissatisfaction with existing conceptions.* A student must be aware of his/her conceptions and recognize some shortcoming in this personal conception. For example, it may fail to explain adequately a particular event, or it may conflict with explanations given by other students or by scientists.

2. *A new conception has to be intelligible.* The student must know what the new idea means, find it to be internally consistent, and be able to construct a representation of it. This does *not* mean the student has to believe it to be true or related to events in the real world. Teachers generally focus instruction solely on this goal of making new conceptions intelligible.

3. *A new conception has to be initially plausible.* The student must find the new conception to be potentially true and believable, consistent with his or her existing view of the world. That is, the student must be able to reconcile the new conception with his or her own prior conceptions. Using the metaphor of Pines and West, the two sources of knowledge, experiential and disciplinary, must be intertwined. This is a step that traditional science instruction *assumes* will happen if conceptions are made intelligible. The studies of instructional failures, however, provide convincing evidence that students do *not* automatically do this.

4. *A new conception has to be fruitful.* If a student is going to incorporate a new conception into his or her schema at the expense of a very comfortable, long-held conceptual ecology, there has to be a convincing reason. Thus, the new conception has to be shown to be more useful than the old conception. A new conception can be viewed as fruitful if it can solve a previously unsolved problem, if it suggests new ideas, or if it gives better explanatory and predictive power than was previously possible. For example, understanding the bouncing nature of light and that we see because light is reflected to our eyes can be useful in explaining a number of everyday phenomena such as why positioning of the light source is important in photography, why it's hard to see in fog, why people dressing in the dark make color matching mistakes, why the sky looks blue, how mirrors work, and so forth. Students must see that the new concept can be useful in explaining real-world phenomena.

Emphasis on Student Construction of Meaning.   The proposed models of conceptual change science instruction build on constructivist views of learning. Learners are viewed not as passive absorbers of information, but as active interpreters of new information and experiences from the perspective of their existing knowledge, or schema. The development of meaningful understandings requires the learner to use his/her schema to assess and interpret new situations. Driver (1986) described this view of the learning process:

> This constructivist view of learning thus places the learner at the centre of the learning process. What is learnt in any programme of work depends on the prior ideas that students bring, the cognitive strategies they have available and also their own particular interests and purposes. (p. 4)

Therefore, instruction for meaningful learning cannot be a simple matter of pointing out to students the conflicts between their own ideas and scientists' ideas. Telling students their ideas are "wrong" and explaining to them why other explanations are better will not engage students in the process of actively constructing meaning. Researchers exploring conceptual change models of instruction emphasize the need to devise ways to engage students in actively thinking and puzzling about the phenomena they are studying.

Classroom Studies Using Conceptual Change/Constructivist Models of Instruction

Researchers interested in meaningful conceptual learning have begun to explore the usefulness and effectiveness of the proposed conceptual change and constructivist models of instruction. Initial studies in this area explored conceptual change instructional models with small, selected groups of students in special settings.

For example, Champagne, Gunstone, and Klopfer (1983) devised an instructional strategy to promote conceptual change about force and motion and studied the effects of this instruction on two small groups of students: 13 academically gifted middle school students who met once a week for 8 weeks and 6 non-physics major science graduates studying to become high school teachers who met for 5 full days over the course of 4 weeks. Hewson (1983), DiSessa (1982), and White (1984) designed computer programs to address misconceptions about force and motion and studied students' conceptual change as they used the programs. Each of these researchers involved students in a series of activities designed to create conceptual conflict and to help students change their conceptual ecologies to accommodate scientific explanations. Studying the effects of such efforts in settings in which the instructional sequence was carefully designed and controlled enabled researchers to pinpoint the impact of specific instructional strategies on individual student understanding. Such approaches to instructional innovation are valuable because of the detailed knowledge they generate about learning-in-progress.

However, more recent research has begun to explore the possibilities of incorporating conceptual change/constructivist models of instruction in regular classrooms. A number of research teams have devised strategies for enabling regular classroom teachers to implement conceptual change models of instruction (Blakeslee & Anderson, 1987; Brook, 1987; Brook & Driver, 1986; Driver, 1987; Erickson, 1987; Kuhn & Aguirre, 1987; Hesse, 1987; Minstrell, 1984; Nussbaum & Novick, 1982b; Roth, 1984, 1987; Scott, 1987; Sieben, 1987; Smith & Anderson, 1987). Despite different approaches in the implementation of conceptual change teaching strategies, these instructional studies reflect shared commitments to meaningful conceptual change learning as a goal of instruction and to teaching approaches that emphasize conceptual conflict and student construction of meaning. There is also a shared view of the teacher as a "cognitive coach" (Collins, Brown, & Newman, in press) who actively negotiates and guides students' interactions with and interpretations of scientific concepts. All of these studies have also paid careful attention to assessment of student learning and students' conceptual change. These shared features of instruction and assessment stand in contrast with traditional modes of science instruction that emphasize broad content coverage and clear teacher presentations of scientific theories and explanations.

In the following paragraphs, examples of teaching strategies used in these studies illustrate how different teachers incorporated the general notions of conceptual conflict, student construction of meaning, and active teacher guidance into their science instruction. These studies illustrate a rapidly growing area of research and development work, and describe some of the instructional strategies that show promise for promoting meaningful conceptual learning.

Teaching Strategies to Engage Students in Conceptual Conflict. Laboratory activities in science teaching are traditionally selected to illustrate and verify central science concepts or to reproduce key experiments in the history of science that demonstrate how new understandings and explanations of phenomena were developed. Thus, the emphasis is on reproducing or confirming scientists' explanations. Instead of selecting laboratory activities to illustrate *scientists'* central concepts, however, teachers using conceptual change teaching approaches in several studies selected laboratory activities based on their potential to engage students in thinking about the shortcomings of their naive explanations. In this approach, teachers spent significant time eliciting student predictions and student explanations, encouraging debate among students about explanations of the observed outcomes of the experiment, and contrasting students' explanations of phenomena and scientists' explanations. The emphasis was on talking about and analyzing the significance of the experimental work as it related to students' ways of thinking.

The teachers in these studies did not rely only on laboratory demonstrations and experiments for creating conceptual conflict. Such conflict was also achieved by posing critical questions or problems to students. For example, fifth-grade teachers in the Anderson and Smith studies used a set of researcher-prepared overhead transparencies (Anderson & Smith, 1982) to pose everyday situations and problems about light and seeing to students. Each transparency included a diagram and a problem for students to explain (e.g., "Why can't the girl see the car on the other side of the wall?"). After eliciting students' explanations, the teachers used an overlay to the transparency that provided a concise scientific explanation for the situation. The most successful teachers encouraged students to compare their own answers to the scientific explanation and guided students in resolving the discrepancies.

Most of the teachers using conceptual conflict as an instructional strategy frequently encouraged students to debate among themselves. They did not easily cave in to students' desires to be told the "right" answer. Instead, the teachers asked questions to help students clarify their explanations and to develop better support for their thinking.

Student writing often played an important role in creating and resolving conceptual conflict. Ms. Kain, a teacher my colleagues and I worked with over a 3-year period (Roth, 1984), had students, at the beginning of a unit on photosynthesis, write down their own ideas about how plants get food. She later had students refer back to their written statements during discussions as the unit progressed, challenging them to think about how their ideas were changing. At the end of the unit, students looked at those statements again and were asked to rewrite their ideas, pointing out ways in which their initial ideas were incomplete, inaccurate, or in conflict with scientific explanations.

Teachers on Erickson's research team also used writing to promote identification and resolution of conceptual conflicts. In Kuhn's classroom (Kuhn & Aguirre, 1987), for example, traditional laboratory reports, with their focus on correct form and the "right" results, were replaced by a more informal journal writing approach. Students were encouraged to write about their own thinking and issues or concepts that were puzzling them. Thus, they were encouraged to identify and write about their confusions and conceptual conflicts.

Teaching Strategies to Promote Student Construction of Meaning.
The creation of conceptual conflict is certainly one approach to engaging
students in actively making sense of scientific concepts, and the teachers
in these studies frequently centered instruction around such conflicts.
However, these teachers also used other strategies to engage students in
actively working through scientific conceptions and making personal
sense of them ("constructing" knowledge).

For example, teachers used a variety of strategies to get students to
construct new links among concepts. One of the teachers in Erickson's
group, Sieben (1987), used the construction and reconstruction of concept maps as a central part of student activity in his classroom. Card sorts
represented another strategy for engaging students in arranging and
rearranging their emerging ideas. One of the middle school teachers
involved in the Smith and Anderson (1987) and Roth (1987) studies also
used card sorts to help students construct meaning. She had students use
cards containing words (food, oxygen, minerals, etc.) and pictures (ar-
rows, the sun, etc.) to construct word-picture "stories" about plants' food
on their desks. The students then talked in pairs, each student explaining his/her "story" and card arrangement to a partner. At the end of the
class period, students were encouraged to make changes in their "stories" and were then required to write down their current explanation.
This activity was repeated twice during the unit on photosynthesis.

Teachers in Driver's group (1987) had students work in small groups
to construct posters illustrating central concepts and the relationships
among them. The posters were then displayed so students could compare how different groups had organized the concepts.

Student writing was used by many of the teachers as a critical way to
involve students in constructing meaning. In our own studies, teachers
have had students write down their own predictions and explanations.
Later, the students looked back at these explanations and tried to use
new scientific concepts to improve/change their explanations. Teachers
in our studies also had students write out answers to a series of application questions toward the end of a unit. Because the questions were
structured to elicit student thinking (not just "right" answers) and because each student constructed an answer ahead of time, a debate-style
discussion of the questions was fostered rather than a "What's the right
answer?" approach.

Classroom discussions replaced teacher lecture as the dominant activity in these classrooms. Both the nature of the questions asked and the
teachers' ways of responding to students supported student construction
of meaning rather than teacher telling of meaning. In traditional science
classes that I have observed, teachers frequently use questions as a way of
involving students in a lecture. Basically, the *teacher* is constructing a

scientific explanation, or "story," and fill-in-the-blank types of questions are asked along the way to make sure students are paying attention and following the story. When students answer these questions, teachers are listening for the correct answer so the story can continue to be developed. "Wrong" answers are disruptive to the class, because they threaten the story line. Teachers pass over them quickly, looking for the correct answer that will enable the story to continue.

In contrast, teachers in these studies tried to elicit *students'* stories and to challenge and push students to clarify, defend, and change their stories based on available evidence and information. Teachers in our own studies, for example, were much more likely to probe student answers for clarification and elaboration, to challenge students to think about experimental evidence, and to push students to recognize gaps and weaknesses in their own explanations. They would ask the tough questions: "Does your explanation tell us *why* the plants died in the dark?" "Compare your answer to Ben's. How are they different?" "Which explanation is better? Why?" Thus, teachers used discussions to guide student thinking and to help them construct meaningful understandings rather than to quiz them on their mastery of scientific facts and definitions.

Impact of Conceptual Change/Constructivist Teaching Approaches on Student Learning

What about student learning in these classrooms? Are students developing meaningful conceptual understandings in these classrooms? In the projects I have been involved with, teachers have been successful in helping students change their misconceptions and develop meaningful understandings of how light enables seeing (fifth graders) (Roth, Anderson, & Smith, 1987) and how plants make their own food (fifth and seventh graders) (Roth, 1984, 1986). For example, when four teachers used their traditional science teaching strategies, only 23% of their fifth grade students understood that we see when reflected light travels to our eyes. However, these same teachers had 86% of their students develop a meaningful understanding of these concepts in the second year of the study when they used the researcher-developed overhead transparency sets to change the nature of classroom discourse (Anderson & Smith, 1983b). Meaningfulness was assessed by asking a number of application questions and analyzing students' consistency in *using* the science concepts to explain novel situations. We have had less success, however, in efforts to promote conceptual change on other topics (cell respiration, matter cycling in ecosystems, color vision).

A number of other researchers have also reported impressive evidence of meaningful conceptual change learning (Champagne et al.,

1982; Minstrell, 1984; Nussbaum & Novick, 1982b) as well as difficulties in achieving the desired student outcomes. In other cases, the research is not yet complete (Driver, 1987).

Clearly this is an area where more research is needed. Additional examples of successful teaching for conceptual change in regular classrooms need to be documented and analyzed. In addition, better understandings of cases where attempts at conceptual change instruction "go wrong" are needed and can be valuable in revising instructional strategies. Such an approach to instructional change was critical in Minstrell's eventual success in teaching about force and motion and in the successes my colleagues and I have had with the teaching of photosynthesis (Smith & Lott, 1983). In one of our studies, an analysis of middle school teachers' failures and successes in implementing conceptual change teaching strategies revealed that critical knowledge of the subject matter, of the learners, and of conceptual change learning theories are necessary for teachers to use recommended teaching strategies effectively (Roth, 1987). This analysis provided important insights into the complexities of conceptual change teaching and suggested that teachers' effective adoption of these strategies will often require a process of conceptual change for the teachers themselves. Understanding where instruction went wrong enabled us to define more clearly what teachers need to know in order to become effective conceptual change teachers. Continued analysis of both successful and less than successful instruction are needed to help us improve and refine conceptual change models of instruction.

It will also be important to study teaching and learning in classrooms where the teacher is not implementing conceptual change teaching strategies for the first time. In most of the studies reviewed here, student learning was assessed in classrooms where teachers were attempting to make critical and difficult changes in their teaching. Lack of dramatic learning improvements in some of these classrooms should not be used as conclusive evidence of the ineffectiveness of the teaching strategies themselves.

Research also needs to identify better ways of assessing learning outcomes. Strategies that can be used in classroom settings to capture the richness of students' conceptual ecologies would enable us to better understand the impact of specific instructional approaches. In addition, it is critical that we begin to assess a fuller range of learning outcomes. Both Driver (1987) and Smith (1987) emphasized at the Second International Conference on Misconceptions and Educational Strategies in Science and Mathematics the need to look beyond *conceptual* change towards other kinds of changes in student learning and thinking. For example, Driver is studying the frequency of student-generated questions and the frequency of female participation in conceptual change classrooms compared with traditional classrooms. She is finding that students in the conceptual change classrooms are much more likely to ask questions and to describe things that are confusing or puzzling to them. Such learning outcomes are important for us to understand.

SUMMARY AND CONCLUSIONS

I: How does this plant get its food?

Evalina: The way it gets its food is from sun, air, and water. But they told me water is *not* food for plant and neither is soil. The sun helps the plant *make* its food. It helps make it in the leaves.

Kevin: Whew, from *lots* of places. From the soil for one, for the minerals and water, and from the air for oxygen. The sunlight for sun and it would change chemicals to sugars. It sort of makes its own food and gets its food from the ground and from air.

I: What would happen if I covered this plant with a box so that only one leaf could get light?

Evalina: I think that the one that's under the box, it would start to die because it needs some light down on it to help it make food. And the one that's probably out in the light, it would probably help feed the plant that's under the box, because if the food is going down the stem like that, it probably would extend to some of the other leaves. But if it didn't, then those under the box, they probably wouldn't live that long, and the one's that out, it would.

Kevin: I imagine it would still keep growing. But, I think it could still only survive off of one leaf, but I doubt it. I don't think so.

Both Kevin and Evalina were students in one of my studies (Roth, 1986) who began instruction holding misconceptions that plants, like people, have multiple external sources of food (including water, fertilizer, etc.). Neither student mentioned on a pretest that plants can get their food by making it themselves out of raw materials taken in from the environment. Neither student distinguished between energy-containing foods and other kinds of nutrients. After taking the pretest, Evalina and Kevin each read a different textbook chapter about photosynthesis. At the end of 3 days of reading, both students could define photosynthesis. However, as the aforementioned quotes suggest, Evalina developed a more meaningful understanding of this concept than Kevin.

Evalina was able to intertwine appropriately the notion of photosynthesis with her everyday knowledge about plants. In the study she read an experimental text (Roth, 1985) that engaged her in puzzling about whether or not the water that her mother "feeds" plants should be considered food. Thus, she struggled to link discipline-based ideas about definitions of food with her own everyday knowledge about plants and food. When she finished reading this text, Evalina had restructured her conceptual ecology about food for plants and incorporated ideas about photosynthesis into that ecology. Her restructuring was a meaningful one as evidenced by her use of photosynthesis concepts to make predictions about the box-over-the-plant question. Kevin, in contrast, did not undergo such conceptual change. After reading a traditional textbook chapter about photosynthesis, he developed an accurate definition of photosynthesis. But he did not use that concept to change his own ways of thinking about food for plants. The two vines of knowledge, his own experiential knowledge (plants take in food from the soil) and the disciplinary knowledge (plants make food), existed side by side but were not appropriately intertwined. When asked about everyday situations involving real-world plants, Kevin used his experiential knowledge vine to come up with predictions and explanations. For example, the disciplinary concept about plants making food was not relevant or useful to him in explaining the question about the box-over-the-plant stated earlier.

I end this chapter by describing the contrasts in the learning of these two students for three reasons. First, the examples bring to life important themes of the line of research on meaningful conceptual learning in science reviewed in this chapter. The cases illustrate, for example, that meaningful conceptual understanding involves the development of rich, conceptual networks that the learner can use to explain and better understand new situations. For such conceptual networks to be meaningful they must be constructed by learners and they must represent an intertwining of students' experiential, "real-world" knowledge with disciplinary knowledge. Kevin ended instruction with two vines of knowledge to choose from in explaining new situations about plants and food. he consistently chose his everyday knowledge vine in answering application questions, and the definition-of-photosynthesis vine was not of much help to him. Evalina, on the other hand, struggled to meaningfully intertwine the two vines of knowledge. Her success in changing her conceptual networks and reorganizing her schema for food for plants was reflected in her ability to draw from this newly organized conceptual ecology to explain new situations in meaningful ways.

Secondly, the cases of Evalina and Kevin suggest that science instruction can be improved so that most students (not just the top 10%) can develop some meaningful conceptual understandings in science classrooms. Although Kevin and Evalina were both seventh graders, Kevin excelled in school and read at the twelfth-grade level whereas Evalina read at the fifth-grade level and frequently experienced difficulties in school. Yet with the help of a text (Roth, 1985) that carefully scaffolded her experiences and encouraged her to make links between her everyday thinking and the disciplinary concepts, Evalina achieved meaningful conceptual change. Kevin's text (Blecha, Gega, & Green, 1979), however, did not provide such support, and despite his intelligence and high interest and confidence in science class, Kevin was unsuccessful in making such links on his own. These cases and the instructional studies reviewed in this chapter suggest that we can do much better in helping average students, like Evalina, develop meaningful conceptual understandings in science.

The third point is that although teaching for conceptual understanding is possible, it will not be easy to change traditional teaching practice. Fundamental changes in the school science curriculum, science curriculum materials, and science teacher education are needed. These will take time to achieve. For example, the text that was so helpful to Evalina was written only after extensive research had been done on students' difficulties in learning about photosynthesis and food for plants. It took patient study to understand the students' conceptions and the impact of instruction on those conceptions. This knowledge was necessary in writing the successful conceptual change text chapter. It will take time and continued research on student conceptions and on the effectiveness of conceptual change teaching strategies to develop the knowledge needed to write curriculum materials that will significantly improve students' conceptual understanding.

Similarly, teachers cannot be expected to adopt conceptual change teaching strategies overnight. Teachers will need to go through their own conceptual change in order to use conceptual change teaching strategies effectively. Understandings of the theoretical underpinnings of the teaching strategies are necessary for successful use of conceptual change models of instruction. Such understandings of the learner, of conceptual change learning theory, and of the subject matter itself will take time and carefully planned educational experiences for teachers to develop. Thus, much further research is needed. We need careful studies of instructional strategies that promote student conceptual change. There is also a need for studies of teacher change and effective strategies for enabling teachers to teach for meaningful conceptual understanding.

REFERENCES

Anderson, C. W., & Smith, E. L. (1982). *Transparencies on light: Teacher's manual* (Research Series No. 130). East Lansing, MI: Institute for Research on Teaching, Michigan State University.

Anderson, C. W., & Smith, E. L. (1983a, April). *Children's conceptions of light and color: Developing the concept of unseen rays.* Paper presented at the annual meeting of the American Educational Research Association, Montreal, Canada.

Anderson, C. W., & Smith, E. L. (1983b, April). *Teacher behavior associated with conceptual learning in science.* Paper presented at the annual meeting of the American Educational Research Association, Montreal, Canada.

Anderson, C. W., & Smith, E. L. (1984). Children's preconceptions and content area textbooks. In G. Duffy, L. Roehler, & J. Mason (Eds.), *Comprehension instruction: Perspectives and suggestions* (pp. 187–201). New York: Longman.

Anderson, C. W., & Smith, E. L. (1987). Teaching science. In V. Richardson-Koehler (Ed.), *Educators' handbook: A research perspective* (pp. 84–111). New York: Longman.

Anderson, R. C., Reynolds, R. E., Schallert, D. L., & Goetz, E. T. (1977). Frameworks for comprehending discourse. *American Educational Research Journal, 14* (4), 367–381.

Anderson, R. C., Spiro, R. J., & Anderson, M. C. (1978). Schemata as scaffolding for the representation of information in connected discourse. *American Educational Research Journal, 15*(3), 433–440.

Applebee, A. N., Langer, J. A., & Mullis, V. S. (1986). *The writing report card: Writing achievement in American schools.* Princeton, NJ: National Assessment of Educational Progress at Educational Testing Service.

Armento, B. J. (1986). Research on teaching social studies. In M. C. Wittrock (Ed.), *Handbook of research on teaching* (3rd ed., pp. 942–951). New York: Macmillan.

Bell, B. F., & Osborne, R. J. (1981). *Interviewing children.* Hamilton, New Zealand: S.E.R.U., University of Waikato.

Biological Sciences Curriculum Study. (1968a). *Biological science: Molecules to man.* Boston, MA: Houghton Mifflin.

Biological Sciences Curriculum Study. (1968b). *High school biology, Green version.* Boston, MA: Houghton Mifflin.

Blakeslee, T., & Anderson, C. W. (1987, April). *Teaching strategies associated with conceptual change in science learning.* Paper presented at the annual meeting of the American Educational Research Association, Washington, DC.

Blecha, M. K., Gega, P. C., & Green, M. (1979). *Exploring science: Green book* (2nd edition). River Forest, IL: Laidlaw Brothers.

Bransford, J. D., & Franks, J. J. (1976). Toward a framework for understanding learning. In G. H. Bower (Ed.), *The psychology of learning and motivation: Advances in research and theory* (Vol. 10). New York: Academic Press.

Brook, A. (1987). Designing experiences to take account of the development of children's ideas: An example from the teaching and learning of energy. In J. D. Novak (Ed.), *Proceedings of the second international seminar on misconceptions and educational strategies in science and mathematics,* Vol. 2 (pp. 49–64). Ithaca, NY: Cornell University.

Brook, A., & Driver, R. (1986). *The construction of meaning and conceptual change in classroom settings: Case study on energy.* Leeds, England: Centre for Studies in Science and Mathematics Education, Children's Learning in Science Project.

Carey, S. (1986). Cognitive science and science education. *American Psychologist, 41,* 1123–1130.

Champagne, A. B., Gunstone, R. F., & Klopfer, L. E. (1983, April). *Effecting changes in cognitive structure among physics students.* Paper presented at symposium on Stability and Change in Conceptual Understanding at the annual meeting of American Educational Research Association, Montreal, Canada.

Champagne, A. B., Gunstone, R. F., & Klopfer, L. E. (1985). Effecting changes in cognitive structures among physics students. In L. H. T. West & A. L. Pines (Eds.), *Cognitive structure and conceptual change* (pp. 163–186). New York: Academic Press.

Champagne, A. B., & Klopfer, L. E. (1977). A sixty-year perspective on three issues in science education: I. Whose ideas are dominant? II. Representation of women. III. Reflective thinking and problem solving. *Science Education, 61*, 431–452.

Champagne, A. B., & Klopfer, L. E. (1984). Research in science education: The cognitive psychology perspective. Reprinted from D. Holdzom & P. B. Lutz (Eds.), *Research within reach: Science education* (pp. 171–189). Charleston, WV: Appalachia Educational Laboratory, Research and Development Interpretation Science.

Champagne, A. B., Klopfer, L. E., & Anderson, J. H. (1980). Factors influencing the learning of classical mechanics. *American Journal of Physics, 48*, 1074–1079.

Champagne, A. B., Klopfer, L. E., & Gunstone, R. F. (1982). Cognitive research and the design of science instruction. *Educational Psychologist, 17*, 13–53.

Champagne, A. B., Klopfer, L. E., Solomon, C. A., & Cahn, A. D. (1980). *Interactions of students' knowledge with their comprehension and design of science experiments* (LRDC Publication 1980/9). Pittsburgh: University of Pittsburgh, Learning Research and Development Center.

Clement, J. (1979). Mapping a student's causal conceptions from a problem-solving protocol. In J. Lochhead & J. Clement (Eds.), *Cognitive process instruction* (pp. 133–146). Philadelphia: Franklin Institute Press.

Clement, J. (1982). Students' preconceptions in introductory mechanics. *American Journal of Physics, 50*(1), 66–71.

Collins, A., Brown, J. S., & Newman, S. E. (in press). Cognitive apprenticeship: Teaching the craft of reading, writing, and mathematics. In L. B. Resnick (Ed.), *Learning & teaching: Essays in honor of Robert Glaser*. Hillsdale, NJ: Lawrence Erlbaum Associates.

Committee on Research in Mathematics, Science, and Technology Education, Commission on Behavioral and Social Sciences Education, National Research Council. (1985) *Mathematics, science, and technology education: A research agenda*. Washington, DC: National Academy Press.

Davis, R. B. (1981). The postulation of certain specific, explicit commonly shared frames. *Journal of Mathematical Behavior, 3*(1), 167–199.

DiSessa, A. A. (1982). On learning Aristotelian physics: A study of knowledge-based learning. *Cognitive Science, 6*, 37–75.

Driver, R. (1986, August). *Restructuring the physics curriculum: Some implications of studies on learning for curriculum development*. Invited paper presented at the International Conference on Trends in Physics Education, Tokyo, Japan.

Driver, R. (1987). Promoting conceptual change in classroom settings: The experience of the Children's Learning in Science Project. In J. D. Novak (Ed.), *Proceedings of the second international seminar on misconceptions and educational strategies in science and mathematics,* Vol. 2 (pp. 97–107). Ithaca, NY: Cornell University.

Driver, R., & Easley, J. (1978). Pupils and paradigms: A review of literature related to concept development in adolescent science students. *Studies in Science Education, 5,* 61–84.

Duncan, I. M., & Johnstone, A. H. (1973). The mole concept. *Education in Chemistry, 10,* 213–214.

Erickson, G. L. (1979). Children's conceptions of heat and temperature. *Science Education, 63*(2), 221–230.

Erickson, G. (1987, April). *Constructivist epistemology and the professional development of teachers.* Paper presented at the annual meeting of the American Educational Research Association, Washington, D.C.

Fey, J. T. (1979). Mathematics teaching today: Perspectives from three national surveys for the elementary grades. In National Science Foundation, Office of Program Integration, Directorate of Science Education, *What are the needs in precollege science, mathematics, and social science education: Views from the field* (pp. 33–41). Washington.

Gilbert, J. K., Osborne, R. J., & Fensham, P. J. (1982). Children's science and its consequences for teaching. *Science Education, 66*(4), 623–633.

Gilbert, J. K., & Watts, D. M. (1983). Concepts, misconceptions, and alternative conceptions: Changing perspectives in science education. *Studies in Science Education, 10,* 61–98.

Gunstone, F. G., & White, R. T. (1981). Understanding of gravity. *Science Education, 65*(3), 291–299.

Helm, H. (1980). Misconceptions in physics amongst South African students. *Physics Education, 15,* 92–105.

Helm, H., & Novak, J. D. (1983). *Proceedings of the international seminar on misconceptions in science and mathematics.* Ithaca, NY: Cornell University.

Hesse, J. J. (1987). The costs and benefits of using conceptual change teaching methods: A teacher's perspective. In J. D. Novak (Ed.), *Proceedings of the second international seminar on misconceptions and educational strategies in science and mathematics,* Vol. 2 (pp. 194–209). Ithaca, NY: Cornell University.

Hewson, P. W. (1983, April). *Microcomputers and conceptual change: The use of a microcomputer program to diagnose and remediate alternative conception of speed.* Paper presented at the annual meeting of the American Educational Research Association, Montreal, Canada.

Hewson, P. W., & Hewson, M. G. (1984). The role of conceptual conflict in conceptual change and the design of science instruction. *Instructional Science, 13,* 1–13.

Hiebert, J. (1984). Children's mathematics learning: The struggle to link form and understanding. *Elementary School Journal, 84*(5), 497–513.

Hiebert, J. (1986). *Conceptual and procedural knowledge: The case of mathematics.* Hillsdale, NJ: Lawrence Erlbaum Associates.

Johansson, B., Marton, F., & Svensson, L. (1985). An approach to describing learning as change between qualitatively different conceptions. In L. H. T. West & A. L. Pines (Eds.), *Cognitive structure and conceptual change* (pp. 233–257). New York: Academic Press.

Johnson, C. N., & Wellman, H. M. (1982). Children's developing conceptions of the mind and the brain. *Child Development, 53,* 222–234.

Kintsch, W. (1974). *The representation of meaning in memory.* Hillsdale, NJ: Lawrence Erlbaum Associates.

Knott, R., Lawson, C., Karplus, R., Their, H., & Montgomery, M. (1978). *SCIIS communities teacher's guide.* Chicago: Rand McNally.

Kuhn, K., & Aguirre, J. (1987). A case study—on the "journal method"—A method designed to enable the implementation of constructivist teaching in the classroom. In J. D. Novak (Ed.), *Proceedings of the second international seminar on misconceptions and educational strategies in science and mathematics,* Vol. 2 (pp. 262–274). Ithaca, NY: Cornell University

Langford, J. M., & Zollman, D. (1982). *Conceptions of dynamics held by elementary and high school students.* Paper presented at the annual meeting of the American Association of Physics Teachers, San Francisco.

Leboutet-Barrell, L. (1976). Concepts of mechanics in young people. *Physics Education, 11*(7), 462–466.

Mali, G. B., & Howe, A. (1979). Development of earth and gravity concepts among Nepali children. *Science Education, 63*(5), 685–691.

Mayer, R. E. (1983). What have we learned about increasing the meaningfulness of science prose? *Science Education, 67*(2), 223–237.

McCloskey, M. (1983). Intuitive physics. *Scientific American, 248*(4), 122–130.

McKnight, C. C., Crosswhite, F. J., Dossey, J. A., Kifer, E., Swafford, J. O., Travers, K. J., & Cooney, T. J. (1987). *The underachieving curriculum: Assessing U.S. school mathematics from an international perspective.* Champagne, IL: Stipes.

Minsky, M. (1975). A framework for representing knowledge. In P. Winston (Ed.), *The psychology of computer vision.* New York: McGraw Hill.

Minstrell, J. (1982). Conceptual development research in the natural setting of the classroom. In M. Rowe (Ed.), *Education in the 80's: Science.* Washington, DC: National Educational Association.

Minstrell, J. (1984). Teaching for the understanding of ideas: Forces on moving objects. In C. W. Anderson (Ed.), *Observing science classrooms: Perspectives from research and practice* (pp. 55–73). 1984 Yearbook of the Association for the Education of Teachers in Science. Columbus, OH: ERIC Center for Science, Mathematics, and Environmental Education.

National Academy of Sciences. (1982). *Science and mathematics in the schools: Report of a convocation.* Washington, DC: Author.

National Assessment of Educational Progress. (1978). *Science achievement in the schools: A summary of results from the 1976–77 National Assessment of Science.* Denver: Education Commission of the States.

National Assessment of Educational Progress. (1979a). *Three assessments of science 1969–77: Technical summary* (pp. 11–14). Washington, DC: National Center for Educational Statistics.

National Assessment of Educational Progress. (1979b). *Mathematical knowledge and skills* (NAER Report No. 09-MA-02). Washington, DC: U.S. Government Printing Office.

National Assessment of Educational Progress. (1979c). *Mathematical applications* (NAER Report No. 09-MA-03). Washington, DC: U.S. Government Printing Office.

National Assessment of Educational Progress. (1979d). *Mathematical understanding* (NAER Report No. 09-MA-04). Washington, DC: U.S. Printing Office.

National Assessment of Educational Progress. (1983). *Reading, science, and mathematics trends: A closer look.* Denver: Education Commission of the States.

National Council of Teachers of Mathematics. (1980). *An agenda for action: Recommendations for school mathematics of the 1980's.* Reston, VA: Author.

National Research Council. (1979). *The state of school science.* Washington, DC: National Research Council.

National Research Council. (1985). *Mathematics, science, and technology education: A research agenda.* Washington, DC: National Academy Press.

National Science Foundation. (1983). *A revised and intensified science and technology curriculum for grades K–12 urgently needed for our future: Recommendation of conference on goals for science and technology education, K–12* (Report to the NSB Commission on Precollege Education in Mathematics, Science, and Technology). Washington, DC: Author.

Novick, S., & Nussbaum, J. (1978). Junior high school pupils' understanding of the particulate nature of matter: An interview study. *Science Education, 62,* 273–282.

Nussbaum, J., & Novak, J. (1976). An assessment of children's concepts of the earth using structured interviews. *Science Education, 60*(4), 535–550.

Nussbaum, J., & Novick, S. (1982a). Alternative frameworks, conceptual conflict and accommodation: Toward a principled teaching strategy. *Instructional Science, 11*(3), 183–200.

Nussbaum, J., & Novick, S. (1982b, April). *A study of conceptual change in the classroom.* Paper presented at the annual meeting of the National Association for Research in Science Teaching, Lake Geneva, IL.

Nussbaum, J., & Sharoni-Dagan, N. (1983). Changes in second grade children's preconceptions about the Earth as a cosmic body resulting from a short series of audio-tutorial lessons. *Science Education, 67*(1), 99–114.

Osborne, R. J., & Wittrock, M. C. (undated). *Learning science: A generative process.* An unpublished paper from Graduate School of Education, U.C.L.A., Los Angeles.

Piaget, J. (1929). *The child's conception of the world.* London: Routledge and Kegan Paul.

Pines, A. L. (1985). Toward a taxonomy of conceptual relations and the implications for the evaluation of cognitive structures. In L. H. T. West & A. L. Pines (Eds.), *Cognitive structures and conceptual change* (pp. 101–115). New York: Academic Press.

Pines, A. L., & West, L. (1983). A framework for conceptual change with special reference to misconceptions. In H. Helm & J. D. Novak (Eds.), *Proceedings of the international seminar on misconceptions in science and mathematics* (pp. 47–52). Ithaca, NY: Cornell University.

Posner, G. J., Strike, K. A., Hewson, P. W., & Gertzog, W. A. (1982). Accommodation of a scientific conception: Toward a theory of conceptual change. *Science Education, 66*(2), 211–227.

Reif, F. (1985). Acquiring an effective understanding of scientific concepts. In L. H. T. West & A. L. Pines (Eds.), *Cognitive structures and conceptual change* (pp. 133–150). New York: Academic Press.

Resnick, L. B. (1983). Mathematics and science learning: A new conception. *Science, 220*, 477–478.

Romberg, T. A., & Carpenter, T. P. (1986). Research on teaching and learning mathematics: Two disciplines of scientific inquiry. In M. C. Wittrock (Ed.), *Handbook of research on teaching* (3rd ed., pp. 850–873). New York: Macmillan.

Roth, K. J. (1984). Using classroom observations to improve science teaching and curriculum materials. In C. W. Anderson (Ed.), *Observing science classrooms: Perspectives from research and practice* (1984 yearbook of the Association for the Education of Teachers in Science). Columbus, OH: ERIC Center for Science, Mathematics, and Environmental Education.

Roth, K. J. (1985). *Food for plants: Teacher's guide*. (Research Series No. 153). East Lansing, MI: Michigan State University, Institute for Research on Teaching.

Roth, K. J. (1986). *Conceptual-change learning and student processing of science texts* (Research Series No. 167). East Lansing, MI: Institute for Research on Teaching, Michigan State University.

Roth, K. J. (1987, April). *Helping science teachers change: The critical role of teachers' knowledge about science and science learning*. Paper presented at the annual meeting of the American Educational Research Association, Washington, DC.

Roth, K. J., Anderson, C. W., & Smith, E. L. (1987). Curriculum materials, teacher talk, and student learning: Case studies in fifth-grade science teaching. *Journal of Curriculum Studies, 19*(6), 527–548.

Roth, K. J., Smith, E. L., & Anderson, C. W. (1983, April). *Students' conceptions of photosynthesis and food for plants*. Paper presented at the annual meeting of the American Educational Research Association, Montreal, Canada.

Rowell, J. A., & Dawson, C. J. (1977). Teaching about floating and sinking: An attempt to link cognitive psychology with classroom practice. *Science Education, 61*(2), 245–253.

Rowell, J. A., & Dawson, C. J. (1980). Mountain or mole hill: Can cognitive psychology reduce the dimensions of conceptual problems in classroom practice? *Science Education, 64*(5), 693–708.

Rumelhart, D. E. (1980). Schemata: Building blocks of cognition. In R. J. Spiro, B. C. Bruce, & W. F. Brewer (Eds.), *Theoretical issues in reading comprehension* (pp. 33–58). Hillsdale, NJ: Lawrence Erlbaum Associates.

Rumelhart, D. W., & Ortony, A. (1977). The representation of knowledge in memory. In R. C. Anderson, R. J. Spiro, & W. E. Montague (Eds.), *Schooling and the acquisition of knowledge* (pp. 99–136). Hillsdale, NJ: Lawrence Erlbaum Associates.

Schank, R. C., & Abelson, R. P. (1977). *Scripts, plans, goals, and understanding*. Hillsdale, NJ: Lawrence Erlbaum Associates.

Scott, P. (1987). The process of conceptual change in science: A case study of the development of a secondary pupil's ideas relating to matter. In J. D. Novak (Ed.), *Proceedings of the second international seminar on misconceptions and educational strategies in science and mathematics*, Vol. 2 (pp. 404–419). Ithaca, NY: Cornell University.

Sieben, G. (1987). Introducing concept mapping in the day to day science curriculum. In J. D. Novak (Ed.), *Proceedings of the second international seminar on misconceptions and educational strategies in science and mathematics* (pp. 436–446). Ithaca, NY: Cornell University.

Sjberg, S., & Lie, S. (1981). *Ideas about force and movement among Norwegian pupils and students.* University of Oslo: Report 81-11, Institute of Physics Report Series.

Smith, E. L. (1987). What besides conceptions needs to change in conceptual change learning? In J. D. Novak (Ed.), *Proceedings of the second international seminar on misconceptions and educational strategies in science and mathematics,* Vol. 1 (pp. 424–433). Ithaca, NY: Cornell University.

Smith, E. L., & Anderson, C. W. (1987, April). *The effects of training and use of specially designed curriculum materials on conceptual change teaching and learning.* Paper presented at the annual meeting of the National Association for Research in Science Teaching, Washington, DC.

Smith, E. L., & Lott, G. W. (1983). Teaching for conceptual change: Some ways of going wrong. In H. Helm and J. Novak (Eds.), *Proceedings of the international seminar on misconceptions in science and mathematics* (pp. 57–66). Ithaca, NY: Cornell University.

Smith, F. (1975). *Comprehension and learning: A conceptual framework for teachers.* New York: Holt, Rinehart & Winston.

Solomon, J. (1983). Thinking in two worlds of knowledge. In H. Helm & J. Novak (Eds.), *Proceedings of the international seminar on misconceptions in science and mathematics* (pp. 127–137). Ithaca, NY: Cornell University.

Stead, B. F., & Osborne, R. J. (1980). Exploring students' concepts of light. Australian Science Teachers Journal, 26(3), 84–90.

Tasker, R. (1981). Children's views and classroom experiences. *Australian Science Teachers Journal, 27*(3), 33–37.

Thorndyke, P. W., & Hayes-Roth, B. (1979). The use of schemata in the acquisition and transfer of knowledge. *Cognitive Psychology, 11*(1), 82–106.

Toulmin, S. (1972). *Human understanding.* Princeton, NJ: Princeton University Press.

Travers, K. J., & McKnight, C. C. (1985). Mathematics achievement in U.S. schools: Preliminary findings from the second IEA mathematics study. *Phi Delta Kappan, 66,* 407–413.

Viennot, L. (1979). Spontaneous reasoning in elementary dynamics. *European Journal of Science Education, 1,* 205–222.

West, L. H. T., Fensham, P. J., & Garrard, J. E. (1985). Describing the cognitive structures of learners following instruction in chemistry. In L. H. T. West & A. L. Pines (Eds.), *Cognitive structure and conceptual change* (pp. 29–50). New York: Academic Press.

White, B. Y. (1984). Designing computer games to help physics students understand Newton's laws of motion. *Cognition and Instruction, 1*(1), 69–108.

Reasoning about Communication and Communicative Skill

Susan L. Kline
University of Washington

Jesse G. Delia
University of Illinois

Although many situations can be seen straightforwardly as calling for one responsive action or another, situations are, in fact, open to multiple responses. Consider the case in which a student leader of a class group is confronted with a classmate who has failed to complete his assigned task. Should the classmate be reprimanded? Should the classmate's understanding of his actions be addressed? How can the classmate's need for self-esteem be acknowledged and affirmed? Considering the complexity and ambiguity of the situation it is not surprising that we have found student responses to range from "You're really irresponsible. Do it over!" to "What's the problem? Can I help? I know you want a good grade on this, too."

The goal of this chapter is to provide a basis for understanding the development of such individual differences in oral communication. We approach this task through a theoretical orientation that places emphasis on the individual's implicit theory of reasoning about communication as a foundation for developing functional communicative skill. In the first part of the chapter we discuss our theoretical perspective on individual differences in the development of communication skills and the foundational developments in person-centered forms of communication. In the second part of the chapter we discuss some discourse practices that promote the development of rhetorical reasoning and person-centered forms of communication. We conclude with a note on teaching oral communication skills in the classroom.

INDIVIDUAL AND DEVELOPMENTAL DIFFERENCES
IN PERSON-CENTERED COMMUNICATION

In this section we outline our conceptualization of oral communication skills and their development. We should note at the outset that we do not see a fundamental divergence in the skills underlying effective communication across various media. There are, of course, distinct skills associated with any particular medium. However, there appear to be important similarities across media in the most fundamental skills (see O'Keefe & Delia, in press). What are these fundamental communicative skills? Although we believe that communication skill involves many components, we believe that coming to control communication means especially acquiring substantial knowledge of discourse, developing interpretive processes for assessing communicative contexts, developing behavioral resources for producing messages, and elaborating a rhetorical system of reasoning about communication.

To become a skilled communicator, one must possess relatively detailed knowledge of the activities that can be accomplished in discourse, and the discourse forms that can bring about particular effects. Oral discourse can assume a variety of purposes, including influencing, informing, and comforting others, resolving interpersonal conflicts, and reaching consensus through discussion. Skilled communicators must be able to differentiate the purposes that discourse serves. Moreover, because oral discourse can accomplish specific purposes, like requesting or promising, skilled communicators must learn the conventional meanings and actions associated with particular speech acts. In this way communicators can know when they are being understood by others and when they obligate their listeners to respond or to act in specific ways.

In addition, because practical activities differ as to their role structures, so oral discourse is shaped by the role structure of its participants. Skilled communicators must differentiate social roles and master the norms and forms of speech typical of specific communicative situations. Moreover, because practical activities emerge as part of the interactional exchange, so too, oral discourse is shaped by interactional history. Skilled communicators are cognizant of past interactions and use such knowledge in designing their messages.

Finally, besides acquiring knowledge of discourse skilled communicators must acquire a sophisticated theory of communication as to how to use talk to accomplish their goals. Speakers produce messages for reasons, usually for multiple reasons. Typically, speakers want to be clear and efficient as they accomplish an instrumental goal (like informing someone about something). Because accomplishing their primary goal typically involves developing a consensus as to the who, what, and why of the communicative encounter, speakers frequently have subsidiary goals as well, such as creating a desirable identity for, and relationship with, their listener. Messages are what speakers produce in order to accomplish their communicative objectives, and the tasks that messages are designed to accomplish differ in complexity. Tasks can become more complex when people recognize obstacles to achieving their goals, or when those goals compete with one another. So, for instance, the task of reprimanding a child is often complicated by the social need to protect the child's feelings. Similarly, comforting someone else becomes a more difficult task when the person distressed has low self-esteem.

All this means is that to be skilled, speakers must be cognizant of the multifunctionality of communication and pursue multiple goals in dealing with others. Skilled communicators also must develop an interpretive system for recognizing and inferring relevant features of the audience's perspective and context so they can determine potential avenues and obstacles to their goals. Finally, all communicators must integrate such diverse knowledge within an implicit theory of reasoning about communication. Such an implicit theory provides a framework for organizing goal-directed action within its own terms.

Individual Differences in the Development of Communication Skills

The acquisition of many of these elements sustaining communication development produce substantial uniformity in communicative skill. Most normal adults in our culture produce and understand grammatical sentences, manage the sequence of utterances in conversation, can follow and construct a coherent narrative, and the like. However, despite this apparent uniformity in verbal skills, we have documented the presence of enormous individual variation in the success with which many communication tasks are managed. As we discuss later, such individual differences have been observed across such diverse processes as reference and description, behavioral regulation, persuasion, conflict–negotiation, comforting, and interpersonal relational issues. All these communicative tasks are what Britton and his associates (Britton, Burgess, Martin, McLeod, & Rosen, 1975) term "transactional," but we have labeled "person-centered" because they intrinsically involve distinctly interpersonal problems and effects. Much, although not all, communication is carried out in a person-centered mode involving the psychological representation of message recipients (see Applegate & Delia, 1980); by contrast, other tasks are appropriately pursued in ways that involve little contact with or recognition of the actual persons involved or of their psychological characteristics and processes.

Role-Taking and the Listener-Adaptation Model. We have, of course, not been alone in our concern with such intrinsically person-centered communication tasks. Most of the traditional research on person-centered communication has reflected a concern with the adaptation of messages to their recipients ("listener adaptation," "recipient design," or "receiver focus"). Indeed, such an idea is central to a variety of important theoretical analyses of communication development (e.g., Flavell, Botkin, Fry, Wright, & Jarvis, 1968; Mead, 1934; Piaget, 1926). The idea has been central to analyses of written as well as oral communication development (e.g., Bereiter & Scardamalia, 1983; Flower & Hayes, 1980).

The predominant model of listener adaptation locates receiver-focused message design in the process of role-taking (e.g., see Flavell et al., 1968). Role-taking or perspective-taking is represented as a covert inference process in which the viewpoint of the message recipient is imaginatively constructed. This viewpoint in its typical form reflects a fusion of Mead's and Piaget's analyses of development as proceeding from egocentrism toward increasing social perspectivism. Yet this view of role-taking and its functions in message design has not fared well in recent years as concepts have been critically analyzed and data amassed. Among the important conclusions suggested by theoretical and empirical analyses have been (a) that role-taking is not a unitary process but an amalgamation of distinguishable mental operations, (b) that role-taking does not operate uniformly across differing inference domains, (c) that communication and role-taking are sometimes positively related and sometimes not, and (d) that successful message design appears to be tied more closely to a set of skills related to the particular message task than to general role-taking (see the discussion in O'Keefe & Delia, in press).

Person-Centered Communication Skills as a Focus. Our research program has been significantly influenced by the general image of message design as audience adaptation, but it has diverged in several important respects from the traditional models emphasizing role-taking. From the outset we sought to avoid communication tasks and situations that were unrealistic and overly simplistic (e.g., as in tasks involving descriptions of novel figures from an array of such figures, single word "messages," or identification of the "distinguishing features" of one object in a set of objects; see reviews of the referential communication literature

by Asher, 1979; Dickson, 1981; and Whitehurst & Sonnenschein, 1985).
As was noted earlier this led us to focus on a variety of potentially
complex, person-centered situations and tasks (e.g., where persons want
to teach or persuade; where the communication focuses on the feelings,
needs, or problems of interactants; where the regulation of an individual's behavior is at issue). Our approach also has been distinctive in (a)
its shift from a concern with role-taking to a concern with general processes of interpersonal interpretation reflecting developments in the
communicator's system of interpersonal constructs (see Delia & O'Keefe,
1979; O'Keefe & Delia, 1986) and (b) the development of systems for
message analyses that involve the hierarchic classification of messages
along an array of dimensions reflecting the development of more complex perceptions of communication situations and behavioral strategies
for achieving goals in those situations.

A similar set of methods has been used in most of our research.
Subjects are typically presented with systematically designed hypothetical situations and asked to deal with the situations. For instance,
parents have been asked how they would act in specific situations requiring them to discipline or comfort their children, managers have been
called upon to regulate the conduct of their subordinates, teachers have
been confronted with situations requiring the disciplining of students,
and children and adolescents have been placed in situations requiring
persuading, comforting, or informing friends and relatives. Most of the
situations presented to subjects have been complex in their creation of
obstacles to goal attainment or competing goals for the speaker. So, for
example, in some situations the target has appeared reluctant to comply
with the speaker, whereas in other situations the speaker's primary task
of reprimand has conflicted with the speaker's desire to protect the target's feelings. In most studies subjects are asked to state exactly what they
would say to accomplish a specified goal, although in some the goal has
been left unspecified to be created by the speaker. Follow-up probes
have frequently been used to elicit particular aspects of communicative
behavior, such as how the speaker would deal with resistance. The speaker's messages are then subjected to our distinctive analysis (for a full
discussion of these methods see Burleson, 1987).

Our analytic approach to message analysis relies on the development
of hierarchically structured coding systems to assess aspects of the "person-centered" quality of communication (Bernstein, 1971). As is elaborated later, "person-centeredness" encompasses such features of the
message as the form of means-end reasoning on which it is premised, the
extent to which the message explicitly acknowledges, legitimates, and
incorporates the listener's views and goals into the speaker's agenda, or
the manner in which multiple goals are integrated in the messages. Be-

cause the way in which such features of person-centeredness are manifested will vary as a function of the communicator's primary task, we
have developed different coding systems to classify persuasive, comforting, regulative, and informative messages (e.g., Applegate & Delia, 1980;
Clark & Delia, 1976). The message practices that are taken to embody
particular levels of person-centeredness are identified, and these features are then hierarchically ordered. Usually the highest degree of person-centeredness exhibited in pursuing a particular instrumental goal is
taken as assessing the individual's capacity to engage in person-centered
communication (again, see the discussion of methods in Burleson, 1987).

   In addition to such measures of person-centered communication we
have also assessed the relative development of the speaker's system of
interpersonal constructs for perceiving people or situations. Construct
system development is typically measured with versions of Crockett's
(1965) Role Category Questionnaire, which asks subjects to describe
their impressions of known peers. Subjects are instructed to concentrate
on describing each peer's "habits, beliefs, mannerisms, ways of treating
others, traits, and personality characteristics" (Burleson & Waltman,
1988, p. 28). These impressions are then analyzed for the number of
constructs contained in the elicited impressions (Crockett, Press, Delia, &
Kenny, 1974), the abstractness or psychological centeredness of the constructs (e.g., Delia, Clark, & Switzer, 1974), or the degree of organization
among the constructs (Crockett et al., 1974). The reliability and validity
of these measures have been well established (e.g., see the review of D.
O'Keefe & Sypher, 1981).

   The results of studies employing these methods have yielded consistent results showing the development of increasing person-centered
communication strategies as a function of increasing age and social experiences. Moreover, such behavioral developments have been revealed to
be substantially related to increases in developments in the interpersonal
construct system and the use of more complex interpretive practices.
Consistent results have been found within populations from preschooler
to mature adults and representing different social and occupational
classes, across a host of communicative tasks (persuading, informing,
comforting, etc.), and across different data collection modalities (oral
and written responses to hypothetical situations). Moreover, the results
of studies using provided hypothetical situations have been consistent
with those requiring actual behavioral responses to situations. Studies
comparing results based on naturalistic observations of situated behaviors and responses to hypothetical situations have also demonstrated the
validity of our general methodological approach (see the methodological
discussions of Delia, B. O'Keefe, & D. O'Keefe, 1982; and Burleson,
1987; Burleson & Waltman, 1988).

Foundational Developments
in Person-Centered Communication

There are several developmental achievements that are central to the general development of person-centered communication that can usefully be distinguished. Outlining these constituent developments simultaneously serves as a vehicle for summarizing much of our research on person-centered communication. We discuss four interrelated aspects of person-centered communication development: (a) the development of increasingly differentiated, articulated and integrated goals for communication; (b) the development of increasingly complex and integrated means-end reasoning for communication; (c) the elaboration of increasing sophistication in representing knowledge of the context as a basis for message formulation; and (d) the acquisition of functional strategies for accomplishing communicative goals.

The Development of Complex Goal Sets. The development of a functional understanding of communication as a medium for doing the work of social life is foundational to communication development. As we noted earlier, this idea is central to the considerable work in the field of communication development and pragmatics that grow out of various speech act theories. Our work suggests, however, that the realization that communication can be organized to pursue specific purposes entails much more than simply learning the conventional forms and meanings of speech acts. Recognition that communication serves functional ends appears to be closely tied to the integrating of premises for reasoning about communication (O'Keefe, 1988). Moreover, it entails the increasing articulation and refinement and the differentiation and integration of goals within complex goal sets (Werner, 1957).

One major manifestation of this development in children's messages is the shift away from unfocused toward planful organization. The messages of young children and some adults appear organized only as a stream of consciousness. Messages of young children and novice writers, for example, appear organized only by a stream of consciousness in which ideas are set forth as they occur to the communicator. By contrast, with development, messages come to show a high degree of planfulness: The pursuit of a central goal or set of goals is sustained through planful organization; this planful organization involves the integration of sets of subgoals; and message elements appear clearly designed to serve the overall goal or subgoals related to it. Bereiter and Scardamalia (1983), Flower and Hayes (1980), and others have shown aspects of this development in written communication skills, and our own research details the developmental elaboration of increasingly goal-directed and planful be-

183

havioral organizational in oral communication situations (e.g., Delia & O'Keefe, 1979).

Another important development reflecting this underlying process of goal articulation is the emergence of control over multifunctional message organization. As O'Keefe and Delia (1982) argued, the development of communicative multifunctionality clearly appears to be a developmental achievement. All behavior does not do the same work, and there are marked developmental and individual differences in the development of the ability to make behavior more productive. As we noted earlier, our research often confronts individuals with complex situations calling for addressing obstacles to the attainment of a goal or requiring the pursuit of multiple or potentially conflicting goals. Older children clearly are more likely than their younger counterparts to address such obstacles, to refine the goal to avoid the obstacle, or to pursue multiple goals either sequentially or through a strategy that integrates multiple goals (see the general discussion of O'Keefe & Delia, 1982).

This issue is addressed most directly in our work on the management of subsidiary aims in discourse. Much of this work has involved presenting subjects with situations involving a conflict between the need to accomplish some instrumental objective and the need to protect the message recipient's face. Brown and Levinson (1978) have cogently argued that every culture has evolved sets of conventional practices for "redressing" the face-threatening nature of actions. Several studies carried out within our framework have examined individual differences in the integration of face protection into messages organized around the pursuit of some potentially face threatening instrumental task of regulation, persuasion, or interpersonal problem solving.

Messages have been analyzed for the degree of face protection in several related ways, all of which reflect developmental processes (Applegate & Delia, 1980; Kline, 1981; O'Keefe, 1988; O'Keefe & Shepherd, 1987). Children and individuals with minimally developed schemas for interpersonal interpretation act more expressively and tend to either explicitly attack the other's face, resolve conflicts between face and task goals by avoiding negative tone or reference to negative content, or avoid the primary communicative task altogether so as to not create a face threat. Unfortunately, the first strategy exacerbates face threat whereas the latter ones avoid effective pursuit of the instrumental goal. Most older children and many adults tend to employ conventional politeness forms such as apologies, hedges, compliments, or excuses to achieve face protection. Such strategies sequentially separate the pursuit of instrumental and face objectives. Adults with the most developed schemas for interpersonal and interpretation and reasoning explicitly redefine the situation to remove the conflict between face and task objectives. These speakers manage face wants by explicitly legitimizing or actively supporting the message target (e.g., "I want to help you out"), by altercasting the target into a desirable identity (e.g., "You can be a fine worker"), and by conveying that the goals and beliefs of the target are consonant with those of the speaker (e.g., "Let's try to work out a solution together because I know you want to get a good grade, too"). O'Keefe and Shepherd (1987) have found that interactants rate these latter integrative methods of managing face wants both as more instrumentally effective and satisfying.

The Development of Reasoning About Communication. It is not enough that communicators acquire the capacity for articulating refined or integrated goal sets, for a goal alone does not provide a model for how to achieve that goal. The communicator must develop, as well, both schemes for reasoning about the connection between communicative means and ends and effective control over the behavioral strategies and routines for enacting this reasoning. O'Keefe has recently argued that individuals differ, not only in their goals, but also in the premises they employ in reasoning about how to achieve their goals through communication.

O'Keefe (1988) suggested that an individual can employ any of three developmentally ordered premises in reasoning from goals to communicative means. Each of these premises is associated with a constellation of beliefs and operations that make relevant different aspects of the communicative context. O'Keefe called each of these three constellations of beliefs and interpretive principles a "message design logic." Each message design logic includes beliefs about what the primary function of messages are, how communication is to be judged, the procedures for translating intentions into message form, and the principles by which messages are deemed internally coherent and meaningful in the speaking context. Each system of reasoning about communication generates messages with characteristic content and structure, including particular methods for integrating conflicting communication goals. In the following paragraphs we describe each of these logics.

Expressive Design Logic. The developmentally simplest premise for reasoning about communication is the belief that "language is a medium for expressing thoughts and feelings" (O'Keefe, 1988, p. 84). People who begin with this premise conceive the process of communication as one in which listeners understand what the speaker is thinking or feeling straightforwardly from the speaker's utterances. The reason why people communicate is to make known their thoughts and reactions to others, and so communication is considered successful when speakers are open and direct and their utterances are clear. Within this view the primary function of messages is to serve the means of self-expression; expressive communicators simply don't appreciate that messages can be designed to serve goals other than self-expression, and that the meaning of a message is influenced by a variety of features of the interactional context (O'Keefe, 1988).

Messages produced with an expressive logic are governed by the simple design principle, "express what you think." This principle, which dictates that speakers should "dump" or pour forth what is on their minds, generates messages that have personal meaning for speakers but may appear pragmatically pointless to hearers. So, for example, expressive messages may contain redundancies, off-task remarks, irrelevant complaints, or nonessential explanations. Expressive messages frequently are reactions to the immediately prior events or thoughts of the speaker, and the semantic and pragmatic connections within expressive messages are subjective and idiosyncratic to the speaker, so the listener usually must have specific knowledge of the speaker to derive the intended interpretation.

Young children are typically expressive but the logic persists as a communication organizing system of reasoning among many adults. O'Keefe (1988) reported that out of 92 undergraduates 22% employed an expressive design logic. She also reported that individuals who receive expressive messages are likely to evaluate them as ineffective and unsatisfying (O'Keefe & McCornack, 1987)

Conventional Design Logic. A second, more advanced system of reasoning about communication begins with a different premise, namely that "communication is a game played cooperatively, according to socially conventional rules and procedures" (O'Keefe, 1988, p. 86). This view essentially conceives communication to be a process of cooperation. Speakers produce messages by acting and following the conventional rules that specify the acceptable means to accomplish their goals, and these messages are interpreted and responded to by hearers in accordance with the same conventional rules. Within a conventional logic, the key function of a message is to secure a desired response. This is accomplished by selecting conventionally defined actions that count as the appropriate way to obligate one's hearer. Thus within this logic communicative competence is equated with appropriateness; one is a successful communicator if both parties enact their roles and follow conventional rules in an appropriate fashion.

Conventional messages are coherent and meaningful to listeners to the extent messages follow the rules and are appropriate enactments, given the roles and norms governing the speaking context. Typically, a coherent conventional message mentions the core speech action, the felicity conditions on the core speech act, the rights or obligations that structure the situation, or the mitigating circumstances operating on those rights or obligations (O'Keefe, 1988).

In her recent analysis, O'Keefe (1988) reported that 46% of 92 undergraduates used a conventional design logic. Conventional messages are rated as moderately effective and satisfying (O'Keefe & McCornack, 1987).

Rhetorical Design Logic. The third system of reasoning about communication is based on a premise that subsumes both the expressive and conventional premises; it is the belief that "communication is the creation and negotiation of social selves and situations" (O'Keefe, 1988, p. 87). This message design logic views meaning not as fixed by conventional forms or the speaking situation, but rather views the speaking context as created and negotiated by the persons involved. From this design logic evolves the view that communication is a recurring attempt to solve the problem of coordination. Because messages themselves create a social reality and because the meanings of messages are not fixed, communication is always a process of coordinating the listener's interpretations and responses with the speaker's intentions and actions. Moreover, because ways of speaking create a social reality, the primary function that messages serve or are seen as serving is negotiation and social consensus. Within this logic, then, success is marked by communication that is smooth and coherent (O'Keefe, 1988).

Rhetorical message producers design their messages principally toward the achievement of goals. Their messages explicitly appear as designed to achieve goals rather than merely reactions or conventional responses to situations. Rhetorical messages are also distinguished by their use of language style to define the speaker's symbolic reality in ways so the listener can make an acceptable interpretation and be motivated to give an acceptable response. Hence rhetorical messages are likely to contain stylistic elements that create definite characters for the speaker and listener, persuasive arguments and appeals to make the speaker's views attractive, and elaborating and contextualizing phrases to make plain the speaker's view of the context.

O'Keefe (1988) found that 32% of 92 undergraduates use a rhetorical design logic. Individuals who receive rhetorical messages were more likely to consider them as both instrumentally effective and satisfying (O'Keefe & McCornack, 1987).

The Development of Context-Sensitive and Receiver-Focused Understanding. A central feature of increasing sophistication in functional communication is its integration with developments that provide detailed, socially shared, and organized understandings of the communicative context and its participants. These developments both reflect and contribute to the decline of expressive reasoning and behavior and the emergence and consolidation of conventional and rhetorical reasoning and behavior. Indeed, considerable research has shown very important consistent positive relationships between the development of more differentiated, abstract, and integrated systems for interpersonal perception and the development of more rhetorically focused communicative reasoning and action (e.g., see Clark & Delia, 1979; Delia & O'Keefe, 1979; O'Keefe, 1988; O'Keefe & Delia, 1986). Moreover, this close relationship between interpretive processes and communicative reasoning and behavior is evidenced early in development and appears to increase in magnitude and significance into adulthood. Research shows that among diverse groups of normal adults (doctors, noncareer mothers, middle managers, etc.), both the use of rhetorically focused communicative reasoning and of highly person-centered behavioral strategies are significantly related to individual differences in the complexity of systems of interpersonal constructs for representing and interpreting persons and social events (e.g., Applegate, 1980b; Burleson, 1983; Clark & Delia, 1977; Delia, Kline, & Burleson, 1979; Kline & Ceropski, 1984; O'Keefe & Shepherd, 1987).

There are many specific aspects of person-centered communication development that are intertwined with developments in constructs for interpersonal perception and interpretation. Here we note only the two most fundamental. First, the integration of communicative reasoning and behavior with advances in social perception processes sustains the development of communicative skills premised on an objective rather than subjective sense of relevance. A number of communication researchers have noted that the messages of unskilled communicators tend to be subjective, personal, and idiosyncratic in their connections to contexts, whereas the messages of skilled communicators are more objective and universal. With unskilled communicators, one must frequently already know or must guess about details of the message producer's personal experiences and past to understand the connections that are being made; skilled communicators come to distinguish their personal experience and knowledge from that which is broadly shared public knowledge and to fashion their messages through connections within this sphere of public knowledge. Second, more developed systems of constructs for interpreting the social world provide knowledge of contexts that are more differentiated and refined, and as a consequence messages can become more individuated to their recipients. Specific knowledge of the particular message recipient is not relevant to successful communication in every situation, but frequently it is. In such cases, communicators who have more developed constructs for person perception are able to find more bases for adaptation and individuation of their messages to the perspective and needs of the listener. Much of our work has shown the important and positive connection between such developments in social perception skill and the development of individuated, receiver-focused communication (e.g., Burleson, 1984; Delia & Clark, 1977; Delia, Clark, & Switzer, 1974; O'Keefe & Delia, 1979). Again it is noteworthy that this close connection between social perception and communicative skills has been observed from early childhood into adulthood.

The Development of Person-Centered Communication Strategies. One can have integrated goal sets, differentiated perceptions of the communicative situation and message recipient, engage in rhetorically-sensitive reasoning, and still be unskilled at communication if the necessary strategies and behavioral routines are not controlled. Just as a message design logic is entwined with the development of interpretive processes for understanding contexts and persons, so is the development of communicative reasoning deeply integrated with the development of particular methods relevant to achieving communication goals. These methods for achieving communicative goals—what we call strategies—are expressed in the communicator's message practices. As was discussed earlier, a central concern of our research program for the past several years has been the development of hierarchic systems for classifying message practices along dimensions reflecting increasing person-centeredness. In this section, we describe some of these ordered schemes of message practices. All of our examples come from the studies we have conducted with children and their mothers, adolescents, college students, and teachers. We briefly overview work in four functional domains: persuasion, comforting, behavioral regulation, and informative communication.

Persuasive Message Practices. One function that messages can serve is to influence others to adopt new ideas or courses of action. In one line of work Clark, Delia, and colleagues analyzed the types of persuasive messages and rationales produced in situations in which the persuadee is reluctant to grant the request (e.g., Burke & Clark, 1982; Clark & Delia, 1976, 1977). In several studies, for example, children were asked how they would gain permission to have an overnight party, or how they would convince a neighbor lady to keep a homeless puppy. From the responses Clark and Delia discovered four developmentally ordered message types: simple requests; elaborated requests that stress the persuader's needs; counterarguing, in which the objections of the persuadee are refuted; and advantage to other, in which the benefits to the persuadee are stressed and the goals of the persuadee incorporated into a common agenda. Delia, Kline, and Burleson (1979) have detailed more specifically the practices associated with each of these message types. In all of the studies the production of higher level messages are positively correlated with increases in intepersonal construct system differentiation and abstractness (e.g., Applegate, 1982; Delia, Kline, & Burleson, 1979; O'Keefe & Delia, 1979).

These message hierarchies reflect the content and structure of messages produced by each of the three message design logics we discussed earlier. The lowest level messages in the hierarchy reflect expressive reasoning: Even in situations where the persuadee is reluctant to accede to the persuasive request, the messages suggest that the speakers are preoccupied with the job of expressing their own needs through the use of simple requests (e.g., "Could I have a party, please?"), pleas and begging (e.g., "Please, pretty please?"), or unadorned statements of desire or need (e.g., "I want a party. Can I have one?"). Messages addressing resistance simply recycle the simple requests or statements of need (e.g., "Oh, please don't say no.") By contrast, higher level messages in the hierarchy reflect conventional and rhetorical reasoning and increasingly receiver-focused concerns. Many of the messages, for example, reflect a conventional design logic in that they recognize the manifest obstacle of the reluctant persuadee and build a case around the conventional conditions and situational norms for requesting. These messages (a) elaborate the necessity, desirability, or usefulness of the request (e.g., "Would you keep this dog safe so he won't run out in the street?") and (b) seek to eliminate the conventionally appropriate reasons for refusing their request (e.g., "Will you please keep this dog for me cause my Mom won't let me keep it." or "Mom, could I have a slumber party for my birthday and *just* invite about five girls?").

Rhetorically designed messages create a context in which the message target can understand the impact, effects, and urgency of a problem that they would also consider their own. These messages construct a persuasive case that either (a) highly individuates the consequences of accepting or rejecting the request, (b) alleviates the negative effects associated with the proposal, (c) actively negotiates a feasible and mutually satisfying action for the persuadee to carry out, or (d) actively takes the persuadee's perspective in articulating specific benefits (e.g., "If I were you and I lived alone, I'd like a good watchdog like this one."). A number of studies show that highly person-centered persuasive messages are more instrumentally effective than less person-centered messages (e.g., Burleson & Fennelly, 1981; Dlugokinski & Firestone, 1974; O'Keefe & Shepherd, 1987).

Comforting Message Practices. Research on situations requiring comforting communication reveal parallel developments in messages designed to relieve another's distress. In a series of studies (e.g., Applegate & Delia, 1980; Burleson, 1980, 1983, 1984; Samter & Burleson, 1984), subjects have been asked to use discourse to comfort someone with hurt feelings. Children have been asked, for example, how they would comfort an upset classmate who had received a bad grade on a test, or how they would comfort a sad friend who was not invited to a particular party.

Messages produced in comforting situations have been classified in a set of nine hierarchically ordered categories that are progressively person-centered. Messages at the lowest levels include expressive reactions that disregard the other's emotional need: such messages comfort by condemning (e.g., "I'd tell her she had no reason to feel that way."), correcting (e.g., "There's nothing to be upset about—it's just an old party."), or ignoring the other's feelings (e.g., "I guess you'd better start studying harder."). Messages at the middle levels of the hierarchy involve the use of conventionally appropriate and polite forms of action for conveying sympathy or relieving distress such as seeking to divert the other's attention ("Do you want to come over to my house and play?") or offering conventionally redressive forms of sympathy ("I'm sorry.").

Messages at the highest levels of the hierarchy use the discourse itself to transform the other's situation and feelings into something better. These message practices include (a) asking about and explicitly acknowledging the feelings of the other, (b) learning about and explaining the reasons for those feelings, (c) legitimizing and creating an in-depth interpretation of those feelings, (d) placing the situation into a larger perspective, and (e) helping the message recipient to reason through the situation and learn from it. Burleson and Samter (1985) have found that people rate the message practices at the lower end of the hierarchy as insensitive and ineffective in providing comfort, whereas the remaining practices are rated as progressively more sensitive and effective.

Regulative Message Practices. A third line of research within our framework has analyzed the discourse of speakers who desire to alter another's behavior (e.g., Applegate, 1980a, 1980b; Applegate & Delia, 1980; Applegate, Burke, Burleson, Delia, & Kline, 1985; Kline, 1988; O'Keefe, 1988). Typically, subjects are placed in positions of authority and given the task of modifying the conduct of an erring subordinate. For example, adolescents in a role of responsibility have been asked to manage the behavior of a classmate, and mothers and teachers have been asked how they discipline their young charges. The situations presented to the subjects are doubly complex because the speaker is faced with an obstacle to their primary objective (the other believes his or her behavior is legitimate) and the social task of protecting the other's self-respect.

Messages and rationales produced in response to these situations have been classified with several related message analytic systems; their degree of "person-centeredness" (Applegate & Delia, 1980), alignment of the listener's views of the problem and proposal (Kline, 1988), and the underlying message design logic (O'Keefe, 1988). Messages at the lowest levels of these systems react to the illegitimate behavior. These messages are often the form of litanies of complaints or recriminations. The speaker either makes no coherent attempt to represent the problem or automatically judges the other's behavior to be wrong. Speakers also make no coherent attempt to advocate an action, instead pronouncing rules, punishments, or issuing ultimatums, commands, or noncontingent threats. Messages produced at the middle levels of the hierarchic analytic systems involve explanations of the impact of the other's actions or explain how the other's actions violate operating norms or principles. Messages at the middle levels also frequently propose and justify "appropriate" solutions, specify some action by which the hearer can successfully meet his or her obligations, and offer reasons for rules, discussing the rights and obligations of compliance and noncompliance and the general principles behind appropriate behavior (e.g., "If you take a nap now you can play with those blocks when you wake up."; or "If you don't take a nap you'll be too tired to go outside and play later.").

The highest level of the regulative message systems shift away from power assertion and concern with rule systems to construct a persuasive case with individuated arguments and appeals. Such message practices depict rhetorical reasoning by (a) framing the problem in terms of both parties' values, feelings, beliefs, and goals, (b) encouraging the other to perceive multiple features of the situation in terms of specific feelings and beliefs, (c) helping the other to make an empathic response by leading him or her to reason through the problem, (d) engaging in procedural negotiations or action facilitation, and (e) helping the other see the rationality of principles of conduct in a larger context (e.g., "I know you picked those flowers because you wanted to do something nice for me and I appreciate it. But Mrs. Jones loves her flowers. She works hard on them. Maybe next time you could pick wildflowers for me. I'd appreciate it just as much.").

Informative Message Practices.   Finally, a small number of our studies have examined the way individuals use discourse to inform and explain (Kline & Ceropski, 1984; Kline & Clinton, 1988; Rowan, 1985). Patient interviews, science fair presentations, and scientific explanations have been analyzed for the extent to which the speaker shows the listener how new information is consistent and/or inconsistent with an objective knowledge base and the listener's existing beliefs. Messages at the lowest levels of our analytic hierarchies condemn, correct, or disregard the other's existing beliefs in conveying the new information. Middle-level messages within the hierarchies reflect use of conventional discourse forms (e.g., naming structures, functions, or processes or using analogies) to convey a context for understanding. Rhetorical reasoning is reflected in the most advanced messages: These messages explicitly (a) identify and legitimate the listener's relevant beliefs, (b) show the listener how to associate new information with the listener's existing beliefs, (c) reject the listener's beliefs if they are wrong and demonstrate how the beliefs are wrong, and (d) replace erroneous beliefs with new information and a explanation that accounts for both the scientific account and why the listener's beliefs seem plausible.

Summary. As can be seen, message design logics manifest themselves in characteristic message practices. Expressive messages appear to be organized by the principle, "Express what you think or feel"; conventional messages are organized by the principle, "Be appropriate," and rhetorical messages are organized by the principle, "Create a satisfying consensus." These different design principles appear to generate consistencies in messages across functional contexts, although the particular types of practices differ depending on the practical activity the speaker is engaged in. Given these consistencies, the problem now becomes to account for their social context of development. Presumably an individual's system of reasoning about communication is acquired in the context of socialization. Parents and teachers, for example, make manifest in their speech beliefs about how communication operates, what discourse is used for, and how discourse is to be evaluated. Exactly what discourse practices facilitate the acquisition of rhetorical reasoning and person-centered communication is the topic of the last section of our chapter.

RHETORICAL REASONING, PERSON-CENTERED MESSAGE PRACTICES, AND THEIR SOCIAL CONTEXT OF DEVELOPMENT

What discourse practices facilitate the acquisition of a rhetorical message design logic and person-centered message practices? We would suggest that children acquire ways of reasoning about communication through the kinds of discourse practices they are exposed to in their families, schools, media, and peer groups. Discourse practices depict reasoning about communication, which, in turn, promotes the acquisition of particular design logics and person-centered discourse practices. In this last section we offer a selective discussion of the discourse practices that clearly depict rhetorical reasoning about communication and that facilitate person-centered messages. We have loosely grouped the discourse practices into two groups: discussion practices that convey rhetorical premises about communication, and instructional practices that overtly display rhetorical reasoning and person-centered forms of talk.

Discussion Practices That Convey Rhetorical Reasoning

There are at least six discourse practices that can be observed to convey rhetorical reasoning. We discuss them briefly, in the following paragraphs.

Discussing the Consequences and Possible Outcomes of Speech. At least two rhetorically based beliefs about speech can be taught by discussing the consequences and effects of speech. One premise is that when one speaks, one always changes the present situation; given this premise, teaching oral communication skills should include discussing the consequences that utterances can have on others and the new situations that are created with one's utterances. A second rhetorical premise about speech is that when one speaks, there can be active movement toward a desired new situation. Hence teaching oral communication skills should include discussing the ways in which children can use speech to solve problems and change situations.

There are at least two systematic lines of research that show the positive effects of discussing consequences and solutions on children's communicative development. One line of work has focused on the effects of parental discipline styles. Much attention has been devoted to studying what Hoffman calls "power assertion" (use of physical punishment or power), "induction" (pointing out consequences of behavior for other involved persons), and "love-withdrawal" (directly expressing anger or disapproval) (e.g., Hoffman, 1977; Hoffman & Saltzstein, 1967). In general, studies show that induction promotes higher levels of social and moral development than the other styles (see the reviews of Brody & Shaffer, 1982; and Grusec & Lytton, 1988).

A second line of research on the effects of discussing consequences and solutions on children's social behavior is that of Shure and Spivack (e.g., Shure, 1981; Shure & Spivack, 1980, 1982; Spivack, Platt, & Shure, 1976). Shure and Spivack have found that measures of a child's social adjustment are positively correlated with the child's ability to conceptualize solutions to their interpersonal problems and to conceive of the consequences their actions have on others (e.g., Marsh, Serafica, & Barenboim, 1981; Shure, Spivack, & Jaeger, 1971; Spivack et al., 1976). They have also found that mothers who help their child articulate their interpersonal problems, explore possible solutions, and discuss consequences are more likely to have daughters with more sophisticated interpersonal problem-solving skills (Shure & Spivack, 1978).

From this research Shure and Spivack have developed programs for parents and teachers to teach interpersonal problem-solving skills to preschool and elementary children (Shure & Spivack, 1978; Spivack & Shure, 1974). The program consists of a sequence of over 40 lessons and activities; initial lessons focus on developing social perception skills, such as becoming aware of individual differences in people and how to find out about these differences, and what makes people feel particular emotions. The final lessons focus on solving hypothetical and actual social dilemmas through dialogues, in which the parent or teacher is taught to question, guide and help the child to (a) define the problem in terms of their own feelings, (b) think of the consequences of their actions, (c) think of their interactant's feelings about the situation, (d) think of alternative solutions to the problem, and (e) pair specific solutions with specific consequences in ways that reconcile both parties' conflicting wants. Shure and Spivack found that parents and teachers who use their training program have improved their children's interpersonal problem solving skills and social adjustment (e.g., Shure, 1981; Shure & Spivack, 1980, 1982). These results appear to be consistent with others' use of the intervention program (see the meta-analysis of Denham & Almeida, 1987).

Discussing the Value and Practice of Negotiating Social Consensus.   A related discourse practice that conveys rhetorical reasoning is to affirm the value of determining what one's listener's desires are and to develop the skill of fitting the listener's desires with one's own goals. Strategic control can be mastered by learning compromising strategies and the lines of argument that can make one's proposal appealing to listeners, such as arguing that one's proposal will solve important problems, yield desirable consequences, or be consistent with the listener's values (Clark, 1984).

One element of Spivack and Shure's training program is to help the child learn to invent arguments that can bring about a social consensus between the parties. However, a program that directly trains children in persuasive and negotiation skills is that of Clark, Willihnganz, and O'Dell (1985). Clark and her colleagues trained fourth graders in three persuasive skills: reconciliation of objectives, generation of consequences, and the construction of persuasive arguments. Children were taught to reconcile conflicting objectives with a set of three compromising strategies: helping (i.e., giving mutual assistance), "part-way" (i.e., showing how the wishes of both parties could be partially satisfied), and "later-way" (i.e., showing how each party could take turns achieving his or her goals). Children were then taught how to consider the consequences of their actions by considering that some consequences primarily affect themselves whereas other consequences affect other people; some consequences are advantages whereas others are disadvantages, and some consequences occur immediately whereas others do not happen until later. Finally, children were taught how to make persuasive arguments by offering advantages to the other and by identifying and answering counterarguments. The instructional procedures for Clark et al.'s teaching unit consisted of introducing the skill and providing a rationale, describing and illustrating the strategies, and having the children rehearse the strategies as a group and individually in two written exercises. Using these procedures Clark and her associates found significant training effects from pre- to posttest.

Using Speech to Provide In-Depth Interpretations of Individual Perspectives. A third discourse practice that conveys rhetorical reasoning is to explicitly focus discussion on the thoughts, goals, and feelings of the parties involved in speaking situations and to teach that one's speech must explicitly connect to the thoughts and feelings of one's listener. The explicit expression of perspectives and feelings makes the psychological domain of experience a manifest feature of reality. Over time, children exposed to these practices should be led to differentiate their construct systems for representing the needs and perspectives of others, and be led to see that people's wants and perspectives are salient aspects of the relevance structure defining the speaking situation. Children should then be led to incorporate others' aims and perspectives directly into their talk. A number of studies within our framework support these notions (Applegate et al., 1985; Applegate & Delia, 1980; Delia, Burleson, & Kline, 1979; Jones, Delia, & Clark, 1981).

Two related sets of beliefs and strategic abilities are implied here. First, children can be taught to use speech to explicitly define one's view of the situation by describing and justifying one's feelings and beliefs. Similarly, children can learn to use speech to elicit the listener's feelings and beliefs and the reasons for those feelings and beliefs. Children can also be taught the value of and use of speech to supply background knowledge so that listeners will be able to reach intended understandings. Second, children could be shown how sylistic features of speech, such as repetition, rhythm, and tone can emphasize a speaker's meanings and render them clearer and more impressive. Hence children could be shown how to describe feelings and beliefs concretely.

Discussing Identity Management. A fourth belief about speech that conveys rhetorical reasoning is that when one speaks, one creates an identity (Goffman, 1969). Part of learning rhetorical reasoning is to learn that what you say gives off images of oneself that may or may not be desired, or that may or may not conflict with other goals one may have. Hence communicative skill involves learning discourse practices that help ensure that listeners will infer intended self-images, such as clarifying one's motives and describing one's beliefs and values (Weinstein, 1966).

Focusing on Arguments. A fifth practice that promotes rhetorical reasoning is to focus on the ability to construct and critique arguments. A host of communicative abilities are implied here, including the ability to (a) produce second-order justifications for one's position, (b) anticipate and refute counterarguments, (c) assess evidence, (d) identify similarities and differences between one's own position and another's, (e) reason about another's reasoning and generate supportive justifications for another's position, (f) generate a common position, and (g) verbally test the various possibilities in a situation with moral principles (Berkowitz, Oser, & Althof, 1987). Knowledge needed to develop argumentation abilities has been systematized by those who teach courses in public speaking and argumentation (e.g., Toulmin, Rieke, & Janik, 1979; Warnick & Inch, 1989).

The role of argument in facilitating advancement in verbal reasoning has been shown by many researchers interested in moral development (e.g., Kohlberg, 1981, 1984). Their work shows that children's advances in verbal reasoning about moral problems can be predicted by particular rhetorical characteristics of the discussions they engage in with their peers, teachers, and parents. In particular, the practice of exposing children to arguments in which moral values and standards are justified in terms of general principles promotes advances in verbal reasoning about moral problems. Presumably, discourse that presents arguments that justify general social principles displays a rationality that the child finds appealing and eventually adopts. In support of this notion it has been found that children understand, prefer, and are more likely to assimilate moral reasoning one level above their own (e.g., Rest, Turiel, & Kohlberg, 1969) and exposing children to advice with arguments one level higher than their own level will promote advanced moral reasoning (e.g., Turiel, 1966).

However, aside from finding that exposure to higher levels of moral reasoning promotes moral development, it appears that learning to ar- gue facilitates moral development. Berkowitz (1985), for example, con- tends that it is the rhetorical act of comparing one's line of reasoning with others, noting their similarities and differences and judging the relative merits of arguments that facilitate advances in verbal reasoning about moral dilemmas. There is empirical support for this notion; in particular, it has been found that encouraging children to discuss contro- versial moral issues is effective in advancing their verbal reasoning abili- ties when (a) the teacher uses a Socratic approach by asking probing questions for the child's reasoning (e.g., Blatt & Kohlberg, 1975), or when (b) children role-play or debate opposing positions with peers who operate at different levels of reasoning (e.g., Berkowitz, Gibbs, & Broughton, 1980; Damon & Killen, 1982). Consistent with these studies, a number of programs for teaching moral reasoning have been devel- oped (e.g., Arbuthrot & Faust, 1981), with emphasis on the use of So- cratic discussion techniques to promote moral reasoning (see the reviews of Colby, Kohlberg, Fenton, Speicher-Dubin, & Leiberman, 1977; Lock- wood, 1978; Mosher, 1980).

Incorporating Identity and Relationship Support With Primary Com- municative Tasks. A final discourse practice that conveys rhetorical reasoning in children is identity and relationship support. Discussion could profitably focus on the recognition that people want to be liked and respected and that certain message strategies conventionally convey liking and respect. Brown and Levinson (1978) found that speakers uni- versally convey liking by attending to the listener's perspective, claiming common points of view, asserting knowledge of and concern for the listener's wants, claiming cooperation, and so on (Brown & Levinson, 1978, p. 107). Speakers convey respect by not presuming or coercing their listeners, by conveying the desire to not impinge on their listeners, and so on (Brown & Levinson, 1978, p. 136). Yet people can also invent ways of speaking that redefine the communicative situation so as to remove its face threatening features.

As already mentioned, studies within our framework have analyzed the degree of identity and relationship support in maternal discipline strategies. By legitimating the child's feelings, perspectives, and desires while simultaneously regulating the child's behavior, parents can ex- plicitly employ a multiple goal set toward the discipline encounter, and display how conflicting intentions (regulation and support) can be recon- ciled. One would suspect that over time the child of such a parent should be led to incorporate identity and relationship support into his message (e.g., Delia, Burleson, & Kline, 1979; Jones, Delia, & Clark, 1981).

Displaying Rhetorical Reasoning
in Instructional Practice

Many instructional practices depict rhetorical reasoning; here we note only three rhetorically oriented practices that are systematically connected to advances in communicative development. The first practice has to do with the way in which the topics just discussed are taught: Rhetorical reasoning can be communicated to students by *showing* how speech creates new situations through its effects on others, *describing* those effects concretely, *showing* how speech creates an image for oneself, *displaying* consideration and respect to students, *assisting* students in message planning, and *reflecting on* the steps in message design. Demonstrating rhetorical premises about communication is itself a rhetorical practice; this practice has implicitly been used in communication training programs (e.g., Clark, Willihnganz, & O'Dell, 1985; Whitehurst & Sonnenschein, 1981).

A second instructional practice that promotes rhetorical reasoning is to collaborate on an understanding of rhetorical reasoning and message design through dialogue. Instructional techniques that depict rhetorical reasoning will seek to identify and replace beliefs of the students that impede their understanding of effective communication. It appears that partial or inaccurate knowledge about oral communication can lead children to construct ineffective messages. For example, in their studies on referential communication skills Whitehurst and Sonnenschein (e.g., 1981, 1985) found that 5-year-olds construct ineffective informative messages because they do not know that an effective informative message should describe differences between potential referents. Whitehurst and Sonnenschein found that an effective training technique is to tell children that they should describe perceptual differences between referents and then in practice-dialogues tell children when they have described such differences. With this technique children come to see the connection between their informative messages and their listener's perceptions; consequently their beliefs about what constitutes an effective informative message is changed. Hence an effective instructional technique is to systematically identify and correct children's erroneous beliefs about how their messages are understood or acted upon by others. Such techniques have also been used in Palincsar and Brown's (in press) related work on reading skills. Palincsar and Brown found that first-graders improve their reading skills when teachers identify their students' erroneous expectations and beliefs about the text and demonstrate, through their talk, more effective beliefs and actions to take in understanding the text.

Finally, it appears that the frequency and variety of the interactions children have are positively correlated with advances in their communicative development. Presumably as individuals experience communication over diverse contexts with different individuals they experience directly how their messages can negotiate a social consensus and produce particular effects rather than merely serve the needs of self-expression. With increased interactions children experience the social need to pay attention to the rights and obligations connected to social roles, and to consider normative expectations. All of these lessons both display and promote rhetorical reasoning.

Throughout his work Piaget (1926, 1932) has argued that peer interactions facilitate the development of the child's communicative abilities. Piaget believed that peer interactions facilitates the child's discovery that their own perspectives are not always shared, and the cognitive conflict from dissonant perspectives facilitates the development of perspective-taking ability and social cognitive concepts, such as cooperation, reciprocity, and mutual respect. Piaget's prediction is supported by a number of studies, which show that children who interact more frequently with their peers develop more sophisticated perspective-taking skills and social concepts (e.g., Dodge, Cole, & Brakke, 1982; Kurdek & Krile, 1982; Strayer & Mashal, 1983). Piaget (1932) also believed that peer interaction provides the context in which children learn to formulate and negotiate social rules, lessons that apparently facilitate verbal reasoning abilities, for children who are more socially involved have higher levels of moral development (e.g., Enright & Sutterfield, 1980; see the review of Brody & Shaffer, 1982). Amount of peer interactions is also positively correlated with referential communication skill (e.g., Deutsch, 1974; Nahir & Yussen, 1977).

Summary

A selective review of research on communicative development reveals several discourse practices that depict and facilitate rhetorical design logic. Discussing consequences and solutions makes salient the effects that discourse has on others' feelings and beliefs. Providing in-depth interpretations of beliefs and feelings and learning to negotiate helps to bring about understanding and social consensus. Assessing the cogency of reasons facilitates the negotiation of mutual agreements about principles governing social conduct. Discussing identity management and support stresses how multiple goals are enacted in discourse. Demonstrating rhetorical premises about communication, assisting students in the acquisition of person-centered communication, and increasing the diversity of students' communicative interactions presumably all help develop children's oral communication skills.

A CONCLUDING NOTE

Our analysis brings us to two points on which we wish to end. First, we suggest that there is a need for studies in communicative development to focus on the recognition of an individual's system of reasoning about communication, and of the complexity of the tasks that are accomplished in and through communication. Second, related to these studies should be the development of coherent curricula for teaching oral communication skills in the classroom.

We believe that teachers should develop activities that will help children develop rhetorical systems of reasoning about communication. This means developing activities that show how discourse itself can change people's minds and social situations. Desirable activities would show how symbols convey multiple meanings and how discourse can create particular emotions or beliefs. Activities that require children to discuss conflicting beliefs and reconcile conflicting goals will enable children to learn how to use discourse to redefine social situations so as to erase disagreements. It is these sorts of communicative activities that can be easily integrated into classroom instruction, and that, we believe, will facilitate the child's development of a rhetorical system of reasoning about communication.

REFERENCES

Applegate, J. L. (1980a). Adaptive communication in educational contexts: A study of teachers' communicative strategies. *Communication Education, 29,* 158–170.

Applegate, J. L. (1980b). Person- and position-centered communication in a day-care center. In N. K. Denzin (Ed.), *Studies in symbolic interaction* (Vol. 3, pp. 59–96). Greenwich, CT: JAI Press.

Applegate, J. L. (1982). The impact of construct system development on communication and impression formation in persuasive contexts. *Communication Monographs, 49,* 277–289.

Applegate, J. L., Burke, J. A., Burleson, B. R., Delia, J. G., & Kline, S. L. (1985). Reflection-enhancing parental communication. In I. E. Sigel (Ed.), *Parental belief systems: The psychological consequences for children* (pp. 107–142). Hillsdale, NJ: Lawrence Erlbaum Associates.

Applegate, J. L., & Delia, J. G. (1980). Person-centered speech, psychological development and the contexts of language usage. In R. St. Clair & H. Giles

(Eds.), *The social and psychological contexts of language* (pp. 245–282). Hillsdale, NJ: Lawrence Erlbaum Associates.

Arbuthnot, J., & Faust, D. (1981). *Teaching moral reasoning: Theory and practice.* San Francisco: Harper & Row.

Asher, S. R. (1979). Referential communication. In G. J. Whitehurst & B. J. Zimmerman (Eds.), *The functions of language and congition* (pp. 175–197). New York: Academic Press.

Bereiter, C., & Scardamalia, M. (1983). Does learning to write have to be so difficult? In A. Freedman, I. Pringle, & T. Yalden (Eds.), *Learning to write: First language/second language.* London: Longman.

Berkowitz, M. W. (1985). The role of discussion in moral education. In M. W. Berkowitz & F. Oser (Eds.), *Moral education: Theory and application* (pp. 197–218). Hillsdale, NJ: Lawrence Erlbaum Associates.

Berkowitz, M. W., Gibbs, J. C., & Broughton, J. M. (1980). The relation of moral judgement stage disparity to developmental effects of peer dialogue. *Merrill-Palmer Quarterly, 26,* 341–357.

Berkowtiz, M. W., Oser, F., & Althof, W. (1987). The development of sociomoral discourse. In W. M. Kurtines & J. L. Gerwirtz (Eds.), *Moral development through social interaction* (pp. 322–352). New York: Wiley.

Bernstein, B. (1971). *Class, codes, and control.* London: Routledge, Kegan Paul.

Blatt, M., & Kohlberg, L. (1975). The effects of classroom moral discussion upon children's level of moral judgment. *Journal of Moral Education, 4,* 129–161.

Britton, J., Burgess, T., Martin, N., McLeod, A., & Rosen, H. (1975). *The development of writing ability (11–18).* London: Macmillan Education.

Brody, G. H., & Shaffer, D. R. (1982). Contributions of parents and peers to children's moral socialization. *Developmental Review, 2,* 31–75.

Brown, P., & Levinson, S. (1978). Universals in language usage: Politeness phenomena. In E. Goody (Ed.), *Questions and politeness* (pp. 56–311). Cambridge, England: Cambridge University Press.

Burke, J. A., & Clark, R. A. (1982). An assessment of methodological options for investigating the development of persuasive skills across childhood. *Central States Speech Journal, 33,* 437–445.

Burleson, B. R. (1980). The development of interpersonal reasoning: An analysis of message strategy justifications. *Journal of the American Forensic Association. 17,* 102–110.

Burleson, B. R. (1983). Social cognition, empathic motivation, and adults' comforting strategies. *Human Communication Research, 10,* 295–304.

Burleson, B. R. (1984). Age, social-cognitive development, and the use of comforting strategies. *Communication Monographs, 51,* 140–153.

Burleson, B. R. (1987). Cognitive complexity. In J. C. McCroskey & J. A. Daly (Eds.), *Personality and interpersonal communication* (pp. 305–349). Beverly Hills, CA: Sage.

Burleson, B. R., & Fennelly, D. A. (1981). The effects of persuasive appeal form and cognitive complexity on children's sharing behavior. *Child Study Journal, 11,* 75–90.

Burleson, B. R., & Samter, W. (1985). Consistencies in theoretical and naive evaluations of comforting messages: Two studies. *Communication Monographs, 52,* 103–123.

Burleson, B. R., & Waltman, M. S. (1988). Cognitive complexity: Using the Role Category Questionnaire Measure. In C. H. Tardy (Ed.), *A handbook for the study of human communication* (pp. 1–35). Norwood, NJ: Ablex.

Clark, R. A. (1984). *Persuasive messages.* New York: Harper & Row.

Clark R. A., & Delia, J. G. (1976). The development of functional persuasive skills in childhood and early adolescence. *Child Development, 47,* 1008–1014.

Clark, R. A., & Delia, J. G. (1977). Cognitive complexity, social perspective-taking, and functional persuasive skills in second-to-ninth grade children. *Human Communication Research, 3,* 128–134.

Clark, R. A., & Delia, J. G. (1979). *Topoi* and rhetorical competence. *Quarterly Journal of Speech, 65,* 187–206.

Clark, R. A., Willihnganz, C., & O'Dell, L. L. (1985). Training fourth graders in compromising and persuasive strategies. *Communication Education, 34,* 331–342.

Colby, A., Kohlberg, L., Fenton, E., Speicher-Dubin, B., & Leiberman, M. (1977). Secondary school moral discussion programs led by social studies teachers. *Journal of Moral Education, 6,* 90–111.

Crockett, W. H. (1965). Cognitive complexity and impression formation. In B. A. Maher (Ed.), *Progress in experimental personality research* (Vol. 2, pp. 47–90). New York: Academic Press.

Crockett, W. H., Press, A. N., Delia, J. G., & Kenney, C. J. (1974). *The structural analysis of the organization of written impressions.* Unpublished manuscript, Department of Psychology, University of Kansas, Lawrence, KS.

Damon, W., & Killen, M. (1982). Peer interaction and the process of change in children's moral reasoning. *Merrill-Palmer Quarterly, 28,* 347–367.

Delia, J. G., Burleson, B. R., & Kline, S. L. (1979, April). *Person-centered parental communication and the development of social-cognitive and communicative abilities.* Paper presented at the annual convention fo the Central States Speech Association, St. Louis, MO.

Delia, J. G., & Clark, R. A. (1977). Cognitive complexity, social perception, and the development of listener-adapted communication in six, eight, ten, and twelve-year-old boys. *Communication Monographs, 44,* 326–345.

Delia, J. G., Clark, R. A., & Switzer, D. E. (1974). Cognitive complexity and impression formation in informal social interaction. *Speech Monographs, 41,* 299–308.

Delia, J. G., Kline, S. L., & Burleson, B. R. (1979). The development of persuasive communication strategies in kindergarteners through twelfth-graders. *Communication Monographs, 46,* 241–256.

Delia, J. G., & O'Keefe, B. J. (1979). Constructivism: The development of communication. In E. Wartella (Ed.), *Children communicating* (pp. 157–185). Beverly Hills, CA: Sage.

Delia, J. G., O'Keefe, B. J., & O'Keefe, D. L. (1982). The constructivist approach to communication. In F. E. X. Dance (Ed.), *Human communication theory* (pp. 147–191). New York: Harper & Row.

Denham, S. A., & Almeida, M. C. (1987). Children's social problem-solving skills, behavioral adjustment, and interventions: A meta-analysis evaluating theory and practice. *Journal of Applied Developmental Psychology, 8,* 391–409.

Deutsch, F. (1974). Observational and sociometric measures of peer popularity and their relationship to egocentric communication in female preschoolers. *Developmental Psychology, 10,* 745–747.

Dickson, W. P. (1981). Referential communication activities in research and in the curriculum: A metaanalysis. In W. P. Dickson (Ed.), *Children's oral communication skills* (pp. 189–204). New York: Academic Press.

Dlugokinski, E., & Firestone, I. J. (1974). Other-centeredness and susceptability to charitable appeals: The effects of perceived discipline. *Developmental Psychology, 10,* 21–28.

Dodge, K. A., Cole, J. D., & Brakke, N. P. (1982). Behavior patterns of socially rejected and neglected preadolescents: The role of social approach and aggression. *Journal of Abnormal Child Psychology, 10,* 389–410.

Enright, R. D., & Sutterfield, S. J. (1980). An ecological validation of social cognitive development. *Child Development, 51,* 156–161.

Flavell, J. H., in collaboration with Botkin, P. T., Fry, C. L., Wright, J. W., & Jarvis, P. E. (1968). *Role-taking and communication skills in children.* New York: Wiley.

Flower, L. A., & Hayes, J. R. (1980). The dynamics of composing: Making plans and juggling constraints. In L. W. Gregg & E. R. Steinberg (Eds.), *Cognitive processes in writing.* Hillsdale, NJ: Lawrence Erlbaum Associates.

Goffman, E. (1969). *Strategic interaction.* Philadelphia, PA: University of Pennsylvania Press.

Grusec, J. E., & Lytton, H. (1988). *Social development.* New York: Springer-Verlag.

Hoffman, M. L. (1977). Moral internalization: Current theory and research. In L. Berkowitz (Ed.), *Advances in experimental social psychology* (Vol. 10, pp. 85–133). New York: Academic Press.

Hoffman, M. J., & Saltzstein, H. D. (1967). Parent discipline and the child's moral development. *Journal of Personality and Social Psychology, 5,* 45–57.

Jones, J. L., Delia, J. G., & Clark, R. A. (1981, May). *Person-centered parental communication and the development of communication in children.* Paper presented at the annual convention of the International Communication Association, Minneapolis, MN.

Kline, S. L. (1981, May). *Construct system development and face support in persuasive messages: Two empirical investigations.* Paper presented at the annual meeting of the International Communication Association, Minneapolis, MN.

Kline, S. L. (1988). Social cognitive determinants of argument design features in regulative discourse. *Argumentation and Advocacy, 25,* 1–12.

Kline, S. L., & Ceropski, J. M. (1984). Person-centered communication in medical practice. In J. T. Wood & G. M. Phillips (Eds.), *Human decision-making* (pp. 120–141). Carbondale, IL: Southern Illinois University Press.

Kline, S. L., & Clinton, B. (1988, May). *The development of informative messages in fourth- through seventh-graders.* Paper presented at the annual meeting of the International Communication Association, New Orleans, LA.

Kohlberg, L. (1981). *Essays on moral development, Volume One: The philosophy of moral development.* San Francisco, CA: Harper & Row.

Kohlberg, L. (1984). *Essays on moral development, Volume Two: The psychology of moral development.* San Francisco, CA: Harper & Row.

Kurdek, L. A., & Krile, D. (1982). A developmental analysis of the relation between peer acceptance and both interpersonal understanding and perceived social self-competence. *Child Development, 53,* 1485–1491.

Lockwood, A. L. (1978). The effects of values clarification and moral development curricula on school-age subjects: A critical review of recent research. *Review of Educational Research, 48,* 325–364.

Marsh, D. T., Serafica, F. C., & Barenboim, C. (1981). Interrelationships among perspective-taking, interpersonal problem-solving, and interpersonal functioning. *Child Development, 28,* 149–159.

Mead, G. H. (1934). *Mind, self, and society.* Chicago, IL: University of Chicago Press.

Mosher, R. L. (Ed.). (1980). *Moral education: A first generation of research and development.* New York: Praeger.

Nahir, N. T., & Yussen, S. R. (1977). The performance of Kibbutz- and city-reared Israeli children on two role taking tasks. *Developmental Psychology, 13,* 450–455.

O'Keefe, B. J. (1988). The logic of message design: Individual differences in reasoning about communication. *Communication Monographs, 55,* 80–103.

O'Keefe, B. J., & Delia, J. G. (1979). Construct comprehensiveness and cognitive complexity as predictors of the number and strategy adaptation of arguments and appeals in a persuasive message. *Communication Monographs, 46,* 231–240.

O'Keefe, B. J., & Delia, J. G. (1982). Impression formation and message production. In M. E. Roloff & C. R. Berger (Eds.), *Social cognition and communication* (pp. 33–72). Beverly Hills, CA: Sage.

O'Keefe, B. J., & Delia, J. G. (1986). Psychological and Interactional dimensions of communicative development. In H. Giles & R. St. Clair (Eds.), *Advances in language, communication, and social psychology* (pp. 41–85). Hillsdale, NJ: Lawrence Erlbaum Associates.

O'Keefe, B. J., & Delia, J. G. (in press). Communicative tasks and communicative practices: The development of audience-centered message production. In B. Rafoth & D. Rubin (Eds.), *The social construction of written communication.* Norwood, NJ: Ablex.

O'Keefe, B. J., & McCornack, S. A. (1987). Message design logic: and message goal structure: Effects on perceptions of message quality in regulative communication situations. *Human Communication Research, 14,* 68–92.

O'Keefe, B. J., & Shepherd, G. J. (1987). The pursuit of multiple objectives in face-to-face persuasive interaction: Effects of construct differentiation in message organization. *Communication Monographs, 54,* 396–419.

O'Keefe, D. J., & Sypher, H. E. (1981). Cognitive complexity measures and the relationship of cognitive complexity to communication. A critical review. *Human Communication Research, 8,* 72–92.

Palincsar, A. S., & Brown, A. L. (in press). Classroom dialogue to promote self-regulated comprehension. In J. Brophy (Ed.), *Teaching for understanding and self-regulated learning: Vol. 1.* Greenwich, CT: JAI Press.

Piaget, J. (1926). *The language and thought of the child.* London: Routledge & Kegan.

Piaget, J. (1932). *The moral judgment of the child.* New York: Free Press.

Rest, J., Turiel, E., & Kohlberg, L. (1969). Relations between level of moral judgment and preference and comprehension of the moral judgment of others. *Journal of Personality, 37,* 225–252.

Rowan, K. E. (1985, November). *Cognitive complexity and explanations of scientific concepts.* Paper presented at the annual convention of the Speech Communication Association, Denver, CO.

Samter, W., & Burleson, B. R. (1984). Cognitive and motivational influences on spontaneous comforting behavior. *Human Communication Research, 11,* 231–260.

Shure, M. B. (1981). Social competence as problem solving. In J. D. Wine & M. D. Smye (Eds.), *Social competence.* (pp. 158–185). New York: Guilford.

Shure, M. B., & Spivack, G. (1978). *Problem-solving techniques in child rearing.* San Francisco, CA: Jossey-Bass.

Shure, M. B., & Spivack, G. (1980). Interpersonal problem-solving as a mediator of behavioral adjustment in preschool and kindergarten children. *Journal of Applied Developmental Psychology, 1,* 29–44.

Shure, M. B., & Spivack, G. (1982). Interpersonal problem-solving in young children: A cognitive approach to prevention. *American Journal of Community Psychology, 10,* 341–356.

Shure, M. B., Spivack, G., & Jaeger, M. (1971). Problem-solving thinking and adjustment among disadvantaged preschool children. *Child Development, 42,* 1791–1803.

Spivack, G., Platt, J. J., & Shure, M. B. (1976). *The problem-solving approach to adjustment.* San Francisco, CA: Jossey-Bass.

Spivack, G., & Shure, M. B. (1974). *Social adjustment of young children.* San Francisco: Jossey-Bass.

Strayer, J., & Mashal, M. (1983). The role of peer experience in communication and role-taking skills. *Journal of Genetic Psychology, 143,* 113–122.

Toulmin, S., Rieke, R., & Janik, A. (1979). *An introduction to reasoning.* New York: Macmillan.

Turiel, E. (1966). An experimental test of the sequentiality of developmental stages in the child's moral judgments. *Journal of Personality and Social Psychology, 3,* 611–618.

Warnick, B., & Inch, E. (1989). *Critical thinking and communication: An introduction to reasoning and argumentation.* New York: Macmillan.

Weinstein, E. A. (1966). Toward a theory of interpersonal tactics. In C. W. Backman & P. F. Secord, (Eds.). *Problems in Social Psychology* (pp. 394–398). New York: McGraw-Hill.

Werner, H. (1957). The concept of development from a comparative and organismic point of view. In D. B. Harris (Ed.), *The concept of development* (pp. 125–146). Minneapolis, MN: University of Minnesota Press.

Whitehurst, G. J., & Sonnenschein, S. (1981). The development of informative messages in referential communication: Knowing when versus knowing how. In W. P. Dickson (Ed.), *Children's oral communication skills* (pp. 127–141). New York: Academic Press.

Whitehurst, G. J., & Sonnenschein, S. (1985). The development of communication: A functional analysis. In G. J. Whitehurst (Ed.), *Annals of child development* (Vol. 2, pp. 1–48). Greenwich, CT: JAI Press.

Reading Comprehension
as a Dimension of Thinking

P. David Pearson
University of Illinois

Taffy E. Raphael
Michigan State University

Obviously, successful readers think as they read. In fact, some reading educators have been bold enough to suggest that reading is nothing more or less than thinking about information that happens to have been presented graphically on a printed page (e.g., Russell, 1961; Smith, Goodman, & Meredith, 1970; Stauffer, 1972). Yet, at a more specific level, we have yet to identify the dimensions of thinking involved in reading and comprehending. To do so involves a thorough understanding of those factors that influence comprehension. From this understanding a clearer set of relationships between comprehension and thinking can emerge.

As a way of grounding the key issues that stand at the interface of comprehending and thinking, we begin with a set of think-aloud protocols from three readers, each with very different abilities, reading the same story; they illustrate how complex the reading–thinking relationship is. They demonstrate that readers vary considerably in how they approach the reading task and how they think about what they read. These variations and the factors that account for them are central to our discussion of the interface between comprehension and thinking.

With the "window" provided by the protocols into the minds of our three readers, we can consider the range of thinking that occurs as they attempt to comprehend the story, *Nate the Great and the Lost List* (see Table 6.1 for a synopsis and sample story segments). In the think-aloud samples that follow, it will become clear that although all three students are "reading" and all are "thinking," they do not all achieve the same degree of success. The first reader, Michael, is quite successful and interactive as

TABLE 6.1
Text and Synopsis of *Nate the Great and the Lost List*

TEXT: I, Nate the Great, am a busy detective. One morning I was not busy. I was on my vacation. I was sitting under a tree with my dog, Sludge, and a pancake. Sludge needed a vacation, too.

My friend Claude came into the yard. I knew that he had lost something. That's the way Claude was.
"I lost my way to your house," he said. "And then I found it."
"What else did you lose?" I asked.
"I lost the grocery list I was bringing to the store. Can you help me find it?"
"I, Nate the Great, am on my vacation," I said.
"When will your vacation be over?"
"At lunch," I answered.

SYNOPSIS: Nate takes on the case of the lost list, making up a map of Claude's route, letting the map blow in the wind to replicate the list's travels, and finally tracing the map to Rosa's house. Rosa is making "cat pancakes" when they arrive. Later, while thinking about the case, Nate makes himself some pancakes and realizes the list of ingredients are much like the list that Claude lost. The only item on this lost list missing from the ingredients for pancakes was tuna fish, an item that Claude had remembered and mentioned to Nate. Nate finds his hunch is correct when he returns to Rosa and finds her cat pancakes are indeed pancakes made with the addition of tuna fish.

Note. From *Ginn Reading Program*, 1985, Level 8, pp. 186–196.

he thinks about the information in the text. Michael's thoughts reveal a focus on rendering text meaningful and awareness of the purposes for which he is reading the selection.

MICHAEL: (Looking at the title). Nate the Great! I love these stories. I wonder if this is like any of the ones in the library. I don't mind having to read this one at all. It'll be fun to talk about. {I, Nate the Great, . . . }. This story is being told by Nate the Great. Vacations are great. I love summer vacation. It must be summer since he's sitting under a tree with his dog— he wouldn't do that in the snow!! Maybe it's Thanksgiving, though—I wonder if it matters.

Claude lost something. Well, Nate the Great always fixes things—I bet this is a story about him finding the list. I was right! Plus, he and Claude must be really good friends—Nate only had vacation until lunch (he must not really have been on vacation, just taking a rest) and he's giving it up to help Claude.

Salt, milk, butter, flour, sugar, and tuna fish . . . this is probably important to remember since that's how I'll know if they found the right list. I know mystery stories always have tricks—they may even think they found a list, but find out it's not Claude's.

Nate is really smart! Dropping the map to see if the wind blows it to the same place the list must have blown. But he also needs luck for it to work.

Rosa is making cat pancakes? I wonder how these would be different from people pancakes? That doesn't make sense. Maybe they have different things in them. What do cats like? Birds! But she wouldn't put birds in a pancake. Oh well, if I keep reading, maybe I'll figure it out.

Notice that Michael is actively involved in reading the text, pausing to think about what he already knows and how it relates to the text, asking questions and wondering about the importance of different information, recognizing features of different genres of stories, and considering strategies that will help him continue to make sense of the story. He predicts upcoming events, makes judgments about the character's relationships, and withholds judgment when appropriate. These mental events represent several of the thinking skills outlined by Kennedy, Fisher, and Ennis (chap. 1 in vol. 2), such as seeking reasons, taking and changing positions based on evidence, and formulating questions. In contrast, our second student, Dennis, is far less active, less reflective, and shows little memory for what he has read.

DENNIS: Nate the Great is a neat rhyming name. V-a-c-a-t-i-o-n, uh, /va ka shun/. Oh! vacation. Yes, I've been on vacation before . . . (student continues reading the words) . . . Who is Rosa? . . . I wonder how they got to her house.

With our "window" into Dennis' thinking during the story, we can see that he is far less actively involved with the text. He pauses to think about vacation (but focuses on decoding the word), then more or less randomly recalls having been on a vacation. Further, his emphasis on decoding unhinges him, and he forgets who one of the main story characters is.

Our third student, Sandy, does not consider reading as a process of comprehending but focuses instead on trying to "get the words right." She is not as successful in decoding as Dennis and has a much lower standard for what constitutes a successful attempt. Because of this, she often does not monitor what she has read to see if it makes sense and, thus, becomes further mired in confusion and misreading of the text.

SANDY: (Reading from text) I, Nate the Great, am a busy deputy. One morning I was not busy. I was on my /vacshun/. I was sitting under a tree with my dog, /sud/, and a pancake. /Sud/ needed a /vacshun/ too. My fired Claude came into the yard. I knew that he likes something. That's the way Claude was.

Umm . . . Claude likes lists. Maybe this is about his favorite food. (Sandy continues reading and reaches the point in the story where Nate and Claude arrive at Rosa's during the making of cat pancakes. Then she reads on:) /Sud/ and I went to Rose's house. Rose opened the door. She looked strong and wild. She was covered with flour.

Ummm . . . Rose must be their friend, but maybe they are afraid of her because she is so strong.

Each of our students is engaged in thinking during reading, but the types of thinking in which each engaged clearly influenced their level of success at constructing meaning from their reading. These variations raise several questions: What influenced our readers as they attempted to comprehend their text? What research is there to support the influence of these variables? How can these findings from research on reading comprehension inform us about the current and future interfaces between comprehending and thinking? The purpose of this chapter is to address each of these questions.

A CONCEPTUAL FRAMEWORK
FOR COMPREHENSION

The conceptual framework we propose represents the contextual nature of reading comprehension. We chose a series of concentric circles (see Figure 6.1) to depict the relationship among these factors in order to minimize the likelihood that anyone might infer that they operate in isolation. For example, readers' goals are influenced by the more general context of the learning environment (e.g., home or school); similarly goals often shape the type of learning task that is selected. For example,

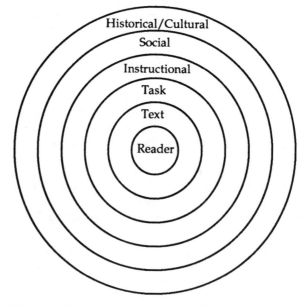

FIG. 6.1.   The contextual nature of reading comprehension.

Michael was clearly aware that the selection he was reading was an assignment from the teacher, yet he drew connections to similar stories he had read. His reflection that he did not mind having to read this and looked forward to the ensuing discussion indicates that he had differential expectations about his level of enjoyment and involvement in assigned readings. In contrast, neither of the other students made distinctions in the tasks, apparently operating under an assumption that reading is a unidimensional activity.

We identify six layers in our conceptual framework of factors that influence comprehension, from the broadest context to the most narrow, including (a) the historical/cultural context, (b) the social context, (c) the instructional context, (d) the task environment, (e) the text, and (f) the reader. Each is embedded in the next to illustrate just how much each factor is influenced by the others; indeed, to pretend that they are truly separable is nothing but a fiction we conveniently adopt so that we can discuss each in turn.

The Historical/Cultural Context

The broadest layer of our conceptual framework is the historical/cultural context; it includes events occurring over time that shape or influence current practices in reading. Gavelek (1986) suggested that "it is within the contexts of schooling that children of most societies acquire, refine, and learn how to make use of their skills of literacy" (p. 3). How schools define what is basic to literacy is determined by the criteria established by the society or culture as a whole. Resnick and Resnick (1977) have documented the changing standards for basic literacy, noting that these standards have become increasingly more demanding. Thus our very notion of comprehension is a dynamic rather than a static concept. According to Gavalek, changing standards may have contributed to our relatively recent discovery of literacy-related learning disabilities; they were not present in the first half of our century simply because we never thought of them as disabilities.

Perhaps the most powerful example of the effects of historical context on instruction and learning in reading comes from the influence of mastery learning concepts on reading curriculum. Prior to the late 1960s, the reading comprehension curriculum of basal reading programs in the United States consisted of some questions in the teachers' manual for teachers to use in story discussions, a few workbook pages devoted to comprehension skills using content related to the most recently read story, and a very occasional "progress check" test, probably also appearing in the teacher's manual (see Pearson & Dole, 1988, for a more elaborate discussion of this period). Then in the late 1960s, armed with the theoretical power of new views of learning for mastery by both Carroll (1963) and Bloom (1968), reading educators began to build new systems for managing reading instruction. Dubbed *skills management systems,* these systems operated on the assumption that most learners can achieve most learning objectives if we as teachers learn more about how to vary aspects of the learning environment.

Advocates of these systems criticized our earlier instructional programs for their inherent unfairness, especially to students for whom learning was difficult. (See Stallard, 1977, for a review of the many systems available in this period; also see Levine, 1985, for more recent reviews.) What we had done, they argued, was to hold instruction constant (treat everyone equal) and allow achievement to vary. What we needed to do, they argued, was to hold achievement constant (by specifying some level of mastery that everyone was to achieve) and allow instruction to vary. As candidates for instructional variation, they suggested such factors as student time on task (more practice), teacher time on task (more of the same instruction), new approaches to instruction, and a re-evaluation of whether prerequisite skills had been learned (see Bloom, 1968).

In the reading field, this mastery learning perspective became operationalized in the early 1970s in what came to be called skills management systems. The logic was as follows:

1. Define the scope and sequence of skills to be learned within the curriculum.
2. For each skill within the curriculum, develop one or more tests to determine whether individuals have mastered it.
3. For each test, identify a set of materials for defining and practicing the skill (to implement the practice of increasing student time on task).
4. Administer pretests to students. Identify those skills for which each student has not achieved mastery.
5. Allow students to practice unmastered skills for some identifiable number of practices.
6. Readminister a mastery test. Either exit to a new skill or set of skills or recycle through still unmastered skills with still more worksheets.

This logic was initially set into operation in either district-developed or commercially available skills management systems (see Stallard, 1977) that were not tied to any particular commercial basal reading series.

However, it did not take long for basal companies to see the wisdom of developing their own series-specific skills management systems; after all, districts who used either their own or a commercially available system were already demanding that basal companies list the workbook pages that corresponded to skills tested in their systems. So, by the late 1970s, virtually every major basal publisher had developed its own internal skills management system. And those occasional progress checks of a decade earlier were replaced by end-of-unit and end-of-book skill mastery tests that served as gateways (or roadblocks, depending on whether a student passed) to the next unit or book. Not surprisingly (and presumably to help those students who did not achieve immediate mastery), with the advent of internal skills management systems came the development of secondary workbooks, ditto packs, and booster activities as ancillary materials in the basal series of the late 1970s.

It was this mastery learning approach to skills instruction in basal series that was in full operation when Dolores Durkin studied comprehension instruction in American schools in the late 1970s (Durkin, 1978–1979). In that study, Durkin spent some 17,997 minutes in intermediate grade reading classrooms looking at what teachers did in the name of comprehension instruction. She found that teachers asking students questions after they read a story (what she called assessment) and students working independently on comprehension skill worksheets (e.g., finding the main idea, sequence of events, cause-effect relations, predicting outcomes, and the like) were what comprised comprehension activity in classrooms; only rarely—a total of 41 minutes—did she observe teachers engaged in any sort of direct teaching of comprehension skills. What she observed was completely consistent with the particular instantiation of mastery learning that occurred in the reading field: Instruction consisted of defining the component skills of a domain, assessing the skills, and providing lots of opportunity for students to practice them.[1] Although there have been some developments in the last decade to suggest that the mastery learning orientation of reading comprehension curricula has diminished slightly, it is still the case, as this chapter is written, that the end-of-unit and end-of-book mastery tests dominate basal readers in American schools.

But the picture is changing. The recent history of reading shows increasing influence of cognitive psychology and the psychology of language. These fields have helped to redefine reading as an interactive

---

[1] We need to distinguish between the mastery learning mentality underlying basal instruction in the late 1970s and early 1980s and mastery learning as it was instantiated in more complete and intentional mastery learning programs (see Jones, Amiran, & Katims, 1985), which seem to share much in common with what we call direct instruction programs.

process emphasizing the goal of comprehension rather than fluent pronunciation (See Anderson, 1977; Pearson, 1986; Rumelhart, 1977). Meaning is constructed by considering the author's intended message and the background knowledge and experiences that the readers bring to the text (Wixson & Peters, 1984). This redefinition has lead to the creation of new measures of comprehension assessment (Valencia & Pearson, 1987; Wixson, Peters, Weber, & Roeber, 1987) that will influence future definitions of what constitutes successful comprehension. Because the way in which we define reading influences the range of tasks that comprise reading, as well as the types of strategies that we teach to our students, the historical context in which reading instruction occurs influences how students think about reading.

Another aspect of the historical context is cultural, as "culture represents the sum of our development historically, whether development is considered broadly (e.g., society's culture) or more specifically (e.g., a given classroom or reading group)" (Raphael, 1986, p. 297). The cultures that influence our students' thinking about comprehension include specialized ones such as the culture of teacher education programs, as well as more traditionally defined cultures such as ethnic and political groups.

Colleges of education help to define the necessary knowledge base of our teachers. Thus, they have a tremendous impact on how we view relationships among different instructional domains. Recently the Carnegie Task Force on Teaching as a Profession (1986) and the Holmes Group (1986) reports have emphasized the importance of critical thinking for teaching. In responding to these reports, teacher educators may create expectations for a separate thinking skills curriculum, and thus, teachers will likely demand it. Conversely, if teacher educators put forward an "integrationist" view and create an expectation that thinking skills should emerge from problem-solving activities embedded within other curricular areas, such as reading and mathematics (see Kennedy et al., chap. 1 in vol. 2, for a good exposition of this issue), teachers will likely demand an integrated thinking skills curriculum. And, the influence of these demands will reach each individual student in our schools because the curriculum largely determines the tasks that students are asked to perform in the name of reading and thinking.

The cultural values that we possess by virtue of membership in ethnic, religious, or national groups influences how we think about what we read (e.g., how we determine levels of importance or how we group information into categories). For example, Steffensen, Joag-dev, and Anderson (1979) examined the effects of cultural background on comprehension by asking college students from the United States and from India to read about an American and an Indian wedding ceremony. The students not only read their native passage more quickly, but they were able to remember more of the important information than did students from the other cultural background. Lipson (1983) found similar effects on Catholic and Jewish students' comprehension when they read texts depicting religiously familiar versus unfamiliar (communion vs. Bar Mitzvah) ceremonies. She found that students remembered more, read faster, and made fewer errors on comprehension measures when reading about the ceremony most familiar to them. Similar effects have been found for both race (Reynolds, Taylor, Steffensen, Shirey, & R. C. Anderson, 1982; Schreck, 1981) and nationality (Pritchard, 1987).

Another example of the relationship between culture and comprehension can be found in the descriptions of the Kamehameha Early Education Program (Au & Mason, 1981; Tharp, 1982). Anthropologists, educators, educational psychologists, and reading specialists have collaborated to identify aspects of native Hawaiian culture that influence students' perceptions of the reading group tasks and goals. They have developed an instructional program consistent with native Hawaiian culture; the new program has led to improved student performance on both informal and standardized measures of reading comprehension.

The Social Context

The social context in which reading occurs also influences readers' thinking as they engage in comprehending texts. The social context includes variable such as where and with whom or what reading occurs. If the reading occurs in a school setting, is it in a reading group, at one's desk, or in the library? If the reading occurs in a reading group, is the focus on learning new reading strategies, discussing a story in a basal, or reacting to a student authored text for the purpose of providing feedback? If the reading occurs at one's desk, is the student voluntarily reading a self-selected book or an assigned chapter from a content area text prior to discussion. Thus, critical to an examination of the social context in which reading occurs is both the general setting and the patterns of interaction that occur between teacher and students and among students (see also Kennedy et al., chap. 1 in vol. 2, for a similar discussion related to the teaching of critical thinking).

The effect of context can be illustrated by considering Sandy, the student who read in order to decode the words accurately (or not so accurately) and was satisfied with constructing a meaning more consistent with her own mispronounced words than with the author's intended message. She thought her goal was to "get done" rather than to understand and learn. Anderson and her colleagues (L. Anderson, Alleman, Brubecker, Brooks & Duffy, etc., 1985) have found this attitude toward independent work to be pervasive among school children. In such a context, Sandy has a lower standard for defining successful comprehension. In another context—reading a note left by her mother explaining where she can find some cookies—Sandy might be more willing or likely to concentrate on the author's intended message. Similarly, if she were reading a story that she herself wrote a week ago, then Sandy would be more likely to suspend her obsession with decoding and getting finished, focusing instead on creating meaning for the written message (see Hansen, 1983).

The social interactions within a given context also influence students' comprehension and thinking. Thus, it matters whether reading is solitary or social. If solitary, meaning is constructed and tested by the reader herself. If social, the final decisions regarding meaning must be negotiated by the members of the group. Further, the social interactions around reading comprehension provide the basis for instruction in comprehension. That is, readers who may not be able to comprehend a text when reading on their own may succeed with support from their peers and teacher.

Wood, Bruner, and Ross (1976) have proposed the metaphor of a scaffold in describing the support provided by more experienced peers or adults. Like the scaffolding used in construction, scaffolded instruction *provides support, is temporary, and is adjustable.* In reading instruction, such scaffolding can be seen when a teacher, or when another student within a discussion group, takes on part of the responsibility for the task so that the less experienced learner can concentrate on acquiring or effectively applying a particular strategy.

Palincsar has conducted a series of studies (Palincsar & Brown, 1983; Palincsar, 1984) that exemplify the concept of scaffolding during reading comprehension instruction. Palincsar termed this instruction "reciprocal teaching." At the basis of reciprocal teaching are four strategies used by students and their teacher as they discuss text, constructing and negotiating the meaning of the text through their dialogue. The four strategies—predicting, summarizing, questioning, and clarifying—support the dialogue that occurs. The teacher serves as facilitator, initially directing students in the appropriate application of these strategies and gradually building students' independent use of the strategies as they take turns leading the discussions. In the case of reciprocal teaching, scaffolding occurs at two levels. First, there is the support the teacher provides following initial instruction in the four strategies. The teacher leads the discussions, helps students to apply the strategies, provides suggestions if students are unable to create relevant questions, and so forth. Second, there is the scaffolding provided by the four strategies. They become, in effect, a shared language to be used to remind students about how to think about the texts they read.

Englert, Raphael, and Anderson's work (Englert & Raphael, 1988; Englert, Raphael, Anderson, Anthony, Fear, & Gregg, 1988) provides a second example of scaffolding, as students learn strategies and skills that can be applied to composing and comprehending informational text. The program, dubbed CSIW for Cognitive Strategy Instruction in Writing, provides scaffolding throughout the range of social interactions that naturally occur in teaching-learning situations: as teachers model effective planning, drafting, and revising strategies; as they guide the students while the students, in turn, plan, draft, and revise informational essays; as they ask students to implement the strategies on their own, composing original essays from a variety of personal knowledge and text resources. Further support is available during this independent stage in the form of "think-sheets." These think-sheets are really a set of curriculum materials with questions or prompts designed to encourage particular thinking activities during different stages of reading or writing. They are quite reminiscent of thinking skill labels. Planning strategies, for example, may include determining one's purpose and brainstorming what is known about a given topic prior to reading or writing about it.

The comprehension instruction that occurs at Kamehameha Elementary Schools provides yet another example of scaffolded instruction, based on patterns of interactions called "talk-story" (Watson-Gegeo & Boggs, 1977), teachers provide instruction that is culturally compatible with the Hawaiian students. A teacher or student poses a question, and in the ensuing discussion, students simultaneously respond, often building on each others' responses without intervention by the teacher. Au (1979) has called the overall instructional framework E-T-R (Experience, Text, Relationship). The framework suggests instruction begin with the building of background knowledge by considering the readers' relevant *Experiences*, leading to a *Text-based* discussion, and finally to building *Relationships* between readers' background knowledge and text information. Often the questions posed by the teacher are beyond the ability of a single child within the group to answer. However, the collaborative nature of activity allows students to jointly construct and negotiate possible answers until they reach a mutually agreeable response. The teacher's role in such an interaction pattern is to provide support when necessary by asking a question that may redirect the students, or by repeating a response made by one or more students during the talk-story exchanges in order to highlight particularly relevant information.

The Instructional Environment

Obviously, the next layer in our conceptual framework, the instructional environment, is greatly influenced by the historical and cultural contexts in which it exists. Over the past 10 years, a great deal of research and rhetoric has been directed at the study of reading comprehension instruction. In the process of conducting that research, we have learned much about the instructional variables that influence the development of comprehension ability, some of which have already been addressed incidentally in unpacking the historical/cultural and social contexts (e.g., the Kamehameha work, reciprocal teaching, CSIW, and the work of Hansen and her colleagues). Although the research on reading comprehension instruction is much too rich, extensive, and (as yet) controversial to permit a complete and authoritative presentation, we can add to the completeness of our framework of reading comprehension by detailing some of the theoretical positions, findings, and unsettled issues.

Direct Instruction. At the most conservative end of the instructional continuum is the direct instruction position (see Gersten & Carnine, 1986, for an extensive review of the comprehension research conducted within this paradigm). It takes as its basic position the idea that children seldom learn what we do not teach them directly. A corollary of this position is that if we leave students to their own devices to develop particular skills and strategies, without benefit of teacher modeling, guided practice, and extensive feedback, they are likely to develop bad habits of reading or thinking. Hence, instruction must be well-planned, deftly executed, and extensively supported with much guided practice, independent practice, feedback, and assessment. Gersten and Carnine (1986) documented a host of skills and strategies that they feel are learned better in a direct instruction setting than in settings in which skills are merely practiced on their own by students (perhaps intended to simulate the kind of *kids-learn-to-comprehend-by-practicing-comprehension-activities* situation which Durkin, 1978–1979, was able to document so easily).

Explicit Instruction. A somewhat less systematic and less controlled version of direct instruction has been labeled explicit instruction by Pearson and his colleagues (Pearson & Dole, 1988; Pearson & Gallagher, 1983) and by Duffy and colleagues (1987). The basic differences between the pure direct instruction position and the explicit instruction position lie in task conceptualization and control over the learning environment. The advocates of explicit instruction see no need to conceptualize skills at a specific level. Indeed because there is so much conceptual overlap among comprehension skills (finding main ideas often entails both drawing inferences and determining cause-effect relationships simultaneously), there is probably both some theoretical merit and some practical benefit (time-savings) to more holistic notions of skill or strategy. An extension of this more holistic perspective is the requirement that skill application always occur with authentic texts instead of texts that were written specifically to facilitate skill application.

They view (see Pearson & Dole, 1988, or Pearson, Dole, Duffy, & Roehler, in press, for a complete discussion) control from more of a shared responsibility perspective than an exclusively teacher responsibility. In fact, the notion of a gradual release of responsibility for task definition and completion from teacher to student is central to the explicit instruction view. Although they raise many unanswered questions about this paradigm, Pearson and his colleagues cite supportive research to establish the efficacy of the explicit instruction position. They include the questioning work of Raphael and her colleagues (e.g., Raphael & Pearson, 1985; Raphael & Wonnacut, 1985), the metacognitive training studies of Paris and his colleagues (see Paris & Winograd, chap. 1 in this volume), and the comprehension skill work of Baumann (1984, 1986) as a part of this tradition.

The typical components in an explicit instructional routine leading to student independence include teacher modeling (making public the secrets of invisible processing), guided practice (a kind of cooperative learning milieu), independent practice (students doing it on their own), consolidation (getting together with students to see if they really have put it all together), and application (to authentic texts). Borrowing from the work of Paris, Lipson, and Wixson (1983), they suggest that the goal of such instruction is to help students get a handle on the WHAT (declarative knowledge), the HOW (procedural knowledge), and the WHEN and the WHY (conditional knowledge) of any skill or strategy worth teaching and learning. Most convincing is the research of Duffy and Roehler (Duffy et al., 1987); they have documented a positive relationship between the degree to which teachers are explicit about explaining the what, how, when, and why and the degree to which students acquire and use comprehension strategies.

Cognitive Apprenticeships. Although it shares much in common with aspects of explicit instruction, the notion of cognitive apprenticeships (see Collins, Brown, & Newman, in press, or Collins, volume 2 of this series) is an interesting alternative to the positions presented thus far. Collins makes several points in discussing the defining characteristics of cognitive apprenticeships. First the basic thesis of the cognitive apprenticeship position is that many of the complex, and ill-structured activities involved in learning school tasks are not well suited to the learning-as-the-transmission-of-knowledge model of Western culture. Instead, such activities are better suited to the apprenticeship model that used to characterize all instruction and continues to characterize instruction for entry into certain crafts and professions. Specifically, what is provided in apprenticeships, but not transmission models, is modeling (Collins has pretty much the same notion as Pearson or Duffy and Roehler), coaching (a more contextually sensitive version of Pearson's notion of guided practice and consolidation), and fading (almost identical to the notion of the gradual release of responsibility).

Second, Collins highlights the importance of the *situated* nature of learning in cognitive apprenticeships; that is, learning is always done in the service of completing genuine tasks (tasks that, for example, a journeyman or master would normally do) rather than tasks especially developed to provide opportunities for novices to practice. The ostensible advantage of situated learning is that the issue of transfer, which has proven to be such a difficult problem in thinking skills research (see Kennedy, Fisher, & Ennis, chap. 1 in vol. 2), is completely finessed.

Third, Collins describes three critical issues related to sequencing instruction within a cognitive apprenticeship framework—complexity, diversity, and the global/local skill distinction. In general, Collins suggests that tasks should increase in complexity over time, although not necessarily in a monotonic fashion. However, at every level of complexity, scaffolding is the mechanism that helps students cope with complexity. Diversity, meeting the same task in new problems and new situations, should also increase over time so that students are able to acquire a "richer set of contextual associations" for the task. In determining the sequence of skills to be taught, Collins suggests that students should complete global before local skills. Notice, this principle is in direct contrast to the mastery learning position described in our discussion of the development of skills management systems for basal readers. When students apply the global skills first, regardless of the amount of scaffolding involved, they begin to build a conceptual map that permits them to attach significance to the later acquired local skills.

As examples of instructional approaches that capture at least some aspects of cognitive apprenticeships, Collins cites Palincsar and Brown's (1983) reciprocal teaching of reading comprehension strategies (discussed earlier in this chapter), Scardamalia, Bereiter's procedural facilitation of writing (1983; also Scardamalia, Bereiter, & Sternbach, 1984), and Schoenfeld's method for teaching mathematical problem solving (1985, in press, in preparation). What all of these approaches have in common, of course, is that they engage students in situated learning while using the principles of modeling, coaching, and fading to learn complex strategies across diverse situations, focusing on teaching of global prior to local skills.

Cognitive apprenticeships, with such an emphasis on scaffolding, highlight the social nature of the learning process. When learning occurs in social situations, be it an apprenticeship or some other form of cooperative learning, learners have to negotiate roles and relationships with others in the environment (see Kline & Delia, chap. 5 in this volume, for a description of how this works in communication situations). In these social learning situations, teachers are given options that might not operate in a knowledge transmission milieu. The availability of scaffolding liberates teachers from the idea that a complex task must be broken down into manageable bits in order to be learned adequately; it does so by offering the alternative of providing support as students proceed with tasks too difficult or complex to complete on their own. With this alternative, teachers recognize that they have to intercede only to provide precisely the minimum assistance necessary for their students to achieve success.

Whole Language. Although the wide-scale research base necessary to support the rapidly spreading whole language movement is sparse, we can think of no recent literacy event that has attracted the attention of the field in the way that whole language has in the past 5 or 6 years (see Altwerger, Edelsky, & Flores, 1988; Goodman, 1986). Furthermore, it provides a perfect ballast for the other end of the continuum that we began with our description of direct instruction; we have moved, with each iteration (to explicit instruction to cognitive apprenticeship), closer to the philosophy underlying whole language.

What distinguishes whole language from the cognitive apprenticeship position is its absolute insistence on authenticity and local control of the learning environment. Everything must be authentic—the purposes for reading or writing, the audiences for whom the task is undertaken, the texts that are read or composed, and the tasks that students are asked to complete in response to reading.

The ultimate authority (and responsibility) for meaning resides with readers, be they 5 or 55 years old. Adults are useful in the learning environment to the degree that they can facilitate the responsible exercise of that authority. Thus, teachers can "demonstrate" their own uses of literacy tools to create meaning, but they cannot "tell" anyone what to do or when to do it. They can share, but they cannot impose, their interpretation of a story. Teachers can point out that communication with others is facilitated by the use of conventions such as spelling and punctuation, but they cannot impose such standards as criteria for judging quality. Clearly on this dimension, there is a difference between the cognitive apprenticeship position and the whole language position.

Much remains to be learned about the effectiveness of the whole language position as a *complete* instructional approach. Currently we have considerable evidence that many of its mandatory features are associated with successful instructional approaches. For example, we have evidence that reading literature enhances reading comprehension to a greater degree than does isolated skill practice (R. C. Anderson, Hiebert, Scott, & Wilkinson, 1985; R. C. Anderson, Wilson, & Fielding, 1988; Taylor & Frye, in preparation). And we know that encouraging students to try to spell words on their own even when they are unsure about a word (what we have come to call invented or inventive spellings) enhances the development of knowledge of letter-sound correspondences (see Clarke). And we know that allowing students to engage in wide-ranging, unfettered writing activities early in their school careers improves both the quality and quantity of writing (Calkins, 1983, 1986; Graves, 1983). What we do not know at present is what kind of either short-term or long-term effect a total whole language program has on student progress.

The Task Environment

Beyond the social context in which the reading task occurs, comprehension is further influenced by the specific tasks and their related goals and purposes. These can be set by the readers themselves, by an external agent such as a teacher, parent, or tutor, or in combination. The three students who were reading about Nate the Great were all apparently engaged in this task for purposes established by an external agent (i.e., teacher) during a reading group. The teacher's goal can be assumed to relate to the development of reading skills, whereas each of the students clearly interpreted the task in terms of their own perceptions. Michael operated as though the goal was understanding and he seemed to enjoy the task. Dennis' goal was to complete the task quickly, reading all the words; Sandy's goal was to decode each word.

The type of task and related purposes and goals also influence the thinking underlying comprehension. A reader who has selected a mystery story to read by the fire on a dreary evening thinks about the task quite differently than a junior high student reading the same story while getting ready for a class discussion; and both of them think differently from another student getting ready for an end-of-chapter test. The research on reader purpose and task environment is replete with examples of just how powerful these influences are (see Carey, Harste, & Smith, 1981; Pearson & Spiro, 1980; Spiro & Myers, 1984; Tierney & Cunningham, 1984).

Perhaps the most influential element of the task environment in today's schools is the testing system that we have built to monitor student progress and/or hold teachers and schools accountable to particular goals and standards. As we suggested earlier in discussing the influence of historical context, the criterion-referenced tests accompanying basal reading programs probably do more to control the types of tasks that occupy the time and energy of students and teachers than any other single curricular force. All one has to do is to note the uncanny similarity between these tests and the ubiquitous worksheets and workbooks accompanying these series in order to document the assertion that assessment drives instruction in American reading programs. The situation is further exacerbated by the fact that all of the basal reading companies do their best to make certain that the skills that appear on the major standardized reading tests are taught and tested in their series; and to make the know even tighter, testing companies, we have learned, now examine the skills taught in the major basals in order to make certain that the skills tested on their tests reflect what is taught in the basals. And the net result of all of this activity is to create an artificial "real world" of reading tasks for students and teachers, which may or may not bear any resemblance to tasks real readers perform when they appreciate good literature or examine text to find information they need to know or to decide whether they agree with an author.

The Text

There is no arguing against the central role played by the text in influencing the thinking required of readers in their attempts to comprehend. The type of text being read is one critical feature of textual influences. Two broad categories of texts are narrative and expository, the former encompassing genres such as fairy tales, historical and realistic fiction, and so forth, whereas the latter includes informational text patterns such as comparison/contrast, explanation, and cause and effect (Meyer, 1975; Meyer & Rice, 1984).

A number of studies have examined the relationship between students' knowledge of how texts are organized and their ability to comprehend these texts. Several researchers (e.g., Neilsen, 1977; Whaley, 1981) have found that students with more fully developed story schemata are more successful in both understanding and remembering text. Similarly, students who are more sensitive to the structures used in expository text are more successful in comprehension and recall of informational text (Raphael & Kirschner, 1985; Taylor, 1980, 1982; Taylor & Beach, 1984).

Different types of texts not only have different underlying structures, they address different types of questions (Armbruster & Anderson, 1984); thus, readers must exhibit flexibility in order to respond appropriately to different texts. In our opening example, Michael immediately recognized that the *Nate, the Great* selection was a mystery story and that he had read other Nate the Great stories. This knowledge allowed him to make several relevant hypotheses (that "mystery stories always have tricks" and that "Nate the Great always fixes things") for which the text became a body of evidence to use in subsequent evaluation. Mystery stories are a particular type of the narrative genre, answering the major question of "Who done (sic) it?" as other questions are considered. These include:

Where is this story taking place?
Who are the main characters?
What is the problem?
What happens?
How is the problem resolved?

These questions stand in contrast to those that might be implicitly (or explicitly) answered in an expository text about the industrial revolution. As an explanation, such a text would likely answer questions like:

What is being explained?
What or who is involved?
What are the steps?

Comparing the industrial revolution in the United States to economic changes in a less developed country may involve answering the questions:

What is being compared?
On what dimensions is the comparison based?
How are they alike?
How are they different?

An important implication for the teaching of both comprehension and thinking skills is that teachers should emphasize how a text can be used to facilitate both. Readers need to understand how texts like this are usually organized, how this one is organized (and whether it is typical), and where information useful for different questions, tasks, or purposes is likely to be located within the text. This is particularly important for students who have difficulty reading and writing informational text (Englert & Raphael, 1988).

Understanding informational text is difficult for students. One reason may be attributed to the lack of experience students have in reading content area material. Most children are quite familiar with narrative text. This is the most frequent type that they hear prior to schooling, and it is the staple of basal reading programs. A second reason why students experience difficulties with informational text is that the texts are often "inconsiderate" of their readers (Anderson, Armbruster, & Kantor, 1980; Armbruster, & Anderson, 1985), lacking clear organization and including few links to readers' experience.

The instructional research on teaching strategies for coping with the structures in different texts is generally positive. Most of this research has been completed within an explicit instructional framework and has shown that highlighting text structures from stories (see Braun & Gordon, 1984; Gordon & Pearson, 1983) or expositions (see Armbruster, Anderson & Ostertag, 1987; Berkowitz, 1986; Taylor, 1982; Taylor & Beach, 1984) facilitates comprehension.

Raphael and Englert's work discussed earlier (Englert & Raphael, 1988; Raphael, Englert, & Kirschner, in press) represents one attempt to provide strategies for identifying potential organizational patterns in which to embed information being read. Students learn to consider the questions authors may wish to address, and the different text structures that may be used to organize the information presented (e.g., comparison contrast, explanation, problem/solution). They first learn to use these questions as guides to their own writing of "pure" texts (e.g., writing an explanation), then they learn to use the different structures in combination, which is the way they are most often found in existing content area texts. Finally, they learn to try to "get into the minds" of the authors of their content area text and determine which questions the author was attempting to answer, what information is available in the text, and what information is missing. Eventually, students can be led through the text analysis, which is often necessary to determine when and why a breakdown in comprehension has occurred: Is the problem in the text presentation, in the readers' lack of background knowledge, or some combination? Such analyses are fundamental aspects of critical thinking, from "dealing in an orderly manner with the parts of a complex whole" to "focusing on a question" to "analyzing arguments" (Kennedy et al., chap. 1 in vol. 2).

The Reader

The sixth factor that influences comprehension is the reader. To appreciate more vividly the importance of the reader as the central figure in an interactive model of reading, consider our three *Nate, the Great* readers. While participating within the identical historical/cultural, social, and task environments, three dramatically different kinds of thinking unfolded as they worked to comprehend the text. These differences can be attributed to the reader. Readers differ from one another on a multitude of variables, the most relevant to our model being background knowledge, conceptual or vocabulary knowledge, and metacognitive knowledge.

There is a plethora of research that has demonstrated the importance of background knowledge to comprehension (see Pearson & Spiro, 1980). One strand of research has examined background knowledge in terms of the readers' perspective, (e.g., Anderson & Pichert, 1978, Carey, Harste, & Smith, 1981). For example, Anderson and Pichert asked adult readers to read a passage about two boys playing hookey and spending the day at one of their homes. Readers were assigned the perspective of a homebuyer or burgler. Homebuyers tended to remember information such as the amount of recent repair to the home, the number of rooms, and so forth, whereas burglers tended to remember the day of the week that the house was unlocked and where valuables were kept. Carey, Harste, and Smith (1981) found similar effects using other ambiguous passages (e.g., escaping from prison vs. escaping from wrestler's grip), though the effect of knowledge was further influenced by the social context (e.g., music building vs. gymnasium) in which the reading took place. The influence of background knowledge was demonstrated directly with children in a study by Pearson, Hansen, and Gordon (1979). They first tested second-grade students on their knowledge about spiders, then divided them into high-knowledge and low-knowledge groups. The students all read an expository selection about spiders and responded to comprehension questions. Not surprisingly, high-knowledge students performed at a higher level, particularly on inferential questions requiring them to integrate text and reader knowledge, that is, to think and read beyond the lines of the text.

The prior knowledge effect has been demonstrated by a number of researchers in a variety of knowledge domains (e.g., Hayes & Tierney, 1982; Marr & Gormley, 1982). However, other research suggests that it is not enough to possess such knowledge, readers must also understand when and how to apply it. Bransford and his colleagues (Bransford & Johnson, 1972; Bransford & McCarrell, 1974) provided evidence as readers read passages purposely written to be ambiguous. Providing hints, such as a title or a picture to invoke particular knowledge, dramatically improved adult readers' performance. Again, similar results have been found in studies with children (e.g., Au, 1979; Hansen & Pearson,

1983). When children engaged in prereading discussions designed to heighten their sensitivity to their own relevant knowledge or to help them build such knowledge, they were able to better comprehend the selections they then read.

One surface index of readers' background knowledge is conceptual or vocabulary knowledge. It is intuitively obvious to suggest that it is difficult to think about concepts that one knows little about. Michael showed how his conceptual knowledge influences thinking about events in *Nate the Great* when he wondered how cat pancakes would differ from people pancakes. This observation may eventually contribute to his solving the case of the missing list. Dennis used vocabulary knowledge as he tried to identify the word, "vacation," recognizing that he too had been on a vacation. However, unlike Michael, he did not tie such knowledge back to the text.

Nagy, Herman, and Anderson (1985) have documented the vast amount of vocabulary knowledge (some 40,000 to 80,000 words) that students develop over the course of the schooling, raising an interesting question of how such knowledge is obtained. It is clear that there is not enough time in the school career to teach the thousands of words that are learned. This research suggests that although some small subset of words can be taught directly, the overwhelming majority must be learned incidentally through context while reading and engaging in normal daily experiences.

But instruction can, and apparently does, help for the small subset of words for which it is feasible to provide instruction. Several instructional studies (e.g., Duin & Graves, 1988; Johnson, Toms-Bronowski, & Pittleman, 1982; McKeown, Beck, Omanson, & Pople, 1985) have shown that rich, conceptually based approaches to vocabulary instruction are superior to no instruction or to instruction that is either definitionally based or contextually based (where context means sentence context). The guidelines evolving from this research suggest that the "context" of the semantic fields of conceptual knowledge readers carry around in their heads is more appropriate than either the "context" of a dictionary or the "context" of a printed page for learning new words. This is not to say that learning from textual context is not important; given the Nagy et al. (1984) findings, it has to be important. A better interpretation is (a) that when vocabulary is taught directly, conceptual approaches are superior *and* (b) when readers acquire new vocabulary knowledge through whatever means they use (including text context), their ultimate task is to get it into the "context in the head."

Schwartz (in press; Schwartz & Raphael, 1985) suggested that an important determinant to students' ability to achieve the ultimate task of getting to the context in the head is their concept of definition. Schwartz has conducted a series of studies in which students learn to identify relevant information from available textual context clues to support their understanding of potentially new concepts. Based on work in semantic networks, Schwartz developed a concept map that helps students focus on identifying superordinates (What is it?), traits or properties (What is it like?), and examples as they build their knowledge of the meaning of words encountered in text. Concept of Definition can be thought of as a metacognitive strategy applicable to vocabulary development.

In addition to readers' backgrounds or conceptual knowledge, successful comprehension is influenced by the readers' metacognitive knowledge. The term, metacognition (for extensive discussion see Paris & Winograd, chap. 1 in this volume; Baker & Brown, 1984; Garner, 1988), has come to be associated with how readers understand and use cognitive processes and strategies and how readers think about and control the reading process. In fact, a popular term used to describe the ideal reader is *the strategic reader*.

Researchers have studied the relationship between learner's metacognitive knowledge about the reading process in general, as well as their knowledge and use of specific strategies and combinations of strategies. For example, positive correlations between knowledge about the process and ability to comprehend have been demonstrated by Paris and his colleagues (Paris & Myers, 1981). They interviewed third- and sixth-grade students, examining their knowledge of person, task, and strategy variables (vis à vis, Flavell & Wellman, 1977), finding that such knowledge increases with both age and ability.

Other researchers have examined the influence of students' knowledge and control of specific aspects of the comprehension process, further substantiating the positive relationship between such knowledge and successful comprehension. For example, Raphael, Englert, & Kirschner (1989) have shown that students' knowledge about how texts are organized is related to their successful composition and comprehension of informational texts. Palincsar and Brown (1983) have demonstrated positive relationships between students' control of four strategies of reciprocal teaching—summarizing, predicting, asking questions, and demanding clarity—and their successful comprehension of expository text.

The three students described in the first section portray the way in which these reader variables affect thinking about text. One can assume that all three were actively involved in trying to successfully complete the task assigned by their teacher, using all the strategies and knowledge they had available. But their different levels of knowledge about the topic, the genre, the words, and the strategies most appropriate for completing the task resulted in very different sorts of comprehension.

Thus, it is when we consider the individual that the full impact of the interactive model of reading that we are advocating can be seen. The model is both deterministic and idiosyncratic. It suggests that every level of the environment in which we engage in literacy events influences our engagement; but it also attributes great authority and responsibility for interpretation to the individual reader and recognizes that individual meaning is as important for self-efficacy as shared meaning is for communication.

THE COMPREHENSION-THINKING INTERFACE

So what does this model suggest about how the respective research and development traditions in reading comprehension and thinking skills can mutually inform one another? We pose three questions to discuss dimensions of thinking as a part of the reading process, each representing one way of considering the relationship between reading comprehension and thinking:

1.   What themes and issues are shared by researchers and theorists in the thinking skills and reading comprehension traditions?

2.   In what ways do thinking and reading comprehension overlap (in spite of different lexical items to describe the same phenomena)?

3.   How can those who are currently shaping the thinking skills curriculum benefit from the mistakes that reading researchers and developers have made in trying to build reading curricula from a base of theory and research?

Common Themes

As we have read other chapters in this volume and other volumes about thinking skills, we have been struck by some common themes, particularly *common influences,* that have been noted by researchers and theorists in both fields. For example, it is clear that although both comprehension and thinking are things that people can do and do do by themselves, both are regarded as social processes. And this social influence is not limited to the context in which they are learned. Both thinking and comprehending are thought of as things that people often do collaboratively; hence, meaning and significance must be negotiated. Both are heavily influenced by cultural phenomena; the ways in which people comprehend, conceptualize problems, solve problems, and weigh evidence vary from culture to culture. In a similar way, both are heavily influenced by the background knowledge that individuals bring to the task; thus, the kind of thinking that experts in a subject matter are able to do may differ from that of novices (see Hirsch, 1987; Simon, 1981). From an instructional point of view, both respond well to scaffolding of the type we have referred to in our *cognitive apprenticeship* model of instruction.

Reading comprehension and thinking are beset by some of the *same thorny conceptual and instructional issues.* For example, the issue of whether thinking skills should be a separate curriculum or embedded within current school subjects is, once one gets beneath the surface differences, the same debate that we have in reading about whether reading comprehension skills can or should be decontextualized from authentic texts in order to deal with the processes underlying them in a clear, pristine manner.

Both are *taxonomic phenomena;* hence, they represent domains that lend themselves to indefinitely more fine-grained analysis. Several questions about infrastructure can be raised for both domains:

- How much must the holistic process of comprehension or thinking be decomposed into more specific components in order to become useful in a curriculum?
- At what point does the further decomposition become counterproductive in the sense that it creates a curricular monster that saps the energies of students and teachers and, in the process, deceives them about the highly interrelated nature of the components?
- Do taxonomies based on logic, intuition, or common sense stand up to statistical tests of construct validity? In other words, do the relational data derived from separate assessments of each of the components corroborate our a priori schemes for decomposition?

In short, both reading comprehension and thinking are highly contextualized activities, and they are plagued by similar instructional debates.

Overlapping Processes

In examining the taxonomies of thinking skills provided by many of the thinking skills theorists in this and other volumes, any reading comprehension researcher is struck by the conceptual—but not the lexical—

overlap between the two domains. There are numerous examples. The generic notion of categorizing is important in almost all of the thinking skills taxonomies; although it is most often called classification in reading curricula (and often gets classified as a vocabulary rather than a comprehension skill), it is a pervasive part of reading comprehension activity in most curricula. The notion of determining levels of importance for ideas within a body of information goes under a variety of names within reading curricula—summarizing, determining the main idea, making generalizations; in thinking skills curricula, it tends to be labeled as identifying premises or conclusions, defining the problem, and the like. Inductive reasoning (reasoning from particulars to the general case) is a cornerstone of thinking skills curricula; in reading, it can be found in many disguises—drawing conclusions, making generalizations, constructing main ideas, drawing inferences (most inference tasks in reading programs are inductive rather than deductive), predicting outcomes, or determining cause-effect relations.

Even critical thinking can be found in reading, as well as writing, programs. In reading, it comes packaged as determining the relevance of information to support an inference, justifying an answer, finding support for a main idea or a generalization, determining the "emotional loading" of certain connotative meanings of words or the "excess baggage" that metaphorical expressions drag along with them. In writing curricula, we believe, it is an inherent feature of the very processes of composition and revision; after all, how can one decide on a change in style, wording, grammar, or even punctuation without thinking about its impact on a potential reader. Hence, writers are always confronted with the question of the validity and impact of their arguments. In thinking skills curricula, critical thinking is often understood as discovering fallacies of reasoning and evaluating the accuracy of information. These are, of course, activities that readers engage in—the kind of "evaluative" activities just described. Hopefully, there are also activities that writers use when they evaluate and revise their own writing.

The point about all of this overlap is that both reading and thinking skills curriculum specialists need to recognize and take advantage of the fact that the overlap exists and provides additional opportunities for curricular reinforcement of important instructional goals within either curriculum.

Lessons to be Learned

As we have developed new reading curricula, using even the best and newest perspectives from reading research and theory, we have made a number of mistakes that we hope need not be repeated by those who develop thinking skills curricula. We close with these lessons in the hope that thinking skills theorists, researchers, and practitioners may travel a straighter and smoother road than we in the reading field have traversed over the last decade or so.

The first piece of advice is to avoid decontextualization of skill instruction, even if the cost is complexity. It is very tempting to generate "clear cut" examples to illustrate how a skill or process ought to apply. But the curriculum specialist who does so, like the scientist examining gravity in a vaccuum, is doomed to misrepresentation; students will learn a lot about skills that can only be used for special examples in specially created workbooks, and they are likely to also learn that these are skills that are not to be used in real reading or thinking situations.

The second piece of advice is to build teacher-reliant, not teacher-proof, materials. We took the teacher-proof approach in reading when we misapplied the notions of mastery learning in building skills management systems for teaching skills. We built a system predicated on the single assumption that practice makes perfect—that what students who have yet to achieve mastery need is more of what they did not get right the first time. Difficult, time-intensive work within the direct instruction, explicit instruction, and cognitive apprenticeship traditions has taught us that good instruction puts both student and teacher at the center of the picture and relies on naturally occurring rather than specially prepared materials.

The third piece of advice is to avoid the decomposition fallacy. Breaking complex processes down into simpler components does not always make it easier for students to master those processes. The danger is that the component subskills, which the curriculum designers may have conceptualized as mere stepping stones (enabling skills) on the way to complex skill mastery, become ends unto themselves. This is especially true in the case of skills management systems, which seduce teachers and administrators into celebrating subskill mastery.

In Conclusion

We want to close by expressing our unbridled enthusiasm for the excitement we see in the thinking skills movement over the past half-decade. And we welcome the opportunity to work with colleagues from many fields in restoring to our educational endeavors at all levels a respect for the dignity and the mystery of the human mind.

REFERENCES

Altwerger, B., Edelsky, C., & Flores, B. M. (1987). Whole language: What's new? *The Reading Teacher, 41*(2), 144–154.

Anderson, L. M., Brubecker, N. L., Alleman-Brooks, J., & Duffy, G. G. (1985). A qualitative study of seatwork in first grade classrooms. *Elementary School Journal, 86*(2), 1–19.

Anderson, R. C. (1977). The notion of schemata and the educational enterprise. In R. C. Anderson, R. J. Spiro, & W. E. Montague (Eds.), *Schooling and the acquisition of knowledge* (pp. 415–432). Hillsdale, NJ: Lawrence Erlbaum Associates.

Anderson, R. C., Hiebert, E. H., Scott, J. A., & Wilkinson, I. A. (1985). *Becoming a nation of readers: The report of the Commission on Reading.* Washington, DC: National Institute of Education.

Anderson, R. C., & Pichert, J. W. (1978). Recall of previously unrecallable information following a shift in perspective. *Journal of Verbal Learning and Verbal Behavior, 17,* 1–12.

Anderson, R. C., Wilson, P. T., & Fielding, L. G. (1988). Growth in reading and how children spend their time outside of school. *Reading Research Quarterly, 23* (3), 285–303.

Anderson, T. H., Armbruster, B. B., & Kantor, R. N. (1980). *How clearly written are children's textbooks? Or, of bladderworts and alfa* (Reading Ed. Rep. No. 16). Urbana: University of Illinois, Center for the Study of Reading.

Armbruster, B. B., & Anderson, T. H. (1984). *Producing considerate expository text: Or easy reading is damned hard writing* (Reading Ed. Rep. No. 46). Urbana: University of Illinois, Center for the Study of Reading.

Armbruster, B. B., & Anderson, T. H. (1985). Producing "considerate" expository text: Or, easy reading is damned hard writing. *Journal of Curriculum Studies, 17,* 247–274.

Armbruster, B. B., Anderson, T. H., & Ostertag, J. (1987). Does text structure/summarization instruction facilitate learning from expository text? *Reading Research Quarterly, 22*(3), 331–346.

Au, K. H. (1979). Using the experience-text relationship method with minority children. *Reading Teacher, 32,* 677–679.

Au, K. H., & Mason, J. M. (1981). Social organizational factors in learning to read: The balance of rights hypothesis. *Reading Research Quarterly, 17,* 115–152.

Baker, L., & Brown, A. L. (1984). Metacognitive skills of reading. In P. D. Pearson (Ed.), *Handbook of reading research* (pp. 353–394). New York: Longman.

Baumann, J. F. (1984). The effectiveness of a direct instructional paradigm for teaching main idea comprehension. *Reading Research Quarterly, 20,* 93–115.

Baumann, J. F. (1986). Teaching third-grade students to comprehend anaphoric relationships: The application of a direct instruction model. *Reading Research Quarterly, 21*(1), 70–90.

Berkowitz, S. J. (1986). Effects of instruction in text organization on sixth-grade students' memory for expository reading. *Reading Research Quarterly, 21*(2), 161–178.

Bloom, B. S. (1968). Learning for mastery. *Evaluation Comment, 1*(2), 1–12.

Bransford, J. D., & Johnson, M. K. (1972). Contextual prerequisites for understanding: Some investigations of comprehension and recall. *Journal of Verbal Learning and Verbal Behavior, 11,* 717–726.

Bransford, J. D., & McCarrell, N. S. (1974). A sketch of a cognitive approach to comprehension. In W. Weimer & D. Palermo (Eds.), *Cognition and the symbolic processes* (pp. 189–230). Hillsdale, NJ: Lawrence Erlbaum Associates.

Braun, C., & Gordon, C. (1984). Writing instruction as a metatextual aid to story schema applications. In J. Niles & L. Harris (Eds.), *Changing perspectives on reading/language processing and instruction* (pp. 61–65). Rochester, NY: National Reading Conference.

Calkins, L. (1983). *Lessons from a child.* Portsmouth, NH: Heinemann.

Calkins, L. (1986). *The art of teaching writing.* Portsmouth, NH: Heinemann.

Carey, R. F., Harste, J. C., & Smith, S. L. (1981). Contextual constraints and discourse processes: A replication study. *Reading Research Quarterly, 16*(2), 201–212.

Carnegie Task Force on Teaching as a Profession. (1986). *A nation prepared: Teachers for the 21st century.* Washington, DC: Carnegie Forum on Education and the Economy.

Carnine, D. W., Kameenui, E. J., & Coyle, G. (1984). Utilization of contextual information in determining the meaning of unfamiliar words. *Reading Research Quarterly, 19,* 188–204.

Carroll, J. (1963). A model for school learning. *Teacher's College Record, 64,* 723–733.

Clarke, L. K. (1988). Invented versus traditional spelling in first graders' writings: Effects on learning to spell and read. *Research in the Teaching of English, 22*(3), 281–309.

Collins, A., Brown, J. S., & Newman, S. E. (in press). Cognitive apprenticeship: Teaching the craft of reading, writing, and mathematics. In L. B. Resnick (Ed.), *Knowing, learning, and instruction: Essays in honor of Robert Glaser.* Hillsdale, NJ: Lawrence Erlbaum Associates.

Duffy, G., Roehler, L., Sivan, E., Rackliffe, G., Book, C., Meloth, M. S., Vavrus, L. G., Wesselman, R., Putnam, J., & Bassiri, D. (1987). Effects of explaining the reasoning associated with using reading strategies. *Reading Research Quarterly, 22*(3), 347–366.

Duin, A. H., & Graves, M. F. (1988). Intensive vocabulary instruction as a prewriting technique. *Reading Research Quarterly, 22*(3), 311–330.

Durkin, D. (1978–1979). What classroom observations reveal about reading comprehension instruction. *Reading Research Quarterly, 14,* 481–533.

Englert, C. S., & Raphael, T. E. (1988). Constructing well-formed prose: Process, structure, and metacognitive knowledge. *Exceptional Children, 54*(6), 513–520.

Englert, C. S., Raphael, T. E., Anderson, L. M., Anthony, H. M., Fear, K. L., & Gregg, S. L. (1988). A case for writing intervention: Strategies for writing informational text. *Learning Disabilities Focus, 3*(2), 90–113.

Flavall, J. H., & Wellman, H. M. (1977). Metamemory. In R. J. Kail, Jr., & J. W. Hagen (Eds.), *Perspectives on the development of memory and cognition* (pp. 3–33). Hillsdale, NJ: Lawrence Erlbaum Associates.

Garner, R. (1988). *Metacognition and reading comprehension.* Norwood, NJ: Ablex.

Gavelek, J. R. (1986). The social contexts of literacy and schooling: A developmental perspective. In T. E. Raphael (Ed.), *The contexts of school-based literacy* (pp. 3–26). New York: Longman.

Gersten, R., & Carnine, D. (1986). Direct instruction in reading comprehension. *Educational Leadership, 43*(7), 70–78.

Goodman, K. (1986). *What's whole in whole language?* Exeter, NH: Heinemann.

Gordon, C., & Pearson, P. D. (1983). *Effects of instruction of listening comprehension research* (Reading Ed. Rep. No. 39). Urbana, IL: University of Illinois, Center for the Study of Reading.

Graves, D. (1983). *Writing: Teachers and children at work.* Portsmouth, NH: Heinemann.

Hansen, J. (1983). The writer as meaning-maker. In J. L. Collins (Ed.), *Teaching all the children to write* (pp. 10–18). Albany, NY: New York Council of Teachers of English.

Hansen, J., & Pearson, P. D. (1983). An instructional study: Improving the inferential comprehension of fourth grade good and poor readers. *Journal of Educational Psychology, 75,* 821–829.

Hayes, D. A., & Tierney, R. J. (1982). Developing readers' knowledge through analogy. *Reading Research Quarterly, 17*(2), 256–280.

Hirsch, E. D. (1987). *Cultural literacy.* Boston: Houghton-Mifflin.

The Holmes Group. (1986). *Tomorrow's teachers: A report of the Holmes Group.* East Lansing, MI.

Johnson, D. D., Toms-Bronowski, S., & Pittleman, S. (1982). *An investigation of the effectiveness of semantic mapping and semantic feature analysis with intermediate grade level children* (Program Report No. 83-3). Madison, WI: Wisconsin Center for Educational Research.

Jones, B. F., Amiran, M. R., & Katims, M. (1985). Teaching cognitive strategies and text structures within language arts programs. In J. Segal, S. F. Chipman, & R. Glaser (Eds.), *Thinking and learning skills: Relating instruction to research* (pp. 259–269). Hillsdale, NJ: Lawrence Erlbaum Associates.

Levine, D. (Ed.). (1985). *Improving student achievement through mastery learning programs.* San Francisco: Jossey-Bass.

Lipson, M. Y. (1983). The influence of religious affiliation on children's memory for text information. *Reading Research Quarterly, 18*(4), 448–457.

Marr, M. B., & Gormley, K. (1982). Children's recall of familiar and unfamiliar text. *Reading Research Quarterly, 18*(1), 89–104.

McKeown, M. G., Beck, I. L., Omanson, R. C., & Pople, M. T. (1985). Some effects of the nature and frequency of vocabulary instruction on the knowledge and use of words. *Reading Research Quarterly, 20* (5), 522–535.

Meyer, B. J. F. (1975). *The organization of prose and its effects on memory.* Amsterdam: North-Holland.

Meyer, B. J. F., & Rice, E. G. (1984). The structure of text. In P. D. Pearson Ed.), *Handbook of reading research* (pp. 319–351 New York: Longman.

Nagy, W. E., Herman, P. A., & Anderson, R. C. (1985). Learning words from context. *Reading Research Quarterly, 20*(2), 233–253.

Neilson, A. (1977). *The role of macrostructures and linguistic connectives in comprehending familiar and unfamiliar written discourse.* Unpublished doctoral dissertation, University of Minnesota, Minneapolis, MN.

Palincsar, A. M. (1984). The quest for meaning from expository text: A teacher-guided journey. In G. G. Duffy, L. R. Roehler, & J. M. Mason (Eds.), *Comprehension instruction: Perspectives and suggestions* (pp. 251–264). New York: Longman.

Palincsar, A. M., & Brown, A. L. (1983). Reciprocal teaching of comprehension-fostering and comprehension-monitoring activities. *Cognition and Instruction, 1* (2), 117–175.

Paris, S., Lipson, M., & Wixson, K. (1983). Becoming a strategic reader. *Contemporary Educational Psychology, 8,* 293–316.

Paris, S., & Myers, M., II. (1981). Comprehension monitoring, memory, and study strategies of good and poor readers. *Journal of Reading Behavior, 13*(1), 5–22.

Pearson, P. D. (1986). Twenty years of research in reading comprehension. In T. E. Raphael (Ed.), *Contexts of school-based literacy* (pp. 43–62). New York: Longman.

Pearson, P. D., & Dole, J. (1988). *Explicit comprehension instruction: A review of research and a new conceptualization of instruction.* Elementary School Journal, 88 (2), 151–165.

Pearson, P. D., Dole, J., Duffy, G. G., & Roehler, L. R. (in press). Developing expertise in reading comprehension: What should be taught? How should it be taught? In S. J. Samuels & A. E. Forstrup (Eds.), *What research says to the teacher* (2nd Edition).

Pearson, P. D., & Gallagher, M. C. (1983). The instruction of reading comprehension. *Contemporary Educational Psychology, 8,* 317–344.

Pearson, P. D., Hansen, J., & Gordon, C. (1979). The effect of background knowledge on young children's comprehension of explicit and implicit information. *Journal of Reading Behavior, 9,* 201–210.

Pearson, P. D., & Spiro, R. (1980). Toward a theory of reading comprehension instruction. *Language Disorders and Learning Disabilities, 1,* 71–88.

Pearson, P. D., & Valencia, S. (1987). Assessment, accountability, and professional prerogative. In S. Baldwin & J. Readance (Eds.), *Research in literacy: Merging perspectives* (pp. 3–16). Rochester, NY: National Reading Conference.

Pritchard, R. (1987). *The effects of cultural schemata on reading processing strategies.* Unpublished doctoral dissertation, Indiana University, Bloomington, IN.

Raphael, T. E. (1986). Contexts of school-based literacy: A look toward the future. In T. E. Raphael (Ed.), *Contexts of school-based literacy* (pp. 295–310). New York: Longman.

Raphael, T. E., Englert, C. S., & Kirschner, B. W. (1986). *The impact of text structure and social context on students' comprehension and production of expository text* (Research Series 177). East Lansing, MI: Michigan State University, Institute for Research on Teaching.

Raphael, T. E., Englert, C. S., & Kirschner, B. W. (1989). Acquisition of expository writing skills. In J. N. Mason (Ed.)., *Reading and Writing Connections* (pp. 261–290). Boston, MA: Allyn & Bacon.

Raphael, T. E., & Kirschner, B. W. (1985). *The effects of instruction in compare/contrast text structure on sixth-grade students' reading comprehension and writing production* (Research Series No. 161). East Lansing, MI: Institute for Research on Teaching, Michigan State University.

Raphael, T. E., & Pearson, P. D. (1985). Increasing students' awareness of sources of information for answering questions. *American Educational Research Journal, 22,* 217–235.

Raphael, T. E., & Wonnacott, C. A. (1985). Heightening fourth grade students' sensitivity to sources of information for answering comprehension questions. *Reading Research Quarterly, 20,* 282–296.

Resnick, D. P., & Resnick, L. B. (1977). The nature of literacy: An historical exploration. *Harvard Educational Review, 47*(3), 370–385.

Reynolds, R. E., Taylor, M. A., Steffensen, M. S., Shirey, L., & Anderson, R. C. (1982). Cultural schemata and reading comprehension. *Reading Research Quarterly, 17*(3), 353–366.

Rumelhart, D. (1977). Toward an interactive model of reading. In S. Dornic (Ed.), *Attention and performance* (pp. 573–604). Hillsdale, NJ: Lawrence Erlbaum Associates.

Russell, D. H. (1961). *Children learn to read.* Boston: Ginn.

Scardamalia, M., & Bereiter, C. (1983). *The development of evaluative, diagnostic, and remedial capabilities in children's composing.* York University, The Ontario Institute for Studies in Education.

Scardamalia, M., Bereiter, C., & Steinbach, R. (1984). Teachability of reflective processes in written composition. *Cognitive Science, 8,* 173–190.

Schoenfeld, A. H. (1985). *Mathematical problem solving.* Orlando, FL: Academic Press.

Schoenfeld, A. H. (in press). On mathematics as sense-making: An informal attack on the unfortunate divorce of formal and informal mathematics. In D. N. Perkins, J. Segal, & J. Voss (Eds.), *Informal reasoning and education.* Hillsdale, NJ: Lawrence Erlbaum Associates.

Schoenfeld, A. H. (in preparation). *Ideas in the air.* (IRL report 88-0011). Palo Alto, CA: Institute for Research on Learning.

Schreck, J. (1981). *The effects of contents schema on reading comprehension for hispanic, black, and white cultural groups.* Unpublished doctoral dissertation, University of Illinois, Urbana, IL.

Schwartz, R. M. (in press). Learning to learn vocabulary in content area textbooks. *Journal of Reading.*

Schwartz, R. M., & Raphael, T. E. (1985)., Concept of definition: A way of improving students' vocabulary. *Reading Teacher, 39,* 198–205.

Simon, H. A. (1981). *The sciences of the artificial* (2nd ed.). Cambridge, MA: MIT Press.

Smith, E. B., Goodman, K. S., & Meredith, R. (1970). *Language and thinking in the elementary school.* New York: Holt, Rinehart and Winston.

Spiro, R., & Meyers, A. (1984). Individual differences and underlying cognitive processes. In P. D. Pearson (Ed.), *Handbook of reading research* (pp. 471–501). New York: Longman.

Stallard, C. (1977). Comparing objective based reading programs. *Journal of Reading, 21*(1), 36–44.

Stauffer, R. (1972). *Directing the reading-thinking process.* New York: Harper & Row.

Steffensen, M. S., Joag-dev, C., & Anderson, R. C. (1979). A cross-cultural perspective on reading comprehension. *Reading Research Quarterly, 15,* 10–29.

Taylor, B. M. (1980). Children's memory for expository text after reading. *Reading Research Quarterly, 15,* 399–412.

Taylor, B. (1982). Text structure and children's comprehension and memory for expository material. *Journal of Educational Psychology, 74,* 323–340.

Taylor, B. M., & Beach, R. W. (1984). The effects of text structure instruction on middle-grade students' comprehension and production of expository text. *Reading Research Quarterly, 19*(2), 134–146.

Taylor, B. M., & Frye, B. J. (1988). *Pretesting: An effective way to minimize time spent on skill work in the intermediate reading class.* Unpublished manuscript, University of Minnesota.

Tharp, R. G. (1982). The effective instruction of comprehension: Results and description of the Kamehameha Early Education Program. *Reading Research Quarterly, 17*(4), 503–527.

Tierney, R. J., & Cunningham, J. W. (1984). Research on teaching reading comprehension. In P. D. Pearson (Ed.), *Handbook of reading research* (pp. 609–655). New York: Longman.

Valencia, S., & Pearson, P. D. (1987). Reading assessment: Time for a change. *The Reading Teacher, 40*(8), 726–732.

Watson-Gegeo, K., & Boggs, S. T. (1977). From verbal play to talk-story: The role of routines, in speech events among Hawaiian children. In S. Erwin-Tripp & C. Mitchell-Kernan (Eds.), *Child discourse* (pp. 27–52). New York: Academic Press.

Whaley, J. F. (1981). Readers' expectations for story structure. *Reading Research Quarterly, 17*(1), 90–114.

Wixson, K. K., & Peters, C. W. (1984). Reading redefined: A Michigan reading association position paper. *The Michigan Reading Journal, 17,* 4–7.

Wixson, K. K., Peters, C. W., Weber, E. M., & Roeber, R. (1987). New directions in statewide reading assessment. *Reading Teacher, 40,* 749–755.

Wood, D., Bruner, J. S., & Ross, G. (1976). The role of tutoring in problem solving. *Journal of Child Psychology and Psychiatry, 17,* 89–100.

7

Individuals and Environments in Writing Instruction

John R. Hayes
Carnegie Mellon University

In this chapter, I focus on a list of six rather diverse factors, each of which has been shown empirically to have an important impact on learning and performance in writing. Of course, there are many important factors. I have chosen these particular six because they are either widely ignored (e.g., spatial factors, perceptual knowledge, and the cultural context) or because there is new, exciting information about them (e.g., the computer environment and the social environment) or for both reasons. We will see that all six of these factors play an important role in our vision of the skilled learner of writing.

FACTOR 1: TASK DEFINITION

Usually, when we design an assignment or a teaching procedure, our attention is focussed squarely on what we want the student to learn, for example, summary writing or revision. We take care to select writing tasks that we believe will give the writer an opportunity to learn the skill we want to teach but we do not focus on the tasks. We view writing tasks as means rather than ends. If some of our students do better than others, we are predisposed to attribute differences in performance to differences in the student's skill in doing the task. We usually do not think to attribute them to differences in the way the students interpret the task. This is because we tend to assume that there *are* no differences in the tasks. After all, as the designers of the assignment, we intended that all participants would do the same task. We know that more advanced students tend to write better than less advanced ones (e.g., tenth grade vs. eighth grade) and we are likely to attribute the differences in performance that we see to differences in skill. Inferences of this sort may be hazardous, though, because there is good reason to believe that younger and older student writers may differ systematically in the way they define the writing tasks to be performed. Thus, differences in writing performance might result from differences in task definition, that is, what the writers think they are supposed to do, rather than from differences in the ability to do the task. In this section, I first discuss evidence that writers who differ in age and experience do define important writing tasks differently. Then I discuss evidence that training procedures may change the writers' task definition.

A number of researchers have reported marked differences in the way experienced and inexperienced writers approach revision. There is considerable evidence that less experienced revisors focus their attention far more locally than do more experienced revisors. Stallard (1974) found that only 2.5% of twelfth-graders' revisions were focused above the word and sentence level. Bridwell (1980), who also studied twelfth graders, found about 11% of revisions above the sentence level.

Sommers (1980) found that college freshmen understand the revision process as a rewording activity, that is, they concentrate on particular words apart from their role in the text. In contrast, experienced writers, (e.g., journalists, editors, and academics) describe their primary objectives when revising as finding the form or shape of their argument. Further, Sommers found that the experienced writers have a secondary objective; a concern for their readership.

Faigley and Witte (1983), who studied writers at various skill levels, found that experts were more likely to change meaning through revision than were novices. They observed that the revisions of inexperienced college writers resulted in changed meaning of 12% of cases; the revisions of experienced college writers, in 25% of cases; and the revisions of experienced adult writers, in 34% of cases.

Hayes, Flower, Schriver, Stratman, and Carey (1987) found that experts and novices differed systematically in their implicit definitions of the revision task. Experts defined revision as a whole-text task. They tended to read the whole text through before beginning revision and created global goals to guide the revision process. Novices, in contrast, saw revision largely as a sentence level task in which the goal was to improve individual words and phrases without modifying the text structure.

Bereiter and Scardamalia (1987) have described differences in task definition that are broader in scope than those just described. They have proposed two general models of the writing process: *knowledge telling*, which characterizes writing processes most usually found in immature writers and *knowledge transforming*, which characterizes writing processes most frequently found in adults and more sophisticated students. In knowledge telling, the writer defines the task of writing as one of reporting knowledge that is relevant to the topic. Thus, the writer who is assigned a topic such as "Should girls and boys play on the same sports teams" will search memory for information suggested by keywords in the topic (e.g., *girls, sports*, etc.) evaluate the relevance of the retrieved information, and then write down whatever retrieved information is judged relevant. Bereiter and Scardamalia (1987) quote a 12-year-old student describing his own composition process as follows:

> I have a whole bunch of ideas and write down until my supply of ideas is exhausted. Then I might try to think of more ideas up to the point when you can't get any more ideas that are worth putting down on paper and then I would end it. (p. 9)

This procedure is simple and effective for many school assignments and for many of the less complex tasks in the adult world, as well.

In contrast to knowledge telling, in which writers write down any information which is judged relevant, knowledge transforming writers define the task of writing as involving the modification of the retrieved information for the purposes of the essay. Retrieved information is reworked to fit with what has been written and what the writer plans to write. What is written, then, is not just what the writer knows but new thoughts as well—thoughts stimulated by the process of writing.

These examples illustrate that writers do differ in their definitions of important writing processes. The interesting possibility is that perhaps we can improve students' writing performance simply by encouraging them to adopt more appropriate definitions of writing tasks. However, it may be that differences in the way writers define tasks simply mirror differences in underlying abilities. Perhaps the junior high school student who defines writing as knowledge telling or the freshman who defines revision as a sentence level task cannot write or revise in any other way. Empirical work by Scardamalia and Bereiter and their colleagues (Bracewell, Scardamalia, & Bereiter, 1978; Burtis, Bereiter, Scardamalia, & Tetroe, 1983) suggests that young writers may, in fact, lack sufficient control over their writing processes to allow them to be successful knowledge transformers. This may not be the case for adult writers, however. Observations by Nelson and Hayes (in press) indicate that college writers can and do modify their definitions of writing tasks to suit the circumstances. For example, a bright college senior, planning a history paper, commented that she could take either of two paths in composing the paper. The easier path involved summarizing her sources and "just shoving in quotes." She would then "tack on some sort of analysis in the last paragraph." The harder path involved analysis of the conflicting accounts to reveal biases and hidden motives in the sources. Her motive here was to get closer to the truth than a simple reporting of the source information would allow. Although this student eventually chose the easier path (because she was "just a science student, not a history major"), she clearly understood that she had the option of transforming knowledge rather than just telling it.

I am really making two points here. First, groups *do* differ in the way they define important writing tasks. Thus, some of the differences in performance that we might attribute to differences in skill may in fact be due to differences in task definition. Second, in some cases at least, task definitions are malleable. That is, some writing performances can be improved simply by making clear to writers what it is that we want them to do. Nelson and Hayes (in press) provide clear evidence supporting this point. (The evidence is discussed later in the section on Social Context.)

Training procedures are intended to improve skills, but they can also have the unintended effect of changing task definition. In evaluating a training procedure, then, we run the risk of confusing increases in skill with changes in task definition. A very insightful study by Smith and Combs (1980) illustrates the point dramatically. At the time Smith and Combs designed their study, there was substantial evidence that a semester's worth of training in sentence combining increased the semantic complexity of a student's writing as measured by mean words per T-unit and mean words per clause (Mellon, 1969). Further, it was believed, and indeed it may be true, that the increased semantic complexity reflected increased linguistic skill imparted by training. However, Smith and Combs (1980) wondered if the increase in complexity might have another cause. Perhaps the changes in performance resulted from covert cues in the training process, which told the students that the task was not just "to write an essay" but rather to "write an essay with long and complicated sentences." To test this hypothesis, Smith and Combs compared three conditions. In the overt cue condition, students were told that the reader of the essay would be a highly intelligent person who is influenced by long and complex sentences. In the covert cue condition, students were given 2 days of sentence combining exercises. Smith and Combs regarded 2 days of training as sufficient to provide cues about how the writing task should be defined, but not sufficient to change skills significantly. In the control condition, students were simply told to write. Results indicated that both the overt and the covert cue conditions resulted in increases in syntactic complexity comparable to those obtained by Swan (1977) and by Morenberg, Daiker, and Kerek (1978) through a semester of training in sentence combining.

The important principle to be derived from the Smith and Combs study is that it is easy to confuse an increase in skill with a change in the way the student defines the task to be performed. When we think that we have a procedure that teaches people a new writing skill, we should always consider comparing the training groups to a control group that receives no training but is asked to try to perform in the way we want the training group to learn to perform. To the extent that "just asking" succeeds, we know that the participants already had the skills we were trying to teach, but the writing task was defined in a way that did not reveal them.

For some writing tasks and for some populations of writers, then, a direct approach to changing writers' task definitions does seem promising. For example, I suspect that freshmen revisors could revise globally if they knew that that was the task they should do. An important objective for researchers and educators, then, is to identify populations of writers whose performance on specific writing tasks could be improved by instruction in appropriate definitions of the tasks.

FACTOR 2: PERCEPTUAL SKILLS

In teaching writing, we focus so much on strategies and rules that we tend to ignore the high-level perceptual skills that underlie skilled writing performance. Although knowledge of topic and genre, a repertoire of strategies, and, indeed, appropriate task definitions are extremely important for skilled performance in writing. I want to argue that this list is not complete because in addition, the writer needs a repertoire of perceptual skills—skills required to recognize problems in the text such as lack of focus, clarity, wordiness, poor diction, and so forth. These skills are essential for the control of the writing process. Writers must be able to perceive problems if they are to fix them or avoid them.

I want to emphasize here that I am concerned with high-level perceptual skills. Educators and researchers have been appropriately attentive to the low-level perceptual skills involved in the visual and auditory recognition of words, but they have not attended to the skills involved in the perception of higher level concepts such as coherence, wordiness, or clarity.

Our revision studies (Hayes et al., 1987) showed that freshmen may be persistently insensitive to problems that more experienced writers would detect easily. For example, one freshman, revising for a freshman audience, read the following sentence four times without finding fault with it. The sentence was "Many naive women possess the assumption that it is necessary to be very skillful to play on varsity teams." On his final reading, he said, "Good! Freshmen would like that." This sort of insensitivity to text problems presents a major difficulty for composition teachers. It is hard to teach students to avoid pitfalls that they can't see.

The best example of a study that focuses on the teaching of high-level perceptual skills was conducted by Schriver (1987). The objective of this study was to determine if training could increase writers' ability to detect aspects of texts that confuse readers. Prior to her teaching study, Schriver created a training text (Schriver, 1984) consisting of 10 two-part lessons. Each lesson contained:

1. *A "problematic" first draft of a text.* For example, one that will give the intended audience difficulties in understanding it. These draft texts did not contain spelling and grammatical errors, but rather had poor definitions, unclear procedures, missing examples, ambiguities, and other "above the word or phrase"level problems. All were written for lay readers.
2. *A reader protocol of a person trying to understand the draft text.* For each of the 10 texts, a "thinking aloud" protocol was collected from a member of the actual audience in the process of trying to understand the text. The protocols revealed a wide variety of understanding problems.

To evaluate the effectiveness of these training materials, Schriver (1987) used a pretest–posttest design. In pretest and posttest, the participants' task was to predict those aspects of a set of texts that would create comprehension problems for the reader. The pretest and posttest materials consisted of six half-page passages that were excerpted from the science and medicine sections of *Time* and *Newsweek* magazines. To determine the accuracy of the writers' predictions of reader problems during pretest and posttest, it was necessary to determine exactly what problems the stimulus texts created for readers. To identify the problems, Schriver collected reading protocols from 30 freshmen trying to understand each of the six texts.

The participants who received training were college juniors and seniors enrolled in ten intact classes in professional writing. Five classes served as the experimental group and five as the control group. Writers in the experimental group were trained with the reader protocol materials over a period of 3 weeks. Writers in the control group were trained in traditional audience analysis heuristics and peer response methods.

The results of the study were quite dramatic. Figure 7.1 shows the hit rates (the mean number of times participants correctly predicted a reader problem) for experimental and control groups on pretest and posttest.

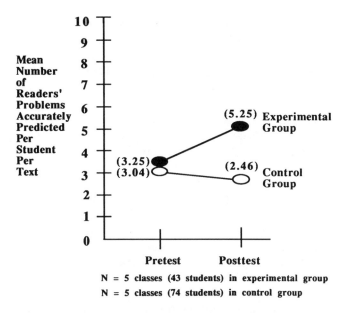

FIGURE. 7.1. The Effect of Reader Protocol Teaching on the Accuracy of Readers' Problems Predicted (Mean Hit Rate).

After training, the experimental group correctly identified significantly more reader problems than before (62% more) whereas the pretest differences between experimental and control groups and the pretest-posttest differences for the control group were not significant.

Schriver's method, then, proved quite successful in teaching writers to detect text features that will cause problems for the reader. One can imagine that the method has considerable promise not just for writers but for training audience sensitivity more generally, for example, for training speakers how their talks will be received and for training literature teachers how their students will respond to assigned texts.

Attention to high-level perceptual skills is important because they are critical in the control of writing processes. If writers do not perceive that their texts lack focus or suffer from wordiness, they will not do anything to solve these problems. The success of Schriver's method suggests that research on and teaching of high-level perceptual skills can have important payoffs.

FACTOR 3: SPATIAL ASPECTS OF TEXT

Discussions of writing tend to focus so strongly on linguistic and rhetorical features that we forget that texts are visual and spatial as well.

Graphic designers, of course, have long been aware that factors such as headings, margins, and white space have very important impact on the clarity, impressiveness, and aesthetics of a text. As writing teachers, though, we do tend to forget these things and are surprised when we encounter evidence of the impact of spatial features of text. My first such surprise was provided in a very clever study by Rothkopf (1971). Rothkopf demonstrated that when people read text, they often remember the spatial location of information that they have read (e.g., "On top of the right hand page about a third of the way through the book.").

Spatial factors also turned up in a study of paragraphing (Bond & Hayes, 1984). In the study, readers were presented with unparagraphed texts and asked to add paragraphing where appropriate. The texts included normal English texts as well as texts that had various categories of words (e.g., nouns, function words) replaced by nonsense words or by x's. Our objective was to identify the semantic and linguistic features of the text, which cued writers to insert paragraphing. As a natural extension of the sequence of text mutilations described earlier, we designed a "control" text in which sentences were replaced by wiggly horizontal lines, Only the beginnings and endings of sentences were preserved in this condition. We expected that with all the lexical and semantic cues removed, participants would be unable to agree as to how the text should be paragraphed. To our surprise, participants agreed with each other in paragraphing the text significantly better than could be expected by chance. We had to conclude that there is a spatial component in paragraphing which can operate independent of linguistic and semantic factors.

Spatial factors also turned up unexpectedly in a series of studies about how people use word processing in writing (Haas & Hayes, 1986). The first study of the series was an interviewing study of 16 experienced computer writers. Almost all of these writers routinely used hard copy printouts at some point in the writing process. When asked why they used hard copy, their most frequent response was that they wanted to get a "better sense of the text." In many cases, the writers used spatial metaphors to describe what they meant by "text sense." For example, one writer said, "I need a hard copy to feel the text's center of gravity." The remaining studies in the series were designed to identify ways in which hard copy might give the writer a better "sense of the text." Recalling the Rothkopf (1971) study discussed earlier, we designed an experiment that measured readers' ability to remember the spatial location of information when it was presented either in hard copy text or in comparable computer screen displays. Participants were asked to read several pages of information either on computer screen or in hard copy. (Computer screens and hard copy pages contained the same number of lines of text and the same number of words per line and were laid out in the same way.) Then the participants were provided with blank pages or screens (depending on whether they had read the text from pages or screens) and asked to point to the locations at which they had read several items of information. We found that readers were significantly better at remembering the location of information when it was presented in hard copy than when it was presented on the computer screen.

In a follow-up experiment, participants were asked to read a text and then to answer questions that required them to search for and retrieve information from the text. As was predicted from the results of the previous experiment, participants took longer to retrieve information when the text was presented on the computer screen than when it was presented on paper.

In a second follow-up experiment, participants were shown texts that had been altered by moving several text lines from their original locations to new locations in the text. The task was to reorganize the text by identifying these lines and their appropriate locations. Significantly less time was required to reorganize texts when they were presented in the paper condition than in the computer condition.

These studies indicate that we represent text spatially as well as linguistically, and that the spatial as well as the linguistic factors are involved in what writers call "getting a sense of the text." When we write, we lay words out in space and when we read, we represent both linguistic and spatial features of the text. Teachers and students should be aware that writing papers entirely on the computer without reference to hard copy print out may degrade the spatial image of the text and make it difficult for the writer to evaluate the text's organization. Encouraging writers to use hard copy for revision appears to be good educational practice.

FACTOR 4: THE PHYSICAL ENVIRONMENT

Some writers have reported very strong preferences about the physical environment in which they write—preferences for particular writing instruments, particular rooms, and particular times of day. (See, for example, Wason, 1980). However, no systematic data have been collected to determine the practical importance of these idiosyncratic preferences. The widespread use of the computer as a new and radically different writing instrument has lead to increased interest in the impact of physical environment on writing. Some, like Daiute (1983) have de-

	Condition	
	pen and paper	computer
Number of planning clauses in protocol divided by total clauses in protocol	.339	.272
Proportion of planning clauses in protocol which occur before anything is written	.426	.283

FIGURE. 7.2.   Planning clauses of protocols.

scribed this impact in largely positive terms. Clearly, word processing provides many useful tools for the writer. However, because word processing systems are occupying an increasingly important role in educational and industrial settings, it is important to have a good understanding of the impact these systems have on the writing process.

Haas (1987) has investigated the planning processes of writers who were composing with computer versus pen and paper. She collected thinking aloud protocols from 10 students and 10 experienced writers, each of whom composed an essay using only computer and another essay using only pen and paper. Haas divided the protocols into clause units and identified those clauses that reflected planning activities. Although experienced writers planned much more than students, both groups showed a greater proportion of planning clauses to total clauses in the pen and paper condition than in the computer condition. Further, writers planned more before starting to write in the pen and paper condition than in the computer condition. These results are shown in Figure 7.2.

In addition, Haas found that the kind of planning that the writers did was influenced by the instrument they used to write. Haas divided planning clauses into several categories including those concerned with sentence level issues (e.g., proposing wording for sentences) and those concerned with conceptual issues (e.g., "Let's see . . . I need to tie this all together in a concluding paragraph"). Haas found a significantly higher proportion of sentence level plans and a significantly lower proportion of conceptual plans when writers used the computer than when they used pen and paper. Mean proportions of total planning clauses are shown in Figure 7.3.

In summary, then, Haas found that when writers wrote with a computer they planned less overall, planned less before beginning to write,

	sentence level		conceptual	
	pen	computer	pen	computer
expert	27.9	36.9	66.2	53.7
novice	22.4	35.4	69.4	50.2

FIGURE. 7.3.   Proportions of low and high level plans.

and planned less at a conceptual level than when they wrote using pen and paper. These findings are clearly of great importance for education and practice in writing. Further research is very definitely in order.

Writers who work with word processing systems, of course, are not constrained to do their writing entirely on the computer. In fact, a study of 16 experienced computer writers by Haas and Hayes (1986) showed that nearly all of these writers made some use of hard copy while composing. To determine what it was that writers were using the hard copy for, Haas (1987) studied six freshmen and five experienced writers over a 4-month period. During that time, the writers were asked to keep process logs when they used word processors to write. They were asked to note especially when they used hard copy and what they used it for, in addition, they were observed while writing in their natural environments. Haas found four major uses of hard copy:

1. Formatting. In many word processing systems, the screen format is different from the hard copy format.
2. Proofreading. Many writers found it easier to search for spelling and punctuation problems with hard copy than online.
3. Reorganizing. Writers expressed a need to examine hard copy to assure themselves that reorganizations done online had had the desired effect on the text.
4. Critical reading. Many writers felt that they could not adequately evaluate the development of their text or "get a sense of the text" unless they read it in hard copy.

Haas found that the distribution of these uses of hard copy by experienced writers was quite different from the distribution for freshmen, as is shown in Figure 7.4. Freshmen were much more likely to use hard copy to check format and spelling, whereas more experienced writers were more likely to use it to evaluate organization and meaning.

Haas divided data for the experienced writers into two sets: one set for "long" texts and one set for "short" texts. The distribution of hard copy

Uses of Hard Copy

	Students	Experienced Writers
Formatting	75%	31%
Proofreading	13%	9%
Reorganization	8%	21%
"Text Sense"	4%	39%

FIGURE. 7.4.   Use of hard copy by students and experienced writers.

use for the short texts resembled that for novice writers, whereas the distribution for long texts resembled that for the experienced writers. The use of hard copy to evaluate organization and meaning then appeared to be restricted to long texts.

Haas has found important differences in the way writers plan when they write on-line rather than with pen and paper. Further, she has found that freshmen and experienced writers make different uses of the computer as a writing tool. These findings suggest that we may want to look very carefully at how we introduce students to the use of word processing and, in particular, how we introduce them to the choices among the writing tools available to them.

Haas' findings may depend on the relative newness of computers as compared to pencil and paper. Future generations, with more advanced equipment and earlier exposure to word processing, may plan as well on-line as off. Although the problems Haas points to may eventually go away, there is no doubt that they are matters that educators should be seriously concerned about now.

Cultural and Social Contexts

The human environment has enormous impact on writing. After all, writing has no point outside of the human environment. I have chosen, rather arbitrarily, to focus here on two aspects of the human environment: the cultural context and the social context. By cultural context, I refer to those persistent beliefs and practices that distinguish one group from another (e.g., the French from the Italians, or working class from upper class). By social context, I refer to the within-culture effects of the people who interact with the writer—the teachers or employers who set goals for the writer and may pass judgment on the resulting text, and the friends and peers who may provide suggestions and comments while writing is in progress.

FACTOR 5: CULTURAL CONTEXT

Culture is an important context for many aspects of human behavior and it seems especially important for linguistic behaviors. When we ignore other cultures, we run a risk close to certainty of interpreting our own cultural choices (e.g., the role of literacy in western culture) as reflecting "human nature." Also, we run a high risk of assuming that what we see in our culture is all there is to see. As Purvis (1988) has pointed out, European educational practices are different from American practices and those differences are instructive. For example, he noted that while American writing assignments are typically limited to 50 minutes, European students are often required to produce a finished essay in 3 hours. We might assume, as indeed I have in designing writing studies, that students would be incapable of writing effectively for more than an hour or so, but European experience seems to indicate that this assumption is false.

The effects of culture are seen quite clearly when individuals must switch between cultures, as do some black children attending a predominantly white school system. Such students learn to adjust their linguistic behaviors to the demands of the current culture. Hymes (1971) illustrated this point by quoting a black mother who said, "You know, I've noticed that when the children play 'school' outside, they talk like they are supposed to in school; and when they stop playing school, they stop" (p. 17). If we observed the children described by Hymes in just one cultural context, whether it be the street or the school or the laboratory, we might not see the full range of language skills that they have available to them.

An interesting study by Stevenson, Lee, Stigler, Hsu, Lucker, and Kitamura (1987), comparing Chinese, Japanese, and American classrooms, illustrates the importance that cultural factors can have for education in mathematics and language arts. The Stevenson et al. study was done in the context of widespread observations that American students perform much more poorly on tests of mathematical computation and problem solving than do oriental students (Crosswhite, Dossey, Swafford, McKnight, & Cooney, 1985). There are also indications that oriental students outperform their American counterparts in language skills as well, but the differences are less dramatic than those in mathematics (Stigler, Lee, Lucker, & Stevenson, 1982). Although some have claimed that these differences in performance are due to differences in innate ability (Lynn, 1982), research has failed to support this claim (Stevenson & Azuma, 1983). To provide information that might account for the observed differences in performance, Stevenson et al. (1987) conducted a very careful study of teacher and student behaviors in a representative sampling of Japanese, Taiwanese, and American first- and fifth-grade classrooms. They found several striking cultural differences in the educational practices of the three countries.

Time in School.   Children in Taiwan and Japan spend more time in school than American children do. Although first graders in all three countries spend about the same amount of time in school each week (about 30 hours), differences appear in the later elementary grades. In fifth grade, American students spend about 31 hours per week in school; Japanese students, about 37 hours per week; and Chinese students about 44 hours per week. Further, the American school year is about three quarters the length of the school year in Japan and Taiwan (170 to 180 days in the U.S. as compared to 230 to 240 days in Japan and Taiwan).

Efficiency.   Class time is used more efficiently in Chinese and Japanese schools than it is in the U.S. in the sense that Chinese and Japanese students spend a larger portion of their class time engaging in academic activities than do American students. Americans spend more time out of class (attending but not in class) and more time in transitional activities (e.g., putting books away, waiting for feedback, etc.) than did the oriental students. Figure 7.5 shows the percent of class time and the estimated total hours per week that children were engaged in academic activity for each grade and each country.

Classroom Organization.   Chinese and Japanese classrooms are much more teacher focused than American classrooms. Students in Taiwan and Japan spend much more time working together as a class than they do working in small groups or as individuals, whereas students in the U.S. spend more time working alone than they do working as a class. American children worked on individual activities 47% of the time; Japa-

	American	Japanese	Chinese
First Grade	20.9	23.4	24.3
Fifth Grade	19.6	32.6	40.4

FIGURE. 7.5.   Hours per week students were engaged in academic activities.

	American	Japanese	Chinese
First Grade			
Language Arts	10.5	8.7	10.4
Mathematics	2.7	5.8	4.0
Fifth Grade			
Language Arts	7.9	8.0	11.1
Mathematics	3.4	7.8	11.7

FIGURE. 7.6. Hours of instruction delivered per week.

nese students, 28% of the time; and Chinese students, 18% of the time. Corresponding to these differences, American teachers spent less time imparting information (21%) than did the Japanese (33%) or the Chinese (58%) teachers. One might argue that the greater emphasis on individual activities is a strength of American schools. However, one should note that within the American schools, Stevenson et al. (1987) found strong and significant negative correlations between the amount of time students work alone and achievement in reading ($r = -.69$) and in math ($r = -.57$).

Distribution of Class Time by Subject. American schools devote a much larger proportion of class time to teaching language arts (41.6%) than to teaching math (18%). In contrast, Chinese and Japanese schools devote about equal time to these two subjects (24%-28%). Figure 7.6 shows Stevenson et al.'s estimates of the numbers of hours of instruction delivered per week in each subject and each school system. These results indicate that American schools are delivering much less instruction in mathematics per week than are Japanese and Chinese schools (less than half as much in fifth grade). Because of the greater length of the oriental school year, these differences would be even more striking if we computed hours of instruction delivered per year.

These results strongly suggest that the relatively poor performance of American versus oriental students could result from cross-cultural differences in educational practice; in particular, differences in classroom organization and in the number of hours of instruction delivered. It is interesting that one of the few areas in which Japanese education is not strong, written composition (Kinosita, 1986), is currently a source of concern to Japanese computer manufacturers. Apparently Japanese companies have lots of employees who can design, build, and program computers, but relatively few who can write clear instructions to customers about how to use them.

FACTOR 6: SOCIAL CONTEXT

Britton, Burgess, Martin, McLeod, and Rosen (1975) have emphasized the importance of social context in writing. As a demonstration of the impact of the student writer's social environment, they point to "the change which comes over adolescent pupils' writing when it is genuinely directed to a peer-audience. Our research has revealed how dramatic this change is" (p. 63).

> "If we look more closely at the context of situation we see that almost all the writing with which we are concerned is in the school domain. The act of written communication in this domain is in many ways unlike other similar acts even when they are apparently identical." . . . "In school, however, the context is one in which this undertaking will be taken as an 'exercise', ... In this context, [the pupil's] audience will overwhelmingly be predetermined and sharply defined; the teacher, a known audience of one."

Laboratory studies of writing typically do not explore issues of social context. Of course, laboratory studies *have* a social context. The social relation between experimenter and participant is a rather special one as Rosenthal (1966) has shown. However, the impact of social context is rarely the focus of laboratory studies of writing. This is not to say that such studies are without value as some have asserted (e.g., Graves, 1980). Laboratory studies are often the most effective way to answer certain kinds of questions. Clearly, laboratory studies such as those of Rothkopf (1971) on spatial memory for text and Haas' studies of writing with word processors yield very valuable information. However, when the researcher's focus is on social context, then ethnographic studies, case studies, and experimental studies in natural contexts seem generally preferable to laboratory studies.

Freedman (1987) showed that student investment in preserving peer social relations can doom an otherwise promising teaching strategy to almost certain failure. She carried out intensive case studies of two ninth-grade classes of two highly successful teachers in schools with outstanding reputations. In both classes, the teachers made use of peer response groups to provide students with feedback about their writing. Freedman tape recorded and analyzed some 60 of these response groups.

In some of the groups, students read their texts aloud and identified problems that they were having in their writing for the group. Members of the group were expected to provide useful comment, but, Freedman found, other students offered advice to the writer in only 12.5% of cases. Even when writers requested help directly, 83% of these requests were ignored.

In other groups, students were asked by the teacher to respond in writing on response sheets by answering questions such as "What words or sentences seem out of place?" and "Is it convincing?" Students almost always refused to provide negative feedback to their peers. Instead, group members worked collaboratively, often with the writer, to compose responses that would preserve peer relations and also satisfy the teacher's explicit instructions. The following is an example of students composing such a response:

> Mike: I'm not going to say anything is out of place. Okay?"
> Donald: "Yeah, everything's great. Perfect!"
> [Both laugh]

Clearly, teachers and researchers who want to develop effective teaching strategies are well advised to keep students' social dynamics in mind, especially for strategies involving student interaction in groups. Unfortunately, this advice is very easy to forget.

In a series of experimental and case studies of students writing in natural college environments, Nelson and Hayes (in press) have shown that social context can shape the writing process in dramatic ways. The authors selected a random sample of eight students in classes that had been assigned to write research papers. These students were asked to keep daily logs of all of the activities involved in writing their assigned papers, for example, library research, planning, and conversations with peers, as well as the actual production of text. The diaries were collected by the researchers at least every other day.

The results indicated that the students differed markedly in their approaches to the assignments, falling into two general groups. One group who employed a "low-effort" strategy and the other group, a "high-effort" strategy. The following are the key features of the low-effort strategy:

1. Students did not start work on their papers until 1 to 3 days before the paper was due.
2. Topic choice was based on the easy availability of information rather than on the student's personal interest in the topic.
3. Students made one trip to the library. Once writing began, no further sources were examined. Thus, the information collected during this one trip determined what the paper could be about.
4. Students summarized and paraphrased sources, page by page and one source at a time.
5. Writing, which was accomplished in one or two sittings, consisted of arranging chunks of notes, each chunk corresponding to a

source text. There was little or no global revision. Most revision involved changes at the word or sentence level.

6. Students disliked writing the assigned paper, describing it as "boring," "tedious," and "busy work."

The following features of the high-effort strategy contrast sharply with those of the low-effort strategy:

1. Students started work on their papers 3 weeks to 1 month before the due date.
2. Topics were chosen on the basis of personal interest.
3. Students returned to the library an average of five times. Searching for information often included "broad background reading" not accompanied by note taking.
4. Notes were typically organized around a predetermined plan rather than summarizing one source at a time.
5. Writing, which was completed over several days or even weeks, showed little direct correspondence with the writer's notes. There was considerable global revision with some students completely abandoning early drafts to start anew.
6. Students did not complain about the writing task or characterized it as "fun" or "interesting."

These differences between students using of high- and low-effort strategies corresponded to differences in the way the teachers of the students managed the writing assignments. Teachers of low-effort students simply specified the assigned topic and the due date. Teachers of high-effort students did one or more of the following things in addition: specified required references, required students to submit drafts, or required students to give in-class talks on their topics. Diary entries suggested that the requirement to give a talk had an important impact on the students. When he learned he would have to give a talk, one student commented, "I can't just write a paper. I've got to understand this topic."

Although these observations are suggestive, they are based on a small sample (eight) in which students were not randomly assigned to conditions. For these reasons, we cannot conclude with any certainty that the teachers management of the writing assignment *caused* the students to choose high- or low-effort writing strategies.

Clearly, the teacher constitutes an important part of the student's social context and can have a major impact on the student's writing process. The observations of Freedman (1987) and of Nelson and Hayes (in press) suggest the variety of ways in which the social contest can influence writing instruction. They also indicate that the magnitude of these social influences may be very large indeed.

The effects of social context are complex and, as yet, not well understood. Researchers and educators will have to work together long and hard before a satisfactory picture of social influences in the classroom begins to emerge. In the meantime, teachers can make use of early results such as those of Freedman (1987) and Nelson and Hayes (in press) if they treat them as suggestions rather than firm conclusions.

THE SKILLED LEARNER

Ordinarily, when I think of skilled learners, I focus on the special characteristics of successful learners without regard to their environment. However, the image of the skilled learner that emerges from the preceding discussion is the image of an individual with special characteristics *working within favorable physical, cultural, and social environments.* Some special characteristics were apparent in the studies we reviewed. Some students spontaneously adopt appropriate task definitions for school tasks and some do not. Some students are "persistently insensitive" to text problems that others detect immediately. The differences are dramatic. If I had to pinpoint the underlying characteristics that made some students more successful in these cases, I would guess that the skilled learners were more alert to cues that they were performing poorly (e.g., failing to comprehend, failing to receive positive feedback, etc.) and that they are more active than others in responding to those cues by asking for feedback, searching for models, and so forth.

The more interesting implication of our discussion, though, is that how well individuals will perform, depends not only on the skills they possess but also on the environments in which they attempt to exercise their skills. A student who writes well with pencil and paper may write disorganized, poorly planned papers in the physical environment of word processing. A student who puts maximum effort into writing papers in the social environment provided by a teacher who "runs a tight ship" may put in minimum effort (and learn very little) with a more laissez-faire teacher. A teaching method may fail if it places the student in a conflict between satisfying the teachers' demands and acting appropriately within the student culture. Finally, cultures that place a high value on academic performance, such as those of China and Japan, appear to lead many more students to become skilled learners than does American culture.

In emphasizing the special characteristics of individuals, as we often tend to do when we discuss skilled learning, we may unintentionally be placing more of the responsibility for good performance on the student and less on ourselves and our culture than is appropriate. More attention to the role of the teacher and the role of our culture in encouraging skill in learning could be quite productive.

CONCLUSION

What implications does this discussion have for teachers? Each of the factors described earlier is, potentially, an answer to the question "Why are my students having difficulty in learning to write?" The first two factors, task definition and perceptual knowledge, although extremely important, may occur to us as potential problems when we are trying to diagnose student problems. As experienced writers, we perceive problems so immediately and we employ our expert task definitions so automatically that we may have difficulty remembering that less experienced writers may not share our skills. As teachers, what can we do about these factors? Two things. First, we should be alert to these problems and prepared to diagnose them. Techniques for diagnosing deficits in perceptual knowledge can be quite simple. Asking student to identify which of several sentences is wordy or which of several paragraphs is disorganized may be sufficient to identify students who fail to perceive wordiness or disorganization. Diagnosing problems in task definition may be more difficult and may require the teacher to observe student closely as they write, possibly through think aloud protocols. The inexperienced revisor, for example, may work through the text one sentence at a time, repairing each sentence in turn, and never consider the relations among the sentences.

After diagnosing problems in perceptual knowledge or in task definition, the teacher must next decide how to help students resolve them. One plausible approach to teaching task definition is to model the behavior of writers with appropriate and inappropriate task definitions. For example, the teacher might think aloud for the class while revising a paragraph—first as an inexperienced writer and then as an experienced writer. Helping students to acquire perceptual knowledge may be more difficult. Schriver's (1987) techniques of training through examples is a good model for perceptual training in general.

The third and fourth factors we discussed concern deficits associated with word processing in the spatial image of the text and in planning. These deficits are especially important to teachers because word processing has become so widely available and because the deficits are so rarely recognized. Students enthused about word processing may abandon hard copy entirely and, in so doing, may create serious writing problems for themselves. Teachers introducing students to word processing should alert them to the potential problems of composing with word processing alone and should indicate the advantages to be gained by mixing word processing and pen and paper technologies.

Our fifth factor, cultural context, is one over which teachers can exercise relatively little control. American culture appears to place much more value on athletic than academic performance. It is much more profitable in America to be a basketball star than a Nobel prize winner. Perhaps teachers can help most by making it clear to students that they admire academic achievement personally. It may also help to make students aware that good performance in studies is much more likely to get them a good job than good performance in athletics.

There is much more that the teacher can do about our final factor, social context, than about cultural context. Teachers are very important part of the social context that influences how students approach writing tasks. The Nelson and Hayes study (in press) suggests that teachers who show that they care about the quality of student writing, perhaps by requiring drafts and talks, or perhaps through other signals that they are attending to the quality of student texts, elicit far more productive effort from students than do other teachers. Teachers, then, can provide positive social support for student writers by indicating plainly and frequently that they care very much about student writing.

In addition, teachers can be sensitive to the realities of social interaction among students so as not to make demands that violate norms for student behavior. One effective way to do this would be to bring students in on the design of instructional assignments. One can imagine going to students with the problem of obtaining useful peer criticism and asking them "What would work?" Bringing students into the design of instructional tasks could help us to avoid tasks that students will not take seriously and might in addition allow students feel that they had a responsible role in their own education.

REFERENCES

Bereiter, C., & Scardamalia, M. (1987). The psychology of written composition. Hillsdale, N. J.: Lawrence Erlbaum Associates.

Bond, S. J., & Hayes, J. R. (1984) . Cues people use to paragraph text. *Research in the Teaching of English, 18,* 147–167.

Bracewell, R., Scardamalia, M., & Bereiter, C. (1976, October). The development of audience awareness in writing. *Resources in Education.* (ERIC Document Reproduction Service No. 154 433).

Bridwell, L. S. (1980). Revising strategies in twelfth grade students' transactional writing. *Research in the Teaching of English, 14*(3), 107–122.

Britton, J., Burgess, T., Martin, N., McLeod, A., & Rosen, H. (1975). *The development of writing abilities (11-18)*. London: Macmillan.

Burtis, P. C., Bereiter, C., Scardamalia, M., & Tetroe, J. (1983). The development of planning in writing. In C. G. Wells & B. Kroll (Eds.), *Exploration of children's development in writing* (pp. 153–176). Chicester, England: Wiley.

Crosswhite, F. J., Dossey, J. A., Swafford, J. O., McKnight, C. C., & Cooney, T. J. (1985). *Second international mathematics study: Summary report for the United States*. Urbana, IL: University of Illinois.

Daiute, C. (1983). The computer as stylus and audience. *College Composition and Communication*, XXXIV, 134–145.

Faigley, L., & Witte, S. (1983). Analyzing revision. *College Composition and Communication, 32*, 400–414.

Freedman, S. W. (1987). Peer response groups in two ninth-grade classrooms (Tech. Rep. No. 12). Center for the Study of Writing, University of California, Berkeley, CA.

Graves, D. H. (1980). Research Update: A new look at writing research. *Language Arts, 57*, 913–919.

Haas, C. (1987). How the writing medium shapes the writing process: Studies of writers composing with pen and paper and with word processing. Doctoral dissertation in rhetoric. Pittsburgh, PA: Carnegie Mellon University.

Haas, C., & Hayes, J. R. (1986). What did I just say? Reading problems in writing with the machine. *Research in the Teaching of English, 20*(1), 20–35.

Hayes, J. R., Flower, L. S., Schriver, K. A., Stratman, J., & Carey, L. (1987). *Cognitive processes in revision.* In S. Rosenberg (Ed.), *Advances in psycholinguistics, Volume II: Reading, writing and language processing* (pp. 176–240). Cambridge, England: Cambridge University Press.

Hymes, D. (1971). Competence and performance in linguistic theory. In R. Huxley & Z. Ingram (Eds.), *Language acquisition: Models and methods,* (pp. 1–23). New York: Academic Press.

Kinosita, K. (1986, May). Address at the Symposium on Document Design for Japanese Academics and Industrialists. Carnegie Mellon University, Pittsburgh, PA.

Lynn, R. (1982). IQ in Japan and the United States shows a growing disparity. *Nature, 297*, 222–223.

Mellon, J. C. (1969). Transformational sentence-combining (NCTE Report No. 10). Urbana, IL: National Council of Teachers of English.

Morenberg, M., Daiker, D., & Kerek, A. (1978). Sentence combining at the college level: An experimental study. *Research in the Teaching of English, 12*, 245–256.

Nelson, J., & Hayes, J. R. (in press). *How the writing context shapes students' strategies for writing from sources.* Technical report for the Center for the Study of Writing at Carnegie Mellon University and the University of California at Berkeley, Berkeley, CA.

Purvis, A. (1968). Research on written composition: A response to Hillocks' report. *Research in the Teaching of English, 22*, 104–108.

Rosenthal, R. (1966). *Experimenter effects in behavioral research*. New York: Appleton-Century-Crofts.

Rothkopf, E. Z. (1971). Incidental memory for location of information in text. *Journal of Verbal Learning and Verbal Behavior, 10,* 608–613.

Schriver, K. (1984). *Revising computer documentation for comprehension: Ten lessons in protocol-aided revision.* (Tech Rep. No. 14). Pittsburgh, PA: Carnegie Mellon University, Communication Design Center.

Schriver, K. A. (1987). *Teaching writers to anticipate the reader's needs: Empirically based instruction.* Doctoral Dissertation in Rhetoric, Carnegie Mellon University, Pittsburgh, PA.

Smith, W. L., & Combs, W. E. (1980). The effects of overt and covert cues on written syntax. *Research in the Teaching of English, 14,* 19–38.

Sommers, N. (1980). Revision strategies of student writers and experienced writers. *College Composition and Communication, 31,* 378–387.

Stevenson, H. W., & Azuma, H. (1983). IQ in Japan and the United States: Methodological problems in Lynn's analysis. *Nature, 306,* 291–292.

Stevenson, H. W., Lee, S., Stigler, J. W., Hsu, C. C., Lucker, G. W., & Kitamura, S. (1987). Classroom behavior and achievement of Japanese, Chinese, and American children. In R. Glaser (Ed.), *Advances in instructions psychology* (Vol. 3, pp. 153–191). Hillsale, N. J.: Lawrence Erlbaum Associates.

Stigler, J. W., Lee, Y. S., Lucker, G. W., & Stevenson, H. W. (1982). Curriculum and achievement in mathematics: A study of elementary school children in Japan, Taiwan, and the United States. *Journal of Educational Psychology, 74,* 315–322.

Swan, M. B. (1977). *The effects of instruction in transformational sentence combining on the syntactic complexity and quality of college level writing.* Unpublished Doctoral Dissertation, Boston University, Boston, MA.

Wason, P. C. (1980). Specific thoughts on the writing process. In L. W. Gregg & E. R. Steinberg (Eds.), *Cognitive processes in writing,* (pp. 129–138). Hillsdale, NJ: Lawrence Erlbaum Associates.

Mathematical and Scientific Problem Solving: Findings, Issues, and Instructional Implications

Edward A. Silver
University of Pittsburgh

Sandra P. Marshall
San Diego State University

In the past two decades, there has accumulated a considerable corpus of research on the learning of mathematics and science and the use of mathematical and scientific knowledge to solve problems. The purpose of this chapter is to briefly summarize several important features of the cognitive theory and related research that are directly relevant to scientific and mathematical problem solving. Because it is not possible to present a complete summary of the themes and findings in this vast literature, our emphasis is on those aspects of the theory and research that might help in designing problem-solving instruction to produce students who are better equipped to use their mathematical and scientific knowledge in solving problems. The interested can find additional summaries and useful information from this literature in other sources (e.g., Frederiksen, 1984; Silver, 1987).

Glaser (1976) identified three essential components of a theory of instruction: (a) description of the competent performances that students should acquire, (b) analysis of the initial states of knowledge and ability with which students enter instructional settings, and (c) explication of the process of learning (i.e., the transition from initial state to desired state) that can be accomplished via instruction. Much of the research on problem solving over the past three decades has related to these three components, and we are therefore in a position to examine this research from the perspective of instructional improvement. Although research has not dealt with these three components with equanimity (Glaser & Bassok, 1989), we find these themes woven throughout the fabric of this chapter. For example, much of the work has dealt with the contrast between experts and novices in a domain, and this research should be relevant to the first two of Glaser's components.

Another general observation worth noting at the outset concerns epistemology. How does a person come to know something? In general, most researchers taking a cognitive science approach agree that individuals *construct* their own knowledge bases; that is, human learning is largely a constructive process. Of course, this notion is not new in the history of psychology. Piaget, for example, developed a constructivist epistemology decades ago, and constructivist roots run deep in the history of philosophy (von Glasersfeld, 1983). But the constructivist perspective has received much attention in recent years. Many cognitive psychologists (e.g., Anderson, 1982), mathematics educators (e.g., Steffe, von Glasersfeld, Richards, & Cobb, 1983), and science educators (e.g., Clement, 1982) have suggested the importance of a constructivist perspective on learning in mathematics and science. According to this constructivist view of the learning process, learners do not simply add new information to their store of knowledge. Instead, learners connect the new information to already established knowledge structures and construct new relationships among those structures. This view implies that mathematical and scientific knowledge is always at least partly created by individual learners. As we shall see in this chapter, a constructivist epistemology implies that designers of effective instruction will need to attend to the underlying organization of knowledge that is constructed by learners, to the preexisting constructions that the learner brings to the instructional setting, and to the instructional conditions and experiences that need to be provided to optimize individual learning. Although some or all of these considerations might be relevant in other epistemological frameworks, they are absolutely essential in current constructivist climate.

This chapter deals with four general areas of research on problem solving: (a) knowledge for problem solving, (b) problem-solving processes, (c) metalevel aspects of problem solving, and (d) instructional characteristics. Our particular focus is on a narrow band within each general area; we concentrate on only a few topics of many on which there has been research of sufficient quality and relevance for instruction. Rather than separate the theoretical, empirical, and practical aspects of this chapter, we have intermingled the instructional suggestions with the discussion of research. We leave it to our readers to construct their own interpretations of our summaries and suggestions.

KNOWLEDGE FOR PROBLEM SOLVING

It hardly needs to be said that an important component of successful problem solving is an adequate store of domain-relevant knowledge.

Herbert Simon (1980) has noted that "research on cognitive skills has taught us . . . that there is no such thing as expertness without knowledge—extensive and accessible knowledge" (p. 82). Certainly, typical instruction in mathematics and science has as a major goal the development of an adequate knowledge base. Nevertheless, it is clear that this instruction succeeds only occasionally in developing adequate knowledge for skillful problem solving. One deficiency in current instruction may be its failure to make explicit certain implicit aspects of the knowledge needed for problem solving. One noteworthy feature of recent cognitive research is that it has generated some explicit hypotheses about tacit knowledge in a variety of areas (Greeno, 1987).

In this section, we consider several implicit aspects of knowledge for problem solving. In particular, we consider a body of research that has examined the intuitions and prior knowledge that students bring to instruction in mathematics and science. This knowledge is appropriately considered implicit, in that it is not explicitly called upon by the demands of the instructional setting, and it is usually not even explicitly formulated and recognized by the learner. Another focus in this section is research on problem solving and expert performance in complex knowledge domains that has identified two aspects of knowledge needed for problem solving that typically remain implicit in traditional mathematics and science instruction. Both involve a form of pattern recognition and organization of stimuli. The first is visual pattern recognition, involving the rapid observation of regularity in patterns of information typically observed in problems. The second implicit aspect is the underlying organization of the knowledge into hierarchies or into clusters of related concepts and procedures.

Informal Knowledge, Intuitions, and Misconceptions

An interesting consequence of the constructive nature of the learning process is that *bugs*—minor systematic flaws in otherwise correct procedures—can occur. Brown and his colleagues (Brown & Burton, 1978; Brown & VanLehn, 1980) have extensively studied the bugs that arise in children's learning of the subtraction algorithm in elementary school. VanLehn (1986) has argued that the extensive data on subtraction bugs not only supports a constructivist view of children's learning but also suggests that the traditional instructional model of "teacher tells student what to do" is not likely to be consistently effective.

Procedures are not the only cognitive entities susceptible to the development of bugs; conceptual information can also be flawed in consistent and predictable ways. These flaws of a conceptual variety are often called *misconceptions*. Many studies in learning and representation of problem solving attempt to identify particular misconceptions held by students. The notion behind many of these studies is that if we are to teach students how to solve problems in science and mathematics, we may first have to "undo" other learning that has taken place. This other learning typically results from students' personal constructions of explanations for commonly observed or experienced phenomena in the real world. Unfortunately, the explanations are often inconsistent with formal, academic scientific theories.

McCloskey and his colleagues examined students' explanation of the trajectories of falling objects (e.g., Caramazza, McCloskey, & Green, 1981; McCloskey, Washburn, & Felch, 1983). Caramazza et al. (1981) presented students with several problems involving a ball tied to a string, moving as a pendulum. The string was to be cut at one of several positions on the pendulum's arc, and the student was asked to describe what would happen to the ball at that point. The researchers observed that many individuals believed the ball would travel forward a short distance then drop directly to the ground. McCloskey et al. (1983) verified this phenomenon, called the "straight-down belief," using several forms of testing, including paper and pencil problems, computer-generated graphics problems, videotaped problems and actual observations of people. They observed the same results for paper-and-pencil tests and dynamic, realistic situations involving people, whether live or videotaped.

McCloskey's experiments confirm that misconceptions of physical motion are consistent with perceptual illusions, but they do not prove that the illusions are the source of the misconceptions. Other researchers argue that a faulty knowledge base underlies the misunderstanding and that the visual perception only serves to reinforce the incorrect knowledge structure. For example, Champagne, Klopfer, and Anderson (1980) evaluated the knowledge base of students entering an introductory college physics course. They reported that untrained students generally had well-developed beliefs about many physics concepts, particularly about motion. These ideas seem to be derived from everyday experiences and apparently were satisfactory for explaining real-world phenomena. To a large extent, they corresponded to Aristotelian notions. Unfortunately, these intuitive ideas were in direct conflict with formal Newtonian physics, thereby presenting the student with two inconsistent explanations for the same phenomenon.

The presence of two conflicting explanations for a phenomenon could provide a powerful learning opportunity. There is evidence, however, that many individuals simply incorporate both explanations into their repertoire—one to be used in solving classroom problems with Newtonian formulas and laws and one to explain everyday phenomena. The Newtonian system describes an idealized world; it is abstract and difficult for students to comprehend (e.g., a frictionless world). On the other hand, as McCloskey and his associates demonstrated, individuals receive daily visual confirmation of their misconceptions. The co-existence of the two systems in the minds of students has been shown by diSessa (1982) in his detailed study of elementary school students and one undergraduate who performed well in the formal problems of the physics class but was unable to relate her knowledge of physics to everyday events. Instead, she relied on a body of intuitive conceptions—remarkably like those expressed by the sixth-grade students diSessa interviewed—that were inconsistent with her formal scientific knowledge but "worked" to explain the observed phenomena.

Taken collectively, the research findings suggest that instruction should directly address the misconceptions commonly held by students. Failure to do so may lead to larger numbers of students who dissociate classroom knowledge from real world situations and problems—students who believe they must use different information to solve classroom problems than they need to solve problems in the real world.

Visual Pattern Recognition

In a classic study, deGroot (1965) asked chess experts (grandmasters and masters) and novices (ordinary chess players) to reproduce the position of the pieces on a chess board. The pieces were either arranged in a midgame position or randomly arranged on the board. For the midgame positions, the experts were able to reproduce the positions of the 20 or 25 pieces almost without error, whereas ordinary players could place only a half-dozen pieces correctly. For the random arrangements, only about 6 pieces were incorrectly placed both by masters and ordinary players.

The performance of the novices on both tasks and of the experts on the random task is in agreement with other research about the capacity limits of short-term memory (cf. Miller, 1956). The findings of deGroot and subsequent research by Chase and Simon (1973) on the ability of the experts to remember positions of 20 or more pieces indicates that experts must "chunk" many pieces together, so that the entire pattern of the board is recognized and remembered. It is important to point out that we are not simply observing an innate difference in perceptual ability between individuals who develop into experts as opposed to novices. Experts are superior only in recognizing meaningful arrangements; they do not have superiority in recalling random patterns. This research on chess experts' ability to recognize patterns of related pieces on the board almost instantaneously and to use these patterns rather than the positions of individual pieces in processing information, has spawned and is consistent with the findings of similar research studies on expert knowledge in other complex task domains.

Several investigators have suggested the importance of pattern recognition in skillful mathematical problem solving. For example, Clement (1983) and Davis (1984) have suggested that visual pattern recognition may be of central importance in the problem-solving behavior of skillful mathematics problem solvers. In particular, Davis and his colleagues (Davis, Jockusch, & McKnight, 1978; Davis & McKnight, 1979) have argued that students' successful solution of algebraic equations and word problems often appears to hinge on generalized pattern recognition. Triggered by the recognition of certain features of a problem, the student selects a solution method—whether or not it "fits" the problem situation. It is likely that pattern recognition skill may involve episodic or imagistic memory representations that are built up through many hours or years of extensive practice in the task domain. Nevertheless, it is also likely that explicit attention to regularities and patterns associated with typical science or mathematics problems could assist students in developing pattern recognition skills that would enhance their problem-solving performance.

Knowledge Organization

George Polya, an eminent mathematician who has written extensively about mathematical problem solving, has asserted that "a well-stocked and well-organized body of knowledge is an asset to the problem solver. Good organization which renders the knowledge readily available may be even more important than the extent of the knowledge" (1973, p. 73). All complex problem solving involves the retrieval of information from one's store of relevant knowledge. Because the efficient retrieval of information during problem solving may depend on the way that information is organized in long-term memory, differences in problem-solving success may be partly attributable to differences in solvers' knowledge organizations.

The notion of a memory schema—a cluster of knowledge that describes the typical properties of the concept it represents—has emerged in the literature to help explain many aspects of human knowledge organization and recall. A schema is usually described as representing a prototypical abstraction of a complex and frequently encountered concept or phenomenon (e.g., Thorndyke & Yekovich, 1980), and it is usually derived from past experience with numerous exemplars of the concept involved. In the past decade or so, a considerable amount of research has been generated on the influence and use of schemas, especially in the area of prose text learning. Schemas have been associated not only with the interpretation and encoding of incoming information but also with the recall of previously processed information (Thorndyke & Hayes-Roth, 1979). Schemas can influence the efficiency with which information is recalled from memory (e.g., Mandler & Johnson, 1977), and they may account for inferences made using incomplete information (e.g., Bransford, Barclay, & Franks, 1972). In short, schemas represent a complex, high level "pattern" of information consisting of conceptual and procedural information.

An explicit link between schema theory and mathematical problem solving was made by Hinsley, Hayes, and Simon (1977), who reported that subjects categorized algebra story problems into standard categories, such as distance-rate-time or age problems, and that subjects were able to categorize a problem almost immediately, usually after hearing only the first few word. In general, Hinsley et al. concluded that their subjects had schemas for standard algebra problems and that the schemas influenced the encoding of information during problem solving.

In another study involving algebra story problems, Mayer (1982) found that problem schemas influenced not only encoding but also retrieval of information in the problems. In particular, he found that subjects recalled relevant information much better than irrelevant details, recalled high frequency problem forms (i.e., common problem types) better than low frequency forms, made recall errors that converted low frequency forms to high frequency forms, and constructed problems that matched standard textbook forms. He interpreted his findings as supporting the hypothesis that students possess schemas for standard algebra problems and that the schemas guide both the encoding and retrieval of problem information.

Another perspective on the importance of schemas in problem solving comes from several studies (Chi, Feltovich, & Glaser, 1981; Chi, Glaser, & Rees, 1981) that have contrasted experts and novices in physics. The experts and novices were asked to categorize problems according to similarities in solution methods. The novices tended to sort on the basis of surface features, such as inclined planes, pulleys, and friction, whereas, the experts categorized problems on the basis of the fundamental principles of physics that were involved, such as conservation of energy or Newton's third law. The greater knowledge and experience of the experts made it possible for them to represent a problem in terms of a schema containing both factual knowledge and procedural knowledge including relevant formulas-of-solution methods for the particular kind of problems involved. The novices apparently had simpler and less complex schemas, generally lacking the relevant procedural knowledge. Experts appeared to focus on principles of the domain that are firmly linked to solution paths. Novices, on the other hand, appeared to focus on surface features of problems, such as the physical objects mentioned in the problem. Novices may have difficulty transferring their learning to new problems because they fail to see the scientific principles underlying the task (Anzai & Yokoyama, 1984).

Similar findings have also been obtained in the area of mathematics. For example, Silver (1979) asked a large number of junior high school students to sort a set of 24 mathematics problems into groups of problems that were mathematically related. The students sorted the problems twice—once before trying to solve the problems and once afterwards. Silver found that successful problem solvers were far more likely than unsuccessful ones to relate and categorize mathematics problems on the basis of their underlying similarities in mathematical structure. Unsuccessful problem solvers were more likely to rely on surface similarities in problem setting or context, or the question asked in the problem, in judging problem similarity. In another study, Schoenfeld and Herrmann (1982) asked mathematics professors (experts) and college students taking advanced mathematics (novices) to sort 32 problems according to the similarity in their solution procedures. The data revealed that the experts had a high degree of agreement on their categorization and that the expert categories were based on structural considerations, such as general solution procedures. The sortings produced by the novices were much more varied and appeared to be driven more by surface features of the problems.

Aspects of the work discussed earlier by Silver and by Schoenfeld and Herrmann have instructional implications. For example, Silver (1979) found that, after students attempted to solve the problems, students who were generally successful problem solvers were far more likely to recognize the mathematical structure of the problems they had solved or tried to solve than were students who were generally unsuccessful problem solvers. This suggests that successful students look for and find structural information in their problem-solving experiences; whereas, unsuccessful students do not. Unless some explicit intervention occurs, the gap between successful and unsuccessful students will be maintained or will widen under the conditions of typical instruction.

Schoenfeld and Herrmann (1982) also had an instructional component to their study. The novices were divided into two groups: an experimental group that received a month-long course in mathematical problem solving and the control group that received a month-long course in computer programming. After instruction, the experimental group showed a greater tendency toward expert-like sorting behavior than the control group. Recent work by Marshall and her colleagues (e.g., Marshall, Pribe, & Smith, 1987) also demonstrates that problem schema information can be explicitly taught to students and that this explicit instruction can help generally unsuccessful problem solvers attain greater success.

A somewhat different, although related, approach to improving learning in science focuses on modifying the organization of information stored in students' long-term memories. Rather than explicitly teaching schema knowledge, most research in this area emphasizes the need to provide more organized instruction that will facilitate the eventual development of schemas. For example, Smith and Goodman (1984) compared linear instruction (essentially unrelated concepts) with two forms of hierarchical instruction (based on related schema knowledge). The domain of interest was electrical circuits. They reported that students receiving hierarchical instruction perform better than those receiving linear instruction on measures such as reading time, verbal recall of the problem, and transfer to other tasks. Eylon and Reif (1984) also contrasted instruction based on a hierarchical organization with a nonhierarchical one. The hierarchical instruction was top-down in nature, stressing the way that concepts were related in the particular physics problems being discussed. The nonhierarchical instruction contained many of the same statements as the hierarchical one but lacked the statements relating the concepts. Eylon and Reif found that students instructed in the hierarchical mode performed better on recall and on problem solving tasks than did students having the nonhierarchical instruction. Taken collectively, these research results strongly suggest that the development of powerful problem-solving schemas is manipulable through instruction.

PROBLEM-SOLVING PROCESSES

As we have seen, schemas provide an interesting and useful way to capture important aspects of knowledge for solving types of problems that are frequently encountered during the course of instruction. In the case of such routine problems, the instructional task is to get the procedural and conceptual knowledge organized so as to be optimally useful. Not all problem solving, however, can be adequately explained solely from the perspective of schemas. Many problems are encountered as if they were unique, or at least as if they were not exemplars of a well-known class. How does problem solving proceed under such circumstances? How can instruction be designed to assist students in solving problems for which they have not yet developed schemas? Some aspects of the processes associated with such problem-solving instruction that might foster flexible problem solving are treated in this section.

Problem Representation Processes

In some ways, each time a person solves a nontrivial problem, the constructivist perspective on learning is exemplified in a microscopic way. In order to solve a complex problem, a person must construct an understanding of the problem that connects his or her store of knowledge with the task requirements of the problem. The confluence of processes associated with this construction of understanding in the context of problem solving is called problem representation.

Although there are some differences among competing theories of problem representation, most researchers agree that the process of problem representation is gradual and constructive. One popular view asserts that the problem solver constructs an initial sparse representation of a particular problem and gradually refines or elaborates it until he or she has a final representation that is adequate for solution (e.g., Larkin, 1983a, 1983b). For example, Larkin, McDermott, Simon, and Simon (1980a, 1980b), who studied the problem solving of experts and novices in the area of physics, noted that experts frequently formed qualitative representations of the problems before attempting any quantitative analyses. White and Frederiksen (1986) studied problem solving in the domain of electricity and found that individuals tended to begin with one or more qualitative representations that were gradually replaced by more detailed quantitative ones. A slightly different, but closely related, view is that individuals construct many successive unstable representations, discarding each in turn until obtaining a final stable one. Lesh's (1985) work involving children solving "applied" mathematics problems has provided some support for this view.

In most current theoretical perspectives, problem representations are viewed as central to the problem-solving process, and problem-solving success is seen as being intimately tied to the adequacy of one's problem representation. The current emphasis on representation is closely tied to the first stage—understand the problem—of Polya's (1957) descriptive model of problem solving. Understanding the problem at the outset of a problem-solving episode is roughly synonymous with constructing an initial problem representation. There is considerable evidence suggesting that failures to solve problems can often be attributed to failures to understand the problem adequately: that is, failures to construct adequate initial problem representations.

Unsuccessful problem solvers are often characterized by their general lack of problem understanding. They often attempt to solve problems without constructing adequate initial problem representations, that is, without understanding the problem. Although it is not trivial to get students to resist the urge to leap into quantitative activity, there is some research (Mestre, DuFresne, Gerace, Hardiman, & Touger, in press) demonstrating that students may benefit from instruction aimed at just such behavior. Mestre et al. developed a computer-based environment that directed novices through a qualitative analysis of physics problems. After a brief period of training with this system, novices showed an increased capability for qualitative analysis and an increased likelihood of engaging in such analysis.

Although novices are often plagued by inadequacies, there are those instances in which apparently naive students succeed spectacularly, beyond all expectations. The research literature documenting these instances suggests a somewhat more sanguine view of naive problem solving. This more optimistic view that is evident, for example, in a close examination of the mathematical problem-solving success of young children suggests that the successes may be traced directly to children's unexpected accomplishments in the areas of understanding and problem representation.

There is evidence that children can invent correct procedures for the performance of a number of tasks without instruction. For example, many children develop correct mental arithmetic strategies without explicit instruction. Moreover, many are able to solve simple addition and subtraction story problems without any formal instruction (Carpenter, 1985). The analysis of successful children's solution processes suggests that they attend to the semantics of the problem situation; that is, they succeed because they construct a representation that is based on an adequate understanding of the problem situation. As Carpenter (1985) has noted:

> Even before they have received instruction in formal arithmetic, almost all children exhibit reasonably sophisticated and appropriate problem-solving skills in solving simple word problems. They attend to the content of the problem; they model the problem; they invent more efficient procedures for computing the answer. Given the limits of their mathematical knowledge, this performance is remarkable. (p. 37)

It is striking that many of these same children will no longer attend to the semantics of the problem after receiving mathematics instruction in school; they apparently prefer instead to choose an arithmetical operation on the basis of the problem's surface features.

The findings on young children's success in solving elementary arithmetic problems also points to a role for "real world" knowledge in mathematical problem solving. Other research on problem solving in arithmetic involving division with remainders (Silver, 1985) and in algebra (Paige & Simon, 1966) has also suggested the power of building mathematical representations that are informed by real world knowledge.

Interestingly, the phenomenon often reported in science research has a different character. For many science problems, everyday understanding is often incorrect in a formal sense and leads to conflicts with formal scientific theories and explanations. As we noted earlier, the science learning literature is replete with studies documenting a large array of misconceptions, each of which apparently interferes with student problem-solving success. Studies of novices shows that untrained individuals are highly unlikely to give correct scientific explanations for common phenomena, such as how a light bulb works or what happens when a ball drops to the ground (e.g., Caramazza et al., 1981; diSessa, 1982).

It is striking that "real world" knowledge appears to have a generally debilitative effect on science problem solving; whereas, it appears to have a generally facilitative effect in the domain of elementary mathematics. It is worth noting that students' misconceptions derived from everyday experience with stochastic phenomena can plague mathematics instruction on more advanced topics, such as probability (Shaughnessy, 1985). Thus, formal school instruction in physical science and mathematical probability is faced with the problem of helping students modify their intuitive, personal explanations and theories to accommodate formal, scientific explanations of commonly observed phenomena. On the other hand, the instructional task in elementary mathematics might be characterized somewhat differently: to teach mathematical formalisms while connecting to a powerful intuitive knowledge base that the learner brings from everyday experience. In general, knowledge derived from everyday experience is an important source of information for students and must be considered carefully in planning problem-solving experiences and instruction.

Other Problem-Solving Processes

Much of the work on mathematics problem-solving instruction has been greatly influenced by the writings of Polya (1957, 1973). Polya's four-phase model for problem solving—(a) understand the problem, (b) devise a plan, (c) carry out the plan, and (d) look back—and his emphasis on the importance of heuristic thinking and reasoning at each phase of problem solving has influenced both curriculum development and research in mathematics education. Although Polya's model is clearly deficient as a description of actual problem-solving behavior, it has been useful in suggesting ways to organize instruction to promote improved problem-solving performance (Kilpatrick, 1985).

In Polya's work, the term *heuristic* is used to describe reasoning that is tentative and incomplete, yet directed generally at productive action toward a problem solution. Actions such as drawing a diagram, thinking of a related problem, and examining special or extreme cases are all heuristic processes because they do not guarantee a successful solution but they may suggest useful directions in which the solution might proceed.

Research on the teaching of general heuristic problem-solving skills and strategies has been conducted at all educational levels. For example, Kantowski (1977) demonstrated that heuristic instruction could be very effective in enhancing the geometry problem-solving performance of secondary school students, Goldberg (1975) found that college students could profit from heuristic instruction, Lee (1978) was able to teach fourth graders to use general heuristic strategies, such as making tables or drawing diagrams, and Putt (1979) found that fifth-grade students could benefit from heuristic instruction so that they were able to use many of the strategies, they developed an appropriate vocabulary for discussing their strategies, and they were able to suggest many questions appropriate for understanding a problem. In fact, Marcucci (1980) used meta-analysis to examine the findings of 33 research studies conducted in elementary school classrooms since 1950. Marcucci concluded that heuristic teaching methods (those emphasizing general heuristic problem-solving strategies and skills) were generally more effective than other instructional approaches.

Some of these heuristic processes, especially those connected with reasoning by analogy, have been shown to be important processes in science problem solving as well. For example, Clement (1983) has demonstrated that reasoning by analogy is a common feature of the thinking of expert problem solvers in physics. Gentner and Gentner (1983) also found analogical processes to be very strong in novice problem solvers in the domain of electricity. It may be that the tendency of learners in a new domain to use analogical problem-solving processes can help students solve problems but interfere with the efficient acquisition of formal knowledge, because the use of analogical reasoning increases the likelihood that misconceptions based on everyday phenomena will be accessed as relevant knowledge for problem solving. This analysis suggests that any attempts to teach effective problem solving through analogical processes, especially in science, should proceed with great care.

META-LEVEL ASPECTS OF PROBLEM SOLVING

We have already seen that two components of success in problem solving are extensive domain-specific knowledge and a wide repertoire of problem-solving skills, particularly representational facility and heuristic processes. It is reasonable to ask what other kinds of knowledge, if any, might be involved in skillful problem solving. Our view of the research literature suggests two possible candidates for types of knowledge needed for problem solving: meta-level processes, such as monitoring and evaluation, and meta-level knowledge, such as beliefs.

Metaprocesses

Several researchers interested in mathematical problem solving (e.g., Lester & Garofalo, 1982; Schoenfeld, 1987; Silver, 1985) have argued for increased attention to metacognitive aspects of problem-solving processes. These metaprocesses—such as initial assessments of personal competence or problem difficulty or managerial decisions regarding allocation of cognitive resources—often appear to be the "driving forces" of a problem solution episode. According to Flavell (1979), metacognition refers to one's knowledge of one's own cognitive processes and products, and of the cognition of others. It also refers to the self-monitoring, regulation,and evaluation of cognitive activity.

Metacognition is not a new idea. Provision for metacognitive functioning has been made in most information-processing models of cognition. Terms like *control processes, executive function,* and *executive scheme* often appear in the description of cognitive models. Although these terms are not necessarily synonymous with metacognition, they all cover to a great extent the area in which metacognition is operative. Although many models of human information processing include metacognitive processes, there has been relatively little empirical investigation of these processes as they relate to mathematical and scientific problem solving. The work that has been done, however, strongly suggests the importance of metacognitive processes in complex problem solving.

Smith and Good (1984) noted differences in metacognitive processes of experts and novices who solved problems in genetics. Specifically, they found that experts were more likely to (a) recheck the problem statement after solution, (b) check that the solution was intuitively reasonable, and (c) monitor whether certain steps had already been carried out elsewhere. In contrast, novices were unlikely to monitor their problem solving, but when they did so, they focused on more specific features of the problem rather than general processes. For example, novices were likely to make frequent checks that the gene number was maintained throughout the procedures they used.

Champagne et al. (1980) also found metacognitive differences between novices and experts in the domain of classical mechanics. They obtained a number of different measures on a group of students enrolled in an introductory college physics course. Protocol analyses of the students' responses to a set of physics problems showed that the more successful students engaged in reflective thinking more often than did the less successful ones. That is, they more often made comments about their own thinking processes and knowledge.

Perhaps the most persuasive work in the area of mathematics has been done by Schoenfeld (1985a, 1985b), who has documented many cases of college and high school students failing to solve problems because of their failure to monitor and evaluate their problem-solving activity. Garofalo and Lester (1985) have also documented similar failures at the elementary school level.

Although the research on this topic has not yet proceeded to a point at which particular instructional recommendations might be made, convincing evidence is beginning to mount that metacognitive processes such as monitoring and evaluation, are important components of problem solving. Because these processes are rarely the explicit focus of typical classroom instruction, it would be wise for instructional planners to consider ways of increasing students' attention to these activities. Rather than developing a check-list approach to monitoring and evaluation, however, we would suggest that attempts be made to immerse students in a problem-solving environment in which reflective, metacognitive activity permeates the atmosphere.

Belief Systems

We have already considered one aspect of belief systems that may influence problem solving in science; namely, beliefs about the nature of commonly observed or experienced phenomena. As we have seen, misconceptions seem, in many cases, to come from common sense notions about how the world works or from common sense intuitions based on the individual's experience in the world. We have seen that intuitions about scientific phenomena are very often technically wrong (e.g., relying on Aristotelian notions to explain forces acting on objects in motion). As mentioned earlier, when very young children are asked to solve simple arithmetic story problems, they are often able to do so by relying on their own world knowledge and experience rather than on the formalisms of arithmetic (Carpenter, 1985). Their knowledge of the real world is often an aid rather than a hindrance to them in solving mathematical problems.

Although students have some knowledge of everyday phenomena that may be helpful in some areas of mathematical problem solving, such as the solution of elementary arithmetic story problems as discussed earlier, there is evidence that students' beliefs about the nature of mathematics and mathematical thinking may generally impede their problem solving. For example, data from the National Assessment of Educational Progress in mathematics (Carpenter, Lindquist, Matthews, & Silver, 1983; Dossey, Mullis, Lindquist, & Chambers, 1988) suggest that students tend to view mathematics as a static, noncreative discipline containing problems that almost always have a single solution and single solution method. Moreover, the process of learning mathematics is seen by students as one of mostly memorizing.

Schoenfeld (1985b) and Silver (1985) have each outlined some issues related to the role that beliefs might play in mathematical problem solving. For example, they commonly observed phenomena that students tend to think that problems should be solved rapidly or not at all, that the solution should depend on recently taught techniques, and that every problem should conform to some model they have been taught to solve, all represent potentially serious impediments to successful problem solving. Although there has been little research that has directly examined the impact of such beliefs on mathematical problem solving, the informal evidence seems quite strong. The instructional suggestion here is that some instructional attention needs to be paid to students' beliefs about the nature of the subject being studied and the nature of problem solving with respect to that subject matter.

One recent study of expert mathematicians (Silver & Metzger, 1989) identified the role that experts' beliefs in certain aesthetic principles, such as elegance, simplicity, and coherence, played in influencing not only their choices during solution of mathematics problems but also their evaluation of personal satisfaction following a problem solution. This study suggests that the role of beliefs as an influence on successful problem solving remains an area that should be studied in detail.

PROBLEM-SOLVING EXPERIENCES

Three decades ago, noted mathematics educators like Henry Van Engen (1959) were suggesting that the best advice that the research literature offered to those interested in the development of students' problem-solving abilities was that problem solving should be taught by giving students lots of problems to solve. Although there is still considerable support for the importance of practice with examples in the learning of problem solving, recent research suggests a much more refined view of the role that examples can play in the acquisition of problem-solving expertise.

The Role of Examples

As noted earlier, VanLehn (1986) has argued that there is strong evidence from research on learning that, at a general level, children do not learn arithmetic procedures by being told how to perform the steps; rather "arithmetic is learned by induction—the generalization and integration of examples" (p. 133). Similar themes have been expressed regarding the learning of problem solving. The first is that expertise develops only after extensive experience in the domain of expertise. A corollary to this theme is that expertise develops over an extended period of time.

Some designers of computer systems that learn have taken both the theme and its corollary into account. For example, Larkin (1983a) developed a program called ABLE, which learned to solve increasingly complex (though fairly elementary) physics problems by using its problem-solving experiences to augment its store of knowledge. ABLE's knowledge consisted of "productions" (condition-action pairs). It utilized this knowledge to solve problems by matching the condition part of a production with the contents of its memory. Beginning with a simple knowledge base, in a version called "Barely ABLE," the system learned to improve its performance by acquiring new productions as a result of its problem-solving experiences with representative problems. Moreover, Larkin's simulations of novices (Barely ABLE) and experts (ABLE) were quite similar in many respects to the behavior of human problem solvers.

The importance of the examples that form the basis of one's experience has been studied by several researchers. For example, Rissland (1978, 1985) has stressed the fundamental role of examples in the teaching/learning process. She suggested a classification scheme for examples and their functions: (a) start-up examples (easily understood and presented cases), (b) reference examples (standard cases), (c) counter-examples (falsifying cases), (d) model examples (paradigmatic cases), and (e) anomalous examples (exceptions and pathologies). Her research demonstrates the critical role that well-chosen examples can play in the teaching-learning process.

The importance of examples is also evident in other analyses of the development of expertise. In their summary of how expertise is acquired, Chase and Chi (1981) emphasized not only the role of examples but also the length of time needed to develop expertise. They suggested that expertise develops when extensive experience with a rich set of examples creates a highly textured knowledge base. They also argued that there appears to be no limit, except for physiological dysfunction, to the extent to which domain-specific cognitive skills can be developed.

Although extensive practice in solving appropriate problems would appear to be a necessary requirement for the development of expertise, research has also produced evidence that practice in solving problems is not sufficient for the development of expertise. For example, Simon and Simon (1978) compared the problem solving of an expert and a novice, each solving two dozen problems from a high school physics test. The performance of the novice did not improve with repeated problem-solving experiences, although over time she relied less on the text and the text examples.

One of the important decisions to be made in designing problem-solving instruction is the number and variety of examples to be included for the learner to solve. Some of our earlier discussion of schema theory and problem representations would be relevant to this decision, as would some consideration of alternate forms of problems, such as worked-out examples for study. Worked-out examples have the virtue that more of them can be accommodated per unit of instructional time than examples that require the learner to generate an original solution. But can learners profit from experience with worked-out examples?

Some recent work on learning from worked-out examples sheds some light on the mechanisms that may underlie learning from examples. For example, Sweller and Cooper (1985) studied the use of worked-out examples as a substitute for problem solving in learning algebra. They found that students who had been presented with worked examples to study made fewer errors on a posttest than students who were given conventional problems in the form of exercises to solve. They suggest that students studying worked examples directly process the relationship between the given initial state and the steps required in order to achieve the goal state, thereby increasing the probability of schema acquisition. Individual differences noted in the Sweller and Cooper study suggested that students' motivation may be an important mediating factor in learning from worked examples. If students' adopt too passive a role in such an instructional setting, they may not achieve success.

Further information concerning individual differences in students' learning from worked examples is provided by Chi, Bassok, Lewis, Reimann, and Glaser (in press). Chi et al. analyzed the self-generated explanations produced by "good" and "poor" students while studying worked examples of mechanics problems. Their data indicate that the learning of "good" students is characterized by their generation of explanations that refine and expand the implicit actions in the example solutions and relate these actions to principles in the textbook. Moreover, these self-explanations are guided by an active, generally accurate monitoring of their understandings. On the other hand, "poor" students do not monitor their understanding and tend to rely heavily on the examples alone to provide the learning.

Taken together these studies of learning from worked-out examples suggest that these kinds of examples may have an important role in problem-solving instruction. They provide a mechanism through which learners could become acquainted with a large number of problem solutions much more rapidly than if all the solutions were generated by the learner. On the other hand, it is clear that students differ in their ability to benefit substantially from worked-out examples. In order to make effective use of worked-out examples, the instructional program would also have to give some attention to the metacognitive skills and intellectual disposition apparently needed to profit from such instruction.

Another kind of problem that should be considered for inclusion in problem-solving instruction is one with a nonspecific rather than a well-specified goal. An interesting cognitive analysis of ill-structured, non-goal-specific problems has been done by John Sweller and his colleagues (Sweller & Levine, 1982; Sweller, Mawer, & Ward, 1983; Owen & Sweller, 1985). Some of Sweller's studies have involved mathematics problems from the domain of geometry and trigonometry. In general, the results of these studies have demonstrated that subjects are far more likely to use means-ends analysis on goal-specific problems (given an angle in a figure, find the value of a particular other angle in the figure) than on non-goal-specific problems (given an angle in a figure, find the measure of as many other angles as you can), and that the non-use of means-ends analysis may have some beneficial effects on subjects' learning. In particular, Sweller's results show that, although means-ends analysis is a powerful problem-solving strategy, the unavailability of means-ends analysis may lead subjects not only to use more *expert-like*, forward-directed problem-solving behavior but also to develop powerful problem-solving schemas. Extrapolating from Sweller's findings, one would predict that students' long-term engagement with non-goal-specific problems and the associated problem posing and conjecture formulation activities may have a dramatic positive effect on their subsequent knowledge or problem solving. This hypothesis remains to be tested either in research or development, but Sweller's research does suggest the value of considering the inclusion of at least some non-goal-specific problems in any problem-solving instructional program.

Social Factors

In addition to considering the types of problems to include in an instructional program, one should also consider the social setting in which the problem solving will be done. What is the nature and amount of interaction that should occur between student and teacher, or among students?/

Metwali's (1979) work suggests the importance of teacher-student discussion as a mediating factor in learning from problem-solving instruction. In fact, Metwali found that the combination of giving students a few problems to solve and discussing the solutions in class was more beneficial than merely giving students many problems to solve. This suggestion is reminiscent of reports (e.g., Easley, 1983) of a highly successful teaching style found in some Japanese elementary schools, in which a teacher and students may spend an entire class period or more actively exploring and discussing the variety of approaches that might be taken to solve a particular problem. This instructional style and its benefits are also evident in the teaching reports provided by Lampert (1986).

Other current research suggests that student-student discussion may also be an important facilitator of growth in problem-solving skills and strategies. Webb (1982a, 1982b) has demonstrated the efficacy of cooperative groups for learning some aspects of the mathematics curriculum. Noddings and her associates (Noddings, 1985; Noddings, Gilbert-Macmillan, & Leitz, 1983) reported that having children work in cooperative small groups to solve mathematics problems resulted in significant growth in the children's problem-solving competence. More recently, Resnick (in press) has presented an argument for the importance of viewing mathematics learning as socially shared cognition. Her thesis rests on a foundation of both modern cognitive analyses of complex cognition and traditional social psychological analyses of cooperative learning. Although the current research evidence is thin, Resnick's analysis suggests that there are many theoretical reasons to expect that this view will reap benefits for problem-solving instruction.

Organization of students into cooperative groups for the purposes of collaborative problem solving appears to hold great potential relative to many of the issues discussed in this chapter. In particular, it is reasonable to expect that the children in a group setting would be more apt to engage in qualitative analyses and better initial problem representations as a direct result of the questions that might be asked during the process. Moreover, the group provides an environment that can promote active monitoring and evaluation of problem-solving activity. Finally, the group can assist individuals to reorganize their knowledge and reassess their intuitive conceptions on the basis of comparison with other group members. Nevertheless, these behaviors will probably not often occur spontaneously in problem-solving groups without some careful attention by the teacher to not only structuring the group and task appropriately but also providing the necessary support.

The general instructional suggestion here is that designers of instruction for problem solving should carefully consider the role and importance of teacher-student and student-student discussions in planning instructional activities. This would appear to be especially true for mathematics, which is often treated instructionally as if it were a subject to be learned in isolation. But this suggestion is also worth considering for science. Although school science laboratories often involve teams of students working together on an experiment, this approach is more likely the result of insufficient equipment than the recognition that science learning might be enhanced by a collaborative social setting. Moreover, the teacher-student dialogue in these science laboratory environments typically concerns experimental procedures not scientific principles or problem-solving strategies. Students in science classes, like their counterparts in mathematics classes, are rarely placed in rich discussion environments or cooperative groups for the purposes of solving the kinds of problems that we have discussed in this chapter. The potential benefits of increased discussion and truly collaborative settings for increasing students' problem-solving competence and learning needs to be explored in science education as well as in mathematics education.

ACKNOWLEDGMENTS

We are grateful to Mary Glick, Steven Leinwand, and Sigmund Tobias for their helpful comments on an earlier draft of this chapter. We also thank Anthony Gabriele for his nontrivial contribution during the process of revision.

REFERENCES

Anderson, J.R. (1982). Acquisition of cognitive skill. *Psychological Review, 89,* 369–406.
Anzai, Y., & Yokoyama, T. (1984). Internal models in physics problem solving. *Cognition and Instruction, 1,* 397–452.
Bransford, J. D., Barclay, J. R., & Franks, J. J. (1972). Sentence memory: A constructive versus interpretive approach. *Cognitive Psychology, 3,* 193–209.
Brown, J. S., & Burton, R. R. (1978). Diagnostic models for procedural bugs in basic mathematical skills. *Cognitive Science, 2,* 155–192.
Brown, J. S., & VanLehn, K. (1980). Repair theory: A generative theory of bugs in procedural skills. *Cognitive Science, 4,* 379–426.
Caramazza, A., McCloskey, M., & Green, B. (1981). Naive beliefs in "sophisticated" subjects: Misconceptions about trajectories of objects. *Cognition, 9,* 117–123.
Carpenter, T. P. (1985). Learning to add and subtract: An exercise in problem

solving. In E. A. Silver (Ed.), *Teaching and learning mathematical problem solving: Multiple research perspectives* (pp. 17–40). Hillsdale, NJ: Lawrence Erlbaum Associates.

Carpenter, T. P., Lindquist, M. M., Matthews, W., & Silver, E. A. (1983). Results of the third NAEP Mathematics Assessment: Secondary school. *Mathematics Teacher, 76,* 652–659.

Champagne, A. B., Klopfer, L. E., & Anderson, J. H. (1980). Factors influencing the learning of classical mechanics. *American Journal of Physics, 48,* 1074–1079.

Chase, W. G., & Chi, M. T. H. (1981). Cognitive skill: Implications for spatial skill in large-scale environments. In J. Harvey (Ed.), *Cognition, social behavior, and the environment* (pp. 111–136). Hillsdale, NJ: Lawrence Erlbaum Associates.

Chase, W. G., & Simon, H. A. (1973). The mind's eye in chess. In W. G. Chase (Ed.), *Visual information processing* (pp. 215–281). New York: Academic Press.

Chi, M. T. H., Bassok, M., Lewis, M. W., Reimann, P., & Glaser, R. (in press). Self-explanations: How students study and use examples in learning to solve problems. *Cognitive Science.*

Chi, M. T. H., Feltovich, P. J., & Glaser, R. (1981). Categorization and representation of physics problems by experts and novices. *Cognitive Science, 5,* 121–152.

Chi, M. T. H., Glaser, R., & Rees, E. (1981). Expertise in problem solving. In R. Sternberg (Ed.), *Advances in the psychology of human intelligence,* Vol. 1, pp. 7–75. Hillsdale, NJ: Lawrence Erlbaum Associates.

Clement, J. (1982). Students' preconceptions in elementary mechanics. *American Journal of Physics, 50,* 66–71.

Clement, J. (1983, April). *Analogical problem solving in science and mathematics.* Paper presented at the annual meeting of the American Educational Research Association, Montreal, Canada.

Davis, R. B. (1984). *Learning mathematics: The cognitive science approach to mathematics education.* Norwood, NJ: Albex.

Davis, R. B., & McKnight, C. C. (1979). Modeling the processes of mathematical thinking. *Journal of Children's Mathematical Behavior, 2,* 91–113.

Davis, R. B., Jockusch, E., & McKnight, C. C. (1978). Cognitive processes in learning algebra. *Journal of Children's Mathematical Behavior, 2,* 10–320.

deGroot, A. D. (1965). *Thought and choice in chess.* The Hague: Mouton.

diSessa, A. A. (1982). Unlearning Aristotelian physics: A study of knowledge-based learning. *Cognitive Science, 6,* 37–76.

Dossey, J. A., Mullis, I. V. S., Lindquist, M. M., & Chambers, D. L. (1988). *The mathematics report card: Are we measuring up?* Princeton, NJ: Educational Testing Service.

Easley, J. (1983). A Japanese approach to arithmetic. *For the Learning of Mathematics, 3,* 8–14.

Eylon, B., & Reif, F. (1984). Effects of knowledge organization on task performance. *Cognition and Instruction, 1,* 5–44.

Flavell, J. H. (1979). Metacognition and cognitive monitoring. A new area of cognitive-developmental inquiry. *American Psychologist, 34,* 906–11.

Frederiksen, N. (1984). Implications of cognitive theory for instruction in problem solving. *Review of Educational Research, 54*, 363–407.

Garofalo, J., & Lester, F. K. (1985). Metacognition, cognitive monitoring, and mathematical performance. *Journal for Research in Mathematics Education, 16*, 163–176.

Gentner, D., & Gentner, D. R. (1983). Flowing waters or teeming crowds: Mental models of electricity. In D. Gentner & A. L. Stevens (Eds.), *Mental models* (pp. 99–129). Hillsdale, NJ: Lawrence Erlbaum Associates.

Glaser, R. (1976). Components of a psychology of instruction: Toward a science of design. *Review of Educational Research, 46*, 1–24.

Glaser, R., & Bassok, M. (1989). Learning theory and the study of instruction. *Annual Review of Psychology, 40*, 631–666.

Goldberg, D. J. (1975). The effects of heuristic methods on the ability to write proofs in number theory (Doctoral dissertation, Columbia University, 1974). *Dissertation Abstracts International, 35*, 4989B.

Greeno, J. G. (1987). Instructional representations based on research about understanding. In A. H. Schoenfeld (Ed.), *Cognitive science and mathematics education* (pp. 61–88). Hillsdale, NJ: Lawrence Erlbaum Associates.

Hinsley, D. A., Hayes, J. R., & Simon, H. A. (1977). From words to equations—meaning and representation in algebra word problems. In M. Just & P. Carpenter (Eds.), *Cognitive process in comprehension* (pp. 89–106). Hillsdale, NJ: Lawrence Erlbaum Associates.

Kantowski, M. G. (1977). Processes involved in mathematical problem solving. *Journal for Research in Mathematics Education, 8*, 163–180.

Kilpatrick, J. (1985). A retrospective account of the past 25 years of research on teaching mathematical problem solving. In E. A. Silver (Ed.), *Teaching and learning mathematical problem solving: Multiple research perspectives* (pp. 1–15). Hillsdale, NJ: Lawrence Erlbaum Associates.

Lampert, M. (1986). Knowing, doing, and teaching multiplication. *Cognition and Instruction, 3*, 305–342.

Larkin, J. H. (1983a). Enriching formal knowledge: A model for learning to solve problems in physics. In J. R. Anderson (Ed.), *Cognitive skills and their acquisition* (pp. 311–334). Hillsdale, NJ: Lawrence Erlbaum Associates.

Larkin, J. H. (1983b). The role of problem representation in physics. In D. Gentner & A. L. Stevens (Eds.), *Mental models* (pp. 75–98). Hillsdale, NJ: Lawrence Erlbaum Associates.

Larkin, J. H., McDermott, J., Simon, D. P., & Simon, H. A. (1980a). Models of competence in solving physics problems. *Cognitive Science, 4*, 317–345.

Larkin, J. H., McDermott, J., Simon, D. P., & Simon, H. A. (1980b). Expert and novice performance in solving physics problems. *Science, 208*, 1335–1342.

Lee, K. S. (1978). An exploratory study of fourth graders' heuristic problem-solving behavior (Doctoral dissertation, University of Georgia, 1977). *Dissertation Abstracts International, 38*, 4004A. (University Microfilms No. 77-29, 779).

Lesh, R. (1985). Conceptual analyses of problem-solving performance. In E. A. Silver (Ed.), *Teaching and learning mathematical problem solving: Multiple research perspectives* (pp. 309–329). Hillsdale, NJ: Lawrence Erlbaum Associates.

Lester, F. K., & Garofalo, J. (1982). *Mathematical problem solving: Issues in research*. Philadelphia, PA: Franklin Institute Press.

Mandler, J. M., & Johnson, N. S. (1977). Remembrance of things parsed: Story structure and recall. *Cognitive Psychology, 9,* 111–151.

Marcucci, R. G. (1980). *A meta-analysis of research methods of teaching mathematical problem solving.* Unpublished doctoral dissertation, University of Iowa, Iowa City, IA.

Marshall, S. P., Pribe, C., & Smith, J. (1987). *Schema knowledge structures for representing and understanding arithmetic story problems* (Tech. Rep. No. N00014-85-K-0661). Washington, DC: Office of Naval Research.

Mayer, R. E. (1982). Memory for algebra story problems. *Journal of Educational Psychology, 74,* 199–216.

McCloskey, M., Washburn, A., & Felch, L. (1983). Intuitive physics. The straight-down belief and its origin. *Journal of Experimental Psychology: Learning, Memory, and Cognition, 9,* 636–649.

Mestre, J. P., Dufresne, R. J., Gerace, W., Hardiman, P. T., & Touger, J. S. (in press). Promoting expert-like behavior among beginning physics students. *American Journal of Physics.*

Metwali, S. M. (1979). *Expressed interest and extent of practice as they affect outcomes in instruction in problem solving.* Unpublished doctoral dissertation, Ohio State University, Columbus, OH.

Miller, G. A. (1956). The magical number seven, plus or minus two: Some limits on our capacity for processing information. *Psychological Review, 63,* 81–97.

Noddings, N. (1985). Small groups as a setting for research on mathematical problem solving. In E. A. Silver (Ed.), *Teaching and learning mathematical problem solving: Multiple research perspectives.* (pp. 345–359). Hillsdale, NJ: Lawrence Erlbaum Associates.

Noddings, N., Gilbert-Macmillan, K., & Leitz, S. (1983, April). *What do individuals gain in small-group mathematical problem solving?* Paper presented at the annual meeting of the American Educational Research Association, Montreal.

Owen, E., & Sweller, J. (1985). What do students learn while solving mathematics problems? *Journal of Educational Psychology, 77,* 272–284.

Paige, J. M., & Simon, H. A. (1966). Cognitive processes in solving algebra word problems. In B. Kleinmuntz (Ed.), *Problem solving: Research, method, and theory* (pp. 51–118). New York: Wiley.

Polya, G. (1957). *How to solve it* (2nd ed.). New York: Doubleday.

Polya, G. (1973). *Induction and analogy in mathematics.* Princeton, NJ: Princeton University Press.

Putt, I. J. (1979). *An exploratory investigation of two methods in instruction in mathematical problem solving at the fifth-grade level.* Unpublished doctoral dissertation, Indiana University, Bloomington, IN.

Resnick, L. B. (in press). Treating mathematics as an ill-structured discipline. In R. Charles & E. A. Silver (Eds.), *Teaching and assessing mathematical problem solving.* Reston, VA: National Council of Teachers of Mathematics.

Rissland, E. L. (1985). Artificial intelligence and the learning of mathematics: A tutorial sampling. In E. A. Silver (Ed.), *Teaching and learning mathematical problem solving: Multiple research perspectives* (pp. 147–176). Hillsdale, NJ: Lawrence Erlbaum Associates.

Rissland, E. L. (1978). Understanding mathematics. *Cognitive Science, 2,* 361–383.

Schoenfeld, A. H. (1985a). *Mathematical problem solving.* New York: Academic Press.

Schoenfeld, A. H. (1985b). Metacognitive and epistemological issues in mathematical understanding. In E. A. Silver (Ed.), *Teaching and learning mathematical problem solving: Multiple research perspectives* (pp. 361–379). Hillsdale, NJ: Lawrence Erlbaum Associates.

Schoenfeld, A. H. (1987). What's all the fuss about metacognition? In A. H. Schoenfeld (Ed.), *Cognitive science and mathematics education* (pp. 189–215). Hillsdale, NJ: Lawrence Erlbaum Associates.

Schoenfeld, A. H., & Herrmann, D. J. (1982). Problem perception and knowledge structure in expert and novice mathematical problem solvers. *Journal of Experimental Psychology: Learning, Memory, and Cognition, 8,* 484–494.

Shaughnessy, J. M. (1985). Problem-solving derailers: The influence of misconceptions on problem-solving performance. In E. A. Silver (Ed.), *Teaching and learning mathematical problem solving: Multiple research perspectives* (pp. 399–415). Hillsdale, NJ: Lawrence Erlbaum Associates.

Silver, E. A. (1979). Student perceptions of relatedness among mathematical verbal problems. *Journal for Research in Mathematics Education, 10,* 195–210.

Silver, E. A. (1985). Research on teaching mathematical problem solving: Some underrepresented themes and needed directions. In E. A. Silver (Ed.), *Teaching and learning mathematical problem solving: Multiple research perspectives* (pp. 247–266). Hillsdale, NJ: Lawrence Erlbaum Associates.

Silver, E. A. (1987). Foundations of cognitive theory and research for mathematics problem-solving instruction. In A. H. Schoenfeld (Ed.), *Cognitive science and mathematics education* (pp. 33–60). Hillsdale, NJ: Lawrence Erlbaum Associates.

Silver, E. A., & Metzger, W. (1989). Aesthetic influences on expert mathematical problem solving. In D. B. McLeod & M. Adams (Eds.), *Affect and mathematical problem solving: A new perspective* (pp. 59–74). New York: Springer-Verlag.

Simon, D. P., & Simon, H. A. (1978). Individual differences in solving physics problems. In R. S. Siegler (Ed.), *Children's thinking: What develops?* (pp. 325–348). Hillsdale, NJ: Lawrence Erlbaum Associates.

Simon, H. A. (1980). Problem solving and education. In D. T. Tuma & F. Reif (Eds.), *Problem solving and education: Issues in teaching and research* (pp. 81–96). Hillsdale, NJ: Lawrence Erlbaum Associates.

Smith, E. E., & Goodman, L. (1984). Understanding written instructions: The role of an explanatory schema. *Cognition and Instruction, 1,* 359–396.

Smith, M. U., & Good, R. (1984). Problem solving and classical genetics: Successful versus unsuccessful performance. *Journal of Research in Science Teaching, 21,* 895–912.

Steffe, L. P., von Glasersfeld, E., Richards, J., & Cobb, P. (1983). *Children's counting types—Philosophy, theory, and application.* New York: Praeger.

Sweller, J., & Cooper, G. A. (1985). The use of worked examples as a substitute for problem solving in learning algebra. *Cognition and Instruction, 2,* 59–89.

Sweller, J., & Levine, M. (1982). Effects of goal specificity on means-end analysis and learning. *Journal of Experimental Psychology: Learning, Memory and Cognition, 8,* 463–474.

Sweller, J., Mawer, R., & Ward, M. (1983). Development of expertise in mathematical problem solving. *Journal of Experimental Psychology: General, 112,* 634–656.

Thorndyke, P. W., & Hayes-Roth, B. (1979). The use of schema in the acquisition and transfer of knowledge. *Cognitive Psychology, 11* 82–106.

Thorndyke, P. W., & Yekovich, S. (1980). A critique of schema-based theories of human story memory. *Poetics, 9,* 23–49.

VanEngen, H. (1959). Twentieth century mathematics for the elementary school. *Arithmetic Teacher, 6,* 71–76.

VanLehn, K. (1986). Arithmetic procedures are induced from examples. In J. Hiebert (Ed.), *Conceptual and procedural knowledge: The case of mathematics* (pp. 133–179). Hillsdale, NJ: Lawrence Erlbaum Associates.

von Glasersfeld, E. (1983). Learning as a constructive activity. In J. C. Bergeron & N. Herscovics (Eds.), *Proceedings of the fifth annual meeting of the international group for the psychology of mathematics education* (pp. 41–69). Montreal: Author.

White, B., & Frederiksen, J. R. (1986). Intelligent tutoring systems based upon qualitataive model evaluations. *Proceedings of AAAI-86; The National Conference on Artifical Intelligence* (pp. 313–319). San Mateo, CA: Morgan Kaufmann Publishers.

Science Education
and the Cognitive Psychology
of Science

Ryan D. Tweney
Bowling Green State University

Bonnie J. Walker
Central State University

The quest for a "science of science education" (Linn, 1986, p. 156) has been the focus of a good deal of effort in the last decade or so, and has proved so promising that discussion has begun on the ways that such knowledge can be incorporated into the professional practice and preparation of science teachers (e.g., Anderson, 1987). Even so, it will be some time before we can speak of a systematic body of knowledge, empirically related to cognitive accounts of science and the learning of science on the one hand and to pedagogical practice and theory on the other hand. No such systematization will be possible, in our view, in the absence of a coherent and psychologically realistic account of the nature of scientific thinking as such. Thus, the major purposes of this chapter are (a) to review certain advances in the cognitive psychology of science and (b) to suggest possible implications for curricular issues and teaching strategies.

Scientific thinking is generally regarded as an essential component in attempts to incorporate thinking skills instruction in the schools (see, e.g., Costa, 1985 and Marzano, in press). Nevertheless, the nature of scientific thinking itself has been largely ignored by educators and continues to be regarded from a standpoint that appears to reflect a number of popular misconceptions about science. According to Mitroff (1974), such misconceptions include the mistaken views that scientific thinking is essentially logical, that scientists approach their task coldly and emotionlessly, stifling their own biases and interests, that scientific thinking is the opposite of the value-laden, multidimensional, creative thought found in the humanities, and that scientists solve problems by virtue of their extensive knowledge of facts. In reality, however, science rests on very different cognitive foundations; although the end result (a finished scientific theory) is, ideally, logically consistent, value-neutral, and tied to a body of factual knowledge, the process by which such theories are created is very different (Tweney, 1987).

In an attempt to review the relevant research in a way that will be maximally useful to applied concerns in science teaching, our review focuses on three broad areas of research. The first concerns the relation between the kind of reasoning that occurs in science and the orthodox categories of formal reasoning that have characterized earlier approaches to the philosophy of science. We see that the "psycho-logic" of science differs rather dramatically from the formal logical descriptions of science that once dominated science studies (and which are still found in our textbooks). Because all science depends on a body of knowledge drawn on as "factual" by the working scientist, our second concern focuses on how specialized "expert" knowledge is utilized in science. Here, we see that there are a number of unresolved issues, but that the principles that are understood can be of great utility for the science educator. Thirdly, we consider recent research on the problem-solving process itself, reviewing certain studies that focus on the role of problem solving in science. In all three sections, we review selected aspects of the "cognitive case studies" of great scientists, partly to show how the principles described actually work, and partly to find unsolved problems.

Throughout the review, we direct our comments toward two related audiences; first, science teachers interested in knowing about science, so as to better characterize its nature for their students, and second, curriculum specialists interested in devising curricula and establishing curricular goals for the better teaching of science. In general, we do not review the large literature directed specifically to research on science teaching. The interested reader can find a useful beginning in Gagne (1985).

PSYCHO-LOGIC OF SCIENCE

Traditional logic and psycho-logic (i.e., the cognitive psychological analysis of logic) agree on one basic point: All science rests heavily on a specific type of proposition known as a conditional inference. "IF Newton's Laws are correct, THEN a given satellite should orbit with velocity v and period T". Observation of specific satellites, such as the moon, can then be used either to confirm or disconfirm the inference. Karl Popper first noticed that, as Hume had suggested, only a disconfirmed inference could be said to be logically correct. If the orbit of a satellite does not agree with the orbit predicted by theory, then something must be wrong with the original proposition. On the other hand, if the orbit does agree with the prediction, there is no assurance that the proposition is correct, because other propositions may also generate the same prediction. This logical asymmetry is the ultimate reason for the continual evolution of scientific ideas; we can never be sure that a given theory is right, only that it has not yet been disconfirmed. Conversely, we can be sure that some theories are wrong (A claim that the earth is flat, say), once they have been disconfirmed by observational evidence.

Popper's emphasis on the importance of disconfirmation has had a major impact on philosophical analyses of science (e.g., Schilpp, 1974). Nevertheless, as clear as his point seems to be *logically,* it has had to be qualified heavily. In practice, no scientific proposition is ever a single, unitary hypothesis. In our earlier example, if a satellite orbit does not agree with Newton's predicted orbit, then *either* Newton's Laws are wrong, *or* our measurements of the orbit are wrong, *or* there is a disturbing force present, *or* . . . It is not hard to see that, in the real world, disconfirmation is not so central as it seemed in Popper's original analysis. As we shall see, there are important implications for science education. Understanding scientific inference (and hence understanding the process by which it is learned and taught) requires careful attention to the role of both confirmation *and* disconfirmation.

Popper's ideas were of great concern to the first researchers in the psychology of science. For instance, Wason (1960) used Popperian falsification principles as a normative base for his studies of conditional inference; studies which, as we see later, give us some of the best insights into how people actually make inferences. In addition, Mitroff (1974) demonstrated that working scientists behaved in ways that did not always conform to Popper's normative rule of disconfirmation. Finally, our own early studies (Mynatt, Doherty, & Tweney, 1977, 1978) were conceived as extensions of Wason's earlier research. Thus, the first step in understanding the psycho-logic of science is to see what is known about "confirmation bias," the tendency to avoid disconfirmation and to seek (apparently illogically) only to confirm a hypothesis.

Confirmation "Bias"

Many psychological studies of inference using various experimental tasks have reported that subjects demonstrate a bias to confirm—a preference for accumulating supporting (confirmatory) evidence for their ideas, rather than actively seeking refuting (disconfirmatory) evidence (e.g., Wason, 1960; Wason & Johnson-Laird, 1970, 1972; Tweney et al., 1980). The general strategy applied in these studies has been to devise a laboratory task that mirrors some aspect of scientific thining, while allow-ing greater control over factors which determine the application of par-ticular problem-solving heuristics. It should be pointed out, however, that such studies must be interpreted carefully; although they can be powerful analytic aids, they may not be wholly representative of what is going on in the real world of science.

Wason's widely used "four-card selection task" bears a certain re-semblance to the task facing the scientist (Wason & Johnson-Laird, 1972). The task involves having subjects determine the truth or falsity of a conditional rule by selecting the relevant evidence. Subjects are shown four cards, two displaying letters (e.g., A and H) and two displaying numbers (e.g., 4 and 7). They are asked to turn over only those cards that can determine the truth or falsity of the conditional rule, "If there is a vowel on one side of a card, then there is an even number on the other side" (If P then Q). Only the "A" and "7" cards should be turned over. The "H" and "4" are irrelevant in testing the truth or falsity of the rule because neither can disconfirm the truth of the rule, no matter what is on the reverse side. Wason found that although most subjects correctly picked the "A" card, the majority failed to pick the "7" card, which could disconfirm the rule, and instead picked "4", which could only confirm the rule. Wason noted that the failure of his subjects to seek the correct evidence violated Popper's normative rule and that the task could there-fore serve as a kind of microcosm for the study of confirmation bias in science. This claim has been contested (e.g., Wetherick, 1962), although the great popularity of the task among experimental psychologists is generally based on the belief that it is analogous to actual scientific think-ing (see, e.g., Evans, 1982; Tweney & Doherty, 1983). Most of the re-search has concerned alternative explanations of why subjects exhibit confirmation bias, and it seems to be the case that a variety of causal factors are at work—there is no simple explanation that applies to all versions of the task or to all subjects.

Two experiments extending the generalizability of the four-card task demonstrated how "reasoning ability is tied to particular schemata relat-ed to particular bodies of knowledge" (Rumelhart, 1978, p. 39). Subjects were given one of two hypothetical jobs: either sorting four labels to insure that labels with a vowel on one side had an odd number printed on the other side or sorting four Sears' sales receipts to insure that all sales over $30 had the manager's approval. In both experiments, the fronts and backs of the labels or receipts correspond to the usual four-card set (P, Q, not-P, not-Q if we represent the conditional in the usual logical symbolism as IF P THEN Q). Although most subjects given the more abstract "label" job failed to select the relevant labels to turn over (selecting only P and Q), a significant number given the "Sears" job selected only the relevant receipts (P and not-Q). Rumelhart posited that a familiar context, such as the "Sears" problem, enables subjects to invoke previously successful problem-solving experiences and solve the task more easily.

A similar context facilitation effect was demonstrated by Griggs and Cox (1982) by having college undergraduates solve a "drinking age" rule problem. Subjects imagine themselves as police officers in a bar enforcing an age-restricting law for drinking beer: "If a person is drinking beer, then the person must be over 19" (Griggs & Cox, 1982, p. 9). To test for violations of the rule, they could choose from four cards representing four people labeled "drinking beer" (P), "drinking Coke" (not-P), "16 years of age" (not-Q), and "22 years of age" (Q). A significant number of subjects picked the correct cards (P and not-Q). Griggs and Cox concluded that the familiar content of the problem cued relevant memories (but see Yachanin, 1986, for a different interpretation).

Tweney and Doherty (1983) argued that the relation between a subject's knowledge of a problem-domain and the inference process was associated in complex ways with performance on such tasks. Wason and Green (1984) found that subject performance on the four-card task depended on the way in which the dimensions of the stimulus cards were combined. Thus, suppose the inference involved colors and shapes, green versus red and round versus triangular. Performance was better when the two dimensions were unified ("If the card is green, then it is round") than when they were disjoint ("If the front of the card is green, then the back of the card has a round shape on it"). It seems that more than just memory retrieval is involved here, because both kinds of cards are equally unfamiliar. Instead, unified stimuli are easier to deal with because it is easier to construct unified mental representations of the problem.

Another laboratory task, Wason's (1960) 2-4-6 rule discovery problem, has frequently been used to study hypothesis testing (Tweney et al., 1980; Walker & Tweney, 1983; Walker, 1985, 1986, 1987; Gorman & Gorman, 1984; Klayman & Ha, 1985; Tukey, 1986). Subjects attempt to discover a general number-sequencing rule, "three ascending numbers," and are given the initial conforming sequence, "2, 4, 6." To test their ideas about the rule, subjects generate additional sequences and are told if these sequences fit the rule or not. Wason (1960) characterized the task as:

> . . . a miniature scientific problem, in which the variables are unknown, and in which evidence has to be systematically adduced to refute or support hypotheses. Generating an instance corresponds to doing an experiment, knowledge that the instance conforms or does not conform, corre-

sponds to its result, and an incorrect announcement corresponds to an inference from uncontrolled data. (p. 139.)

Wason found that a majority of the subjects initially proposed one very specific hypothesis, such as "three even numbers" or "numbers separated by two," and conducted only confirmatory tests, trying sequences consistent with their idea, such as "even numbers—6, 8, 10." Thus, most subjects declared rules that were sufficient to explain the obtained evidence, but which did not specify both the necessary *and* sufficient conditions for all the possible evidence.

Recent research using Wason's 2-4-6 task has revealed how complex these issues become: Although most subjects are misled by conducting a high proportion of confirmatory tests, in certain circumstances the strategy is actually beneficial. Thus, Tweney et al. (1980) asked subjects to find two interrelated rules rather than one, substituting the titles of "Dax" and "Med" for Wason's traditional "Right" or "Wrong" response categories. For example, if the rule was "three ascending numbers," the sequence, "2, 4, 6," was considered a "Dax" and the sequence, "6, 4, 2," a "Med." Even though subjects made predominately more confirmatory tests than in the usual task, solving for two rules was significantly easier. Tweney et al. suggested that disconfirming data that might otherwise have been ignored as a "wrong" answer for the "Dax" hypothesis became, in effect, data relevant to the "Med" hypothesis.

Confirmation Heuristics

Using confirmatory tests early in the solution process appears to be a generally beneficial strategy. Gorman and Gorman (1984) used Wason's task, but some subjects were taught how to disconfirm their hypotheses and no subjects were told until the end of the experiment whether or not their rule announcements were correct. Those subjects shown how to disconfirm their hypotheses began the solution process by first confirming an initial idea and then subsequently conducted disconfirming tests. The combination of early confirmatory testing, followed by later disconfirmatory tests, significantly increased correct solution rates. Similarly, Tweney, Doherty, and Mynatt (1981) argued that confirmation "bias" may actually serve as a powerful heuristic in the early stages of inference. For some tasks, a confirmatory strategy may be the single most powerful heuristic. As Klayman and Ha (1987) pointed out:

> . . . many phenomena of human hypothesis testing can be understood in terms of a general "positive test strategy." According to this strategy, you test a hypothesis by examining instances in which the property or event is

expected to occur (to see if it does occur), or by examining instances in which it is known to have occurred (to see if the hypothesized conditions prevail). (p. 4-5)

Thus, the use of such a strategy, although illogical from Popper's point of view, may be highly adaptive and useful across a wide variety of situations. Tweney, et al. (1981) have also questioned the utility of disconfirmation as an "optimal inference technique" (p. 123) and argued that although disconfirmatory strategies are logically rational, they may not always be effective. The results of Mynatt, et al.'s (1977, 1978) artifical universe studies, complex and open-ended inference tasks, indicated that subjects who attempted to use disconfirmation early in the solution process were misled by the results and entirely abandoned hypotheses that were partially correct.

Several analyses of research involving both the four-card and the 2-4-6 task (Klayman & Ha, 1987; Tweney & Doherty, 1983) have suggested that the strategies used in solving such inference tasks are complex and dependent on the "semantic, syntactic, and pragmatic context of the inference problem at hand" (Tweney & Doherty, 1983, p. 139). Furthermore, recent studies of the 2-4-6 task have reported that under certain conditions subjects attempt to solve the task not only by using a mixture of confirmatory and disconfirmatory tests, but also by testing alternative hypotheses and conducting exploratory tests to develop new hypotheses (Tukey, 1986; Walker, 1985, 1986). For instance, analyses of protocols when subjects were asked to "think aloud" while performing the 2-4-6 task (Walker, 1986) revealed that specific hypotheses were not always being tested. In some cases, when a subject's most viable hypothesis had been disconfirmed, exploratory tests were conducted to develop new ideas. Similar strategy findings were reported when subjects were asked to label the dominant types of problem-solving heuristics they used to solve the 2-4-6 task (Tukey, 1986). Subjects sometimes chose confirmatory and disconfirmatory categories, but a significant number also chose exploratory and discovery-centered categories to describe their strategies.

In general, then, in tasks designed to mirror the normatively logical structure of scientific inference, subjects perform in ways that deviate substantially from Popperian normative rules. It is not the case that these deviations represent *"biases"* in the strict sense of the term. Instead, they appear to represent applications of generally powerful heuristics, which do not always serve the subject well in the restricted context of a laboratory task. In the real world, things are different. Thus, by examining the notebooks of the physicist Michael Faraday, Tweney (1985) was able to show that Faraday frequently ignored disconfirmatory evidence, particularly during the early stages of an investigation. It would be inappropriate to call this a bias, however. Instead, it appears to have been a part of a powerful heuristic based on initial pursuit of confirming evidence, followed in the last stages of inference by systematic attempts to find alternative explanations. If these systematic attempts failed, then Faraday could be sure he had a well-supported finding. One point follows immediately for science education: Leading students to an appreciation of scientific inference should rest on the exploration of multiple perspectives. It is not sufficient to teach students how to confirm a single perspective (nor how to disconfirm a single perspective). It is interesting to note that such a strategy is at odds with the usual classroom laboratory experiment that emphasizes getting the "right" answer, and that treats deviations from the right answer as mistakes on the part of the student.

In sum, then, we have seen that a particular logical inference in science, the "If . . . Then . . . " conditional, plays a central role in scientific thinking. Although the logic of such propositions is clear-cut, the psycho-logic is not. In general, people (including scientists) simply do not rely on the normative logical rules for evaluating such propositions. Instead, they rely much more heavily on confirmatory attempts than on the seemingly more appropriate logic of disconfirmation. And yet, as we have seen, such confirmatory "biases" turn out to have great heuristic value in real-world inference. Scientific thinking (and science education) needs to be regarded with these facts in mind.

EXPERT KNOWLEDGE IN SCIENCE

Enormous strides have been made in our understanding of the nature of knowledge in recent years. Of special interest for science education is the large body of research findings based on how expert knowledge differs from the knowledge possessed by novices. Clearly experts "know more" than novices; that is part of what it means to be an expert in the first place. Scientists know more about science than non-scientists, as we should expect. The interesting differences between expert and non-expert go deeper than this, however. Studies of chess expertise provide some hints about what we might expect to be true in science.

Many studies have been done on chess expertise since the pioneering study of deGroot (1965). By comparing expert players (actually, in the nomenclature of chess, "master" players) to relatively less experienced players (actually "experts" in chess nomenclature), deGroot showed that few differences existed between the two in knowledge of the game rules, memory capability, or the number of moves considered prior to selecting a particular move (the so-called "depth of search"). However, expert players were substantially better than novices in correctly recalling a briefly presented chess configuration. Chase and Simon (1973) showed that the superior recall was dependent on the larger "chunks" used by expert players; faced with a chess position, experts encode more chess pieces per chunk than do novices. Newell and Simon attributed the difference to the much larger number of positions recognized as meaningful by expert players; their greater experience led to the storage of a greater number of patterns. Experts thus "see" more than novices (Eisenstadt & Kareev, 1977).

Similar differences were found by Berliner (Brandt, 1986) in a study comparing expert teachers to novice teachers. Thus, when briefly shown a photograph of a classroom and asked to describe what is happening, expert teachers frequently noticed two children in the back of the room who were not attending to the teacher, whereas novices rarely noticed such patterns and focused instead on details of physical setting, clothing, and other less relevant characteristics.

Although there have been few formal studies comparing expert and novice scientists along similar lines, there are several case studies that suggest that similar factors are at work. The well-known story of Fleming's discovery of penicillin (Austin, 1978) is a case in point. His serendipitous discovery of the drug was based on his ability to recognize the significance of a lack of bacterial growth surrounding a plate contaminated by blue bread mold. Such recognitions are likely to be dependent on the greater number of stored patterns, which in turn permit more meaningful organization of perceived realities; "Serendipity favors the prepared mind" (see also Perkins, 1981). Biographies of scientists support this view. Thus, Goodfield's (1981) portrait of an anonymous cancer researcher reveals an almost obsessive accumulation of knowledge by a productive scientist. Gruber's (1974) analysis of Darwin's scientific notebooks reveals a similar characteristic. It is interesting to note also that Anne Roe's classic studies of the personalities of biological and physical scientists found only one factor that characterized all of her scientist-subjects—an immersion in their work over a period of many years, frequently to the exclusion of anything else (Roe, 1949, 1951).

What Do Experts Know?

Much recent work seems to show that experts differ from novices in *how* their knowledge is organized and used, even when the amount of knowledge is equated. This has enormous implications for science education because it suggests that we may be able to arrange the order of acquisition of scientific knowledge in a way that leads students more quickly to the kind of organization that experts manifest. Clearly, we have here a fruitful area for further research.

In the previous section of this chapter, we saw that even the most austerely defined problem-solving or inference tasks could not avoid the fact that human beings rely on previous knowledge in drawing inferences or solving problems. The same is true of science, of course, but the challenge is to ask just exactly what knowledge is drawn upon, how it is organized, and how it is used in scientific thinking. Chi and her colleagues (Chi, Feltovich, & Glaser, 1981; Chi, Glaser, & Rees, 1982) found that expert physicists and novice physics students categorized physics problems in different ways. Whereas experts relied on general principles to group different problems (e.g., "These all involve the conservation of momentum"; "These can all be solved using Newton's Second Law"), novices categorized on the basis of superficial aspects of problems (e.g., "These all involve inclined planes"). This is particularly relevant because such categorizations, like the chunks used by chess masters, seem to determine the initial approaches taken to actually solving the problem. Experts begin with the general principles and look for ways to concretize them in the specific task at hand, whereas novices begin with the specifics and look for formulas that incorporate both the goal of the problem and the specifics mentioned by the problem. Ironically, novice physics students seem to rely *more* on equations than do the experts!

Larkin (1981) found differences that extend throughout the problem-solving task between expert and novice physicists. Whereas novices solved problems by "working backwards" (starting with the goal state and setting up subgoals that would connect the goal with the initial state), experts "worked forward" (by starting with the general principles and elaborating a path from the principles to the goal state). Similar differences have been observed in a variety of domains of expertise: chess, medical diagnosis, social science reasoning, and more. Chi et al. (1982) also found that, for equivalent amounts of knowledge, experts incorporate procedural rules directly in their knowledge, whereas novices' declarative knowledge is relatively devoid of such procedural specifications. Thus, experts seem to approach inclined plane problems by using rules of the form "IF plane is not smooth, THEN use work done by friction" whereas novices use rules of the form "IF plane is not smooth, THEN determine coefficients of static and kinetic friction." Whereas the expert rule directly relates a broad principle of physics, the novice rule directly invokes a specific equation.

Workers in artifical intelligence have relied on these characterizations of expert/novice differences in the construction of computerized expert systems (Barr & Feigenbaum, 1981, chap. 7; Stillings et al., 1987). Most such systems are programmed by tapping the knowledge of a human expert. Initially, the expert's knowledge is represented to the computer in the form of production rules, "If-then" statements that specify a particular operation to be carried out if a particular input condition is met— much like the rules derived by Chi et al. in their study of physics students and experts. The hardest part of constructing a computerized expert system is getting the system to recognize specific problem situations that call for special treatment, just as we might expect from the studies by Larkin, Chi, and Simon.

The computerized expert system can be given a specific knowledge base "ab initio," in the assurance that, although perhaps incomplete, the starting knowledge base at least contains no misinformation. The same is not true of the human student. As Carey (1986) pointed out, the task in science teaching involves a restructuring of already existing knowledge, because students attempting to learn physics, say, already possess a set of concepts concerning physical reality. The task facing the student thus parallels that of the scientific discoverer, who must also reconceptualize a domain of knowledge. In a broad sense, then, learning science resembles a series of paradigm shifts; the effective teaching of science must in turn be based on empirically based knowledge of the intuitive conceptualizations of the student. Cognitive scientists and educators have begun to address these questions (e.g., Disessa, 1982; Driver, Guesne, & Tiberghien, 1985; Kuhn, Amsel, & O'Laughlin, 1988; McCloskey, et al., 1980; Wiser & Carey, 1983) although much more research needs to be done.

Skill Expertise in Science

Scientific expertise often relies on specific skills from other domains of knowledge, specifically, from mathematics, the most notorious stumbling block in science education. What is often lost sight of, however, is that mathematics is a *tool* in science. In our opinion, many science textbooks misuse mathematics by presenting it in a way that is rarely found in actual scientific practice. In scientific practice, mathematical statements are frequently used as a means of representing phenomenal reality; a derivational role is much less frequent. Chi's and Larkin's studies are again relevant; students were more likely to use mathematical expressions as the starting point of problem solving, whereas physicists used equations only as a last, fairly superficial, computational device. Similarly, Einstein described his creative thinking as dependent on visual intuition which, as a last step only, needed to be turned into mathematical expressions for communication purposes (Tweney et al., 1981). Although mathematics does sometimes play a central derivational role in

science (as in the case of Maxwell's demonstration of the relation between light and electromagnetic phenomena) we believe Einstein's procedure to be more common (see also Langley & Simon, 1986; Shepard,
1978).

To the extent that mathematics is a notoriously problematic classroom
subject in itself, it is not surprising that teaching the use of mathematics
in science is perhaps the most problematic part of science education.
Partly this is due to inadequate conceptualizations of what it is that
students need to learn in mathematics, as Rissland (1985), for example,
suggested. However, the problem is partly due to a failure to fully exploit
the tool-like aspects of mathematics. Thus, Wollman (1987) found that
junior high school students had no conceptual relation between their
physical knowledge of density and their formal knowledge of the density
formula $D = M/V$. More surprisingly, these students' teachers did not
believe that such relational knowledge could be taught, even though
Wollman was able to do so with a relatively straightforward use of
prompts. Representation of mathematically expressed relations is apparently the key factor here. Thus Ranney (1987) found that perception of
algebraic strings by college students was dependent in complex ways on
the syntax of the strings, utilizing a kind of "grammar" of algebra. Yet
little is known about how such grammars are mapped onto conceptual
knowledge outside mathematics. Although computation skills have been
the focus of much research (e.g., Gagne, 1985, chap. 9), conceptual skills
need to be addressed as well (see also Schoenfeld, 1985).

The use of imagery of certain types is an essential skill at least some of
the time in science, and the issues also seem relevant to science education. A hotly debated issue among cognitive scientists is whether or not
imagery plays a functional role in thinking. Some (e.g., Kosslyn, 1983)
have argued for such a role, although others (e.g., Pylyshn, 1981) have
argued that no independent evidence can be found that supports such a
claim. However that debate is resolved, many scientists do report using
visual images in their thinking (see the section on imagery in Tweney et
al., 1981), and there are numerous historical case studies that strongly
suggest the importance of imagery in science, Kekule's dream being the
classic example (Shepard, 1978 discussed this and other examples).
Gruber (1974) has stressed the centrality of certain very specific images
in Darwin's creative thought, as have Nersessian (1984) and Tweney
(1985) for the case of Faraday. Miller (1984) has even argued that the
history of modern physics since the mid-19th century has been dependent on a shift in the role of imagery, changing from a direct, pictorial
function to a more abstract function in which the format of an image
serves to represent a non-visualizable relationship. Miller quoted the
following intriguing statement made by Heisenberg in 1976:

If we wish to compare the knowledge of modern particle physics with any of the old philosophies, the philosophy of Plato appears to be the most adequate: The particles . . . are representations of symmetry groups, . . . and to that extent they resemble the symmetrical bodies of the Platonic doctrine. (Miller,1984, p. 173)

As with images, analogies and metaphors find frequent uses in science. Nersessian (1984) has stressed the productive role of analogies as "articulating devices" that serve to give temporary meaning to a vague unarticulated construct. Gooding (1986) has similarly stressed the importance of understanding the process by which vague "construals" become fully articulated, socially communicable concepts. Sternberg (1985) has argued that analogies are based on a fundamental set of cognitive operations that map one set of structures onto another, and are thus central to an understanding of all inductive reasoning. In real-world science, analogies are frequently mentioned in biographical accounts, or even in the published results of scientific inquiry, for example in Bohr's planetary model of the atom. Clement (in press) has found evidence for the use of analogies in the think-aloud protocols of scientists asked to solve a difficult mechanics problem. Science texts frequently employ analogies to present new concepts, and it is plausible to think that they can be powerful pedagogical devices. Given this, it is surprising how little research has been directed to this topic (but see Gentner & Gentner, 1983).

The expert, in sum, differs from the novice in more than simply sheer *amount* of knowledge. There are also major differences in how the knowledge is organized and in how it is used. Further, as we have seen, scientific expertise involves a wide range of cognitive devices (images, analogies, etc.), which seem to play a central role in scientific thinking. Science educators, like educators in any domain, need to be aware of these findings, for they suggest new and powerful ways to conceptualize the goal of science education.

PROBLEM SOLVING IN SCIENCE

Cognitive scientists generally conceptualize problem solving as a search process: Given some initial state, a set of allowable "rules," and an end state, the task is to find a path from the initial state to the goal state by specifying a sequence of applications of the rules. An anagram task, for example, starts with a sequence of letters, RHTAE say (the initial state), and requires that the letters be rearranged (the rules) to form a common English word (the goal state). A great deal has been learned in recent years concerning the methods that people use to solve such problems and the conditions under which the process is efficient, that is, likely to lead to solution in a reasonable time. For many problems solution algorithms can be specified, that is to say, the problem is guaranteed to be solved by repetitive application of a particular rule. In the case of an anagram, one could start with the first given letter (R) and try all possible arrangements of the other four letters (RHTEA, RHETA, etc.). If the solution is not found try the second letter (HRTEA, HRETA, etc.) and so on. Although people do use such algorithmic procedures for some tasks (e.g., long division), they are hard to learn (ask any teacher!) and sometimes exceedingly slow for human problem solvers. In science, algorithmic procedures for problem solving play a minor role in the thought processes of scientists themselves, hence the constant pressure to move such procedures "out of the jellyware and into the hardware," as the recent proliferation of computers bears witness.

Most human problem solving relies, not on algorithms, but on heuristics, generalized strategies that limit the space of possibilities that needs to be searched. Faced with the anagram RHTAE, for example, one might choose to search for a two-syllable word, RATEH, RETAH, and so forth. In this case the goal of finding an English word made out of five letters is reduced to the subgoal of finding an English word of the form _ E _ A _ given the three letters, R, H, and T. If the subgoal fails to generate a solution, one might then seek a new subgoal and try again: Find an English word of the form _ E A _ _, and so on. (Actually, the second pattern usually leads quickly to the solution.) The heuristic procedure of finding subgoals has been shown to resolve itself into a fairly small set of characteristic types, for example, seek a subgoal that will minimize the difference between the initial and goal state. In our example, the initial anagram might appear similar to the word RATHER; one could thus look for an English word with one less letter to reduce the difference between the goal and the given (which, in this case, is not a productive strategy).

Unlike algorithms, heuristics need not be successful; they can lead to no answer or to a wrong answer. On the other hand, heuristics sometimes quickly succeed and prove to be much faster than the corresponding algorithm. The true power of heuristics is especially evident in complex problem solving. Thus, algorithmic approaches to playing the game of chess are certainly possible, but have proved to be overwhelmingly tedious even for the fastest computers. Workers in artifical intelligence have therefore focused on the task of providing computers with heuristic devices modeled after human chess players, and have been much more successful with this approach (see Stillings et al., 1987, chap. 5, for an overview of recent AI approaches to problem solving).

Heuristics in Science

Scientific problem solving, like all complex human problem solving, depends on a variety of heuristics only some of which have been described. The confirmatory/disconfirmatory heuristics described earlier are clear examples, and the use of imagery and analogy can be construed as heuristics as well. In general, scientific thinking requires the consideration of multiple alternatives (Baron, 1985; Platt, 1964) yet it is known that this is difficult for human beings (e.g., Doherty, Mynatt, Tweney, & Schiavo, 1979). In everyday problem solving there is a strong tendency to ignore multiple alternatives, concentrating on only one alternative that "makes sense" (Perkins, in press). Scientists, however, frequently use heuristics to regulate the consideration of alternatives, changing, for example, the confirmation bias of ordinary thinking into a confirmation heuristic that postpones but does not ignore the need to consider alternatives (Tweney et al., 1981). Goodfield's (1981) wonderful account of the inner world of a molecular biologist makes this clear; the "imagined world" of her scientist-subject was frequently self-challenged by the subject herself.

It follows from the aforementioned that one important part of the process of socialization in science must focus on the acquisition of heuristics. Note that consideration of alternatives is frequently *dis*couraged in textbooks and laboratory exercises that tend to focus on reinforcing the "right" answer rather than having the student appreciate the processes by which wrong answers can be considered and dismissed. In addition to short-changing the importance of heuristics, such materials have a further pedagogical disadvantage in that they create the false impression that successful scientists somehow intuit the "right" answer, which they can prove to be correct. In reality, successful scientific accounts depend at least as much on repeated attempts to *dis*prove the correctness of hypotheses, as Popper (1934/1959) emphasized.

Problem solving in science has been directly studied only in restricted domains. Langley, Simon, Bradshaw, and Zytkow (1987) constructed detailed accounts of how data are used to discover and generate lawful relationships, and were able to simulate on a computer the process by which lawful generalizations are developed from data (although Gorman, 1987, has argued that their simulations are inaccurate when compared to the historical record of the actual discovery). Kulkarni and Simon (1988) have used a similar approach to construct a computer simulation that models the discovery of the urea cycle of Hans Krebs. Their simulation is especially striking because it reacts to unexpected data, and proposes experiments to generate more data, in a fashion similar to the one revealed in Krebs's own laboratory notebooks. Klahr and Dunbar (1988) characterized scientific problem solving as involving a two-fold search, through a space of possible experiments and through a space of hypotheses. Their model worked well as an account of how adult subjects discovered and explored the operation of an electronic device. Here also, the observed heuristics corresponded to those observed in traditional problem-solving tasks. The classical description of such heuristics is by Newell and Simon (1972; the interested reader might prefer the more accessible account of Mayer, 1983).

CONCLUSION

In actual fact, no single model of problem solving is likely to capture all of the richness of scientific practice. Thus, although Faraday relied heavily on certain heuristics to discover induction (Tweney, 1985), other strategies were used in other contexts. What appears to have guided his choice of a particular strategy is not always clear: influences ranging from his religious beliefs, to his specific visual style of thinking have been identified (Gooding & James, 1985); there is no reason to expect a complete picture to be anything except highly complex. Gruber (1974) and Wallace and Gruber (1989) suggested that such complexity is essential: Science is based on a network of enterprise in which diverse interests and methods interact. Similar claims have been made for creative thinking in general (e.g., Perkins, chap. 13 in this volume). Perhaps the most general lesson for the educator is to be found here; good science teaching must ultimately also rest on a multiplicity of approaches and on a healthy respect for the variety of characteristics of science. Educators must, in short, expand their conceptions of what science really is.

Thinking in science is a diverse process. In these few pages, we have singled out a role for heuristics, for important aspects of the organization and use of knowledge, for specific strategies involving the use of images and analogies in problem solving. The list is far from complete, but is long enough to suggest that no account of science that concentrates on just one kind of thinking is likely to be correct. A full understanding of the process of science must reflect this diversity. And so must a full pedagogy of science education.

ACKNOWLEDGMENTS

Grateful acknowledgment is made to the editors and to Michael O'Loughlin for their comments on an early draft of this chapter.

REFERENCES

Anderson, C. W. (1987, April). *Three perspectives on cognition and their implications for science teaching.* Paper presented at the Annual Meeting of the American Educational Research Association, Washington, DC.

Austin, J. H. (1978). *Chase, chance, and creativity.* New York: Columbia University Press.

Baron, J. (1985). *Rationality and intelligence.* Cambridge, England: Cambridge University Press.

Barr, A., & Feigenbaum, E. A. (1982). *Handbook of artificial intelligence* (Vol. 2). Stanford, CT: HeurisTech Press.

Brandt, R. (1986). On the expert teacher: A conversation with David Berliner. *Educational Leadership, 44*(2), 4–9.

Carey, S. (1986). Cognitive science and science education. *American Psychologist, 41,* 1123–1130.

Chase, W. G., & Simon, H. A. (1973). Perception in chess. *Cognitive Psychology, 4,* 55–81.

Chi, M. T. H., Feltovich, P. J., & Glaser, R. (1981). Categorization and representation of physics problems by experts and novices. *Cognitive Science, 5,* 121–152.

Chi, M. T. H., Glaser, R., & Rees, E. (1982). Expertise in problem solving. In R. S. Sternberg (Ed.), *Advances in the psychology of human intelligence.* (Vol. 1., pp. 7–75). Hillsdale, NJ: Lawrence Erlbaum Associates.

Clement, J. (in press). Observed methods for generating analogies in scientific problem solving. *Cognitive Science.*

Costa, A. L. (Ed.). (1985). *Developing minds: A resource book for teaching thinking.* Alexandria, VA: Association for Supervision and Curriculum Development.

deGroot, A. D. (1965). *Thought and choice in chess.* The Hague: Mouton.

Doherty, M. E., Mynatt, C. R., Tweney, R. D., & Schiavo, M. D. (1979). Pseudodiagnosticity. *Acta Psychologica, 43,* 111–121.

Eisenstadt, M., & Kareev, Y. (1977). Perception in game playing: Internal representation and scanning of board positions. In P. N. Johnson-Laird & P. C. Wason (Eds.), *Thinking: Readings in cognitive science* (pp. 548–564). Cambridge, England: Cambridge University Press.

Evans, J. St. B. (1982). *The psychology of deductive reasoning.* London: Routledge & Kegan Paul.

DiSessa, A. A. (1983). Phenomenology and the evolution of intuition. In D. Gentner & A. Stevens (Eds.), *Mental models* (pp. 15–34). Hillsdale, NJ: Lawrence Erlbaum Associates.

Driver, R., Guesne, E., & Tiberghien, A. (Eds.). (1985). *Children's ideas in science.* Milton Keynes, England: Open University Press.

Gagne, E. D. (1985). *The cognitive psychology of school learning.* Boston, MA: Little, Brown.

Gentner, D., & Gentner, D. R. (1983). Flowing waters or teeming crowds: Mental models of electricity. In D. Gentner & A. Stevens (Eds.), *Mental models* (pp. 99–130). Hillsdale, NJ: Lawrence Erlbaum Associates.

Goodfield, J. (1981). *An imagined world.* New York: Harper.

307

Gooding, D. (1985). "In nature's school": Faraday as an experimentalist. In D. Gooding & F. A. J. L. James (Eds.), *Faraday rediscovered* (pp. 105–135). New York: Stockton.

Gooding, D., & James, F. A. J. L. (Eds.). (1985). *Faraday rediscovered: Essays in the life and work of Michael Faraday, 1791-1867.* New York: Stockton.

Gorman, M. E. (1987). Will the next Kepler be a computer? *Science & Technology Studies, 5,* 63–65.

Gorman, M. E., & Gorman, M. E. (1984). A comparison of disconfirmatory, confirmatory, and a control strategy on Wason's 2-4-6 task. *Quarterly Journal of Experimental Psychology, 36A,* 629–48.

Griggs, R. A., & Cox, J. R. (1982). The elusive thematic-materials effect in Wason's selection task. *British Journal of Psychology, 73,* 407–20.

Gruber, H. E. (1974). *Darwin on man.* New York: Dutton.

Klahr, D., & Dunbar, K. (1988). The psychology of scientific discovery: Search in two problem spaces. *Cognitive Science, 12,* 1–48.

Klayman, J., & Ha, Y. W. (1987). Confirmation, disconfirmation, and information in hypothesis testing. *Psychological Review, 94,* 211–228.

Kosslyn, S. M. (1983). *Ghosts in the mind's machine: Creating and using images in the brain.* New York: Norton.

Kuhn, D., Amsel, E., & O'Loughlin, M. (1988). *The development of scientific thinking skills.* New York: Academic Press.

Kulkarni, D., & Simon, H. A. (1988). The processes of scientific discovery: The strategy of experimentation. *Cognitive Science, 12,* 139–176.

Langley, P., Simon, H. A., Bradshaw, G. L., & Zytkow, J. M. (1987). *Scientific discovery: Computational explorations of the creative process.* Cambridge, MA: MIT Press.

Larkin, J. H. (1981). Cognition of learning physics. *American Journal of Physics, 49,* 534–541.

Linn, M. C. (1986). Science. In R. F. Dillon & R. J. Sternberg (Eds.), *Cognition and instruction,* (pp. 155–204). New York: Academic Press.

Marzano, R. J. (Ed.). (in press). *Dimensions of thinking: A framework for curriculum and instruction.* Alexandria, VA: Association for Supervision and Curriculum Development.

Mayer, R. E. (1983). *Thinking, problem solving, cognition.* San Francisco, CA: W. H. Freeman.

McClosky, M., Caramazza, A., & Green, B. (1980). Curvilinear motion in the abence of external forces: Naive beliefs about the motion of objects. *Science, 210*(5), 1139–1141.

Miller, A. I. (1984). *Imagery in scientific thought: Creating twentieth century physics.* Boston: Birkhauser.

Mitroff, I. (1974). *The subjective side of science.* Amsterdam: Elsevier.

Mynatt, C. R., Doherty, M. E., & Tweney, R. D. (1977). Confirmation bias in a simulated research environment: An experimental study of scientific inference. *Quarterly Journal of Experimental Psychology, 29,* 85–95.

Mynatt, C. R., Doherty, M. E., & Tweney, R. D. (1978). Consequences of confirmation and disconfirmation in a simulated research environment. *Quarterly Journal of Experimental Psychology, 30,* 395–406.

Nersessian, N. (1984). *Faraday to Einstein: Constructing meaning in scientific theories.* Dordrecht: Martinus Nijhoff.

Newell, A., & Simon, H. A. (1972). *Human problem solving.* Englewood Cliffs, NJ: Prentice-Hall.

Perkins, D. N. (1981). *The mind's best work.* Cambridge, MA: Harvard University Press.

Perkins, D. N. (in press). Informal reasoning in everyday thinking. In J. F. Voss, D. N. Perkins, & J. Segal (Eds.), *Informal reasoning and education.* Hillsdale, NJ: Lawrence Erlbaum Associates.

Platt, J. R. (1964). Strong inference. *Science, 146,* 347–353.

Popper, K. R. (1959). *The logic of scientific discovery.* New York: Basic Books. (Original work published 1934).

Pylyshn, Z. W. (1981). The imagery debate: Analogue media versus tacit knowledge. *Psychological Review, 87,* 16–45.

Ranney, M. (1987). The role of structural context in perception: Syntax in the recognition of algebraic expressions. *Memory & Cognition, 15,* 29–41.

Rissland, E. L. (1985). The structure of knowledge in complex domains. In S. F. Chipman, J. W. Segal, & R. Glaser (Eds.), *Thinking and learning skills, Vol. 2: Research and open questions* (pp. 107–125). Hillsdale, NJ: Lawrence Erlbaum Associates.

Roe, A. (1949). Psychological examinations of eminent biologists. *Journal of Consulting Psychology, 13,* 225–246.

Roe, A. (1951). A psychological study of physical scientists. *Genetic Psychology Monographs, 43,* 121–239.

Rumelhart, D. E. (1978). *Schemata: The building blocks of cognition* (Tech Rep. No. 79). San Diego, CA: University of California, Center for Human Information Processing.

Schilpp, P. A. (Ed.). (1974). *The philosophy of Karl Popper.* LaSalle, IL: Open Court.

Schoenfeld, A. H. (1985). *Mathematical problem solving.* New York: Academic press.

Shepard, R. N. (1978). Externalization of mental images and the act of creation. In B. S. Randhawa & W. E. Coffmann (Eds.), *Visual learning, thinking, and communication* (pp. 133–190). New York: Academic Press.

Sternberg, R. J. (1985). *Beyond IQ: A triarchic theory of human intelligence.* Cambridge, England: Cambridge University Press.

Stillings, N. A., Feinstein, M. H., Garfield, J. L., Rissland, E. L., Rosenbaum, D. A., Weisler, S. E., & Baker-Ward, L. (1987). *Cognitive science: An introduction.* Cambridge, MA: MIT Press.

Tweney, R. D. (1985). How Faraday discovered induction: A cognitive approach. In D. Gooding & F. A. J. L. James (Eds.), *Faraday rediscovered* (pp. 189–210). New York: Stockton.

Tweney, R. D. (1987, April). *What is scientific thinking?* Paper presented at the Annual Meeting of the American Educational Research Association, Washington, DC (ERIC# ED 283 675, 7 pp.).

Tweney, R. D. & Doherty, M. E. (1983). Rationality and the psychology of inference. *Synthese, 57,* 139–61.

Tweney, R. D., Doherty, M. E., & Mynatt, C. R. (Eds.) (1981). *On scientific thinking*. New York: Columbia University Press.

Tweney, R. D., Doherty, M. E., Worner, W. J., Pliske, D. B., Mynatt, C. R., Gross, K. A., & Arkkelin, D. L. (1980). Strategies of rule discovery in an inference task. *Quarterly Journal of Experimental Psychology, 32,* 109–23.

Tukey, D. D. (1986). A philosophical and empirical analysis of subjects' modes of inquiry in Wason's 2-4-6 task. *Quarterly Journal of Experimental Psychology, 38A,* 5–33.

Walker, B. J. (1985). *Instructional effects on strategy choice and solving efficiency in the Wason 2-4-6 rule discovery task.* Unpublished master's thesis, Bowling Green State University, Bowling Green, OH.

Walker, B. J. (1986, October). *Variations in problem-solving styles in the Wason 2-4-6 rule discovery task.* Paper presented at the first annual Ohio University Conference, Athens, OH.

Walker, B. J. (1987). A comparison of the psychological effects of the possibility of error and actual error on hypothesis testing. Unpublished dissertation, Bowling Green State University, Bowling Green, OH.

Walker, B. J., & Tweney, R. D. (1983).*Comparison of one and two-rule conditions in the Wason 2-4-6 rule discovery task.* Unpublished manuscript, Bowling Green State University, Department of Psychology, Bowling Green, OH.

Wallace, D. B., & Gruber, H. E. (Eds.). (1989). *Creative people at work.* Oxford: Oxford University Press.

Wason, P. C. (1960). On the failure to eliminate hypotheses in a conceptual task. *Quarterly Journal of Experimental Psychology, 12,* 129–40.

Wason, P. C., & Johnson-Laird, P. N. (1972). *Psychology of reasoning: Structure and content.* Cambridge, MA: Harvard University Press.

Wason, P. C., & Green, D. W. (1984). Reasoning and mental representation. *The Quarterly Journal of Experimental Psychology, 36A,* 597–610.

Wason, P. C., & Johnson-Laird, P. N. (1970). A conflict between selecting and evaluating information in an inferential task. *British Journal of Psychology, 61,* 509–15.

Wetherick, N. E. (1962). Eliminative and enumerative behavior in a conceptual task. *Quarterly Journal of Experimental Psychology, 14,* 246–9.

Wiser, M., & Carey, S. (1983). When heat and temperature were one. In D. Gentner & A. Stevens (Eds.), *Mental models.* (pp. 267–298). Hillsdale, NJ: Lawrence Erlbaum Associates.

Wollman, W. (1987, April). *Relating formal and physical knowledge.* Paper presented at Annual Meeting of the National Association for Research in Science Teaching, Washington, DC.

Yachanin, S. A. (1986). Facilitation in Wason's selection task: Content and instruction. *Current Psychological Research & Reviews, 5,* 20–29.

Teacher Decision Making[1]

Hilda Borko
University of Maryland

Richard J. Shavelson
University of California, Santa Barbara

This chapter explores the decisions that teachers make while planning and carrying out instruction. We assume that underlying teaching behavior are complex cognitive processes, and that planning and interactive decision making are central aspects of teacher cognition. The conception of teaching as a cognitive process has had a significant impact on the educational research community's approach to the study of teaching. This impact is attested to by the large number of studies of teachers' thoughts, judgments, plans, and decisions conducted within the past 15 years (e.g., Clark & Peterson, 1986). However, despite the inherent appeal of this view of teachers and the recent attention it has received, Shulman (1986) contended that "little that is remarkable has emerged from these studies" (p. 24). He suggested as one reason for this problem the lack of attention to much of the cognitive psychological work of the 1970s, which uses "key terms such as schema, script, frame, metacognitive strategy, and other words to describe those mental tools or structures employed by learners to make sense of what they are being taught" (p. 25).

This chapter addresses Shulman's concern by examining the research on teacher decision making through the lens of cognitive psychology. The purposes of the chapter are to: (a) review recent research on teacher

---

[1]Much of the chapter is based on our earlier reviews of the research on teachers' plans and interactive decisions (Borko & Niles, 1987; Shavelson, 1983; Shavelson & Stern, 1981). We have also drawn upon the very comprehensive review of research on teachers' thought processes by Clark and Peterson (1986).

planning and interactive decision making; (b) present a cognitive psychological framework for analyzing teacher thinking; (c) examine research on teacher decision making from the perspective of this framework; and (d) suggest implications for future research on teaching and for teacher education.

ASSUMPTIONS UNDERLYING RESEARCH ON TEACHER DECISION MAKING

The conception of teaching as a cognitive process rests on two fundamental assumptions (Shavelson & Stern, 1981). The first assumption is that teachers are professionals who make reasonable judgments and decisions in a complex, uncertain environment. Given the limited information-processing capabilities of the human mind, teachers, like all persons attempting to solve complex problems, construct simplified models of the actual situation and then behave rationally with respect to these simplified models. This view of teachers as operating rationally within the limits of their information-processing capabilities leads to the assumption that they make reasonable (rather than rational) judgments and decisions.

The second assumption is that, in teaching, there is a relationship between thought and action. More specifically, we assume that teachers' behavior is guided by their thoughts, judgments, and decisions. Thus, an understanding of the teaching process depends on both a description of teachers' thoughts, judgments, and decisions, and an understanding of how these cognitions are translated into action.

These assumptions are clearly reflected in a report to the National Conference on Studies in Teaching (National Institute of Education, 1975), which served as the impetus for funding research on teacher thinking:

> It is obvious that what teachers do is directed in no small measure by what they think. . . . To the extent that observed or intended teacher behavior is "thoughtless," it makes no use of the human teacher's most unique attributes. In doing so, it becomes mechanical and might well be done by a machine. If, however, teaching is done and in all likelihood will continue to be done by human teachers, the questions of the relations between thought and action become crucial. (p. 1)

Thus, to understand what is uniquely human about the process of teaching, we must study teachers' thinking—their planning and interactive decisions.

TEACHER PLANNING

Planning is that component of teaching in which teachers formulate a course of action for carrying out instruction over a school year, a term, a week, a day, or a lesson. Researchers have examined a number of issues related to planning, issues involving both the thought processes of teachers and the outcomes of these processes. The examination of these issues has proven to be a somewhat difficult task. Most teachers do produce written plans that are fairly easily accessible as data sources in the study of planning. However, a large portion of planning is mental—mental dialogues in which teachers engage, often spontaneously, throughout the day. Much of the result of this mental planning never appears on paper. As Clark (1983) noted, planning is one of the usually invisible and solitary parts of teaching—characteristics that do not easily lend themselves to investigation.

Despite these difficulties, a number of researchers have made a contribution to our understanding of planning. These researchers on teacher planning have used a variety of methods including questionnaires, interviews, ethnography, simulations, "think-aloud" protocols, and content analysis of written plans. (Discussion of these methods is beyond the scope of this chapter. Detailed descriptions and discussions can be found in chapters of the *Handbook of Research on Teaching* (Wittrock, 1986) by Erickson (1986); Evertson & Green (1986); Linn (1986); and Shavelson, Webb, & Burstein (1986).) The different methods have revealed different aspects of the planning process. These findings are addressed within this section, organized according to four major topics: (a) reasons for planning; (b) how teachers plan; (c) factors that affect planning, and (d) planning of experienced and inexperienced teachers.

Reasons for Planning

Not surprisingly, teachers report that they plan for many different reasons. To some extent, planning is internally motivated. Clark and Yinger (1979) categorized 78 teachers' written responses to the question of why they plan into three clusters, each representing a different set of internally motivated reasons. These teachers planned in order to: (a) meet immediate psychological needs (e.g., reduce anxiety and uncertainty, find a sense of direction, confidence, and security); (b) prepare themselves, mentally and physically or instrumentally, for instruction (e.g., learn the material, collect and organize materials, organize time and activity flow); and (c) guide the interactive processes of instruction (e.g., organize students, get an activity started, provide a framework for instruction and evaluation). The 12 elementary teachers who participated in McCutcheon's (1980) study reported similar reasons for planning (reasons which could also be placed into Clark and Yinger's categories)— for example, to feel more confident about teaching content, to better learn the subject matter, to help the lesson run more smoothly, to envision and circumvent potential problems.

Planning is also motivated by external sources. For example, a major reason for the written plans developed by the teachers in McCutcheon's study was to meet their schools' administrative requirements that plans be turned in to the school principal or supervisor of instruction on a regular basis. A second reason reported by several teachers was to provide guidance to substitute teachers.

Types of Plans. In addition to these general reasons for planning, some researchers have reported that teachers make different types of plans and that these different types of plans serve different functions. Yinger (1980) studied the planning decisions of a single first/second - grade teacher over a 5-month period. Using a case study approach that included extensive classroom observation, interviews, and process tracing methods, he identified five types of plans that this teacher made: yearly, term, unit, weekly, and daily.

Borko, Lalik, and colleagues (Borko, Lalik, Livingston, Pecic, & Perry, 1986) followed two fifth-grade teachers through their first year of teaching to examine the process of learning to teach. As one component of her case study, Borko examined the teacher's planning of reading and language arts instruction. Like the teacher with whom Yinger worked, this first year teacher engaged in yearly, unit, weekly, and daily planning. She did not, however, make term plans.

The 78 teachers in Clark and Yinger's (1979) study described three examples of their own plans representing the three most important types of planning that they did during the school year. Analysis of these descriptions revealed eight distinct types of planning (listed in order of the frequency with which they were mentioned): weekly, daily, unit, long-range, lesson, short-range, yearly, and term. Unit plans were most often identified as the most important type of plan, followed by weekly and daily plans. Only 7% of the teachers listed lesson plans among the types of plans most important to them.

Long-range plans made early in the school year generally focus on setting up the physical environment of the classroom, establishing the classroom social system, assessing student ability, fitting the curriculum (framed by the school system curriculum objectives) to the unique teaching situation, developing a general sequence and schedule, and ordering and reserving materials. They typically are not concerned with organizing or sequencing specific sets of learning activities (Clark & Elmore, 1979; McCutcheon, 1980; Yinger, 1980). Clark (1983) suggested that the major function of these early plans is to define a "problem space" within which teachers and students will operate throughout the year. This problem space sets the boundaries within which subsequent planning and decision making will occur.

Yinger (1980) reported the functions served by other types of planning engaged by the teacher in his study. Term plans detailed content to be covered during the 3-month period and established a weekly schedule of activities and times for that period. In planning units, the teacher developed a sequence of well-organized learning experiences, specified according to content and activities. In her weekly plans, she laid out the week's activities and entered them into her plan book, organized into four daily instructional blocks. Daily planning served the purposes of making any last minute changes in the day's schedule, setting up and arranging the classroom and materials, and preparing the students by writing the day's schedule on the board.

Unit, weekly, and daily plans served similar functions for the teacher Borko studied (Borko et al., 1986). In reading and language arts, most planning was done on a weekly basis, and consisted of selecting and ordering activities and entering them into her planbook. Daily planning consisted primarily of revising and fine-tuning weekly plans, gathering and preparing materials, and writing objectives and activities on the board. Unit planning was done primarily for units outside of normal basal instruction. It typically included library research, selecting and designing activities, finding and gathering resources, and creating artwork (e.g., bulletin boards). Not surprisingly, as both of these teachers moved from yearly to daily planning, the focus of their plans became more specific, shifting from general outlines of instructional sequences to actual details of activities, materials, and teaching strategies.

How Teachers Plan

Until recently, much of the writing on how teachers plan has been prescriptive in orientation. Typically, prescriptions advocated some version of the objectives-based, means-end model first proposed by Tyler in 1950. This model describes planning as a four-step process: specifying behavioral objectives, choosing appropriate learning activities, organizing and sequencing the chosen activities, and selecting evaluation procedures. It has been advocated for use by teachers of all levels and all subject areas, and taught to thousands of preservice teachers over the past 35 years. In this section, we address the question of how well this model fits with research-based descriptions of how teachers plan. We focus first on the planning that occurs during structured time periods. We then consider the less formal aspects of planning, sometimes referred to as mental planning.

Steps in the Planning Process. Several studies have examined the components of instruction teachers consider when planning and the order in which they consider these components. These studies explored aspects of planning such as the development of course syllabi (Taylor, 1970), decisions typically made prior to teaching (Zahorik, 1975), and planning for specific experimenter-prescribed lessons (Morine-Dershimer & Vallance, 1976; Peterson, Marx, & Clark, 1978). They used a variety of methods including content analysis of course syllabi and written lesson plans, questionnaires completed by teachers, discussions with small groups of teachers, and think-aloud protocols recorded during planning periods.

Despite the diversity of issues and methods, a consistent pattern is apparent in findings from these studies, namely that Tyler's model does not fit well with research-based accounts of the planning process. These research-based descriptions differ from Tyler's model in both the relative prominence of the four planning steps and the sequence in which they occur.

Planning seems to focus primarily on content and activities. The first planning decision usually made by teachers involves subject matter content. The most frequent planning decisions involve content and activities. The most commonly reported practice for preparing written plans is to begin by identifying the subject matter to be covered and an activity to be used, and then to consider other elements such as materials, goals, objectives, and evaluation procedures. In terms of frequency of mention, objectives are not a particularly important component of the planning process. They are also seldom the starting point for planning. In fact some teachers report that they do not actually write down objectives unless they are required to do so by the principal. Because objectives are implied in activities and are typically listed in manuals that accompany texts, to write them down is seen as an unnecessary expenditure of time and energy.

An Alternative Model of the Planning Process. As one component of his case study of a first/second-grade teacher's planning, Yinger (1980) developed a three-stage cyclic model to represent this teacher's approach to the planning of instructional activities (the basic structural units of her daily and weekly planning). During the problem finding state, the teacher derived an initial conception of the planning problem, based on a consideration of content, goals, and her own knowledge and experience. In the problem formulation and solution stage, she designed instructional activities by repeatedly cycling through a process of elaboration, investigation (mental testing), and adaptation. The third stage consisted of implementation and evaluation of the activities in the actual classroom setting. As a result of these processes, activities were either rejected or modified and (if effective) eventually incorporated into the teacher's repertoire of knowledge and experience to be used in future planning.

Clark and Yinger (1979) found that a similar cyclic model could be used to describe unit planning. They asked five teachers to plan a 2-week unit on writing, keep journals for 3 weeks to document their planning, and participate in interviews with the researchers twice during the week. Each teacher began with a general idea and proceeded through phases of successive elaboration and modification. They differed in the extent to which they developed instructional activities (i.e., engaged in problem finding and problem formulation/solution stages) prior to implementing and evaluating them within the actual classroom situation. (Clark and Yinger characterized this difference as incremental versus comprehensive planning.) However, all participated, to some extent, in each of the three stages described in Yinger's study.

Both of these studies suggest another way in which research-based descriptions of planning differ from the models typically presented in teacher education programs. Models presented in teacher education programs recommend that teachers identify several alternatives and then select among the alternatives the one best suited to the objectives and learners. In contrast, teachers appear to pursue one idea from the outset. They generally begin with ideas that have worked in the past and spend the limited time available for planning, elaborating and embellishing these ideas (see also McCutcheon, 1980).

Mental Planning. The studies just described focus primarily on planning that occurs during structured planning periods and is recorded in the form of written plans. However, teachers report that a large part of their planning occurs spontaneously throughout the day, and is never written down. McCutcheon (1980) characterized this planning as mental dialogues. For the teachers in her study, mental dialogues covered a wide range of concerns including the teaching of particular skills and concepts to individuals or groups, handling of behavior problems, and tying together of different subject matter areas. They helped the teachers to articulate and short-circuit potential problems, elaborate written plans, learn the subject matter to be presented, and feel more confident about teaching.

Morine-Dershimer (1979) made a similar point that planning is seldom fully reflected in teachers' written plans. Written plans are nested within more comprehensive mental plans or lesson images, and the fact that certain planning elements are not part of written plans should not lead to the conclusion that they are not important components of planning. For example, although objectives were not part of her teachers' written plans, they did seem to be part of their lesson images. Similarly, in a study by Smith and Sendelbach (1979), the principal product of unit planning for sixth-grade science instruction was a mental picture of the unit to be taught, including a sequence of activities and students' probable responses. Notes that accompanied the teachers' mental plans were sketchy, typically consisting of lists of important points to remember.

McCutcheon (1980) pointed out that mental planning is not recognized by theoreticians or teacher educators as an important or legitimate part of planning. Because of this, she suggested, teachers and administrators may not recognize mental planning as an important, legitimate professional activity. Yet, "mental planning is probably the part of teaching that has the potential for being the most professional activity of teaching, for it gives teachers the opportunity to relate theoretical knowledge to particular cases" (McCutcheon, 1980, pp. 8–9). Although we know little about mental planning, we do know enough to suggest that it is an aspect of the planning process that warrants further attention by educational researchers and practitioners.

Factors That Influence Teachers' Plans

As we have seen, research-based descriptions characterize planning as a process of selecting and elaborating instructional activities, strategies, and techniques. The decision-making conception suggests that teachers have many instructional tools at their disposal and that they select and elaborate these with the intent of helping students to reach some goal (usually academic achievement). The conception further suggests that their decisions are affected by a variety of factors including information about their students, the nature of the instructional task, their own personal characteristics, and institutional constraints. Research findings concerning each of these factors are summarized in the sections that follow.

Information About Students. Teachers often report that information about students is the most important factor in determining their planning. This information appears to be particularly salient early in the school year, as they are getting to know their students and forming instructional groups (Mintz, 1979; Morine-Dershimer, 1979). Shavelson and Stern (1981) reported several student characteristics to be important in the majority of studies of teacher judgment and decision making they reviewed: students' general ability or achievement, gender, class participation, self-concept, social competence, independence, classroom behavior, and work habits. The characteristic that has the greatest impact on planning decisions is ability; non-academic characteristics are taken into account to a lesser extent.

A series of studies by Borko and Niles (1982, 1983, 1984) illustrates this pattern. Policy-capturing and process-tracing methods were used to examine teachers' planning strategies for grouping students—hypothetical students as well as children in their own classrooms—for reading instruction. In all three studies, participants formed groups primarily on the basis of reading ability. Non-academic characteristics, particularly class participation, motivation, work habits, and maturity, were considered when decisions about the best placements for individual students were not easily made, solely on the basis of ability.

Nature of the Instructional Task. Shavelson and Stern (1981) described the instructional task as the basic unit of planning and action in the classroom. For teachers, the task consists primarily of subject matter (content and structure), activities, and materials. Although conceptually distinct, these components are closely linked in actual classroom instruction and planning for instruction.

Often, teachers' consideration of subject matter focuses more on the content of the subject matter than on the structure. They accept the textbook as the major, and often only, source of content and frequently do little to modify its orientation to, or relative emphasis on, various components of the curriculum (e.g., Clark, 1978-1979). Thus, once a textbook has been selected (a decision typically not made by the individual teacher or even the individual school), subject matter concerns in planning translate into concerns about presentation of textbook-prescribed content.

Planning about presentation of content typically focuses on activities and materials. Here too, textbooks and associated materials, especially teachers' manuals, play a major role. Several studies have reported that teachers rely on manuals accompanying prescribed textbooks as the primary source of instructional activities and materials (e.g., Clark & Elmore, 1981; McCutcheon, 1980; Smith & Sendelbach, 1979). As an illustration, 85% to 95% of the reading and mathematics activities used by teachers in McCutcheon's study were based on suggestions in teachers' manuals. The figure was somewhat lower in other subject areas, in large part because of time constraints on instruction, which necessitated choosing among topics and limited the kinds of activities that teachers could plan. Also, teachers were more likely to introduce their own interests into areas such as social studies, science, language, and art.

The reliance on textbook series can be explained, in part, by institutional constraints on teachers' decision making. At one school system in McCutcheon's (1980) study, teachers were not permitted to use any supplementary materials until the end of the year, when the textbook had been completed. Similarly, the beginning teacher whom Lalik followed (Borko et al., 1986) was expected to complete 2 years of basal instruction during 1 academic year and to report progress in the program to building administrators on a weekly basis. Teachers in the study of second-grade reading conducted by Borko, Eisenhart, and colleagues (Borko, Eisenhart, Kello, & Vandett, 1983) were permitted more flexibility than these extreme cases; however, students were expected to complete all textbooks, workbooks, and worksheets provided by the basal programs.

Nonetheless, although institutional constraints clearly provide some limitations, many teachers do not exercise as much decision-making responsibility as they have available with regard to the instructional program. For example, the beginning teacher whom Borko followed (Borko et al., 1986) reported that her school administration did not dictate teachers' instructional programs. Yet, she followed the basal reading program very closely, in part because she liked it and in part because of limited time and energy to plan alternative activities. Thus, even in situations where close adherence to textbook programs is not required, teachers may rely on basal materials in order to keep the time spent planning and preparing manageable.

Teachers' reliance on textbooks and associated teachers' manuals when selecting and organizing instructional tasks may negatively affect the quality of instruction. Teachers may assume that textbooks and manuals are structured to provide for continuity across lessons when, in fact, they may not be. Further, textbooks may be based on assumptions that differ from teachers' beliefs regarding issues such as the role of the teacher or the nature of the learning process. Such discrepancies between instructional programs and teachers' beliefs or styles may also result in a lack of continuity (McCutcheon, 1980).

The Context of Instruction. Requirements concerning textbook use are not the only external conditions that affect teachers' planning decisions. Studies of extra-classroom pressures on teacher planning indicate that a variety of pressures originating outside the classroom significantly affect planning. For example, Floden, Porter, Schmidt, Freeman and Schwille (1981) used a laboratory policy-capturing approach to study the effects of external constraints (textbooks, media, central division and building administration, other teachers, and parents) on teachers' decisions to incorporate new topics into the mathematics curriculum. The most notable aspect of teachers' responses was their willingness to change content, whatever the pressure for change.

Several naturalistic investigations support the conclusion that external pressures affect planning. For example, in McNeil's (1980) study of high school economics courses, teachers planned instruction in a teacher-directed lecture format, with no reading or writing, little student discussion, and very little use of the school's resources. Their intent was to avoid as many management problems as possible, in order to meet the goals of an administration that expected them to enforce rules of discipline, but which rarely backed them on that enforcement.

Both McCutcheon (1980) and Borko and colleagues (1984) reported effects of school-level and central administration policy beyond the previously cited restrictions on curriculum and materials. Administratively based influences on planning included policies about class size, scheduling, grouping, and promotion and retention. For example, McCutcheon (1980) reported that the policy of grouping across classes for reading and mathematics instruction constrained teachers to adhere more closely to a schedule and resulted in a greater focus on isolated subject matter rather than integrated subjects. For teachers in the school Borko and colleagues (1984) studied, county and school guidelines specified when reading, language arts, and mathematics would occur during the school day and how much time each subject was allocated. Building administrators further influenced planning by assigning all students to reading and mathematics groups within classrooms. However, despite this clear influence of external forces on the nature of instructional programs, teachers found room within these constraints for planning and decision making, which led to programs which varied greatly across classrooms.

Teacher Characteristics.   Several researchers have hypothesized that characteristics of teachers such as their conceptions of teaching, beliefs about particular subject areas, and professional experience affect their instructional planning. In a number of studies, these hypothesized relationships have not been strongly supported. For example, Russo (1978) reported that teachers' progressive and traditional educational beliefs were not related to their grouping of students for reading and mathematics or to their decisions about lesson plans for the groups. She speculated that specific conceptions of reading or mathematics, rather than global views of education, might be associated with differences in planning for these two subject areas. However, Borko and Niles (1982) found that teachers' content-oriented and pupil-oriented conceptions of reading contributed little to their strategies for forming reading groups. Similarly, although Borko (1978) found some relationship between traditional and progressive views of education and teachers' organizing and structuring of educational experiences, the influence of beliefs on planning was small.

Planning of Experienced and Inexperienced Teachers

In contrast to other teacher characteristics, level of experience or expertise does seem to affect planning. Educational researchers consistently have found differences between the planning of "experts" (typically experienced teachers) and "novices" (typically student teachers).[2] These differences are in both the nature of plans and the planning process.

Experienced teachers' plans typically are more detailed than the plans of novices, and include more information about instructional strategies and activities and a greater number of instructional and management routines (e.g., Housner & Griffey, 1985; Leinhardt, 1986; Warner, 1987). These differences are illustrated in Housner and Griffey's (1985) study, which compares the planning and interactive decision making of experienced physical education teachers and preservice teachers. Experienced teachers in this study made over twice as many planning decisions about strategies for implementing instructional activities (e.g., management of instruction, assessment and feedback, equipment use). They also made twice as many adaptation decisions—contingency plans for potential problem situations.

Further illustration of these differences in the plans of expert and novice teachers is found in the research by Leinhardt and colleagues on the cognitive structures and processes of teaching (e.g., Leinhardt, 1986; Leinhardt & Greeno, 1986; Leinhardt & Smith, 1985). Defining "agendas" as operational plans that include goals, objectives, actions, and operational routines, Leinhardt and colleagues found several differences in the agendas reported by expert and novice teachers. Experts' agendas were richer; they contained more detail and displayed more detail when

---

[2]The issue of what constitutes expertise in teaching is one which has not yet been resolved. While "mere experience is simply not believed by most people to correlate highly with expertise in teaching" (Berliner, 1986), we have no established criteria for distinguishing expertise from mere experience. Criteria which typically are employed include nomination by colleagues or administrators, observations by researchers, and standardized test scores of students. While reputational measures, observation and standardized tests have clear limitations as indicators of pedagogical expertise, they are the best measures we have. Given this state of affairs, we adopt Berliner's position in this chapter, "Thus, the terms 'experienced' and 'expert' are used throughout this discussion as if they were interchangeable. We know they are not, but cannot yet untangle them, so we must ask for patience in resolving the this situation." (p. 9).

verbally presented. Three aspects of experts' reported agendas were indicators of this richness: greater explicit reference to student actions, the mention of planning of test points (checks during the lesson on student understanding or performance), and the inclusion of over twice as many instructional moves. Experts' agendas were also richer in connectedness, with an overarching goal that orders actions, a hierarchical structure of subplans and routines, and an instructional logic that seems to drive the flow of the lesson. Leinhardt captured many of these differences by characterizing an expert's agenda as "a conceptual roadmap that keeps the lesson flowing in a particular direction" (1986, p. 19).

Several investigations of the planning process indicate that experienced teachers plan more quickly and efficiently than do novices. They are, at the same time, more selective in their use of information and able to incorporate more instructionally relevant information into their deliberations (e.g., Berliner, 1986; Borko & Niles, 1982, 1983; Housner & Griffey, 1985; Sardo, 1982; Warner, 1987). Two studies of teachers' grouping decisions by Borko and Niles (1982, 1983) illustrate these characteristics of the planning process. In a policy-capturing study to identify student characteristics that predict teachers' placement of students in reading groups, experienced teachers tended to use more complex strategies than did student teachers. Specifically, although most student teachers considered only formal and informal assessments of reading ability, most experienced teachers used a decision strategy that also included one non-academic characteristic (usually class participation; Borko & Niles, 1982). In a subsequent process-tracing study, in-depth analysis of think-aloud protocols for one experienced teacher and one student teacher indicated that the experienced teacher used clearer decision rules and applied them with less deliberation. Further, she made decisions based more on student characteristics, with less feeling of being constrained by structural concerns such as number and size of instructional groups (Borko & Niles, 1983). Similarly, in the study by Housner and Griffey (1985) the experienced teachers requested more information from the researchers than did the preservice teachers when planning instruction, particularly information about student experience and the instructional facility.

A planning simulation used by Berliner, Carter and colleagues in their research program to examine pedagogical expertise points out further differences in the planning of experienced/expert classroom teachers, minimally experienced/novice teachers, and inexperienced/postulant teachers (i.e., subject matter experts who are interested in teaching but have no teaching experience; e.g., Berliner, 1986, 1987; Carter, Sabers, Cushing, Pinnegar, & Berliner, 1987). Participants in the simulation were given information left by the previous teacher, about a class they had been assigned 5 weeks into the school year, and were asked to plan for their first 2 days of instruction. Expert teachers did not seem to believe that specific information about students would be salient to their task of taking over a new class and remembered less of this information than did novices or postulants in a recall task. In contrast, experts did attend to the number of students in the class; apparently they viewed this information as having important instructional implications. Experts also defined the task differently than did novices or postulants. Their intention was to start over, to create a new beginning. Their plans incorporated routines for beginning the school year, including strategies for gathering information about what students knew and could do. In contrast, novices and postulants typically planned to take over where the previous teacher left off. Not surprisingly, the information they planned to collect focused on where in the text to begin instruction. These and other differences between the groups led Berliner (1987) to conclude that "experience as a classroom teacher leads to changes in cognition— in perception, memory and thought—in ways that seem more sophisticated, more efficient, and more useful" (1987, p. 76).

Studies by Sardo (1982) and Warner (1987) provide evidence for two additional contrasts in the planning processes of experienced and inexperienced teachers: greater attention to long-term planning and less attention to Tyler's (1950) means-ends model by experienced teachers. Sardo examined planning styles of four junior high teachers. For the least experienced teacher (with 2 years of teaching experience), planning consisted primarily of daily and lesson plans. This teacher also followed Tyler's means-ends model more closely than the others. For the more experienced teachers, planning was less systematic, utilized less time, and focused more on the flow of activities for an entire week rather than the details of individual lessons. Similarly, experienced Home Economics teachers in Warner's study focused more on long-term planning than did Home Economics student teachers. When planning daily lessons, the experienced teachers also used Tyler's model less frequently than did the student teachers.

The pattern that emerges from this diverse group of studies is one that characterizes experienced teachers' plans as richer and more detailed than inexperienced teachers', and their planning process as more efficient. Recent work within cognitive psychology on the cognitive characteristics of expertise provides one explanation for this pattern. Expert teachers have more elaborate cognitive schemata (or systems) for organizing and storing their knowledge of teaching and of subject matter than do novices. These better-developed schemata enable them to determine what information is relevant to their planning tasks and to plan more efficiently. (The role of cognitive schemata in teachers' decision making is considered further in the final section of this chapter.)

TEACHERS' INTERACTIVE DECISIONS

Interactive decision making refers to decisions teachers make while interacting with their students. These decisions differ from planning decisions in that they are "in-flight" or "real-time" decisions, typically made without the luxury of time to reflect or to seek additional information. Researchers have defined interactive decision making in several ways and have examined a variety of issues related to the nature, causes, and consequences of interactive decisions. Their conceptualizations and research findings are addressed in this section, organized according to four major topics: (a) definitions of interactive decision making; (b) research on teachers' interactive decision making; (c) models of teachers' interactive decision making; (d) interactive decisions of experienced and inexperienced teachers.

Definitions of Interactive
Decision Making

Clark and Peterson (1986) reviewed definitions of interactive decisions used by a number of researchers and concluded, "These investigators have converged on a definition of an interactive decision as a deliberate choice to implement a specific action" (p. 274). Defined in this way, an interactive decision is a conscious choice between continuing to behave as before and behaving in a different way; it does not require the consideration of alternative courses of action. Using this definition, Clark and Peterson calculated that across five studies that provide information on the frequency of teachers' reported interactive decisions, the estimated number of decisions is remarkably consistent, ranging from .5 to .7 decisions per minute (Fogarty, Wang, & Creek, 1982; Marland, 1977; Morine & Vallance, 1975; Shroyer, 1981; Wodlinger, 1980). Based on this estimate, Clark and Peterson concluded, "Thus, these data suggest that the decision-making demands of the classroom are relatively intense" (p. 274).

Not all researchers agree with Clark and Peterson's definition of interactive decision making or their conclusion about its prominence in teachers' interactive thinking. For example, both Marland (1977) and Warner (1987) argued that the definition combines two types of interactive thinking that should be considered separately because of differences in their patterns of occurrence in classrooms. The first, which they label "interactive decision making," entails explicit reference to consideration of alternatives and selection of one of the alternatives. The second, which they label "deliberate action," occurs when a teacher sees a need for some action or response, but considers only one course of action. Warner suggested that conscious, deliberate actions comprise the majority of experienced teachers' information processing in the classroom. Interactive decision making occurs much less frequently, primarily when a routine action is not immediately available for dealing with unexpected classroom events. He argued that although deliberate action is a major characteristic of the interactive information processing of experienced teachers, interactive decision making is not.

Although the arguments offered by Marland and Warner are compelling, the fact remains that most researchers of teachers' interactive thinking have not distinguished between deliberate actions and interactive decisions. Further, many issues and research findings apply equally to both types of thought processes. Therefore, in this chapter we combine the two processes in our discussion of interactive teaching. However, for cases in which patterns of findings differ, we discuss these differences and their implications for understanding teacher thinking.

Research on Teachers' Interactive Decision Making

Most investigations of teachers' interactive decision making have used stimulated recall interviews to elicit teachers' self-reports of their thoughts and decisions while working with students. Although the format of stimulated recall sessions varies considerably across investigations, studies typically include audiotaping or videotaping a lesson (or series of lessons), playing it back for the teacher, and asking the teacher to describe his or her mental activities that were taking place during the lesson. Interviews are audiotaped and transcribed. Responses are coded by categorizing thought units and then counting the number of thought units within each category. Issues addressed in these analyses include the role of plans and routines, nature of interactive decision making, and antecedents of interactive decisions. (See Shavelson, Webb, & Burstein, 1986 for a discussion of these methods.)

Role of Plans and Routines. Teachers' interactive decisions are greatly influenced by their plans. These plans are often in the form of mental "scripts" (cf. Schank & Abelson, 1977) or "images" (cf. Morine-Dershimer, 1978-1979) rather than written lesson plans. For experienced teachers, they typically include a number of routines that are enacted during the course of the lesson.

Several recent investigations have pointed to the centrality of routines in teachers' interactive thinking (e.g., Leinhardt & Greeno, 1986; Warner, 1987). "Routines are recurring activities that become established within a particular classroom as predictable sequences or 'scripts' for teacher and student behavior. From a management perspective, routines are activities for which the probable level of student cooperation is known in advance" (Doyle, 1979, p. 61). Routines are an important aspect of the "planfulness" of experienced teachers, despite the fact that they may not be part of verbal reports of planning, or even of conscious planning efforts (Leinhardt & Greeno, 1986).

Routines minimize conscious decision making during interactive teaching. They reduce the amount of information teachers have to consider and the decisions they have to make by rendering the timing and sequencing of activities and student behavior predictable within the activity flow of the lesson (Shavelson & Stern, 1981). When routines are being enacted, teachers' information processing consists primarily of monitoring cues that are indicators of potential problems or unexpected events. These cues (discussed further in the section on antecedents of interactive decisions) include individual students (Conners, 1978; MacKay, 1977; MacKay & Marland, 1978; Marland, 1977; Morine-Dershimer, 1978-1979; Warner, 1987), and specific instructional processes (e.g., Conners, 1978; Marland, 1977; Peterson & Clark, 1978; Warner, 1987).

In general, then, teachers follow their mental scripts while teaching, enacting well-established routines for the various activities they have planned. This pattern is broken only when monitoring indicates potential problems or unexpected events. It is in these instances, when routines are not going as planned, that teachers engage in interactive decision making. However, even in these situations, teachers are reluctant to change their lessons. Changes that do occur typically are minor adjustments or fine-tuning, rather than major deviations from plans (Clark & Yinger, 1979; Joyce, 1978-1979; Peterson & Clark, 1978).

Existing research does not reveal why teachers are reluctant to change their plans. Shavelson and Stern (1981) speculated on several possible reasons. One explanation is that during planning, the teacher selected the best (or perhaps only) available routine. A routine selected hastily during interactive teaching could not be expected to fare as well. A second possibility is that changing routines during a lesson increases uncertainty for both teacher and students. This higher level of uncertainty increases the information processing demands on the teacher, making him or her less able to monitor student involvement and behavior. It also increases the probability of student misbehavior and classroom management problems (Doyle, 1979).

In sum, teachers' major concern during interactive teaching is to maintain the flow of the activity. To do this, they rely on routines that are part of their mental scripts or images, and monitor the lesson to detect potential problems or unexpected events. They make interactive decisions only when their monitoring indicates that the lesson is not proceeding according to the script.

Nature of Interactive Decision Making. When teachers make interactive decisions, they tend to consider only a few courses of action. MacKay (1977) reported that teachers seldom considered more than two alternatives. Morine and Vallance (1975) reported that the mean number of alternatives considered for each decision was between 2.2 and 3.2, across lesson taught by the 40 teachers in their investigation.

Marland (1977) and Warner (1987) contended that we should not consider a choice between continuing with the lesson and changing direction as a choice among alternatives unless the teacher considers more than one new direction. They further contended that unless alternatives are considered, the choice is not an interactive decision. According to these criteria, the vast majority of teachers' conscious choices do not entail selection among alternatives. Thus, teachers in Warner's study reported only 21 instances that he categorized as interactive decisions, contrasted to 96 that he classified as deliberate actions. According to their criteria, teachers rarely consider alternative actions when making choices during interactive teaching.

Despite disagreements over definitions, Clark and Peterson (1986) concurred about the relative infrequency with which teachers consider alternative courses of action during interactive teaching. In their own research (Peterson & Clark, 1978), teachers reported considering alternatives in only 20% to 30% of the cases, across 3 days of instruction. Not only do teachers consider few alternatives; they also tend not to evaluate alternatives critically. Rather, they seek confirmation for their choices (MacKay, 1977, MacKay & Marland, 1978).

Antecedents of Teachers' Interactive Decisions. Two related lines of research have addressed the question of what cues inform teachers' interactive decisions. The first is research on the content of teachers' interactive thoughts. The second focuses specifically on antecedents of their interactive decisions.

Clark and Peterson (1986) reviewed 6 studies that described the content of teachers' interactive thoughts (Colker, 1982; Conners, 1978; Marland, 1977; Marx & Peterson, 1981; McNair, 1978-1979; Semmel, 1977), and noted a fairly consistent pattern of findings. Across all 6 studies, the largest percentage of teachers' reported interactive thoughts were concerned with the learner. The percentage of thoughts that focused on learners ranged from 39% to 50% in the 5 studies with normal learners, and was 60% for Semmel's study of teachers of exceptional children. Teachers reported thinking about a variety of learner attributes including understanding, involvement, attention, and behavior.

The second largest category of teachers' reported interactive thoughts focused on the instructional process. Teachers reported thinking about instructional processes and strategies such as the nature of their explanations, questions, reinforcement, review and practice exercises, sequencing and pacing of activities, and transitions between activities. Across the 6 studies, the percentage of teachers' stimulated recall statements that were classified in this category ranged from 20% to 30%. Relatively small percentages of teachers' statements about their interactive thoughts dealt with content or subject matter (5% to 14%) or with instructional objectives (0% to 14%).

Warner's (1987) recent investigation of the thinking of Home Economics teachers revealed a similar pattern in the experienced teachers' reports of their interactive thoughts. These teachers reported that most of their thoughts while teaching related to students, either individual students (38%) or small groups (16%). Other major categories of their interactive thoughts were the instructional process (22%), teacher questions (18%), and plans or lesson content (10%).

Using a slightly different focus, several investigators asked teachers specifically about events or cues that prompted their interactive decisions (Fogarty et al., 1982; Housner & Griffey, 1985; Marland, 1977; Warner, 1987; Wodlinger, 1980). The types and percentages of cues they reported are similar to those for the more general issue of interactive thinking. Student cues were most frequently identified as antecedents for interactive decisions (percentages ranged from 38% to 85%). Teachers reported basing decisions on factors such as disruptive behavior; inattentiveness; incorrect, unsatisfactory, or incomplete responses or work; and apparent lack of understanding.

Aspects of the instructional process were also identified by the teachers as antecedents of their interactive decisions. For example, both Marland (1977) and Warner (1987) reported that a large percentage of teachers' reported deliberate actions were related to questioning strategies and the selection of student respondents. Other deliberate actions included in this category focused on the selection of specific teaching strategies and appropriate examples.

The teacher in Wodlinger's (1980) study reported that many of her interactive decisions (35%) were triggered by environmental factors such as instructional materials and equipment, interruptions, and time constraints. She also noted that her own cognitive and affective states stimulated interactive decisions (16%).

A Model of Teachers' Interactive Decision Making

The model of teachers' interactive decision making proposed by Shavelson and Stern (1981) represents many of the research findings and conclusions discussed earlier. This model is reproduced in Figure 10.1. It characterizes teachers' interactive teaching as the carrying out of well-established routines. While carrying out routines, the teacher monitors the classroom, seeking cues that indicate whether or not a routine is proceeding as planned. When the teacher observes a cue that is outside the range of tolerance (e.g., unacceptable student behavior), the teacher must decide whether immediate action is necessary. If it is, then the teacher determines whether a routine is available. If an appropriate routine is available, it is initiated. If not, the teacher takes some other action to correct the situation. If immediate action is not required, the teacher considers whether or not delayed action is called for. If it is, the teacher makes a mental note and continues teaching. If it is not, he or she decides whether or not to remember the information and then continues teaching.

Shavelson's (1983; Shavelson & Stern, 1981) discussions of this model focus on student behaviors and characteristics as the cues that teachers monitor. However, within the model, monitoring need not be limited to student cues; other aspects of the lesson (e.g., time, instructional materials) could also serve as indicators that the lesson is not proceeding as planned.

The model also posits a "threshold mechanism" whereby observed cues trigger interactive decision making only when they are judged to be outside of the teacher's tolerance. As Clark and Peterson (1986) noted, no research has been conducted to determine whether or not such a threshold mechanism is at the core of teachers' interactive decisions. It may be that some decisions are triggered by unexpected events that fall outside the range of a teacher's tolerance (e.g., students' off-task behavior). However, other decisions may be part of the normal enactment of routines (e.g., selecting student respondents during recitation activities). Thus, although this model accounts for many of the research findings about teachers' interactive decisions, it may not accurately represent all types of decisions or all situations in which they are made. Indeed as

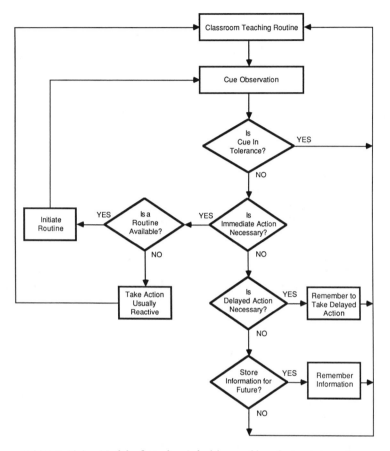

FIGURE 10.1.   Model of teachers' decision making during interactive
teaching (from Shavelson & Stern 1981, p. 483).

Shavelson (1986) suggested, recent work in cognitive psychology, addressed later in this chapter, provides a set of concepts that may help us
to revise and broaden the model.

Interactive Decisions of Experienced
and Inexperienced Teachers

As was the case with planning, several researchers have compared the
interactive thinking and decision making of experienced and inexperienced teachers. Although these researchers have examined a variety
of aspects of thinking, their findings consistently suggest differences in
the information experienced and inexperienced teachers attend to when

teaching and in the knowledge they draw on when making interactive decisions.

Differences in the information experienced and inexperienced teachers attend to while teaching suggest different concerns and priorities about classroom life. For example, in their study of elementary physical education teachers, Housner and Griffey (1985) found that both experienced teachers and preservice teachers attended primarily to student performance, involvement and interest. However, whereas experienced teachers reported attending primarily to performance cues, preservice teachers placed greater emphasis on student interest. Similarly, when asked to identify cues that caused them to alter their lessons, experienced teachers identified student performance as the primary cue whereas preservice teachers identified student interest and verbalizations or requests. Additionally, experienced teachers attended more to individual student behavior whereas preservice teachers gave more attention to class behavior patterns. Housner and Griffey interpreted these findings (together with the findings about planning differences reported earlier) as evidence for experienced teachers' better-formulated instructional strategies and greater attention to students' acquisition of motor skills, compared to preservice teachers' greater emphasis on ensuring that students are happy, busy, and well-behaved.

Differences in cues that reportedly were the basis of experienced and preservice teachers' interactive decisions in a study by Fogarty and colleagues (1982) are consistent with Housner and Griffey's interpretation. Preservice teachers focused most frequently on students' disruptive behavior (27% of the cues); for experienced teachers, disruptive behavior comprised only 6% of the reported cues.

Findings from a series of studies within Berliner, Carter, and colleagues' research program (Berliner, 1986, 1987; Carter, Cushing, Sabers, Stein & Berliner, 1988) provide further evidence for differences in patterns of attention and selection. Expert, novice and postulant teachers reacted to a standard set of slides depicting classroom life. Experts were more selective than novices or postulants in the information they recalled. They seemed to focus on information that they deemed to be important, information that had instructional significance. For example, they more often identified the means of instruction, recalled types of instructional activities, and attended to classroom work arrangements than did either novices or postulants. In contrast, many novices and postulants did not seem to have a sense of what visual information was worth focusing on, and there are fewer clear patterns in the information they recalled.

A second pattern of differences between the interactive thinking of experienced and inexperienced teachers relates to the meaning they bring to the analysis of classroom situations. When discussing their own or other teachers' classrooms, experienced teachers are able to draw upon their personal knowledge of classrooms and students. They can therefore predict, identify, and deal with classroom problems more quickly and routinely than can novices. Two studies by Calderhead illustrate this pattern. In the first study (Calderhead, 1981), experienced teachers and student teachers were asked to report on information they would need and strategies they would use in responding to common critical incidents in classrooms. The experienced teachers described similar situations that they considered typical of their own classrooms and commented on how they would normally deal with them. They also often reported taking pupil characteristics into account. In contrast, the student teachers distinguished far fewer situations, reported focusing on features such as time of day and importance of the lesson, and responded more often with overall "blanket" reactions. The second study focused on experienced teachers', first year teachers', and student teachers' perceptions of students. Experienced teachers evidenced a large quantity of knowledge about children and an awareness of the range of knowledge, skills, and problems to expect in the classroom. Calderhead (1983) concluded that "Experienced teachers in a sense 'know' their new class even before they meet it" (p. 5).

The research by Berliner, Carter, and colleagues (e.g., Berliner, 1987; Carter et al., 1988) also supports this pattern of differences. When responding to questions about the slides, expert teachers clearly related the classroom scenes to their own classrooms. Their responses were more interpretive, drawing on their personal knowledge of classrooms to attribute meaning to the classroom scenes and explain the phenomena depicted. Their responses also displayed more of a sense of typicality; they spontaneously identified slides that were out of order and spent mental energy attempting to make sense of the atypical. The researchers suggest that expert teachers draw on their classroom experience and knowledge to look for meaning and attribute meaning to what they observe. In contrast, novices and postulants provided comparatively "flat" descriptions, and did not offer explanations or develop meanings for what they saw.

Warner's (1987) comparative study of experienced and inexperienced Home Economics teachers' thinking about teaching provides the most direct evidence for differences in interactive decision making. In stimulated recall exercises following episodes of their own teaching, experienced teachers reported fewer interactive decisions but a greater number of deliberate actions during instruction than did inexperienced teachers. Warner explained this difference by suggesting that experienced teachers had available in their teaching repertoires a number of routine action responses. When they determined that change was necessary, they often were able to draw on an appropriate routine within their repertoire, rather than considering two or more alternative courses of action. Further, automaticity was a more important feature of the classroom behavior of experienced teachers; that is, their responses to a greater number of classroom events occurred without conscious awareness. Experienced teachers also reported processing less information than novices during interactive teaching and focusing their attention more exclusively on individual students. Warner suggested that experienced teachers' better developed conceptual systems enable them to discriminate more effectively between features of the classroom that do and do not require attention. Experienced teachers' interactive thinking, like their planning, is characterized by a greater economy of management of information to be processed.

A number of patterns emerge from these studies of teachers' interactive thinking. Experienced and inexperienced teachers seem to find different types of information useful to their interactive decision making. Inexperienced teachers attend more to information that is relevant to behavior and classroom management concerns; experienced teachers focus more on information that has instructional significance. Experienced teachers appear to be more selective in their attention and more efficient in their processing of information during interactive teaching. Further, experienced teachers draw on their experience and knowledge of classroom life to attribute meaning to what they observe and determine the typicality of events as they unfold. This enables them to act quickly and with automaticity during interactive teaching, particularly when events are typical and routine action sequences seem appropriate.

Several researchers on teaching have noted that these differences in the thinking patterns of experienced and inexperienced teachers parallel differences reported in other areas of expertise such as chess playing and physics problem solving (e.g., Berliner 1986; Leinhardt & Greeno, 1986; Shavelson, 1986; Warner, 1987). They suggest that concepts and principles derived from recent work in cognitive psychology, used to explain expertise in these areas (cf. deGroot, 1965; Larkin, McDermott, Simon, & Simon, 1980), can similarly help explain many characteristics of pedagogical expertise. In the final section of this chapter, we explore the application of several of these concepts and principles to patterns of teacher planning and interactive decision making. First, however, we examine the relationship between teachers' decisions and student outcomes.

TEACHERS' DECISIONS AND STUDENT OUTCOMES

Most studies of teachers' planning and interactive decision making are descriptive in nature. However, some researchers have begun to examine the role that plans and interactive decisions play in classroom processes and student attitudes and achievement. A study of social studies instruction by Peterson et al. (1978; also Clark & Peterson, 1981; Marx & Peterson, 1981; Peterson & Clark, 1978) is unique in its tracing of teaching from initial information, through teacher characteristics and cognitive processes, to planning and interactive teaching and the effects of these components of teaching on students' achievements and attitudes. Twelve teachers taught a social studies unit (not previously taught by the teachers) to three different groups of eight junior high students whom they did not know and on whom they had no other information. With respect to planning, Peterson et al. (1978) reported that planning directed primarily to content and objectives was associated with "subject-matter focused" teacher behavior and with a somewhat rigid pattern of instruction. In contrast, planning that dealt with the learner was positively related to teacher behaviors classified as "group focused."

During interactive teaching, teachers used information about student participation and involvement in the lesson to judge how well their lessons were progressing. They considered alternatives only when teaching was going poorly and changed strategies in about half the problematic situations. Their changes usually were not major ones; they are probably best characterized as fine-tuning of the original plans (Peterson & Clark, 1978).

Correlations between a measure of the complexity of teachers' interactive decisions and measures of student achievement and attitude were negative. Specifically, students' achievement and attitude scores were lower in situations where teachers reported considering alternative teaching strategies and deciding not to change their behavior. However, as is often the case, the teachers who considered alternative teaching strategies were those whose lessons were not going as planned and whose routines were not maintaining the flow of activity. Further, the teachers who decided not to change their behaviors were those whose planning was focused primarily on objectives and content. Their decisions not to change led to Peterson et al.'s (1978) interpretation of rigidity in their teaching. In this study, the skill of planning accurately to maintain the activity flow and the willingness to change direction when activities are not proceeding as planned both play a role in the observed link between teacher behavior and student outcomes.

Although no other study has traced the teaching process through all phases examined by Peterson, Marx, and Clark, several studies that explored relationships among some of the phases produced results that support patterns they discovered. For example, in his study of the teaching of a fifth-grade mathematics unit, Carnahan (1980) found a relationship between instructional planning and the general structure and focus of interactive teaching. Specifically, he reported a positive relationship between emphasis in written plans on individuals or small groups and the extent to which a teacher used small groups in classrooms. He did not, however, find a relationship between plans and the specific details of verbal behavior. Carnahan suggested that the limited relationship of plans to the general organization of teaching is appropriate. Because student responses during interactive teaching are unpredictable, verbal dialogue is not a profitable focus for teacher planning.

Zahorik's (1970) study of teacher planning supports the relationship between planning directed to content and objectives and rigid patterns of instruction. This study compared the effects of structured planning with the absence of structured planning on teachers' classroom behavior in a lesson on credit cards. Six teachers were given partial lesson plans 2 weeks in advance; six were asked to reserve 1 hour of instructional time and were told just before that hour what they were to teach. Teachers who were given structured lesson plans did not encourage or develop students' ideas as much as the teachers who did not have the opportunity to plan. They also did not foster discussion as well. One possible explanation for this finding is that teachers without the chance to plan had no choice but to explore student ideas and experiences whereas those who knew the topic in advance were able to focus on content rather than the students. However, when considered together with findings reported by Peterson, Marx, and Clark, this study also suggests that when planning becomes too structured or too task-oriented, it can lead to instruction that is rigid and unresponsive to students.

Like Peterson, Marx, and Clark, Morine and Vallance (1975) used student achievement scores to differentiate effective and ineffective teachers in their study of interactive decision making. During stimulated recall interviews, more effective teachers mentioned fewer items of information that they used in making their decisions than did less effective teachers. They also mentioned fewer specific aspects of the interactive decisions. Clark and Peterson (1986) suggested that the conceptual systems of the more effective teachers may have been better-developed than those of the less effective teachers. As a result, the more effective teachers were better able to reduce the cognitive complexity of the classroom by engaging in simplifying processes such as chunking, differentiation, and selectivity. These observed differences in patterns of interactive decision making, and the hypothesized differences in conceptual systems, are similar to differences between experienced and inexperienced teachers examined earlier in this chapter. Theoretical and empirical support for the proposed facilitative role of conceptual systems (or cognitive schemata) in the planning and interactive decision making of effective teachers and experienced teachers is provided by an analysis of teaching from the perspective of cognitive psychology.

A COGNITIVE ANALYSIS OF TEACHING

Shavelson (1985) suggested that "there is provocative evidence that the concepts in cognitive psychology provide potentially powerful tools for studying teaching" (p. 7). Taking this notion a step further, Leinhardt and Greeno (1986) characterized teaching as "a complex cognitive skill" which "requires the construction of plans and the making of on-line decisions" (p. 75) and suggested that these plans and on-line (i.e., interactive) decisions can be described and analyzed using concepts in cognitive psychology. In this final section of the chapter we present the concepts that have been identified by Shavelson (1985, 1986) and Leinhardt and Greeno (1986), and continue with the task they have begun, that of interrelating these concepts with our knowledge of teacher thinking.

The concept of *schema* is central to a cognitive analysis of teaching. In fact, Leinhardt and Greeno (1986; see also Leinhardt & Smith, 1985) suggested that the main feature of a teacher's knowledge structure is a set of interrelated schemata for teaching activities. As R. Anderson (1984) has defined the term, "A schema is an abstract structure of information. It is abstract in the sense that it summarizes information about many particular cases. A schema is structured in the sense that it represents relationships among concepts" (p. 5).

Schemata for Teacher Thinking

Three types of schemata seem to characterize teacher thinking: scripts, scenes, and propositional structures (Shavelson, 1986). A script is a knowledge structure that summarizes information about familiar, everyday experiences. Relationships in a script are temporal. Experienced teachers have scripts for common global teaching activities such as correcting homework, presenting new information, providing guided practice, and conducting class discussions. They also have scripts for routines—smaller, more specific sets of teacher and student behavior such as distributing paper and bringing students together for small group instruction.

Scenes are structures that represent teachers' knowledge of people and objects in common classroom events. Relationships in scenes are spatial. Experienced teachers have scene schemata for classroom activities such as whole group instruction, small group work, and independent seatwork. These schemata enable them to store a great deal of information about the relationships among people and objects in recurring classroom activities, and to rapidly recognize common activity structures.

Propositional structures represent teachers' factual knowledge (i.e., "knowing that"; J. Anderson, 1976) about components of teaching such as the students in their classrooms, subject matter, and pedagogical strategies. For example, experienced teachers' propositional structures for storing information about their students probably include mental representations of student ability, knowledge, motivation, and behavior patterns.

Many differences in the thinking of experienced and inexperienced teachers can readily be explained using the concepts of script, scene, and propositional structure. In fact, a single assumption underlines most of these explanations, namely that cognitive schemata change in predictable ways as people develop expertise in a given area. For example, the cognitive schemata of experts typically are more elaborate, more complex, more interconnected and more accessible than those of novices. In the following paragraphs, we provide several examples to demonstrate how concepts from cognitive psychology explain differences between experienced (or expert) and inexperienced (or novice) teachers. We are not the first people to make this connection. We have already mentioned the work of Leinhardt and colleagues (e.g., Leinhardt & Greeno, 1986; Leinhardt & Smith, 1985). Berliner, Carter, and colleagues (e.g., Berliner, 1986, 1987; Carter et al., 1987; Carter et al., 1988) designed their research program with the specific intent of exploring pedagogical expertise from the framework of cognitive psychology. Our first example is drawn from their research.

Across the series of tasks in which participants responded to slides of classroom life (Berliner, 1987; Carter et al., 1988), experts focused on information that had instructional significance, and seemed to draw on their knowledge of classrooms to ascribe meaning to the people and objects depicted. Experts also noticed aspects of the slides that appeared to be unusual or atypical. Novices were less focused in the information that they recalled, and provided "flat" descriptions without explanations or interpretations for what they saw. One explanation for these differences is based on the premise that participants compared the slides to their mental *scenes* of classrooms. Experts have learned what aspects of classroom life are salient to teaching and learning. Their schemata or scenes for classrooms reflect this knowledge by having categories or "slots" for instructionally relevant dimensions of classrooms. When they view slides, they selectively attend to information that will fit into these slots (e.g., work arrangements, types of instructional activities). They also ascribe meaning to the slides based on these comparisons,and spend mental energy attempting to make sense of atypical visual stimuli. In contrast, novices' less well-developed mental scenes of classrooms impose less structure and less meaning on their responses to the slide tasks.

A similar interpretation can be made for Calderhead's (1983) findings regarding teachers' perceptions of students, in this case using the construct of *propositional structures*. Experienced teachers have more elaborate propositional structures for characteristics of students than do novices. These schemata have categories for student characteristics that the teachers have found to be important to classroom life. The information about specific students and classes that they have stored in these propositional structures over years of teaching enables them to predict likely configurations of student attributes such as ability, knowledge, skills, behavioral characteristics, and social interaction patterns. Given this wealth of stored information and the predictions they can make based on the information, they do, in some sense, know a new class before they meet it.

The construct of *scripts* is central to an explanation of Warner's (1987) finding that experienced teachers reported fewer interactive decisions (choices among alternatives) but a greater number of deliberate actions (changes based on the consideration of a single course of action) than did novices. When an unexpected event occurs in a classroom and the teacher determines that some response is required, the teacher may engage in either deliberate action or interactive decision making. Warner suggested that deliberate action is the more desirable option because it is much less cognitively demanding than is interactive decision making. He further suggested that teachers engage in the consideration of alternatives primarily when a routine action is not immediately available for dealing with the unexpected situation. Experienced teachers have a greater number of scripts for routine actions than do novices and their scripts generally are more flexible and adaptable to a greater number of situations. They will therefore be faced with the need to engage in interactive decision making much less frequently than will novices. Thus, we speculate that the availability of a larger repertoire of scripts for common classroom activities reduces the cognitive demands of teaching for the experienced teacher.

As a final, more elaborate example, we examine teacher planning using concepts from cognitive psychology. The match between research-based descriptions of planning and concepts such as script, scene and propositional structure is not made as easily as was the case for studies of experienced and inexperienced teachers. Our analysis should be viewed as an initial step in merging these two bodies of literature.

In their cognitive analysis of teaching, Leinhardt and Greeno (1986) characterized teachers' plans as agendas that guide subsequent actions in the classroom. They hypothesized that agendas include traditional lesson plans, activity structures, operational routines, and decision elements. Activity structures, the schemata for major segments of lessons, are a central feature of agendas, and the feature on which we focus first. They consist of interrelated, hierarchically organized sets of scripts and scenes. Like other cognitive schemata, these scripts and scenes are abstract structures with slots to be instantiated or filled in as the teacher develops an agenda or operating plan for a particular lesson. The teacher fills in these slots by drawing on information stored in relevant propositional structures. In a mathematics class, for example, the agenda for a typical lesson includes activity structures for segments such as homework check, presentation, guided practice, and seatwork. The activity structure for presentation includes a script for explanation as well as a scene for the instructional format to be used (e.g., whole class, small group). As the teacher develops an operational plan or agenda for the lesson, that teacher will instantiate the explanation script by selecting specific instructional content, strategies, and materials appropriate to the scene (e.g., the students and instructional format). To do this, the teacher will draw on information stored in propositional structures for students, subject matter, and pedagogical strategies.

This conceptualization of planning provides a framework for understanding some aspects of descriptive research on teacher thinking. For example, research-based descriptions of factors that influence teachers' plans can easily be incorporated into the conceptualization. Specifically, the research reviewed in this chapter suggests that the major factors that influence teachers' plans are characteristics of students and the instructional task. We can think of information about these factors as being stored in the propositional structures that teachers draw on when developing agendas for particular lessons. More specifically, the characteristics of students and tasks that teachers consider are those that have slots or categories in their respective propositional structures. Descriptive research suggests that, in the case of students, these typically are general ability or achievement, gender, class participation, self-concept, social competence, independence, classroom behavior, and work habits. Major characteristics of the instructional task are content, activities, and materials (Shavelson & Stern, 1981).

Similarly, descriptions of antecedents of teachers' interactive decisions are easily incorporated by the cognitive analysis of teaching. As Leinhardt and Greeno (1986) suggested, skilled teaching requires interactive decisions, such as decisions about whether or not to proceed with the next component of the lesson. Decision elements are built into an agenda to accomplish these decisions. More concretely, decision elements are checkpoints, designed to permit continuous updating and revision of the lesson based on factors such as individual students' readiness for new material and the likelihood that students will succeed in solving instructional problems. Antecedents of interactive decisions can be thought of as the information sources to which teachers turn when they arrive at these checkpoints. Not surprisingly, descriptive research indicates that the largest category of antecedents reported by teachers is learner attributes, including understanding, involvement, attention, and behavior. The second largest category is instructional strategies including explanations, questions, reinforcement, review and practice exercises, sequencing and pacing of activities, and transitions between activities (Clark & Peterson, 1986). Clearly, these are the sources one would expect a teacher to consider when deciding whether to proceed with a lesson.

Not all features of teacher thinking addressed in the descriptive research can be as easily incorporated into the cognitive analysis of teaching. For example, the framework, in its current stage of development, does little to extend our understanding of the reasons teachers plan or the different types of plans they develop. It may be that as the cognitive analysis of teaching proceeds, it will expand to include these and other facets of teacher thinking.

CONCLUSION

We seem to be on the verge of a significant accomplishment in research on teacher thinking. As we bring together the tools from cognitive psychology and the rich base of descriptive research on teacher thinking, we are beginning to formulate a theory and develop a language that will enable us to formally describe teacher thinking. One implication of our progress to date is that the previously useful distinction between preactive and interactive thinking (Jackson, 1968) now seems inappropriate. Preactive and interactive decision making are not conceptually distinct processes. Rather, they are interrelated components of a more broadly conceived process of developing and enacting agendas based on teaching schemata. Other implications will undoubtedly emerge as we continue to develop, and begin to empirically test, formal models of teacher cognition.

REFERENCES

Anderson, J. (1976). *Language, memory and thought*. Hillsdale, NJ: Lawrence Erlbaum Associates.
Anderson, R. C. (1984, November). Some reflections on the acquisition of knowledge. *Educational Researcher, 13*, 5–10.
Berliner, D. C. (1986). In pursuit of the expert pedagogue. *Educational Researcher, 15*(7), 5–13.

Berliner, D. C. (1987). Ways of thinking about students and classrooms by more and less experienced teachers. In J. Calderhead (Ed.), *Exploring teachers' thinking* (pp. 60–83). London: Holt, Rinehart & Winston.

Borko, H. (1978, March). *An examination of some factors contributing to teachers' preinstructional classroom organization and management decisions.* Paper presented at the annual meeting of the American Educational Research Association, Toronto, Ontario.

Borko, H., Eisenhart, M., Kello, M., & Vandett, N. (1984). Teachers as decision markers versus technicians. In J. A. Niles & L. A. Harris (Eds.), *Changing perspectives on research in reading/language processing and instruction: Thirty-third yearbook of the National Reading Conference* (pp. 124–131). New York: The National Reading Conference.

Borko, H., Lalik, R., Livingston, C., Pecic, K., & Perry, D. (1986, April). *Learning to teach in the induction year: Two case studies.* Paper presented at the annual meeting of the American Educational Research Association, San Francisco.

Borko, H., & Niles, J. A. (1982). Factors contributing to teachers' judgments about students and decisions about grouping students for reading instruction. *Journal of Reading Behavior, 14,* 127–140.

Borko, H., & Niles, J. A. (1983). Teachers' cognitive processes in the formation of reading groups. In J. A. Niles & L. A. Harris (Eds.), *Searches for meaning in reading/language processing and instruction: Thirty-second yearbook of the National Reading Conference* (pp. 282–288). New York: The National Reading Conference.

Borko, H., & Niles, J. (1984, April). *Teachers' strategies for forming reading groups: Do real students make a difference?* Paper presented at the annual meeting of the American Educational Research Association, New Orleans.

Borko, H., & Niles, J. (1987). Descriptions of teacher planning: Ideas for teachers and researchers. In V. Koehler (Ed.), *Educators' handbook: Research into practice* (pp. 167–187). New York: Longman.

Calderhead, J. (1981). A psychological approach to research on teachers' decision making. *British Educational Research Journal, 7,* 51–57.

Calderhead, J. (1983, April). *Research into teachers' and student teachers' cognitions: Exploring the nature of classroom practice.* Paper presented at the annual meeting of the American Educational Research Association, Montreal, Canada.

Carnahan, R. S. (1980). *The effects of teacher planning on classroom processes* (Tech. Rep. No. 541). Madison, WI: Wisconsin R & D Center for Individualized Schooling.

Carter, K., Cushing, K., Sabers, D., Stein, P., & Berliner, D. (1988). Expert-novice differences in perceiving and processing visual classroom stimuli. *Journal of Teacher Education, 39*(3), 25–31.

Carter, K., Sabers, D., Cushing, K., Pinnegar, S., & Berliner, D. (1987). Processing and using information about students: A study of expert, novice, and postulant teachers. *Teaching and Teacher Education, 3,* 147–157.

Clark, C. M. (1978-1979). A new question for research on teaching. *Educational Research Quarterly, 3,* 53–58.

Clark, C. M. (1983). Research on teacher planning: An inventory of the knowledge base. In D. C. Smith (Ed.), *Essential knowledge for beginning educators* (pp.

5–15). Washington, DC: American Association of Colleges for Teacher Education.

Clark, C. M., & Elmore, J. L. (1979). *Teacher planning in the first weeks of school* (Research Series No. 56). East Lansing, MI: Michigan State University, Institute for Research on Teaching.

Clark, C. M., & Elmore, J. L. (1981). *Transforming curriculum in mathematics, science, and writing: A case study of teacher yearly planning* (Research Series No. 99). East Lansing, MI: Michigan State University, Institute for Research on Teaching.

Clark, C. M., & Peterson, P. L. (1981). Stimulated-recall. In B. R. Joyce, C. C. Brown, & L. Peck (Eds.), *Flexibility in teaching: An excursion into the nature of teaching and training* (pp. 256–261). New York: Longman.

Clark, C. M., & Peterson, P. L. (1986). Teachers' thought processes. In M. C. Wittrock (Ed.), *Handbook of research on teaching* (3rd ed.) (pp. 255–296). New York: Macmillan.

Clark, C. M., & Yinger, R. J. (1979). *Three studies of teacher planning* (Research Series No. 55). East Lansing, MI: Michigan State University, Institute for Research on Teaching.

Colker, L. (1982). *Teacher's interactive thoughts about pupil cognition.* Unpublished doctoral dissertation, University of Illinois at Urbana-Champaign.

Conners, R. D. (1978). *An analysis of teacher thought processes, beliefs, and principles during instruction.* Unpublished doctoral dissertation, University of Alberta, Edmonton, Canada.

deGroot, A. D. (1965). *Thought and choice in chess.* The Hague: Mouton.

Doyle, W. (1979). Making managerial decisions in classrooms. In D. L. Duke (Ed.), *Classroom management* (Yearbook of the National Society for the Study of Education) (pp. 42–74). Chicago, IL: University of Chicago Press.

Erickson, F. (1986). Qualitative methods in research on teaching. In M. C. Wittrock (Ed.) *Handbook of research on teaching* (3rd ed.) (pp. 119–161). New York: Macmillan.

Evertson, C., & Green, J. (1986). Observation as inquiry and method. In M. C. Wittrock (Ed.) *Handbook of research on teaching* (3rd ed.) (pp. 162–213). New York: Macmillan.

Floden, R. E., Porter, A. C., Schmidt, W. H., Freeman, D. J., & Schwille, J. R. (1981). Responses to curriculum pressures: A policy-capturing study of teacher decisions about content. *Journal of Educational Psychology, 73,* 129–141.

Fogarty, J. L., Wang, M. C., & Creek, R. (1982, March). *A descriptive study of experienced and novice teachers' interactive instructional decision processes.* Paper presented at the annual meeting of the American Educational Research Association, New York City.

Housner, L., & Griffey, D. (1985). Teacher cognition: Differences in planning and interactive decision making between experienced and inexperienced teachers. *Research Quarterly for Exercise and Sport, 56,* 45–53.

Jackson, P. W. (1968). *Life in classrooms.* New York: Holt, Rinehart & Winston.

Joyce, B. R. (1978-1979). Toward a theory of information processing in teaching. *Educational Research Quarterly, 3*(4), 66–77.

Larkin, J. H., McDermott, J., Simon, D. P., & Simon, H. (1980). Models of competence in solving physics problems. *Cognitive Science, 4,* 317–345.

Leinhardt, G. (1986, September). *Math lessons: A contrast of novice and expert competence.* Paper presented at the Psychology of Mathematics Education Conference, East Lansing, MI.

Leinhardt, G., & Greeno, J. G. (1986). The cognitive skill of teaching. *Journal of Educational Psychology, 78,* 75–95.

Leinhardt, G., & Smith, D. (1985). Expertise in mathematics instruction: Subject matter knowledge. *Journal of Educational Psychology, 77,* 247–271.

Linn, R. (1986). Quantitative methods in research on teaching. In M. C. Wittrock (Ed.), *Handbook of research on teaching* (3rd ed.) (pp. 92–118). New York: Macmillan.

MacKay, A. (1977). The Alberta studies of teaching: A quinquereme in search of some sailors. *CSSE News, 3,* 14–17.

MacKay, D. A., & Marland, P. W. (1978, March). *Thought processes of teachers.* Paper presented at the annual meeting of the American Educational Research Association, Toronto, Canada.

Marland, P. W. (1977). *A study of teachers' interactive thoughts.* Unpublished doctoral dissertation, University of Alberta, Edmonton, Canada.

Marx, R. W., & Peterson, P. L. (1981). The nature of teacher decision making. In B. R. Joyce, C. C. Brown, & L. Peck (Eds.), *Flexibility in teaching: An excursion into the nature of teaching and training* (pp. 236–255). New York: Longman.

McCutcheon, G. (1980). How do elementary school teachers plan? The nature of planning and influences on it. *Elementary School Journal, 81,* 4–23.

McNair, K. (1978-1979). Capturing inflight decisions. *Educational Research Quarterly, 3*(4), 26–42.

McNeil, L. M. (1980, April). *Knowledge forms and knowledge content.* Paper presented at the annual meeting of the American Educational Research Association, Boston, MA.

Mintz, S. L. (1979, April). *Teacher planning: A simulation study.* Paper presented at the annual meeting of the American Educational Research Association, San Francisco, CA.

Morine, G., & Vallance, E. (1975). *Special study B: A study of teacher and pupil perceptions of classroom interaction* (Tech. Rep. No. 75-11-6). San Francisco, CA: Far West Laboratory.

Morine-Dershimer, G. (1978-1979). Planning and classroom reality: An in-depth look. *Educational Research Quarterly, 3*(4), 83–99.

Morine-Dershimer, G. (1979). *Teacher plan and classroom reality: The South Bay study: Part 4* (Research Series No. 60). East Lansing, MI: Michigan State University, Institute for Research on Teaching.

Morine-Dershimer, G., & Vallance, E. (1976). *Teacher planning* (Beginning Teacher Evaluation Study, Special Report C). San Francisco, CA: Far West Laboratory.

National Institute of Education. (1975). *Teaching as clinical information processing* (Report of Panel 6, National Conference on Studies in Teaching). Washington, DC: National Institute of Education.

Peterson, P. L., & Clark, C. M. (1978). Teachers' reports of their cognitive processes during teaching. *American Educational Research Journal, 15,* 555–565.

Peterson, P. L., Marx, R. W., & Clark, C. M. (1978). Teacher planning, teacher behavior, and student achievement. *American Educational Research Journal, 15,* 417–432.

Russo, N. A. (1978, March). *Capturing teachers' decision policies: An investigation of strategies for teaching reading and mathematics.* Paper presented at the annual meeting of the American Educational Research Association, Toronto, Ontario.

Sardo, D. (1982, October). *Teacher planning styles in the middle school.* Paper presented to the Eastern Educational Research Association, Ellenville, NY.

Schank, R. C., & Abelson, R. (1977). *Scripts, plans, goals and understanding.* Hillsdale, NJ: Lawrence Erlbaum Associates.

Semmel, D. S. (1977, April). *The effects of training on teacher decision making.* Paper presented at the annual meeting of the American Educational Research Association, New York City. (ERIC Document Reproduction Service No. ED 138 558).

Shavelson, R. J. (1983). Review of research on teachers' pedagogical judgments, plans and decisions. *Elementary School Journal, 83,* 392–413.

Shavelson, R. J. (1985, April). *Schemata and teaching routines: A historical perspective.* Paper presented at the annual meeting of the American Educational Research Association, Chicago, IL.

Shavelson, R. J. (1986). *Interactive decision making: Some thoughts on teacher cognition.* Invited address, I Congreso Internacional, "Pensamientos de los Profesores y Toma de Decisiones," Seville, Spain.

Shavelson, R. J., & Stern, P. (1981). Research on teachers' pedagogical thoughts, judgments, decisions, and behavior. *Review of Educational Research, 51,* 455–498.

Shavelson, R., Webb, N., & Burstein, L. (1986). Measurement of teaching. In M. C. Wittrock (Ed.), *Handbook of research on teaching* (3rd ed.) (pp. 50–91). New York: Macmillan.

Shroyer, J. C. (1981). *Critical moments in the teaching of mathematics: What makes teaching difficult?* Unpublished doctoral dissertation, Michigan State University, East Lansing, MI.

Shulman, L. S. (1986). Those who understand: Knowledge growth in teaching. *Educational Researcher, 15*(2), 4–14.

Smith, E. L., & Sendelbach, N. B. (1979, April). *Teacher intentions for science instruction and their antecedents in program materials.* Paper presented at the annual meeting of the American Educational Research Association, San Francisco, CA.

Taylor, P. H. (1970). *How teachers plan their courses.* Slough, Berkshire, England: National Foundation for Education Research.

Tyler, R. W. (1950). *Basic principles of curriculum and instruction.* Chicago, IL: University of Chicago Press.

Warner, D. R. (1987). *An exploratory study to identify the distinctive features of experi-*

enced teachers' thinking about teaching. Unpublished doctoral dissertation, The University of New England, Armidale NSW 2351, Australia.

Wittrock, M. C. (Ed.) (1986). *Handbook of research on teaching* (3rd ed.). New York: Macmillan.

Wodlinger, M. G. (1980). *A study of teacher interactive decision making.* Unpublished doctoral dissertation, University of Alberta, Edmonton, Canada.

Yinger, R. J. (1980). A study of teacher planning. *The Elementary School Journal, 80,* 107–127.

Zahorik, J. (1970). The effects of planning on teaching. *Elementary School Journal, 71,* 143–151.

Zahorik, J. (1975). Teachers' planning models. *Educational Leadership, 23,* 134–139.

Learning Strategies for Acquiring Useful Knowledge

Sharon J. Derry
Florida State University

Much of today's classroom instruction is directed toward three general types of goals: (a) acquiring the ideas and facts fundamental to disciplines such as science, literature, and history; (b) acquiring basic procedural skills that underlie various curricular disciplines—skills such as reading and using language, and use of problem-solving procedures; and (c) improving higher-order thinking capabilities that enable students to access and apply basic curricular knowledge to the solution of meaningful problems. The chapters in this volume are concerned primarily with goal (c)—improvement of higher-order thinking capabilities. Yet it is readily apparent that the authors represented here believe that an important key to mature thinking is the capacity to access and employ basic information and skills that are taught in the school curriculum. Some argue that development of general thinking capability requires that fundamental curricular knowledge be learned in a form that renders it memorable and useful for whatever problem-solving situations may occur in later courses and throughout life (e.g., Bransford, Franks, Vye, & Sherwood, 1986; Bransford, Sherwood, Vye, & Rieser, 1986; Bransford, Vye, Kinzer, & Risko, chap. 12 in this volume). It seems that educators who wish to promote general reasoning capability must not only teach practical thinking skills, but also must insist that fundamental curricular knowledge is "well constructed." Otherwise, such knowledge can remain inert and useless, even if it is "learned" (e.g., Bransford, Franks, et al., 1986; Bransford, Sherwood, et al., 1986; Bransford, Franks, & Sherwood, 1987).

Recent research in cognitive psychology has taught us a great deal

347

about the nature of usable knowledge. We know that factual information is likely to be called into service only if it is understood and stored within well-structured, well-elaborated networks that render ideas memorable in situations where they will be needed. Procedural skills are likely to be accessed and used spontaneously only if they have properly evolved through practice, and if conditions that indicate their applicability are clearly understood. We also know that by using various *learning strategies,* people can intentionally influence the form and quality of the knowledge they do acquire (e.g., Biggs, 1979; Cook & Mayer, 1983; Mayer, 1987; Mayer & Bromage, 1980). This chapter examines the learning strategies concept in terms of a theoretical framework that distinguishes between declarative and procedural knowledge, and between inert and useful learning. One theme of this chapter is that teachers and students should be made aware of the nature and form of useful knowledge, and of learning strategies that are likely to facilitate its creation. The argument will be made that strategies for useful learning should be devised by teachers and taught in school classrooms.

WHAT IS A LEARNING STRATEGY?

There is much confusion in the current literature concerning the mean-ing of the term *learning strategy.* The term has been used in reference to particular learning skills, such as rehearsal, imaging, and outlining (e.g., Cook & Mayer, 1983; Levin, 1986), to more general types of self-man-agement activities such as planning and comprehension monitoring (e.g., Pressley, Borkowski, & Schneider, 1987), and to complex plans that combine several specific techniques (e.g., Derry & Murphy, 1986; Snow-man & McCown, 1984). The definition adopted for this chapter draws a distinction between *specific* learning tactics and more general learning strategies. Whereas a learning strategy is viewed as a complex plan one formulates for accomplishing a learning goal, a learning tactic is de-scribed as any single processing technique one uses in service of the plan (Derry & Murphy, 1986; Paris & Lindauer, 1982, p. 339; Snowman & McCown, 1984). That is, a learning strategy is seen as the application of one or more specific learning tactics to a learning problem.

This view of learning strategies is compatible with the definition of strategy given by Marzano et al. (1988) in *Dimensions of Thinking,* a curricu-lum framework for teaching higher-order thinking skills in public schools. They proposed that eight types of higher-order thinking processes be taught: comprehending, problem solving, and composing are three ex-amples. These higher processing abilities depend on prerequisite learn-ing of certain core skills and subskills. For example, organizing informa-tion is a useful core skill that requires the subskills representing and comparing. Marzano et al. assumed that these skills can be performed in various ways by using various mental techniques, or strategies. Therefore, in accordance with their definition, a learning strategy is a technique that a person uses to perform a learning skill. For example, rehearsal plus imaging could be the strategy used to perform the skill of memorization.

Can Learning Strategies
Improve Thinking Skill?

Learning strategies in the classroom can improve general thinking skills in two ways. First, they can be evoked as tools for helping students properly encode the subject matter at hand. For example, to help students identify and recall important key ideas for essay examinations in history, an informed teacher could devise and assign a study strategy that combines the tactics of goal setting and reward (for motivation to complete the readings), outlining (for identifying and organizing main ideas), and use of elaboration memory techniques (for recalling key topics). In addition, when teachers take time to explain how assigned strategies work and why they are beneficial, and when they provide feedback on written assignments that document strategy use, students may also acquire general learning capability in the form of metacognitive knowledge about memory and the learning process itself (Campione, Brown, & Ferrara, 1982; Flavell, 1979, 1981; Pressley, Borkowski, & O'Sullivan, 1984).

Metacognition refers to learners' awareness and knowledge of their own learning processes, as well as their abilities and tendencies to control those processes during learning. Research has shown that a major difference between mature and less able learners is that the former exhibit greater metacognitive sophistication concerning learning and memory processes (e.g., Pressley et al., 1984). Students who possess a large store of knowledge about learning strategies and their uses are better prepared to cope with a wide variety of learning situations. Given the amount of time that most people spend in school, in job-related training, and in acquiring knowledge associated with their interests and hobbies, it can easily be argued that the ability to find good solutions to many types of learning problems is one of the most important general thinking abilities.

Different Strategies for
Different Types of Knowledge?

Like all problems, learning tasks possess characteristics that render some strategies more feasible and more likely to work than others. First, there are task characteristics that define the learning situation in terms of its *beginning state.* This beginning state is partly defined by: (a) the student's available knowledge of the to-be-learned material (Is the student familiar or unfamiliar with the subject material?); and (b) partly by the nature and condition of the to-be-processed information (Is it text or computer-assisted instruction? Easy or difficult to comprehend?). Second, each task also has a goal characterized by the type of cognitive structure the learner must acquire in order to render the knowledge useful (Is the student acquiring factual knowledge or procedural skill? Will the student need to know a lot of detail, or just the gist?). There are different learning tools for different learning jobs (Levin, 1986). One major goal of learning-strategies research is to equip teachers and students with useful, prescriptive theory that can guide them in evaluating their learning situations and selecting potentially successful strategies.

Recently I have found it interesting and useful to view this issue in the context of cognitive learning theories that draw a distinction between declarative versus procedural learning (E. Gagne, 1985). Although not all researchers accept this distinction (e.g., Rumelhart & McClelland, 1986; Rumelhart & Norman, 1981), it is a classic distinction (e.g., Winograd, 1975) that is fundamental to the learning theories of Robert Gagne (1985), John Anderson (1983) and others. The basic idea is that much of what is learned in classrooms enters long-term memory as either declarative or procedural knowledge. Declarative knowledge, which can be called "knowledge that," is exemplified by the organized collections of facts and concepts that help comprise many disciplines such as history, English literature, and science. Procedural skills, or "knowledge how," are performance *capabilities* involving symbol manipulation, such as the ability to write, read, or solve algebra problems. Although different courses often emphasize the importance of one particular knowledge form over the other, it is evident that expertise in most subject-matter domains requires facility with both declarative knowledge and procedural skills. It will be argued that these two different types of learning require very different types of learning strategies.

LEARNING AND REMEMBERING
DECLARATIVE KNOWLEDGE

In order to learn declarative knowledge, the student must first engage in comprehension processes that abstract meaning from incoming instructional material. A well-established fact in learning psychology is that students cannot develop useful memories for ideas they do not understand (e.g., Bransford & Johnson, 1972). In general, instruction will be meaningful if: (a) the student actually possesses the prior knowledge and vocabulary that the writer of instruction assumes the student will possess; and (b) the instruction is reasonably well-structured and devoid of ambiguities or misleading statements. In addition, students must have developed the comprehension skills involved in identifying important themes and concepts that should be studied, and in separating these from less important instructional details that need not be remembered (e.g., Meyer, 1977). However, work by Brown (e.g., 1978, 1980) suggests that the ability to see what one should learn from instruction is a problem for some learners. In addition, some researchers (e.g., Jones, Amiran, & Katims, 1985) have pointed out that students routinely encounter a variety of "implicit" and "inadequate" text conditions, both in and out of school, and that some require great "effort after meaning" (Bartlett, 1932).

Assuming that the comprehension process is successful, students do not learn the exact words they hear or read, but instead encode abstract representations of the ideas gleaned from the instrucitonal presentation. We do not know exactly how these ideas are represented in the mind. For now we will assume only that the individual ideas is an abstract encoding roughly equivalent to a single proposition containing a subject and predicate phrase. The declarative knowledge residing in a person's long-term memory is often conceptualized as a large, tangled network of such ideas (e.g., Anderson, 1983; Minsky, 1985; Spiro, Vispoel, Schmitz, Samarapungavan, & Boerger, 1987). Within this network, semantically related ideas are stored with stronger connections to one another than are semantically unrelated ideas.

At any single point in time, most ideas in the network are inactive; only the few that a person is thinking about at that moment are receiving strong enough activation to be conscious in working memory. However, most researchers assume that previously processed ideas that are connected to the active thoughts in working memory also receive some degree of stimulation through a process that Anderson (1983) called "spreading activation." Because ideas closely related to thoughts in working memory receive greatest activation, these can be brought into conscious attention with relative ease. However, information that is not related in meaning to currently active thoughts may be difficult or impossible to recall. Thus, it is important to help students establish appropriate connections among the ideas they learn in school, because these connections help determine peoples' abilities to think of needed information at appropriate times, and to recognize conceptual relationships and analogies.

Anderson (1983) and E. Gagne (1985) postulated that learning of new declarative knowledge takes place when new ideas become linked to prior knowledge in an existing propositional network. They suggested that the connection between new and old ideas is most likely to take place within the small attentional space called working memory. That is, when two logically related ideas enter conscious attention simultaneously, there is substantial likelihood that the connection between them will be encoded by the learner. According to this view, working memory always contains two types of information during learning. Part of working memory is occupied by new, to-be-learned information—ideas presented to the student by printed text, verbally, or by other media. The other part is occupied by the prior knowledge to which the new ideas must be connected—ideas in that part of the long-term memory network the student is currently thinking about. It would seem important for teachers and students to realize that this conscious thinking space, in which much of our formal learning occurs, can hold only a few ideas at a time. Teachers can and should help influence which ideas come together in memory as students learn, think, and solve problems.

Learning of usable ideas proceeds in working memory by connecting the new ideas to prior knowledge, and is greatly facilitated by a process called *elaboration*. Elaboration occurs when students think about new ideas and prior knowledge together so that this thinking stimulates the generation of additional ideas about how new information and prior knowledge are related. Elaborations are often spontaneously generated by the student; they need not be prompted by the instructional material. Thus, elaboration is a process of adding to the information that is being learned. "The addition could be a logical inference, a continuation, an example, a detail, or anything else that serves to connect information" (E. Gagne, 1985, p. 83).

For example, suppose a student were learning about Matthew Arnold and reads that he was a British poet of the 19th century. Knowing already that the 19th century is the Victorian era, the student might generate linking elaborations by imaging Arnold as a character in Victorian scenes, in the presence of Queen Victoria, and so forth. Such images need not be present explicitly in the instructional material, but can be generated spontaneously as a means of fitting a new item into the appropriate prior knowledge network. In general, if the connection is difficult to imagine, more time and effort will be required by the elaboration process, and more assistance from the teacher may be needed.

New ideas can more easily be recalled and used later if they are stored with connections to a contextual network that the student will think about when the new ideas are needed. For example, when the student later enters a discussion or takes a test and wants to recall poets of the Victorian era, that student will likely recall that area of the knowledge network that contains information about Victorian poets. If Matthew Arnold is stored elsewhere without connections to other concepts associated with poetry and the 19th century, the likelihood of retrieval probably will be very low.

CHARACTERISTICS OF USEFUL DECLARATIVE KNOWLEDGE

Elaboration

Declarative knowledge is useful only to the extent that it can be recalled when needed. Many theorists believe that recall is greatly aided by the formation of well-elaborated knowledge structures (see Reder, 1980, for review). Students who generate elaborations by imaging, making deductions, and drawing inferences while they are learning create additional ideas that are added to the network as recall cues. Such elaborations, if *appropriate and specific* (e.g., Stein et al., 1982), form helpful connections and access pathways to ideas in the network, increasing the probability that affected ideas can be retrieved. In addition, elaborative information may help students "construct" (diSibio, 1982; E. Gagne, 1985) appropriate responses whenever required information is not actually present in the network. For example, a student who has encoded reactions to and thoughts about the somber tone of a poet's work might be able to "figure out" an answer to the following test item: "Provide an example of a 19th century 'graveyard poet'." Many problems in life call for information that is not actually encoded within long-term memory, but that can be derived from whatever information is present about the topic. In generating *constructed responses,* people apply general reasoning skills to an existing knowledge base in order to produce a new idea that is not actually encoded in the network. A well-elaborated network provides a rich, intertwined knowledge source that supports both constructive recall and recall by retrieval.

Organization

In addition, research suggests that recall of needed information is greatly aided when a student's idea network is planfully organized. Many researchers have documented the benefits of hierarchical organization (e.g., Frase, 1973; Meyer, 1977; Thorndyke, 1977), although others have argued that complex knowledge domains are inherently ill-structured and thus cannot be so neatly arranged (e.g., Spiro et al., 1987). Yet searching for a detail embedded somewhere within a loosely organized knowledge structure may be like trying to locate a needle in a haystack.

This problem is seemingly exacerbated by the small capacity of human working memory, which permits the student to *consciously* examine only one or two ideas at a time.

E. Gagne (1985) suggested that hierarchically organized idea networks allow students to manage the search process by first accessing appropriate higher-level idea sets and then searching through a limited number of chosen sets. For example, consider a test question that requires students to identify the author of a certain piece of "period poetry." Student A has organized her knowledge about poets within a structure that groups poets according to the time periods in which they wrote. Thus she accesses the name *Matthew Arnold* by first considering evidence that the author is from the Victorian era, and then by searching only through her knowledge about the poets in that period. Student B, whose knowledge structure reflects only his own personal preferences in poets, may have to search randomly and extensively through a larger set of poets in order to answer the test question. The absence of a well-differentiated hierarchical structure precludes the possibility of controlled search.

In sum, it has been suggested that a useful idea is one that can be retrieved or constructed at the time it is needed to answer a question or solve a problem. All situations that create a need for information (e.g., a test question) contain words or other contextual cues that can trigger activation of particular parts of the memory network. One way to help insure an idea's usefulness is to integrate it into the memory network that is likely to be activated when the idea is required. The likelihood of retrieving or constructing the idea is further enhanced if the network is both well-elaborated and well-structured.

LEARNING STRATEGIES FOR USEFUL DECLARATIVE KNOWLEDGE

The notion of useful declarative knowledge as a learning outcome is similar to a concept that Mayer (1987) and others have called *meaningful learning*. According to this concept, an idea's meaning can be measured in terms of its relationships to other, previously learned ideas. Thus, a highly meaningful idea is one that has been integrated into a relevant body of prior knowledge. In a similar sense, useful ideas also must be part of a well-structured body of prior knowledge that can provide cues and access pathways for recall at appropriate times.

Mayer's (1987) experiments have indicated that meaningful learning differs in form and structure from rote learning. Whereas the rote memory structure may contain many ideas, most of these are neither internally connected to one another nor externally connected to prior knowledge structures. Meaningful knowledge, on the other hand, is tightly structured with many internal and external connections, but may not contain as many ideas. This type of knowledge structure produces relatively high performance on conceptual questions and on problem-solving tasks requiring use of main ideas, but relatively low performance on immediate recall of verbatim and detailed information. Rote learning, on the other hand, produces higher immediate verbatim recall and detailed memories, but relatively low conceptual understanding and problem-solving performance. Apparently, students who engage in meaningful learning are more selective about the ideas they choose to study. They also systematically organize these ideas and integrate them with prior knowledge.

This section focuses on learning strategies that can be taught to students to help them develop declarative knowledge that is both useful and meaningful. I do not attempt an exhaustive review, but focus on some important principles and concepts of strategies instruction for declarative knowledge. A selection of example strategies illustrates these principles and concepts.

Focusing Attention

Some learning strategies simply assist students in locating and focusing extra attention on potentially useful ideas that are present in instruction. In situations where the instructional material is well-structured and relatively easy, and particularly if learners are able readers, advising students to write down, highlight, or underline important information might harness attention. For example, Richards and August (1975) found that students who were asked to underline sentences in a passage subsequently recalled more information than did control subjects who simply read the passage. However, one potential problem with simple focusing tactics is that they do not insure emphasis on important information. A second is that students may fail to see important conceptual relationships that help give the instruction its meaning.

Focusing on Structural Importance. Research by Meyer (e.g., 1975, 1977) has shown that school-type text has a hierarchical content structure that render's some ideas more important than others to each passage's overall meaning. An idea's position within the passage's content structure has been shown to be a major determinant of its memorability. However, research also indicates that some students are insensitive to content structure and even to other more obvious clues (e.g., headings, topic sentences) that point to important ideas and their interrelation-ships (e.g., Brown, 1978, 1980). Such students might benefit from being trained in how to use text structure as an aid in locating and organizing key material. For example, Dansereau (1985) and Meyer (1977) have taught students to heed headings, topic sentences, and other cues to content structure provided by authors or instructional designers. Unfor-tunately, many instructional materials are "implicit," "inconsiderate," or "inadequate," and thus may lack good structural cues (e.g., Jones et al., 1985). In fact, difficult text is the rule rather than the exception in advanced courses, wherein students are expected to employ reasoning skills and prior knowledge to "figure out" some of the important infor-mation (e.g., Cook & Mayer, 1983; Jones et al., 1985; Wittrock, 1984).

Schema Training

Challenging or inadequate learning materials require learners to impose their own structural knowledge as a basis for extracting or constructing major themes. *Schema training* is a general term that refers to a range of methods for helping learners develop and use such structural knowl-edge. With schema training, a student is provided with an abstract pro-totype representing a hierarchically structured set of concepts, objects, events, questions, and so forth. The student is taught to impose that structure on instructional text as a basis for identifying what the well-informed reader should know.

For example, Dansereau (1985) taught college students to use a theo-ry schema as a study aid for scientific text. The schema specified six general categories of information about scientific theories: description, inventor/history, consequences, evidence, other theories, and X-tra in-formation. These main categories were further divided into 13 sub-cate-gories. An investigation of this technique was conducted in which experi-mental subjects studied using the theory schema, while control subjects studied with no schema. The experimental group performed signifi-cantly better than the control group on an essay examination, but perfor-mance on other types of tests was equal. This schema-training approach could be adapted to almost any course of study, although other types of text would require different schemas. For instance, short stories would lend themselves to schemas based on "story grammars" (Kintsch, 1977), which include components for theme, plot, resolution, and so forth.

Another type of schema-based approach focuses not on fitting pas-sage ideas into general categories, but on analyzing the internal organi-zation of a text or lesson. Weinstein and Mayer (1985) and Mayer (1987) reported a dissertation study by Cook (1982), which provided a complex form of schema training to some students and no training to others. Students in the training group were taught to recognize different kinds of structures found in science texts and how to create different outlines for each. The five structures were:

Generalization—The passages explains, clarifies, or extends a main idea.

Enumeration—The passage lists facts sequentially.

Sequence—The passage describes a connected series of events or steps in a process.

Classification—The passage groups material into categories.

Compare/Contrast—The passage examines relationships between two or more things.

In Cook's study, trained subjects recalled more conceptual information, but less other information, as compared to controls. However, trained students also showed large advantage on ability to solve problems using the passage information.

Some forms of schema training, such as Dansereau's (1985) scientific theory schema previously described, are content-dependent learning strategies. That is, a schema is designed that is appropriate only for a particular domain of study. Other schema approaches, such as Cook's (1982), are based on more generally useful schemas. A highly general schema-training technique appropriate for any discipline is *networking* (Dansereau, 1978; Dansereau et al., 1979). Networking focuses students' attention directly on logical connections among ideas present in instruction. Learners analyze the instructional passage and construct explicit node-link maps representing the passage's meaning. Constructing a node-link map involves identifying important ideas and representing them on paper as "nodes." "Links" are drawn between nodes to represent interrelationships among ideas. The schema training associated with this technique consists of teaching students to recognize six types of idea links that occur in expository instruction. These are:

Part link—Several subordinate ideas are parts that make up a superordinate category.

Type link—Subordinate ideas are type examples of a superordinate category.

Leads-to link—One idea leads to or causes another.

Analogy link—One idea is compared with another.

Characteristic link—A subordinate idea is a characteristic trait of a superordinate idea.

Evidence link—One idea provides evidence that another idea is true.

Research has shown that networking facilitates recall of conceptual information, rather than detail, and is most successful with lower-ability learners. However, McKeachie (1984) pointed out that the technique is time consuming and difficult to learn.

Schema Training Versus Signaling. Schema training can be contrasted with alternative "lesson-controlled" (Derry & Murphy, 1986) techniques, which explicitly point out the content and structure of what is to be learned. One such method, called "signaling," provides supplementary outlines and headings that spell out the main ideas and organization of instruction. Loman and Mayer (1983) and Mayer, Dyck, and Cook (1984) compared learning by students who read signaled versions of passages with learning by those who read normal versions. Although verbatim recall was slightly decreased for students who received signalling, these students outperformed control subjects on tests of conceptual information and transfer. The major advantage of signalling over schema training is that it is an efficient means of helping students identify what the teacher wants the student to know. However, a primary advantage of schema training is that it encourages students to be autonomous, active leaners.

Elaboration Strategies

The schema-based techniques described in preceding paragraphs are "omnibus" (Dansereau, 1985) learning strategies—strategies that combine multiple processing tactics in support of multiple cognitive learning processes. These schema techniques "work" partly because they encourage students to focus on important information, and partly because schemas help organize the material. However, merely comprehending this "content structure" (Meyer, 1977) is not a sufficient condition for meaningful learning. The creation of functional knowledge goes beyond comprehension, because additional effort must be made to integrate new ideas into well-elaborated networks that provide pathways of retrieval throughout long-term memory. When the goal is usable declarative knowledge, learning strategies must also incorporate elaboration tactics to help insure that students effectively integrate their new ideas.

Most schema-based learning strategies do encourage some elaboration. The schemas themselves are higher-order prior knowledge structures to which incoming material is connected. As such, schemas can serve as mnemonics that guide recall. For example, if science facts are needed to solve a problem, the student whose learning has followed a schema pattern could access her set of theory schemas, then systematically search through sub-categories containing theory summaries, lists of researchers and studies, and so forth. In addition to serving a mnemonic function, schemas also can encourage learners to elaborate on incoming information in a way that causes new knowledge to become associated with prior experience. Such elaboration can occur naturally as a result of needing to fill slots in a schema. For example, if a text is vague regarding the theme, plot, or climax of a story action, the student would have to infer or imagine ways to fill those slots.

Nevertheless, as Levin (1986) has pointed out, it is important to distinguish between strategies that primarily facilitate comprehension (with learning as an incidental by-product), versus those that purposefully create or update elaborated knowledge structures. Although most schema-based strategies will tend to produce some elaboration, it is also possible to deliberately construct strategies that will strongly enhance this important phase of learning. One method is to incorporate proven elaboration tactics into the omnibus learning strategies that are assigned by teachers or used spontaneously by students. Examples of such tactics include question answering (including self-questioning), paraphrasing, summarizing, creating analogies, generative notetaking, and generating imagery. Research suggests that all of these activities increase elaborative encoding and improve recall and transfer (Dansereau, 1985; Mayer, 1987; Palincsar & Brown, 1983; Reder, 1980; Weinstein & Mayer, 1985).

Self-questioning, believed to be a powerful elaboration technique, has been incorporated into a great many omnibus learning strategies. For example, self-questioning is an integral part of the K-W-L strategy developed by Ogle (1986). Using this strategy, the student asks three questions about the reading material: What do I know about this topic? What do I want to know? and What have I learned? Questioning is also an integral part of reciprocal teaching (Palincsar & Brown, 1983), a successful reading strategy in which students take turns at being a teacher that asks important questions. The process of question answering appears to encourage inferencing and generation of new information, thus creating elaborative links between old and new knowledge.

The power of having students generate their own analogies and images during instruction has been illustrated by Linden and Wittrock (1981). In their study, children who received instructions to generate analogies and images for stories were better able to remember main ideas and answer conceptual question than were children who received regular classroom instruction. Similar results have been reported by Mayer

(1976, 1980), who instructed college students to read information segments in a computer manual and then restate each segment in terms of a familiar idea representing a concrete model. Mayer (1987) also reviewed research on generative notetaking (e.g., having students rewrite information in their own words), which produces a pattern of results consistent with the "useful knowledge" hypothesis. In sum, students who elaborate while studying not only tend to understand the ideas better, but are better able to recall conceptual information later when it is required.

Elaboration tactics, such as generating images and self-questioning, can be incorporated naturally and easily into schema-based learning strategies. For example, students using networking or outlining could be instructed to elaborate on their written summaries by generating connecting images and analogies for each idea. Marzano et al. (1988) suggested the use of "frames," schematic sets of generic questions that are developed by experts, but that can be used by students to guide their self-questioning strategies. Appropriately constructed frames could enhance focusing, structuring, and elaboration within a single omnibus learning strategy. A related example is Wittrock's (1984) questioning strategy, which not only requires students to think about passages in terms of a "Who?, What?, Where?, When?, How?, and Why?" schema, but also to generate passage summaries based on those questions. This strategy has proved effective with Army recruits.

It is not difficult to imagine many ways in which elaboration activities could be combined with schema-based learning tactics within a single, omnibus learning strategy to help produce both meaningful comprehension and useful declarative knowledge. A categorical summary of declarative learning tactics is shown as Table 11.1.

PROCEDURAL KNOWLEDGE

Much of the learning strategies research to date has focused exclusively on mental techniques for acquiring declarative knowledge. Another very important type of knowledge acquired in school is *procedural skill*. Expertise in basic subjects, like reading, writing, and mathematics, is largely a matter of having knowledge of procedures: procedures for word recognition, procedures for forming written numeric symbols and alphabetic characters, procedures for adding and subtracting multi-digit numbers, procedures for solving word arithmetic problems, and so forth. Relatively little is known about learning strategies for acquiring these types of capabilities.

According to many theorists (e.g., Anderson, 1983; E. Gagne, 1985;

TABLE 11.1
Learning Tactics That can be Used in Strategies
for Acquiring Declarative Knowledge

Tactic Category	Examples	Some Conditions of Use	Strengths or Weaknesses
Simple attentional focusing	Highlighting. Underlining.	Structured, easy materials. Good readers.	No emphasis on importance or conceptual relations of ideas.
Structured focusing	Look for headings, topic sentences. Teacher-directed signalling.	Poor readers. Difficult but considerate materials.	Efficient, but does not promote active elaboration, depth thinking.
Schema building	Use of story grammars, theory schemas. Networking	Poor text structure. When goal to encourage active analysis.	Inefficient, but develops higher-order thinking skills.
Elaboration techniques	Self questioning. Imaging. Finding analogies.	Goal is to remember ideas.	Powerful, easy to combine. Difficult for some students. unassisted. Will not insure focus on what is important.

R. Gagne, 1985), procedural knowledge differs dramatically from declarative knowledge in a number of ways. Whereas declarative knowledge represents knowing *that* something is the case, procedural knowledge represents the ability to *do* something. The result of activating procedural knowledge is not simple recall, but operations on and transformations of information. Procedural skills also differ from declarative knowledge because, when procedures are well-learned, they can be accessed and used quickly and automatically. Although activation of declarative information is relatively slow and conscious, well-learned procedural skills can be performed rapidly with little conscious effort. Consider, as examples, the speed involved in decoding printed text during reading, in generating speech during a conversation, or in applying car brakes to avoid an accident.

In previous sections of this chapter, declarative knowledge was characterized in terms of propositional networks. However, many researchers employ a different representational construct for describing how procedural knowledge resides in long-term memory. Procedural knowledge is often represented as systems composed of *condition-action rules* also called *productions* (e.g., Anderson, 1983; E. Gagne, 1985). Individual productions have an IF-clause, which specifies what conditions must be met, and a THEN-clause, which specifies the action that is taken when the conditions are met. In complex problem-solving domains, such as science and mathematics, higher-order thinking requires access to hundreds of productions. Collectively, the memory representation of all productions available for use within a performance domain is called a *production system*. Like propositional networks, production systems are viewed as abstract cognitive constructs that bear no relation to how the brain is structured in a neurophysical sense.

According to Anderson (e.g., 1983), procedural skill systems contain two basic types of productions: (a) pattern-recognition and (b) action-sequence procedures. Pattern-recognition procedures enable people to recognize conceptual patterns within their environment, that is, to "conceptualize" (Klausmeier, chap. 3 in this volume; Marzano et al., 1988). Seeing that a particular type of math problem represents a multiplicative relation is an example of pattern recognition, as is realizing the appropriate time in a tennis game to execute a lob or a forehand volley. On the other hand, action-sequence procedures underlie our abilities to actually carry out sequences of operations, such as those involved in multiplying complex numbers or executing a tennis swing.

Although in early stages of learning it is useful to separate them, the skills of conceptualizing and executing action sequences are closely related during actual performance. Klausmeier (chap. 3 in this volume) states: "Conceptualizing is considered a most basic learning process in that concepts provide the vital link between sensing environmental events and acting on what we have sensed." During problem solving, particular action sequences are needed for particular purposes, and thus they must be executed when particular cueing patterns signal that appropriate conditions exist. According to Anderson's theory (1983; Anderson et al., 1986), patterns activated in a persons' conscious working memory, and recognized by pattern-recognition productions, provide the signalling that calls particular action-sequence productions into use. This is possible because each action-sequence production is believed to be stored in long-term memory along with the conditions that signal its applicability. Thus, when conceptual patterns activated in working memory are recognized, and when these match conditions of particular productions, then an action sequence will be executed.

When the goal is to solve a complex problem, many individual productions must be selected and connected together in order to produce a problem-solving strategy. Productions are linked during performance through flow of control. Control is passed from one production to another whenever the activation of one production creates the pattern conditions needed for calling another. For example, recognizing a tennis situation requiring a forehand volley would set up conditions for executing the volley, which in turn could create conditions for rushing the net.

The learning strategies needed for acquiring the procedural skills that underlie complex performances differ markedly from those used in learning declarative knowledge. The nature of this procedural learning process will next be examined for both concept/pattern-recognition and action-sequence procedures.

LEARNING NEW PROCEDURES

Concept/Pattern Recognition

Klausmeier (chap. 3 in this volume) has proposed CLD, a comprehensive theory of *con*cept *l*earning and *d*evelopment (CLD) that has a sound foundation in research. CLD describes how a given conceptual pattern can be attained at four successively higher levels of understanding: concrete, identity, classificatory, and formal. At the concrete level, the student attends to and discriminates a pattern as an entity different from its surrounds. At the identity level, the student in addition develops the ability to recognize, as an entity, the same pattern when it is encountered in different contexts. The ability to identify differing patterns as examples of the same concept indicates concept attainment at the classificatory level. Formal understanding of a concept enables a person to define and analyze concepts in terms of their relevant and non-relevant attributes.

According to Klausmeier (chap. 3 in this volume), the ability to conceptualize is based on a set of core skills. One skill critical to all four levels is that of attending selectively to concepts and their defining attributes and rules. Another important skill at all levels is discrimination, the ability to perceive two patterns as different and to respond differently to them. A third skill, one especially important in acquiring the classificatory level of concept recognition, is generalization, which occurs whenever a person responds in a similar manner to two patterns that are different from one another, but that are alike in the sense that they represent a single concept.

Finally, two skills needed for developing formal conceptual understanding are hypothesizing and meaningful reception learning. Hypothesizing refers to a learning strategy whereby a best guess is made as to what concept is represented by a pattern. Then this hypothesis is tested against reality, leading to acceptance or rejection of the guess. Meaningful reception learning refers to the process of acquiring or refining conceptual understanding through the processing of explanatory information about the concept.

It has already been noted that in problem-solving situations, concept/pattern recognition supplies the triggering mechanism that signals usefulness of particular action-sequence productions. To insure that students recognize the full range of situations to which an action-sequence production applies, it is clear that problem-solving concepts must be acquired at least to the classificatory level. According to Klausmeier's analysis, the capability that distinguishes the classificatory level of concept development from lower levels is the ability to generalize that two or more different examples of a concept are equivalent. At the beginning of this level, only some defining attributes of a conceptual pattern may be learned, and thus sometimes the pattern will not be detected. At a more mature level, all defining attributes of a pattern have been learned so that very few instances of the concept pattern are missed. When the formal level is reached, the learner is able to analyze and describe the concept in terms of its defining attributes. A formal level of concept attainment would help insure even greater usefulness of procedural knowledge, because formal capabilities would enable students to critically analyze and produce responses even for less obvious, non-routine conceptual patterns.

Klausmeier (chap. 3 in this volume) argues that we cannot assume that concept-acquisition skills are learned by students receiving typical school instruction. He outlines several instructional procedures that can be used to help learners develop these processing skills for concept attainment. These will be mentioned again later.

Learning Action-Sequence Procedures

The learning of action sequences is a slow process, characterized by many errors. According to Anderson's theory (1983; E. Gagne, 1985), this form of procedural learning proceeds through three phases. The initial phase is to create a declarative representation for each step in the procedure. For example, the student might first learn to log onto a computer by memorizing a series of steps or rules as declarative knowledge. At this stage of learning, performance is very slow, conscious, and prone to error.

As the learner attempts to execute and practice the procedure, performance gradually becomes faster and more accurate. Anderson (1983) argued that this performance change indicates that a new form of memory code is evolving. This process of changing from a declarative to a performance-based representation involves two subprocesses: proceduralization and composition. Proceduralization, the second phase of learning action sequences, is the creating of productions, procedural encodings that no longer rely heavily on reminders and cues from declarative knowledge. One production is developed for each step in the procedure.

The third learning phase, composition, involves collapsing some of the simple, discrete productions to create larger, more efficient productions. A series of discrete productions is a less efficient means of accomplishing an action than is a single, "composed" production system. Efficient productions are not easy for learners to acquire. One reason is that the capacity of working memory limits learners' conscious awareness to about 7 (plus or minus 2) information "chunks," and this probably translates to no more than one or two productions at a time (e.g., Fletcher, 1986; E. Gagne, 1985; Miller, 1956). Thus, composition involves gradually building up large action sequences in a stepwise fashion, which is accomplished by thinking about and combining only two or three productions at a time. A second reason for difficulty is that composition requires the learner to know all component productions that will make up the final, complex procedure. Often, students do not possess the prerequisite skills that are required for learning the more complicated performance.

There are advantages and disadvantages to creating highly efficient, composed production systems. A major advantage is that learners can execute composed action systems easily without devoting much conscious attention. This frees attentional resources for other activities. For example, driving a car involves using a number of highly composed procedures that coordinate clutching, braking, and accelerating. These systems of behavior are so highly coordinated that most people can perform them effortlessly while listening to the radio or carrying on a conversation with passengers. However, one disadvantage of composition is that it can lead to inflexible performance, which can be detrimental in many situations. For example, proper braking during a skid differs from normal procedure. If individuals learn to habitually solve a given type of problem in one way, they may be unable to deal with less common problem variations that require modifications to the procedures as originally learned.

THE IMPORTANCE OF USEFUL
PROCEDURAL KNOWLEDGE

I have talked recently to several scholars and teachers who appear to be downplaying the role of basic procedural learning in classrooms that emphasize higher-order problem solving. One current trend in problem-solving instruction favors approaches based on deliberate reflective thinking, described by Baron (1981) as ". . . a type of thinking that considers options and reasons before choosing a course of action or adopting a belief" (p. 291). Although I applaud this trend, I am also concerned that the current emphasis on reflection may tempt some into viewing procedural skills as lowly routine performances that are relatively easy to learn, and that should take a back seat in modern curricula to the so-called higher-order thinking capabilities.

This would be a mistake for several reasons. First, it must be recognized that although many real-world problem situations do call for reflective thinking, there also are many, many problems for which reflective thinking is highly inappropriate. In general, reflective thinking will be a viable problem-solving strategy when there is adequate time for it. In reality, however, people are required to perform both routine and non-routine tasks with a high degree of accuracy and speed. That is, they are expected to respond like experts, not only on specialty tasks associated with their jobs, but also on everyday problems, like determining the best buy on fabric softener. Consider the time pressures faced daily by pilots, surgeons, air-traffic controllers, nuclear power-plant operators, soldiers, classroom teachers, even parents. Consider the rate of response expected of these people in emergency situations! Not all problems merit reflective thinking, and time constraints may even prohibit it. Unfortunately, the luxury of time may be available only after many decisions have been made, when people have an opportunity to reflect on their successes and mistakes and hopefully to learn from them.

In this sense, it is argued that a very important response system in everyday living is *reflexive,* as compared with reflective, thinking. Reflexive thinking is characterized by the rapid construction and execution of action sequences that provide optimizing solutions to complex problems. Reflexive thinking often must produce adequate, even creative, solutions to complicated problems. Everyday competence requires the ability to think reflexively. Schools can help students develop reflexive capabilities by helping them develop rapid execution of many useful procedural skills, including concept-recognition and action-sequence skills. These skills should be practiced both individually and in realistic problem-solving situations that require their timely integration. In addition, students

might be taught learning strategies that will help them acquire procedural knowledge throughout life as autonomous learners.

LEARNING STRATEGIES FOR ACQUIRING
USEFUL PROCEDURAL KNOWLEDGE

Can students be trained to employ learning strategies that will facilitate
acquisition of basic procedural skills? This question is on the current
learning-strategies research agenda, but has not yet been fully investigated. Although hundreds of studies have examined the effects of learning-
strategies training on acquisition of declarative knowledge, few have
looked at procedural learning in that light. Nevertheless, some guiding
principles can be derived from instructional research, which has increased our knowledge of learning practices that facilitate procedural
learning. The types of procedural learning strategies suggested by this
research are summarized in Table 11.2 and discussed in the following
sections.

Strategies for Concept Learning

When students learn new concepts in any subject, they are acquiring
pattern-recognition procedures that can be used in problem solving.
Teachers and instructional materials can enhance the concept-learning
process in a number of different ways, as reported by Klausmeier in his
chapter. For example, concept learning is enhanced when the examples
that are used to help teach the concept are controlled (e.g., E. Gagne,
1985; Klausmeier & Feldman, 1975). When learners are given concept
examples that are very different from one another, except on the specific
relevant attributes that define the concept, generalization at the classificatory level is encouraged. On the other hand, discrimination learning
is encouraged by comparing examples of a concept to non-examples. In
early phases of discrimination learning, examples and non-examples
should differ only on those important critical attributes that define the
concept. For instance, the concept of rectangle is more easily discriminated from the concept of triangle if drawings of the two concepts are
identical on every respect, except for the number of sides.
    Although a number of successful instructional techniques have been
developed for concept acquisition, less is known about the efficacy of
teaching students concept learning strategies to employ on their own as
autonomous learners. However, there is some evidence that teaching

TABLE 11.2

Categories of Learning Tactics for Acquiring Procedural Knowledge

Tactic Category	Examples	Some Conditions of Use	Strengths or Weaknesses
Hypothesizing	Student reasons and guesses why particular pattern is or is not example of concept.	Goal is to learn attributes of concepts and patterns.	Inefficient unless feedback given. Encourages independent thinking.
Seeking reasons for actions	Student seeks explanations why particular actions are or are not appropriate.	Goal to determine which procedures required in which situations.	Develops metacognitive knowledge. Inefficient if not guided. If too guided, might not promote thinking skills.
Using examples and nonexamples	Student asked to identify examples and nonexamples of concept pattern.	Goal to promote generalization and discrimination of concept patterns.	If student selects examples, slow, inaccurate learning possible. Feedback essential.
Algorithms	Student is taught algorithm for identifying concept.	Student having difficulty with particular pattern.	Possible rote learning with no holistic understanding of idea. Does not encourage automaticity.
Reflective self-instruction	Student compares reification of own performance to expert model.	Goal is to tune, improve complex skill.	Develops understanding of quality performance. May increase self-consciousness, reduce automaticity.
Part practice	Student drills on one specific aspect of performance.	A few specific aspects of a performance need attention.	Develops subskill automaticity. Does not encourage subskill integration.
Whole practice	Student practices full performance without attention to subskills.	Goal to maintain or improve skill already acquired, or to integrate subskills.	May consolidate poorly executed subskills. Helps develop smooth whole performance, provided prerequisites learned.

368

concet-learning strategies could be beneficial. Klausmeier (chap. 3 in this volume) reports a study in which experimental subjects benefited from being taught an algorithmic strategy for determining whether an instance was or was not a concept. He also suggests that training students to formulate and test hypotheses about concepts can help them acquire formal understanding. In sum, providing students with metacognitive knowledge in the form of rules and strategies for concept acquisition may help encourage higher levels of conceptualizing. More research is sorely needed in this area.

Strategies for Acquiring Action Sequence Procedures

Collins (1987) and Lesgold and Magone (1987) suggested that students be encouraged to reflect on and analyze their performances as they learn to combine procedures in complex problem-solving situations. Lesgold and Magone speculated that students who develop this strategy may eventually be able to teach themselves, so long as they have an expert model. Both researchers have developed computer-based instructional systems designed to encourage and facilitate this self-instructional process. Collins' system monitors students as they attempt to solve geometry problems. The system presents two reifications on the screen: one of the student's problem-solving session and one that represents the performance of an expert problem solver. Students are encouraged to evaluate their performance by comparing it with the expert approach. The purpose of this method is to help students acquire metacognitive knowledge that will lead to better problem-solving strategies. This method is compared to common practice in sports psychology, whereby players analyze videotapes of their own performance and compare them with videotapes of experts.

In fact, similar procedures could be used in the classroom, without the aid of a computer or videotaping equipment. Teachers and instructional materials could provide performance models or reifications for students to emulate. It should be possible to train students to take better advantage of these classroom models. More research on the benefits of reflective self-instruction is needed.

Practice

Reflectively analyzing one's own performance style by comparing it to expert performance may prove to be an excellent learning strategy for acquiring problem-solving capability in a complex domain. However, in all but the most trivial subject areas, this training procedure alone will not create experts. Even after a problem-solving performance is thoroughly understood in a declarative sense, it must be proceduralized. In any non-trivial domain of performance (e.g., chess, tennis, mathematics, composing), true expertise can follow only from many years of actually performing. Even the most talented of experts spend much of their lives in practicing their specialties. The expert performance style that results is characterized by smooth, rapid, and automatic processing, as distinguished from the deliberate, slower performance of an "expert novice" (Heller & Hungate, 1985). As every sports coach knows, the most powerful pedagogical technique for building this expertise is practice. Practice is equally essential for developing expertise in cognitive domains.

Two types of practice strategies are possible: part drills and whole drills (Schneider, 1985). With part drills, one attempts to improve a complex performance by practicing individual subskills that are used in that performance. For example, students might practice their multiplication or square root tables as a strategy for improving their performance in algebra. Or they might practice their tennis backhand in an attempt to improve their tennis. The basic idea underlying part practice is to improve subskill automaticity. To the extent that subskills can be executed without much effort, more working-memory resources are made available for concentrating on the higher-order aspects of performance.

Another drill strategy is whole training, which involves practicing variations of whole, complex tasks, often under mild speed stress. For example, students in air-traffic controller training practice on simulators that create real-world problem situations. The purpose of whole training is to develop facility in accessing and combining lower-order subskills, and in using them to produce rapid solutions to real-world problems.

There are several things that students should be taught about practice. First, that it is an extremely important activity. If one wishes to develop expertise in any complex performance domain, then practice is essential. Second, expertise does not develop automatically, nor does it develop in one session. Schneider (1985) has argued that automation of even fairly simple subskills can require thousands of practice trials, and this number increases substantially for complex skills. However, this practice must be spaced out over a period of time, rather than massed into a few sessions. Intuitively we know that expertise at chess, tennis, or mathematics often develops slowly, over an entire lifetime. But students should be reminded of the common sense notion that skill comes easily for no one. Becoming an expert at anything means very hard work.

AUTONOMOUS LEARNING

The focus thus far has been on strategies for acquiring traditional subject matter in a form that renders it both meaningful and useful. I now ask whether there are strategy-training methods that can insure the usefulness of the learning strategies themselves. Useful strategy knowledge creates autonomous learners who can recall and utilize previously learned strategies whenever appropriate conditions warrant.

Autonomous learning is a complex activity involving: (a) analysis of learning situations; (b) production of appropriate learning strategies; (c) evaluating the success of each learning effort; and (d) when necessary, revising learning strategies. Researchers agree that a problematic goal for schooling is to produce autonomous learners. Unfortunately, it is often the case that students who can correctly execute learning strategies when instructed to do so will fail to use them spontaneously when appropriate situations arise outside of class (Brown & Campione, 1984; Deshler, Schumaker, & Lenz, 1984). The search for instructional methods that can produce self-regulated learners is also part of our current research agenda in cognitive psychology, and interesting new teaching concepts are emerging as a result of this search.

Informed Training. One idea gaining wide acceptance is the notion of "informed strategies training." According to Campione et al. (1982) and Pressley et al. (1984), this procedure enhances direct strategy instruction with training on the utility of target strategies and on how and when they should be used. Deshler, Schumaker, Lenz, and Ellis (1984) reported evidence that even poor students can learn to analyze learning situations and generate their own strategies. Studies have shown that informed training is superior to "blind training" (Campione et al., 1982) in producing transfer and use of specific learning tactics (Pressley et al., 1984). Throughout this chapter it has been suggested that teachers can help develop students' learning skills by devising, assigning, and explaining learning strategies, and by providing feedback on strategy use. These established classroom practices would seem to be excellent vehicles for conveying information about the utility of strategies and when they should be employed.

Prompting. It is now widely accepted that metacognitive knowledge about when to use particular strategies is a prerequisite for self-regulated learning (e.g., Pressley et al., 1984). However, Derry and Murphy (1986) argued that although utility information may be necessary, it will not always be sufficient condition for insuring spontaneous strategy initiation, especially for learning-disabled and low-achieving students. They believe that the skills of self-regulation evolve slowly through intensive, long-term practice. Thus, students must be provided with opportunities for selecting their own learning tactics in a variety of learning situations, and for receiving corrective feedback concerning selection as well as execution.

Derry and Murphy (1986) recommended a practical instructional procedure based on fading prompts. Prompts are brief reminders, inserted into regular classroom instruction, for the purpose of helping students recall previously learned strategies at times when their use is appropriate. During early phases of training, the teacher explicitly points out situations that call for particular types of strategies, and instructs students to use these strategies. Gradually over time, the level of instructional support is faded, so that students are encouraged toward autonomous strategy initiation. Derry, Jacobs, and Murphy (1987) pointed out that additional research on this technique is needed. However, their study indicated that prompting does not interfere with learning of primary instructional material, and that it may enhance the efficiency of the instructional process.

Deshler's Teaching Method.   Deshler, Schumaker, and Lenz (1984) described an eight-step teaching model that has led to maintenance and transfer of learning strategies taught to learning-disabled adolescents. The steps in this model are:

1. Pretest on target learning strategy.
2. Provide rationale for learning strategy.
3. Describe target strategy.
4. Model use of strategy.
5. Induce verbal rehearsal of strategy.
6. Provide for controlled practice.
7. Give positive and corrective feedback.
8. Posttest learning strategy.

Deshler et al. (1984) also recommended that strategy instruction emphasize the characteristics of settings in which learning skills are likely to be useful. They noted that there are various levels of strategy transfer, and that casual efforts to induce transfer will not be successful with learning-disabled students.

General Learning Models.   A fourth procedure for encouraging autonomous learning involves teaching students to view each learning situation as a problem to be solved, and to apply a general problem-solving procedure to help them devise a learning strategy. Such general prob-lem-solving procedures are taught in addition to specific learning tactics and strategies, and are viewed as methods for helping students orches-trate the specific skills. Many researchers (e.g., Baron, 1981; Bransford & Stein, 1984; Polya, 1957) believe that intelligent problem solving in general proceeds according to a plan with the following steps: (a) prob-lem analysis; (b) developing a plan; (c) carrying out the plan; (d) evaluat-ing the results; and if necessary, (e) modifying the plan. Thus, a general plan for studying might reflect these stages. For example, Derry et al. (1987) taught soldiers to utilize the 4C's to develop plans for reading and solving word problems. The 4C's stood for: Clarify situation, Construct strategy, Carry out strategy, and Check results. In their program, stu-dents also were taught specific processing tactics that could be used to help implement each stage of the general plan.

One presumed advantage to such plans is that they remind students to stop and think reflectively about each learning situation prior to pro-ceeding with the task (Baron, 1981). Also, the plan is supposed to serve as a mnemonic device that will help students recall previously learned specific tactics associated with each step (Derry & Murphy, 1986, p. 8). However, more research on use of such plans is needed. There is some support for the idea. For example, Belmont, Butterfield, and Ferretti (1982) reviewed 121 studies of attempts to teach cognitive skills to chil-dren, only 7 of which provided training in a general problem-solving plan. Six of these 7 studies reported maintenance and transfer of cog-nitive skills in new situations, whereas the other studies reported no transfer.

On the other hand, although many strategies training programs have included a general problem-solving plan in the course of instruction (e.g., Dansereau et al., 1979; Derry et al., 1987), few have examined the added advantage explicitly due to that plan. A dissertation experiment recently conducted by John Jacobs, one of my graduate students, failed to demonstrate that adding a general study plan increased performance over what occurred as a result of informed training. Furthermore, work by Derry and Kellis (1986) suggests that adequate general plans are spontaneously generated by both low- and high-ability adult learners. The major difference between these groups occurs in their choice of specific learning tactics.

In sum, four instructional procedures have been suggested for help-ing students become autonomous learners. These are: informed train-ing, which embellishes direct strategies instruction with information about when to use specific types of learning techniques; fading prompts that remind students to recall and use previously-learned strategies; an

8-step teaching technique that includes steps for explanation, modeling, and practice of strategies; and instruction in general problem-solving models that remind students to analyze their learning situations, and to devise, carry out, and check their strategies. Although further evaluation of these techniques is called for, all represent potentially useful approaches that might conveniently be implemented during classroom instruction.

CONCLUDING COMMENTS

In order for knowledge to be usable, it must be well constructed. Learning strategies for acquiring declarative knowledge can help students:

1. Focus on main ideas.
2. Organize these ideas within hierarchically structured networks.
3. Connect main ideas to one another and to prior knowledge through elaboration.

Such well-structured, well-elaborated declarative knowledge is likely to be recalled in a usable form when it is needed.

More research is needed to develop better learning strategies for acquiring useful procedural knowledge. We do know that:

1. Well-learned conceptualizing and action-sequence procedures are important because they enable students to think reflexively in situations that demand accurate, rapid response.
2. Learning strategies that engender appropriate use of examples during learning may help students acquire important concept-recognition procedures.
3. Reflective self-instruction and strategic practice may be able to help students acquire action sequence procedures.

Teachers can train students to employ learning strategies while accomplishing their classroom assignments. In addition, students can be moved toward the goal of spontaneous initiation of learning strategies. I have reviewed a number of principles and example techniques that researchers have used to stimulate the learning of useful declarative and procedural knowledge. As Ellen Gagne (1985) has pointed out, however, the list of available procedures that can be generated from these principles is limited only by the knowledge and imagination of the teacher or the designer of instruction.

ACKNOWLEDGMENTS

This work was partially supported by NSF Grant No. IST-851094.

REFERENCES

Anderson, J. R. (1983). *The architecture of cognition.* Cambridge, MA: Harvard University Press.
Anderson, J. R., Boyle, C. F., Corbett, A., & Lewis, M. (1986). *Cognitive modelling and intelligent tutoring* (Tech. Rep. No. ONR-86-1). Pittsburgh, PA: Carnegie-Mellon University.
Baron, J. (1981). Reflective thinking as a goal of education. *Intelligence, 5,* 291–309.
Bartlett, F. C. (1932). *Remembering.* Cambridge, MA: Cambridge University Press.
Belmont, J. M., Butterfield, E. C., & Ferretti, R. P. (1982). To secure transfer of training instruct self-management skills. In D. K. Detterman & R. J. Sternberg (Eds.), *How and how much can intelligence be increased* (pp. 147–154). Norwood, NJ: Ablex.
Biggs, J. B. (1979). Individual differences in study processes and the quality of learning outcomes. *Higher Education, 8,* 381–394.
Bransford, J. D., Franks, J. J., & Sherwood, R. S. (1987, April). *Knowledge and thinking.* Paper presented at annual meeting of the American Educational Research Association, Washington, DC.
Bransford, J. D., Franks, J. J., Vye, N. J., & Sherwood, R. D. (1986, June). *New approaches to instruction: Because wisdom can't be told.* Paper presented at a Conference on Similarity & Analogy, University of Illinois; Champaign-Urbana.
Bransford, J. D., & Johnson, M. K. (1972). Contextual prerequisites for understanding: some investigations of comprehension and recall. *Journal of Verbal Learning and Verbal Behavior, 11,* 717–26.
Bransford, J., Sherwood, R., Vye, N., & Rieser, J. (1986). Teaching thinking and problem solving. *American Psychologist, 41,* 1078–1089.
Bransford, J. D., & Stein, B. S. (1984). *The ideal problem solver: A guide for improving thinking, learning, and creativity.* New York: Freeman.
Brown, A. L. (1978). Knowing when, where and how to remember: A problem of metacognition. In R. Glaser (Ed.), *Advances in instructional psychology* (Vol. 7, pp. 55–113). Hillsdale, NJ: Lawrence Erlbaum Associates.
Brown, A. L. (1980). Metacognitive development and reading. In R. J. Spiro, B. C. Bruce, & W. F. Brewer (Eds.), *Theoretical issues in reading comprehension* (pp. 453–481). Hillsdale, NJ: Lawrence Erlbaum Associates.
Brown, A. L., & Campione, J. C. (1984). Three faces of transfer: Implications for early competence, individual differences, and instruction. In M. Lamb, A. Brown, & B. Rogoff (Eds.), *Advances in developmental psychology* (Vol. 3, pp. 143–192). Hillsdale, NJ: Lawrence Erlbaum Associates.
Campione, J. C., Brown, A. L., & Ferrara, R. A. (1982). Mental retardation and

intelligence. In R. J. Sternberg (Ed.), *Handbook of human intelligence* (pp. 392–490). Cambridge, England: Cambridge University Press.

Collins, A. (1987, April). *Cognitive apprenticeship and instructional technology.* Paper presented at the annual meeting of American Educational Research Association, Washington, DC.

Cook, L. K. (1982). *Instructional effects of text structure-based reading strategies on the comprehension of scientific prose.* Unpublished doctoral dissertation, University of California, Santa Barbara.

Cook, L. K., & Mayer, R. E. (1983). Reading strategies training for meaningful learning from prose. In M. Pressley & J. R. Levin (Eds.), *Cognitive strategy research: Educational applications* (pp. 87–126). New York: Springer-Verlag.

Dansereau, D. F. (1978). The development of a learning strategy curriculum. In H. F. O'Neill, Jr. (Ed.), *Learning strategies* (pp. 1–29). New York: Academic Press.

Dansereau, D. F. (1985). Learning strategy research. In J. W. Segal, S. F. Chipman, & R. Glaser (Eds.), *Thinking and learning skills* (Vol. 1, pp. 209–240). Hillsdale, NJ: Lawrence Erlbaum Associates.

Dansereau, D. F., Collins, K. W., McDonald, B. A., Holley, C. D., Garland, J. C., Diekhoff, G. M., & Evans, S. H. (1979). Development and evaluation of an effective learning strategy program. *Journal of Educational Psychology, 79,* 64–73.

Derry, S. J., Jacobs, J., & Murphy, D. A. (1987). The JSEP learning skills training system. *Journal of Educational Technology Systems, 15* (4), 273–284.

Derry, S. J., & Kellis, A. (1986). A prescriptive analysis of low-ability problem-solving behavior. *Instructional Science, 15,* 49–65.

Derry, S. J., & Murphy, D. A. (1986). Designing systems that train learning ability: From theory to practice. *Review of Educational Research, 56* (1), 1–39.

Deshler, D. D., Schumaker, J. B., & Lenz, B. K. (1984). Academic and cognitive Interventions for LD adolescents: Part I. *Journal of Learning Disabilities, 17,* 108–117.

Deshler, D. D., Schumaker, J. B., Lenz, K., & Ellis, E. (1984). Academic and cognitive interventions for LD adolescents: Part II. *Journal of Learning Disabilities, 17,* 170–179.

diSibio, M. (1982). Memory for connected discourse: A constructivist view. *Review of Educational Research, 52,* 149–174.

Flavell, J. H. (1979). Metacognition and cognitive monitoring: A new area of psychological inquiry. *American Psychologist, 34,* 906–911.

Flavell, J. H. (1981). Cognitive monitoring. In W. P. Dickson (Ed.), *Children's oral communication skills* (pp. 35–60). New York: Academic Press.

Fletcher, C. R. (1986). Strategies for the allocation of short-term memory during comprehension. *Journal of Memory and Language, 25,* 43–58.

Frase, L. T. (1973). Integration of written text. *Journal of Educational Psychology, 65,* 252–261.

Gagne, E. D. (1985). *The cognitive psychology of school learning.* Boston: Little, Brown.

Gagne, R. M. (1985). *The conditions of learning* (4th ed.). New York: Holt, Rinehart & Winston.

Heller, J. I., & Hungate, H. N. (1985). Implications for mathematics instruction of research on scientific problem solving. In E. A. Silver (Ed.), *Teaching and learning mathematical problem solving: Multiple research perspectives* (pp. 83–112). Hillsdale, NJ: Lawrence Erlbaum Associates.

Jones, B. F., Amiran, M., & Katims, M. (1985). Teaching cognitive strategies and text structures within language arts programs. In J. W. Segal, S. F. Chipman, & R. Glaser (Eds.), *Thinking and learning skills* (Vol. 1 pp. 259–297). Hillsdale, NJ: Lawrence Erlbaum Associates.

Kintsch, W. (1977). On comprehending stories. In M. A. Just & P. A. Carpenter (Eds.), *Cognitive processes in comprehension* (pp. 33–62). Hillsdale, NJ: Lawrence Erlbaum Associates.

Klausmeier, H. J., & Feldman, K. V. (1975). Effects of a definition and varying numbers of examples and nonexamples on concept attainment. *Journal of Educational Psychology, 67,* 174–178.

Lesgold, A., & Magone, M. (1987, April). *Procedural skills of thinking and problem solving.* Paper presented at the annual meeting of American Educational Research Association, Washington, DC.

Levin, J. R. (1986). Four cognitive principles of learning-strategy instruction. *Educational Psychologist, 21* (1 & 2), 3–17.

Linden, M., & Wittrock, M. C. (1981). The teaching of reading comprehension according to the model of generative learning. *Reading Research Quarterly, 17,* 44–57.7.

Loman, N. L., & Mayer, R. E. (1983). Signaling techniques that increase the understandability of expository prose. *Journal of Educational Psychology, 75,* 402–412.

Marzano, R. J., Brandt, R., Hughes, C., Jones, B. F., Presseisen, B., Rankin, S., & Suhor, C. (1988). *Dimensions of thinking: A framework for curriculum and instruction.* Alexandria, VA: Association for Supervision and Curriculum Development.

Mayer, R. E. (1976). Some conditions of meaningful learning for computer programming: Advance organizers and subject control of frame sequencing. *Journal of Educational Psychology, 68,* 143–150.

Mayer, R. E. (1980). Elaboration techniques that increase the meaningfulness of technical text: An experimental test of the learning strategy hypothesis. *Journal of Educational Psychology, 72,* 770–784.

Mayer, R. E. (1987). Instructional variables that influence cognitive processes during reading. In B. Britton & S. Glynn (Eds.), *Executive control processes in reading* (pp. 201–216). Hillsdale, NJ: Lawrence Erlbaum Associates.

Mayer, R. E., & Bromage, B. K. (1980). Different recall protocols for technical texts due to advance organizers. *Journal of Educational Psychology, 72,* 209–225.

Mayer, R. E., Dyck, J., & Cook, L. K. (1984). Techniques that help readers build mental models from science text: Definitions, training and signalling. *Journal of Educational Psychology, 70,* 514–522.

McKeachie, W. J. (1984). Spatial strategies: Critique and educational implications. In C. D. Holley & D. F. Dansereau (Eds.), *Spatial learning strategies: Techniques, applications, and related issues* (pp. 301–312). Orlando, FL: Academic Press.

Meyer, B. J. F. (1975). *The organization of prose and its effects on memory.* New York: American Elsevier.

Meyer, B. J. F. (1977). The structure of prose: Effects on learning and memory and implications for educational practice. In R. C. Anderson, R. J. Spiro, & W. E. Montague (Eds.), *Schooling and the acquisition of knowledge* (pp. 179–200). Hillsdale, NJ: Lawrence Erlbaum Associates.

Miller, G. A. (1956). The magical number seven plus or minus two: Some limits on our capacity for processing information. *Psychological Review, 63,* 81–97.

Minsky, M. (1985). *The society of mind.* New York: Simon & Schuster.

Ogle, D. (1986). The K-W-L: A teaching model that develops active reading of expository text. *The Reading Teacher, 39,* 564–70.

Palincsar, A. S., & Brown, A. L. (1983). *Reciprocal teaching of comprehension-monitoring activities* (Tech. Rep. No. 269). Urbana, IL: Center for the Study of Reading, University of Illinois.

Paris, S. G., & Lindaur, B. K. (1982). The development of cognitive skills during childhood. In B. Wolman (Ed.), *Handbook of developmental psychology* (pp. 333–349). Engelwood Cliffs, NJ: Prentice-Hall.

Polya, A. (1957). *How to solve it.* Garden City, NY: Doubleday-Anchor.

Pressley, M., Borkowski, J. G., & O'Sullivan, J. T. (1984). Memory strategy instruction is made of this: Metamemory and durable strategy use. *Educational Psychologist, 19,* 94–107.

Pressley, M., Borkowski, J. G., & Schneider, W. (1987). Cognitive strategies: Good strategy users coordinate metacognition and knowledge. In R. Vasta & G. Whitehurst (Eds.), *Annals of child development* (Vol. 4, pp. 80–129). Greenwich, CT: JAI Press.

Pressley, M., Goodchild, F., Fleet, J., Zajchowski, R., & Evans, E. D. (in press). The challenges of classroom strategy instruction. *Elementary School Journal.*

Rankin, S., & Hughes, C. (1987, April). *The Rankin-Hughes list of selected thinking skills and its implications for curriculum and instruction.* Paper presented at the annual meeting of American Educational Research Association, Washington, DC.

Reder, L. M. (1980). The role of elaboration in the comprehension and retention of prose: A critical review. *Review of Educational Research, 50,* 5–53.

Rickards, J., & August, G. J. (1975). Generative underlining strategies in prose recall. *Journal of Educational Psychology, 67,* 860–865.

Rumelhart, D. E., & McClelland, J. L. (1986). *Parallel distributed processing: Explorations in the microstructure of cognition* (Vol. 1). Cambridge, MA: MIT Press.

Rumelhart, D. E., & Norman, D. A. (1981). Analogical processes in learning. In J. R. Anderson (Ed.), *Cognitive skills and their acquisition* (pp. 335–360). Hillsdale, NJ: Lawrence Erlbaum Associates.

Schneider, W. (1985). Training high-performance skills: Fallacies and guidelines. *Human Factors, 27,* 285–300.

Snowman, J., & McCown, R. (1984, April). *Cognitive processes in learning: A model for investigating strategies and tactics.* Paper presented at the annual meeting of the American Educational Research Association, New Orleans, LA.

Spiro, R. J., Vispoel, W. P., Schmitz, J. G., Samarapungavan, A., & Boerger, A. E. (1987). Knowledge acquisition for application: Cognitive flexibility and transfer in complex content domains. In B. K. Britton & S. M. Glynn (Eds.), *Executive control processes in reading* (pp. 177–200). Hillsdale, NJ: Lawrence Erlbaum Associates.

Stein, B. S., Bransford, J. D., Franks, J. J., Owings, R. A., Vye, N. J., & McGraw, W. (1982). Differences in the precision of self-generated elaborations. *Journal of Experimental Psychology: General, 111,* 399–405.

Thorndyke, P. W. (1977). Cognitive structures in comprehension and memory of narrative discourse. *Cognitive Psychology, 9,* 77–110.

Winograd, T. (1975). Frame representations and the declarative/procedural controversy. In D. G. Bobrow & A. Collins (Eds.), *Representation and understanding:* Studies in cognitive science (pp. 185–210). New York: Academic Press.

Wittrock, M. C. (1984). *Teaching reading comprehension to adults in basic skills courses* (Vol. 2). (MDA 903-82-C-0169). Alexandria, VA: U.S. Army Research Institute.

Weinstein, C. E., & Mayer, R. E. (1985). The teaching of learning strategies. In M. C. Wittrock (Ed.), *Handbook of research on teaching* (3rd ed.) (pp. 315–327). New York: Macmillan.

Teaching Thinking and Content Knowledge: Toward an Integrated Approach

John D. Bransford, Nancy Vye,
Charles Kinzer, Victoria Risko
Vanderbilt University

In 1979, Lochhead and Clement edited a volume on *Cognitive Process Instruction* and began their preface with the following quotation from a college student: "They should have a course to teach you how to learn . . . all they have is courses on what to learn" (p. iii). Lochhead and Clement went on to explain that their volume represented the thinking of people who were" . . . reawakening the 19th century belief that education can improve the functioning of the mind through training, and that the role of the University is not just to pass on information . . ." (p. iii). They argued that a major function of universities—and presumably of all forms of schooling—is to help students improve their abilities to learn productively and think more clearly (see also Derry, this volume). As Mann noted in his history of cognitive process training (1979), this latter belief has a long and distinguished history.

In 1987, several authors published books that emphasized the need for culturally relevant knowledge (e.g., Hirsch, 1987; Ravitch & Finn, 1987). They also argued that schools were failing to provide students with knowledge of their cultural heritage. For example, Ravitch and Finn (1987) discussed the existence of serious gaps in 17-year-olds' knowledge of history and literature. The authors of these books suggested that a major reason for these gaps was that many curricula were based on faulty educational theories that over-emphasized the teaching of general processes and skills and that involved "content neutral" lessons (e.g., Hirsch, 1987). In general, these authors argue that more attention should be paid to *what* students learn.

Our goal in this chapter is to explore relationships between general processes of thinking and learning and specific knowledge of particular content. Our discussion is divided into three parts. First, we provide a brief overview of the literature indicating the importance of specific knowledge for thinking and learning. Our discussion will be brief because excellent reviews of this literature are available elsewhere. This literature is important because it illustrates the powerful roles that specific knowledge plays.

In the second portion of this chapter we address the following question: If specific knowledge is so important for thinking, why not simply emphasize the acquisition of new content knowledge? We argue that this approach to instruction will not suffice. The major reason is that the acquisition of factual content by no means guarantees that students will develop organized knowledge structures that guide subsequent thinking. They therefore fail to use relevant knowledge even though it could help them solve subsequent problem-solving tasks.

In the third section of this chapter we explore the possibility of emphasizing general processes and specific content in ways that mutually strengthen one another. We do so by discussing the principles of an approach to instruction that we call anchored instruction—an approach designed to teach accessible knowledge. Some illustrations of our initial attempts to use anchored instruction to merge content and process are discussed.

THE IMPORTANCE OF SPECIFIC KNOWLEDGE

A passage adapted from one written by McCarrell and Brooks (cf. Bransford & Stein, 1984) provides an excellent illustration of the role of specific knowledge in guiding language comprehension. Read it through once and try to understand it.

> Sally first let loose a team of gophers. The plan backfired when a dog chased them away. She then threw a party but the guests failed to bring their motorcycles. Furthermore, her stereo system was not loud enough. Obscene phone calls gave her some hope until the number was changed. It was the installation of blinking neon lights across the street that finally did the trick. Sally framed the ad from the classified section and now has it hanging on her wall. (p. 51)

Most people have difficulty understanding the passage about Sally. If you are in this situation, it is instructive to notice what effects this can have. One is that it is relatively difficult to remember what Sally did.

Another is that you are unable to answer a host of inference questions. For example:

1. Where did Sally put the gophers?
2. Why did Sally want the guests to bring motorcycles?
3. Whose number was changed?
4. Who probably made the calls?
5. What did the advertisement say?

If you fail to understand the letter about Sally, it is extremely difficult to answer such questions.

The passage becomes much more comprehensible when one is supplied with appropriate information. This information allows people to remember more effectively as well as to answer inference questions. The information required to understand the passage about Sally involves information about her goal, namely, that she is trying to get a neighbor to move. Given this information, it is instructive to read the passage again and to then try to answer inference questions such as those just noted.

ADDITIONAL ILLUSTRATIONS OF THE
ROLE OF CONTENT KNOWLEDGE

The passage about Sally was specially designed to let people experience the changes in their own comprehension processes before and after the activation of relevant knowledge (see also Bransford & Johnson, 1972; Dooling & Lachman, 1971). Even though the passage was specially designed, it is important to note that a great deal of research suggests that the availability of relevant knowledge to guide inferences that fill in the gaps in messages is important for any type of communication (e.g., R. Anderson, 1984).

Consider a story taken from a fourth-grade reader. The story contained statements like the following: "The Indians of the Northwest Coast lived in slant-roofed houses built of cedar plank. . . . Some California Indian tribes lived in simple earth-covered or brush shelters. . . . The Plains Indians lived mainly in teepees. . . ."

The story provided no information about why certain Indians chose certain houses, and no attempt was made to explain how the area where Indians lived related to the kinds of houses they built. Adults reading this story might be able to make these assumptions on their own, but children are likely to have difficulty doing so. Without this extra information, the relationships between particular Indian tribes and their houses seem arbitrary, and we should expect story comprehension and memory to suffer.

Specific knowledge is also necessary for problem solving. As an illustration, consider a problem discussed by Sherwood, Kinzer, Bransford, and Franks (1987). In the movie, *Raiders of the Lost Ark*, Indiana Jones attempts to remove a golden idol from a cave. The idol is booby trapped, so he tries to compensate for its weight by replacing it with a small bag of sand. If we assume that the idol is solid gold and that its volume is approximately 2,000 cubic centimeters (about the size of a $\frac{1}{2}$-gallon carton of milk), how might we get a relatively precise estimate of its weight without using any gold objects or a scale?

This problem can be solved by referring to a table of densities. The latter will indicate that the density of solid gold is 19.3 grams per cubic centimeter; it is an extremely dense metal (the density of lead is only 11.2 grams per cubic centimeter). On earth, a solid gold idol with a volume 2,000 cubic centimeters would weight approximately 60 pounds.

People who know nothing about density would be unable to solve the golden idol problem. Slight variations of the problem (e.g., the goal might be to determine the weight of the idol on the moon or under 10 feet of water on the earth) require even more knowledge. In general, specific knowledge is extremely important for most problems that people confront (e.g., Newell, 1980; Simon, 1980).

As we noted earlier, there is a vast research literature on the role of content knowledge in problem solving. Much of the research on the role of knowledge in learning has explored the importance of scripts and schemas for comprehension (e.g., Anderson, 1984; Anderson & Pearson, 1984; Bransford, 1984; Nelson, Fivush, Hudson & Lucariello, 1983; Pearson & Raphael, this volume; Schank & Abelson, 1977). Other researchers have begun to develop theories of how activated knowledge is used to create mental models that guide processes of comprehension, inference and reasoning (e.g., Brewer & Nakamura, 1984; Johnson-Laird, 1985; Kintsch, 1979; Van Dijk, 1987). In addition, the literature on differences between experts and novices in particular domains shows clearly that a major reason for these differences involves the nature and organization of people's knowledge (e.g., Chase & Simon, 1973; Chi, Feltovich, & Glaser, 1981; see Bransford, Sherwood, Vye, & Rieser, 1986; Glaser, 1984 for an overview of this research). Many researchers also argue that the knowledge available to individuals is more important for predicting their success in jobs and everyday settings than are their scores on traditional intelligence tests (e.g., Ceci & Liker, 1986; Wagner & Sternberg, 1986). Overall, the evidence is overwhelming that people's abilities to think and solve problems is affected considerably by the nature and organization of the knowledge that they have already acquired.

ACCESS AND THE PROBLEM OF INERT KNOWLEDGE

Given the importance of specific content knowledge for thinking and problem solving, it seems reasonable to assume that the best course for educators is to teach content directly. This is hardly a novel idea, of course; educators have been trying to do this for centuries. An important question is whether current research can tell us anything new about ways to teach knowledge.

We argue that modern research does indeed contain some new information. It provides guidance in arranging learning experiences so that students acquire usable knowledge rather than what Whitehead (1929) called inert knowledge (knowledge that is not used in new problem-solving contexts even though it is relevant). These ideas are explored shortly. First, however, it is useful to try to use your own knowledge (in this case your knowledge of fractions) to solve a problem. Please work the following problem as quickly as you can.

A Problem Involving Fractions

A spy wants to hide a roll of secret film that he has reduced to $\frac{1}{8}$ inch in diameter and $2\frac{1}{4}$ inches in length. Looking at the bookshelf (see Figure 12.1) he notices the two-volume desk-top encyclopedia series. The spy uses a drill that is $\frac{1}{4}$ inch in diameter. He begins on page 1 of volume 1 and drills straight through to the last page of volume 2. Assume that the cover on each book is $\frac{1}{4}$ inch thick and that each book without its cover is 1 inch thick. Will the microfilm fit? How long is the hole?

We have given this problem to over 100 college students, the majority of whom missed it. Their difficulties did not stem from a lack of knowledge; instead, it stemmed from a failure to access relevant information that they actually knew quite well.

The most frequent mistake made by our students is that they overestimated the length of the hole because of failure to consider their knowledge of how pages are arranged in a book. Look at volume 1 in Figure 12.1. The first page is on the right side of the book as you are viewing it. Similarly, the last page of Volume II is on its left side. Therefore, the spy only drilled through the two covers. The hole is too short for the film.

Studies of Access

The preceding study illustrates a failure to access knowledge that is relevant for problem solving. When people reflect on their own experiences, most agree that there are many instances where they fail to reason

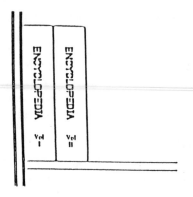

FIG. 12.1.   Encyclopedia Problem.

effectively or solve problems because of a failure to access previously
acquired knowledge (e.g., Bransford & Nitsch, 1978). People may fail to
think of "obvious" (in hindsight) counterexamples to their arguments
(counterarguments that they already knew about); or they may answer
someone's questions and only later realize that they knew other information that would have been much more relevant. People may also fail to
use relevant strategies that, on reflection later, would have been appropriate to use (Borkowski, Carr, Rellinger & Pressley, this volume; Bereiter, 1984; Paris & Winograd, this volume).

In recent years, several groups of researchers have begun to conduct
controlled studies of access in laboratory settings—studies that involve a
different methodology from the more typical ones that simply ask students to recognize or recall previously acquired information. An experiment by Gick and Holyoak (1980) represents a case in point.

Gick and Holyoak presented college students with the following passage about a general and a fortress:

> A general wishes to capture a fortress located in the center of a country.
> There are many roads radiating outward from the fortress. All have been
> mined so that while small groups of men can pass over the roads safely, a
> large force will detonate the mines. A full-scale direct attack is therefore
> impossible. The general's solution is to divide his army into small groups,
> send each group to the head of a different road, and have the groups
> converge simultaneously on the fortress. (p. 309)

Students memorized the information in the passage and were then
asked to use it to solve the tumor problem that is illustrated next.

You are a doctor faced with a patient who has a malignant tumor in his stomach. It is impossible to operate on the patient, but unless the tumor is destroyed the patient will die. There is a kind of ray that may be used to destroy the tumor. If the rays reach the tumor all at once and with sufficiently high intensity, the tumor will be destroyed. At lower intensities the rays are harmless to healthy tissue, but they will not affect the tumor either. What type of procedure might be used to destroy the tumor with the rays, and at the same time avoid destroying the healthy tissue? (p. 307–308)

Few college students were able to solve this problem if they were not provided with hints. In contrast, when students were asked to use the information in the fortress problem to solve the ray problem, over 90% were able to solve the problem. These students perceived the analogy between dividing the troops into small units and using a number of small-dose rays that each converge on the same point—the cancerous tissue. Each ray is therefore too weak to harm tissue except at the convergence point.

Guided Versus Spontaneous Access

Note that the group in the Gick and Holyoak study that scored 90% on the ray problem was *explicitly informed* that information about the fortress was relevant. In most problem-solving situations we do not have the luxury of someone telling us which aspect of our knowledge is relevant. If we cannot access relevant knowledge spontaneously, it does us little good.

From the perspective of spontaneous access, the most interesting part of the Gick and Holyoak study involved a group of college students who also memorized the fortress story and were then presented with the ray problem. However, students in this group were not explicitly told to use the information about the fortress to solve the problem involving rays. For this group of students, the solution rate for the ray problem was only 20%. These results illustrate the value of using the "spontaneous access" methodology (see also Asch, 1969; Stein, Way, Benningfield, & Hedgecough, 1986; Weisberg, DiCamillo, & Phillips, 1978). People may be able to retrieve and use knowledge when explicitly asked to do so yet fail to spontaneously access it or use it. Under these conditions, the knowledge does them little good.

It is not difficult to imagine a number of situations in which knowledge can be explicitly recalled but not spontaneously used. In history, for example, people can learn to recall facts on demand. However this provides no guarantee that they will spontaneously use lessons from history to solve current problems that they face.

Additional Studies of Access

The analogy between the fortress problem and the ray problem is not as direct as it could be. For example, the low intensity rays are used to protect the healthy tissue. In contrast, in the fortress problem the smaller groups of soldiers are used to protect the soldiers themselves rather than any innocent people (analogous to healthy tissue) in the enemy camp.

Because of the indirect analogy, it is possible that the Gick and Holyoak study overestimates the degree to which relevant knowledge remains inert. A study conducted by Perfetto, Bransford, and Franks (1983) was designed to explore issues of access with materials that were much more directly related to the problems to be solved.

College students were asked to solve problems such as the following:

1. Uriah Fuller, the famous Israeli superpsychic, can tell you the score of any baseball game before the game starts. What is his secret?

2. A man living in a small town in the U.S. married twenty different women in the same town. All are still living, none of them has divorced him and he has never divorced any of them. Yet, he has broken no law. Can you explain?

Most college students have difficulty answering these questions unless provided with clues. Before solving the problems, some students were given clues that were clearly relevant to each problem's solution. These students first received statements such as "Before it starts, the score of any game is 0 to 0"; "A minister marries several people each week." The students were then presented with the problems and explicitly prompted to use the clue information (which was now stored in memory) to solve them. Their problem-solving performance was excellent. Other students were first presented with the clues and then given the problems but they were not explicitly prompted to use the clues for problem solution. Their problem-solving performance was very poor; in fact, it was not significantly better than that of baseline students who never received any clues. These findings were very surprising to Perfetto et al., (1983) but they have been replicated many times.

A number of researchers have also found that knowledge of general *strategies* may remain inert unless people are explicitly prompted to use them. For example, children may be taught to (a) organize lists of pictures and words into common categories, (b) rehearse the category names during learning, and (c) use the names as retrieval cues at time of test. Data indicate that, when the children are explicitly encouraged to use such strategies, their memory performance improves. However, when later provided with new lists and asked to learn them, the children frequently fail to spontaneously use their clustering strategies unless they are explicitly prompted to do so. Their knowledge of relevant strategies therefore remains inert. (Borkowski et al., this volume; Brown & Campione, & Day, 1981; Lodico, Ghatala, Levin, Pressley, & Bell, 1983; Paris, Newman, & McVey, 1982; Paris & Winograd, this volume).

Reasons for Access Failures

Why might human information processing systems frequently produce access failures? Are human systems simply inefficient, or are there good reasons why we often fail to gain access to information that was previously acquired?

One answer to the preceding question is that, in general, a lack of access to previously acquired information is adaptive. Access needs to be selective. It would hurt us if we always had to consciously think through everything that we know.

This point can be clarified by considering research with experts such as chess masters (Chase & Simon, 1973; deGroot, 1965). They found that masters did not think of a greater number of possible moves than did the lesser skilled players. The masters' thoughts differed in terms of quality rather than quantity. For the masters, the best set of potential moves seemed to be accessed; they simply seemed to "come to mind."

Imagine what would happen if the experts' ability to access relevant information had not been selective. They would have thought of every possible move at each point in the game. Because of limitations on their working memory, they would have had to search through each of these moves in order to separate the good ones from the poor ones. This is a very inefficient process that takes a great deal of attentional capacity and time.

As another illustration of advantages of selective access, imagine talking with a friend whom you see nearly every day. If you tried, you could undoubtedly retrieve a number of memories about experiences that the two of you have shared recently, but you do not want such memories to automatically come to mind every time you see your friend. If they did you would be deluged with information that would interfere with your current thoughts.

The Importance of Conditionalized Knowledge

Overall, research on spontaneous access illustrates the importance of what Simon (1980) calls "conditionalized knowledge." Theorists such as J. Anderson (1987), Larkin (1979), Newell (1980) and Simon (1980) argue that an extremely important aspect of learning involves knowledge about the conditions under which knowledge is applicable. Without knowledge of these conditions, knowledge does us little good and is often misapplied.

Imagine a person who could remember, and provide accurate paraphrases for, a long list of proverbs. Proverbs contain wise advice that can be very useful, but the mere ability to remember and paraphrase these proverbs is a far cry from wisdom. The wise individual knows when each proverb is applicable. This becomes especially clear when one notes that many proverbs contradict one another. Examples include "Many hands make light work" versus "Too many cooks spoil the broth"; "He who hesitates is lost" versus "Haste makes waste." Wise individuals have conditionalized their knowledge. They know when to do what.

Selective Access Versus No Access

Note that there are presumably no occasions when people have absolutely no access in a situation. We always activate some aspect of our knowledge that is potentially relevant, we may simply fail to access those aspects of our knowledge that are especially relevant. This may be a major reason why erroneous but habitual ways of viewing various events (these are often referred to as misconceptions) are often so difficult to change (e.g., Eaton, Anderson, & Smith, 1984; Roth, this volume; Silver & Marshall, this volume; Tweney & Walker, this volume). It is one thing to be able to explicitly retrieve a newly-taught theory or model for interpreting various phenomena. It is a different matter to spontaneously access that knowledge when thinking about everyday events. These events are more likely to provide cues for accessing old knowledge that, despite being a misconception from a scientific perspective, has provided a useful way of thinking about the world.

FACILITATING ACCESS

So far in this chapter we have made two general arguments. The first is that specific content knowledge is necessary in order to comprehend and reason effectively and to solve problems. The second is that attempts to teach new knowledge as facts are not sufficient. Factual information can often be recalled when it is specifically requested, but this by no means guarantees that it will be used spontaneously in new situations.

Our goal in this section is to discuss some approaches to instruction that are designed to teach specific content knowledge in the context of problem solving. Our argument will be that this helps students acquire content knowledge in a way that renders it more accessible in later, transfer situations. In addition, this approach to instruction can help students learn general procedures for learning and thinking that can help them continue to learn about new domains.

An Experimental Demonstration
of Problem-Oriented Learning

Experiments conducted by Adams, Kasserman, Yearwood, Perfetto, Bransford, and Franks (1988) and Lockhart, Lamon, and Gick (1988) illustrate how procedures that help students experience the usefulness of information can facilitate access. These experiments represent an extension of the Perfetto et al. (1983) studies that were discussed earlier. Recall that in these earlier studies, college students did not spontaneously access relevant information even though it had just been presented. For example, despite having just learned the answer (i.e., that the score of a game before it begins is 0 to 0), students were unable to state how a superpsychic could predict the score of any game before it began.

In the original experiment by Perfetto et al., students first studied statements such as "The score of any game before it begins is 0 to 0." Imagine a slight change in the learning situation. In the new situation students are presented with statements in the following manner: "It is easy to guess the score of any game before it begins; the score is 0 to 0." This mode of presentation should help students identify and define a problem; namely, that it is not clear why it should be easy to guess the score of any game. After the initial problem identification, the answer "the score is 0 to 0" becomes a tool for solving the problem rather than a mere fact.

Data from Adams et al. (1988) and Lockhart et al (1988) show that, given this latter learning situation, students were much more likely to spontaneously access relevant knowledge than were those who received the information in the original format. By being helped to see the conditions under which knowledge was useful, the students were much more likely to use it spontaneously later on.

Experiencing the Value of Information

Problem-oriented learning situations can also help students appreciate the value of information. More specifically, it can help students understand differences between "knowing X" and "thinking to use X." In a recent paper (Bransford, Sherwood, Hasselbring, Kinzer, & Williams, in press) we discuss a situation in which college students were asked to rate the usefulness (on a 7-point scale) of factual statements such as the following: "The score of any game before it begins is 0 to 0"; "A minister may marry several people each week" (Bransford et al., in press). Not surprisingly, students indicated that these facts were not all that useful. Their ratings tended to be: "Not useful—I knew this already."

Contrast the preceding findings with ones in which the same sets of facts were rated. However, this time the facts were presented in the context of problem solving. One of the problems that students were trying to solve was: "A superpsychic can predict the score of any game before it begins. How is this possible?" A second problem was "A man living in a small town in the U.S. married several different women in the same week yet he divorced none of them and broke no laws. Explain." When the facts just noted were presented in these contexts, students rated them as very valuable (the ratings tended to be "Extremely useful: They produced an insight"). The students were able to experience the difference between "knowing X" and "thinking to use X." They realized that they had not spontaneously accessed this knowledge when they were attempting to solve the problems during the first part of the task.

The Importance of Multiple Perspectives

It is instructive to note that, even in the successful access studies that used problem-oriented acquisition (Adams et al., 1988; Lockhart et al., 1988), there was a definite similarity between the acquisition experiences and the test situations involving transfer. In general, access seems to be strongly affected by similarity between acquisition and test (Bransford et al., in press; Gick & Holyoak, 1983; Stein et al., 1986).

The fact that access is affected by similarity between acquisition and test makes it especially important for students to have the opportunity to experience the same problem from a variety of perspectives. For examples, consider a problem such as finding ways to reduce the number of bruises on tomatoes (Adams, 1979). A mechanical engineer's approach might be to make the mechanical tomato pickers less likely to bruise tomatoes. A transportation expert might try to find ways to protect tomatoes during shipping. A biologist might try to create a strain of tomatoes that is less likely to be bruised. A fourth approach might be to develop an extremely fast-growing tomato seed that can be shipped directly to the consumer. The ability to take multiple perspectives on a problem (to define it from a variety of perspectives) is an especially important aspect of problem solving (e.g., Bransford & Stein, 1984). Different ways of presenting information affect the probability that students will spontaneously view new problems from multiple points of view.

We recently conducted a study in which college students were first exposed to a variety of perspectives such as the four previously mentioned (Vye, Bransford, & Franks, in preparation). Students in one group read about each perspective in a different context. Better methods of shipping were discussed in the context of watermelons, the idea of creating a fast growing product that could be shipped to consumers as seeds was discussed in the context of peaches, and so forth. Students in a second group read about the application of each perspective to a single context (i.e., watermelons).

Following an acquisition phase, all the students were given a problem about reducing bruises on tomatoes and asked to generate as many ideas as possible. The test measured spontaneous access; students were not explicitly prompted to use the information from the first part of the experiment. Students who had read about each perspective in a single context (the watermelon context) generated ideas that represented twice as many perspectives as did subjects in the other group.

Problems With Many Curricula

At one level the results of the multiple perspectives study seems obvious. Students who have had the opportunity to see how a variety of different ideas each affect their thinking about a single problem should be more likely to take multiple perspectives given subsequent problems.

We noted earlier that there are important differences between "knowing X" and "thinking to use X." The idea of multiple perspectives appears to be an intuitively obvious idea, but it also appears to be an idea that often is not used in the design educational curricula. Curricula often introduce different ideas in different contexts. In most basal readers, for example, students are introduced to different components of story grammars. Each component is often introduced in a different story rather than in a single story. Similarly, in many attempts to teach learning and problem-solving skills, different components (e.g., how to memorize, categorize, compare, etc.) are taught in the context of different examples. At a more general level, traditional curricula are organized so that science, mathematics, reading, writing, and so forth all tend to be taught in different contexts rather than integrated into single contexts (Bransford et al., in press). Research in the area of access suggests that these approaches to instruction may be much less optimal than they need to be.

THE CONCEPT OF ANCHORED INSTRUCTION

Recently, we have been working with a number of colleagues at Vanderbilt (especially Bob Sherwood, Ted Hasselbring, Susan Williams, Laura Goin, & Tom Sturdevant) to develop design principles for instruction that facilitate the acquisition of useful knowledge. Our current work is exploring the value of anchoring instruction in rich macro-contexts that permit problem finding, exploration, and discovery (Bransford et al., in press). The goal of the anchor is to enable students to identify and define problems and to attempt to construct their own ideas about problems to be solved and strategies for solving them. Students can then be introduced to information that is relevant to their anchored perceptions; they therefore are able to see whether they thought to use an idea or concept even though they may have known it already (see the earlier discussion of knowing X vs. thinking to use X). *The major goal of anchored instruction is to let students experience the changes in their perception and understanding of the anchor as they view the situation from multiple points of view.* We also want the students to experience the effects of *sustained thinking* about a problem area over a reasonably long period of time (e.g., a minimum of weeks).

Theorists such as Dewey (1910) and N. R. Hanson (1970) noted that opportunities to experience changes in perceiving and understanding are common to experts in a discipline. They have been immersed in phenomena and are familiar with how they have been thinking about them. When introduced to new theories, concepts, and principles, they can experience the changes in their own thinking that these ideas afford (this also allows them to elaborate on and evaluate the new information). For novices, however, the introduction of concepts and theories often seem like the mere introduction of new facts to be memorized. Because the novices have not been immersed in the phenomena being investigated, they are unable to experience how the new information can guide their thinking in new ways.

An Illustration of Anchored Instruction

As an illustration of an initial use of anchored instruction in the classroom, consider a study with college honors students (freshman and sophomores at Vanderbilt). We wanted to work with honors students because we believe that anchored instruction can be extremely valuable even for students who do well in traditional, academic settings. As part of an assignment, the students were asked to read an article entitled "Reactions to Response-Contingent Stimulation in Early Infancy" (Watson & Ramey, 1972). A sample is provided here:

When a stimulus consistently follows an individual's response, the situation is set for instrumental learning. If the stimulus is rewarding and the individual is capable of learning, the response should become more frequent. Thus, the traditional learning analysis would ask whether the response is affected by the situation (e.g., does the response become more frequent, stronger, etc.). In this paper, we shall ask this standard learning question in an analysis of the effectiveness of a special learning situation which was arranged for young infants.

The paper continued with a description of the contingency situation set up for infants in the experimental group (i.e., a movement-activated mobile) and control groups (a non-contingent mobile). Results were then discussed.

Vanderbilt students—especially honors students—are certainly able to learn from the article. They can paraphrase what the issue was, what was measured, and what was found. Nevertheless, the students essentially learn a set of facts about what someone else had done (in Dewey's terminology, they learned about records of others' accomplishments).

Consider an alternate approach to uses of the Watson and Ramey article. The goal of this approach was to help students experience the processes involved in attempting to learn about learning in infants. In order to achieve this goal, we attempted to recapture some of the experiences that would be available to an expert in learning research or in infant research. A major advantage available to the expert is that she or he can imagine the situation being studied; he or she has a rich mental model of the phenomenon and the difficulties in designing and interpreting the results of various experiments. Furthermore, experts know how they have been thinking about the area and hence are in a better position to appreciate and evaluate the ideas about the area that others may suggest. Novices try to imagine these types of situations but, because of a lack of knowledge, their mental models are impoverished. This makes learning less effective and less fun.

We asked some honors students at Vanderbilt to first study a videodisc of a 6-month-old infant who was exposed to a voice-activated mobile. The students were able to experience the changes in the infant's reactions to the mobile over time and to try to decide whether the infant actually caught on to the contingency. Because the video was on a videodisc, the students could easily return to various sections of the video and explore the actions and expressions in considerable detail.

All the students concluded that they could not be sure whether the infant had learned the contingency. Even more difficult was the decision about whether the infant understood the contingency between the actions of the mobile and her voice (the mobile moved and played a tune for 12 seconds and then stopped). The students were then asked to state how they would conduct experiments to convince themselves that infants could learn a contingency and understand what they were doing. Finally, they read articles like the Watson and Ramey article that was quoted earlier.

The presence of the video had very positive effects—even for the honors students who were quite skilled at learning from text. The students were able to experience first-hand the difficulties of interpreting the behavior of the infant in the video, and their attempts to design their own studies provided them with an excellent basis for comparison when they finally read the research literature. In general, the students who first saw the video were able to experience a complex problem (how to decide whether the infant learned and understood) and experience the changes in their own thinking as they were attempted to clarify the situation for themselves and as they were introduced to others' thinking. In contrast, students in the "read only" group essentially memorized basic statements. They did not have the opportunity to first experience a complex problem and to then experience the changes in their own noticing and understanding that came about through discussion with their peers and then through the readings.

Essays from students in the videodisc group were very interesting, in part, because they contained insightful discussions of the strengths and weaknesses of the articles that they read. For example, the students in the video group were very appreciative of some of the elegant design principles that Watson and Ramey thought of (the students' initial design ideas were often less elegant). Thus, Watson and Ramey used a very simple way to measure responses, and they used a response and mobile-type that was different from the ones shown on the videodisc. Students noted these details and were able to compare them with the procedures on the videodisc. The students were also excellent at determining the kinds of conclusions that were warranted by the data gathered by Watson and Ramey. The students' initial experiences with the infants' gestures and gazes in the video (they were trying to use this gauge "understanding") helped them realize that the Watson and Ramey article provided no information about whether the infants really understood the contingency. The only information was that response frequency had increased.

Some Design Principles in Anchored Instruction

Several aspects of the design of the preceding instruction are noteworthy. First, the instruction began with a video that enabled students to experience the difficulty of interpreting learning and insight. This is very different from beginning a lesson with typical educational video that simply illustrates the activities of scientists. The goal in anchored instruction is to help students identify and define their own problems. Rather than being an "advance organizer" (Ausubel, 1960, 1968), the video might be considered an "advance disorganizer" that is designed to stimulate questions and puzzlement (Bransford, 1984).

A second point about the video can be appreciated by considering it as a prereading exercise that is given prior to reading the Watson and Ramey article. In typical prereading exercises, students are verbally prompted to access knowledge that is relevant for a passage or story they are reading (e.g., Spiegel, 1981). Prior to reading the Watson and Ramey article, we could have asked students to state what they believed about infants' learning, what they thought might be problems in studying infants, and so forth. A problem with this approach is that students who have not had a great deal of experience studying infants do not have detailed knowledge of the phenomenon; therefore, there is little to access. An additional problem is that the teacher asks the questions rather than the students. In the videodisc context, our students were given the opportunity to notice whatever they felt was important. Different students noticed different things, but they for the most part noticed information that was valid and interesting to note.

A similar point about the importance of knowledge for the phenomenon being studied is relevant to the use of teaching procedures such as reciprocal teaching (Palincsar & Brown, 1984). Our college honors students had excellent skills of summarizing, predicting, and so forth. However, even for these students, if one were to ask them to take the role of teacher and lead a class discussion, they could do so in a much more effective manner if everyone in the class had a rich knowledge of the phenomena being discussed.

One additional point about our use of the infant videodisc anchor is that, ideally, the goal is to approach it from a variety of perspectives rather than only one perspective. For example, our students read additional articles. Some introduced new ideas about experimental design (e.g., the use of a within subject design rather than the between subject design used by Watson & Ramey) but did so in the context of studies with animals. Other articles introduced ideas about individual differences and ways that they might be measured by dynamic learning tasks but the articles involved experiments on 4-year-olds rather than infants. Other articles explored the value of learning contingencies for subsequent transfer. For students in the control group, readings such as these are not seen as closely related to one another. For students in the anchored group, each reading suggested new issues and questions about the video. Students could see how their thinking changed as they approached the issue from multiple points of view.

Varieties of Anchors

We do not mean to imply that the anchors in anchored instruction must always be based on video. Case-based approaches to instruction provide an excellent illustration of anchored instruction that relies on a verbal mode. These have been used in business schools for some time, and for many of the reasons that we discussed earlier. In 1940, Gragg lamented that traditional forms of instruction failed to prepare business students for action. The students knew a lot of facts and concepts but failed to use them to make effective business decisions. In case-based approaches, students first begin with cases that represent problems-to-be-solved. As they are introduced to new concepts and frames for thinking, they see the effects of this information on the problems they confront.

Programs such as Lipman's "Philosophy for Children" (Lipman, 1985) and Wales and Stager's "Guided Design" (1977) are also excellent illustrations of anchored instruction. Lipman's program is centered around novels involving children who encounter a number of problems in their everyday lives and at school. They learn to use a variety of methods from philosophy for exploring these problems. In "Guided Design", students are introduced to relevant knowledge from experts; the knowledge is also presented in the context of working on interesting, complex problems that the instructors present.

We like video-based anchors because they appear to have a number of advantages. The most important is that they contain much richer sources of information than are available in the printed media (and also than in many computer programs that have limited graphics). In the video, gestures, affective states, scenes of towns, music, and so forth always accompany the dialogue. Therefore, there is much more to notice. This increase in opportunities for noticing is especially important for increasing the possibility of finding relevant issues that are embedded in the video—it provides an opportunity to encourage problem finding and problem representation (e.g., Bransford & Stein, 1984) rather than to always provide preset problems to students. In addition, the richness of information to be noticed increases the opportunity to help students appreciate how their perception and comprehension change as they are helped to view the video from multiple points of view.

The reader may see some similarities between anchored instruction and "unit instruction," an approach popular in the 1950s and 1960s (Beauchamp, 1959). They share Dewey's (1910) notion that education is more than the transmission of knowledge, that it involves understanding the utility and consequence of knowledge. In addition, both use "theme-based" instruction instead of the separate-subject approach (i.e., math, social studies, science) that is typically used in schools. However, there are some major differences between the approaches. One obvious difference relates to the use of video in the anchored approach. Perhaps more importantly, a closer look at what constitutes a theme and its associated activities reveals fundamental differences. Anchored instruction is problem-oriented and activities are logically related to the problem. Unit instruction, as we have seen it instantiated, is topic-oriented (e.g., What are some types of transportation?), and as a result, the choice of unit activities appears more arbitrary (e.g., take a bus trip, learn to recognize different kinds of airplanes). We suspect therefore that the unit approach would be less effective for developing usable knowledge.

THE NEED TO DECONTEXTUALIZE

An important assumption underlying anchored instruction is that, eventually, there is a need to decontextualize the learning by helping students bridge from the anchored context to other contexts. Nevertheless, we assume that students first need to develop relatively firm expertise in the initial context before this bridging takes place.

Research by Nitsch (1977) provides useful information about the advantages of contextualized learning followed by attempts to bridge to other contexts. Working with college students, Nitsch taught concepts that were potentially applicable to a wide variety of contexts. For example, the concept *crinch* was defined as: "To make someone angry by performing an inappropriate act." This concept was applicable to a variety of contexts such as (a) restaurants (The man argued about the prices on the menu); (b) antique stores (The customer flicked cigarette ashes on the newly refinished antique chest), (c) races (The spectator at the dog races jumped up on his seat and blocked the view of the people seated behind him) and so forth.

Another concept was *minge,* which was defined as: "To gang up on a person or thing." This was also applicable to a variety of contexts. In the restaurant context, for example, an illustration might be "The customers surrounded the sleeping cook." For the racing context an example would be "The spectators all booed the judges' long-delayed decision."

In one of her experiments, Nitsch investigated the effects of learning in same context versus varied context conditions. For all conditions, students first heard the 6 concept definitions and then received a set of examples (e.g., The diner failed to leave a tip). They indicated which concept each example represented (in this case crinch) and received feedback about the correct answer. This method of learning proceeded until each student could correctly identify all 24 examples that were used during training (6 concepts and 4 examples of each).

Students in the same versus varied context conditions received different types of examples during training. For those in the same context conditions, each of the 4 examples of a concept were in the same context. Thus, all examples of crinch involved restaurants, all examples of minge involved cowboys, and so forth. This condition is illustrated in the top half of Table 12.1.

Students in the varied context condition received examples of each concept that came from a variety of contexts. Examples of varied-context training items used for crinch and minge are illustrated in the bottom half of Table 12.1.

After all students had learned to correctly identify the training exam-

TABLE 12.1
Same-Context and Varied-Context Examples

Same-Context Examples:

Crinch: Originally used by waitresses
         To make someone angry by performing an inappropriate act.
    The diner failed to leave a tip.
    The man argued about the prices on the menu.
    The customer deliberately knocked the ketchup on the floor.
    The man complained because the waitress was too slow.

Minge: Originally used by cowboys.
        To gang up on a person or thing.
    The three riders decided to converge on the cow.
    Four people took part in branding the horse.
    They circled the wolf so it could not escape.
    All six cowboys fought against the rustler.

Varied-Context Examples:

Crinch: Originally used by waitresses
         To make someone angry by performing an inappropriate act.
    The cowboy did not remove his hat when he went into the church.
    The spectator at the dog races jumped up on his seat and blocked the
        view of the people seated behind him.
    The customer flicked cigarette ashes on the newly refinished antique
        chest.
    The man complained because the waitress was too slow.

Minge: Originally used by cowboys
        To gang up on a person or thing
    The band of sailors angrily denounced the captain and threatened a
        mutiny.
    A group in the audience booed the inept magician's act.
    The junk dealer was helpless to defend himself from the three thieves.
    All six cowboys fought against the rustler.

NOTE. Adapted from Nitsch (1977).

ples (e.g., to correctly state that "All six cowboys fought against the rustler" was an example of minge), they were given a transfer test. This test included examples of concepts that had not occurred during training. Thus, a new test item might be "The students surrounded the lazy professor" and students would indicate which concept is represented (minge). Results indicated that the two types of training had powerful effects on transfer. Students in the varied context condition were excellent at correctly identifying new examples of each concept. In contrast, the performance of students in the same context condition was quite poor.

The fact that students in the varied context group showed better transfer is not particularly surprising. It seems obvious that people need to experience variability in examples in order to acquire useful concepts. Nevertheless, Nitsch also found a large disadvantage for varied context training.

Recall that Nitsch trained all her participants until they learned to correctly identify each of the 24 training items (4 examples for each of 6 concepts). Only after achieving initial learning were they given the transfer test (you cannot transfer if you have not learned). We noted that the varied context group performed well on the transfer test, but students in this group had a much more difficult time learning than did students in the same context group. In the varied context group, students kept getting various concepts confused. After the experiment, they reported that the experience was very frustrating to them.

In one study, Nitsch created a *hybrid group* that was designed to facilitate initial learning as well as transfer. First, all students learned in the same context condition. After they could identify the contextualized concepts relatively effortlessly, they were given a few trials with varied context examples. Following this they received the transfer test. Students in the hybrid group did extremely well on the transfer test. Furthermore, they learned easily during initial acquisition. They were spared the strong sense of confusion and frustration that had been experienced by students in the varied context group.

THE YOUNG SHERLOCK PROJECT

We close this chapter by describing an ongoing project that uses anchored instruction to help students learn skills of problem finding, problem solving, and reasoning while also learning relevant content. The students involved in the project were fifth-grade students. The content we taught involved social studies (including geography and history), language arts, and science. The project has gone on for approximately 1 year and still needs refinement. Nevertheless, it provides an interesting anchor for future analysis and thought.

We call our project the Young Sherlock Project because it is anchored primarily in the movie (on videodisc) *The Young Sherlock Holmes*. Sherlock provides an excellent model of problem solving. He is a master at attending to significant details in order to solve crimes. In addition, the Young Sherlock film provides a model of a story that can be compared to other stories, including written mysteries. Furthermore, the setting for the movie is turn-of-the-century Victorian England. This provides an opportunity to help students develop a mental model of what it is was like to live during this time in history. The goal of helping student acquire a useful mental model is different from merely getting them to remember an isolated set of historical facts (e.g., the dates of the Victorian Era, the name of Victoria's Prime Minister, etc.).

Some of the design principles underlying the Young Sherlock Project become clearer if we contrast them with other possibilities. Imagine, therefore, that we had merely shown the students the movie a number of times so that they could recall its various aspects. Assume that students could recall (a) the overall story; (b) ways that Sherlock modeled good problem solving; and (c) facts about turn-of-the-century England. All this information could be useful. Nevertheless, data on spontaneous access suggest that this type of information would probably not be spontaneously used in new problem-solving contexts. Thus, it is doubtful that the students would become better problem solvers simply because they could remember characteristics of good problem solving that Sherlock exhibited. Similarly, it is doubtful that the ability to recall facts about Victorian England would have a powerful effect on the information students noticed when reading a book or seeing a video about turn-of-the-century America. These ideas are elaborated in the following discussion.

BEING A DETECTIVE VERSUS
LEARNING FACTS ABOUT A DETECTIVE

We asked our students to be detectives rather than simply learn about the characteristics of detectives. Movies and books about Sherlock Holmes are not explicitly designed to do this—readers and viewers do not get the opportunity to notice clues before Sherlock finds them. We are treated to his successes but rarely have a chance to test ourselves.

The availability of Young Sherlock on videodisc allows us to ask our students to "play Sherlock" and explore a number of features. One of our goals was to get students to use targeted vocabulary words that were useful for describing scenes in the video—words such as *perceptive, imaginative, pompous,* and so forth. Note that an emphasis on using words to describe scenes is different from the experience of simply being asked to supply definitions when presented with words. Part of our goal was to get students to spontaneously use words rather than merely be able to define them when explicitly asked.

We also asked students to check the details of the Sherlock movie for authenticity. This provides an excellent opportunity for them to notice problems and opportunities and to learn content as well. For example, early in the Sherlock film a young Watson notes that he is in London in December in the middle of the Victorian Era. This 10-second scene contains a number of clues that students can explore in more detail. For example, where is London? (Ideally all middle school students know, but unfortunately many do not.) Does it really snow in London, and if so, does it snow in December? (Students can read the geography sections of many of their texts to find out about climate.) What was the Victorian Era and when was its height? (This brings in relevant information about history.) Assuming that the date is the 1880s to 1890s, is it accurate for Watson to be riding in a horse-drawn carriage rather than using other transportation such as a car? Does the movie begin as a true Sherlock story should (i.e., with Watson as the narrator)?

Other scenes invite inquiry into the nature of dress in England in the 1880s, the type of lighting (when was electric lighting invented?), and the types of schools (Watson attends a boarding school). Still other scenes show a pedal-powered airplane (clearly a fantasy but a nice prompt for reading about the history of aviation plus about modern pedal-powered planes), a chemistry lesson (which according to our expert is factually and historically accurate), a gym class that involves fencing, scenes just outside of London that involve mountains, and so forth. The movie provides a wealth of issues that can be explored.

To help them view the setting from multiple content perspectives, we introduced the students to a frame for guiding their noticing (e.g., Jones, Palincsar, Ogle, & Carr, 1987). The frame was our "Steps Toward Greater Comprehension" Framework (abbreviated as the STEPS plus G framework). The framework was designed to help students learn what to look for in order to increase the richness of their comprehension of texts and movies.

As was true with our vocabulary instruction (shown earlier), we assumed that our STEPS plus G framework had to be used rather than merely memorized. Students were asked to revisit the Watson scene and other relevant scenes from young Sherlock in order to look for and categorize clues according to Social information (e.g., clothes, customs), Technological information (e.g., transportation, electric lights), Economic information (e.g., natural resources, products manufactured), Political information (e.g., system of government, voting rights), Scientific information (e.g., advances in medicine), and Geographic information (e.g., weather, climate). The students and teachers shared their clues and discussed how they assigned information to the content categories. Students found this task to be highly motivating, in part because it is impossible for anyone to notice every detail in a video. Students were able to see how ideas from their peers changed their perceptions of a situation that they had previously seen.

EVALUATING ACCURACY AND COMMUNICATING IDEAS

Issue-finding activities such as the ones just discussed provide a meaningful goal for reading about the Victorian era. Students were asked to use multiple text passages that we collected relevant to the Victorian Era to verify the accuracy of the information they generated from the film. The goal for this activity was to determine if the director of the film was accurate in his representation of London in the winter of the Victorian Era. The students worked in small groups to view video scenes again and study relevant texts.

Students in our middle school project were encouraged to "play Sherlock" and check the details of the Sherlock movie for authenticity. This provided an excellent opportunity for them to notice problems and opportunities and to learn content as well.

Each group presented the results of its "investigations" to the other class members. At the end of the unit, students were asked to develop multi-media presentations by combining text with the videodiscs. This made the presentations extremely interesting to watch (the students' teachers were surprised at the attentiveness of all students for the others' presentation). In addition, it allowed students to become familiar with some of the more powerful tools of the 20th century: the computer coupled with the videodisc. Projects included a travelogue for Victorian England and a video diary of a person transported back through time to the height of the Victorian Era. In another project, students produced a newscast set in the 1880s. Each group member was a reporter and reported on different components of the STEPS plug G framework (one student was the economics reporter). The students did an outstanding job of capturing the newscast genre.

WRITING WELL-FORMED STORIES

We also used the Young Sherlock anchor to provide a context for help-ing students learn about the structural elements necessary to construct cohesive and meaningful stories. Part of this work involved instruction in the story grammar elements that underlie well-formed narratives.

In most basal readers, students are introduced to story grammar ele-ments. However, we noted earlier that each element is often introduced in the context of a different story. For example, students may read a folk tale and be asked to focus on examples of characteristics differentiating the personality traits of the protagonist and antagonist. In another lesson, students may read a mystery and discuss the concept of setting. After reading a different story, an adventure story for example, students may be asked to sequence the plot events. In such a curriculum, story elements are taught in different and unrelated contexts. This is the type of situation that we want to avoid.

We used the Young Sherlock anchor to illustrate the relatedness of story structure elements. In one episode, for example, Watson meets Sherlock for the first time at the private boarding school they are both attending. Before Watson can introduce himself, Sherlock displays his perceptive abilities by relying on visual and physical clues to describe Watson's parentage, place of residence before coming to school, eating habits, and goals for education. Watson then verifies the accuracy of Sherlock's hypotheses. From this episode, the setting of the school was examined, the personality traits of Sherlock were identified, and the plot structure was traced—from the initiating event of Watson entering Sher-lock's room, to establishing Sherlock's goal to characterize Watson, and to the goal resolution and Watson's subsequent reaction. Our students then read related texts to identify story elements that they contained. Students later used story grammar elements as a frame for writing their own mysteries.

OVERVIEW OF DIFFERENCES BETWEEN EXPERIMENTAL AND CONTROL GROUPS

Our Young Sherlock anchored instruction project was conducted with several classes of fifth-graders three times a week for an hour at a time for a total of 7 months. We also taught comparable control classes (stu-dents were randomly assigned to experimental or control groups) who received the same content in the instruction but did not receive the overall Sherlock anchor. For example, when learning vocabulary, our control class received example sentences that were unrelated to one another rather than all related to a common context. Similarly, when instructed in elements of story grammars, our control class learned each component in the context of a different story (analogous to the format of many basal readers as described earlier) rather than in a coherent context. Furthermore, students in our anchored group learned the STEPS plus G framework in one context whereas those in the control group were exposed to information about economics, social customs, and so forth in different contexts. Finally, because the control group did not have video, they could not engage in problem-finding activities such as those used in the anchored group.

Other than the use of a coherent video context, we tried very hard to make the control group instruction as effective as we knew how to make it. For example, the students had the same number of writing assignments (which they liked) and the same opportunities to work in cooperative learning groups (which they also liked). Further, the instructional time spent teaching particular units to each group was comparable. Teachers' observers confirmed that instruction for the control group was of high quality and was consistent with instruction normally found in fifth-grade classrooms.

INITIAL DATA

Several aspects of our data are noteworthy. First, at the end of the school year we conducted individual interviews with the students. Students in both the experimental (anchored) and control groups liked the classes, and they especially liked writing assignments and small group work (they reported rarely doing this in other classes). The students in the anchored group were especially enthusiastic about the group work; they mentioned that they were especially appreciative of information that their peers had noticed that had escaped their attention.

In one aspect of our assessment we asked students to describe the personality characteristics of people they had studied during the lessons on story characters. These lessons had occurred 6 months earlier so we were particularly interested in the students' abilities to remember what they had learned. Students in the control group were able to recall story characters but they were poor at remembering personality characteristics of these characters. Only 13% of the students were able to describe any personality traits of any characters they remembered. In contrast, 90% of the students in the anchored instruction group were able to provide rich descriptions of personality traits (theirs were of characters in *Young Sherlock*). The anchored instruction students' lessons that explicitly focused on personality traits had also occurred 6 months earlier. They continued to explore the Young Sherlock movie throughout the semester, but the subject of personality traits was never again the explicit focus of a lesson. The opportunity to remain immersed in the movie had a powerful effect on the students' abilities to describe characters in rich detail.

It is also noteworthy that, in several of our assessment tests, there were opportunities for students to use vocabulary that had been introduced during the school year (e.g., punctual, pompous). Although the overall base rate for purely spontaneous usage was relatively low, differences between experimental and control groups were extremely large. In addition, in a multiple-choice test of vocabulary (students had to match words with definitions), the anchored group showed no forgetting after a several month delay whereas the control group did show forgetting. Note that the groups had not differed in their performance on this test when it was administered immediately following the unit. It seems therefore that anchored instruction promoted long-term retention and spontaneous use of vocabulary.

Data on students' writings samples also revealed differences between the experimental and control students. Students in the video group produced stories that were quite different from the ones produced by their nonvideo peers. Stories written by students in the video group were causally cohesive stories—stories bound by goal identification and goal resolution. Stories written by students in the nonvideo group were collections of action statements that were not integrated or tied to a plot structure. One way in which the two groups did not differ was in their ability to identify story grammar (i.e., setting, goal, resolution) components in stories that they read. Both groups improved in this regard, but not differentially.

When asked to identify kinds of information to look for in a film or story that takes place in the 1800s, students in the anchored instruction group generated a wealth of information (social customs, methods of transportation, clothing, housing conditions, economic conditions, political systems, and educational conditions) they would rely on to learn about that historical period. Conversely, students in the nonvideo group tended to rely on only two factors (i.e., methods of transportation and clothing) to study the historical information. Seventy percent of the video students were able to recall the content areas assigned to the STEPS plus G categorization system that we taught them in the Victorian unit.

Overall, the differences between the experimental and control groups

were large. Furthermore, they were large despite the fact that, in our
control group, we taught the same basic knowledge for the same time
period, patterned after methods that were enhanced from suggestions
focused in the relevant teachers' guides. We also taught in a manner that
was as effective and interesting as we could make it, but without using an
anchor.

Our Young Sherlock anchor allowed us to help students integrate
knowledge that otherwise is often taught in piecemeal fashion. This had
a number of positive effects on their abilities to remember and use what
they learned. We noted earlier that instruction often proceeds in a non-
integrated, piecemeal fashion. In many approaches to teaching thinking,
each component is taught in the context of a different example. In many
approaches to teaching comprehension strategies, stories to be com-
prehended are unrelated to one another (or often only weakly related) so
that there is no chance to develop an organized set of knowledge about a
complex area. Our data suggest that there are definite advantages to
helping students become deeply involved in the exploration of interesting, complex domains. They were better able to write stories, use vocabulary, and generate categories of information that could help them comprehend new domains.

As an additional comment on the Young Sherlock project, consider
the modality of the anchor. We noted earlier in this chapter that anchors
can be verbal as well as visual. Young Sherlock is available in text form
and we could have used this for our anchor. It would have allowed us to
capture the advantages of some of our lesson designs, but not of others.
In particular, the videodisc provides a richness of information for noticing, evaluating, and describing that exceeds the level available in the text
version. The video also allows students to create multi-media presentations (in essence, enhanced and illustrated language experience products) that are highly motivating for their peers and their teachers to
watch. We think that the provision of videodisc-based anchors add a
value to education that is worth the relatively low cost.

Clearly, there is much more that could be done to make the Young
Sherlock curriculum even more effective. An important addition will be
to put greater emphasis on activities designed to decontextualize knowledge learned in the Sherlock context. We will also focus more explicitly
on skills of reasoning (e.g., Ennis, 1987; Paul, this volume; Perkins, this
volume). Similarly, we plan to work on reading comprehension skills
using procedures such as those implemented in reciprocal teaching (Palincsar & Brown, 1984). In each of the latter two cases, however, we
believe that the use of semantically rich anchors will facilitate students
abilities to acquire useful knowledge.

SUMMARY AND CONCLUSIONS

We began this chapter by noting that some authors urge that we teach general thinking skills whereas others emphasize the need for content. We argued that this is not an either/or issue, and we tried to explain why.

We acknowledged that content knowledge indeed plays an extremely important role in thinking and problem solving. This leads to the question: If knowledge is so important, why not simply focus on it? Our answer elaborated on the insights of Whitehead (1929) plus others (e.g., Gragg, 1940) who emphasized the inert knowledge problem. Many ways of teaching produce knowledge that can be explicitly recalled under specific conditions but that is not spontaneously used.

We discussed a series of laboratory experiments that explored ways to overcome the inert knowledge problem, and we discussed an approach to instruction—called anchored instruction—that attempts to use design principles derived from research to create effective learning environments. The anchored instruction research that we and our colleagues have conducted to date has attempted to explore the effects of three features: (a) The emphasis on problem-oriented learning experiences; (b) The importance of taking a multi-disciplinary perspective on a single problem area; and (c) the value of sustained thinking about a problem area. When these occur together, they seem to help students develop rich, organized knowledge structures plus acquire useful skills such as the ability to find important issues and write interesting and informative stories and lessons.

We noted that research on the general concept of anchored instruction has a long history (e.g., Dewey (1910) emphasized the importance of theme-based projects; Gragg (1940) emphasized the importance of case-bearing learning). Nevertheless, there is a great deal of research that remains to be done in this area. The availability of modern videodisc technology (the players are not all that expensive) make it possible to create anchors that provide especially rich environments that students and teachers can explore.

ACKNOWLEDGMENTS

The research reported in this chapter was supported in part by G008710018-88 from OERI and by MDA903-84-C-0218 from the Army Research Institute.

We are indebted to the following colleagues and students who are working to develop the concept of anchored instruction; Bob Sherwood,

Ted Hasselbring, Susan Williams, Laura Goin, Tom Sturdevant, Brigid Barron, Laurie Furman, Betsy Montavon, Kim McLarty, Jennifer Goodman, Holly Martin, Ann Dupree, Dorothy Fuller, Dale Yount and Joanna Hampton. We are also indebted to Beverly Conner and Faapio Po'e for their excellent editorial help. Finally we wish to thank the students and teachers who assisted us in our research.

REFERENCES

Adams, J. L. (1979). *Conceptual blockbusting* (2nd ed.). New York: Norton.
Adams, L., Kasserman, J., Yearwood, A., Perfetto, G., Bransford, J., & Franks, J. (1988). The effects of facts versus problem-oriented acquisition. *Memory & Cognition, 16,* 167–175.
Anderson, J. R. (1987). Skill acquisition: Compilation of weak-method problem solutions. *Psychological Review, 94,* 192–210.
Anderson, R. C. (1984). Role of reader's schema in comprehension, learning and memory. In R. Anderson, J. Osborn, & R. Tierney (Eds.), *Learning to read in American schools: Basal readers and content texts.* Hillsdale, NJ: Lawrence Erlbaum Associates.
Anderson, R. C., & Pearson, P. D. (1984). A schema-theoretic view of basic processes in reading comprehension. In P. David Pearson (Ed.), *Handbook of reading research* (pp. 255–291). New York: Longman.
Asch, S. E. (1969). A reformulation of the problem of associations. *American Psychologist, 24,* 92–102.
Ausubel, D. P. (1960). The use of advance organizers in the learning and retention of meaningful verbal material. *Journal of Educational Psychology, 51,* 167–272.
Ausubel, D. P. (1968). *Educational psychology: A cognitive view.* New York: Holt, Rinehart & Winston.
Beauchamp, G. A. (1959). *Basic dimensions of elementary method.* Boston: Allyn & Bacon.
Bereiter, C. (1984). How to keep thinking skills from going the way of all frills. *Educational Leadership, 42,* 75–77.
Bransford, J. D., & Johnson, M. K. (1972). Contextual prerequisites for understanding: Some investigations of comprehension and recall. *Journal of Verbal Learning and Verbal Behavior 11,* 717–726.
Bransford, J. D. (1984). Schema activation versus schema acquisition. In R. C. Anderson, J. Osborn, & R. Tierney (Eds.), *Learning to read in American schools: Basal readers and content text* (pp. 259–272). Hillsdale, NJ: Lawrence Erlbaum Associates.
Bransford, J. D., & Nitsch, K. E. (1978). Coming to understand things we could not previously understand. In J. F. Kavanagh & W. Strange (Eds.), *Speech and language in the laboratory, school and clinic* (pp. 267–307). Cambridge, MA: MIT Press.

Bransford, J. D., & Stein, B. S. (1984). *The IDEAL problem solver.* New York: W. H. Freeman.

Bransford, J. D., Sherwood, R., Hasselbring, T. S., Kinzer, C. K., & Williams, S. M. (in press). Anchored instruction: why we need it and how technology can help. In D. Nix & R. Spiro (Eds.), *Advances in computer-video technology.* Hillsdale, NJ: Lawrence Erlbaum Associates.

Bransford, J. D., Sherwood, R., Vye, N. J., & Rieser, J. (1986). Teaching thinking and problem solving: Research foundations. *American Psychologist, 41*(10), 1078–1089.

Brewer, W. F., & Nakamura, G. V. (1984). The nature and functions of schemas. In R. S. Wyer & T. K. Srull (Eds.), *Handbook of social cognition* (Vol. 1, pp. 119–160). Hillsdale, NJ: Lawrence Erlbaum Associates.

Brown, A. L., Campione, J. C., & Day, J. (1981). Learning to learn: On training students to learn from texts. *Educational Researcher, 10,* 14–24.

Ceci, S. J., & Liker, J. (1986). Academic and nonacademic intelligence: An experimental separation. In R. J. Sternberg & R. K. Wagner (Eds.), *Nature and origins of competence in the everyday world* (pp. 119–142). Cambridge, England: Cambridge University Press.

Chase, W. G., & Simon, H. A. (1973). The mind's eye in chess. In W. Chase (Ed.), *Visual information processing* (pp. 215–281). New York: Academic Press.

Chi, M. T. H., Feltovich, P. J., & Glaser, R. (1981). Categorization and representation of physics problems by experts and novices. *Cognitive Science, 5,* 121–152.

deGroot, A. (1965). *Thought and choice in chess.* The Hague: Mouton.

Dewey, J. (1910). *How we think.* Boston: D. C. Heath.

Dooling, D. J., & Lachman, R. (1971). Effects of comprehension on retention of prose. *Journal of Experimental Psychology, 88,* 216–222.

Eaton, J. E., Anderson, C. W., & Smith, E. L. (1984). Students' misconceptions interfere with science learning: Case studies of fifth-grade students. *Elementary School Journal, 84*(4), 365–379.

Ennis, R. (1987). What is critical thinking? In J. Baron & R. Sternberg (Eds.), *Teaching thinking skills: Theory and practice* (pp. 9–26). New York: W. H. Freeman.

Gick, M. L., & Holyoak, K. J. (1980). Analogical problem solving. *Cognitive Psychology, 12,* 306–365.

Gick, M. L., & Holyoak, K. J. (1983). Schema induction and analogical transfer. *Cognitive Psychology, 15,* 1–38.

Glaser, R. (1984). Education and thinking: The role of knowledge. *American Psychologist, 39,* 93–104.

Gragg, C. I. (1940). Because wisdom can't be told. *Harvard Alumni Bulletin.*

Hanson, N. R. (1970). A picture theory of theory meaning. In R. G. Colodny (Ed.), *The nature and function of scientific theories.* Pittsburgh: Pittsburgh University Press.

Hirsch, E. D. (1987). *Cultural literacy: What every American needs to know.* Boston, MA: Houghton Mifflin.

Johnson-Laird, P. N. (1985). Deductive reasoning ability. In R. J. Sternberg

(Ed.), *Human abilities: An information-processing approach* (pp. 173–194). New York: W. H. Freeman.

Jones, B. F., Palincsar, A. S., Ogle, D. S., & Carr, E. G. (1987). *Strategic teaching: Cognitive instruction in the content areas.* Alexandria, VA: Association for Supervision and Curriculum Development.

Kintsch, W. (1979). On modeling comprehension. *Educational Psychologist, 14,* 3–14.

Larkin, J. H. (1979). Information processing models and science instruction. In J. Lochhead & J. Clement (Eds.), *Cognitive process instruction: Research on teaching thinking skills* (pp. 109–118). Philadelphia, PA: Franklin Institute Press.

Lipman, M. (1985). Thinking skills fostered by philosophy for children. In J. Segal, S. Chipman, & R. Glaser (Eds.), *Thinking and learning skills: Relating instruction to basic research* (Vol. 1, pp. 83–108). Hillsdale, NJ: Lawrence Erlbaum Associates.

Lochhead, J., & Clement, J. (Eds.). (1979). *Cognitive process instruction: Research on teaching thinking skills.* Philadelphia, PA: Franklin Institute Press.

Lockhart, R. S., Lamon, M., & Gick, M. L. (1988). Conceptual transfer in simple insight problems. *Memory & Cognition, 16,* 36–44.

Lodico, M. G., Ghatala, E., Levin, J. R., Pressley, M., & Bell, J. A. (1983). Effects of meta-memory training on children's use of effective memory strategies. *Journal of Experimental Child Psychology, 35,* 263–277.

Mann, L. (1979). *On the trail of process: A historical perspective on cognitive processes and their training.* New York: Grune and Stratton.

Nelson, K., Fivush, R., Hudson, J., & Lucariello, J. (1983). Scripts and the development of memory. In M. T. H. Chi (Ed.), *Trends in memory development search* (pp.). Basel, Switzerland: Karger.

Newell, A. (1980). One final word. In D. T. Tuma & F. Reif (Eds.), *Problem solving and education: Issues in teaching and research* (pp. 175–189). Englewood Cliffs, NJ: Prentice-Hall.

Nitsch, K. E. (1977). Structuring decontextualized forms of knowledge. (Doctoral dissertation, Vanderbilt University, Nashville, TN). *Dissertation Abstracts International, 38B,* 3935.

Palincsar, A. S., & Brown, A. L. (1984). Reciprocal teaching of comprehension-fostering and comprehension monitoring activities. *Cognition and Instruction, 1,* 117–175.

Paris, S. G., Newman, R. S., & McVey, K. A. (1982). Learning the functional significance of mnemonic actions: A microgenic study of strategy acquisition. *Journal of Experimental Child Psychology, 34,* 490–509.

Perfetto, B. A., Bransford, J. D., & Franks, J. J. (1983). Constraints on access in a problem solving context. *Memory & Cognition, 11,* 24–31.

Ravitch, D., & Finn, C. E. (1987). *What do our 17 year-olds know? A report on the first national assessment of history and literature.* New York: Harper & Row.

Schank, R. C., & Abelson, R. P. (1977). *Scripts, plans, goals, and understanding: An inquiry into human knowledge and structures.* Hillsdale, NJ: Lawrence Erlbaum Associates.

Sherwood, R. D., Kinzer, C. K., Bransford, J. D., & Franks, J. J. (1987). Some benefits of creating macro-contexts for science instruction: Initial findings. *Journal of Research in Science Teaching, 24,*(5), 417–435.

Simon, H. A. (1980). Problem solving and education. In D. T. Tuma & R. Reif (Eds.), *Problem solving and education: Issues in teaching and research* (pp. 81–96). Hillsdale, NJ: Lawrence Erlbaum Associates.

Spiegel, D. L. (1981). Six alternatives to the Directed Reading Activity. *The Reading Teacher, 34*(8), 914–920.

Stein, B. S., Way, K. R., Benningfield, S. E., & Hedgecough, C. A. (1986). Constraints on spontaneous transfer in problem-solving tasks. *Memory & Cognition, 14*(5), 432–441.

van Dijk, T. A. (1987). Episodic models in discourse processing. In S. J. Samuels (Ed.), *Comprehending oral and written language* (pp. 161–196). New York: Academic Press.

Vye, N., Bransford, J. D., & Franks, J. (in preparation). *Effects of multiple perspectives on access.* Manuscript in preparation, Vanderbilt University, Nashville, TN.

Wagner, R. K., & Sternberg, R. J. (1986). Tacit knowledge and intelligence in the everyday world. In R. J. Sternberg & R. K. Wagner (Eds.) *Nature and origins of competence in the everyday world* (pp. 51–83). Cambridge, England: Cambridge University Press.

Wales, C. E., & Stager, R. A. (1977). *The guided design approach.* Englewood Cliffs, NJ: Educational Technology Publications.

Watson, J. S., & Ramey, C. T. (1972). Reactions to response-contingent stimulation in early infancy. *Merrill-Palmer Quarterly of Behavior and Development,* Vol. 18, No. 3, pp. 218–227.

Weisberg, R., DiCamillo, & Phillips, D. (1978). Transferring old associations to new situations: A nonautomatic process. *Journal of Verbal Learning and Verbal Behavior, 17,* 219–228.

Whitehead, A. N. (1929). *The aims of education.* New York: Macmillan.

The Nature and Nurture
of Creativity

D. N. Perkins
Harvard Graduate School of Education

SALIERI'S SYNDROME

We all have opportunities to deploy creative thinking in everyday life. Before looking seriously at research on creative thinking and its teaching, let me mention two cases in point. A friend and colleague, Steve Schwartz of the University of Massachusetts, Boston, recently told me of a situation where he needed to cut a piece of cheese, with no knife at hand. He wondered if he had something knifelike—and an answer occurred to him. He drew his wallet out of his pocket, his credit card out of the wallet, and cut the cheese with the credit card. "Don't leave home without it!"

Another friend and colleague, Abigail Lipson of the Bureau of Study Counsel at Harvard, showed an alert eye by noticing and photographing this wonderful sign on a Cambridge building:

RAGE WAREHOUSE
  IRE PROOF

Such a warehouse seems to be an excellent idea; you can store away all your rage, with assurance that none of it will escape this "ire proof" facility to do any mischief. Of course, the sign actually reads "Storage Warehouse, Fire Proof," but a wing of the building juts forward on the left, so that, seen from the proper angle, the partly occluded sign appears as just shown. Hundreds walk by daily without noticing the accidental transformation, but Abigail did.

Unimportant though these incidents are in the annals of invention, they aptly illustrate two characteristics of creative thinking. Steve's success with the credit card reveals freedom from what psychologists call "functional fixedness." By and large, people tend to think of objects only in terms of their conventional functions; credit cards, for instance, are for charging expenses. To see a credit card as a cutting instrument is to demonstrate a flexibility that cuts across conventional categories. The Rage Warehouse episode relates to a somewhat similar mental trap: reading in. As anyone who has ever proofread a document knows, your knowledge of how words are spelled often misleads; you tend to read them as correct even when they are not. Likewise, most people would simply know that the sign reads "Storage Warehouse, Fire Proof," having seen it a hundred times. To perceive the "Rage Warehouse" instead is to read out an unexpected message rather than reading in the expected one.

Not only do these cases illustrate flexible thinking, they also demonstrate creativity in the small. They tell us that creative thinking is within reach. When many people ponder creative thinking, they consider only the towering figures of invention such as Mozart, who, to Salieri's dismay, wrote music out of his head with no corrections on the manuscript page. Too many people become victims of this "Salieri's syndrome," imagining that they lack creativity because they do not measure up to their culture megaheroes. It is all the more important, then, that we understand what creative thinking is, how creative thinking is a potential for anyone, and how schooling can help learners to realize that potential.

WHAT IS THE OUTER NATURE
OF CREATIVE THINKING?

To understand creative thinking, we first need to understand what it looks like from the outside. The outer nature of creative thinking is what we see that leads us to identify an episode of thinking as creative. Broadly speaking, we consider thinking creative when it produces creative outcomes. The broadest possible sense of outcomes is intended here, including poems, paintings, scientific theories, business plans, jokes, flower arrangements, cakes, games, and conversations. To be considered creative, such outcomes must be both original and appropriate to their context.

For instance, to be a creative way of cutting cheese, the credit card idea must be both novel and appropriate. If a reader of this chapter later cuts cheese with a credit card, this lacks originality and does not count as creative. If a credit card plainly could not possibly cut cheese, the original idea would be inappropriate to the context and not creative. Attention to the way we talk about creative things shows that originality and contextual appropriateness are our tacit criteria for considering an outcome creative. But when do we call an episode of thinking creative? Just when it produces an outcome that is, or at least seems to be, original and appropriate. In short, first and foremost, our criterion for creative thinking concerns the sorts of results it yields.

WHAT IS THE INNER NATURE OF CREATIVE THINKING?

The outer nature of creative thinking does not explain how it occurs. What we really want to unveil is the inner nature of creative thinking—the patterns of thought, attitude, and skill that enable and encourage it. But thinking usually is a private affair. Although we can see the outer manifestation of creative thinking directly—the results it yields—we can only know the inner nature of creative thinking indirectly, through evidence that links reports of processes of thought and various psychological traits to the kinds of outcomes a person produces.

The techniques psychologists and others have used to prove the inner nature of creative thinking have been diverse. "Think aloud" process tracing methods have been employed to track the course of thought during episodes of creating and problem solving (e.g., Newell & Simon, 1972; Patrick, 1935, 1937; Perkins, 1981). In the psychometric approach, correlations have been sought between various test-like performances and biographical measures of creative productivity (see, for instance, the review by Mansfield & Busse, 1981). Psychoanalytic and related "depth psychology" perspectives have been brought to bear (e.g., Arieti, 1976; Rothenberg, 1979). Some have suggested that the kind of discovery involved in creativity involves problem-solving processes that can be modeled by computer, and have offered computer models to illustrate the point (e.g., Langley, Bradshaw, & Simon, 1983; Lenat, 1983). Behaviorist interpretations of creative thinking exist, including a charming essay in which B. F. Skinner argued that a poet produces a poem much as a hen lays an egg, all determined by genetic and individual history and the external contingencies of reinforcement (Skinner, 1972). Although this is not the place to review in detail the diverse concepts and methods that have been employed in the study of creativity (cf. Perkins, 1981, 1988), perhaps it is fair to say that, at one time or another, most of the arsenal of recent psychology has been brought to bear on the problem.

Although many exceptions could be cited, broadly speaking three

very different ways of thinking about the inner nature of creative thinking appear in the literature. They might be called a "potency" viewpoint,
a "patterns of thinking" viewpoint, and a "values" viewpoint. A potency
viewpoint suggests creative results depend on the efficacy of certain basic
mental operations. A viewpoint emphasizing patterns of thinking suggest that creative results depend on how basic mental operations are
organized into patterns. A values viewpoint suggests that creative results
depend on the values by which one selects goals, methods, and solutions.
Let us consider each in turn.

Does Creative Thinking Reflect Potencies?

By definition, a psychological potency is a power to do something. One
common view of the inner nature of creative thinking is that creative
thinking depends on a power to generate original appropriate ideas.
Idea generation is treated as a particular cognitive operation that can
work with more or less power. If we can measure this power, we can
measure the person's potential to think creatively. "Ideational fluency"
and "ideational flexibility" are the best known examples of potency concepts supposedly underlying creative thinking. Ideational fluency is the
ability to generate quickly a large number of appropriate ideas—many
uses for an ordinary brick, for example. Ideational flexibility is the ability
to generate *varied* uses for the brick, rather than uses of a very similar
kind. For instance, if all your uses employed a brick as some sort of
weight, that would not display great flexibility (Guilford, 1967; Guilford
& Hoepfner, 1971; Wallach, 1970; Wallach & Kogan, 1965).

According to this potency viewpoint, using a credit card as a knife and
recognition of the Ire Proof Rage Warehouse sign reflect potencies of
ideational fluency and flexibility. If well-supplied with such potencies, a
person will often think creatively and produce outcomes of striking inventiveness. Perhaps effort and practice can even improve ideational
fluency and flexibility, making people more creative. There are other
notions also that amount to potency theories of creative thinking. The
notion of "remote associates" developed by Mednick (1962) suggests that
creative minds have a "flat associative hierarchy" that yields further
flung associations and consequent creative syntheses. Another very
straightforward potency view holds that creative thinking simply reflects
general intelligence. According to this view, people with high IQ's tend
to be more creative, people with lower IQ's less creative.

Despite the popularity of the fluency, flexibility, and remote associates
models, empirical research has largely disconfirmed potency theories of
creative thinking. Any candidate potency has to pass the test of correlat-

ing with outer performance: Those who score high on tests of the potency in question should have better creative track records in their personal or professional lives. This generally has not turned out to be the case. For instance, measures of ideational fluency and flexibility rarely correlate with real world creative achievement (Crockenberg, 1972; Mansfield & Busse, 1981; Mansfield, Busse, & Krepelka, 1978; Wallach, 1976a, 1976b). As to IQ, considerable research has consistently shown that real-world achievement, creative or otherwise, within a field such as physics, math, or business bears little relation to general intelligence, which has much more predictive power for school performance than for productivity in life in general (Baird, 1982; Barron, 1969; Wallach, 1976a, 1976b). More detailed reviews of these matters can be found in Mansfield and Busse (1981) and Perkins (1981, 1988), among other sources.

Does Creative Thinking Reflect Patterns of Thinking?

Because potency theories appear not to account for creative thinking, we need to consider alternatives. One option looks to the *ways* creative people deploy whatever cognitive operations they use—with what selection, emphasis, timing, and direction. Such ways might be called patterns of thinking. The question becomes not whether certain cognitive operations are powerful, but how a person organizes whatever powers are possessed into patterns of thinking that yield creative results.

One relevant pattern of thinking identified by Jacob Getzels and Mihalyi Csikszentmihalyi (1976) is called *problem finding*. The authors argued that, although problem *solving* is important, creative thinkers are most conspicuous for their problem *finding* behavior—their more extensive search for problems worth solving and their greater flexibility in defining problems. Investigating the working patterns of student artists in a laboratory experiment, these researchers found that some much more than others invested time in exploring what sort of work to attempt, remained ready to change directions when an alternative direction suggested itself for a work already underway, and displayed other related behaviors.

For instance, a problem finder given some materials to arrange into a still life, would explore many possibilities, set aside some objects, and bring back others before settling on an arrangement. An artist less inclined to problem finding would quickly assemble an arrangement and commence to draw it. Later, when both artists were in the midst of their renderings, the problem finder would be more likely to reconceive the direction of the drawing, altering it substantially or rearranging the materials. The problem finders' products were rated as more creative by their teachers and an independent panel. The problem finders also proved more professionally successful as practicing fine artists in follow-up studies conducted 7 and 18 years later (Csikszentmihalyi & Getzels, in press; Getzels & Csikszentmihalyi, 1976).

In what sense is problem finding a distinctive pattern of thinking? In the sense that the problem finders invested unusual time and effort in certain phases of the artistic process—finding an initial direction and pursuing a change in direction. The same pattern also appears in the work of creative scientists, who pay keen attention to the character of the problems and projects they undertake, tackling those that seem most pivotal and pregnant with possibilities for new discovery (Mansfield & Busse, 1981; Roe, 1952a, 1952b, 1963). The notion of problem finding also suits the credit-card-as-knife episode well. One might initially define the problem, as "Where can I get a knife?" But such a formulation does not find the real problem, which is more like "Where can I get something *knifelike*—thin and rigid." This broader formulation of the problem fits credit cards and suggests several other solutions besides.

Another characteristic of creative thinking that might be considered a pattern of thinking has been identified by the psychoanalyst Albert Rothenberg (1979). Rothenberg held that inventive people tend to think in opposites and contraries, bringing them together in new syntheses. He termed this style of thought *Janusian thinking,* after the Greek god Janus who had two faces and so looked both ways at once.

The general notion that creative thinking depends on Janusian thinking suffers from a weakness of logical circularity. Anything original, crossing boundaries as it must to be original, almost always joins opposites in some sense. However, Rothenberg presented some intriguing empirical evidence for the reflexive Janusian tendency of creative minds. He reported that people identified as creative on other measures also showed a spontaneous tendency to think in contrasts and opposites on simple word association tests. This, like problem finding, might be considered an ingrained pattern of thinking. Anyone can adopt a mental set to think in opposites momentarily, but perhaps creative thinkers have a persistent mental set to discern contraries and put them together, even when the task at hand is one that in no obvious way invites creativity, as with the word association test. Janusian thinking may figure in the recognition of the Ire Proof Rage Warehouse, which requires openness to a variant meaning.

Many other patterns of thinking may be important to creative thinking. For instance, several features of the well-known "brainstorming" technique pioneered by Osborn (1953) might figure in the spontaneous creativity of gifted individuals. For example, brainstorming systematically defers criticism in the belief that early criticism inhibits the flow of ideas. Perhaps this is a pattern of thinking that many creative individuals use, whether they have heard of brainstorming by name or not. Unearthing and questioning one's tacit assumptions is another commonplace tactic of creative thinking that, again, might well be prominent in creative thinking, whether the thinker has read the books or not.

Such simple thinking strategies or *thinking frames* as they might better be called (Perkins, 1986b), probably abet creative thinking significantly. The problem is that only in a couple of cases, such as problem finding and thinking in opposites, has any research documented the relation between patterns of thinking that supposedly figure in getting creative results and the person's track record of creative results. Research of this sort is not easy to do, so perhaps it is not surprising that so little has occurred. Despite the need for more research, the findings that exist encourage the view that at least some patterns of thinking directly promote creative results. Whereas the evidence on potency perspectives tended to be negative, we have at least some evidence supporting a *patterns of thinking* perspective.

Does Creative Thinking Reflect Values?

The clearest evidence of all demonstrates the connection between creative thinking and values broadly construed—a person's commitments and aspirations. Not surprisingly, creative people tend to have creative values. They display autonomy, resist conformity. They *enjoy* originality, taking delight in its freshness and expending effort to find or create it. These value tendencies in both creative scientists and creative artists have been well-documented (Barron, 1969, 1972; Getzels & Csikszentmihalyi, 1976; Mansfield & Busse, 1981; Roe, 1952a, 1952b, 1963). To recall our examples, Steve *enjoyed* the clever use of the credit card, not feeling in the least embarrassed about so strange a strategy, as some people would. Likewise, Abigail *enjoyed* the Ire Proof Rage Warehouse, rather than thinking it simply silly, as some might. Enjoying originality is just as important as recognizing it; for instance, some people prove able to discriminate originality in paintings but dislike the originality (Getzels & Csikszentmihalyi, 1976).

Not only affinities but tolerances seem important to creative thinking. The same sources just cited give evidence that creative scientists and artists appear to have a high tolerance for ambiguity, disorganization, and asymmetry. Whereas some people find ambiguous, disorganized, and asymmetric situations upsetting and shun them, creative people appear to enjoy the challenge of coping with them. In science, very often the core challenge is to deal with a maze of ambiguities and forge a new unity.

Intrinsic motivation is yet another feature of creative values. Intrinsic motivation involves valuing something for its own sake, rather than for extrinsic rewards such as a high salary or a prize. The psychologist Teresa Amabile (1983) has built a compelling argument for the relevance of intrinsic motivation to creative thinking. People tend to function most creatively on those endeavors where they feel high intrinsic motivation. For instance, creative scientists feel a deep-seated investment in their work—an investment that often makes familial and other relations secondary (Mansfield & Busse, 1981; Roe, 1952a, 1952b, 1963). Likewise, many poets and artists report an impressive dedication to their craft (Barron, 1972; Perkins, 1981). And certainly, as anyone close to the world of art knows, none of the fine arts make for especially promising careers if the extrinsic rewards of condominiums, summer cottages, and Jacuzzis are most on one's mind.

It hardly seems surprising that creative people cherish originality, tolerate ambiguity, experience intrinsic motivation, and so on. But we might be surprised by what this value profile probably means. Although one could think of these traits as consequences of creativity, more likely that are causes. That is, a person is more or less creative due to the values the person embraces. I have argued extensively in *The Mind's Best Work* that people all too easily view creative thoughts as bubbling up spontaneously from some ineffable inner source (Perkins, 1981). Instead, conspicuous creativity often emerges because the person in question is *trying* to be creative—trying to produce things original and appropriate. Much more than we usually suppose, creating is an intentional endeavor shaped by the person's values.

HOW DOES CREATIVE THINKING RELATE TO EXCEPTIONAL ABILITY?

Many people think of creative thinking as a matter of talent. This is just a potency theory under a different name. As already outlined, the research argues that the inner nature of creative thinking depends deeply on a person's value profile—what the person commits to, tolerates, hungers after. Also, creative thinking appears to involve certain patterns of deploying one's abilities—problem finding, Janusian thinking, challenging assumptions, and so on. Creative thinking so conceived has little to do with great ability such as might be measured by IQ or domain-specific tests in music, the visual arts, mathematics, and so on.

This may seem almost paradoxical. How can talent not matter? Well, of course it matters, but key to the question of creative thinking is *how* it matters. Certainly a person with greater natural ability at mathematics has an advantage because that ability may enable greater creative achievements in mathematics. But the ability is not the creativity. The same ability, in a person without the appropriate values or patterns of thinking, might lead only to conventional though technically adroit accomplishments.

One could put the matter this way: Abilities merely enable a certain level of achievement without promoting it, just as being tall enables one to get baskets more easily without necessarily motivating one to be a basketball player. In contrast, the value and thought patterns discussed actively promote creative results, encouraging a person to use whatever abilities he or she possesses to creative ends. The inner nature of creative thinking therefore has most to do with certain values and patterns of thinking. Actual magnitude of achievement inevitably depends on values, patterns, and ability too.

DOES CREATIVE THINKING
DEVELOP WITH MATURATION?

A popular if somewhat broad question motivates considering the developmental course of creativity: Do youngsters start creative and lose the knack, or, in contrast, develop toward creativity? As to the latter, common sense suggests that people develop toward nearly any sort of sophisticated performance. As to the former, many people find in the behavior of children an open spontaneity that they often do not see in adolescents and adults. What has been lost in all but a few, they suggest, is creativity.

Naturally it is difficult to resolve such a sweeping issue with precision. Nonetheless, the present framework provides a basis for making some progress on it. First of all, in light of the analysis of creative thinking offered here, should we consider creative thinking to be something that needs to develop? Plainly, yes. One side of creative thinking involves patterns of thinking. We could hardly expect these patterns to be in place from birth; they must be acquired in the course of development. Perhaps even more important than patterns are various attitudes conducive to creative thinking. Here it seems plausible to say on the basis of informal experience that some children begin with somewhat different attitudes than others; some are more exploratory and open, some less so. At the same time, it is plainly the case that attitudes develop as well as patterns of thinking. They are in part shaped by what peers, parents, and others value and reward, for example. One would not expect to find in most children the kind of mature attention to matters aesthetic, tolerance of ambiguity, savoring of originality, and so on, that marks a developed creative individual, although one might indeed find precursors of it.

If creative thinking indeed *has* to develop, how can we understand the seeming creativity of children and its seeming loss by many children? Here we encounter a subtle mix of myth and reality. It is surely a myth that *most* children are conspicuously creative. A more seasoned view is that children, like adults, come with many different dispositions. Equally dubious is the notion that all of children's seemingly creative behavior should be counted as genuinely creative. For instance, sometimes children cross boundaries an adult would not because they do not know the rules or conventions. Whereas an adult exploring beyond those boundaries might be considered creative, the same criterion hardly applies to children. For another example, the sheer and often chaotic energy of some children may lead them to creative outcomes that reflect chance rather than real creative thinking.

Moreover, we must remember both the originality and the appropriateness criteria for creativity. We often delight in the originality of children while viewing with tolerance the degree to which their ideas and products function well. It is easy to think of "being original" as the hardest part of creativity, but this may be deceptive. Being original in a way that works is considerably harder than just being original. Youngsters may look more creative than they are exactly because we are so much more generous in applying the "appropriateness" standard to them than to adults.

All this argues that our vision of children as outstandingly creative may be somewhat misleading. Nonetheless, the evidence is clear that, at least by contemporary cultural standards, children tend to lose something around age 9 or 10. The loss and its complexities have been particularly well documented in the case of drawing and painting. Youngsters' freely imaginative, dynamic, and colorful works tend to become staid and studied as they attempt to learn the technicalities of "correct" representation (Winner, 1982, chap. 5). At the same time, however, tests of sensitivity to stylistic nuance and expressiveness reveal that younger children are actually *less* alert to these important dimensions of drawing and painting, arguing that the more aesthetic performance of the youngsters is not something they are in any sense in creative command of, but rather a consequence of their mental makeup during that period of development (Carothers & Gardner, 1979; Gardner & Winner, 1982; Winner, 1982).

What is the significance of the "conventional stage" that youngsters enter around their tenth year? It may be that the delving into the rigors of representational conventions is a necessary stage in development toward mature artistry. It may also be that this "conventional stage" is a product of a culture and system of schooling that pays little heed to the arts and, after the first years of a child's life, becomes less and less rewarding of divergence. Both could even hold true at once. The fact remains, however, that during the first years of the second decade of childhood, many students become very self-critical and never again evince a spontaneous interest in drawing or painting.

Accordingly, children in general plainly need more help in finding their way through this period if certain facets of their creativity are to develop. Such help probably should involve at least two aspects. First of all, children should receive some of the technical guidance they thirst for; often in the visual arts such guidance actually is withheld in the name of creativity. Second, efforts should be made to preserve, or restore, the playful originality more commonly found earlier, but in more mature forms. None of this should be seen as efforts to preserve an early but deeply authentic creativity; remember the evidence that younger children are not really in command of what they are doing—they just do things that way. Nonetheless, there is a loss of playfulness that would benefit from careful attention and ultimate restoration if youngsters are to develop toward a mature creativity.

HOW DOES CREATIVE THINKING RELATE TO THE DIMENSIONS OF THINKING?

The *Dimensions of Thinking* model introduced in Marzano et al. (1988) and elaborated by the chapters in this volume highlights five dimensions:

- Metacognition
- Critical and creative thinking
- Thinking processes
- Core thinking skills
- The relationship of content-area knowledge to thinking

It is natural to ask how creative thinking, one aspect of the second dimension, connects to the rest of the model. The following comments make no effort to review or critique the concepts or terminology of the *Dimensions of Thinking* framework itself, but rather take the framework as given and seek to relate creativity to it.

Dimension 1: Metacognition

Metacognition refers to cognition about one's own thinking and learning. We know things about, and have skills for guiding, our own cognitive processes. For instance, most people know a number of practical things about how well their memories work, under what conditions remembering is likely to be difficult, and how to handle such situations. All this is part of their metacognitive knowledge, part of metacognition.

The very category, metacognition, seems at odds with one perspective on creativity. The vision of creative thinking we inherit from the Romantics presents a remarkably passive view of the inventive mind. To be sure, the creative person may have to labor long and hard to prepare his or her mind for creative moments. But, whatever the mindful preparation, moments of invention themselves supposedly "bubble up" from some subterranean combustion. Venerable sources such as Coleridge's famous account of the writing of "Kubla Khan" (Lowes, 1927) and contemporary sources too (Grumbach, 1986) project such a view.

However, the general model of creative thinking outlined here demonstrates ample room for mindfulness and control in creative thinking; for metacognition, in short. The individual can be mindful of the factors that figure in creative thinking—such as attention to matters aesthetic, for instance—and can control the process of creative thinking to a significant extent by deploying various patterns of thinking that abet creative results. To be sure, one should not expect miracles from mindfulness about creative thinking, any more than one should from a metacognitive approach to any intellectual endeavor. Nonetheless, creative thinking seems as much an appropriate domain for metacognition as any other sort of thinking. The concluding section of this chapter will urge that, in fact, creative thinking as we know it is steadily becoming *more* metacognitive and changing in character as it does so.

Dimension 2: Critical and Creative Thinking

Creative thinking is one of two broad ways of thinking identified in the *Dimensions of Thinking* framework. The need therefore is to examine the distinction between creative thinking and its sibling way of thinking, critical thinking. The contrast is not so sharp as one might suppose at first. Although in everyday parlance we speak of critical and creative thinking as two different sorts of things, in fact they have a good deal to do with one another.

The first step in relating critical and creative thinking must be to deal with an ambiguity in the current use of the term *critical thinking*. Some authors employ the term in a broad sense that includes not only creative thinking but effective thinking of nearly any sort. On such an understanding of critical thinking, creative thinking is a subtype rather than a sibling of critical thinking. However, other authors use the term critical thinking in a narrower sense that does not treat it as a generic label for good thinking but rather, in the spirit of *Dimensions of Thinking,* as a particular way of thinking. The narrower sense also seems closer to everyday usage. In keeping with *Dimensions of Thinking* and everyday usage, we will focus on the narrower meaning here.

The main relation to draw between creative and critical thinking seems to be this: The two contrast much more in their objectives than in their processes. Considering objectives, critical thinking aims to produce an assessment of things, beliefs, and courses of action (cf. Ennis, 1981, 1986). Creative thinking, as discussed earlier, aims to produce a creative outcome. The same point can be made using the notion of the "outer nature" of creative thinking, discussed earlier. The outer symptoms by which we identify in a person an episode of creative versus critical thinking contrast: For the one, we look for an outcome that is creative. For the other, we look for an outcome that involves a sound assessment of things, beliefs, or courses of action.

Of course, sometimes the two sorts of outcomes meld into one. An assessment of something certainly can be creative. For example, the most brilliant literary criticism is without question creative. But the overlap between the objectives of creative and critical thinking is modest. In particular, critical assessments often and unproblematically fail the originality criterion for a creative outcome. A good assessment of a play, a business plan, or a holiday spot may be, but does not need to be, particularly original. Emphasis falls on the soundness of the assessment, not on its originality. Likewise, a creative outcome may happen to be, but is not typically, an assessment. Such paradigmatic creative outcomes as paintings, poems, scientific theories, and inventions are not usually in themselves assessments of something.

Although the outer natures of creative and critical thinking show considerable contrast, the same cannot be said for their inner natures. When we turn to the processes of creative thinking or critical thinking, we find that the two infuse one another. Creative thinking, even when its principal product is not an assessment, inevitably involves innumerable episodes of assessment. Abigail preserved the photographic record of the "Rage Warehouse" because she assessed it as surprising and provocative; Steve proceeded to cut the cheese with his credit card because he thought the idea would work. Likewise, a poet again and again assesses the developing poem, pondering the power of a word or phrase, examining the rhythm and structure, and so on (cf. Perkins, 1981, chap. 4). Just as good creative thinking depends on numerous episodes of assessment, good critical thinking typically depends on numerous episodes of invention, where the skilled critical thinker "breaks set" and sees through to factors pro and con that others might miss (Perkins, 1985).

Finally, it should be noted that creative and critical thinking merge totally in the richest and most far-reaching episodes of thinking. The ferment in physics during the turn of the century offers a case in point. The old regime of classical Newtonian and Maxwellian physics was in trouble. Alternatives were devised—relativity and quantum mechanics. Different versions were aired and critiqued. Was all this creative thinking or critical thinking? Plainly both deeply joined. The critical insights were highly creative and the creative ideas rigorously critical and rigorously criticized.

In summary, the contrast between creative and critical thinking has some substance. Looking at outcomes of modest scope—the typical poem or the typical movie review—we can see the earmarks of thinking aimed at a characteristically creative or critical outcome. However, the contrast usually is overdrawn. Looking to the inner processes and examining especially far-reaching courses of thought, we find creative and critical thinking inextricably interlocked.

Dimension 3: Thinking Processes

This dimension identifies a number of thinking processes—concept formation, principle formation, comprehension, problem solving, decision making, research, composition, and oral discourse. Certain of these are traditional contexts for the exercise of creative thinking—problem solving, research, and composition. Steve's experience with the credit card, for example, naturally classifies into the problem-solving category. However, a little thought quickly discloses that the other categories present equally appropriate occasions for creative thinking. As just stressed in discussing critical thinking, when one is making a decision, one often does well to challenge assumptions, revise viewpoints, and undertake other operations with a creative spirit. For another example, Abigail's experience with the "Rage Warehouse" is an instance of comprehension contrary to expectation. Likewise, forming a sound concept of something may demand one's full creative resource to see through to a new way of organizing the information available.

Just as the various thinking processes can be undertaken more or less creatively, so also they all routinely figure in episodes of creative thought. For example, the writing of an inventive novel plainly involves not only composition of the text, but decision making to determine which direction the plot will take at various points, concept formation to create personalities, comprehension to develop the fictional world of the novel and the characters' motivations, and so on. In summary, creative thinking is an important contributor to, and also a client of, the thinking processes identified.

Dimension 4: Core Thinking Skills

This dimension from the *Dimensions of Thinking* framework relates to creative thinking much as does the previous. Again, certain of the categories of skills identified as part of the skills dimension display an obvious connection to creative thinking: formulating questions, inferring, and restructuring, for example. At the same time, other skills that at first thought seem less related to creativity plainly contribute importantly to the process of creative thinking. Setting goals is a case in point. As noted earlier, the research of Getzels and Csikszentmihalyi (1976; Csikszentmihalyi & Getzels, in press) argues that special investment in exploring and selecting goals is characteristic of creative thinking. Likewise, activities such as observing or recalling can be crucial to a creative endeavor and also can be creative subendeavors in themselves.

Dimension 5: The Relationship
of Content-Area Knowledge to Thinking

This theme raises a provocative and not easily resolved question: Does a particular individual's creativity *depend on* particular content mastery or should we view it as a more general and crosscutting attribute. Favoring the dependency view is the commonplace observation that notable creative figures generally have been masters of the crafts of their disciplines. Beethoven and Mozart were superb technical musicians. Picasso, known for his adventurous explorations of the resources of imagery, in his youth attained a prodigious grasp of conventional representational painting techniques. A body of contemporary research arguing for the importance of an extensive content-specific repertoire in skilled performance of any sort also supports the view that creative productivity may depend on mastery of particular content. This research on expertise has addressed such areas as chess play (Chase & Simon, 1973), physics problem solving (Chi, Glaser, & Rees, 1982; Larkin, McDermott, Simon, & Simon, 1980), mathematical problem solving (Schoenfeld & Herrmann, 1982), and computer programming (Schneiderman, 1976; Soloway & Ehrlich, 1984).

On the other hand, the characteristics of creative thinking identified earlier have a fairly apparent cross-disciplinary cast. The dispositions to search out problems, to challenge assumptions, or to attend to the aesthetic dimensions of something are tendencies that at least seem as though they should be cross-disciplinary. Moreover, it is often said that too much knowledge may inhibit creativity. There is even a psychological basis for this notion. As expertise accumulates, more and more knowledge becomes "compiled" into highly context specific automatized forms (Anderson, 1983) that consequently resist scrutiny and challenge.

Although no strong empirical evidence on the exact question appears to exist, it seems reasonable to suggest the following resolution. The broad values and patterns of thinking characteristic of creativity have at least a somewhat cross-disciplinary character. A person creative in one domain is likely to be creative in other domains that he or she knows something about. However, a professional order of creativity in a domain generally calls for considerable mastery of that domain, which is a context-specific matter of talent, will, and extensive experience. It is possible that one might "overmaster" a domain and become trapped by a repertoire of reflexive beliefs and procedures. However, plainly this does not always happen, because so many notably creative individuals have been undisputed masters of their crafts and innovative nonetheless.

CAN WE TEST FOR CREATIVITY?

When the importance of an aspect of human behavior is recognized, interest in measuring it follows quickly behind. The importance of creative thinking is hardly in question, and the relations drawn between creative thinking and the other elements of the *Dimensions of Thinking* model emphasize the significance of creative thinking all the more. With these points in mind, it is natural to ask whether we can test for creativity.

The discussion so far implies a positive answer to this question. The potential and tendency to think creatively reflects a number of values that can be tested. For instance, many personality instruments measure the kinds of values characteristic of creative thinking. Creative patterns of thinking such as problem finding also can be detected, as in the work of Getzels and Csikszentmihalyi (1976; Csikszentmihalyi & Getzels, in press). Finally, biographical inventories, where one actually examines a person's track record of creative achievements, provide a rather direct "outer" measure of creative thinking, in terms of creative outcomes.

"What test should I use?" is the inevitable next question. Unfortunately, this query is not so easily answered. Most of the commercially available tests of creativity invest heavily in the ideational fluency and flexibility tradition. As noted earlier, validation studies of these measures have not in general favored them. One of the few tests showing some predictive validity is the Torrance Tests of Creative Thinking (Torrance, 1966, 1974). This battery evaluates a person on four dimensions: fluency, flexibility, originality, and elaboration. Validation studies done on general populations have yielded correlations of the order of .5 between Torrance test scores and biographical measures of creative achievement applied a number of years later (Torrance, 1972b, 1980, 1981; Torrance & Wu, 1981). For a conventional psychometric test, the Torrance battery is a reasonable bet.

But there are dilemmas to be faced. The Torrance Tests appear to be somewhat redundant with IQ, although Torrance and his colleagues rightly argue that they are not entirely so (Torrance, 1981; Torrance & Wu, 1981). Moreover, the Torrance Tests are very much in the ideational fluency and flexibility tradition. How is it, then, that they show some validity whereas the others do not? One possible reason is that they do not really measure ideational fluency and flexibility, despite their outer appearance, as a factor analysis conducted by Plass, Michael, and Michael (1974) suggests. Another is that the correlations obtained may reflect the varied population in the validation sample: The Torrance battery was validated against a general school population. Validation studies for many other tests have used professional populations, and professional engineers, physicists, or whatever, are much more uniform in their general ability and personality profiles, making correlations harder to come by (Mansfield & Busse, 1981). Accordingly, the Torrance Tests may not be sensitive enough to differentiate levels of creativity within professional and other special populations.

From the educational standpoint, another problem is much more serious. A test that correlates with people's creativity does not necessarily make a good instrument for evaluating instruction, because the instruction often teaches to the test and spoils its validity. Teaching to a test can work fine providing the test measures exactly what you want; if you have a test that directly gauges good essay writing, you may teach to it with aplomb. But most creativity tests, including the Torrance Tests, measure neither the inner nature nor the outer nature of creative thinking directly. That is, they neither measure process nor outcome directly. Rather, they only measure indirect correlates of creative thinking. Accordingly, teaching to the test may improve test scores without improving what you really want. One cannot view improved Torrance Test scores as sound evidence of the effectiveness of an intervention designed to boost creative thinking, especially when the instruction fairly directly addresses issues of fluency and flexibility as it usually does.

All this adds up to something of a paradox: Although creativity can be measured to some extent, a good test of it is hard to come by, especially a test suitable for program evaluation. So what should one do? If you are undertaking descriptive research, you can use a combination of measures, including personality indices, biographical reviews, and the Torrance Tests. If you are evaluating an instructional program, matters become more difficult. You need to use measures of actual creative accomplishments, for instance originality and appropriateness ratings (preferably broken down into relevant subscales) on complex products produced by students, products that afford an opportunity for invention. For example, if the instruction has emphasized art, the students might do works of art, if writing, short short stories.

A more ambitious measurement plan requires a biographical inventory of recent productive activities of control and treatment students conducted at least half a year after the instruction has terminated. Such an approach is not very convenient, but it does probe for maintenance and transfer of any habits of creative thinking acquired during the instruction. One might add personality measures and the Torrance Test, but the latter alone certainly would not make the case. It is unfortunate that we face a serious measurement problem here, but face it we do.

CAN CREATIVE THINKING BE TAUGHT?

This question, like the previous, earns a confident "yes" on the basis of theory. It has been argued that creative thinking involves certain values and patterns of thinking. Values can be conveyed to some extent, and patterns of thinking can be taught directly or encouraged in other ways. Therefore, creative thinking can be taught. To be sure, one does not expect to be able to manufacture Mozarts, but to find that disappointing would be to fall into the Salieri Syndrome mentioned earlier. We should be happy to boost creative thinking somewhat by shifting learners' values and patterns of thinking in the direction of creativity.

How have educators sought to accomplish this? One approach has been to emphasize the building of skills of fluency and flexibility (cf. Torrance, 1972a). On the basis of the research questioning a potency account of creative thinking, the appropriateness of this approach to instruction can be questioned. However, often instruction in fluency and flexibility may offer patterns of thinking, not just practice, to enhance flexibility and fluency; these patterns may well help. In addition, it is reasonable to think that while students are exercising their abilities of fluency and flexibility they may at the same time be assimilating values that foster creative thinking. Therefore, although a fluency and flexibility approach cannot be viewed as ideal from the standpoint of the present analysis, it might nonetheless yield positive results.

Fluency and flexibility aside, many approaches to the teaching of creativity emphasize a variety of patterns of thinking that assist in breaking set and constructing ideas and things. To mention just a few examples from an abundance of sources, Edward de Bono has offered a number of set breaking strategies under the general label "lateral thinking" (de Bono, 1970). Adams (1974) has reviewed various cognitive and affective blocks that he suggests stand in the way of creative thinking, with recommendations for remedying them. Gordon (1961) and others have urged that generating metaphors and analogies is an important tactic for creative thinking. "Brainstorming," which was mentioned earlier, is a technique for group and individual use designed to defer criticism and encourage the free exploration of ideas (Osborn, 1953). More recently, an approach to fostering creative thinking has been developed around the concept of design (Perkins, 1984, 1986a; Perkins & Laserna, 1986).

Although the foregoing examples illustrate some broad approaches that might be taken to fostering creative thinking, optimal results in developing this, or any other, sort of thinking depend on much more than the strategies and values promoted by the instruction. Perkins (1986b) argued that many efforts to develop thinking skills falter for lack of respecting important pedagogical constraints. For instance, explicit articulate attention to patterns of thinking enhances their learning more than tacit encouragement, where students are supposed to "soak up" the patterns of thinking through exposure. For another example, thinking skills commonly do not transfer beyond the context of learning unless the instruction directly addresses the problem of transfer and encourages students to monitor their own use of a skill and seek to apply it widely. For yet a third, often students receive insufficient practice with a strategy to internalize it, and so, feeling uncomfortable with the skill, do not use it. To be sure, sometimes instruction does attend to some of these factors, and even instruction that does not do so explicitly may have some success. Nonetheless, it is important to recognize that, from the standpoint of theory, good pedagogy as well as a good choice of patterns of thinking and values is important to effectiveness.

That in theory creative thinking can be taught is nice to know, but naturally one would like direct empirical evidence of success. Urfortunately, there is only a little suggestive evidence rather than a critical mass of supportive results. There are two reasons for this shortfall. First of all, most of the familiar approaches to enhancing creative thinking have never been formally evaluated. Although this may seem odd, it is symptomatic not just of the teaching of creative thinking but the teaching of thinking in general, a field that suffers from chronic underevaluation (Nickerson, Perkins, & Smith, 1985). It is not that there has been no evaluation, but that there has not been nearly enough.

The second reason for the shortfall is that, by and large, those evaluations that have been conducted reflect the problems of testing discussed earlier. To be sure, a number of teaching experiments have yielded gains in measures of creativity (cf. Torrance, 1972a). However, these experiments typically suffer from the problem of teaching to the test, so the improvements in test scores cannot be taken as adequate evidence.

A few experiments have demonstrated improvement on actual creative performance. For example, Catalina Laserna and I developed and tested a unit on inventive thinking as part of Project Intelligence, a 1-year thinking course for seventh-graders in Venezuela (Perkins & Laserna, 1986). This course, including the inventive thinking sequence, is now available in English under the title *Odyssey*. We evaluated the impact of the inventive thinking lessons by one of the methods mentioned earlier: various rating scales applied to a complex product. The instruction emphasized analysis and creation of designs, and the posttest asked the students, as well as control students, to design a table for a very small apartment. The students who had received the lessons produced designs incorporating about twice as many solution ideas, presented their designs in much more detail, and in general outshone the control group students on a number of measures (Bolt, Beranek, & Newman, 1983; Herrnstein, Nickerson, Sanchez, & Swets, 1986).

Another relevant finding comes from Alan Schoenfeld's research on mathematical problem solving. Alan Schoenfeld reports a 1-month intensive instructional sequence that very substantially improved the mathematical problem-solving ability of participating college students (Schoenfeld, 1982; Schoenfeld & Herrmann, 1982; see also Schoenfeld, 1985). Not only did the students show much more success with problems similar to those employed in the instruction, but also they approached problems of a rather different character more effectively. This flexibility suggests an improvement in their mathematical creative thinking in general.

Both the design and the mathematical problem-solving results benefit from a common feature: Gains were evaluated by holistic meaningful tasks of the sort one wants the students to handle better. For neither, therefore, is teaching to the test the major issue it becomes with the Torrance Test and like instruments. On the other hand, these findings and others like them certainly are very limited. Students more creative at designing gadgets or solving mathematical problems may not be more creative in activities of different or wider scope. For instance, although becoming better mathematical problem solvers, Schoenfeld's students might not have become better mathematical problem finders. I know of no empirical evidence one way or another about broad-spectrum improvements in creative thinking. Nonetheless, for the theoretical reasons stated earlier, such improvement should be possible.

CAN SCHOOLS FOSTER CREATIVE THINKING?

Conventional schooling does not serve the needs of creative thinking very well. However, instruction can fairly readily be redesigned to foster the development of such thinking. To see why and how, first of all we have to recognize a fundamental but surmountable barrier: atomism in instruction. Most tasks that students engage in emphasize what I like to call "short answer problems"—the sums of columns of numbers, the verb form to fill in the blank, and so on. Practice with such tasks may be important, but it does not afford much opportunity to develop creative thinking. Not only do such tasks usually have one right answer, but they do not involve the students in understanding or producing complex wholes.

In contrast, virtually all significant invention in real life involves designing complex wholes—a poem, an essay, a painting, a scientific theory, an operating business, an advertising campaign. Complex wholes provide the occasion and elbow room for creativity—and critical thinking too, as outlined in my recent *Knowledge as Design* (Perkins, 1986a; see also Perkins, 1984). Accordingly, education should be organized to a much greater extent around the production and appreciation of complex wholes, with the complexity tailored to the maturity of the learner, of course. Teachers should encourage students to invest themselves in such activities, taking responsibility for and pride in what they do.

With that basic point about content in mind, let us revisit the themes of values and patterns of thinking. The treatment of values showed that creative thinking is an intensely aesthetic matter, involving appreciation of originality, parsimony, elegance, and so on. Outside the arts proper, conventional schooling does little to highlight the aesthetics of knowledge or products of mind. When was the last time you saw students of mathematics encouraged not just to learn but to *admire* the Pythagorean Theorem? Yet teachers can easily find opportunities to celebrate the aesthetic dimensions of mathematics, physics, history, even grammar, much more than it does.

Creative values also included intrinsic motivation. The research on intrinsic motivation argues that it is much more easily undermined than fostered. Typical educational practices tend to reduce intrinsic motivation—heavy grading, minimal informative feedback, little choice of activities, constant scrutiny of work, and so on. First and foremost, education for creative thinking needs to avoid spoiling intrinsic motivation by limiting or modifying such practices. Of course, this cannot be done naively. Informative feedback can be extremely valuable and may not undermine intrinsic motivation, some examination of student works is often essential, and so on. But teachers certainly can take the sharp edge off the factors that work against intrinsic motivation during those parts of the instruction that seek to emphasize creativity.

If matters of value could be handled better, the same holds for patterns of thinking conducive to creative thinking. As noted earlier, a number of patterns of thinking popular in books on creativity promote mobility of thinking. Examples include brainstorming, the use of metaphor and analogy, seeking alternative ways of solving the same problem, paying heed to the other side of the case in developing arguments, and the use of random associations to stimulate thought. Such strategies are almost never taught in conventional instructional settings, but they easily could be. A note of warning, though: To teach *only* strategies of ideational fluency and flexibility is to buy into the ideational fluency tradition, where a broader conception of creative thinking would serve better.

Part of that broader conception involves attention to problem finding, another pattern of thinking. Problem-finding activities play hardly any role in conventional education. Students rarely formulate their own problems, nor are they encouraged in other acts of mind that exemplify problem finding—identifying and challenging assumptions and seeking new problem representations, for instance. Yet, again, one can readily design lessons that ask students to find their own problems within specified boundaries.

One might feel that younger students do not know enough yet to appreciate the aesthetics of a subject matter or engage in problem finding. This simply is not so. Even elementary arithmetic and reading, for example, afford opportunities to celebrate the beauty and cleverness of designs. The decimal number system and the alphabet are marvelously clever designs, and even younger students can appreciate something of their elegance and inventiveness if it is artfully highlighted. Further, the ordinary subject matters make ample room for problem finding by students. Children can, for example, make up arithmetic problems of various types and solve one another's problems. Notice how this converts a task involving short answer problems to a task involving designing wholes.

These are relatively simple accessible ideas, and many more are easily found. For instance, in *Knowledge as Design,* a number of tactics for saturating the subject matters with attention to creative and critical thinking are explored (Perkins, 1986b). With various frameworks at hand for treating the subject matters more creatively, the principal barriers to a more creative education become communication and conservatism. Teachers need to learn about such resources and to overcome others', and sometimes their own, conservative mindsets about how to teach, in order to take the opportunity. These are not easy problems, but at least the opportunity is there. This immanence of the creative and occasions to create in the most ordinary and elementary contexts is our primary counter to Salieri's Syndrome, that sees creative thinking as an elevated endeavor exclusively for those sufficiently elevated to attempt it.

AGENDAS FOR INQUIRY

I have tried to describe some of what we know about creative thinking and some implications for the practice of education. But none of this implies that the book is closed on the nature of and prospects for creative thinking. Indeed, any such attitude would be shockingly contrary to the spirit of creative thinking itself. Inevitably, ample room for inquiry on several fronts remains. Three in particular seem to have special importance in the present context: characteristics of creative thinking, the pedagogy of creative thinking, and the practicality of creative schooling. A few comments follow on each of these in turn.

Characteristics of Creative Thinking

The centrality of values, the importance of patterns of thinking, and the questionable role of potencies have been emphasized here. Although this picture reflects current findings, further testing and refinement certainly is in order. For example, some might argue that the values profile of a creative individual is far more important than patterns of thinking, urging that patterns of thinking relatively automatically develop out of an appropriate values profile. It would be interesting to try to operationalize and test such a position. For another example, as emphasized earlier, many of the patterns of thinking thought to be important in creativity have never been validated, either as presences in the thinking process of individuals of known creativity or as helpful guides that demonstrably boost the creative results of students following the patterns. The promise of such patterns rests on plausibility, not empirical evidence.

For yet a third example, whether creative thinking is a cross-disciplinary trait of a person, or a trait only principally manifested in a person's specialty, is an issue fairly readily investigated through close-grained biographical studies and other means. The development of creative thinking also deserves more careful scrutiny. For instance, cross-cultural studies could help to illuminate the role of the "literal period" in development. Such themes as these do no more than sample the many matters that could be explored.

The Pedagogy of Creative Thinking

As emphasized earlier, there is a dearth of solid empirical evidence showing that creative thinking can be developed through instruction, even though theory argues affirmatively and a few suggestive findings exist. One problem is the lack of a refined testing methodology for documenting gains without being vulnerable to an accusation of teaching to the test. Demonstrating an adequate pedagogy for creative thinking calls for development work toward such a methodology. Problems of measurement aside, the importance of internalization and transfer of creative values and patterns of thought was emphasized earlier. Although conditions likely to foster internalization and transfer have been discussed in Perkins (1986b) and elsewhere, formal inquiry is needed to confirm that these suffice or, if they do not, to spur the development of more powerful instructional models.

Even if students develop creative values and patterns of thought, these are not likely to survive and thrive unless the continuing instruction encourages their continued use. Accordingly, inquiry is needed into the opportunities for the exercise of creative thinking inherent in the teaching of the conventional subject matters. It was urged earlier that this was very feasible. However, such an assertion stands some way from a chart of possibilities or a systematic strategy that can help teachers to locate such possibilities for themselves.

The Practicality of a Creative Curriculum

The aforementioned themes deal with creative thinking and its pedagogy in principle—what is creative thinking really like, what sort of teaching would develop creative thinking if ideally implemented, and related questions. However, inquiry also is needed into the practicalities of a creative curriculum, a curriculum in which students in many, perhaps most, school settings have a good chance of acquiring the values and patterns of thinking characteristic of creativity. Here, for example, issues of preservice and in-service teacher education arise. How can entrenched "right answer" attitudes be changed? How can teachers learn the new styles of interaction between teacher and student that can abet the development of students' creative thinking? What can be done in climates seemingly unconducive to the development of creative thinking—for examples, a ghetto school with distrust between the students and faculty?

It may seem odd to view such questions as matters of research. To be sure, they call for very "hands on" research, where approaches are tried, probing the realities of practical circumstances. Nonetheless, a quest for a systematic understanding of such situations and the barriers they pose to success is as important a part of the battle for effective education as laboratory research. Indeed, many seemingly sound educational innovations have finally foundered on the seemingly secondary problem of getting teachers and students to adopt the methods that in principle should serve so well. Consequently, an agenda for research on creative thinking should not neglect a look at the classroom realities and ways to cope with and transform those realities.

CREATIVE THINKING AS AN EVOLVING PHENOMENON

These comments on what we know, and what more we would like to know, about creative thinking and its development should at least suggest that we are on the right track, and indeed have come some way along it. A fitting close to this review may be a final reflection on the phenomenon we are contemplating. To be sure, that phenomenon is creative thinking, but how constant a character does it really have? We tend to assume that creative thinking is a phenomenon with a stable nature—the same for us as for cave men. Creative thinking is there in the world, like trees, stars, and molecules. We want to understand it better and garner more of it, so we try to discover its inner nature and put that inner nature to work.

Let me suggest that this picture of creative thinking is subtly mistaken. Creative thinking is not a phenomenon with a constant nature at all. Perhaps it was a few hundred years ago, but the development of contemporary art shows how the phenomenon of creative thinking has changed and is still changing. In most cultures and at most times, art has not been a radically creative activity but more a refined craft. However, since the impressionists, and perhaps since the Renaissance, Western artists have become self-conscious innovators. It is plain that nearly any mid-20th century artist of note did not just happen upon a new genre but strove to create one. Genuine creative thinking in art came to mean not merely devising new works but calculatedly inventing new idioms.

A less flamboyant but similar self-consciousness can be seen occasionally in the scientific community today. Since the work of Thomas Kuhn (1962) on the history of scientific revolutions, at least some scientists have become acutely aware of the difference between work within a paradigm, extending its logic, and research of a more ground-breaking character that entails a shift in paradigm. Sometimes scientists writing about their own fields of expertise even discuss their and other work in just such terms. Having notions like paradigm change at hand does more than afford an opportunity for refined reflection; it allows a scientist to formulate personal objectives more sharply.

Likewise in any creative context, those who know something about creative thinking know better how to think of their own endeavors. One can ask oneself reflectively, "How original is this? How parsimonious is it? How elegant is it?" One can urge oneself, "Define the problem. Challenge your assumptions. Find the real problem." Strategies like these do not promise instant invention, of course. But they bring to bear in a self-conscious way values and patterns of thinking that nudge one's thinking along creative paths. Choosing a creative path was more difficult before, because the look of the path was not so clear.

What is the moral of this tale? The kind of creative thinking we often see today is more articulate, directed, and self-conscious. It is therefore a somewhat different phenomenon from what might be called "innocent" creativity. Some might feel wary of this new awareness, but I do not, because I think that a more knowing creativity gains in leverage and focus. We are, in a perfectly real sense, creating creative thinking, evolving the concept further even as we study it. Who knows what may result—perhaps credit cards will become the versatile Swiss army knives of an electronic age or we will have microchip Rage Warehouses for convenient Ire Proof storage of our passions. Creative thinking not only seems within reach, but may reach further than we yet imagine.

REFERENCES

Adams, J. L. (1974). *Conceptual blockbusting: A guide to better ideas.* New York: W. H. Freeman.

Amabile, T. M. (1983). *The social psychology of creativity.* New York: Springer-Verlag.

Anderson, J. R. (1983). *The architecture of cognition.* Cambridge, MA: Harvard University Press.

Arieti, S. (1976). *Creativity: The magic synthesis.* New York: Basic Books.

Baird, L. L. (1982). *The role of academic ability in high-level accomplishment and general success* (College Board Rep. No. 82–6). New York: College Entrance Examination Board.

Barron, F. (1969). *Creative person and creative process.* New York: Holt, Rinehart & Winston.

Barron, F. (1972). *Artists in the making.* New York: Seminar Press.

Bolt, Beranek, & Newman, Inc. (1983). *Final report, Project Intelligence: The development of procedures to enhance thinking skills.* Cambridge, MA: Author.

Carothers, T., & Gardner, H. (1979). When children's drawings become art: The emergence of aesthetic production and perception. *Development Psychology, 15,* 570–580.

Chase, W. C., & Simon, H. A. (1973). Perception in chess. *Cognitive Psychology, 4,* 55–81.

Chi, M. T. H., Glaser, R., & Rees, E. (1982). Expertise in problem solving. In R. Sternberg (Ed.), *Advances in the psychology of human intelligence* (pp. 7–75). Hillsdale, NJ: Lawrence Erlbaum Associates.

Crockenberg, S. B. (1972). Creativity tests: A boon or boondoggle for education? *Review of Educational Research, 42*(1), 27–45.

Csikszentmihalyi, M., & Getzels, J. W. (in press). Creativity and problem finding in art. In F. H. Farley & R. W. Neperud (Eds.), *The foundations of aesthetics, art, and art education.* New York: Praeger.

de Bono, E. (1970). *Lateral thinking: Creativity step by step.* New York: Harper & Row.

Ennis, R. H. (1981). Rational thinking and educational practice. In J. Soltis (Ed.), *Philosophy and education* (Vol. 1, Eightieth yearbook, pp. 143–183). Chicago: National Society for the Study of Education.

Ennis, R. H. (1986). A taxonomy of critical thinking dispositions and abilities. In J. B. Baron & R. S. Sternberg (Eds.), *Teaching thinking skills: Theory and practice* (pp. 9–26). New York: W. H. Freeman.

Gardner, H., & Winner, E. (1982). First intimations of artistry. In S. Strauss (Ed.), *U-shaped behavioral growth.* New York: Academic Press.

Getzels, J., & Csikszentmihalyi, M. (1976). *The creative vision: A longitudinal study of problem finding in art.* New York: Wiley.

Gordon, W. J. (1961). *Synectics: The development of creative capacity.* New York: Harper.

Grumbach, D. (1986). The literary imagination. In R. M. Caplan (Ed.), *Exploring the concept of mind* (pp. 121–131). Iowa City, IA: University of Iowa Press.

Guilford, J. P. (1967). *The nature of human intelligence.* New York: McGraw-Hill.

Guilford, J. P., & Hoepfner, R. (1971). *The analysis of intelligence.* New York: McGraw-Hill.

Herrnstein, R., Nickerson, R., Sanchez, M., & Swets, J. (1986). Teaching thinking skills. *American Psychologist, 41,* 1279–1289.

Kuhn, T. (1962). *The structure of scientific revolutions.* Chicago, IL: University of Chicago Press.

Langley, P., Bradshaw, G. L., & Simon, H. A. (1983). Rediscovering chemistry with the BACON system. In R. S. Michalski, J. G. Carbonell, & T. M. Mitchell (Eds.), *Machine learning: An artificial intelligence approach* (pp. 307–330). Palo Alto, CA: Tioga.

Larkin, J. H., McDermott, J., Simon, D. P., & Simon, H. A. (1980). Modes of competence in solving physics problems. *Cognitive Science, 4,* 317–345.

Lenat, D. B. (1983). Toward a theory of heuristics. In R. Groner, M. Groner, & W. Bischof (Eds.), *Methods of heuristics* (pp. 351–404). Hillsdale, NJ: Lawrence Erlbaum Associates.

Lowes, J. L. (1927). *The road to Xanadu*. Boston, MA: Houghton Mifflin.

Mansfield, R. S., & Busse, T. V. (1981). *The psychology of creativity and discovery*. Chicago, IL: Nelson-Hall.

Mansfield, R. S., Busse, T. V., & Krepelka, E. J. (1978). The effectiveness of creativity training. *Review of Educational Research, 48*(4), 517–536.

Marzano, R. J., Brandt, R. S., Hughes, C. S., Jones, B. F., Presseisen, B. Z., Rankin, S. C., & Suhor, C. (1988). *Dimensions of thinking: A framework for curriculum and instruction*. Alexandria, VA: Association for Supervision and Curriculum Development.

Mednick, S. A. (1962). The associative basis of the creative process. *Psychological Review, 69*, 220–232.

Newell, A., & Simon, H. (1972). *Human problem solving*. Englewood Cliffs, NJ: Prentice-Hall.

Nickerson, R., Perkins, D. N., & Smith, E. (1985). *The teaching of thinking*. Hillsdale, NJ: Lawrence Erlbaum Associates.

Osborn, A. (1953). *Applied imagination*. New York: Scribner.

Patrick, C. (1935). Creative thought in poets. In R. Woodworth (Ed.), *Archives of Psychology, 178*.

Patrick, C. (1937). Creative thought in artists. *Journal of Psychology, 4*, 35–73.

Perkins, D. N. (1981). *The mind's best work*. Cambridge, MA: Harvard University Press.

Perkins, D. N. (1984). Creativity by design. *Educational Leadership, 42*(1), 18–25.

Perkins, D. N. (1985). Reasoning as imagination. *Interchange, 16*(1), 14–26.

Perkins, D. N. (1986a). *Knowledge as design*. Hillsdale, NJ: Lawrence Erlbaum Associates.

Perkins, D. N. (1986b). Thinking frames. *Educational Leadership, 43*(8), 4–10.

Perkins, D. N. (1988). Creativity and the quest for mechanism. In R. S. Sternberg & E. Smith (Eds.), *The psychology of human thought* (pp. 309–336). Cambridge, England: Cambridge University Press.

Perkins, D. N., & Laserna, D. (1986). *Inventive thinking* (Lesson sequence in *Odyssey: A curriculum for thinking*). Watertown, MA: Mastery Education.

Plass, H., Michael, J. J., & Michael, W. B. (1974). The factorial validity of the Torrance tests of creative thinking for a sample of 111 sixth-grade children. *Educational and Psychological Measurement, 34*, 413–414.

Roe, A. (1952a). A psychologist examines 64 eminent scientists. *Scientific American, 187*(5), 21–25.

Roe, A. (1952b). *The making of a scientist*. New York: Dodd, Mead.

Roe, A. (1963). Psychological approaches to creativity in science. In M. A. Coler & H. K. Hughes (Eds.), *Essays on creativity in the sciences*. New York: New York University.

Rothenberg, A. (1979). *The emerging goddess: The creative process in art, science, and other fields*. Chicago, IL: University of Chicago Press.

Schneiderman, B. (1976). Exploratory experiments in programmer behavior. *International Journal of Computer and Information Sciences, 5*, 123–143.

Schoenfeld, A. H. (1982). Measures of problem-solving performance and of problem-solving instruction. *Journal for Research in Mathematics Education, 13* (1), 31–49.

Schoenfeld, A. H. (1985). *Mathematical problem solving.* New York: Academic Press.

Schoenfeld, A. H., & Herrmann, D. J. (1982). Problem perception and knowledge structure in expert and novice mathematical problem solvers. *Journal of Experimental Psychology: Learning, Memory, and Cognition, 8,* 484–494.

Skinner, B. F. (1972). A lecture on "having" a poem. In *Cumulative record: A selection of papers, Third edition* (pp. 345–355). New York: Meredith Corporation.

Soloway, E., & Ehrlich, K. (1984). Empirical studies of programming knowledge. *IEEE Transactions on Software Engineering, SE-10*(5), 595–609.

Torrance, E. P. (1966). *The Torrance tests of creative thinking: Norms-technical manual.* Princeton, NJ: Personnel Press.

Torrance, E. P. (1972a). Can we teach children to think creatively? *Journal of Creative Behavior, 6*(2), 114–143.

Torrance, E. P. (1972b). Career patterns and peak creative achievements of creative high school students twelve years later. *Gifted Child Quarterly, 16,* 75–88.

Torrance, E. P. (1974). *The Torrance tests of creative thinking: Norms-technical manual.* Bensenville, IL: Scholastic Testing Service.

Torrance, E. P. (1980). Growing up creatively gifted: A 22-year longitudinal study. *The Creative Child and Adult Quarterly, 5,* 148–159.

Torrance, E. P. (1981). Predicting the creativity of elementary school children (1958–80)—and the teacher who "made a difference." *Gifted Child Quarterly, 25,* 55–62.

Torrance, E. P., & Wu, T. (1981). A comparative longitudinal study of the adult creative achievements of elementary school children identified as highly intelligent and as highly creative. *The Creative Child and Adult Quarterly, 6,* 71–76.

Wallach, M. A. (1970). Creativity. In P. H. Mussen (Ed.), *Carmichael's manual of child psychology* (Vol. 1, pp. 1211–1266>). New York: Wiley.

Wallach, M. A. (1976a). Psychology of talent and graduate education. In S. Messick & Associates (Eds.), *Individuality in learning.* San Francisco: Jossey-Bass.

Wallach, M. A. (1976b). Tests tell us little about talent. *American Scientist, 64,* 57–63.

Wallach, M. A., & Kogan, N. (1965). *Modes of thinking in young children.* New York: Holt, Rinehart & Winston.

Winner, E. (1982). *Invented worlds: The psychology of the arts.* Cambridge, MA: Harvard University Press.

Critical and Reflective Thinking: A Philosophical Perspective

Richard W. Paul
Center for Critical Thinking and Moral Critique
Sonoma State University

In this chapter I lay the foundation for a philosophy-based, in contrast to a psychology-based, approach to teaching critical thinking across the curriculum. I both lay out the general theory and provide some examples of how the theory could be used to transform classroom instruction and activities. Nevertheless, I want to underscore the point that I do not have the space to cover my subject comprehensively. Interested readers must independently pursue the leads I provide, if they are to grasp the power and flexibility of philosophy-based approaches to critical thinking instruction. I must content myself with the attempt to provide some insight into the style of thinking and thinking about thinking characteristically philosophical and some sense of the potential strength and usefulness of such an approach.

There are three overlapping senses of *philosophy* that can play a role in explicating the nature of philosophical thinking: philosophy as a field of study, philosophy as a mode of thinking, and philosophy as a framework for thinking. In what follows, I focus on philosophy as a mode of and framework for thinking and say least about it as a field of study. Nevertheless, some characterization of the field of philosophy is useful.

Philosophy is a field steeped in dialogical and dialectical thought. Philosophy is an art rather than a science, a discipline that formulates issues that can be approached from multiple points of view, and that invites critical dialogue and reasoned discourse between conflicting viewpoints. Critical thought and discussion are its main instrument of learning. More so than any other field, philosophy requires all participants to think their own way to whatever system of beliefs come ultimately to constitute their thought within the field. This entails that all philosophers develop their own unique philosophies. As a point of contrast, science students are not expected to construct their own science. Sciences have emerged because of the possibility of specializing: collecting, differentiating, and quantifying empirical knowledge of the laws of nature. Science is a cooperative, collaborative venture between participants who agree to limit strictly the range of issues they consider and their mode of considering them. Philosophy, on the other hand, is an individualistic venture wherein participants do not agree, except in the broadest sense, on the range or nature of the issues they will consider. Philosophers have traditionally been concerned with big questions, root issues that organize the overall framework of thinking itself, in all, not just one, domain. Philosophers do not typically conduct *experiments*. They do not typically form *hypotheses* or make *predictions* in the scientific sense of these activities. What philosophical tradition gives us is a historical tapestry rich in the development of individualistic syntheses of ideas across multiple subject domains: syntheses carefully and precisely articulated and elaborately argued. There is a reason for this basic difference between the history of science and that of philosophy. Some questions by their nature admit of collaborative treatment and solution; some do not. We do not need, for example, to individually test for the chemical structure of lead or individually determine the appropriate theory of that structure; we can rely on the conclusions of those who have done so. But we cannot learn the structure of our own lives or the best way to plan for the future by looking up the answer in a technical manual or having an answer determined for us by a collaborative scientific effort. We must each analyze these questions, if we are to obtain rationally defensible answers. There is always a variety of ways in which human lives can be analyzed and a variety of possible ways of devising strategies for living them. In virtually all cases, no answer or answers to philosophical questions can be validated by one person for another.

The method of philosophy, or, if you will, the mode of thinking characteristic of philosophy, is that of critical discussion, rational cross examination, and dialectical exchange. Every person who would participate in that discussion must learn how to create and elaborate rational defenses for alternative ways of thinking about things. This discipline in the mode of thinking characteristic of philosophy is rooted in the ideal of learning to think with a clear sense of the ultimate foundations of one's own thinking, of the essential logic of one's own thought, and of significant alternative competing ways of thinking.

To put this point differently, consider philosophical thinking as a framework for thought. When one engages in philosophical thinking, one develops a unique *framework*. One thinks philosophically within some self-constructed network of assumptions, concepts, defined issues, key inferences, and insights. To think philosophically as a liberal is to think within a different framework of ideas than conservatives do. To think philosophically, in this sense, is to know that one is thinking within a different framework of ideas than other thinkers. It is to know the foundations of liberalism in comparison to those of conservatism.

PHILOSOPHICAL AND UNPHILOSOPHICAL MINDS: PHILOSOPHY AS A MODE OF THINKING AND A FRAMEWORK FOR THINKING

Perhaps the best way to show what lies at the heart of the uniqueness and power of philosophy is to consider the contrast in general between unphilosophical and philosophical minds. In doing so, I present the two as idealized abstractions for the purpose of clarifying a paradigm; I realize that no living person will perfectly illustrate these idealizations.

The unphilosophical mind thinks without a clear sense of the foundations of its own thought, of the most basic concepts, aims, assumptions, and values that define and direct it. In other words, the unphilosophical mind is unaware that it thinks within a system, within a framework, within, if you will, a *philosophy*. As a result, the unphilosophical mind is trapped within the system it uses, unable to deeply understand alternative or competing systems. The unphilosophical mind tends toward an intra-system closed-mindedness. The unphilosophical mind may learn to think within different systems of thought, if the systems are compartmentalized and apply in different contexts, but it cannot compare and contrast whole systems because at any given time it thinks within a system without a clear sense of what it means to do. This kind of intra-system thinking can be skilled, but because of its unphilosophicalness, it lacks foundational self-command. It functions well when confronted with questions and issues clearly defined within one or another system in which it can think, but it is at its worst when facing problems that cross systems, require the revision of a system, or presuppose a deep understanding of the system used.

Unphilosophical liberals, for example, would be hard pressed to think clearly and accurately within a conservative point of view, and hence would not do well with an issue like "What are some of the most important insights of conservatism?" Unphilosophical psychologists, to take another example, would find it difficult to integrate sociological or economic insights into their thinking. Indeed, to think unphilosophically in almost any discipline is to think reductionistically with respect to insights outside of one's field. One either reduces them to whatever can be absorbed into the established concepts in one's field or ignores them entirely. It should be clear by now, that in my view there are people who would not describe themselves as philosophers who nevertheless think philosophically.

An unphilosophical mind is at its best when routine methods, rules, or procedures function well and there is no need to critically reconceptualize them in the light of broad understanding of one's framework for thinking. If one lacks philosophical insight into the underlying logic of those routines, rules, or procedures, one lacks the ability to mentally step outside of them and conceive of alternatives. As a result, the unphilosophical mind tends toward conformity to a system without grasping clearly how the system came to be what it is or how it might have been otherwise.

The philosophical mind, in contrast, routinely probes the foundations of its own thought, realizes that its thinking is defined by basic concepts, aims, assumptions, and values. The philosophical mind gives serious consideration to alternative and competing concepts, aims, assumptions, and values, enters empathically into thinking fundamentally different from its own, and does not confuse its thinking with reality. By habitually thinking in a global way, the philosophical mind gains foundational self-command, and is comfortable when problems cross disciplines, domains, and frameworks. A philosophical mind habitually probes the basic principles and concepts that lie behind standard methods, rules, and procedures. The philosophical mind recognizes the need to refine and improve the systems, concepts, and methods it uses and does not simply conform to them. The philosophical mind deeply values gaining command over its own fundamental modes of thinking.

The discipline of philosophy is the only one at present that routinely fosters the philosophical mind, although there are philosophical minds at work in every discipline. The philosophical mind is most evident in other disciplines, in those working on foundational concepts and problems. In everyday life, the philosophical mind is most evident in those who deeply value doing their own thinking about the basic issues and problems they face and giving serious reasoned consideration to the ideas and thinking of others. In everyday life, the philosophical mind is most evident in those not afraid to probe conventional thought, rules, mores, and values, those skeptical of standard answers and standard definitions of questions and problems.

In teaching, the philosophical mind is most evident in those who routinely raise fundamental issues through Socratic questions; who routinely encourage students to probe the foundation and source of their own ideas and those of others; and who routinely encourage students to develop their own philosophy or approach to life or learning based on their own disciplined, rational thought. Need I add that philosophical thinking is not habitual in most people?

WHY CHILDREN NEED
TO THINK PHILOSOPHICALLY

Everyone has a philosophy in one sense, because human thought and actions are always embedded in a framework of foundational concepts, values, and assumptions which define a philosophy. Humans are by their nature inferential, meaning-creating animals. In this sense, all humans use philosophies and even in some sense create them. Even the thinking of very young children presupposes philosophical foundations, as Piaget so ably demonstrated. Of course, if by philosophy we mean the explicit and systematic reflection on the concepts, values, aims, and assumptions that structure thinking and underlie behavior, then in that sense most children do not philosophize. One can have a philosophy, in other words, without thinking one's way to it. Nevertheless, in this sense most children have the impulse to philosophize and for a time seem driven by a strong desire to know the most basic *what* and *why* of things.

Of course, parents or teachers rarely cultivate this tendency. Usually, children are given didactic answers in ways that discourage, rather than stimulate, further inquiry. Many parents and teachers seem to think that they or textbooks have appropriate and satisfactory answers to the foundational questions that children raise, and the sooner children accept these answers the better. Thus, they unwittingly encourage children to assent to, without truly understanding, those answers. In effect, we teach answers to philosophical questions as though they were like answers to questions about chemistry. Usually children lose the impulse to question as they learn to mouth the standard answers of parents, peers, and other socializing groups. How many of these mouthed answers become a part of children's "gut" belief systems is quite another matter.

To approach this point another way, children learn behaviors as well as explanations. They learn to act as well as to speak. And this includes coming to behave in ways inconsistent with much of their conscious talk and thought. Children learn to live, as it were, in different and only partially integrated worlds. They develop unconscious worlds of meaning, for example, that do not square completely with what they are told or think they believe. Some of these meanings become a source of pain, frustration, repression, fear, and anxiety. Some become a source of harmless fantasizing and day-dreaming. Some are embedded in action, albeit in camouflaged, or in tacit, unarticulated ways.

In any case, the process of unconsciously taking in or unknowingly constructing a variety of meanings outstrips the child's initial impulse to reflect on or question those meanings. In one sense then, children become captives of the ideas and meanings whose impact on their own thought and action they do not themselves determine. They have in this sense two philosophies (only partially compatible with each other): one verbal but largely unlived; the other lived but typically unverbalized. This split continues into adulthood. On the emotional level, it can lead to anxiety and stress. On the moral level, it is the basis for hypocrisy and self-deception. On the intellectual level, it results in a condition in which gut-level beliefs and spontaneous thought are unintegrated with school learning, which in turn is ignored in "real life" situations.

As teachers and parents, we seldom consider the plight of children from this perspective. We tend to act as if there were no real need for children to reflect deeply about the meanings they are absorbing. We do not tend to note the conflicting meanings they absorb, the double messages they are caught-up in. Typically we are more concerned that they absorb the meanings that we think are *correct* and act in ways that we approve of. Reflecting on their thoughts and actions seems important to us only to get them to think or act correctly, that is, as we think and act. We seldom question whether they deeply agree or even understand. Whether conflicting meanings and double messages become an on-going problem in their lives is not in the foreground of our parental attention.

In some sense, we act as if we believed, and doubtless many consciously do believe, that children have no significant capacity, need, or right to think for themselves. Many adults do not think that children can participate mindfully in the process by which their own minds and behavior are shaped. Of course, at the same time we often talk to our children as though they were somehow responsible for, or in control of, the ideas they express or act on. We need to deal explicitly with this contradictory attitude toward children.

I believe that children have the need, the capacity, and the right to freedom of thought and that the proper cultivation of that capacity requires an emphasis on the philosophical dimension of thought and action. Again, by the philosophical dimension I mean precisely the kind of deliberative thought that gives to thinkers the on-going disposition to mindfully create, analyze, and assess their own most basic assumptions, concepts, values, aims, and meanings; in effect to choose the very framework in which they think and on the basis of which they act. I would not go so far as to say, as Socrates was reputed to have said, that the unreflective life is not worth living, but I would say that an unreflective life is not a truly *free* life and is often a basic cause of personal and social problems.

I claim at least this much, that philosophical thinking is necessary to freedom of thought and action. I also hold that freedom of thought and action are good in themselves and should be given a high priority in schooling. They are certainly essential for a democracy. How can the people rule if they do not think for themselves on issues of civic importance? And if they are not encouraged to think for themselves *in* school, why should they do so once they *leave* school?

Let me now discuss whether children are in fact capable of this sort of freedom of thought, reflection on ultimate meanings, values, assumptions, and concepts. The question is both conceptual and empirical. On the conceptual side, the issue is one of *degree*. To the degree children are encouraged in supportive circumstances to reflect philosophically, to that degree only will they develop proficiency in such reflection. Because very few parents and teachers by and large value this sort of reflection or are adept at cultivating it, it is understandable that children soon give up on their instinctive philosophical impulses (the basic *why* and *what* questions). It would be foolish to assume that it is the *nature* of children to think and act unreflectively when indeed our experience indicates that they are socialized into unreflectiveness. Because we do not encourage children to philosophize, why should they do so? Furthermore, in many ways we penalize children for philosophizing. Children will on occasion innocently entertain an idea in conflict with the ideas of their parents, teachers, or peers. Typically, such ideas are ridiculed and the children made to feel ashamed of their thoughts. It is quite common, in other words, to penalize unconventional thought while rewarding conventional thought. When we think only as we are rewarded to think, however, we cease to think freely or deeply. Why should we think for ourselves if doing so may get us into trouble and if teachers, parents, and powerful peers provide authoritative didactic answers for us? Before we decide that children cannot think for themselves about basic ideas and meanings, we ought to give them a real and extended opportunity to do so. No society has yet done this. Unless we are willing to exercise some faith in freedom of thought, we will never be in a position to reap the benefits of it or discover its true limits, if any.

Let me now explore the conceptual side of the question further by suggesting some kinds of philosophical issues embedded not only in the lives of children but in the lives of adults as well:

Who am I? What am I like? What are the other people around me like? What are people of different backgrounds, religions, and nations like? How much am I like others? How much am I unlike them? What kind of a world do I live in? When should I trust? When should I distrust? What should I accept? What should I question? How should I understand my past, the pasts of my parents, my ethnic group, my religion, my nation? Who are my friends? Who are my enemies? What is a friend? How am I like and unlike my enemy? What is most important to me? How should I live my life? What responsibilities do I have to others? What responsibilities do they have to me? What responsibilities do I have to my friends? Do I have any responsibilities to people I don't like? To people who don't like me? To my enemies? Do my parents love me? Do I love them? What is love? What is hate? What is indifference? Does it matter if others do not approve of me? When does it matter? When should I ignore what others think? What rights do I have? What rights should I give to others? What should I do if others do not respect my rights? Should I get what I want? Should I question what I want? Should I take what I want? Should I take what I want if I am strong or smart enough to get away with it? Who comes out ahead in this world, the strong or the good person? Is it worthwhile to be good? Are authorities good or just strong?

I do not assume that children ought to reflect on all or even most of the questions that professional philosophers consider—although the preceding list contains many concepts that professional philosophers tackle. To cultivate philosophical thinking, one does not force students to think in a sophisticated way before they are ready. Each student can contribute to a philosophical discussion thoughts that help other students orient themselves within a range of thoughts, some of which support or enrich and some of which conflict with other thoughts. Different students achieve different levels of understanding. There is no reason to try to "force" any given student to achieve any given level of understanding. In any case, it is possible to lead young students into philosophical discussions, which help them begin to:

1. Get a sense of the significance and relevance of basic philosophical questions to understanding themselves and the world about them.
2. Understand the problematic character of human thought and the need to probe deeply into it.
3. Gain insights into what it takes to make thinking more rational, critical, and fair-minded.
4. Organize their thinking globally across subject matter divisions.
5. Achieve initial command over their own thought processes.
6. Come to believe in the value and power of their own minds.

In the transcript that follows an average fourth-grade class is led to discuss a variety of basic ideas: how the mind works, the nature of mind, why different people interpret the same events differently, the relationship of happiness and sadness to mental interpretations, the nature and origin of personality, nature versus nurture, peer group influence on the mind, cultural differences, free will versus determinism, the basis for ethical and unethical behavior, the basis for reputation, the relation of reputation to goodness, mental illness, social prejudice and sociocentrism, and the importance of thinking for oneself. This transcript represents the first philosophical discussion this particular class had and although it is clear from some of their answers that their present degree of insight into the ideas being discussed is limited, it is also clear that they are capable of pursuing those insights and of articulating important philosophical ideas that could be explored at greater and greater depth over time.

Transcript
Fourth-Grade Socratic Discussion

How does your mind work?

Where's your mind?

Student: "In your head." (numerous students point to their heads)

Does your mind do anything?

Student: "It helps you remember and think."

Student: "It helps, like, if you want to move your legs. It sends a message down to them."

Student: "This side of your mind controls this side of your body and that side controls this other side."

Student: "When you touch a hot oven it tells you whether to cry or say ouch!"

Does it tell you when to be sad and when to be happy?

How does your mind know when to be happy and when to be sad?

Student: "When you're hurt it tells you to be sad."

Student: "If something is happening around you is sad."

Student: "If there is lightning and you are scared."

Student: "If you get something you want."

Student: "It makes your body operate. It's like a machine that operates your body."

Does it ever happen that two people are in the same circumstance but one is happy and the other is sad? Even though they are in exactly the same circumstance?

Student: "You get the same toy. One person might like it. The other gets the same toy and he doesn't like the toy."

Why do you think that some people come to like some things and some people seem to like different things?

Student: "Cause everybody is not the same. Everybody has different minds and is built different, made different."

Student: "They have different personalities?"

Where does personality come from?

Student: "When you start doing stuff and you find that you like some stuff best."

Are you born with a personality or do you develop it as you grow up?

Student: "You develop it as you grow up."

What makes you develop one rather than another?

Student: "Like, your parents or something."

How can your parent's personality get into you?

Student: "Because you're always around them and then the way they act if they think they are good and they want you to act the same way then they'll sort of teach you and you'll do it."

Student: "Like, if you are in a tradition. They want you to carry on something that their parents started."

Does your mind come to think at all the ways the children around you think? Can you think of any examples where the way you think is like the way children around you think? Do you think you behave like other American kids?

Student: "Yes."

What would make you behave more like American kids than like Eskimo kids?

Student: "Because you're around them."

Student: "Like, Eskimo kids probably don't even know what the word 'jump-rope' is. American kids know what it is."

And are there things that the Eskimo kids know that you don't know about?

Student: "Yes."

Student: "And also we don't have to dress like them or act like them and they have to know when a storm is coming so they won't get trapped outside."

O.K., so if I understand you then, parents have some influence on how you behave and the kids around you have some influence on how you behave. . . . Do you have some influence on how you behave? Do you choose the kind of person you're going to be at all?

Student: "Yes."

How do you do that do you think?

Student: "Well if someone says to jump off a five-story building, you won't way O.K. You wouldn't want to do that . . ."

Do you ever sit around and say, "Let's see shall I be a smart person or a dumb one?"

Student: "Yes."

But how do you decide?

Student: "Your grades"

But I thought your teacher decided your grades. How do you decide?

Student: "If you don't do your homework you get bad grades and become a dumb person but if you study real hard you'll get good grades."

So you decide that, right?

Student: "And if you like something at school like computers you work hard and you can get a good job when you grow up. But if you don't like anything at school you don't work hard.

Student: "You can't just decide you want to be smart, you have to work for it."

Student: "You got to work to be smart just like you got to work to get your allowance."

What about being good and being bad, do you decide whether you're good or you're bad? How many people have decided to be bad? (3 students raise their hands) To first student: Why have you decided to be bad?

Student: "Well, I don't know. Sometimes I think I've been bad too long and I want to go to school and have a better reputation but sometimes I feel like just making trouble and who cares."

Let's see, is there a difference between who you are and your reputation? What's your reputation? That's a pretty big word. What's your reputation?

Student: "The way you act. If you had a bad reputation people wouldn't like to be around you and if you had a good reputation people would like to be around you and be your friend."

Well, but I'm not sure of the difference between who you are and who people think you are. Could you be a good person and people think you bad? Is that possible?

Students: Chorus of "NO!"

So some people are really good at hiding what they are really like. Some people might have a good reputation and be bad; some people might have a bad reputation and be good.

Student: "Like, everyone might think you were good but you might be going on dope or something."

Student: "Does reputation mean that if you have a good reputation you want to keep it just like that? Do you always want to be good for the rest of your life?"

I'm not sure . . .

Student: "So if you have a good reputation you try to be good all the time and don't mess up and don't do nothing?"

Suppose somebody is trying to be good just to get a good reputation— why are they trying to be good?

Student: "So they can get something they want and they don't want other people to have?"

Student: "They might be shy and just want to be left alone."

Student: "You can't tell a book by how it's covered."

Yes, some people are concerned more with their cover than their book.

When teachers approach their subjects in a philosophical way, they make it much easier for students to begin to integrate their thinking across subject matter divisions. In the preceding discussion, for example, the issues considered involved personal experience, psychology, sociology, ethics, culture, and philosophy. The issues, philosophically put, made these diverse areas relevant to each other. And just as one might inquire into a diversity of issues as a result of asking a basic philosophical question, so one might proceed in the other direction: first asking a question within a subject area and then, by approaching it philosophically, exploring the relations between that subject and others. These kinds of transitions are quite natural and unforced in a philosophical discussion because all dimensions of human study and experience are indeed related to each other. We would see this if we could set aside the blinders that usually come with conventional discipline-specific instruction. By routinely considering root questions and root ideas philosophically, we naturally pursue those connections separate from these blinders.

As teachers teaching philosophically, we are continually interested in what the students themselves think on basic matters and issues. We continually encourage students to explore how what they think about X relates to what they think about Y and Z. Of necessity this requires that students' thought moves back and forth between their own basic ideas and those being presented in class by other students, between their own ideas and those expressed in a book, between their thinking and their experiences, between ideas within one domain and those in another. This *dialogical* process (moving back and forth between divergent domains and points of view) will sometimes become *dialectical* (some ideas will clash or be inconsistent with others). The act of *integrating* thinking is deeply tied to the act of *assessing* thinking, because, as we consider a diversity of ideas, we discover that many of them are in fact incompatible with each other. Teachers should introduce the critical analytic vocabulary of English (to be discussed presently) into classroom talk, so that students increasingly sense standards and tools that they can use in making their integrative assessments. Skilled use of such terms as *assumes, implies,* and *contradicts,* is essential to rational assessment of thinking.

It would be unrealistic to expect students to suddenly and deeply grasp the roots of their own thinking, or to immediately be able to honestly and fair-mindedly assess it; to instantly weed out all beliefs to which they have not consciously assented. In teaching philosophically, one is continually priming the pump, as it were, continually encouraging responsible autonomy of thought, and making progress in degrees across a wide arena of concerns. The key is continually to avoid "forcing" the student to acquiesce to authoritative answers without understanding them. To the extent that students become submissive in their thinking, they stop thinking for themselves. When they comply tacitly or passively without genuine understanding, they are set back intellectually.

To cultivate students' impulse to think philosophically, we have to continually encourage students to believe that they can figure out where they stand on root issues, that they themselves have something worthwhile to say, and that what they have to say ought to be given serious consideration by the other students and the teacher.

Thus, all subjects can be taught philosophically or unphilosophically. Let me illustrate by using the subject of history. Because philosophical thinking tends to make explicit our most basic ideas and assumptions, by using it we can better orient ourselves toward the subject as a whole and integrate mindfully the parts into that whole.

Students are introduced to history early in their education, and that subject area is typically a requirement through high school and into college, and with good reason. But the unphilosophical manner in which history is often taught fails to develop students' ability to think historically for themselves. Indeed, history books basically tell students what to believe and what to think about history. Students have little reason in the typical history class to relate what is said to the framework of their own ideas, assumptions, values, and so forth. Students do not know that they have a philosophy and even if they did, it is doubtful that without the stimulation of a teacher who approached the subject philosophically, they would initially see the relevance of history to it.

But consider the probable outcome of teachers raising and facilitating discussions on questions such as the following:

What is history? Is everything that happened part of history? Can everything that happened be put into a history book? Why not? If historians have to select some events to include and leave out others, how do they do this? If this requires that historians make value judgments about what is important, is it likely that they will all agree? Is it possible for people observing and recording events to be biased or prejudiced? Could a historian be biased or prejudiced? How would you find out? If events, to be given meaning, have to be interpreted from some point of view, what is the point of view of the person who wrote our text?

Do you have a history? Is there a way in which everyone develops an interpretation of the significant events in his or her own life? If there is more than one point of view that events can be considered from, could you think of someone in your life who interprets your past in a way different from you? Does it make any difference how your past is interpreted? How are people sometimes harmed by the way in which they interpret their past?

Obviously all of these questions would not be asked at once. Rather they would be the *kind* of question routinely raised as part of stimulating students to take history seriously, to connect it to their lives, minds, values, and actions. After all, many of the most important questions we face in everyday life do have a significant historical dimension, but that dimension is not given by a bare set of easily isolated facts. For example, arguments between spouses often involve disagreements over how to interpret events or patterns of past events or behavior. And often how we interpret events in our lives depends on our basic values, assumptions, and so forth. Few of us are good historians or philosophers in the matter of our own lives. But then, no one has encouraged us to be. No one has helped us to grasp these kinds of connections or relate to our own thought or experience in this way. We do not see ourselves as shaping our experience within a framework of meanings, because we have not learned how to isolate and identify the central ideas of our lives. Rather we tend to believe, quite egocentrically, that we directly and immediately grasp reality. The world must be the way we see it because we see nothing standing between us and the world. We seem to see it directly and objectively. We do not really see the need therefore to give serious consideration to other ways of seeing or interpreting it. As we identify our philosophy, framework, or ideas, however, and deliberately put those ideas to work in interpreting our world, including giving serious consideration to competing ideas, we are freed from the illusion of absolute objectivity. We begin to recognize lack of objectivity as a serious problem in human affairs. Our thought begins to grapple with that problem in a variety of ways. We begin to discover ways in which our fears, insecurities, vested interests, frustrations, egocentricity, ethnocentricity, prejudices, and so forth blind us. We begin to develop intellectual humility. We begin in short to think philosophically. Children have this need as much as adults, for children often imbibe and construct meanings that come to constrain and frustrate their development and alienate them from themselves as well as from healthy relationships to others.

VALUES AND INTELLECTUAL TRAITS

Philosophical thinking, like all human thinking, is infused with values. But those who think philosophically make it a point to understand and assent to the values that underlie their thought. One thinks philosophically because one *values* figuring out the meaning and significance of one's life. If we do so sincerely and well, we recognize obstacles along the way that challenge us to decide the kind of person we want to be, including deciding the kind of mind we want to have. We have to make a variety of value judgments about ourselves regarding, among other things, fears, conflicts, and prejudices. This requires us to come to terms with the traits of mind we are developing. For example, to be truly open to knowledge, one must become intellectually humble. But this intellectual trait is connected with other traits, such as intellectual courage, intellectual integrity, intellectual perseverance, intellectual empathy, and fairmindedness. The intellectual traits characteristic of our thinking become for the philosophical thinker a matter of personal concern. Philosophical reflection helps to heighten this concern.

To illustrate, consider this excerpt from a letter from a teacher with a Master's degree in Physics and Mathematics:

> After I started teaching, I realized that I had learned physics by rote and that I really did not understand all I knew about physics. My thinking students asked me questions for which I always had the standard textbook answers, but for the first time made me start thinking for myself, and I realized that these canned answers were not justified by my own thinking and only confused my students who were showing some ability to think for themselves. To achieve my academic goals I had memorized the thoughts of others, but I had never learned or been encouraged to learn to think for myself.

This is a good example of intellectual humility and, like all intellectual humility, it is based on a philosophical insight into the nature of knowing. It is reminiscent of the ancient Greek insight that Socrates himself was the wisest of the Greeks because only he knew how little he really understood. Socrates developed this insight as a result of extensive, deep questioning of the knowledge claims of others. He had to think his way to this insight and he did so by carrying through on the basic *what* and *why* questions that children often ask. We as teachers cannot hand this insight to children on a silver platter. All persons must do for themselves the thinking that leads to it. Unfortunately, although intellectual virtues cannot be conditioned into people, intellectual failings can. Because of the typically unphilosophical way in which most knowledge is presented, intellectual arrogance rather than humility is fostered, particularly in those who have a retentive memory and an ability to repeat back what they have heard or read. Students are rewarded for giving standard textbook answers and encouraged to believe that they understand what has never been justified by their own thinking. To move toward intellectual humility, most students (and teachers) would need to think philosophically (broadly, deeply, and foundationally) about most of what they have "learned," as the teacher in the preceding example did, but such questioning in turn requires a certain amount of intellectual courage, perseverance, and faith in their own ability to think their way to understanding and insight from the perspective of their own point of view.

My point here is that genuine intellectual development requires people to develop particular intellectual traits, traits acquired only by thinking one's own way to a set of basic philosophical insights. Certain kinds of philosophical thinking lead to insights, which in turn infuse and inform basic skills of thought. Skills, values, insights, and intellectual traits are mutually and dynamically interrelated. It is the whole person who thinks, not a disassociated portion of a person's brain.

For example, intellectual empathy requires the ability to reconstruct accurately the viewpoints and reasoning of others and to reason from premises, assumptions, and ideas other than our own. But if one has not developed the philosophical insight that different people often think from divergent premises, assumptions, and ideas, one will never appreciate the need to entertain them. One will never grasp the basic truth that reasoning from assumptions and ideas other than our own will seem absurd to us precisely to the degree that we are unable to step back philosophically and recognize that differences exist between people in their very framework for thinking. These kinds of philosophical differences are common, even in the lives of small children. Children often reason from the assumption that their needs and desires are more important than the needs and desires of anyone else, to the conclusion that they ought to get what they want in this or that circumstance. It may seem absurd to them that they are not given what they want. They are trapped in the egocentric viewpoints, see the world from within them, and unmindfully take their viewpoints (their philosophies, if you will) to define reality. To work one's way out of this intellectual entrapment requires time and much philosophical reflection.

To develop a consciousness of the limits of our knowledge we must have the **courage** to face our own prejudices and ignorance. To discover our own prejudices and ignorance in turn we often have to **empathize** with and reason within points of view toward which we are hostile. To achieve this end we must typically **persevere** over an extended period of time, for it takes time and significant effort to learn how to emphatically enter a point of view against which we are biased. That effort will not seem justified unless we have the **confidence in reason** to believe we will not be tainted or taken in by whatever is false or misleading in this opposing viewpoint. Furthermore, the belief alone that we can survive serious consideration of alien points of view is not enough to motivate most of us to consider them seriously. We must also be motivated by an **intellectual sense of justice.** We must recognize an intellectual **responsibility** to be fair to views we oppose. We must feel **obliged** to hear them in their strongest form to ensure that we do not condemn them out of ignorance or bias.

If we approach thinking or teaching for thinking atomistically, we are unlikely to help students get the kind of global perspective and global insight into their mind, thought, and behavior which a philosophical approach to thinking can foster. Cognitive psychology tends to present the mind and dimensions of its thinking in just this atomistic way. Most importantly, it tends to leave out of the picture what should be at its very center: the active, willing, judging agent. The character of our mind is one with our moral character. How we think determines how we behave and how we behave determines who we are and who we become. We have all of us a moral as well as an intellectual responsibility to become fairminded and rational, but we will not become so unless we cultivate these traits through specific modes of thinking. From a philosophical point of view, one does not develop students' thinking skills without in some sense simultaneously developing their autonomy, rationality, and, if you will, their character. This is not fundamentally a matter of drilling the student in a battery of skills, although some drilling may help. Rather it is essentially a matter of orchestrating activities to continually stimulate students to express and to take seriously their own thinking: what it is, what it assumes, what it implies, what it leads to, what it is compatible and incompatible with, and so forth; and to help the student do this with intellectual humility, intellectual courage, intellectual empathy, intellectual perseverance, and fairmindedness.

DIFFERENCES BETWEEN THE TRADITIONS
OF PHILOSOPHY AND COGNITIVE PSYCHOLOGY

Failure to address the attitudinal and normative dimensions of thinking results in an imbalance in perspective. There are important differences between those features of thinking highlighted by philosophers working in the critical thinking movement and the general approach to thinking fostered by cognitive psychologists and educators influenced by them. And although there is much that each field is beginning to learn from the other, learning can fruitfully take place only if some of the significant differences between these two traditions are set out in clear relief and due emphasis is given to both traditions.

In thinking of the relationship between the traditions of cognitive psychology and philosophy, I am reminded of a couple of remarks by the great 19th-century educator-philosopher John Henry Newman (1912) in his classic *Idea of a University:*

> I am not denying, I am granting, I am assuming, that there is reason and truth in the "leading ideas," as they are called and "large views" of scientific men; I only say that, though they speak truth, they do not speak the whole

truth; that they speak a narrow truth, and think it a broad truth; that their
deductions must be compared with other truths, which are acknowledged
to be truths, in order to verify, complete, and correct them. (p. 178)

If different studies are useful for aiding, they are still more useful for
correcting each other; for as they have their particular merits severally, so
they have their defects. (p. 176)

In this case, the "scientific" views of cognitive psychologists need to be
corrected by the insights of philosophers, if the whole truth is to be
apprehended.

It is only when we are aware of the differing emphases, assumptions,
and concepts, even the differing value priorities of the two disciplines
and see how these are reflected in the work of those interested in critical
thinking that we can begin to appreciate the distinctive contributions of
both cognitive psychology and philosophy to instruction for thinking.
Few K-12 educators and their education department counterparts recognize the possible contribution of philosophy to instruction for thinking
because their own educational background was heavily biased in favor of
psychologically and scientistically oriented courses. Rarely were they expected to articulate a philosophical perspective, to reason and synthesize
across disciplinary lines, rarely were they expected to formulate their
philosophy, and, what is more, most do not feel comfortable with philosophical argumentation and counter-argumentation as a means of establishing probable truth. Well-reasoned philosophical essays do not seem
to them to be research, properly so called, because empirical studies are
not typically cited in such essays. With these thoughts in mind, let us
examine 24 contrasting emphases between these two disciplines (see Figure 14.1). I do not assume, of course, that all 24 are always present, but
that, on the whole, there is a gestalt-like pattern of differences between
the writings of *most* cognitive psychologists and *most* philosophers.

There are, in other words, significant differences between the style,
direction, and manner in which one aims for improvement in thinking
when one's own thinking about thinking is shaped more or less deeply by
scholars working in one or the other of these two rich traditions. It
should be added that inevitably problems of misunderstanding and mutual prejudice remain as residues of the historical separation of psychology from the discipline of philosophy. That psychologists are sometimes
skeptical of philosophical approaches to teaching for thinking is poi-
gnantly demonstrated by Al Benderson (1984) of the Educational Testing Service. In characterizing "The View From Psychology" (on philosophy's contribution to teaching for thinking) Benderson said:

Psychologists, who have their roots in research into mental processes, tend

| | Tendencies of: | |
With respect to:	Cognitive Psychologists	Philosophers
1. Approach to thinking	Approach thinking descriptively.	Tend to approach thinking normatively.
2. Methodology	Focus on empirical fact-gathering. (This is not to imply that cognitive psychologists do not formulate theories or engage in conceptual analysis.)	Focus on the analysis of cases of "well-justified" thinking in contrast to cases of "poorly justified" thinking.
3. Modes of thinking studied	Focus on expert versus novice thinking, intra-disciplinary thinking, and monological thinking.	Focus on rational reflective thinking, on interdisciplinary thinking, and on multilogical thinking.
4. Value emphasis	Emphasize the value of expertise.	Emphasize the values of rationality, autonomy, self-criticism, open-mindedness, truth, and empathy.
5. Authority	Make the authority of the expert central.	Play down the authority of the expert and play up the authority of independent reason.
6. Language used	Generate more technical terminology and make their points in a technical fashion.	Take their terminology and concepts more from the critical/analytic vocabulary of a natural language (e.g., assumes, claims, implies, is consistent with, contradicts, is relevant to).
7. Role of values in thinking	Separate the cognitive from the domain of (a) value-choices of the thinker and (b) the overall world view of the thinker (at least when discussing basic mental skills and processes).	Emphasize the role in thinking of values and the overall conceptual framework of the thinker; hence, the significance of identifying and assessing points of view and frames of reference.

(continued)

	Tendencies of:	
With respect to:	Cognitive Psychologists	Philosophers
8. Place of dialogue	Play down the significance of dialogical and dialectical thinking.	Play up the significance of dialogical and dialectical thinking; view debate and argumentation as central to rational thinking.
9. View of affect	Underemphasize the affective obstacles to rational thinking: fear, desire, prejudice, bias, vested interest, conformity, self-deception, egocentrism, and ethnocentrism.	Emphasize the affective obstacles to rational thinking (this emphasis is correlated with the emphasis on the philosophical ideal of becoming a rational person).
10. Role of teacher	Play down the role of the teacher as autonomous critical thinker (this is perhaps an emerging issue in cognitive psychology).	Make central the role of the teacher as autonomous critical thinker, the need to question her own biases, prejudices, point of view, and so forth.
11. Classroom climate	Play down the need to develop classrooms as communities of inquiry wherein dialogical and dialectical exchange is a matter of course.	Play up the need to develop classrooms as communities of inquiry where students learn the arts of analyzing, synthesizing, advocating, reconstructing, and challenging each others' ideas.
12. Place of intelligent skepticism	Ignore or play down the significance of the student as Socratic questioner, as intelligent skeptic (this too may be an emerging issue).	Make central the significance of questioning; view intellectual advancement more in terms of skill in the art of questioning than in the amassing of an unquestioned knowledge base (the thinker as questioner is connected by philosophers with the disposition to suspend judgment in cases in which the thinker is

464

With respect to:	Tendencies of:	
	Cognitive Psychologists	Philosophers
		called upon to accept beliefs not justified by his or her own thinking).
13. Place of empirical research	Play up the significance of empirical research in settling educational issues.	Skeptical of empirical research as capable of settling significant educational issues without argumentation between conflicting educational viewpoints or philosophies on those issues.
14. View of the teaching process	Give more weight to the significance of teaching as embodying step-by-step procedures (although there is increasing dissent within cognitive psychology from this orientation).	Play up the significance of dialogical approaches that involve much criss-crossing and unpredictable backtracking in teaching and thinking; skeptical of step-by-step procedures in teaching and thinking.
15. Identified micro-elements in thinking	In analyzing the micro-elements in thinking, emphasize such categories as recalling, encoding and storing, and identifying relationships and patterns—all of which admit to empirical study.	In analyzing the micro-elements in thinking, emphasize identification of issues, assumptions, relevant and irrelevant considerations, unclear concepts and terms, supported and unsupported claims, contradictions, inferences and implications—all of which shed light on thought conceived as the intellectual moves of a reasoning person.
16. Place of micro-skills	Separate the analysis of micro-skills from normative considerations.	Link the analysis of micro-skills with normative considerations since, for philosophers, micro-skills are intellec-

(continued)

	Tendencies of:	
With respect to:	Cognitive Psychologists	Philosophers
		tual moves which can be used to clarify, analyze, synthesize, support, elaborate, question, deduce, or induce.
17. View of macro-processes	View macro-processes from the perspective of categories of research in cognitive psychology: problem solving, decision making, concept formation, and so forth.	View macro-processes from the perspective of the overall reasoning needs of rational person: ability to analyze issues and distinguish questions of different logical types, ability to Socratically question, ability to engage in conceptual analysis, ability to accurately reconstruct the strongest case for opposing points of view, the ability to reason dialogically and dialectically (each use of a macro-process is a unique orchestration of some sequence of micro-skills in the context of some issue, problem, or objective).
18. Teaching as a science or art	Present teaching for thinking as a quasi-science, with the assumption that there is a discrete body of information that can be "added up" or "united" and passed on "as is" to the teacher.	Present teaching for thinking as an intellectual art; play down the significance of technical empirical information as necessary to skill in that art.
19. Place of philosophy of education	Ignore or play down the significance of teachers developing a philosophy of education into which rationality, autonomy, and self-criticism become central values.	Emphasize the importance of each teacher developing an explicit philosophy of education which is openly stated in the classroom; tend to encourage students to do the same,

466

	Tendencies of:	
With respect to:	Cognitive Psychologists	Philosophers
		especially in relation to their philosophy of life.
20. Obstacles to rational thinking	Ignore the problem of prejudice and bias in parents and the community as possible obstacles to teaching for rational thinking.	Sensitive to the dangers of community and national bias as possible obstacles to teaching for rational thinking.
21. Place of virtues and passions	Underemphasize the significance of rational passions and intellectual virtues.	Emphasize the significance of rational passions (developing a passionate drive for clarity, accuracy, fair-mindedness, a fervor for getting to the bottom of things, to the deepest root issues, for listening sympathetically to opposing points of view, a compelling drive to seek out evidence, an intense aversion to contradiction and sloppy thinking, a devotion to truth as against self-interest) and intellectual virtues (intellectual humility, intellectual courage, intellectual integrity, intellectual empathy, intellectual perseverance, intellectual faith in reason, and an intellectual sense of justice).
22. Specialized vs. mundane thinking	Orient themselves toward domain-specific thinking, with the "good" thinker often associated with the successful business or professional person, or with a specialist working within a discipline.	Emphasize the link between an emphasis on rational thinking and the goals of a traditional liberal education, of the ideal of the liberally educated person and on mundane generalizable skills such as

(continued)

	Tendencies of:	
With respect to:	*Cognitive Psychologists*	*Philosophers*
		proficiency in the art of reading the newspaper critically in detecting propaganda and bias in public discourse, in advertising, in textbooks, and in rational reorientation of personal values and beliefs.
23. Place of ethics of teaching and the rights of students	Lay insufficient stress upon the relation of teaching for thinking to the ethics of teaching and the rights of students.	Emphasize the link between teaching for critical thinking and developing moral insight and with the rights of students; in this case, with the student's "right to exercise his independent judgement and powers of evaluation"; as Siegel (1980) puts it:"To deny the student this right is to deny the student the status of a person of equal worth."
24. Thinking and one's way of life	Lay insufficient stress upon the relation of modes of thinking to fundamental ethical and philosophical choices concerning a way of life.	Link emphasis on critical thinking with an attempt to initiate students, as Israel Scheffler (1965) puts it, "into the rational life, a life in which the critical quest for reasons is a dominant and integrating motive."

FIG. 14.1.   Two contrasting approaches to thinking.

to view thinking from a different perspective than do philosophers. ETS Distinguished Research Scientist, Irving Sigel, a psychologist, views philosophers who claim to teach thinking skills as encroaching upon a field in which they have little real expertise. "These philosophers are imperialists," he charges. "They don't know the first thing about how kids think." (p. 10)

R. S. Peters and C. A. Mace (1967), two philosophers in turn commenting on the separation of psychology from philosophy for the *Encyclopedia of Philosophy*, said:

> The trouble began when psychologists claimed the status of empirical scientists. At first the philosophers were the more aggressive, deriding the young science as a bogus discipline. The psychologists hit back and made contemptuous remarks about philosophical logic-chopping and armchair psychology. The arguments were charged with emotion and neither side emerged with great credit. . . . Not all issues between philosophers and psychologists have been resolved, but there has been notable progress toward a policy of coexistence, and here and there some progress toward cooperation has been made. (p. 26)

In the field of teaching for thinking there has been, in my view, much more coexistence than cooperation. The largest and oldest conference tradition in the field (the Sonoma Conferences: two national and six international conferences, the last with a registration of over 1,000 with over 100 presenters and 230 sessions) has had only token participation by cognitive psychologists. The conference on *Thinking* at Harvard, in turn, had only token participation by philosophers. There are, it appears to me, few psychologists or philosophers who read widely in the other tradition. Furthermore, the field of education has been dominated by various psychologically based rather than philosophically based models of instruction. It is understandable, therefore, why *Dimensions of Thinking* (Marzano et al., 1988), a recent publication from the Association for Supervision and Curriculum Development, written by a team that included no philosophers, fails to successfully represent the approach or include the insights of philosophy in the thinking skills movement.

Virtually all of the research cited, the concepts and terminology used, and the recommendations made for implementation in *Dimensions of Thinking* are taken from the writings of scholars working principally in the tradition of cognitive psychology. The work and perspective of many of the philosophers concerned with thinking is minimally reported. Those whose work is not significantly used include for example:

Michael Scriven, Harvey Siegel, Mortimer Adler, John Passmore, Israel Scheffler, Mark Weinstein, R. S. Peters, Ralph Johnson, J. Anthony Blair, Stephen Norris, John Dewey, Vincent Ruggiero, Edward D'Angelo, Perry Weddle, Sharon Bailin, Lenore Langsdorf, T. Edward Damer, Howard Kehane, Nicholas Rescher, Paulo Freire, Robert Swartz, Max Black, James Freeman, John Hoaglund, Gerald Nosich, Jon Adler, Eugene Garver . . . (to name some who come readily to mind).

I might also mention in passing that virtually nothing is done to illuminate significant philosophical contributions to our understanding of thinking from the great philosophers of the last 300 years. There is no mention of Immanuel Kant's work on the mind's shaping and structuring of human experience, of Hegel's work on the dialectical nature of human thought, of Nietzsche's illumination of self-delusion in human thought, or of Wittgenstein's work on the socio-linguistic foundations of human thought.

Another perspective conspicuously absent from *Dimensions of Thinking* is that of affective and social psychology, especially those studies that shed light on the major obstacles or blocks to rational thinking: prejudice, bias, self-deception, desire, fear, vested interest, delusion, illusion, egocentrism, sociocentrism, and ethnocentrism. The significance of this omission should be clear. The point behind the thinking skills movements (in both cognitive psychology and philosophy) is not simply to get students to think; all humans think spontaneously and continuously. The problem is to get them to think *critically* and *rationally* and this requires insight by students into the nature of uncritical and irrational thinking. There is a massive literature in affective and social psychology that bears on this problem and hence its seminal insights and concepts should be a significant part of any adequate framework for understanding how to reform education so as to cultivate rational, reflective autonomous, empathic thinking. Philosophers, I might add, are often as guilty as cognitive psychologists in ignoring the work of affective and social psychologists.

THE SKILLS AND PROCESS OF THINKING

Philosophers, as I have emphasized, do not tend to approach the micro-skills and macro-processes of thinking from the same perspective as cognitive psychologists. Intellectual skills and processes are approached, not from the perspective of the needs of empirical research, but from the perspective of personal, rational control. The philosophical is, as I have suggested, a person-centered approach to thinking. Thinking is always the thinking of some actual person, with some egocentric and sociocentric tendencies, with some particular intellectual traits, involved in the problems of a particular life. This need to understand one's own mind, thought, and action cannot be eliminated with information from empirical studies about aspects or dimensions of thought. The question foremost in the mind of the philosopher is not "How should I conceive of the various skills and processes of the human mind so as to be able to conduct empirical research on them?" but "How should I understand the elements of thinking so as to be able to analyze, assess, and rationally control my own thinking and accurately understand and assess the thinking of others?" Thinking is viewed from the perspective of the needs of the thinker attempting to achieve or move toward an intellectual and moral ideal of rationality and fairmindedness. The tools of intellectual analysis used are the results of philosophy's 2,500 years of thinking and thinking about thinking.

Since thinking for oneself is a fundamental presupposed value for philosophy, the micro-skills philosophers use are intellectual moves that a reasoning person continually makes, independent of the subject matter of thought. Hence, whenever one is reasoning, there is some issue or problem that one is reasoning about (hence a family of skills derived from analyzing and clarifying issues and problems). Likewise, whenever one is reasoning, one is reasoning from some point of view or within some conceptual framework (hence a family of relevant skills derived from analyzing and clarifying interpretations or interpretive frameworks.) Finally, whenever one is reasoning, one is, in virtue of one's inferences, coming to some conclusions from some beliefs or premises which are, in turn, based on some assumptions (hence a family of relevant skills derived from analyzing, clarifying, and evaluating beliefs, judgments, inferences, implications, and assumptions). There is, from the philosophical point of view, a range of interrelated processes that one needs to engage in (all of which constitute unique orchestrations of these various micro-skills) in virtually every case. Hence, from the philosophical point of view, the fundamental question is not whether one is solving problems or making decisions or engaging in scientific inquiry or forming concepts or comprehending or composing or arguing, precisely because one is typically doing all of the above (excluding possibly scientific inquiry) in each and every case. Problem solving, decision making, concept formation, comprehending, composing, and arguing are in some sense common to all reasoning. What we need to do as reasoners, from the philosophical point of view, is not to decide which of these things we are doing, but rather to use with good judgment any or all of the following macro-processes:

1. *Socratic Questioning:* Questioning ourselves or others in such a way as to bring out into the open the salient features of our thinking:
   (a) What precisely is at issue?
   (b) From what point of view are we reasoning? Are there alternative points of view from which the problem or issue might be approached?
   (c) What assumptions are we making? Are they justified? What alternative assumptions could we make instead?

(d) What concepts are we using? Do we grasp them? Their ap-
     propriateness? Their implications?
(e) What evidence have we found or do we need to find? How
     dependable is our source of information?
(f) What inferences are we making? Are those inferences well
     supported?
(g) What are the implications of our reasoning?
(h) How does our reasoning stand up to competing or alter-
     native reasoning?
(i) Are there objections to our reasoning we need to consider?

2. *Conceptual Analysis.* If there are problematic concepts or uses of
   terms, they need to be analyzed and their basic logic set out and
   assessed. Have we done so?

3. *Analysis of the Question-at-Issue.* Whenever one is reasoning, one
   is attempting to settle some question at issue. But in order to
   settle a question, one must understand the kind of question it is.
   Different questions require different modes of settlement. Do
   we grasp the precise demands of the question-at-issue?

4. *Reconstructing Alternative Viewpoints in Their Strongest Forms.*
   Because, whenever one is reasoning, one is reasoning from a
   point of view or within a conceptual framework, it is necessary
   again and again to practice identifying and reconstructing
   those views. Have we empathically reconstructed the relevant
   points of view?

5. *Reasoning Dialogically and Dialectically.* Because it is almost always possible to imagine some range of alternative lines of reasoning with respect to a given issue or problem, and because a
   reasonable person sympathetically considers alternative lines of
   reasoning, it is necessary again and again to practice dialectical
   reasoning. Have we reasoned from a variety of points of view
   (when relevant) and rationally identified and considered the
   strengths and weaknesses of these points of view as a result of
   this process?

Implicit in the macro-processes, as I have suggested earlier, are identifiable micro-skills. These constitute moves of the mind in attempting to
think in a philosophical, and hence in a rational critically creative way.
The moves are implied in the critical-analytic vocabulary of English (presumably every natural language—French, German, etc.,—has equiv-
alents for them). Hence in Socratically questioning someone we are engaging in a *process* of thought. Within that process we make a variety of
moves. We make those moves explicit by using analytic terms such as:

claims, assumes, implies, infers, concludes, is supported by, is consistent with, is relevant, is irrelevant, has the following implications, is credible, plausible, clear, in need of analysis, without evidence, in need of verification, is empirical, is conceptual, is a judgment of value, is settled, is at issue, is problematic, is analogous, is biased, is loaded, is well confirmed, is theoretical, hypothetical, a matter of opinion, a matter of fact, a point of view, a frame of reference, and a conceptual framework.

To put the point another way, in order to gain command of our thinking we need to be able to take it apart and put it back together in the light of its logic, the patterns of reasoning that support it, oppose it, and shed light on its rational acceptability. We do not need a formal or technical language to do this, but we do need a command of certain critical-analytic terms available in ordinary English. Their careful use helps discipline, organize, and render self-conscious our ordinary inferences and the concepts, values, and assumptions that underlie them.

PHILOSOPHICAL AND CRITICAL THINKING

Those familiar with some of my other writings will recognize that what I am calling here philosophical thinking is very close to what I have generally called *strong sense critical thinking*. The connection is not arbitrary. The ideal of strong sense critical thinking is implicit in the Socratic philosophical ideal of living a reflective life (and thus achieving command over our own mind and behavior). Instead of absorbing their philosophy from others, people can, with suitable encouragement and instruction, develop a critical and reflective attitude toward ideas and behavior. Their outlook and interpretations of themselves and others can be subject to serious reflection. As we so reflect and integrate the insights we discover, our beliefs become more our own creation, rather than the product of our unconscious absorption of others' beliefs. Such basic ideas as history, science, drama, mind, imagination, and knowledge become organized by the criss-crossing paths of one's reflection. They cease to be thought of as compartmentalized subjects. The philosophical questions one raises about history cut across those raised about the human mind or about science or knowledge or imagination. Only the depth that philosophical questioning and honest criticism provide, protects us from the danger of *weak sense critical thinking*. When we think critically merely in a weak sense, we question only within the parameters of a fundamentally unquestioned point of view. We tend to use our intellectual skills merely to defend and buttress those concepts, aims, and assumptions already deeply buried in our thought.

The roots of thinking determine the nature, direction, and quality of thinking. If teaching for thinking does not help students understand the roots of their thinking, it will fail to give them real command over their minds. They may simply make the transition from uncritical thought to weak sense critical thought. They may make the transition from being unskilled in thinking to being narrowly skilled, to being close-mindedly skilled.

David Perkins (1986) has highlighted this problem from a somewhat different point of view. In studying the relationship between people's scores on standardized IQ tests and their open-mindedness, as measured by their tendency to construct arguments against their points of view on a public issue, Perkins found that:

> Intelligence scores correlated substantially with the degree to which subjects developed arguments thoroughly on their own sides of the case. However, there was no correlation between intelligence and elaborateness of arguments on the other side of the case. In other words, the more intelligent participants invested their greater intellectual endowment in bolstering their own positions all the more, not in exploring evenhandedly the complexities of the issue. (p. 3)

Herein lies the danger of an approach to thinking that relies fundamentally, as cognitive psychology often does, on the goal of technical competence, without making central the deeper philosophical or normative dimensions of thinking. Student skill in thinking may increase, but whatever narrowness of mind or lack of insight, whatever intellectual closed-mindedness, intellectual arrogance, or intellectual cowardice the students suffer, will be supported by that skill. It is crucial therefore that this deeper consideration of the problem of thinking be highlighted and addressed in a significant and global manner. Whether one labels it "philosophical" thinking or "strong sense critical thinking" or "thinking that embodies empathy and open-mindedness" is insignificant. A similar point can be made about the thinking of teachers if we merely provide teachers with exercises for their students that simply promote technical competence in thinking, if inservice programs are not designed to challenge the thinking of teachers, they will likely inadvertently pass on their own deeply seated prejudices to their students. Teachers will not see the quality of their own thinking as relevant to classroom instruction. They will assume their thinking is adequate, rather than seriously inquire into whether it is sensitive to root ideas, to alternative frames of reference, and to the logic of what is said. The fact is, however, that the thinking of teachers is deeply involved at every level of teaching. Left unreformed by self-analysis and critique, little will change in the students' thought.

Unfortunately a general case for the contribution of philosophy to thinking and to teaching for thinking, such as this one, must of necessity lack in a good deal of the concrete detail regarding how one would, as a practical matter, translate the generalities discussed here into action in the classroom or in everyday thinking. There are two basic needs. The first is an ample supply of concrete models that bridge the gap between theory and practice. These models should come in a variety of forms: video tapes, curriculum materials, handbooks, and so forth. Second, most teachers need opportunities to work on their own philosophical thinking skills and insights. These two needs are best met in conjunction with each other. It is important for the reader to review particular philosophy-based strategies in some detail.

The most extensive program available is *Philosophy for Children,* developed by Matthew Lipman in association with the Institute for the Advancement of Philosophy for Children (Lipman, Sharp, & Oscanyan, 1980). It is based on the notion that philosophy ought to be introduced into schools as a separate subject and philosophical reflection and philosophical ideas used directly as an occasion for teaching thinking skills. The program introduces philosophy in the form of children's novels. Extensive teachers' handbooks are provided and a thorough inservice required in order to ensure that teachers develop the necessary skills and insights to encourage classroom discussion of root ideas in such a way that students in turn achieve philosophical insights and reasoning skills. In a year-long experiment conducted by the Educational Testing Services, significant improvements were recorded in reading, mathematics, and reasoning. *Philosophy for Children* achieves transfer of reasoning skills into the standard curriculum but is not designed to directly infuse philosophical reflection into it.

In contrast, the Center for Critical Thinking and Moral Critique at Sonoma State University in California is developing a philosophy-based approach focused on directly infusing philosophical thinking across the curriculum (see Paul, Binker, & Charbonneau, 1987 and Paul, Binker, Jensen, & Kreklau, 1987). Handbooks of lesson plans K-12 have been remodeled by the Center staff to demonstrate that, with redesign, philosophically based critical thinking skills and processes can be integrated into the lessons presently in use, if only teachers gain the requisite training and practice in remodeling the lessons they presently use. Thirty-one strategies are used. They represent ways of helping students to use:

STRATEGIES FOR INFUSING CRITICAL THINKING

A.   Affective Strategies

S-1.	to think independently	(See below.)
S-2.	to develop insight into ego/socio-centricity	i.e., to encourage children to question their own immediate beliefs and those of their peer group, discuss the discrepancies between self or group image and self or group behavior, explore self-justifying or group-justifying thought
S-3	to exercise fair-mindedness/reciprocity	e.g., to encourage children to role play the thinking of parents or other children
S-4	to explore thoughts underlying feelings	i.e., to encourage children to think about as they do and how to recognize how their feelings can illuminate their thought
S-5	to suspend judgment	i.e., to encourage children to distinguish what they know from what they do not

B.   Cognitive Strategies—Macro-Abilities

S-6	to avoid oversimplification	e.g., to encourage children to explore other causes contributing to an event which had been previously overlooked by them or by their text
S-7	to transfer ideas to new contexts	i.e., to encourage children to apply a newly learned idea or skill to a variety of phenomena or situations
S-8	to develop one's perspective	i.e., to present opportunities for children to develop their own ideas, through discussion or written work
S-9	to clarify issues and claims	i.e., to have students discuss how they could settle questions or verify claims
S-10	to clarify ideas	i.e., to encourage children to give examples and opposite cases and discuss what a term implies
S-11	to develop criteria for evaluation	i.e., to give children practice setting up standards or ideals, and discussing how they might use them to test or evaluate something, to encourage them to make the standards they use explicit
S-12	to evaluate source credibility	e.g., to distinguish legitimate from illegitimate authorities, or evaluate the reliability of observers or reporters of events
S-13	to raise and pursue root questions	i.e., to encourage children to explore

in-depth the basic issues or important questions underlying a subject area, or those raised in or by course material

S-14 to evaluate arguments i.e., to give children experience in evaluating which reasons are better

S-15 to generate or assess solutions i.e., to give children the opportunity to suggest solutions, before presenting solutions to them; to encourage extended and fairminded comparison of all suggested solutions

S-16 to evaluate actions and policies e.g., to discuss and evaluate the actions of story characters or historical figures

S-17 to clarify or critique text i.e., to encourage children to question, clarify, and evaluate what they read

S-18 to make interdisciplinary connections i.e., to encourage children to compare and explore the relationships between the various subject areas and explore issues and phenomena from the perspective of more than one discipline

S-19 to engage in Socratic discussion i.e., to create an open-minded, curious atmosphere in the classroom wherein each person's ideas are considered worthy of exploration; to ask clarifying and probing questions of children regarding their ideas; to provide opportunities for children to question others

S-20 to practice dialogical thinking i.e., to engage children in exploring and comparing multiple perspectives in extended discussion

S-21 to practice dialectical thinking i.e., to allow children to pit conflicting perspectives against each other in extended discussion, in order to test their relative strengths and weaknesses

C. Cognitive Strategies—Micro-Skills

S-22 to distinguish facts from ideals e.g., to give children practice in identifying the difference between what is so from what they wish were so

S-23 to use critical vocabulary i.e., to give children practice using such words as assume, infer, criteria, perspective, relevant, distinguish, contradict, interpret, etc.

S-24 to distinguish ideas e.g., to have children distinguish and compare the ordinary and the scientific concept of 'work'

S-25 to examine assumptions i.e., to encourage children to recog-

		nize and evaluate beliefs they and others take for granted
S-26	to distinguish relevant from irrelevant facts	i.e., to ask children to explain which information is relevant to a question or problem, which is not, and why
S-27	to make plausible inferences	e.g., to ask children what can justifiably be inferred about a character from his actions and statements
S-28	to supply evidence for a conclusion	i.e., to routinely ask children *why* they say what they say, how they know what they know
S-29	to recognize contradictions	i.e., to give children practice in telling which pairs of statements couldn't both be true and why, or in exploring inconsistencies between word and deed, or in discussing double standards
S-30	to explore implications and consequences	e.g., to give children statements and ask them, "If this were true, what else would have to be true?"
S-31	to refine generalizations	i.e., to encourage children to qualify generalizations—e.g., to say 'many,' 'often,' 'seldom,' 'In *this* kind of case . . .'

Each strategy is embodied in a principle and its application explained and illustrated with a variety of specific lesson-plan examples. For instance, the first strategy, practicing independent thinking is explained in the following way:

S-1 Exercising Independent Thought
Principle:
Critical thinking is autonomous thinking, thinking for oneself. Many of our beliefs are acquired at an early age, when we have a strong tendency to accept beliefs for irrational reasons (because we want to believe, because we are rewarded for believing). Critical thinkers uses critical skills to reveal and eradicate beliefs to which they cannot rationally assent. In formulating new beliefs, critical thinkers do not passively accept the beliefs of others; rather they analyze issues themselves, reject unjustified authorities, and recognize the contributions of justified authorities. They do not accept as true, or reject as false, beliefs they do not understand. They are not easily manipulated.

Application:
A critical education respects the autonomy of the student. It appeals to rationality. Students should be encouraged to discover information, and use their knowledge, skills, and insights to think for themselves. In science, for example, students could put their own headings on charts or graphs

they make, or decide what kind of graph would be most illuminating. Merely giving students "facts" or telling them the "right way" to solve a problem hinders the process of critiquing and modifying preexisting beliefs with new knowledge. Allowing students to think things through deepens student understanding of material studied.

Rather than simply having students discuss ideas in their texts, the teacher can have them brainstorm ideas and argue among themselves, for instance, about problems and solutions to problems. Before reading a section of text that refers to a map, chart, time-line, or graph, have students read and discuss what the map, or the rest, shows. Have students develop their own categories instead of providing them with categories. For example, remodel "Types of Literature" lessons by having students discuss and group writings they have read.

When giving written assignments, those assignments should provide many opportunities for the student to exercise independent judgment: in gathering and assembling information, in analyzing and synthesizing it, and in formulating and evaluating conclusions. Have students discuss how to organize their points in essays.

Students could review material themselves, rather than relying on their texts for summaries and review questions. The class could brainstorm about what they learned when studying a lesson or unit. Only after they have exhausted their memories should the teacher try to elicit any crucial points neglected.

Eighteen lesson plans in the K-3 handbook, and 24 lessons in the 4-6 handbook are then cited to which a teacher can refer to see how the general strategy can be applied.

We provide a "before" and "after," (the lesson plan before it was remodeled and after it was remodeled); a critique of the unremodeled lesson plan to clarify how the remodel was achieved; a list of specific objectives; and the particular strategies used in the remodel. Here is one such example.

Two Ways to Win

(Language Arts—Second Grade)

Objectives of the Remodeled Lesson

The student will:

- use analytic terms such as: assume, infer, imply
  - make inferences from story clues

- discuss and evaluate an assumption about making friends
- clarify "good sport" by contrasting it with its opposite, "bad sport"

Original Lesson Plan

Abstract

Students read a story about a brother and sister named Cleo and Toby. Cleo and Toby are new in town and worried about making new friends. They ice skate at the park every day after school, believing that winning an upcoming race can help them make new friends (and that they won't make friends if they don't win). Neither of them win; Cleo, because she falls, Toby, because he forfeits his chance to win by stopping to help a boy who falls. Some children come over after the race to compliment Toby on his good sportsmanship and Cleo on her skating. Most of the questions about the story probe the factual components. Some require students to infer. Questions ask what "good sport" means and if Cleo's belief about meeting people is correct. (From *Mustard Seed Magic*, Theodore L. Harris et al. Economy Company. (c) 1972, pp. 42–46)

Critique

There are a number of good questions in the original lesson that require students to make inferences, for example, "Have Toby and Cleo lived on the block all their lives?" THe text also asks students if they know who won the race. Because they do not, this question encourages students to suspend judgment. Although good sportsmanship is a good idea for students to discuss, the text fails to have students practice techniques for clarifying ideas. Instead, they ask students to list the characteristics of a good sport (a central idea in the story) with no discussion of what it means to be a bad sport. The use of opposite cases to clarify ideas helps students develop fuller and more accurate ideas. With such practice a student can begin to recognize borderline cases as well; for example, where someone was a good sport in some respects, bad in others.

Strategies Used to Remodel

S-10 clarifying ideas

S-28 supplying evidence for a conclusion

S-23 using critical vocabulary

S-25 examining assumptions

Remodeled Lesson Plan

Where the original lesson asks, "What does 'a good sport' mean?," we suggest an extension (**S-10**). The teacher should make two lists on the board of the students' responses to the question "How do good sports and bad sports behave?" Students could go back to the story and apply the ideas on the list to the characters in the story, giving reasons to support any claims they make regarding the characters' sportsmanship (**S-28**). In some cases there might not be enough information to determine whether a particular character is a good or bad sport. Or they might find a character who is borderline, having some characteristics of both good and bad sports. Again, students should cite evidence from the story to support their claims. The students could also change details of the story to make further points about the nature of good and bad sportsmanship. (If the girl had pushed Cleo down in order to win the race, that would have been very bad sportsmanship.) To further probe the idea of good sportsmanship, ask questions like the following: How did Toby impress the other children? Why did they think he did a good thing? If you had seen the race, what would you have thought of Toby? Why do we value the kind of behavior we call good sportsmanship? Why don't we like bad sportsmanship? Why are people ever bad sports?

There are a number of places in the lesson where the teacher could introduce, or give students further practice using critical thinking vocabulary **S-23**. Here are a few examples: What can you infer from the story title and picture? What parts of the story imply that Toby and Cleo will have some competition in the race? What do Toby and Cleo assume about meeting new people and making new friends? **S-25** Is this a good or bad assumption? Why? Why do you think they made this assumption? Have you ever made similar assumptions? Why? What can you infer that Cleo felt at the end of the story? How can you tell?

After close examination of specific classroom materials and teaching strategies, one comes to understand how to translate philosophically based approaches into classroom practice. Only then is one in a reasonable position to assess the value and power of such approaches.

THE PHILOSOPHY-BASED APPROACH TO TEACHING

A strong case can be made for a philosophically based approach to thinking and teaching for thinking. Such an approach differs fundamentally from most cognitive psychology-based approaches. Philosophy-based approaches reflect the historic emphases of philosophy as a field, as a

481

mode of thinking, and as a framework for thinking. The field is historically committed to certain intellectual and moral ideals, and presupposes the capacity of people to live a reflective life that enables them to
achieve an understanding of and command over the most basic ideas
that rule their lives. To achieve this command, people must critically
examine the ideas on which they act and replace those ideas when, in
their own best judgment, they can no longer rationally assent to them.
Such an ideal of freedom of thought and action requires that individuals
have a range of intellectual standards by means of which they can assess
thought. These standards are partially given by the critical-analytic terms
that exist in every natural language, but they must also be applied in a
certain spirit—a spirit of intellectual humility, empathy, and fair-mind-
edness. To develop insight into proper intellectual judgment, one must
engage in and become comfortable with dialogical and dialectical thinking. Such thinking is naturally stimulated when one asks basic questions,
inquires into root ideas, and invites and honestly considers a variety of
responses. It is further stimulated when one self-reflects. The reflective
mind naturally moves back and forth between a variety of considerations
and sources. The reflective mind eventually learns how to inwardly generate alternative points of view and alternative lines of reasoning, even
when others are not present to express them.

A teacher who teaches philosophically brings these ideals and practices into the classroom whatever the subject matter, for all subject matter is grounded in ideas which in the last analysis must be understood
and related to ideas preexisting in the students' minds. The philosophically oriented teacher wants all content to be critically and analytically
processed by each and every student in such a way that students can
integrate it into their own thinking, rejecting, accepting, or qualifying it
in keeping with the honest thinking of that student. All content provides
grist for the philosophical mill, an opportunity for students to think
further, to build upon their previous thought. The philosophically oriented teacher is careful not to require the students to take in more than
they are capable of intellectually digesting. The philosophically oriented
teacher is keenly sensitive to the ease with which minds become passive
and submissive and reiterate without deeply understanding what they
"learn." The philosophically oriented teacher is more concerned with
the global state of students' minds (Are they developing their own thinking, points of view, intellectual standards and traits, etc.?) than with the
state of the students' minds within a narrowly defined subject competence. Hence it is much more important to such a teacher that students
learn how to think historically (how to look at their own lives and experience and the lives and experiences of others from a historical vantage
point) than that they learn how to recite information from a history text.

History books are read as aids to historical thought not as ends-in-themselves.

The philosophically oriented teacher continually looks for deeply rooted understanding and encourages the impulse to look more deeply into things. Hence, the philosophically oriented teacher is much more impressed with how little we as humans know than with how much information we have collected. They are much more apt to encourage students to believe that they, as a result of their own thinking, may come to better answers to life's problems than have yet been devised, than they are to encourage students to submissively accept established answers.

What stands in the way of successful teaching for thinking in most classrooms is not fundamentally the absence of technical, empirical information about mental skills and processes, but a lack of experience of and commitment to teaching philosophically. As students, most teachers, after all, were not themselves routinely encouraged to think for themselves. They were not exposed to teachers who stimulated them to inquire into the roots of their own ideas or to engage in extended dialogical and dialectical exchange. They have not had experience in Socratic questioning, in taking an idea to its roots, in pursuing its ramifications across domains and subject areas, in relating it critically to their own experience, or in honestly analyzing it from other perspectives.

To appreciate the power and usefulness of a philosophy-based approach, one must understand, not only the general case that can be made for it, but also how it translates into specific classroom practices. One will achieve this understanding only if one can for a time step outside the framework of assumptions of cognitive psychology and consider how thinking, thinking about thinking, and teaching for thinking might be reappropriated from a very different and fresh perspective. If we look at thinking only from the perspective of cognitive psychology, we will likely fall into the trap that Gerald W. Bracey (1987) recently characterized as:

> . . . the long and unhappy tendency of American psychology to break learning into discrete pieces and then treat the pieces in isolation. From James Mill's "mental mechanics," through Edward Titchener's structuralism, to behavioral objectives and some "componential analysis" in current psychology. U.S. educators have acted as if the whole were never more than the sum of its parts, as if a house were no more than the nails and lumber and glass that went into it, as if education were no more than the average number of discrete objectives mastered. We readily see that this is ridiculous in the case of a house, but we seem less able to recognize its absurdity in the case of education. (p. 684)

In thinking, if nowhere else, the whole is greater than the sum of its parts, and cannot be understood merely by examining its psychological

leaves, branches, or trunk. We must also dig up its philosophical roots
and study its seed ideas as ideas: the "stuff" that determines the very
nature of thought itself.

CONCLUSION: TOWARD RAPPROCHEMENT

Cognitive psychologists and philosophers have typically failed to appropriate the strengths, and correct for the weaknesses, of their two traditions. Despite this failure, there are some signs of emerging common
themes in the two traditions that may prove to be the basis for integration. Representatives of both traditions are developing a profound critique of what I would call a "didactic" theory of knowledge, learning, and
literacy and framing a "critical" alternative. Behind this critique and
reconstruction is a growing common sense of how the didactic paradigm
is impeding the scholastic development of critical thinkers. I recently
summarized this picture as follows:

> Most instructional practice in most academic institutions around the world
> presupposes a didactic theory of knowledge, learning, and literacy, ill-
> suited to the development of critical minds and literate persons. After a
> superficial exposure to reading, writing, and arithmetic, schooling is typ-
> ically fragmented thereafter into more or less technical domains each with
> a large technical vocabulary and an extensive content or propositional
> base. Students memorize and reiterate domain-specific details. Teachers
> lecture and drill. Active integration of the students' daily non-academic
> experiences is rare. Little time is spent stimulating student questions. Stu-
> dents are not typically encouraged to doubt what they hear in the class-
> room or read in their texts. Students' personal points of view or philoso-
> phies of life are considered largely irrelevant to education. Classrooms with
> teachers talking and students listening are the rule. Dense and typically
> speedy coverage of content is typically followed by content-specific testing.
> Interdisciplinary synthesis is ordinarily viewed as a personal responsibility
> of the student and is not routinely tested. Technical specialization is con-
> sidered the natural goal of schooling and is correlated with getting a job.
> Few multi-sided issues or problems are discussed or assigned, and even
> fewer teachers know how to conduct such discussions or assess student
> participation in them. Students are rarely expected to engage in dialogical
> or multi-sided reasoning, and few teachers are proficient analysts of such
> reasoning. Knowledge is viewed as verified intra-disciplinary propositions
> and well-supported intra-disciplinary theories. There is little or no discus-
> sion of the nature of prejudice or bias, little or no discussion of metacogni-
> tion, little or no discussion of what a disciplined, self-directed mind or self-
> directed thought require. The student is expected to develop into a literate
> educated person through years of what is essentially content memorization
> and ritual performance.

	Theory of Knowledge, Learning, and Literacy	
Assumption about	Didactic Theory	Critical Theory
1. The fundamental needs of students	That the fundamental need of students is to be taught more or less what to think, not how to think (i.e., that students will learn how to think if they can only get into their heads what to think).	That the fundamental need of students is to be taught how, not what to think; that it is important to focus on significant content, but this should be accomplished by raising live issues that stimulate students to gather, analyze and assess that content.
2. The nature of knowledge	That knowledge is independent of the thinking that generates, organizes, and applies it.	That all knowledge of "content" is generated, organized, applied, analyzed, synthesized, and assessed by thinking; that gaining knowledge is unintelligible without engagement in such thinking. (It is not assumed that one can think without some content to think about, nor that all content is equally significant and useful.)
3. Model of an educated person	That an educated literate person is fundamentally a repository of content analogous to an encylcopedia or data bank, directly comparing situations in the world with "facts" that he or she carries about fully formed as a result of an absorptive process; that an educated person is fundamentally a true believer, that is, a possessor of truth, and therefore	That an educated literate person is fundamentally a repository of strategies, principles, concepts, and insights embedded in processes of thought rather than atomic facts. Experiences analyzed and organized by critical thought, rather than facts picked up one-by-one, characterize the educated person. Much of what is "known" is constructed by the

(continued)

	Theory of Knowledge, Learning, and Literacy	
Assumption about	Didactic Theory	Critical Theory
	claims much knowledge.	thinker as needed from context to context—not prefabricated in sets of true statements about the world; that an educated literate person is fundamentally a seeker and questioner rather than a true believer, and therefore cautious in claiming knowledge, being aware of many unknowns.
4. The nature of knowledge	That knowledge, truth, and understanding can be transmitted from one person to another by verbal statements in the form of lectures or didactic teaching.	That knowledge and truth can rarely, and insight never, be transmitted from one person to another by the transmitter's verbal statements alone; that one person cannot directly give another what he has learned—one can only facilitate the conditions under which people learn for themselves by figuring out or thinking things through.
5. Relative importance of listening	That students do not need to be taught skills of listening in order to learn to pay attention and this is fundamentally a matter of self-discipline achieved through will power. Students should therefore be able to listen on command by the teacher.	That students need to be taught how to listen critically—an active and skilled process that can be learned by degrees with various levels of proficiency. Learning what another person means by what she/he says requires questioning, trying on, testing, and, hence, engaging in public or private dialogue with him or her, and this involves critical thinking skills.

486

Assumption about	Theory of Knowledge, Learning, and Literacy	
	Didactic Theory	*Critical Theory*
6. The relationship of basic skills to thinking skills	That the basic skills of reading and writing can be taught without emphasis on higher order critical thinking skills.	That the basic skills of reading and writing are inferential skills that require critical thinking; that students who do not learn to read and write critically are ineffective readers and writers, and that critical reading and writing involve dialogical processes in which probing critical questions are raised and answered (e.g., What is the fundamental issue?, What reasons, what evidence, is relevant to this issue? Is this source or authority credible?, Are these reasons adequate? Is this evidence accurate and sufficient? Does this contradict that? Does this conclusion follow? Is another point of view relevant to consider?)
7. The status of questioning	That students who have no questions typically are learning well, while students with a lot of questions are experiencing difficulty in learning; that doubt and questioning weaken belief.	That students who have no questions typically are not learning— while having pointed and specific questions, on the other hand, is a significant sign of learning. Doubt and questioning, by deepening understanding, strengthen belief by putting it on more solid ground.
8. The desirable classroom environment	That quiet classes with little student talk are typically reflective of	That quiet classes with little student talk are typically classes with lit-

(continued)

Assumption about	Theory of Knowledge, Learning, and Literacy	
	Didactic Theory	*Critical Theory*
	students learning while classes with a lot of student talk are typically disadvantaged in learning.	tle learning while student talk, focused on live issues, is a sign of learning (provided students learn dialogical and dialectical skills).
9. The view of knowledge (atomistic vs. holistic)	That knowledge and truth can typically be learned best by being broken down into elements, and the elements into sub-elements, each taught sequentially and atomically. Knowledge is additive.	That knowledge and truth is heavily systemic and holistic and can be learned only by many on-going acts of synthesis, many cycles from wholes to parts, tentative graspings of a whole guiding us in understanding its parts, periodic focusing on the parts (in relation to each other) shedding light upon the whole, and that the wholes that we learn have important relations to other wholes as well as their own parts and hence need to be frequently canvassed in learning any given whole. (This assumption has the implication that we cannot achieve in-depth learning in any given domain of knowledge unless the process of grasping that domain involves active consideration of its relation to other domains of knowledge.) That each learner creates knowledge.
10. The place of values	That people can gain significant knowledge without seeking or valuing it, and hence that education can take	That people gain only the knowledge they seek and value. All other learning is superficial and transitory. All

488

	Theory of Knowledge, Learning, and Literacy	
Assumption about	Didactic Theory	Critical Theory
	place without significant transformation of values for the learner.	genuine education transforms the basic values of the person educated, resulting in persons becoming lifelong learners and rational persons.
11. The importance of being aware of one's own learning process	That understanding the mind and how it functions, its epistemological health and pathology, are not important or necessary parts of learning. To learn the basic subject matter of the schools one need not focus on such matters, except perhaps with certain disadvantaged learners.	That understanding the mind and how it functions, its health and pathology, are important and necessary parts of learning. To learn the basic subject matter of the schools in-depth requires that we gain some insight into how we as thinkers and learners are processing that subject matter.
12. The place of misconceptions	That ignorance is a vacuum or simple lack, and that student prejudices, biases, misconceptions, and ignorance are automatically replaced by their being given knowlege.	That prejudices, biases, and misconceptions are built up through actively constructed inferences embedded in experience and must be broken down through a similar process; hence, that students must reason their way dialogically and dialectically out of their prejudices, biases, and misconceptions. Thus, students need many opportunities to express their views in class no matter how biased and prejudiced those views might be and a non-threatening enviroment to argue their way out of their internalized misconceptions.

(continued)

	Theory of Knowledge, Learning, and Literacy	
Assumption about	Didactic Theory	Critical Theory
13. The level of understanding desired	That students need not understand the rational ground or deeper logic of what they learn to absorb knowledge. Extensive but superficial learning can later be deepened.	That rational assent is an essential facet of all genuine learning and that an in-depth understanding of basic concepts and principles is an essential foundation for rational concepts and fact. That in-depth understanding of root concepts and principles should be used as organizers for learning within and across subject matter domains.
14. Depth vs. breadth	That it is more important to cover a great deal of knowledge or information superficially than a small amount in depth.	That it is more important to cover a small amount of knowledge or information in depth (deeply probing its foundation) than to cover a great deal of knowledge.
15. Role definition for teacher and student	That the roles of teacher and learner are distinct and should not be blurred.	That we learn best by teaching or explaining to others what we know, and so students need a lot of opportunities to teach what they know to others, to formulate their understanding, in different ways, and to respond to diverse questions from other learners.
16. The correction of ignorance	That the teacher should correct the learner's ignorance by telling her or him what she/he does not know.	That students need to learn to distinguish for themselves what they know from what they do not know. Much of what students are presently learning should be recognized by the students as content that they do not genuinely

	Theory of Knowledge, Learning, and Literacy	
Assumption about	Didactic Theory	Critical Theory
		know or comprehend, but have merely memorized. Self-directed recognition of ignorance is necessary to learning.
17. The responsibility for learning	That the teacher has the fundamental responsibility for student learning.	That, progressively, the student should be given increasing responsibility for his or her own learning. Students need to come to see that only they can learn for themselves and that they will not do so unless they actively and willingly engage themselves in the process.
18. The transfer of learning to everyday situations	That students will automatically transfer the knowledge that they learn in didactically taught courses to relevant real-life situations.	That most knowledge that students memorize in didactically taught courses is either forgotten or rendered "inert" by their mode of learning it, and that the most significant transfer is achieved by in-depth learning which focuses on experiences meaningful to the student and aims directly at transfer.
19. Status of personal experiences	That the personal experience of the student has no essential role to play in education.	That the personal experience of the student is essential to all schooling at all levels and in all subjects; that it is a crucial part of the content to be processed (applied, analyzed, synthesized, and assessed) by the student.

(continued)

Assumption about	Didactic Theory	Critical Theory
20. The assessment of knowledge acquisition	That a student who can correctly answer questions, provide definitions, and apply formulae while taking tests has proven his or her knowledge/understanding of those details.	That students can often provide correct answers, repeat definitions, and apply formulae while yet not understanding those questions, definitions, or formulae. That proof of knowledge/ understanding is found in the students' ability to explain in their own words, with examples, the meaning and significance of the knowledge, why it is so, and to spontaneously recall and use it when relevant.
21. The authority validating knowledge	That learning is essentially a private, monological process in which learners can proceed more or less directly to established truth, under the guidance of an expert in such truth. The authoritative answers that the teacher has are the fundamental standards for assessing students' learning.	That learning is essentially a public, communal, dialogical, and dialectical process in which learners can only proceed indirectly to truth, with much "zigging and zagging" along the way, much back-tracking, misconception, self-contradiction, and frustration in the process. In this process, authoritative answers are replaced by authoritative standards for engagement in the communal, dialogical process of enquiry.

FIG. 14.2. Assumptions of the didactic vs. the critical approach to learning.

492

The above dominant pattern of academic instruction and learning is based on an uncritical theory of knowledge, learning, and literacy that is coming under increasing critique by those concerned with instruction fitted to new interpretations of the emerging economic and social conditions and changing conditions for human survival.

What follows is a set of 21 contrasting assumptions about knowledge, learning and literacy. The first set represents the assumptions of the dominant, traditional perspective; the second represents the emerging common ground of assumptions held by many philosophers and cognitive psychologists. (Paul, in press)

Perhaps a growing joint recognition of the need for both cognitive psychologists and philosophers to make common cause against the didactic theory of education will be the impetus for an ongoing fruitful exchange of ideas across these rich traditions. It is certainly in the interest of all those who consider the ability to think critically to be at the heart of education rightly conceived, for this rapprochement to take place.

REFERENCES

Benderson, A. (1984). The view from psychology. *Critical Thinking: Focus 15.* Princeton NJ: Educational Testing Service.

Bracey, G. W. (1987, May). Measurement-driven instruction: Catchy phrase, dangerous practice. *Phi Delta Kappan, 68*(9), 683–688.

Harris, T. L. (1972). *Mustard Seed Magic.* City: Economy Company.

Lipman, M., Sharp, A. M., & Oscanyan, F. S. (1980). *Philosophy in the classroom.* (2nd ed.). Philadelphia, PA: Temple University Press.

Marzano, R. J., Brandt, R. S., Hughes, C. S., Jones, B. F., Presseisen, B. Z., Rankin, S. C., & Suhor, C. (1988). *Dimensions of thinking: A framework for curriculum and instruction.* Alexandria, VA: Association for Supervision and Curriculum Development.

Newman, J. H. (1912). *The idea of a university.* London: Langman's Green.

Paul, W. (in press). Critical thinking in North America: A new theory of knowledge, learning and literacy. *Argumentation: North American Perspectives on Teaching Critical Thinking.* Boston: D. Reidel Publishing Co.

Paul, R. W., Binker, A. J. A., & Charbonneau, M. (1987). *Critical thinking handbook: K-3, a guide for remodeling lesson plans in language arts, social studies, and science.* Rohnert Park, CA: Center for Critical Thinking and Moral Critique.

Paul, R. W., Binker, A. J. A., Jensen, K., & Kreklau, H. (1987). *Critical thinking handbook: 4th - 6th grades, a guide for remodeling lesson plans in language arts, social studies, and science.* Rohnert Park, CA: Center for Critical Thinking and Moral Critique.

Perkins, D. (1986, April). *Reasoning as it is and could be: An empirical perspective.*

Paper presented at the conference of the American Educational Research Association, San Francisco, CA.

Peters, R. S. and Mace, C. A. (1972). Article on "Psychology", *The Encyclopedia of Philosophy*. New York: MacMillan, Inc.

Scheffler, I. (1965). *The conditions of knowledge*. Chicago, IL: Scott Foresman.

Siegel, H. (1980, November). Critical thinking as an educational ideal. *Educational Forum, 45*(1), 7–25.

Dimensions of Thinking: A Critique

Raymond S. Nickerson
Bolt Beranek and Newman Inc.

PURPOSE

There appears to be a consensus among educators that a major objective of education should be to teach thinking. It is less apparent that there is a consensus regarding what this means. If one examines specific programs to teach thinking, one is struck by the variation from program to program in focus and emphasis and the lack of a unifying perspective in terms of which to relate them. The authors of *Dimensions of Thinking: A Framework for Curriculum and Instruction* (Marzano, Brandt, Hughes, Jones, Presseisen, Rankin and Suhor, 1988) take the lack of an organizing framework for the field as their point of departure, and the development of such a framework as their goal. They are careful to note that "framework" is a considered choice of term and that their intent is not to develop a theory or model of cognition or intelligence, but rather to identify, within the work of others in the field, "dimensions that appear to be threads running through both research and theory—perspectives that can be used to analyze various approaches to teaching thinking and to provide direction for planning curriculum and instruction" (p. 3). The dimensions they identify are these:

- Metacognition
- Critical and creative thinking
- Thinking processes
- Core thinking skills
- The relationship of content-area knowledge to thinking

The authors' intent for the framework is that it be used "in designing staff development programs for teachers and other educators and as the basis for curriculum planning at all levels" (p. xiv). The book is organized in terms of the five dimensions identified, with a chapter devoted to each, and ends with a discussion of how the framework might be applied in the areas of curriculum, instruction, and assessment.

The assignment that I accepted for this chapter was to take a critical look at the *Dimensions* framework as a whole, and that is what I will attempt to do. But before discussing what I see to be some problematic aspects of *Dimensions,* I want to applaud the willingness of the authors to undertake the daunting task of organizing a large, complicated, and diffuse literature in such a way as to give teachers of different subjects and at different levels "a common knowledge base and a common language for teaching thinking." I wish to note too that, in my view, the resulting book has many positive features. These include a great deal of information about recent research on the teaching of thinking and pointers to numerous sources of more, recognition of the importance of domain knowledge to effective thinking, promotion of the idea that teachers have a dual agenda that includes the development in all students of a rich knowledge base and a repertoire of thinking abilities that will enable them to use that knowledge in meaningful ways, recognition that the teaching of thinking is a concern of education at all levels from kindergarten through college and beyond, many suggestions for classroom activities that can be used to highlight and develop specific aspects of thinking, acknowledgment of the importance of attitudes as major determinants of the quality of thought, presentation of critical and creative thinking as complementary types of thinking, recognition of the importance of teachers serving as role models of critical and creative thinkers, highlighting of the importance of maintaining classroom climates that are conducive to good thinking, and stress on the need for work on evaluation.

The problems I see in *Dimensions* fall roughly into four categories, which I will refer to for convenience as (a) problems of terminology, (b) problems of perspective, (c) the risk of reification, and (d) neglected issues.

Problems of Terminology

The title of the book—*Dimensions of Thinking*—is problematic in my view for two reasons. First, it invites the reader to view the framework that is proposed as a representation of how thinking itself is organized. The authors are explicit in asserting that this is not their intent, but then why select a title that lends itself so readily to this interpretation? It seems to me unlikely that the disclaimers will suffice to dissuade all readers from taking the framework as a structural representation of thinking as opposed to a convenient way of organizing a body of literature pertaining to thinking and the teaching thereof. And this concern is amplified by the fact that the discussion of specific dimensions often reinforces this interpretation.

The second difficulty I have with the use of "dimensions, both in the title and in the body of the book, is that to many people the word conveys a meaning that could have a very interesting application to thinking but is not what is intended here. In a footnote to the Preface of *Dimensions* the authors credit me with pointing out that their use of the term is inappropriate because they do not mean by it measurable extensions in space. This comment is correct, but is open to misinterpretation taken out of the context in which it was originally made, because in isolation "extensions in space" may be taken to refer to the 3-dimensional space in which we live. The objection as originally stated referred to the more abstract mathematical notion of space and noted that in its most familiar mathematical usage, "dimension" connotes one of a set of n axes (n can be any number) by reference to which the "location" of an entity can be specified. Every object in such a space has a value on every dimension and the set of values associated with an object uniquely defines its location in that space. Distances between entities in such a space can be defined, measured, and compared. It makes sense, for example, to say that two specified points in this space, say A and B, are closer to each other than are two other points, say D and E; or to say that A is closer to B than to C along dimension X, but closer to C than to B along dimension Y. As noted in *Dimensions,* "dimension" has no such connotation; the dimensions identified are not intended—at least I believe they are not intended—to define a space in terms of which either cognitive entities or approaches to the teaching of thinking can be located.

This observation is made the more significant by the fact that it would be possible, and possibly useful, to conceptualize thinking in terms of such a space. We may imagine what an attempt to describe thinking in terms of a set of dimensions—in the more conventional sense of continua, or properties that can vary in degree—would produce. Candidate dimensions, in this sense, might include such properties as complexity, structuredness, creativeness, criticalness, automaticity, reflectiveness, and domain-dependence. I do not mean to suggest that this is the best possible set in terms of which to define a "thinking space," but I believe these are useful for purposes of illustration, which is to say it should be possible to come up with examples of thinking that differ noticeably with respect to each of them. The following table is the result of an attempt to do that.

	Low	High
Complexity	Sorting socks into matching pairs; deciding which flavor of ice cream to buy	Planning a business venture; assessing the benefits and risks of a new medicine
Structuredness	Composing a poem; choosing a vocation	Determining the structure of a molecule; evaluating the validity of a formal argument
Creativeness	Summarizing a written document; solving for the unknown(s) in a well-formed algebraic equation	Designing a logo for a letterhead; generating a new hypothesis to account for some scientific data
Criticalness	Memorizing a phone number; generating a wish list of vacation possibilities	Weighing the evidence in a court proceeding; editing a manuscript
Automaticity	Baking a cake for the first time; diagnosing a malfunctioning appliance	Finding one's way home from school or work; inferring the referents of pronouns in a straight-forward reading
Reflectiveness	Analyzing some data with a prescribed algorithm; memorizing the outline of a speech	Evaluating the acceptability of one's progress on an ongoing research project; introspecting on one's reasons for holding a particular opinion
Domain-dependence	Assessing the safety of a child's toy; figuring out how to mediate an interpersonal dispute	Determining the solvability of a differential equation; judging the plausibility of an assertion about the Lascaux cave paintings

One can imagine individual thinking episodes being located in a space defined by dimensions such as these. Figuring out what to do about a burned-out light bulb, for example, would probably be considered low on complexity, creativeness, and reflectiveness, high on structuredness and perhaps somewhere between the extremes on the other dimensions. Designing an experiment to test a new scientific hypothesis would occupy a quite different location in this space.

There are well known techniques for doing dimensional analyses of complex conceptual or cognitive variables that do not require the prior identification of the dimensions of interest but take that identification as the goal of the analyses. These are the multidimensional scaling methods that take as input large numbers of rating judgments or pairwise comparisons and from them infer the dimensionality of the space involved. To my knowledge such techniques have not been applied to thinking on any very extensive scale, but an effort to apply them in this domain could be instructive.

I do not mean to suggest by these comments that "dimensions" is meaningless as used in *Dimensions,* but just that it is not the most appropriate term. The word has a well-established connotation that is not exploited in *Dimensions,* and its use there is suggestive of an analysis that was not done.

It will be noted that two of the dimensions used to define the imaginary thinking space above—criticalness and creativeness—are used in *Dimensions.* It seems appropriate to refer to an episode of thinking as more or less critical or as more or less creative, and we can imagine each of these properties as varying continuously over a large range. My problem with the way these terms are used in *Dimensions* is that speaking of critical and creative thinking as *a* dimension of thinking invites the reader to conceptualize a single dimension with critical on one end and creative on the other. According to this view, a high degree of criticalness would be represented thus

<pre>
        critical   creative
    —X——————————————————————————————————————
</pre>

and a high degree of creativeness so

<pre>
        critical   creative
    ——————————————————————————————————————X—
</pre>

the implication being that to be high on criticalness means being low on creativeness, and conversely.

The authors of *Dimensions* are careful to note that this is not their intent and that they see critical and creative not as opposites but as complementaries. I believe this view would be clarified if instead of speaking of critical and creative thinking as one dimension, we conceptualized criticalness as one dimension and creativeness as another, (as shown below), thereby quite explicitly recognizing the possibility that thinking—at least any extended episode of thinking—may be both critical and creative (or neither the one nor the other) at the same time. Thus the points 1 through 4 on the figure would represent examples of thinking that are, respectively, critical but not creative, creative but not critical, neither critical nor creative, and both critical and creative. Inasmuch as both criticalness and creativeness are assumed to vary in degree, points could appear anywhere on the graph. As a matter of empirical fact, it may be that examples of thinking that are represented by 1 and 2 (and, alas by 3) are more easily found than those represented by 4, but, as the authors of *Dimensions* would argue, 4 should be the target; we want both criticalness and creativeness, and not one at the expense of the other.

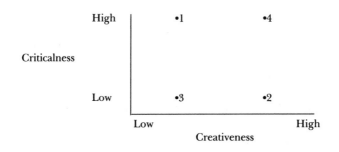

Another terminological difficulty relates to the use of the terms "skills" and "processes," which, in *Dimensions* are given connotations that are more restrictive than, and somewhat at odds with, the uses of these terms both in common parlance and in the research literature. Both of these words are common ones, which is not to say that they have precise, universally agreed-upon meanings, but they do have fairly well-established patterns of use. "Process" is a generic term. One dictionary definition of it is "something going on." The writing of a letter is a process, the preparing of a meal is a process, falling asleep is a process, growth is a process. In contrast, "skill," as the term is most commonly used, connotes an ability of a specific kind and, in particular, one that has been acquired, perhaps through training. We think of a skill as something one does or does not possess. We would say that one *has*, or one *lacks*, such and such a skill. It would be unusual to use "process" in that way. It would not seem strange, however, to say that one had become skillful or skilled at some process. We might say, for example, that one had become skilled at writing letters, or at preparing meals. Unfortunately—inasmuch as it complicates the task of using unambiguous terminology—we might also say that one had acquired the skill of letter writing or of cooking. In other words, we sometimes refer to specific processes as skills. This does not mean that the two concepts are synonymous (we would probably not refer to growth, which is a process, as a skill), but it should make us cautious about employing these words to connote two distinctive types of mental operations.

Problems of Perspective

The question of terminology aside, a more substantive problem involving the process-skill distinction relates to what might be called a componential view of thinking. Thinking is complex and not well understood. In trying to understand it, we find it useful to make simple conceptual models. One approach to conceptualization that has been popular among investigators who are interested in the teaching of thinking and the development of materials and approaches for doing so, involves the decomposition of thinking into components. The components are variously referred to as processes, skills, abilities, competencies, among other things. Diagrams are often drawn to show how components relate to one another. Sometimes these diagrams are hierarchies showing how components at a given level of complexity combine to form superordinate components or expand into subordinate ones. Sometimes these diagrams are intended to represent temporal relationships and to indicate the sequence in which components occur in an episode of thought. The goal seems to be to reduce thinking to its basic constituents, the assumption being that if one can identify those constituents, one will then know how to improve thinking as a whole. If one believes, for example, that classification is an essential element of thinking, then one objective in a program to teach thinking is likely to be to make sure that students can classify, and to teach them how to do so if they cannot.

Perhaps the attempt to identify the components of thinking is motivated by the assumption that the reductionism that has worked so well in the physical sciences will prove to be equally useful in psychology, and that, like the material universe, the mind is successively decomposable into ever more basic building blocks until one arrives ultimately at what can be considered the primitives, from which all more complicated instances of thinking can be built. But it is possible that the mind is not that type of entity and that the reductionist approach is not appropriate in this context.

Skills are viewed in *Dimensions* as relatively low-level or basic cognitive operations that, when mastered, can be executed quickly and relatively automatically and that function as components in higher-level processes. Processes are seen as more complex than skills. They are assumed to take longer to complete and to make use of skills in their execution. According to the *Dimensions* view, the execution of a process may require the exercise of several skills, and the same skill may be critical to several processes. Twenty-one skills are identified in *Dimensions* and eight processes.

One difficulty with this conceptualization stems from the fact that each of the terms representing skills/processes in these lists, as it is used in common parlance, refers to a type of cognitive activity that can vary in complexity over an enormous range. The following examples make the point. The first three are skills within the *Dimensions* framework and the fourth a process.

Representing.   A stick figure can be a representation of a person; Andreas Vesalius' incomparable anatomy drawings are also representations of a person. The simple drawing below is a representation of the moon's orbit about the earth as the earth revolves about the sun.

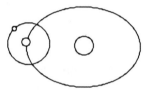

So is the equation that took Charles Delaunay twenty years to develop and check, and filled two volumes when he was done (Pavelle, Rothstein, and Fitch, 1981).

Classifying.   When I say this is a rectangle and that is a triangle, I am classifying. When I say this is an instance of music and that is an instance of visual art, I am also classifying. And I am classifying when I say this is an instance of early Italian Baroque music and that of late French Impressionism or that this is a mazurka and that is an Irish jig.

Setting goals.   Goals vary greatly in complexity and function at all levels. Chipman (1986) emphasizes the role of goal hierarchies in the orchestration of lower-level skills, and illustrates their multi-level nature by reference to the writing of a piece of exhortatory prose. This may involve a top-level goal of persuading the reader to adopt a particular point of view or to behave in a certain way; subordinate to this, the somewhat lower-level goal of constructing a compelling argument; still more specific, the goal of finding a way to relate a premise of the developing argument to the circumstances of the assumed reader; and at a lower level still, the goal of producing a clear and grammatical sentence, or of finding just the right word to use at a particular place in it. Obviously, it is important that while working toward lower-level goals, one not lose sight of the higher-order ones, else behavior that makes sense in the microcosm may be pointless from a more macroscopic perspective.

Problem solving. One is solving a problem when one turns the thermostat up to raise the heat in one's house, when one replaces a burned-out light bulb with one that works, when one ties two short pieces of string together to get a piece long enough for a particular use. One is also solving a problem when one negotiates a labor-management dispute, when one discovers a polio vaccine, or when one designs an instrument that will produce pictures of structures too small to be resolved by visible light.

The point is, it is possible to think of instances of any of the skills or processes identified in *Dimensions* that are sufficiently complex as to involve many of the other skills and processes in their execution. Thus one can give an example of *problem solving* that requires the use of *representations,* but one can just as well give an example of *representing* that requires a good bit of *problem solving;* and I suspect the same point can be made with respect to any other combination of skills or processes that one might consider. In some sense, each of them can and does use and support each of the others. How, for example, can one compare without observing or recalling? How can one classify without comparing? How can one represent without identifying relationships and patterns? How can one identify errors, or summarize, without comprehending? How can one set goals without making decisions? How can one represent or restructure without composing? How can one identify relationships and patterns or attributes and components without forming concepts?

The notion that thinking is decomposable into atoms that can be combined to make molecules of thought is an appealing one, because of its simplifying implications for the teaching of thinking. But this conceptualization runs into problems, because no matter what one identifies as an atom, it will not behave itself as a building block should. In particular, it will, on occasion, require those things it is supposed to be a component of as components of itself. This puts each component in the position of being subordinate and superordinate to the same entities, which is to say, of being its own grandfather, as it were.

Does this mean that we cannot talk about observing, classifying, setting goals, problem solving, decision making, and the like? Not at all. But what we have to avoid, I believe, is creating the impression that thinking can be neatly partitioned into such activities. In our use of words such as observing, classifying, and so on, we have to recognize not only the fluidity of language but the many-faceted, multi-level nature of thought. We can talk of thinking skills and processes, and even of specific thinking skills and processes, but we have to recognize that our language is only marginally descriptive of that to which it refers, and we must not be surprised when the entities we identify in our models or frameworks of thinking persist in jumping out of the boxes in which we have put them.

A further concern relating to *Dimensions'* skills and processes involves the rationale for including certain operations in these lists and not others. It is not apparent to me on what basis the specific skills and processes were selected from among the much larger set of possibilities. Is it apparent that the criteria mentioned for inclusion admit these while precluding others of a like sort that might have been considered, such as organizing, interpreting, describing, generalizing, evaluating, planning, abstracting, estimating, hypothesizing? Where do counting and computing fit in this framework? Is the validity of the lists testable? What evidence can be presented that the lists do not omit items that are more important than those they contain?

The Risk of Reification

Organizing frameworks—theories, models, taxonomies, themata, paradigms, and the like—play a paradoxical role in influencing the way we think. The paradox stems from the fact that the questions "What is good about organizing frameworks?" and "What is bad about organizing frameworks?" have the same answer: They channel (direct, constrain) thinking.

Organizing frameworks help us interpret sensory input, make connections, fit concepts together and maintain a view of the world that has some coherence. Without such frameworks in terms of which to interpret what we see and hear in our daily lives, our cognitive experiences would be hopelessly kaleidoscopic. The important role that such frameworks have played in the history of science has been described and discussed by various scholars, notably Kuhn (1970) and Holton (1973).

Organizing frameworks can also have negative effects on thinking. The difference between a channel and a rut is somewhat a matter of perspective. While organizational structures guide our thinking, and facilitate it in a sense, the guidance can become restrictive and the facilitation may be bought at the expense of oversimplification. When our thinking is highly constrained by a particular framework, we fail to notice things that do not fit that framework, or, worse, unwittingly distort perceptions to make them fit. Although a structure evokes certain questions, it can decrease the likelihood that certain others will be asked. If one accepts the *Dimensions* framework, one's thinking about thinking may be facilitated somewhat by virtue of having a structure; on the other hand, it may be constrained to stay within that structure. If the conceptualization is seriously wanting, the cost of its constraining aspects could outweigh the value of the benefits derived.

It is not my intention to argue that an organizing framework must be "correct" in order to be useful. Such an argument would be silly in view of the fact that few, if any, of the major frameworks that have been so central to the progress of science could be considered correct in an absolute sense. Whitehead (1938) points out that oversimplifications, which obviously distort reality, have sometimes been very useful indeed. "Great advances in thought are often the result of fortunate errors. These errors are the result of oversimplification. The advance is due to the fact that, for the moment, the excess is not relevant to the simplified notions. One of the chief examples of this truth is Aristotle's analysis into genus, species and sub-species" (p. 21). Aristotle was wrong, Whitehead suggests, inasmuch as there are not clear divisions among genera, among species, or anywhere else; but he was right for practical purposes in that he provided a useful conceptual structure in terms of which to think about the living world.

But from the fact—if we accept it as such—that a framework need not be an accurate reflection of reality in order to be useful, it does not follow that all frameworks are equally useful, or even that any framework is always better than none at all. I confess to some ambivalence on the question of whether an organizing framework is really what the literature that relates to the teaching of thinking needs at the present. This ambivalence stems in large part from the fact that frameworks can constrain thinking about a topic, as noted above, and from the belief that we do not yet know enough about thinking and how to teach it that we can afford to have our thinking about it much constrained. Of course we need to structure discussions of the topic in order to give them some coherence, but the challenge will be to recognize any such structure as a conceptual convenience, to be kept only so long as it proves to be useful, and to be discarded happily as soon as a better one comes along.

The great risk in any organizing framework, it seems to me, and especially one that relates to an emerging field, as does *Dimensions,* is that it will be taken too seriously. This is the problem of reification; what was intended to serve as a conceptual expedient soon becomes perceived as reflecting "the way things really are." The authors of *Dimensions* are sensitive to this risk and are careful to point out the tentativeness of their structure and the fact that they do not intend for it to be taken as a model of how the mind works. I believe the risk is still there, however, and that it is a serious one. Frameworks are not always used only in the ways their developers intended; they are likely either to be ignored or to take on a life of their own. Some people *will* take them more seriously than they should, and it is well to aware of that fact. We tend to want answers—simple, understandable answers, no matter how complex the questions. And in our eagerness to get them, we find it exceedingly easy to confuse assumptions with conclusions, to turn hypotheses into facts, to ignore caveats and disclaimers and permit conceptual conveniences to become dogma.

The identification in *Dimensions* of eight thinking processes and 21 thinking skills that underlie them lends itself much too readily to being interpreted as a neat and simple answer to the question of what constitutes thinking and as a prescription for teaching it. The authors are to be commended for noting that this interpretation is not what they intend; I believe the risk exists in spite of that.

Neglected Issues

A neglected issue in discussions of metacognition—in *Dimensions* and elsewhere—relates to the question of how best to allocate limited cognitive resources. When a person has a cognitively demanding task to perform, that task will require the application of some portion of the individual's total cognitive resources. If the task is sufficiently demanding, it may require all, or nearly all, of them. The monitoring, management, and evaluation of one's own performance also require cognitive resources, and to the degree that those resources are applied to these functions, they are not available for use on the problem of interest. Metacognitive activities are overhead functions, as it were. The question is how much of one's limited resources should be used up in this way. How much of one's cognitive capacity should one devote to thinking about how one is performing the task, or about how effectively one is monitoring one's performance of the task, as opposed to thinking about the task per se?

Another way to frame the same issue is in terms of attention-sharing in a dual-task situation. The secondary task in this case is the monitoring of performance on the primary task. We know from extensive research that unless at least one of two simultaneous tasks is highly automated, the need to share attention between them usually has a detrimental effect on the performance of one or both of them. If this principle holds when one of the tasks is self monitoring, then a reasonable rule of thumb might be: if the primary task is very demanding and not highly automated, the monitoring task should be kept simple; or conversely: if intensive monitoring is desired and monitoring itself is not highly automated, then the primary task should be kept simple or should be bitten off in small chunks. This is a subject that needs some research. A specific question of interest is that of the extent to which metacognitive processes can and should become automated.

I agree wholeheartedly with *Dimensions'* acknowledgment of the importance of attitudes but would like to have seen a much greater emphasis on them. We want students not only to feel good about themselves (when they should feel good about themselves) and to persevere (reasonably) at tasks; we also want them to respect the truth, to be inquisitive, to value learning, to respect opinions that differ from their own, to enjoy cooperating with others, and so on. No mention is made in *Dimensions* of the relationship between attitudes and values. I believe this is a serious omission. Many of our most important attitudes are rooted in values, and they are not likely to be changed independently from changes in the values from which they stem. Respect for opinions that differ from our own, for example, presupposes certain beliefs about human rights and the dignity and intrinsic worth of individual human beings.

Setting goals is discussed in *Dimensions* as one of the core skills identified in Chapter 5, and the importance of students setting learning goals for themselves is stressed. Much more attention should be given to the ways in which goals relate to thinking, in my view, because it is a key consideration and one that has been generally neglected relative to the attention it deserves. "Goal-directed thinking" is a familiar term in the literature on cognition. The term is ambiguous in an interesting way. It could be taken to mean either thinking directed *by* goals or thinking directed *at* goals. In the former case the thinker sees the problem as that of figuring out how to attain some goal, the goal itself being a given; in the latter case the goal is the focus of thought, the problem here is deciding whether the goal is a reasonable one to pursue. In the first case the question is: How can I best accomplish X. In the second case: What should I try to accomplish? I believe that the term "goal-directed thinking" is typically used in the former sense, and have suggested elsewhere that thinking directed *at* goals may be somewhat less straightforward as an educational objective, but extremely important nonetheless (Nickerson, 1986). High-level goals deserve special emphasis in any account of thinking, or of the teaching of thinking, that is intended to be relatively comprehensive, because they play such critical roles in defining who each of us is as an individual. The desire and ability to be reflective about personal goals before deciding to pursue them must be among the most important aspects of what it means to be a rational human being.

Ironically, although *Dimensions* stresses the importance of critical thinking, the book is not very critical in its discussion of work on the teaching of thinking. It reports what various people have said on the topic, but seldom questions the tenability of the assertions that people have made or conclusions they have drawn. It describes approaches to the teaching of thinking but offers little in the way of evidence regarding the effectiveness of these approaches, nor does it reflect an attitude of healthy skepticism toward approaches the effectiveness of which remains undocumented. All sources that are cited seem to be given about the same degree of credence. In short, *Dimensions* fails to give the reader as much help as one would like in distinguishing what should be viewed as conclusions based on solid empirical or theoretical work from what must be considered assumptions or conjectures.

Final Comment

I realize that the foregoing comments have been predominantly critical; I hope they have been constructively so. It is difficult to imagine a question that is more worthy of the attention of educators and educational researchers than that of how to teach thinking. *Dimensions* represents a very significant effort on the part of its authors to figure out what the research literature has to say about the teaching of thinking, and to put whatever that is into a form that will make it accessible to teachers, curriculum developers, and others who have the awesome responsibility of determining what happens in the classroom from day to day. The degree to which this effort has been successful must be a matter of opinion, at least for the present, but the very fact that it was made is a testament to the strong desire of some educational leaders to bridge the gap between research and practice, especially with respect to thinking and the improvement of it through instruction. One must hope that this desire will spread and that as a consequence both of further research and of continuing efforts to make the results of that research accessible to the practitioner community we will get an increasingly better understanding of what it means to think well and of how to make the classroom a place where thinking ability, in the broadest sense, is effectively enhanced.

REFERENCES

Chipman, S. (1986). What is meant by higher order cognitive skills. In G. Miller (Ed.) *Assessing cognitive skills and mathematics and science*. Princeton, NJ: Spencer Foundation.

Holton, G. (1973). *Thematic origins of scientific thought*. Cambridge, MA: Harvard University Press.

Kuhn, T. S. (1970). *The structure of scientific revolutions*, 2nd Edition. Chicago: University of Chicago.

Marzano, R. J., Brandt, R. S., Hughes, C. S., Jones, B. F., Presseisen, B. Z., Rankin, S. C., & Suhor, C. (1988). *Dimensions of thinking: A framework for curriculum and instruction*. Alexandria, VA: Association for Supervision and Curriculum Development.

Nickerson, R. S. (1986). Why teach thinking? In J. B. Baron & R. J. Sternberg (Eds.), *Teaching thinking skills: Theory and practice.* New York: W. H. Freeman and Company.

Pavelle, R., Rothstein, M., & Fitch, J. (1981). Computer algebra. *Scientific American, 245*(6), 136–152.

Whitehead, A. N. (1938). *Modes of thought.* Cambridge: The University Press.

Conclusions

In the Introduction, we stated that one purpose for developing this Volume was to provide an overview of research on the various dimensions of thinking. Because so many researchers focus on specific dimensions of thinking, it was important to examine what is known about all the dimensions: The whole may be much greater than the sum of the parts. A second purpose was to link recent research on thinking with the movement to restructure schools. Specifically, we argued that all too often restructuring focuses on reorganizing school governance structures to provide site-based management, teacher empowerment, and parent involvement; changing the fundamentals of schooling to improve thinking, teaching, and achievement in the classroom are rarely included. This collection of papers provides state-of-the-art descriptions of recent research on thinking and its implications for classroom instruction, teacher education, and restructuring.

Altogether, six dimensions of thinking were discussed:

1. Metacognition
2. Seven cognitive processes (conceptualizing, comprehending, composing, communicating, problem solving, enquiry research, and teaching)
3. The role of domain-specific knowledge
4. Learning strategies and skills
5. Creative thinking
6. Critical thinking

These six dimensions were selected based on an organizational framework developed by Marzano et al., (1988). As stated in the Introduction, this framework is not intended to form a taxonomy or hierarchy with mutually exclusive categories.

Research on thinking is inherently an entangled domain with many overlapping categories and perspectives. Indeed, the development of this book has caused many authors to consider perspectives and fields of research that they typically do not address. This is evident in Perkins' analysis of how each of the dimensions relates to creative thinking, in the extensive references to psychological literature in the chapters by Paul and Ennis (Volume 2), in the discussion of critical thinking skills and perspectives in O'Flahavan and Tierney (Volume 2), and other chapters.

No doubt, too, there will be considerable debate about the meaning of such an organizational framework. Nickerson argues, disclaimers notwithstanding, that the dimensions of thinking framework may be perceived as a structural representation of thinking, not just a convenient way of organizing research; and once implemented, such frameworks take on a life of their own. He fears, as we do, that this framework may be used to teach thinking skills as ends in themselves. Nickerson also disagrees with some of our categories and labels, and these criticisms are all well taken. Nevertheless, we believe that these dimensions are not merely artifacts of research interests or convenience of organization.

To the contrary, the capability to summarize across a variety of perspectives is a powerful vantage point. First, Spiro (1989) argued that, when trying to understand a complex phenomenon, a single representation would be misleading; therefore, it is very useful to study it from multiple perspectives thereby forming multiple representations. Second, each dimension represents a distinctive source of knowledge that is important to understand and address for schooling and teacher education. Third, the dimensions of thinking concept provides a useful framework for identifying and analyzing the multiple sources of knowledge and perspectives. Finally, there are important trends in conceptualizing thinking across the dimensions.

Our conclusions address the following questions. What does this volume uniquely contribute to understanding the nature of thinking, summarizing across all the dimensions? What is the vision of skilled learning suggested by these descriptions? What do these findings imply for classroom instruction, teacher education, and the movement to restructure schools? A central thesis is that this analysis represents a greatly expanded view of thinking, one which accepts the multiple sources of knowledge and multiple aspects of the learner.

MULTIPLE KNOWLEDGE SOURCES

For any given task, thinking is situated within and draws upon multiple knowledge sources. That is, for any given event of sustained thinking, the learner might call upon knowledge from cognition, from metacognitive states and decisions, from experiences in various environments, and from beliefs about the self. That is, there are general and domain-specific sources of knowledge; metacognitive judgments, beliefs, and values; knowledge of environments; self systems and dispositions, and finally, declarative and procedural knowledge. These categories are not mutually exclusive and some sources of knowledge seem to be nested in others.

General and Domain-Specific Knowledge Sources

Throughout this decade, researchers have debated the relative importance of general versus domain-specific knowledge, and this volume is no exception. Thus, many authors argue that successful learners have extensive bodies of domain-specific knowledge; that in most instances, knowledge of the domain is required for effective strategy use, and that general knowledge has little transfer value (Bransford, et al.; Hayes; Klausmeier; Pearson & Raphael; Roth; Silver & Marshall; Tweney & Walker). For example, in order to use a general skill like pattern recognition in chess, the learner must have a great deal of knowledge of chess, and knowledge of that strategy in chess has little value for using it in other domains. Additionally, Bransford et al. directly criticized approaches that emphasize the importance of acquiring new content knowledge; in their view, acquisition of factual content in no way guarantees that students will develop organized knowledge structures that guide subsequent thinking.

In spite of the prominence of this perspective, there is a new and noticeable "softening" in attitude toward the uses of general strategies among those emphasizing domain-specific instruction. In fact, Bransford et al., emphasized that general processes such as problem solving and content knowledge must mutually reinforce each other. Moreover, there are numerous examples of general strategies throughout these chapters: knowing that effort is required to complete a task (Borkowski et al), thinking about a topic before reading about it (Paris & Winograd), general problem solving strategies (Bransford et al; Silver & Marshall), and using organizational frames (Perkins). We would also include here the broad range of strategies for critical thinking and reasoning such as challenging assumptions and recognizing bias which may be used in learning from text, oral communication, and argumentation in any domain (Ennis, Volume 2; Kline & Delia; Paul). We return to this issue in the section on successful learning (see also Alexander & Judy, 1988; Perkins & Salomon, 1989, for additional debate).

Metacognitive Knowledge: Judgments, Beliefs, and Values

Thinking is also situated in various sources of metacognitive knowledge. Traditionally, metacognitive knowledge has referred primarily to self-appraisal and self-management. Self-appraisal refers to knowledge of cognitive states and processes. Self-management refers to knowledge of the self in action: the plans that students make before doing a task, the adjustments they make as they work, and the changes they make afterwards. Paris and Winograd argue that questions about effort, expectations, difficulty, and outcomes necessarily include social interactions, motivational dispositions, and consequences of learning. Therefore, they propose to redefine metacognitive knowledge to include the affective and motivational characteristics of thinking (see also Borkowski et al.). Specifically, they argue that metacognitive knowledge is comprised of judgments and beliefs about the learning situation that determine which tasks students find worthwhile that lead students to make choices bout how much effort they will expend. These beliefs reflect affective biases and misconceptions such as tendencies to attribute success to luck, self-concepts, and motivational dispositions. Further, metacognition is embedded in ongoing thinking and problem solving and therefore is a functional means to learning rather than a goal in itself in their view.

Knowledge of Environments

Underlying these metacognitive beliefs, and partly driving them, are students' explicit and implicit knowledge of the classroom as a physical, social, and cultural community. In making metacognitive judgments, students may draw upon their knowledge of the attitudes and beliefs of the teacher about topics and persons, perceived goals of instruction, his or her system of rewards and punishments, and personal preferences, (Ames & Ames, Volume 2; Barr & Anderson, Volume 2; Hayes; Paris & Winograd; Pearson & Raphael; Roth). Students' metacognitive judgments may also be influenced by their knowledge of the affective and cognitive characteristics of other students in the classroom as well as by knowledge of their own status in relation to others socially and academically (Hayes; Ames & Ames, Volume 2; Barr & Anderson, Volume 2). Even very young students are aware of procedures and language use in the classroom (Florio, Volume 2; Green, Kantor, & Rogers, Volume 2). Indeed, an important function of early instruction is to teach students, for example, the multiple meanings of a word such as "okay" including "yes," "stop" (as in "that's enough"), or "it's your turn."

Self Systems and Dispositions

In the process of acting within and upon the various knowledge sources described above, the learner constructs over-arching belief structures, which direct metacognitive development and influence the quality of academic performance. The most important of these belief structures is the self-system. According to Borkowski et al., these self-systems include (cognitive) constructs such as self-efficacy, self-esteem, locus of control, achievement, and motivation. These systems are strongly directed by attributional beliefs, especially attributions about the causes of success and failure. A second over-arching set of belief structures that operates at all times and in all domains are dispositions to be critical and creative; among other things, these dispositions structure academic work, social interactions with others, and our feelings about ourselves. Other belief structures that influence performance across domains are the specific message design logics that govern communication with others (Kline & Delia). These are closely tied to social and cognitive development and determine much of our success in achieving our goals.

Thus far, we have discussed various categories of knowledge that appear to be loosely defined but equivalent categories; domain-specific and general knowledge, metacognitive knowledge, experiential knowledge, self-systems, and dispositions. That is, in a given moment of thinking, the learner may call upon each of these types of knowledge. Declarative and procedural knowledge, discussed in the section below, appears to be of a somewhat different order.

Declarative and Procedural Knowledge

Declarative knowledge, "knowing that," includes knowledge of concepts, propositions, events, and states as well as definitions of strategies, skills, and cognitive processes (Derry). A strong generalization emerging from these chapters is that there are many sources of errors in declarative knowledge. In particular, declarative knowledge may contain inaccurate information and "buggy" algorithms (Silver & Marshall), opinions and personal bias taken as facts (Paris & Winograd; Paul), idiosyncratic perceptions (Hayes), inappropriate definitions of comprehension (Pearson & Raphael), incorrect attributions regarding success and failure (Borkowski et al; Paris & Winograd), and misconceptions about the world (Roth). It is vital for teachers to anticipate these problems.

Procedural knowledge, "knowing how," is comprised of capacities to conduct certain tasks such as how to decode words in reading, how to solve a type of arithmetic problem, and how to use a particular strategy in a given situation. Procedural knowledge also refers more broadly to cognitive processes such as knowing how to comprehend, how to compose, and so·on. A common theme is that many students do not spontaneously acquire either type of procedural knowledge (e.g., Derry; Borkowski et al.; Paris & Winograd). Therefore, it is imperative that procedural instruction be provided for students who need it.

What is somewhat different about declarative and procedural knowledge is that they are orthogonal to these loosely defined and sometimes overlapping categories. That is, general and domain-specific knowledge may be stored as declarative or procedural knowledge; metacognitive knowledge may also be stored in both ways; so can experiential knowledge, self-system knowledge, and knowledge of critical and creative thinking. Thus, each of the other sources of knowledge is nested in *both* declarative and procedural propositions.

To summarize, knowledge is located in various domains simultaneously. That is, any act of thinking may involve knowledge that is general or domain specific, metacognitive, experiential, dispositional, or self-defining—all at the same time. Moreover, each of these sources of knowledge is nested within declarative and procedural knowledge. Thus, each of the dimensions of thinking is situated in multiple knowledge bases and multiple environments, yielding multiple representations and perspectives.

This idea that learning is situated in multiple knowledge bases and contexts is related to, but separate from, other definitions of situated learning discussed in these volumes and elsewhere. Bransford and his colleagues argue that students are able to access their knowledge when instruction is driven by problems situated in contextually rich environments. Additionally, Collins and his colleagues argue that situations produce knowledge through activities. That is, according to Brown, Collins, & Duguid (1989, p. 32), "knowledge is in part a product of the activity, context, and culture in which it is developed" (see also Collins, Brown, & Newman, 1989). Brown et al. have proposed that the concept of situated cognition as an alternative to conventional models of learning. We believe that the dimensions of thinking concept developed here offers a useful framework for analyzing the multiple knowledge bases and contexts in which knowledge is situated.

Expanded Views of Thinking

The notion that thinking is situated in multiple knowledge bases represents expanded views of thinking, compared to conceptions of thinking offered in behaviorism and information processing models. In these earlier perspectives, cognitive states and processes are often defined in isolation from other aspects of the learner, and context primarily means purpose, sometimes cultural context. Moreover, until now the study of thinking has generally been conducted in separate strands, each relatively insulated from the other. In contrast, this characterization represents three major shifts in our understanding of thinking. First, the concept of *thinking* has been expanded to include the whole person. Thus, thinking involves understanding affective, motivational, social, and cultural characteristics of the individual as well as cognitive characteristics. Second, the concept of *context* has been expanded to include multiple physical, social, and cultural environments. That is, the learner derives cognitive meanings, values and beliefs, attributions, motivation, dispositions, and self-systems from various environments, which determine specific choices and actions. Thus, in an important sense, thinking is defined partially by these contexts, and they have strong influences on learning in the classroom. Third, this means that our notions of *constructing meaning* have expanded to include these contexts. Therefore, sustained thinking must involve the orchestration of multiple dimensions simultaneously and sequentially in a dynamic flow in various environments. The integration of physical, affective, social, cultural, and cognitive aspects of learning provides a holistic perspective that has not been present in previous models.

This holistic perspective supports more emphasis on ethnographic studies of thinking than has been the case to date. This approach is currently used for studies of expert teaching (e.g., Duffy, Roehler, & Rackliffe, in press; Leinhardt & Greeno, 1986), learning outside of school (e.g., Lave, 1988; Schon, 1987; Spiro, 1989) and increasingly learning in school (Bransford et al. Hayes; see also Green, Kantor, & Rogers; O'Flahavan & Tierney, in Volume 2). We believe there would be many benefits for adapting a holistic perspective for learning in schools as a complement to more narrowly defined studies. This approach would:

- conceptualize the learner as a complex whole operating within multiple knowledge bases and environments, each of which influences and is influenced by, the learner as well as others;
- focus on the complex tasks of schooling which involve integrating information from multiple sources over a period of days or weeks;

517

- plot the interplay of judgments, beliefs, and choices made in complex paths that might extend over hours, days, or even weeks—sometimes in class, sometimes elsewhere; and
- yield multiple representations of information, co-existence of contradictions and inconsistencies, changes in perceptions and conceptual growth, changes in expectations and values, and development of specific skills and knowledge bases.

A VISION OF SUCCESSFUL LEARNING

Just as views of thinking have been expanded, our vision of the successful learner has been enriched by recent research. In 1987, Jones and her colleagues described successful learning as oriented to constructing meaning and independent learning, organized, and strategic (Jones, Palincsar, Ogle, & Carr, 1987; cf. Resnick, 1987). The work in this Volume suggested (1) that this vision of learning is essentially shared among many strands of research and (2) that there have been some important shifts of language and focus. In this section, we discuss four attributes of successful learning and changes of focus for each attribute: depth of purpose, organization of knowledge, quality of cognitive strategies and skills, and self-regulated behavior.

Choice and Self-Determination

In the past, purpose has been defined both in very broad terms such as solving a problem or constructing meaning and in specific terms such as analyzing a play to learn something about one's culture and values. In either case, purposes and goals were essentially cognitive in nature, and much attention has been given in the literature on thinking about the need for purposes to be authentic, that is, that there should be a real audience for an essay such as a fellow student or pen pal (Resnick, 1987). Although purpose has not been a major focus of attention in this volume, there were numerous references to successful learning as being guided by a specific choices and self-determination that go beyond striving to make sense out of the new information. Thus, Roth, for example, describes the rare fifth grader who, unlike her peers, is aware that the disciplinary view contradicts her prior knowledge and strives for clarity and consistency and ultimately achieves conceptual change. Similarly, Paul characterizes the critical thinker in the "strong sense" as having faith in reason as well as strong values for intellectual humility, courage to face one's own prejudices, and motivation to fight injustice. Perkins discusses creative thinkers as persons who enjoy being original (as part of their self-concept). Tweney and Walker describe expert scientists as having a passion for acquiring knowledge. Speaking metacognitively, Borkowski et al. argue that children are driven by inherent needs for self-determination and self-development as part of their sense of self-worth. Successful learners seem better able to harness this energy for academic learning, compared to less successful learners. Paris and Winograd characterize the proficient learner as strategic, using cognitive tools to accomplish the craft of schooling.

In each of these descriptions, purposes encompass very deep-seated and broad-based dispositions that have both cognitive and emotional components. In essence, the definition of purpose has been expanded to include metacognition and self-systems in much the same ways as our understanding of the nature of thinking.

Organization of Knowledge

While debate continues about exactly what constitutes expert and novice performances (Silver & Marshall), there is increasing consensus that successful learning depends heavily on an extensive body of relevant prior knowledge that is well-elaborated in terms of knowledge structures or schemata (Derry; Pearson & Raphael). But what are the characteristics of these structures? How are they organized? Interestingly, successful learners in one domain appear to use similar processes in other domains.

In mathematics and science, for instance, there is substantial evidence to suggest that success in problem solving depends heavily on constructing an adequate initial problem definition and problem representation (Silver & Marshall; Tweney & Walker). However, this does not occur immediately; knowledge is organized in successively richer and more refined problem representations. Moreover, successful learners organize what they know in terms of fundamental principles, concepts, and patterns that are both meaningful and accessible (Bransford et al.; Tweney & Walker). This extensive knowledge and experience makes it possible to represent a problem in terms of a schema containing both factual and procedural knowledge (Silver & Marshall). This high-level knowledge also enables the learner to identify and focus on what is important and relevant as well as to understand underlying similarities and differences among phenomena. During the process of problem solving, successful problem solvers typically begin with general principles and look for ways to concretize them and are more persevering about aligning new information with prior knowledge where there are inconsistencies and contradictions (Roth; Silver & Marshall; Tweney & Walker).

Similarly, in reading, writing, and conceptualizing, it is evident that successful learners have well-developed capabilities to represent fundamental and global information about text structures, tasks, genres, and strategies as well as concepts and principles about specific topics (Hayes; Pearson & Raphael). Successful writers, for example, define the task of revision as a whole-text task, reading the whole text through and creating global goals, rather than focusing immediately on words and sentences. Successful readers use examples in the paragraph to attain the macrostructure, the global concept of the paragraph (Klausmeier). To attain concepts, highly successful students work through a process of successive hypothesis testing that seems to be closely parallel to the development of successive refinements of problem representations discussed by Silver and Marshall. Also, as in science and mathematics, it is not enough merely to have extensive background knowledge; good readers understand when and how to apply it effectively (Pearson & Raphael).

This emphasis on representation and constructing high-level knowledge structures is also present in research on thinking in other areas. Expert teachers organize representations of people and objects in classroom events, components of teaching such as subject matter, and "scripts" for familiar instructional procedures such as correcting homework (Borko & Shavelson). These representations of knowledge are then used to organize lesson plans and classroom activities. Similarly, skilled communicators must possess both knowledge of discourse forms and a sophisticated theory of communication as to how to use talk to accomplish their goals, according to Kline and Delia. This means that they must be able to recognize and interpret audience patterns and perspectives as well as integrate diverse knowledge sources. This implicit theory is then used for organizing goal-directed action. Finally, learners may use both general and domain-specific frames to organize both declarative and procedural knowledge (Perkins).

We see a paradox in these descriptions. Earlier, it was emphasized that extensive domain-specific prior knowledge is needed to become expert. Also, when experts in one area are given an unfamiliar task, they no longer have that knowledge from which to draw. At the same time, it is apparent from these descriptions that successful learners are using similar mental processes to represent their knowledge across various disciplines. Thus, while the knowledge that they acquire in one discipline or topic may be domain specific, and therefore not transferable, there do appear to be some core processes of constructing schemata, finding and defining problems, and testing hypotheses that are common to successful learning in diverse situations. That these processes are less effective when used in unfamiliar situations should not deny their limited effectiveness in unfamiliar situations (cf, Perkins & Salomon, 1989; Rumelhart, 1980; Spiro, 1980).

This organized, meaningful learning used by more proficient learners is in sharp contrast to the attributes of less proficient learners. Roth, for example, demonstrates that less proficient learners typically engage in rote memorization (adding isolated bits of information to prior knowledge without linking it to existing structures), and distorted learning (relying on prior knowledge and ignoring the disciplinary information altogether, and ignoring it when it contradicts prior knowledge). Other authors refer to less successful learners' focus on decoding (Pearson & Raphael) and "knowledge telling" in writing (Hayes). Bransford et al., argue that this unorganized or poorly-organized information is inert, essentially unaccessible for useful applications. This type of learning is sometimes called "conceptual capture" because bits of information are captured and integrated inappropriately. Similarly, in Paul's view, "the unphilosophical mind is trapped within the system it uses, unable to understand alternative or competing systems."

Quality of Strategies and Skills

In the preceding section, we described some global processes for organizing meaningful knowledge. In this section, we describe specific skills and strategies to organize meaningful knowledge. In an important sense, these strategies are cognitive tools that successful students use to create and design knowledge structures as architects construct blueprints (Paris & Winograd; Perkins). Four strategies were outstanding: elaborating information from various sources to each other and to prior knowledge, inventing or imposing broad-stroke organizational patterns, engaging conceptual change strategies, and generating causal explanations.

First, there are various strategies for integrating new ideas into existing knowledge structures. Learning usable ideas occurs largely by focusing attention on what new information is important and elaborating it with ideas already in prior knowledge (Derry). Elaboration involves linking or bonding bits of information in various ways: making a logical inference, generating an example, detail, visual image, analogy or metaphor; recalling an association from natural language or experience. Elaboration may also be accomplished by self-questioning, articulating the attributes of a concept (Klausmeier), identifying key events or categories of information (Bransford et al.; Tweney & Walker), and summarizing to consolidate what is learned. Thus, elaboration is fundamentally integrative and additive; it does not necessarily involve systematically reorganizing information structurally.

Second, students may invent or learn specific "big picture" organizational structures to organize what they know. For example, students may identify or impose a specific text structure or genre while reading (Pearson & Raphael) or writing (Hayes); generate a complex mnemonic or

generic organizational structure (Derry; Perkins); develop highly ab-
stracted, generalized routines or frames for thinking or decision making
within a domain (Borko & Shavelson; Perkins); or design specific argument structures (Ennis; Kline & Delia; Paul). Other examples include
problem finding and problem defining (Bransford et al.; Perkins).

Third, to develop contextually-rich knowledge structures in ill-structured domains, it may be necessary to go beyond inventing or imposing a
broad organizational structure systematically. That is, it may be necessary to alter existing structures substantially to align prior knowledge
with the new information so that conceptual change occurs. This may be
accomplished by examining a topic or problem in multiple contexts,
thereby building multiple perspectives. Bransford et al., for example,
argue that to develop highly conditionalized knowledge in ill-structured
domains, students must experience changes in perception and understanding of a concept as they view it from multiple perspectives.

Sometimes this process involves fine-tuning through careful editing,
analysis, revision of specific points, as well as effortful restructuring of an
existing knowledge structure, especially where a misconception is involved. Examples of fine-tuning include perceiving a lack of clarity and
organization in written texts (Hayes; Pearson & Raphael), adjusting the
meaning of a concept as additional examples and nonexamples are assimilated (Klausmeier), as well as debriefing after completion of a task
and applying a principle to new examples to test comprehension (Collins, Volume 2; Silver & Marshall). At other times, restructuring includes
struggling to purge bits and pieces of outdated notions or concepts from
prior knowledge as the disciplinary view becomes assimilated (Roth; Silver & Marshall) and revising your point of view substantially in relation
to new information (Kline & Delia; Paul). Paul, for example, lists five
macro-level strategies for these purposes: socratic questioning, conceptual analysis, analysis of the question-at-issue, reconstructing alternative
viewpoints in their strongest form, and reasoning dialogically and dialectically. These are supported by various micro-level strategies such as
evaluating source credibility, avoiding oversimplification, and suspend-
ing judgment.

What characteristics make some students engage in fine-tuning and
structural restructuring? According to Hayes, skilled writers are more
alert to cues that they are performing poorly such as failing to comprehend, and they are more active than others in responding to those
cues by asking for feedback, searching for models, and other activities.
Pearson and Raphael extend this argument when they note that skilled
learners are more metacognitively aware of themselves as learners and
aware of the task demands. However, these sensitivities may also be a
function of the disposition to be critical discussed by Paul, or they may be
motivated by the various purposes discussed above.

Fourth, for learning action sequences, students may seek reasons and explanations for actions (why they are appropriate and when to use them), engage in reflective self-instruction comparing personal performance to that of an expert, practice specific aspects of performance, and practice the procedure as a whole (Derry). This applies to acquiring specific strategies as well as to understanding complex sequences of events such as causal chains. At the same time, there comes a time in learning many action sequences when such reflection is inappropriate, according to Derry. Air traffic control procedures, for example, require immediate decisions and performance of routine and nonroutine tasks with accuracy and speed. In such instances, she argues for reflexive responses that are characterized by the rapid construction and execution of action sequences. She worries that the movement to teach thinking may devalue teaching for automaticity in favor of reflecting systematically through reasons and options before choosing a course of action; we should have both reflection and reflexivity when each is appropriate.

This repertoire of thinking strategies and skills is very different from those of less proficient learners. These learners are either unaware of contradictory and conflicting information and inadequate causal understanding or they are aware of these limitations in their knowledge but are unwilling or unable to attend to them. Thus, many elementary science students believe, on the one hand, that the plant makes its own food, and on the other, that fertilizer and sun are "plant food." Similarly, unphilosophical students do not seem to be aware of inadequate information, illogical reasoning, and so on (Paul). Bransford et al., refer to students who have critical knowledge, but it is inert because it was encoded as isolated facts rather than organized for applications and use.

To summarize, successful students seem to have different criteria for processing information compared to less successful students. To return to Hayes' comment: Successful students seem to be more aware of when they do not understand something and persevere until they address what they do not understand. Toward these ends, they have developed a repertoire of strategies to elaborate and integrate bits of related knowledge, to align prior knowledge to new information, and to restructure and finetune for clarity and conceptual change, to organize knowledge for application and use, and to understand the causes of things through questioning and self-questioning.

Self-Regulated Learning

A significant outcome of self-determination, organization of knowledge, and use of strategies is the capability for self-regulated learning. Borkowski et al. argue that there are three dimensions of metacognitive strategies. First, knowledge of specific strategies includes the procedures and conditions for its use. Second, metamemory acquisition procedures are strategies that operate on other strategies; these include comparing strategies with each other, self testing, and conducting personal experiments. Third, general strategy knowledge and attributional beliefs include understanding that success takes effort, that planning and monitoring are helpful.

It is this more general level of knowledge and use that has motivational properties, according to them. Different attributional beliefs evoke different emotional responses. Achievement distress (self-blame, humiliation, and self-derogation) follow from the belief that one is unable to manage events that others seem to control. This sense of failure leads to decreasing effort and to learned helplessness (see also Paris & Winograd).

To summarize, the vision of successful learning emerging from this volume involves *having deep values and beliefs regarding the purposes of learning*—self-determination, understanding complex concepts and multiple perspectives, applying and using knowledge, developing philosophical foundations. Proficient learning involves *working actively to organize knowledge* so that new information is well-elaborated and consistent with prior knowledge, with details and factual information well-structured by general principles and concepts. Proficient learning involves *reflection in action* by managing the progress of learning on-line while it is taking place, and by constantly adjusting and changing as new information is assimilated—sometimes thinking backwards to previous experiences and acquired information, sometimes thinking forward to anticipate and estimate. Proficient learning involves *strategic orchestration* of multiple knowledge bases and environments in a dynamic flow.

THINKING INSTRUCTION AND RESTRUCTURING SCHOOLS

Dimensions of Cognitive Instruction

A fundamental assumption throughout Volume 1 and Volume 2 is that models of instruction must reflect what is known about learning and thinking. Just as conceptions of thinking and learning have been expanded, so too have conceptions of cognitive instruction. In contrast to the deluge of narrowly-focused training studies emphasizing specific thinking strategies in previous research, recent approaches to cognitive instruction are multi-dimensional. Specific approaches emphasized in these volumes include the concepts of anchored instruction (Bransford et al.), cognitive apprenticeship (developed by Collins, see Volume 2; also described by Pearson & Raphael), conceptual change strategies defined by Roth, reciprocal teaching (described by Paris & Winograd; Pearson & Raphael; Collins, Volume 2), and cognitive strategy instruction (Borkowski et al.; Derry; Paris & Winograd; Paul; Pearson & Raphael; Perkins).

First, each of these approaches to cognitive instruction emphasizes some variation of a dual agenda in which general strategies and processes are taught as a means to teaching domain-specific objectives (see below for discussion of variations). And there is increasing agreement that strategies should be taught through scaffolded instruction by cycles of modeling, coaching, and fading in the context of dialogue and collaboration. In most of these approaches, instruction is situated in rich domain-specific contexts that permit problem finding, reflection, sustained exploration, and discovery (Bransford et al.). Accordingly, students can experience changes in their perception as they view the situation from multiple points of view and develop increasingly refined representations. There is also a strong emphasis on knowledge use and applications. Where misconceptions are involved, Roth argues that successful instruction must somehow make the student dissatisfied with the existing conception, make the disciplinary conception meaningful, and explicitly compare and contrast the two views to revise the outdated conception.

Second, all of these cognitive approaches include important metacognitive components. This includes the values and beliefs that support sustained enquiry and conceptual change. Moreover, this is not a matter of adding to the curriculum as much as it is the focus on modeling, dialogue, and collaboration that occurs with scaffolding. So many teachers assume that asking questions and receiving answers is dialogue, when it is essentially recitation. Dialogue, as defined throughout Volumes 1 and 2, always involves collaboration in which the teacher and students work together to probe the foundations of their thinking, in which students are encouraged to formulate questions and work cooperatively to find answers. It is through this type of dialogue that students develop the values, beliefs, attributions, and goals that characterize proficient learning, as well as learn the crucial procedural and conditional knowledge needed for achievement.

Third, given this focus on collaboration and dialogue, these approaches communicate a new and refreshing conceptualization of the classroom environment. In this collaborative classroom, the roles and responsibilities of students have essentially been redefined. Responsibility for learning is shared. Initially, it is the responsibility of the teacher but as time progresses, students assume increasing responsibility, not only for learning but also for assessment. The teacher is no longer information giver, but model and mediator; in these approaches, students learn to ask questions and formulate problems themselves,

Fourth, these new approaches to cognitive instruction pay very close attention to the ways that learners view themselves and their motivational states. Particularly important in these approaches are the judgments and beliefs that students have about the place of learning and schooling in their lives as well as attributions about success and failure. Issues such as these are usually mediated through thinking aloud strategies and dialogue.

Thus, there is considerable consensus about the importance of each of these four dimensions of cognitive instruction: the dual agenda of general and domain-specific strategies in the service of content objectives, metacognition, dialogue and collaboration, and relating learning to self-systems.

Issues Related to Strategy Instruction

What is debated here and elsewhere is the specific location of strategy instruction and the emphasis given to domain-specific knowledge. On the one hand, the cognitive strategy approach emphasizes the value of teaching general strategies and organizational patterns explicitly in adjunct skills courses. This means that although skills may be addressed to content objectives, the sequencing of instruction is skills driven. In this type of instruction, a unit on listening comprehension strategies might be followed by some problem solving activities. This instruction may be helpful for students at risk who may need extensive modelling, coaching, and guided practice, as well as attention to providing procedural, conditional knowledge, and transfer training. At the same time, just as there has been a softening of attitude among domain-specific proponents to strategy instruction, there has been a parallel recognition of the importance of domain-specific knowledge among cognitive strategy proponents and therefore more attention to the domain-specific components of strategy instruction and transfer.

On the other hand, the other approaches discussed above such as anchored instruction emphasize teaching various dimensions of thinking, including instruction for less proficient students, embedded in content-rich courses taught by content teachers. That is, thinking skills would not merely be presented by content teachers as a separate strand of instruction, as is the case in many school programs and new commercial materials in the content areas. To the contrary, specific processes and strategies would be presented when they played a functional role to learn some specific content. In this way, both general processes and specific strategies are infused in ongoing thinking and problem solving, rather than become ends in themselves. This means structuring the teaching of reading, writing, oral communication, and critical thinking across the curriculum as well as metacognition, problem solving, decision making, and creating thinking in a dynamic flow to teach specific objectives.

There are several arguments for embedding strategy instruction within content areas. First, Pearson & Raphael argue strongly that the movement to teach thinking should avoid the mistake made within the reading community, namely, decontextualizing skills instruction. Second, all too frequently strategies taught separately become ends in themselves, learned without the rich procedural and conditional knowledge to make them effective in subject disciplines. Third, with some noteworthy exceptions which are mostly in colleges rather than schools, there is little evidence that thinking skills programs transfer the acquired skills to other domains (Resnick, 1987; see also Marzano et al., 1988).

How explicit strategy instruction should be and to what extent should specific strategies be decomposed for instruction is also controversial. Borkowski et al., for example, argue that explicit strategy instruction is the heart of motivating students and recommend that teachers be motivated and equipped to teach effective strategies effectively, providing adequate procedural and conditional knowledge. Whereas others in this Volume might not see explicit strategy instruction as the key to motivating students, there is additional support for it among cognitive strategy instruction proponents.

Others *seem* to prefer implicit strategy instruction relying on modeling and coaching with little attention to decomposing skills. Specifically, there is very little mention of explicit strategy instruction in the chapters by Roth, Bransford et al., and Collins in Volume 2. It would, therefore, be easy to assume that there was little focus on it in theory or in the practices flowing from it. However, a close examination of the instructional approaches upon which the concepts of cognitive apprenticeship and anchored instruction are built reveals that in fact they have much explicit strategy instruction. Reciprocal teaching, for example, is one of those approaches and involves considerable discussion of strategy labels, purposes, and conditions for use. Much the same can be said for the other strategies upon which anchored instruction is founded.

Finally, there is the question of cognitive instruction and development. There is consistent evidence in this volume that younger children and less proficient students can be taught the same processes and strategies as those used by more successful learners. Reciprocal teaching, anchored instruction, and conceptual change strategies have been tested with younger children and children with special academic needs. So have many of the strategies taught as cognitive strategy instruction such as summarizing and self-questioning (Pearson & Raphael). Thus, there is little support for the notion that strategies for understanding and conceptual change should be taught in a hierarchy such as mastering basic definitions, literal meaning, and computational skills before engaging in analysis and problem solving.

To summarize, until recently, narrowly focused cognitive strategy instruction was the predominant method of cognitive instruction. As our understanding of learning and thinking has been enhanced, instructional strategies have added new dimensions. Specifically, there is much more attention to domain-specific knowledge, even among cognitive strategy proponents; extensive metacognitive components; a strong focus on collaborative classroom environments through dialogue and scaffolding; and finally, attention to self-systems and motivation. Differences among these strategies revolve around the sequencing of skills (whether they are ends in themselves or content driven) and their decomposition. At the same time, these differences are diminishing.

Implications for Restructuring Schools

To improve teaching and learning in ways suggested in this volume requires ultimately changing multiple dimensions of schooling and teacher education: curriculum, instruction, and assessment and the model of schooling that drives both practice and policies; the treatment of less proficient students, staff development and teacher education, and models of instructional leadership (Jones, 1988; see also Levine & Cooper, Volume 2).

Clearly, fundamental restructuring of schools is needed. Decentralizing governance structures, teacher empowerment, and parental involvement may indeed be necessary beginnings to redefining schooling, but they are not sufficient. To improve student achievement, it is crucial to redefine the conditions for teaching and learning as well for students and teachers.

The vision of proficient learning and teaching reflected in these chapters calls for a model of learning that recognizes the importance of acquiring and organizing domain-specific knowledge so that students can apply and use it in diverse contexts. Such a model would recognize the importance of the many sources of knowledge and the dynamic orchestration of these multiple sources in sustained thinking over long periods of time. Schools would see the learner holistically reflecting cognitive, affective, and physical characteristics in multiple environments that influence and guide the process of learning as well as what is learned.

In this vision, curricula would strive toward a dual agenda of domain-specific knowledge and thinking processes/strategies including collaborative skills and the development of productive self-systems. In such curricula, instruction would be designed to address authentic problems and questions. Reading, writing, problem solving, reasoning, and oral communication would be integrated across the disciplines to address these questions and problems.

In the classroom, students would collaborate with teachers and other students with much attention paid to teacher and student modeling, coaching, dialogue, explanations, guided practice, generating questions, and self-questioning. Teachers would see themselves as mediators, actively working to help students construct meaning; think strategically; become self-regulated learners; develop values and beliefs that support nurturing attitudes, critical enquiry, and lifelong learning; and persevere in spite of competing interests, inadequate and inconsistent information, and loosely-defined constraints.

This vision of schooling contrasts sharply with virtually every aspect of traditional schooling. Most fundamentally, it contrasts with the assembly model of learning that underlies traditional schooling and traditional teacher education, emphasizing learning basic skills and isolated facts. It also contrasts with traditional teaching with its focus on assessment of learning and didactic methods. Thus, while much of the new instruction described above was derived from observations of expert teaching in and out of school, *most* teachers do not teach in ways that are consistent with this research.

There are good reasons for this. First, traditional preservice and inservice institutions do not provide the knowledge base for teachers or administrators. This includes not only knowledge of content and specific strategies, but the other knowledge bases in which learning is situated: the multi-dimensional character of thinking and instruction; the values, beliefs, assumptions, attributions, and purposes associated with proficient learning; the knowledge of physical, social, and cultural environments; and the dynamic flow over time. Nor do many teachers have opportunities for practice and feedback that would enable them to apply this research.

Second, the vision of thinking and instruction emerging here is fundamentally at odds with existing values, beliefs, and policies in schools. For example, the idea that teachers help students construct meaning and engage in dialogue that allows students to control the questioning is in conflict with long-standing norms of the teacher as information giver and teacher-directed instruction. Additionally, most teachers are so isolated that they lack the social skills to engage in collaborative activities. These conflicts are explored in Volume 2 (Florio; Greene, Kantor, & Rogers; Marzano). Assessment is another example of conflict. Assessment drives instruction. As long as our assessment measures focus on measuring isolated skills and facts, teachers are unlikely to change (see Linn, Volume 2).

Third, the research in this volume requires that we truly believe that most children can learn, including most less proficient children. Many teachers and administrators do not believe this, and these beliefs are buttressed by federal and state regulations for remedial and special education and by local practices involving tracking (Allington; Barr & Anderson, Feuerstein et al., Secada, Volume 2). That is, until recently, policies for Chapter 1 and special education not only segregated low-achieving students from contextually rich social and academic environments but also functionally prohibited "higher order thinking" instruction. Under these conditions, even those who "succeed" at achieving the low level of outcomes expected are ill-equipped for the needs of an information society. In the light of these considerations, remediation is the problem, not the students. Yet there are massive vested interests in these outdated practices, interests which ultimately sap the productive capability of increasing numbers of students destined to be disconnected from the means to function effectively in a rapidly changing society.

In spite of these problems, there is much room for optimism and enthusiasm. There is increasing evidence that the tide is turning toward fundamental change. Everywhere there is dissatisfaction with existing curricula. More important, there are new state and national guidelines that do reflect recent research in various dimensions of thinking: the new definition of reading developed in California, Illinois, Michigan, and Wisconsin, (Idol, Jones, & Mayer, Volume 2); as well as new guidelines in mathematics (National Council of Teachers of Mathematics, 1989), science (American Association for the Advancement of Science, 1989), and technology (Technology Education Advisory Council, 1989). Additionally, there are numerous instructional programs in schools and preservice contexts that are effective and promote teaching for understanding (Collins; Ennis; Idol, Jones, & Mayer; Marzano; O'Flahavan & Tierney, Volume 2). It is also heartening to see reform for administrators (National Policy Board for Educational Administration, 1989), teacher education (Lanier & Featherstone, 1988), national school networks (e.g., Education Commission of the States, 1989), and designs for future schools that reflect fundamental change (e.g., Reigeluth, 1987). At the same time, we are concerned that many of the reforms for teachers and administrators, outside these noteworthy networks and reform states, are not aligned with research on learning, cognitive instruction, and expert teaching. Particularly, there seems to be little effort in schools, state departments, national certification boards, or institutions of higher education to require knowledge or use of this research for teachers or administrators. We hope that these volumes may be used to address this misalignment.

Education is at a critical juncture. On the one hand, traditional patterns are resistant to change through inertia, fear, and vested interests. If we do not use this research to implement changes on a large scale, the nation may lose faith in public education, the profession of teaching altogether, and the movement to teach thinking. Too many of our citizens will not be prepared for life in an information society, a global economy, and rapid change. In the short term, this could result in a highly polarized society with increasing numbers of the disconnected and poorly prepared living within severe constraints while the well-educated become increasingly segregated in private schools and foreign soils, taking ever more of the nation's wealth.

On the other hand, the long-term human and economic costs of this bipolarization are too high to continue along the old roads. Much of the knowledge and technology that is needed for fundamental reform is in place for this generation of researchers and educators to collaborate in transforming our schools on a large scale. The roads to fundamental reform will be fraught with difficulties, as were the pathways that the pioneers forged to build a new society. Yet, we have the knowledge to restructure our schools to promote lifelong learning among communities of learners. If we use this opportunity to reconnect the disengaged to the heart of schooling and to align America's schools with the needs of society, we may harness untold constructive energies.

REFERENCES

Alexander, P. A., & Judy, J. E. (1988). The interaction of domain-specific and strategic knowledge in academic performance. *Review of Educational Research, 58,* 375–404.

American Association for the Advancement of Science. (1989). *Science for all Americans.* Washington, DC: American Association for the Advancement of Science.

Brown, J. S., Collins, A., & Duguid, P. (1989). Situated cognition and the culture of learning. *Educational Researcher, 18,* 32–42.

Collins, A., Brown, J. S., & Newman, S. (1989). Cognitive apprenticeship: Teaching students the craft of reading, writing, and mathematics. In L. B. Resnick (Ed.), *Knowing, learning, and instruction: Essays in honor of Robert Glaser,* pp. 453–494. Hillsdale, NJ: Lawrence Erlbaum Associates.

Duffy, G. G., Roehler, L., & Rackliffe, G. (in press). Constraints on teacher change. *Journal of Teacher Education.*

Education Commission of the States. (1989). *Re: Learning from schoolhouse to statehouse.* Washington, DC: Education Commission of the States.

Jones, B. F. (1988). Redefining curriculum and instruction for students at risk. In B. Z. Presseisen (Ed.), *Students at risk and thinking: Issues and research perspectives* (pp. 76–103). Washington, DC: National Education Association.

Jones, B. F., Palincsar, A. S., Ogle, D. S., & Carr, E. G. (Eds.). (1987). *Strategy and learning: Cognitive instruction in the content areas.* Alexandria, VA: Association for Supervision and Curriculum Development.

Lanier, J. E., & Featherstone, J. (1988). A new commitment to teacher education. *Educational Leadership, 46*(3), 19–22.

Lave, J. (1988). *Cognition in practice.* New York: Cambridge University Press.

Leinhardt, G., & Greeno, J. G. (1986). The cognitive skill of teaching. *Journal of Educational Psychology, 78,* 79–95.

Marzano, R., Brandt, R., Hughes, C., Jones, B. F., Presseisen, B. Z., Rankin, S., & Suhor, C. (1988). *Dimensions of thinking: A framework for curriculum and instruction.* Alexandria, VA: Association for Supervision and Curriculum Development.

National Council of Teachers of Mathematics. (1989). *Curriculum and evaluation standards for school mathematics.* Reston, VA: National Council of Teachers of Mathematics.

National Policy Board for Educational Administration. (1989). *Improving the preparation of school administrators: An agenda for reform.* Charlottesville, VA: National Policy Board for Educational Administration.

Perkins, D., & Salomon, G. (1989). Are cognitive skills context-bound? *Educational Researcher, 18,* 16–25.

Reigeluth, C. M. (1987). Search for meaningful reform: A third-wave educational system. *Journal of Instructional Development, 10,* 3–14.

Resnick, L. B. (1987). *Education and learning to think.* Washington, DC: National Academy Press.

Rumelhart, D. E. (1980). Schemata: The building blocks of cognition. In R. J. Spiro, B. C. Bruce, & W. F. Brewer (Eds.), *Theoretical issues in reading comprehension* (pp. 35–38). Hillsdale, NJ: Lawrence Erlbaum Associates.

Schon, D. A. (1987). *Educating the reflective practitioner.* San Francisco: Jossey-Bass Press.

Spiro, R. J. (1980). Constructive processes in prose comprehension and recall. In R. J. Spiro, B. C. Bruce, & W. F. Brewer (Eds.), *Theoretical issues in reading comprehension* (pp. 245–278). Hillsdale, NJ: Lawrence Erlbaum Associates.

Spiro, R. J. (1989, March). *Professional cognition: Management of complexity.* Paper presented at the annual meetings of the American Educational Research Association, San Francisco.

Technology Education Advisory Council. (1989). *Technology: A national imperative.* Reston, VA: Technology Education Advisory Council.

Author Index

I

K

J

Subject Index